# The Second
# Anglo-Sikh War

AMARPAL SINGH SIDHU was born in the Punjab, India. He spent over twenty years working in the software industry before turning to his real interest in military history and the exploration and analysis of battlefields. His first book, *The First Anglo-Sikh War*, has been well received. Amarpal has appeared and collaborated on history programs for several TV channels.

FIELD MARSHAL SIR JOHN LYON CHAPPLE GCB, CBE was a career British Army officer in the second half of the twentieth century. He served as Chief of the General Staff, the professional head of the British Army, from 1988 to 1992. Early in his early military career he saw action during the Malayan Emergency and again during the Indonesia–Malaysia confrontation and later in his career he provided advice to the British Government during the Gulf War.

# The Second Anglo-Sikh War

Amarpal Singh

AMBERLEY

*Dedicated to my father (1930–2012)*

First published 2016
This edition published 2017

Amberley Publishing
The Hill, Stroud
Gloucestershire, GL5 4EP

www.amberley-books.com

British Library Cataloguing in Publication Data.
A catalogue record for this book is available from the British Library.

ISBN 978 1 4456 7113 0 (print)
ISBN 978 1 4456 5024 1 (ebook)

Typesetting and Origination by Amberley Publishing.
Printed in the UK.

# Contents

# Foreword by Field Marshal
# Sir John Lyon Chapple

It is said that wars are fought by many yet written about by few. This is evident in the case of the Anglo-Sikh wars. As British military historians concede, these conflicts were important in that they were the final campaigns fought by the East India Company on Indian soil and thus completed the conquest of India. These wars also happened to be the most difficult campaigns the company had to face on the Subcontinent. Both Ferozeshah in the first war and Chillianwala in the second were close-run encounters with results that could have gone either way. Sadly in some respects, these wars have been overshadowed by the events of 1857 and have therefore received much less research and attention than warranted.

These wars form only a small part of our shared Anglo-Sikh history. It was in 1809 that the first treaty between the British East India Company and Maharajah Ranjit Singh of the Sikh Empire was signed. The relationship between the British and the Sikh people is therefore more than two hundred years old. As President of the Indian Historical Military Society, I have had very great pleasure in closely working with Harbinder Singh Rana and the Maharajah Duleep Singh Centenary Trust in helping fostering and promoting this friendship and shared history.

I had great satisfaction in reading this new work on the Second Anglo-Sikh War. There has been no significant work published on this campaign for far too long. I recall being present at the Royal Geographical Society in Kensington on 7 September 2010 when Amarpal released his inaugural book on the First Anglo-Sikh War. In this account of the subsequent campaign, he again presents a compelling insight into the military and political backdrops against which they need to be considered to be fully understood. Most accounts to date have failed to convey both the political intrigue which precipitated the wars and also the scale of the gallantry displayed by the Sikhs. The book is a commendable interweaving of accounts from both whilst remaining objective. Perhaps this is because the author is a 'British Sikh' who has over time been imbued with a perspective which has hitherto eluded others. In any event this book is a welcome and valuable addition to a critical phase in our common history.

Field Marshal Sir John Lyon Chapple GCB, CBE

# List of Maps

# Chronology

**1757**
23 Jun.    Battle of Plassey establishing British control over Bengal

**1780**
13 Nov.   Birth of Ranjit Singh

**1801**
12 Apr.   Ranjit Singh crowned Maharajah of Lahore

**1818**
?            Birth of Maharani Jind Kaur

**1838**
6 Sep.    Birth of Duleep Singh

**1839**
27 Jun.   Death of Ranjit Singh
8 Oct.    Kharak Singh, oldest son of Ranjit Singh, overthrown

**1840**
5 Nov.    Death of Kharak Singh of slow poisoning
6 Nov.    Death of Prince Nau-Nihal Singh
2 Dec.    Chund Kaur, his mother, becomes regent

**1841**
20 Jan.   Shere Singh becomes regent

**1843**
16 Sep.   Maharajah Shere Singh assassinated, succeeded by Duleep Singh
18 Sep.   Duleep Singh proclaimed Maharajah

**1845**
11 Dec.   Sikh army crosses the Sutlej River, forming the border between the Sikh and East India
            Company possessions

| | |
|---|---|
| 18 Dec. | Battle of Mudki |
| 21 Dec. | Battle of Ferozeshah |

**1846**

| | |
|---|---|
| 21 Jan. | Battle of Bhudowal |
| 28 Jan. | Battle of Aliwal |
| 10 Feb. | Battle of Sabraon |
| 11–13 Feb. | British cross the Sutlej into the Punjab |
| 14 Feb. | Hardinge communicates conditions for peace to Lahore |
| 14 Feb. | Gulab Singh leaves Lahore to visit Hardinge |
| 18 Feb. | Formal submission of Maharajah Duleep Singh at British camp at Lullianee |
| 20 Feb. | British force reaches Lahore and encamps under the walls of the city |
| 22 Feb. | British occupy part of the Lahore fort, Badshahi mosque, Hazuri Bagh |
| 9 Mar. | Treaty of Lahore signed |
| 11 Mar. | Additional articles added to Treaty of Lahore |
| 15 Mar. | Gulab Singh made Maharajah of Kashmir |
| 16 Mar. | Treaty of Amritsar signed, transferring Kashmir to Gulab Singh |
| 1 Apr. | Henry Lawrence appointed as Governor-General's agent at Lahore |
| 13 Apr. | The commandant of the Kangra fortress refuses to surrender it to the British |
| 21 Apr. | The 'cow row' – a European wounds several cows in Lahore, causing disturbance |
| 24 Apr. | Two ringleaders in the 'cow row' hanged under orders of Henry Lawrence |
| 3 May | Henry Lawrence reaches Kangra fort |
| 28 May | Surrender of Kangra fortress to the British (Henry Lawrence) after a six-week standoff |
| 26 Jul. | Lal Singh writes two letters to Sheikh Imam-Ud-Deen, the Governor of Kashmir, to delay handing over the territory to Gulab Singh |
| 2 Oct. | Sikh army leaves Lahore to enforce the handover of Kashmir to Gulab Singh |
| 15 Oct. | Sir John Littler marches from Lahore towards Kashmir |
| 16 Oct. | Henry Lawrence departs for Kashmir for the transfer of the province to Gulab Singh |
| 1 Nov. | Sheikh Imam-Ud-Deen reaches Thana and give himself up to Henry Lawrence |
| 9 Nov. | Gulab Singh enters Srinagar as new Maharajah of Kashmir |
| 3 Dec. | Trial of Lal Singh begins |
| 4 Dec. | Lal Singh found guilty |
| 9 Dec. | Frederick Currie tells Lahore Durbar that British garrison at Lahore will depart soon |
| 13 Dec. | Lal Singh transported to Ferozepore and into exile in British territory |
| 15 Dec. | Currie asks Lahore government members if they wish the British garrison to stay at Lahore |

16 Dec.   Lahore government agrees to British terms for a new treaty
26 Dec.   Treaty of Bhyrowal signed by Governor-General and Duleep Singh, making British presence permanent in the Punjab

**1847**
12 Feb.   Prema plot to assassinate Henry Lawrence thwarted

3 Mar.    Sikh guns captured in First Anglo-Sikh War paraded at Fort William

7 Aug.    Tej Singh made a raja with Duleep Singh refusing to cooperate
19 Aug.   Maharani Jind Kaur removed to Sheikhupura
21 Aug.   Henry Lawrence leaves Lahore, John Lawrence becoming temporary resident

16 Dec.   Dewan Mulraj meets John Lawrence to inform him of his resignation

**1848**
12 Jan.   Lord Dalhousie lands in India to become new Governor-General
18 Jan.   Henry Lawrence and previous Governor-General Hardinge depart Calcutta for England

9 Mar.    Currie begins appointment as British resident at Lahore
16 Mar.   Mulraj writes to Currie confirming his wish to resign

4 Apr.    Agnew and Anderson leave for Multan to assume control
17 Apr.   Agnew's party reaches Raj Ghat opposite Multan
18 Apr.   Agnew and Mulraj have meeting at Eidgah
19 Apr.   Agnew travels to Multan Fort to assume control of province
20 Apr.   Agnew and Anderson killed at Eidgah
22 Apr.   Agnew's letter for help reaches Herbert Edwardes at Dera Futteh Khan
23 Apr.   Edwardes reaches the right bank of Indus
25 Apr.   Edwardes reaches and occupies the city of Leia
25 Apr.   Currie receives news of Agnew and Anderson's deaths
29 Apr.   Shere Singh's column begins move from Lahore to Multan

8 May     May Conspiracy ringleader Khan Singh and others arrested in Lahore
9 May     Lahore conspirators tried and sentenced to death
11 May    Lahore conspirators hanged
14 May    Jind Kaur exiled to Benares

**18 Jun.   BATTLE OF KYNEERIE**
20 Jun.   Edwardes occupies Soojabad and Kote
20 Jun.   Currie sends out force from Lahore to intercept the preacher Bhai Maharaj
26 Jun.   Fort of Secunderabad surrenders to Edwardes
28 Jun.   Sheikh Imam-Ud-Deen joins forces with Edwardes with 4,000 men

1 Jul.    Currie orders three Sikh columns north of Multan to advance to the city
**1 Jul.    BATTLE OF SADOOSAM**

| | |
|---|---|
| 6 Jul. | Shere Singh reaches Multan |
| 10 Jul. | Currie orders General Whish with British force to Multan |
| 21–24 Jul. | British troops from Ferozepore and Lahore begin move to Multan |
| | |
| 2 Aug. | Maharani Jind Kaur arrives at Benares |
| 6 Aug. | Murder of the American Canora and beginning of Hazara insurrection led by Chutter Singh |
| 18-19 Aug. | British columns under Whish reach Multan |
| | |
| 1 Sep. | Whish carries out reconnaissance of fortress prior to siege |
| 4 Sep. | British siege train of heavy guns arrives at Multan |
| 5 Sep. | Whish sends proclamation to city asking for unconditional surrender |
| 5 Sep. | Grand parade of British force and allies held in front of fortress |
| 5 Sep. | Siege of Multan begins |
| | |
| 7 Sep. | Formal operations begin against city |
| 7 Sep. | Capture of Ram Tirath |
| 8 Sep. | Attack on enemy outposts outside the city walls |
| 12 Sep. | General assault against outworks in suburbs |
| 13 Sep. | Hummund Ghurree, the last Multan outpost outside city walls, is captured |
| 14 Sep. | **Shere Singh's army openly declares for the nationalist cause at Multan** |
| 15 Sep. | Whish suspends siege of city and retreats towards Suraj Khund |
| 17 Sep. | Golab Singh, brother of Shere Singh, arrested in Lahore |
| 18 Sep. | Currie orders four more arrests related to alleged conspiracy |
| | |
| 7 Oct. | Festival of Dussehra; a planned attack by Mulraj on the British force fails to happen |
| 9 Oct. | Shere Singh leaves Multan for the north of the country |
| 11 Oct. | Dalhousie leaves Calcutta for the Punjab |
| 11–12 Oct. | Shere Singh crosses the Ravi and marches towards Ramnuggar |
| 23–24 Oct. | Peshawar troops hear of Shere marching north and also rebel |
| | |
| 5 Nov. | British Commander-in-Chief Gough arrives at Ferozepore |
| **7 Nov.** | **BATTLE OF SURAJ KHUND** |
| 9 Nov. | Gough leaves Ferozepore with army off the Punjab and enters Punjab |
| 13 Nov. | Gough reaches Lahore |
| 16 Nov. | Gough leaves Lahore to join British vanguard near the Chenab River |
| 21 Nov. | Gough reaches British vanguard |
| 21 Nov. | First batch of Bombay force under Dundas moves off from Roree to Multan |
| **22 Nov.** | **BATTLE OF RAMNUGGAR** |
| 30 Nov. | British siege train reaches Gough's force at Ramnuggar |
| | |
| 1 Dec. | Thackwell leaves Ramnuggar with large force to cross the Chenab upstream |
| **3 Dec.** | **BATTLE OF SADULPORE** |
| 10–26 Dec. | Bombay reinforcements begin reaching Multan to strengthen Whish's force |
| **25 Dec** | **Whish commences second siege of Multan** |
| 27 Dec. | First attack of combined Whish and Bombay force on city suburbs |

| | |
|---|---|
| 30 Dec. | Grand magazine inside Multan fortress explodes causing immense damage |

**1849**

| | |
|---|---|
| 1 Jan. | Large elements of Dost Mohammad's force reach Attock fortress |
| 2 Jan. | Assault on Multan begins. City is captured |
| 2 Jan. | Attock fortress falls to Dost Mohammad |
| **13 Jan.** | **BATTLE OF CHILLIANWALA** |
| 22 Jan. | Walls of Multan fort breached. Whish orders assault for this day. Garrison surrender. |
| 25 Jan. | Chutter Singh joins Shere Singh at Chillianwala |
| 26 Jan. | News reaches Chillianwala of the fall of Multan |
| 1 Feb. | Henry Lawrence again becomes Resident |
| 12 Feb. | Shere Singh begins moves from Rasul to Gujrat |
| 13–20 Feb. | Elements of Whish's force begin joining Gough's army |
| 14 Feb. | Shere Singh and the Sikh army reaches Gujrat |
| 15 Feb. | Gough's army moves of from Chillianwala to Lussoorie |
| 18 Feb. | Gough reaches Kungah |
| 20 Feb. | Gough advances to Shadiwal |
| **21 Feb.** | **BATTLE OF GUJRAT** |
| 3–4 Mar. | Trial of Goojur Singh at Multan |
| 14 Mar. | Chutter Singh and Shere Singh surrender near Rawalpindi |
| 20 Mar. | Gilbert advances to Nowshera |
| 21 Mar. | Gilbert advances to Peshawar and terminates campaign |
| 28 Mar. | Henry Elliot informs Lahore Government members of Governor-General's decision to annex the Punjab |
| **29 Mar.** | **Duleep Singh holds his last court at Lahore, at which he signs away all claims to the rule of the Punjab** |
| 31 Mar. | Dalhousie creates a board of control to administer the Punjab |
| 6 Apr. | John Login appointed guardian of Maharajah Duleep Singh and commander of citadel of Lahore |
| 6 Apr. | Maharani Jind Kaur moved from Benares to Chunar fortress |
| 18 Apr. | Maharani escapes from fortress of Chunar and proceeds to Nepal |
| 29 Apr. | Maharani reaches Nepal |
| 31 May | Mulraj trial begins |
| 22 Jun. | End of Mulraj trial |
| 31 Jul. | Mulraj told Governor-General has remitted his death sentence but he will be exiled abroad |
| 1 Oct. | John Lawrence orders arrest of Shere Singh and Chutter Singh at Attari for breaking parole along with other Sikh officers |

| 7 Dec. | Dalhousie takes receipt of Koh-i-noor to be sent to Queen Victoria |
| 21 Dec. | Duleep Singh sent to reside at Fatehgarh outside the Punjab |

**1850**

| 13 Feb. | Auction of jewellery captured at Multan commences |
| 6 Apr. | Koh-i-noor leaves India aboard the HMS *Medea* |
| 29 Jun. | HMS *Medea* reaches Portsmouth |
| 3 Jul. | Koh-i-noor is presented to Queen Victoria |

**1851**

| 17 Jan. | Shere Singh and Chutter Singh, among other prisoners, reach Calcutta for incarceration at Fort William |
| May–Oct. | Koh-i-noor exhibited at the Great Exhibition in London |

**1853**

| 8 Mar. | Duleep Singh, aged fourteen, becomes a Christian at Fatehgarh |

**1854**

| 5 Mar. | Duleep Singh leaves Fatehgarh for Calcutta |
| 19 Apr. | Duleep Singh leaves for England from Calcutta |
| 1 Jul. | Queen Victoria gives special audience to Duleep Singh |
| 4 Sep. | Minority of Duleep Singh ends but Dalhousie extends the period for two more years |

**1863**

| 1 Aug. | Death of Jind Kaur in London |

**1886**

| 25 May | Duleep Singh reconverts to Sikhism |

**1893**

| 22 Oct. | Death of Duleep Singh |

# Prologue

# 'The Last Lahore Durbar'

At the appointed hour of 7 a.m. on the morning of 29 March 1849, a small party of Europeans rode up the ramp leading to the fort and palace of Lahore. Heading the group were Henry Lawrence, the British Resident in the city, and Henry Miers Elliot, Foreign Secretary of the British Government of India. Other British officials of the Residency along with an armed escort accompanied them. The ten-year-old Maharajah of the Punjab, Duleep Singh, and his courtiers awaited them at the fort entrance. There were the usual greetings and pleasantries and a brief exchange of presents took place. The two parties then walked together into the Hall of Audience in the palace where a hushed assembly of courtiers, officials and onlookers had gathered.

Word had spread of the last Durbar, the customary reception by the Indian prince, and most of the Europeans in the city had turned up to witness the occasion. The right-hand side of the hall had been reserved for them, and such was the interest that there was room for no more. The left was full of Sikh members of the Durbar and others who wished to witness the occasion. The Sikh courtiers wore sombre clothes, in keeping with the nature of the event, with none of the jewels and rich clothes usually apparent in the Durbar. British soldiers lined the room on all sides and there was an oppressive quietness in the chamber as all waited for what was to come.

The Maharajah was conducted to a seat at the end of the hall. A chair had been set aside on either side of his for Lawrence and Elliot. The audience looked on silently as they settled into their seats. The young Maharajah appeared comfortable, it was noted. Whether he realised the purpose of the gathering was unclear, although Elliot seemed to think so. 'The Maharajah, who is endued with an intelligence beyond his years, and cannot be supposed to have been ignorant of the purpose for which the Durbar was now convened for the last time, conducted himself throughout with cheerfulness and self-composure,' he reported later to the Governor-General of India, the Earl of Dalhousie.

The event was formal but short on ceremony. A declaration prepared by the Governor-General was read out, first in Persian and then in Hindustani by Elliot. 'For many years, while the wisdom of Maharajah Ranjit Singh ruled the people of the Punjab, friendships and unbroken peace prevailed between the British nation and the Sikhs,' it began, before launching into a savage criticism of the present Lahore Government, its inability to control the Sikh army and the consequences of the first war three years earlier. The British Government had been generous in allowing the continuation of the state after the first war, he declared. Despite the extended hand of friendship, the reparations due to the East India Company for the previous war had not been paid, but had rather grown. Instead a second war had been waged, with British officers and political agents held captive and others murdered. The Sikh army was avowedly nationalist and incapable of change. 'They proclaimed their purpose to be the extirpation of the British power, and the destruction of the British people; and they have struggled fiercely to effect it.' Not only this, but the Sikh army had been joined by members of the Lahore Government, thus flouting the recent treaty whereby the government of the country had been willingly passed to the British. A costly and unprovoked war had resulted. However, the Sikh army had been defeated and its guns taken in the recent conflict, and although the British Government had no desire for further conquest, there could be no guarantee that the Lahore state and its people would cease their warlike activities. The Maharajah must be responsible for the lawless actions of his subjects. 'Wherefore, the Governor-General, as the only effectual mode which now remains of preventing the recurrence of national outrage, and the renewal of perpetual wars, has resolved upon declaring the British Sovereignty in the Punjab, and upon the entire subjection of the Sikh nation, whom their own rulers have long been unable to control, who are equally insensible to punishment or forbearance, and who, as past events have now shown, will never desist from war so long as they possess the power of an independent kingdom.'

The country was to be annexed into British possessions, and the Sikh Empire was no more. There was no talk for several minutes as the news was absorbed. One of the senior members of the Lahore Government present in the audience, Dewan Deena Nath, then spoke up. He said the decision was just and should be obeyed, but hoped that the Maharajah and his servants would be given allowances to live comfortably; but that if France, after the defeat of Napoleon Bonaparte, was given back to the legitimate emperor, surely British clemency would allow the Punjab to be restored as well. 'The time of concession and clemency is gone,' Elliot replied. The terms, which had been agreed previously, must be adhered to and the declaration should now be made public knowledge. Silence followed. With no other comment, the ceremony was continued. The document detailing the pension arrangements for the Maharajah was produced in duplicate. Several of the leading Lahore Government members present then signed the papers. The copies were then given to the seated Maharajah. He wrote his initials in English on both. Elliot then gave him one copy and kept the other. Among the financial details of his settlement, one condition stood out. It was a demand for the surrender of the famous Koh-i-noor, the largest diamond in the world.

This was the end of the ceremony. The Durbar was dissolved and those who had assembled quietly left the Hall of Audience. No words of conversation or whispers were heard. Lawrence and Elliot walked out of the palace too, and orders were given for the final formalities.

'As I left the palace,' recorded the Foreign Secretary, 'I had the proud satisfaction of seeing the British colours hoisted on the citadel under a Royal salute from our own artillery at once proclaiming the ascendency of British rule and sounding the knell of the Khalsa Raj.'

# Preface

# The Katalgarh – The House of Slaughter

… strong in national faith and feeling, dangerous from perfect discipline and desperate through starvation.

George Buist on the redundant Khalsa soldiers, *Annals of India for the Year 1848*

Perfect tranquillity prevails at present throughout all the territories under the Lahore Government and I have no reason to think that the apparent contentment of the people is other than real.

Frederick Currie, Resident at Lahore, to Government of India, 6 April 1848

Less than three months before the last Lahore Durbar, the Battle of Chillianwala had taken place. Any modern visitor to London caring to explore the grounds of the Royal Hospital Chelsea, home of the Chelsea Pensioners, will undoubtedly come across the Chillianwala monument, a memorial to that battle. This prominent obelisk was constructed in memory of the losses to HM 24th regiment during the short but sanguinary contest fought on the banks of the River Jhelum in the Punjab. Another similar obelisk stands nearly 6,500 kilometres away, a few kilometres from the Jhelum itself and close to the village of Chillianwala in what is now Pakistan. A simple epitaph marks the sandstone structure and addresses the dead of both sides.

In this battle, fought on 13 January 1849 A.D., where British forces were led by Lord Gough and the Sikh Army by Raja Sher Singh, both sides fought valiantly and fearlessly and countless were killed in action. May God illuminate their souls with divine light and their names shine in the world.

There is a plot around the obelisk, which marks the mass graves of the British participants who died in the battle. The village locals refer to it is as the Katalgarh, the House of Slaughter.

\*\*\*

HM 24th Regiment suffered the worst casualties among the British force during the battle. Unbeknown to them, they had been facing the Bannu troops of the Khalsa army, the sturdiest and most battle-hardened men that remained of Ranjit Singh's Sikh army in 1849. As the regiment had pushed through the wooded area adjacent to the river, clearing the trees in some confusion, they had come into full sight of the Sikh line. In that instant the Sikh infantry and guns fired fast and accurately, and with devastating results, tearing terrible gaps into the British line as it advanced and forcing the regiment to pull back down the incline they had recently traversed, leaving large numbers dead.

Chillianwala was a swift and brutal battle. Only three hours after the initial British advance, as darkness covered the field of battle, over two and a half thousand men in the British line lay dead or wounded, with half the line meeting a bloody repulse. Sir Hugh Gough, the Commander-in-Chief of the British forces in India and personally leading the army, contemplated a disaster during the night as his army lay vulnerable to a counterattack. Orders were given to build defensive entrenchments and breastworks round the camp over the following days, the first time a British force in India had resorted to these measures. Only the caution of Shere Singh, the Sikh commander, and his ignorance of the confusion in the British ranks during the hours after the battle would save Gough from a worse predicament.

In London and beyond, besides the monument, there are several other prominent reminders of the conflict that was the Second Anglo-Sikh War. The Koh-i-noor diamond, demanded as part of the pension agreement agreed for the dethroned young Maharajah after the annexation of the Punjab, now resides in the Tower of London and is seen by thousands of people every day trooping past to see the Crown Jewels collection. The throne of Ranjit Singh, the founder of the Sikh Empire, sits in the Victoria and Albert Museum and there are reminders in the form of the tulwars (Sikh swords), muskets, cannon and standards of the Sikh army scattered around museums throughout the country.

***

A year prior to Chillianwala, during the early months of 1848, there had been rumours of war against the British in the Punjab. Frederick Currie, the former Foreign Secretary to the Government of India and member of the Supreme Council of India, had been appointed the new Resident at Lahore with the incumbent Henry Lawrence taking sick leave at the tail end of 1847. While travelling towards the city during the month of February to take up his position, his suspicions had been aroused in the Jalandhar district, an area recently annexed by the British after the First Anglo-Sikh War. Lt Lake, one of the political agents in the area, had warned him the area was ripe for insurrection against the British. 'I found him fully impressed with the belief that a rising would take place before many months were over, which was the result, not of any particular tangible circumstance, but of the feeling which he had observed, and the hints which had at different times been thrown out in his presence,' recalled Currie later in correspondence with the government in Calcutta. No proof was available, just the feeling that something may happen. John Lawrence, the Commissioner of the Jalandhar district, had also heard of these rumours but since no proof was forthcoming had paid no heed to them. There were certain other signs as well, however. Sirdar Lehna Singh Majithia, a prominent but un-soldierly Sikh nobleman, had left the Punjab. He had been given charge of the Manjha district, the heartland of the Sikh population and thus the most likely place for an outbreak. This would put the mild-mannered man in a difficult position. His departure was taken as a sign that something was definitely afoot.

Some weeks after Currie had settled into his role at Lahore, Major Napier employed at that time in surveying various parts of the Punjab had also written to him about the attitude he found prevailing in the Punjab. The people he encountered, the Sikh soldiers forming his escort and his servants, talked 'of the inutility of their work, as the Europeans would not be allowed to remain much longer in the Punjab; a few months would see them across the Sutlej'. These perceptions and utterances he had noticed everywhere he went and from many people of varied backgrounds. His assistants, too, had noticed this 'insolent' attitude. So frequent were these expressions, in fact, and so widespread were these beliefs, that he had decided to inform the Resident at Lahore. Capt. Abbott, in Hazara, the province neighbouring Peshawar, to the north-west of Lahore, had also heard much of an insurrection and had written to Lahore regarding his suspicions. It was generally felt the Maharani of Lahore, Jind Kaur, was the focus and inspiration of these perceptions and the financier for any plot to expel the British from the Punjab.

Rumours and suspicions aside, however, the first few months of 1848 prior to the breakout of the Second Anglo-Sikh War, like the last few months of 1847, proved to be an exceptionally quiet time in the Punjab and beyond. So quiet, in fact, that the newspapers found themselves now struggling to find anything worthy of printing about the country. This was in marked contrast to the period during and after the end of the first war. There had been attempted rebellions, first the Governor of the Kangra Fortress and then the Governor of Kashmir. Then there had been the subsequent trial and exile of the Vizier of the Punjab in 1846, followed by the plot to kill the British Resident in Lahore in February of the previous year. The exile of the Queen Regent and mother of the Maharajah from the palace in Lahore in August 1847 had received significant coverage among many other pieces of news. Since that event, however, nothing of importance had happened in the country and news from the state had tailed off dramatically. 'Everything continues perfectly quiet in the Punjab,' Viscount Henry Hardinge, the previous Governor-General, had stated in a letter to the Secret Committee in November of the previous year, shortly before departing for England. This was echoed into the New Year by the newspapers searching for newsworthy items. So little news was now emanating from the Punjab, in fact, that newspaper editors virtually threw their hands up in surrender. 'The news by the present mail is as gratifying as the most ardent lover of peace could desire. The Punjab is as tranquil as it has ever of late been,' wrote *Allen's Indian Mail* on 5 October 1847.

Several months later, the state of apparent tranquillity was seen to continue. 'The Punjab, so long the chief source of expectation and excitement, does not furnish, by the mail just arrived, a scrap of intelligence worth recording,' the same publication wrote on 6 December 1847, showing perhaps a trace of frustration and disappointment.

This was the situation that continued into the first quarter of the New Year as well. In the absence of real political or military turmoil, attention turned elsewhere and news that would otherwise figure deeper in newspapers surfaced on its front pages. There was speculation that the ruler of Oudh was misgoverning his territory. The Maharani at Gwalior had offered a bribe of 2 lakh (a lakh is 100,000) rupees to a Major Stevens. The Nizam of Hyderabad owed a large amount of money to the East India Company and there was speculation on the expected British interference in Hyderabad affairs in consequence. Smallpox had also broken out in Hyderabad. Further afield in Afghanistan, Dost Mohammad, the ruler of Kabul, was having the usual and interminable problems with rivals to the throne and family and was rumoured to be seeking asylum within British India.

On the commercial front, the opium trade with China was booming and a strong speculative rise in opium prices was developing. Opium exports from Calcutta alone were impressive. 21,649 chests had been exported the previous season, and this season (1848) 28,705 had been sent – an increase of more than 30 per cent. There had been thoughts in certain quarters that the speculators bidding up the prices in Calcutta bore similarities to the Tulip mania or the South

Sea Bubble of earlier times. At Calcutta, the seat of British power, the absorbing topic was still the failure of the Union Bank of Calcutta and its consequences. Sir T. Turton, the Ecclesiastical Registrar of Calcutta, had also been making headlines having embezzled, it was said, upwards of £180,000 of public money.

Nevertheless there remained significant interest in the Punjab, the vast state now being effectively ruled by a British Resident, a consequence of the First Anglo-Sikh War two years earlier. In the absence of more important news, anecdotes and smaller trivia from the Punjab were dissected. There was less fear of attacks on lone Europeans in the city of Lahore, it was reported. British soldiers were now allowed to walk singly throughout the city. In Peshawar and other provinces, the holding of the local Durbar on Sunday had been abandoned in deference to British religious tastes by the Sikh Governor. Tej Singh, the Commander of the Sikh army, had even proposed, irrespective of Hindu belief, that cows should be allowed to be slaughtered at Lahore for the consumption of Europeans despite no request from Henry Lawrence, the Resident. The Azan, the loud Muslim call for prayer from the minarets of mosques, was being allowed in the Sikh capital again by the Durbar following a suggestion by the Resident. Another speculative issue being mooted in the absence of more important news was whether the introduction of windmills into the plains of the Punjab for raising underground water in the more arid areas would be profitable.

Attention sometimes turned to the political agents that now ruled the state and their enviable position. So little was there to do in Lahore that a correspondent of the *Delhi Gazette* in the city wrote during the month of April a rather damning indictment of how easy the lives of the Resident's assistants at Lahore could be. Describing the political agents being 'enthroned' in chairs under fans, he said that 'they give audiences to dependent princes and dictate a *sab acha* diary to a clerk while quietly picking teeth after breakfast' (*sab acha* meaning all is fine). Although life wasn't quite so idyllic and there were some criticisms of the article, it nevertheless suggested a life of indolence in a conquered country with its bureaucracy entirely oriented to receiving orders from the thin British layer of administrators that had been imposed on it over the last year.

British political agents and administrators had spread out to rule the Lahore provinces after the recent war, frequently on their own and with no British force to back them, the country seemingly so well pacified as to allow of this. Only one of the Sikh provinces did not have a British political agent. That was the province of Multan in the far south, ruled by the governor Dewan Mulraj. This was to change shortly. In relation to this, the *Delhi Gazette* featured a quite small and innocuous report on 12 April 1848 regarding the progress of two British officers travelling to Multan city. 'Mr P. Vans Agnew accompanied by Lieut Anderson had left for Mooltan,' the report read. 'They will have a hot season and the usual hard work, which we have attempted elsewhere to describe, to encounter and have no house to get into.' The Governor of Multan had decided to resign. This was an opportune moment to assign a British political agent to the province and Frederick Currie, the new British Resident, had despatched one of his assistants, Patrick Vans Agnew, and an assistant to effectively govern the province. The hot season was beginning and as the temperature inexorably rose, many of the Europeans across India were considering packing for their annual trip to the hill stations to escape the heat and dust of the summer. Multan was one of the hottest places in India during summer. An arid climate far from the cooling effect of the sea ensured extreme temperatures, averaging nearly 50 °C and regularly topping this. It was a long journey, and on 4 April the two British officers had set out in leisurely fashion on boats down the Ravi River from Lahore to avoid the heat and dust of an overland journey and to unwittingly trigger a war.

'Anyone but a civilian would have foreseen that to send Vans Agnew and Anderson down to Multan at the time, and in the manner selected, was almost sure to produce an ebullition of feeling, and of violence. It was very like rolling a live shell with a lit fuse into a well-stored magazine, the chances in both cases being very decidedly in favour of an explosion', the *Calcutta Review* later declared confidently, albeit with hindsight. But despite the murmurings of war, at the time it was anything but obvious that the spark for conflict would come from this city and at this time; Multan was far away, and the grievances of the city garrison little known or cared about in the Sikh capital of Lahore or in British Calcutta. Herbert Edwardes, one of the British political agents operating in the Punjab and directly involved in the opening encounters of the war, summed it up in frustration: 'There are things in this rebellion hard to be understood.' This was a feeling no doubt shared by many at the time. For if Agnew and Anderson, or in fact any of the other main protagonists on either side in the coming war, had been asked as to the probability of a breakout of hostilities a few days hence, they would have regarded it as practically non-existent. Below the surface, however, resentment against the present state of matters had been growing steadily around Multan and around the country.

***

The Sikh Empire had been founded by Ranjit Singh, a one-eyed, diminutive teenager and inheritor of a few villages in turn-of-the-century Punjab. Capturing Lahore in 1799 while not yet nineteen years of age and making it his capital, Ranjit would rapidly consolidate his hold over the entire Punjab region and Kashmir during the three decades. His misfortune, perhaps, was that the East India Company had already laid claim over the rest of India by this stage. If this had not been the case, the general consensus in British circles in India was that Ranjit Singh would have undoubtedly reached both Calcutta in the east and Mysore to the south and made himself sole master of India in his own lifetime.

Ranjit Singh had never contemplated expanding southwards across the Sutlej River, for this would bring him into conflict with the massive resources of the East India Company. The East India Company, too, never mooted any adventures north of the Sutlej. Governor-Generals, Commander-in-Chiefs, British diplomats and other assorted visitors alike were beguiled by the self-made Maharajah and his natural charm, invariably referring to him as 'the great Ranjit' or the 'Lion of the Punjab'. From a military perspective they realised his army was formidable and they preferred him as an ally and a strong bulwark against any supposed French, Russian or Afghan tribal intrusions into India. The relationship between the two states therefore remained cordial. Ranjit died in 1839, leaving the legacy of a powerful organised state, a full treasury and a remarkable army, trained and drilled to Western standards and able to compete on par with a European equivalent. The years following his death had not been favourable for the Lahore state, however. Without his guiding strength, the vitality of the state vanished. None of his sons inherited his character and all but one died in the intrigues and power struggles that followed his death. Bureaucrats and opportunists without the necessary wherewithal and skills to control the army inherited the kingdom. Endlessly called in by different factions to help tip the scales, the army increasingly held power, with the Sikh garrison in the capital becoming a new praetorian guard.

There was a general dread of the 'punchayts', the republican army committees, who by 1845 decided all affairs in Lahore politics, usually with the musket and bayonet. The Vizier, or Prime Minister of the state, Lal Singh, in desperation had thrown the Sikh army across the border in order to occupy the praetorians with a war against the British power. A liberal amount of treachery was used by Lal Singh and the Sikh Commander-in-Chief Tej Singh to ensure victories for the British at the battles of Mudki, Ferozeshah and Sabraon. But while the subsequent Treaty of Lahore of March 1846 had weakened the state, the more recent Treaty of Bhyrowal, signed in January 1847, had gone much further. The new treaty had effectively handed over the governing of the state to the British Resident.

There was increasing discontentment at the developing British influence in the country among the general population. It was generally agreed in the towns and villages that the British were taking the country 'by degrees'. Slowly and surely, the concessions of the listless Lahore Durbar had left the British Resident and his collection of assistants with all the power. Indeed, John Lawrence and Frederick Currie, the later Residents, rarely called in the Lahore Durbar ministers now except to inform or discuss decisions already made regarding the running of the state.

A vast number of former Sikh soldiers, now unemployed, could be seen all round the country, begging for food or turning to the plough for which they had little training or desire. Superlative soldiers and gunners, weaned and trained by Ranjit Singh and his generals for many years, they looked with enthusiasm on any opportunity that could bring back the glories of the Ranjit years and throw off the developing British yoke at the same time.

Henry Lawrence, the first Resident at Lahore, appears to have been generally liked and he in turn had an open empathy for the Sikh nation. But Lawrence had assistants who were delegated power. These political agents spread through the Punjab after the recent treaty and became the effective viceroys of the Resident by the beginning of 1848. They were sole military command, deputy judge advocate, sessions judge and revenue settlement officer all rolled into one. With control of military, financial and judicial command of these provinces, they effectively replaced the Sikh governors, although these were left in place as titular heads.

The exploits, as it were, of Lawrence's young men, as they were called, were highly visible and made newspaper headlines during the year of 1847. Frequently travelling alone and without a British force with them, they confidently made all decisions, ignoring the Sikh hierarchy, causing as yet silent resentment with the regional governors and local officials. For the Sikh soldiers, too, being commanded by lone British officers and agents was galling. This was especially so in the more westerly provinces like Bannu, Peshawar and Hazara, which had not seen a conquering British army. Not all were impressed with their stories and the effect these men had in the Punjab.

'I was not surprised at what had occurred,' wrote George Campbell, one of the political assistants in the Cis-Sutlej Sikh states already under British supremacy and later Lt Governor of Bengal. 'I had always prophesied that the arrangement of 1848 would not succeed. The native government leaders and army were maintained, but they were wholly overridden by a set of young political who magnified their exploits in their communications to the press, but irritated and alienated the Sikhs.'

George Clerk, the Governor of Bombay, and formerly the agent at Ferozepore, responsible for much diplomacy with the Punjab, had predicted this policy would end in trouble and that a greater military force should always be sent with the political agents. Sir Hugh Gough, the British Commander-in-Chief, in retrospect had misgivings on the imposition of the new de facto governors without a sufficiently strong accompanying British military force to awe the population and local Sikh garrisons. 'This policy of such interference may be very questionable, as any attack upon our people must involve us; and such attack becomes not only possible but probable, when the object is unpopular and those ordered to carry it out wholly unprotected,' he wrote in his private letters after the killing of Agnew and Anderson in Multan.

The situation would not be helped by the change in Residents in late 1848 when the ailing but warm Henry Lawrence left the Punjab and the businesslike but cold John Lawrence and latterly Frederick Currie took his place in turn. There was a general perception that had Henry Lawrence stayed the war would never have taken place, his more diplomatic touch being sufficient to smooth any ruffled feathers.

There were other reasons as well. One of the most emotive issues in the Punjab at this time was the incarceration of the Maharani of Lahore, Jind Kaur, in mid-1847 and her eventual exile into British territory the following year. Accused of intrigues against the British, who had by now made themselves comfortable at Lahore, she had been banished from the palace and was being kept under close guard in a provincial town 40 km west of the capital. This had been taken as a national insult around the country, the Maharani being a widow of Ranjit Singh, a firm friend of the British during his lifetime. Her exile to British territory would be used as a rallying cry to encourage soldiers to defect to the nationalist cause over the coming months. In the eyes of many, only one step remained for the British to end the pretence of a Sikh government; this was for the British to throw the mask off and assume power openly, for the Lahore Government had been totally eclipsed by this time, and what the population feared and discussed was the eventual dethronement of the young Maharajah.

And lastly there were the curious prophesies among the more superstitious of the population that the end was nigh for British rule in Punjab, prophecies and rumours that had begun reaching British ears also. These had begun circulating widely in the Punjab in early 1848, forecasting the end of British domination exactly two and a half years after the end of the first war. No one knew of the origins of these prophesies, but before the events at Multan and in the wake of them they became common talk, and seemed to capture the public imagination. Some mentioned Mulraj, the Governor of Multan, as the person who would free the state from the Firangis (Europeans). Some even named dates on which the insurrection would begin.

\*\*\*

The reasons for the outbreak of the Second Anglo-Sikh War are complex. In order to make the tale clearer to the reader, therefore, I have decided to begin the narrative at an appropriate point, specifically the end of the First Anglo-Sikh war. When it did break out, the conflict was almost a year in length, including long intervals, and would be fought in two major theatres, in the province and city of Multan and near to Lahore, 400 km upstream from Multan between the Chenab and Jhelum rivers. There were also several minor theatres, for rebellions in Jalandhar, Hazara, Peshawar and Bannu provinces occurred in parallel with events unfolding elsewhere. All these events fall into several distinct phases of time, however, and therefore I have organised the book chapters in four separate sections. Specifically these are 'Prelude', 'Insurrection', 'War' and 'Dissolution'. The first section, 'Prelude', begins with the cessation of the first war in February 1846 and ends with resignation of Dewan Mulraj, the Governor of Multan, in April 1849. This period encompassed two years of developing British control of the Lahore state, countered by plots and intrigues by nationalists with opposing motives. There would be the aborted rebellions in Kangra and Kashmir and the subsequent trial and exile of Lal Singh, the Vizier of the Lahore state by the British Government. Brought in effectively to destroy the overbearing and untrusted Sikh army, the East India Company representatives found it relatively easy to dominate the timorous Lahore Durbar. Threatened with a removal of the stabilising British garrison, the Lahore Durbar would surrender all power when, in December 1846, the Treaty of Bhyrowal was signed. The treaty effectively made the British Resident all powerful in every department of state. In the oft-quoted words of the chronicler John Clark Marshman, 'an officer of the Company's artillery became, in fact, the successor to Ranjit Singh'. The only establishment outside of the government that could challenge this turn of events was the Sikh monarchy. The Maharani, Jind Kaur, therefore quickly became the focus and financier for nationalist elements in Lahore. Information of her intriguing with these cliques reaching the British Resident would lead to her exile from Lahore Fort and virtual incarceration in mid-1847.

The second section, 'Insurrection', deals with the five-month period beginning mid-April 1848 and commences with the arrival of the two British officers, Agnew and Anderson, at Multan ostensibly to take over the running of the province. An unexpected altercation between a drug-addled soldier and the two officers in the city fortress would lead to their murders and a trigger for the discontented city garrison to commence an unplanned insurrection.

Intimidated by his soldiery, the Governor of Multan, Dewan Mulraj, would become the rather unlikely leader of an even more unlikely rebellion. A Hindu Khatri (trader caste) cum bureaucrat with a rather nervous disposition, a less-than-imposing physique and with no military experience, he had none of the dash, imposing features and aristocratic connections the bulk of the Sikh soldiers envisaged in a champion of the Khalsa army. Consequently, his wealth attracted the more mercenary elements to his cause but never the veteran Sikh soldiers of the army in any quantity. 'A fish caught in a strong current' was the popular, and largely correct, perception of him in the British press in India during this time as he vacillated between surrender and boldly riding the tiger of his own unruly troops.

Interestingly enough, there never would be a proper enquiry into the murders of the two officers. It was mooted later that many of the high Multan officials and officers who had enthusiastically sided with Mulraj and the garrison early in the conflict only to desert him later for the British side would be implicated. Bringing these allies to trial would cause embarrassment for the British Government of India.

The first five months of the conflict turned out to be a curious war by proxy. Herbert Edwardes, the British political agent in the trans-Indus area of the Derajat, immediately countered Mulraj's mercenaries with an equally ragtag bunch of his own Muslim mercenaries as well as receiving aid from the irregular army of Bhawulpore, a pro-British Muslim state across the Sutlej River. The fact that neither Mulraj nor the killer of Agnew and Anderson were Sikh was one of the more curious features of the war at this time, and was remarked upon by no few people in high circles both in the Lahore Durbar and in Calcutta. Mulraj and the assassin were Hindus in what was an overwhelmingly Muslim section of the Punjab. The garrison of the city too had few Sikh soldiers. Perhaps because of this, it was never clearly identified as a new Anglo-Sikh War in its initial stages, rather it was designated a local insurrection. This designation would actually remain from the first shot to the last, the war being carried out by the East India Company, for public consumption at least, in the name of the Maharajah of Lahore, its ally, against 'rebels' to the authority of the Lahore Government.

Ally or not, the Earl of Dalhousie, the Governor-General, was nevertheless determined that heavy reparations would have to be paid by the Lahore Durbar for the insult to the British Government. The annexation of the Multan province from Punjab was mooted, or alternatively a severe financial penalty on the Sikh state for its inability to control its soldiers. The fact that the state, to all intents and purposes, was being governed by the British cut no ice with Dalhousie.

During the months following the murders there would be various manoeuvres by the armies of Mulraj and Edwardes, ending in the battles of Kyneerie and Sadoosam. The rebellion faded as a victorious Herbert Edwardes moved with his force towards the city and prepared for a siege. Only the British siege guns necessary to batter the city into submission delayed the ending of the insurrection at this point, and these guns duly arrived along with a British force under General Whish. By the end of August 1848, therefore, five months after the killing of the two British officers, a large and motley collection of Muslim mercenary tribesmen from the trans-Indus region under Herbert Edwardes, irregular Muslim troops from Bhawulpore under Lt Lake, Sikh army regulars sent from Lahore under General Shere Singh, European regulars of the East India Company and their Bengal sepoy counterparts under General Whish encircled the city as a formal siege was begun. The suburbs were largely captured, and the fall of the walled city and fortress was expected shortly.

With the city expected to fall in a matter of days, attention unexpectedly turned 500 km to the north of Multan. Here, in the hilly province of Hazara, Chutter Singh, the Sikh governor and father of General Shere Singh, had begun his own insurrection in early August. In due course Shere Singh would decide to aid his father in the nationalist cause. This happened in dramatic fashion on 14 September 1848 and caused the immediate lifting of the siege at Multan and the retreat of the besieging British force. It also definitively signalled the beginning of a clear war as opposed to rebellion, as much of the Sikh army at Bannu and Peshawar, previously unwilling to commit to Mulraj, now began flocking to the banner of the popular Sikh general.

The third, and largest, section of the book covers the war, the period between 14 September 1848 and 21 March 1849. Two smaller encounters at Ramnuggar and Sadulpore between the Sikh and British forces foreshadowed the dramatic and confused battle at Chillianwala. Subsequent to this and the fall of Multan, the union of the two British armies of Whish and Gough would prove far too irresistible. Lack of food, supplies and funds forced Shere Singh into a risky gamble, a march to Lahore. With the river crossings controlled by British forces, however, this proved impossible. At the decisive Battle of Gujrat, called the 'battle of the guns' for its reliance on heavy artillery, Gough with his superior resources comfortably beat the Sikh army. The brought an end to the war, with the surrender of the main Sikh army at the city of Rawalpindi to Major-General Sir Walter Gilbert.

This section also covers what had now become very much the secondary theatre of battle, covering both the preparations and the subsequent second siege and capture of Multan by the British. Besieged by 15,000 British troops and as many allies, the city and fortress were subjected to perhaps the heaviest bombardment of any city in the nineteenth century. Over seventy pieces of heavy artillery would throw over 40,000 pieces of shot and shell into the doomed city and fortress before the garrison capitulated.

The fourth section, 'Dissolution', covers the period immediately following the war and the winding up of the Lahore state by the British. Annexation had already been decided on by Dalhousie, and the Punjab passed into the maw of the East India Company, less than ten years after the passing of its founder. Elaborating on the fate of the royal family of Lahore after the war would fill a book in itself. The narrative, however, would not be complete without an insight into the unfortunate lives of its two main individuals, the young Maharajah and his mother. Both experienced a tragic existence after the war, the former dying alone and in penury in a modest Paris hotel. At the age of ten he had been separated from his mother and brought up in European society in Fatehgarh, an exclusive British outpost in Uttar Pradesh. Influenced by those around him, he would convert to Christianity and move to England. There he would spend the bulk of his time living the carefree life of a dispossessed aristocrat on an East India Company pension. It was only many years later that his thoughts returned to re-establishing himself as the Maharajah of Lahore. After an abortive journey to India and a fruitless attempt to enlist the aid of the Russians, a penniless Duleep Singh died in France at the age of fifty-five.

His mother, the Maharani Jind Kaur, had a shorter and equally tragic life. After being divested of power after the Treaty of Bhyrowal, she would attempt to help nationalist groups in plots against the British at Lahore, resulting in incarceration by the British authorities. Escaping and receiving sanctuary in Nepal, she would spend eleven years in Kathmandu as an unwanted guest living on a modest pension. Brought together with her son in 1861, she would travel with him to London where, with her health sapped, she died a premature death, half-blind and with her legendary beauty gone, at the age of forty-six.

\*\*\*

An understanding of the terrain of the Punjab allows for a better grasp of the reasons for the movements of troops and the nature of the war in general. The First Anglo-Sikh War had been fought entirely in the flat lands south of the Sutlej River, which marked the effective boundary between Sikh and British possessions. The lay of the land and demographics of the Punjab, though, would become much more of an issue in the second war. While the Punjab is largely flat in its centre, this is not strictly the case towards the west as one heads across the Jhelum River and the mountains of Afghanistan or northwards towards Jammu and Kashmir. There, the ground becomes progressively more hilly and difficult.

The Punjab (*Punj-ab* literally meaning land of five rivers) can be divided conveniently into six distinct sections or doabs (a piece of territory between two rivers). From east to west, the Sutlej, Beas, Ravi, Chenab and Jhelum rivers merge into the all-powerful Indus. The Sutlej, the easternmost river, formed the boundary between the Sikh Empire of Ranjit Singh and the East India Company for well-nigh forty years. The Sikh states south of the Sutlej who had accepted British supremacy were commonly called the Cis-Sutlej states. Fearful of being swallowed up by the much bigger Sikh state to their north, they preferred the safety of British hegemony and played no part both in the first and second wars. The Manjha doab, the area between the Sutlej and the Beas River, was the richest and best cultivated territory of the Punjab. This had been annexed by the East India Company after the first war. Marking its east was the hilly territory of the Kangra area, effectively the foothills of the Himalayas further east and where there were few roads. To the west of the Manjha lay the Bari doab, the territory between the Beas/Sutlej combination and Ravi River. This territory was also well developed and contained the principal cities of Lahore (the capital), Amritsar and Multan much to the south. Still further west, between the Ravi and the Chenab, was the Rechna doab. This, too, was prime farming territory, with much ground under cultivation although to the south there was more jungle. Beyond the Chenab and bounded by the Jhelum River was the Jech doab, where much of the campaign would take place. This otherwise flat doab is scarred by a 50 km-long piece of hilly territory beginning north of Chillianwala and Rasul and heading north-east towards Bhimber, the first signs of the progressively more uneven ground to the west. Only the Kharian Pass, roughly midway, allows easy access to the territory west and the Jhelum. Otherwise a traveller must head either south or north to bypass the hilly ground, thereby losing several days in the process.

The Sind Sagur doab between the Jhelum and the Indus River, the largest of the doabs, has a quite different nature to the easterly doabs, being the home of the Salt Range mountains. Across the Indus lies the rich circular vale of Peshawar, its western end marked by the famous Khyber Pass, the natural boundary between India and mountains of Afghanistan. 19 km east of the pass is the city of Peshawar and the territory's administrative centre. The city and area had formerly been an Afghan stronghold until, a dozen years previously in 1836, the Afghans had been ejected by Ranjit Singh's armies. The area was fertile and along with the city of Peshawar, with a population of 50,000, provided good revenue. Also providing good revenue was the well-cultivated valley of Bannu, south across the mountains from Peshawar; likewise the province of Hazara to the north-east of Peshawar, across the Indus. Much of the territory here is hilly and many of its roads utilised narrow passes which, if defended properly, could easily stop the progress of larger forces. The main city in this province was Haripur, 35 km north of Hassan Abdul. Further to the north of Hazara lay Jammu and Kashmir, formerly of the Sikh Empire but now carved off and made independent after the First Anglo-Sikh War. A former tributary of Ranjit Singh, Gulab Singh, had been made Maharajah of the territory by the British after the First Anglo-Sikh War.

By far the most well-known route cutting through the Punjab from the mountains of the Khyber to the metropolis of Lahore and into India was the ancient road now known as the Grand Trunk Road (or GT road). From Lahore, the road passed through the Kharian Pass and across the Jhelum River to Jhelum town. From here the route passed the imposing fortress of Rhotas to Dina and on through the narrow defile of the Bakrala Pass before traversing the Salt Range Mountains and reaching Rawalpindi. Leaving Rawalpindi, the road crossed the Margalla (or 'cut-throat') Pass to reach Hassan Abdul and Attock. Across the Indus, the route headed due west to the cities of Nowshera and Peshawar and on to the Khyber Pass. Used by numerous invaders in the previous centuries moving east towards Lahore and Delhi, it would be used again by the Sikh commander Shere Singh, the Afghan army under the Kabul ruler Dost Mohammad and a pursuing General Gilbert, in charge of the British force during the closing stages of the war.

While the plains of the Punjab had little if any difficult terrain, the rivers were an entirely different matter. The Sutlej, Beas, Rabi, Chenab and Jhelum all move in a broadly south-westerly direction into the Indus and complicate the advance or retreat of an army, each stream providing, in military terms, an obstacle or strong defensive line as may be the case. The knowledge and control of fords or the command of boats on these rivers was therefore essential and an important part, as in previous centuries, in gaining an advantage over an enemy.

In terms of demographics, the bulk of the population of the Punjab at the time lay in the richer, more cultivated Manjha, Bari and Rechna doabs to the east with much smaller populations westwards and northwards into Hazara and Peshawar. The Manjha territory, along with the Bari doab, formed the heartland of the Sikh population, and from here Ranjit Singh used to draw the flower of the Sikh army. Beginning from the Rechna doab, the more westerly the area, the heavier the proportion of its Muslim population and the more lawless and inimical to Sikh rule. This reached its zenith in the wild, distant western mountainous areas of Bannu, Peshawar and Derajat across the Indus, where the concept of submitting to taxation and government was largely alien. Kidnap, murder and other sorts of violence were rampant, with robbers and cut-throats frequenting the highways. The people here were largely Pathan and, as the chronicler Sir William Lee-Warner amusingly put it, 'sworn enemies to civilisation'.

\*\*\*

The Second Anglo-Sikh War, unfortunately, would be one of the last major conflicts not comprehensively covered by the new discipline of battlefield photography. It was in 1847, just a year prior to events at Multan, that the first grainy daguerreotypes were being taken of the American–Mexican War, far away on another continent. The wars that followed shortly afterwards would suffer no such problem. Roger Fenton and James Robertson just four years later in the Crimean War (1853–6) and Felice Beato in the aftermath of the Indian Mutiny of 1857 proved to be the pioneers of this new field. Nevertheless, some tantalising glimpses into the period both prior to and during the war survive, remarkably including some portraits of several of the protagonists. It was to be the forty-three-year-old Scot John McCosh, an amateur photographer who had entered the East India Company's army as an assistant surgeon in 1831, who would take the first images of Punjab and Lahore. McCosh had begun dabbling in photography in the period between 1843 and 1844. However, his chance to move into the Punjab came after the end of the First Anglo-Sikh War in 1846 when he moved into the newly annexed Jalandhar territory. He was transferred to British-controlled Ludhiana later, before moving to Lahore during the eve of the outbreak of the Second Anglo-Sikh War. McCosh served with the 31st Bengal Native Infantry (NI) and later the 2nd Bengal European Regiment, to whom he was appointed surgeon on 1 March 1849, and he was present at the battles of Sadulpore, Chillianwala and Gujrat. Unfortunately none of his photographs, if he ever took any of the battlefields, survive. In the National Army Museum lies an album of his original works. The photographs include the only extant portrait of Dewan Mulraj, the Governor of Multan, as well as one of Patrick Vans Agnew, the political agent whose death would trigger the conflict, taken at either Jalandhar or Ferozepore before he left for Lahore and on to his mission to Multan on 31 March 1848. The album contains a space marked 'Chutter Singh and his sons', although the image is sadly missing. Chutter Singh and his son Shere Singh were instrumental in turning the Multan rebellion into war and leading the main Sikh army. One of McCosh's other images includes a view of Lahore Fort complete with British sentries, perhaps inadvertently capturing the coming state of things. McCosh undoubtedly attempted to capture more images of the Sikh leaders and other prisoners but was refused permission by Frederick Currie, the Lahore Resident at the time, who did not want the prisoners 'bothered'. The image of Mulraj that survives was perhaps taken without the Resident's permission.

***

The political repercussions of the war and the subsequent annexation of the Punjab would be profound, not just in the Punjab but in the whole Indian subcontinent. After the war, for the next hundred years the East India Company would find a fresh new source of soldiers, more reliable and more trustworthy than the sepoys used during the previous century of its rule. Sikh and Punjabi soldiers would form the new backbone of the British army in India. The fall of the last independent kingdom in India meant British possessions now stretched from Bengal to the natural frontier of India at the Khyber Pass and gave Governor-General Dalhousie the impetus to consolidate and expand British acquisitions on the subcontinent, something that would unwittingly lead to the Indian Mutiny eight years later.

The geographic Punjab which formed the core of the Sikh Empire lies divided now. The vast bulk of it falls into what could be described as northern Pakistan. Peshawar, Bannu and the North-Western Frontier areas wrested from the Afghans by Ranjit Singh are still as turbulent as they were when the Sikh army patrolled them over 170 years ago. The province of Kashmir, awarded to Gulab Singh after the first war, is divided between Pakistan and India and still being contested. The Sikh possessions east of Kashmir have been reclaimed by China. The Manjha, the Jalandhar doab and the hill states, along with the other Cis-Sutlej states, are now the only segments that fall into the Indian Punjab.

The battlefields – excluding the more minor affairs in Jalandhar, Kangra, Bannu, Hazara and the Derajat – lie exclusively in what is now Pakistan, forming a triangle in the Jech doab between the Chenab and Jhelum rivers. Ramnuggar (now called Rasulnuggar), Sadulpore and Gujrat lie on the banks of the Chenab River, around 100 km north-west of Lahore, while Chillianwala lies a further 45 km to the north-west of Ramnuggar. Multan lies around 350 km to the south-west of Lahore.

The great fortress of the city where the initial spark for the war was lighted no longer exists. What was left of the tottering remains was demolished by the British a few years after the war. A large park exists in its place, however, preventing encroachment or new development and thus making it easy for a visitor to imagine the structure. Wandering around the park's circumference, a visitor can still sense and make out where the gates of this powerful fortress would have been and where the altercation between an angry local soldier high on cannabis and an imperious British political agent took place.

# PRELUDE

There is not, in my judgement, the slightest trust to be placed in any person or any party here. There is an utter want of truth and honour in all; every man is ready to plot, to intrigue, to cabal against his neighbour – there is no oath and no bond which they will not take, and take in order to be the better able to deceive.

John Lawrence, Resident at Lahore in 1848, later Viceroy of India

The majority of the servants of the Durbar, and of the Durbar itself, are mere creatures of circumstance, utterly without nationality.

George Campbell, Deputy Commissioner of Cis-Sutlej Sikh states, 1849

# Treaties and Banquets

Beginning on the evening of 10 February 1846 and continuing for the next three days, long lines of British East India Company troops could be seen streaming across a pontoon bridge to the right bank of the Sutlej River. Over 20,000 strong in all, they were accompanied by an army of camp followers four times as large, plus horse artillery guns, heavy siege guns pulled by elephants and over 100,000 bullock and cattle pulling baggage wagons and ammunition hackeries. As the night grew colder and the light faded, numerous torches and campfires quickly lit up the banks of the river on both sides. The Sutlej River, in the north of India, formed the border between the possessions of the Sikh Empire and those of the East India Company. From where they were crossing, at Khoonda Ghat, close to the nearby British base of Ferozepore, a straight road led to the Sikh capital of Lahore, less than 70 km away to the west.

The Battle of Sabraon, the final conflict of the First Anglo-Sikh War, had taken place earlier the same day with the Sikh army defeated. Events would move rapidly after the British crossing of the river. By the night of the 10th, the vanguard of the army was encamped at the small town of Kasur, a march of 15 km from the river. Here, the village fort was occupied. The next day, the bulk of the units that had fought at Sabraon began making their crossing. On the 12th, more units crossed after an eleven-gun salute to Major-General Sir Robert Dick, who had fallen in the battle. The rest of the army crossed over on the 13th, along with Sir Hugh Gough, the British Commander-in-Chief in India. The following day, the Governor-General of India, Sir Henry Hardinge, who had accompanied the British force through the recent battles, crossed the river to join Gough in his advance to Lahore. There was no opposing force on the right bank of the river. Intrigue and treachery had hampered the Sikh army's efforts in its conflict with the East India Company during the previous two months.

Ever since the death of Ranjit Singh, the founder of the Sikh Empire seven years earlier, the state had been racked with internal problems. A catalogue of poor successors had taken the throne and positions of power with the help of the army, becoming both dependant on its support and ensuring its transformation into a new praetorian guard. Shortly before the outbreak of the First Anglo-Sikh War, the army held all power and, on a whim, soldiers had summoned and casually killed the previous Vizier or prime minister of the state. On the parade ground of the army, in front of thousands of watching soldiers, silent and in perfect order, the Vizier offered a huge bribe of money for his life. Seconds later, he had been dragged off his elephant and shot dead. The Lahore treasury was bare from the inducements offered to the soldiers in recent years. A new Vizier, Lal Singh, and a new Commander-in-Chief of the army, Tej Singh, had recently been chosen. These men, anxious not to fall victim to the soldiers' caprices, had actively encouraged the Sikh army to cross the Sutlej, hoping to weaken or destroy it in a war with the East India Company. The ruling clique preferred British supremacy and the accompanying stability and safety to the rough attentions of their own soldiers.

Despite these handicaps, the Sikh army had come near to overpowering the East India Company forces at the Battle of Ferozeshah seven weeks earlier, part of a bitterly fought campaign of five battles. Only the unnecessary withdrawal of both Sikh armies had saved Gough's force, which had run out of ammunition and found itself in desperate straits. In the final battle at Sabraon, however, re-energised by reinforcements and fresh supplies, Gough had comprehensively defeated the Sikh army posted on the left bank of the Sutlej. With the Sikh army's capacity now largely destroyed, the Lahore Government made preparations to surrender the Punjab to the advancing British.

Hardinge had already made his mind up as to what he would demand from the Lahore Government as reparations to bring the war to a conclusion. Waging an extended war to annex the whole state would be impossible in the present situation for a whole host of reasons. Not all the Sikh army had been engaged, and many fresh Sikh army units still remained to the west of Lahore. These could decide to continue the war along with the remaining Sikh force north of Sabraon. The Sikh army, despite its losses, still had an arsenal of well over 250 guns available. Ranjit Singh during his lifetime had also taken care to construct or maintain major fortresses and strongpoints like Gobindgarh at Amritsar, Multan, Attock and Jamrud to guard the country. These, along with hundreds of lesser forts dotted around the country and the major fortified cities, posed a significant problem for any would-be invader, slowing any advance to a crawl. The advance through the Punjab proper would be very different from the recent fighting south of the Sutlej.

There was also the question of protecting the already long and vulnerable supply lines from Meerut and Delhi through hostile territory. The British force was exhausted and the European regiments, the backbone of the army, had taken substantial casualties in the recent battles along the Sutlej. Only 3,200 of the more than 7,500 Europeans previously available were now in a fit state to continue a protracted war, if this was to be the case. The accumulation of the European regiments in the north of India and any potential continued absence left the British hold on its Indian possessions to the south in a vulnerable state. The territory of Kashmir to the north, where an advance might be required, posed its own problem. A mountainous territory difficult to traverse with its narrow mountain passes, it could easily be defended by a small force. During the wintry six months of the year, the deep snow made many of the passes impossible.

Not least of the problems on Hardinge's mind was the approach of the hot season, when the European regiments, not used to the heat, tended to prove vulnerable. The last issue was one of finance. The war had proved costly, and with the East India Company treasury as empty as the one at Lahore, a continuation of the war would be ruinous. This was a point which the Court of Directors of the East India Company in London would make as well. Their wish was to end the war as soon as possible so that the business of profit could be addressed. 'The Sikh army may rally, declaring the terms to be degrading, & shut themselves up in their fortified towns. I have very scanty means for one or two sieges, & the season is far advanced,' wrote Hardinge on 16 February in his private letters. Mulling over these thoughts prior to and after the Battle of Sabraon, Hardinge was conscious of the necessity of bringing the war to a quick close. In any case there was no need for further war. The alternative and easier prospect was to settle for a peace treaty with a compliant Sikh government content to be subordinate to the British and demand a weakening of the state and its army as far as possible so that it posed no future risk to British power and ambitions.

Hardinge had decided to demand the Jalandhar doab, the area immediately north of the Sutlej and the richest and most well-developed section of the Punjab state. The portion would be easy to maintain, being adjacent to the current British territory and the outposts of Ludhiana and Ferozepore. In addition, the border would be easily defendable, with the Beas River being the new frontier with Lahore. The Kashmir province of the Sikh Empire would also be carved off. 'It was necessary last March to weaken the Sikhs by depriving them of Kashmir. The distance from Kashmir to the Sutlej is 300 miles of very difficult mountainous country, quite impracticable for six months. To keep a British force 300 miles from any possibility of support would have been an undertaking that merited a strait-waistcoat and not a peerage,' Hardinge mused later on the difficulties of occupying this territory. The next best thing was to award it to Gulab Singh, the ruler of the state of Jammu, a nominal Lahore vassal who had signally failed to help the army of his superiors during the recent war. An ambitious and opportunistic man, he was a better choice than a Sikh governor made independent. The Jalandhar doab also bordered Kashmir, making the new tributary well connected to its new paramount power and ensuring his good behaviour. On top of this, large reparations that would hamstring the already bankrupt Lahore state would be demanded.

At Kasur, shortly after crossing the Sutlej, the frontier, Hardinge summed up his demands:

A diminution of the strength of such a warlike nation on our weakest frontier seems to me to be imperatively required. I have therefore determined to take a strong and fertile district between the Sutlej and Beas. This will cover Ludhiana and bring us within a few miles of Amritsar with our back to the hills. In a military sense it will be very important – it will weaken the Sikhs and punish them in the eyes of Asia. I shall demand one million and a half in money as compensation; and if I can arrange to make Gulab Singh and the hill tribes independent including Kashmir, I shall have weakened this warlike republic. Its army must be disbanded and reorganised. The numbers of the artillery must be limited. The Maharajah must himself present the keys of Govindghar and Lahore where the terms must be dictated and signed.

Nevertheless, a Sikh government and army, albeit heavily weakened, was strongly desired by the Governor-General at the same time. Hardinge was hesitant in having any Muslim powers or tribes in the ascendancy anywhere in the Punjab or allowing the Afghans to extend their control across the Khyber Pass by overly crippling the Sikh state. Some 200 km west of Lahore began a sea of Islam stretching all the way to Europe, and he had no intention of allowing that border to move eastwards from the Indus to the Sutlej. The Punjab was to be reduced to a buffer state, strong enough to keep the unruly tribes along the Indus at bay but incapable of ever challenging the British again. Thus the Sikh Kingdom would continue to police the dangerous and financially draining border areas with Afghanistan at no cost to the East India Company.

The first meeting between Sikh emissaries from Lahore and the British party was on 15 February. Raja Gulab Singh, the ruler of Jammu, had been given the role of plenipotentiary and asked to open negotiations with the British Government by the Lahore Durbar. Gulab Singh, prior to leaving the capital, had insisted any agreement he brokered with Hardinge must be accepted by the Lahore Government without question, a demand that had been readily accepted. He came accompanied by finance minister Dewan Deena Nath, senior courtier and diplomat Fakeer Nur-Ud-Deen, Dost Mohammad's brother Sultan Mohammad Khan, and various other dignitaries. The party reached the British camp, arriving inexplicably four and a half hours late for the meeting. Presents were offered, a horse with a gold saddle for Hardinge and a horse with a silver saddle for Gough. Gulab Singh was treated very coldly, however, and his presents were not accepted by Hardinge. 'I received the Rajah in Durbar as representative of an offending government, omitting the forms and ceremonies usually observed on the occasion of friendly meetings, and refusing to receive, at that time, the proffered nuzzurs [tributes] and complimentary offerings,' explained Hardinge. Friendly relations would only be restored once the terms of the treaty Hardinge had decided on were accepted. Hardinge's address to Gulab Singh and the other emissaries was in English, being translated into Persian at the same time by a secretary. 'I briefly explained to the Rajah and his colleagues,' recorded Hardinge, 'that the offence which had been committed was most serious, and the conduct of the chiefs in the army was most unwarrantable; that this offence had been perpetrated without the shadow of any cause of quarrel on the part of the British government, in the face of an existing treaty of amity and friendship, and as all Asia had witnessed the injurious conduct of the Sikh nation, retributive justice required that the proceedings of the British government should be of a character which would mark to the whole world that insult could not be offered to the British government, and our provinces invaded by a hostile army, without signal punishment.'

Hardinge directed Gulab Singh to Frederick Currie, the Chief Secretary to Government, and Henry Lawrence, the political agent, for further details of the agreement that was to be signed. Gulab Singh, having already been promised the large province of Kashmir and the higher title of Maharajah as a reward for his neutrality during the war, had nothing to gain by bargaining hard with the British party. Rather it was in his interest, too, to weaken the powerful Sikh army. Nevertheless, the negotiations between Gulab Singh and Currie were extended to several hours for no particular reason other than to give the event some gravitas and assure the Lahore Durbar that Gulab Singh had done his best to preserve the country's honour. The British demands were non-negotiable, and in any case Gulab Singh was quite ready to accept what was offered. Hardinge's terms were severe. Aside from the annexation of the Jalandhar doab, 1.5 million lakh rupees would be demanded as compensation for the war. Of this, half a million was to be paid immediately on the signing of the treaty despite the bare Lahore treasury. The Sikh army was to be severely reduced, from over 80,000 strong to 20,000 infantry and 12,000 cavalry. The surrender of all guns still with the Sikh army (twenty-five in total) and used in the recent war was also demanded. In addition, the country would be ruled by a council of state. A British force would stay for several months to maintain peace while the new government was established, with Henry Lawrence deputed to stay as the representative of the British Government. 'I entirely concur in the policy of Sir H. Hardinge. Ample reparation is made and compensation given for our vast outlay, while we have a power sufficiently strong to repel them (yet not strong enough again to threaten us) between us and the unruly Afghans,' commented Gough on the military implications of the agreement.

Another issue arranged was that the Maharajah of Lahore, Duleep Singh, a young boy only seven years old at the time, must come and submit to the Governor-General the following day in person at the village of Lullianee, the scheduled next stop of the British force as it continued its advance towards Lahore. The message was communicated to Lahore and Duleep Singh was brought to Gulab Singh's camp on the 17th ready to meet Hardinge the next day.

The British force reached the little mud-walled village, a place of cornfields surrounded by jungle 35 km from Lahore, on the 18th. On that evening, Duleep Singh was escorted to the British camp by Gulab Singh, Dewan Deena Nath, Fakeer Nur-ud-Deen and around a dozen other notables of the Sikh Government. No salutes were fired at his arrival, Hardinge having intimated to Gulab Singh that submission by the Maharajah must be tendered in person before he could be received in friendly fashion. The young Maharajah accordingly threw bags of money at Hardinge's feet as a sign of that submission. Duleep Singh was kept with the Governor-General for around an hour and a half. Hardinge refused to discuss the terms of the treaty with him, he being of too tender an age. The discussion instead centred on the fame and wisdom of his father, the late and famous Ranjit Singh, and Hardinge expressed his hopes that Duleep Singh would follow in his footsteps and keep cordial relations with the British. Presents were now offered in return, a musical box with a bird along with fifty trays of other presents.

Thrust into the limelight for the first time in his life, Duleep Singh seemed to have handled it well, although whether he knew the implications of what was going on around him is unlikely. 'The Maharajah,' recorded Gough, 'is a very interesting boy, and showed great nerve, very different from the Gwalior Rajah.' With negotiations, inasmuch as they were, reaching a friendly end, Duleep Singh left the British camp with Hardinge ordering a royal salute on his departure from twenty-one of the British 24-pounders the army had brought with them across the Sutlej. On being asked by Gulab Singh what he wished to do with Duleep Singh, Hardinge decided the Maharajah should accompany the British force to the capital and he was therefore left by the Sikh party with the British force. Meanwhile Gulab Singh had ordered the Sikh army to remain stationary at Raeban, around 30 km east of Lahore, while the British force advanced and occupied the capital. Muslim troops were put in possession of the gates of Lahore with orders that no Sikh contingents from the army at Raeban were to be allowed entry.

The following day the British advance continued and at the village of Kuna Kulch, 15 km west of Lullianee, heavy firing from Lahore was heard for nearly an hour. This happened to be the Lahore Durbar ordering the firing of seven rounds from every gun in the city in celebration of the meeting of the Maharajah and the Governor-General and the restoration of amicable relations. At noon on the 20th, the British force reached Lahore and began setting up camp on the plain of Meean Meer, the parade ground of the Sikh army. A grand procession as part of the entry into the fort of Lahore was planned. The British camp being set up on the south-east of the city and the fort being situated on the north-west, a route through the city was initially planned. However, it was thought the narrow streets would not allow for easy progress and in any case a route round the city's perimeter and a large train of British troops escorting the Maharajah and the British party back to the fort would impress locals further and prove more regal. Two regiments of European cavalry, two regiments of native cavalry, one regiment of irregular horse and two troops of horse artillery under Brig. Cureton were readied.

At 2 p.m., the British party, mounted on elephants, set off in slow and stately fashion from the Governor-General's tent towards the Maharajah's tent 2 km away. The party was headed by Frederick Currie along with Major Lawrence; William Edwardes, the Under Secretary of the Foreign Department; Robert Cust, assistant secretary to the Foreign Department; Charles Hardinge, the Governor-General's son and private secretary; Lt-Col Wood, military secretary to the Governor-General; Capt. Cunningham; Capt. Hardinge; Capt. Napier; and other officers. Before reaching the Maharajah's camp they were met by Gulab Singh and other chiefs halfway. Word was then sent for the Maharajah to be readied by the time the British procession reached his camp. On reaching the camp, Duleep Singh's elephant came forward along with elephants of various other dignitaries of the Lahore court and the two columns merged into one in their travel to the fort. Drawing big crowds, the scene was captured in one of Charles Hardinge's famous sketches made during his stay in Lahore. 'The procession of the Maharajah in his circuit round the city was unique in effect. The colours of the dresses, the line of elephants, contrasting with the display of troops, were a sight not easily to be effaced from our recollection,' he would recall.

A twenty-one-gun salute was fired by the accompanying horse artillery as the joint party reached the fort and alighted from the elephants. They then proceeded into the fort and to the inner chambers of the palace where, in a packed assembly hall Frederick Currie addressed the assembled Sikh courtiers. 'I then observed to the Maharajah and chiefs,' noted Currie, 'that by order of the Right Hon. The Governor-General, I had thus brought the Maharajah, conducted by the British army, to his palace, which his Highness had left for the purpose of tendering submission to the British Government, and of placing himself, his capital and his country, at the mercy of the Governor-General, and requesting pardon for the insult that had been offered; and that the Governor-General had thus restored him to his palace as a mark of favour which he desired to show to the descendant of the late Maharajah Ranjit Singh.'

After concluding the Durbar, a twenty-one-gun salute was fired by the accompanying British horse artillery to mark the occasion. The British party then returned back to their camp but circled the other half of the city that had not been travelled to allow the rest of the population to see the victors. Thus the whole city had been circumvented. 'We did not see one gun upon any part of the walls; all their embrasures were empty,' Currie pointed out as they travelled back to the British camp.

The following day, the Governor-General ordered the chief engineer and his officers to enter the fort for inspection and for the gates of the city and other strongpoints to be marked out for occupation. Strict orders were given for British soldiers not to enter the city as yet to avoid panic, many inhabitants having left the city with their possessions for fear of plundering by the invading army. Only a few soldiers were given passes to visit the city but with escorts by Sikh horsemen.

Early on the morning of 22 February, sections of the Lahore Fort were ordered to be cleared and British troops sent to garrison these strong points to make it apparent to all who controlled the capital and seat of power. Along with the fort, British troops now occupied the Badshahi Masjid, the main city mosque located opposite the fort and eminently defendable due to its high walls, and the Hazuri Bagh, the garden which connected these two structures. The British troops were ordered to be on their best behaviour to instil a confidence in the people of Lahore that the occupation would be a peaceful one and to allow provisions to be forthcoming. 'Supplies of all sorts are willingly brought into our camp and punctually paid for,' Gough would inform Hardinge, 'and I believe that by every class of persons in this vicinity the presence of our troops is felt to be a national benefit; none certainly have had real cause to lament it as a calamity.' On the same day Lal Singh, the inept Vizier, conspicuously absent from the negotiations and meetings at Lullianee, arrived in Lahore and proceeded to give himself up to the British force, mounted on an elephant and with a train of followers. Tej Singh, Commander-in-Chief of the Sikh army, would follow in a day or two.

***

Hardinge would stay in Lahore for another two weeks while preparations for the signing of the treaty were being made, the time largely spent on meetings, parties in the palace with the Lahore Government members, return parties in the British camp and visits to the considerable sights of the historic city. On 23 February Hardinge toured the fort, the Badshahi Masjid and the Hazuri Bagh, where a summer building used by Ranjit Singh was situated.

Although the Lahore Durbar had consented to British demands, the population of Lahore and the environs were unsubdued and several assaults on the soldiers of the British force were already reported during these days. 'It is by no means safe to go about alone far beyond the limits of the camp,' James Coley, one of the chaplains accompanying the British force, recorded, 'The Seekhs in the city and villages around are still as insolent as possible; and, inasmuch as they are practised ruffians and cut-throats, they are not pleasant people for a lonely Faringee to meet with.' A day earlier, a European soldier had gone too far out of the British camp and had been set upon by local villagers and killed. Two British sepoys had also gone into the city, the restrictions on venturing into the city having been lifted by this time, and had been severely assaulted, complete with sabre wounds, although allowed to live. 'The Seekhs are very far from being subdued in spirit; and it is very possible they may rise again next winter or the winter after and give us some more work,' Coley continued, his prediction being closer to the truth than perhaps he would himself have thought.

On the other hand, trade was booming with the British force; the local shopkeepers and businessmen were anxious to take advantage and make money from the huge influx of British soldiers and camp followers, and food supplies and goods were readily forthcoming. It was noted a large number of old Greek coins made of gold, silver and brass were being traded with the British soldiers who had any leanings towards numismatics. It was strongly rumoured in the British camp that the Jewish community in Kabul had set about counterfeiting these coins such was the demand in British circles of that time for any old Greek coins left behind by the departing Macedonians two millennia before. Meanwhile, British strength in Lahore was supplemented on 3 March by the arrival of Charles Napier's force at Lahore from the Sind to the south of the Punjab. For the occasion, a grand dinner was organised by the Governor-General in his tent on 5 March. Sitting with Gough on his right and Napier on the left and with all his officers present, Hardinge eulogised the two men and the army for their conduct during the recent war and numerous toasts and speeches followed, with many loud exclamations of 'Hip, Hip, Hip, hurrah!'

The actual treaty as per British demands was signed on 8 March in Henry Lawrence's tent and was attended by all the ministers of the Lahore Durbar. Duleep Singh was not present but a letter in his name was read out to the assembly asking for British troops to be stationed at Lahore for a further period so that stability could be assured. Lal Singh, the Vizier, had no confidence that he could keep the army under control and the state on an even keel. Having betrayed the Sikh army in the recent war, and conscious of his unpopularity, he was fearful the British force may depart before he could re-establish himself. Hardinge in turn communicated to the Durbar that their proposal must be put in writing. This being agreed to, the meeting was at an end with the signing of the new treaty. The proposal would duly come. There was expressed in a letter from the Vizier an 'earnest and sincere desire of the Durbar that British troops with intelligent officers should, for some months, as circumstances seemed to require, be left at Lahore for the protection of the Maharajah, and his Government'.

The following day at 4 p.m., another ostentatious Durbar was held in Hardinge's state tent for the ratification of the new treaty. With Gough, Napier and a host of European civilians and officers seated on the right half of the tent and Sikh sirdars and Durbar members seated on the left, Hardinge took his place in centre stage seated on a throne. Duleep Singh was brought in by Lal Singh and Gulab Singh, along with around thirty other Durbar members and leading sirdars. He was given a seat on Hardinge's right. Waldemaar, the Prince of Prussia, who had travelled up with the British army and witnessed the recent great battles, was given a seat on his left. Outside, the Governor-General's band played while the proceedings continued. Charles Hardinge, the Governor-General's son, was also at the Durbar. 'The scene was a striking one. The little prince, loaded with Oriental jewellery and with the Sikh aigrette in his turban, looked on with perfect calmness. Whether his intelligence could grasp the peculiarity of his position could not be fathomed; but when the Governor-General rose to address the chiefs his dark eyes became animated, and were fixed on the Lord Sahib dictating terms to the descendant of the great Ranjit.'

In his address, Hardinge laid out his plans for the dismemberment of the Punjab and the limitations to be imposed on the Lahore Army. After each sentence, Currie would translate the words into Persian for the benefit of the Sikh visitors before Hardinge continued. 'For forty years it was the policy of Ranjit Singh to cultivate friendly relations between the two governments; and during the whole of that period the Sikh nation was independent and happy. Let the policy of that able man towards the British Government, be the model for your future imitation,' he declared before specifying British troops would stay in Lahore no longer than the end of the year. This was followed by the obligatory nuzzurs and ceremonies and a salute fired from the British 24- and 32-pounders. A dinner party followed with more speeches and toasts.

The treaty, then, had been amended. The Governor-General had consented to occupy the capital and its fort so that the Lahore Government could get itself in order and reorganise the army and bring stability to the country. There were critics of the policy on both sides. No shortage of people in Lahore would find the extended British stay in Lahore irksome and damaging to the country and it's doubtful that the support of the British troops lent any further gravitas to the Lahore Durbar. For many it gave the opposite impression, that of foreign troops propping up an impotent assembly, treacherous towards its own armed forces.

On the British side there also were doubts over this policy. Sir Charles Napier among others felt the installation of a force at Lahore had too many parallels with what had happened in Kabul a few years earlier and which was still fresh in most people minds. A British garrison could easily be overwhelmed by the Sikh army should it decide to rebel against the new order. Napier, thinking of the risks, volunteered to command the garrison, an offer that was turned down by Hardinge on the grounds of Napier's poor health at the time. For others it was seen as an opportunity; the Lahore Government was patently unfit to rule the country and certainly the nine months remaining would probably be insufficient to put the state on an even keel, allowing for more British intervention in the state. 'This treaty is looked upon by many as a thing patched up for present expediency, to be broken by the Seekhs at the first opportunity,' summed up James Coley, the chaplain with the army. 'It strikes me however that this is the first step to our sovereign possession of the Punjab.'

The celebration over the signing of the treaty was replicated by the Maharajah, a Durbar for the Governor-General being held in his tent and camp on 10 March. One of the things the British officers were most curious about was the famous Koh-i-noor diamond, the largest precious stone in the world, and the diamond was duly asked for and brought out to be shown around to the British party and was the subject of much conversation and attention.

Hardinge had determined to display a show of power at this occasion. All the 110 guns and the 22,000-strong British force that had crossed the Sutlej was paraded before the Maharajah, the Vizier and sirdars along with Gulab Singh and the Lahore population. Hardinge, hearing of his detractors in the policy of not continuing the war to wholly conquer the Punjab, on seeing the troops was heard to utter, 'See those men? There are only 3,200 fit for duty.' He had had nearly 8,000 European troops during the war, he would argue. Continuing the war would have been impossible even had he wished to and if the Lahore Durbar had been unwilling to surrender. Two days after the initial treaty, additional articles were added to the treaty as requested by Lal Singh. Three of the articles formed the core of the changes. The first article allowed for a British force to stay at Lahore for up to a year 'adequate for the purpose of protecting the person of the Maharajah and the inhabitants of the City of Lahore, during the reorganisation of the Sikh Army, in accordance with the provisions of Article 6 of the Treaty of Lahore'. The second article would leave the capital and its fortress in full possession of the British, with the Lahore state paying for the privilege of being occupied and any and all elements of the Sikh army to be expelled from the neighbourhood of the city. The third article called for the reorganisation of the Sikh army, a euphemism for its reduction. Lal Singh, the Vizier, had felt unable to reduce it unless with the backing of the British in the form of a treaty. The expulsion of the Sikh army elements in Lahore allowed free reign to Lal Singh, who had already begun to recruit Muslim militia men to control the city while beginning the organising of the disbandment of Sikh regiments round the country.

The British force that would occupy Lahore would consist of HM 80th Foot with eight native regiments (the 6th, 12th, 27th, 42nd, 43rd, 45th, 47th and the 68th) with Day's troop of horse artillery, Horseford's battery, Fordyce's battery, two 18-pounders and two 8-inch howitzers along with additional companies of foot artillery and cavalry in the form of a wing of the 2nd Irregular Cavalry and two companies of sappers and miners. This force was to be commanded by Major-General Sir John Littler. This was thought to be strong enough not to be overwhelmed. In any case a strong additional force was set aside for the occupation of the now annexed Jalandhar doab also close by. In addition, the British base at Ferozepore was not far should reinforcements be required.

On 11 March a trip to the famous Shalimar gardens a few kilometres outside Lahore was arranged, the last engagement before Hardinge concluded the merry-go-round of ceremonies, banquets and formal occasions and headed off to see the holy city of Amritsar and the Golden Temple. There he would sign the Treaty of Amritsar with Gulab Singh, whom he described in his private papers as 'the greatest rascal in Asia' but politically, at least for now, a good friend of the British. Charles Napier left for his own province the next day. Large elements of the British force also began returning to British territory across the Sutlej.

*** 

The Treaty of Amritsar had come about because the British demand of reparations of 1.5 million rupees could not be paid by the Lahore Government on account of the empty treasury. This gave the excuse for the separation of Kashmir from the Punjab and its award to Gulab Singh for he had offered to 'buy' the province for £750,000. This money would then be given directly to the British as part payment of the Lahore state's reparations. Thus Gulab Singh, a Lahore vassal who had stayed out of the recent conflict, could be rewarded indirectly. This act of paying of a former humble cavalryman – a scheming and treacherous one at that – with an independent kingdom sat uneasily with many in British society in India. 'The transaction scarcely seems worthy of the British name and greatness, and the objections become stronger when it is considered that Gulab Singh had agreed to pay 68 lakhs of rupees (£680,000) as a fine to his paramount, before the war broke out, and that the custom of the East as well as of the west requires the feudatory to aid his Lord in foreign war and domestic strife. Gulab Singh ought thus to have paid the deficient millions of money as a Lahore subject, instead of being put in possession of the Lahore

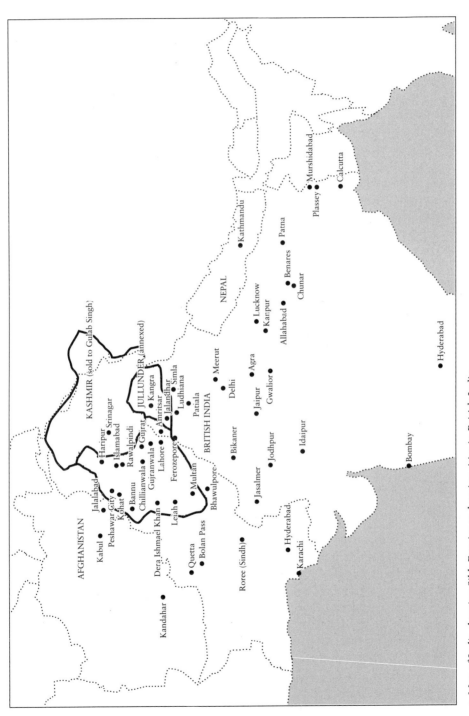

1. Map of India showing Sikh Empire and major cities in British India

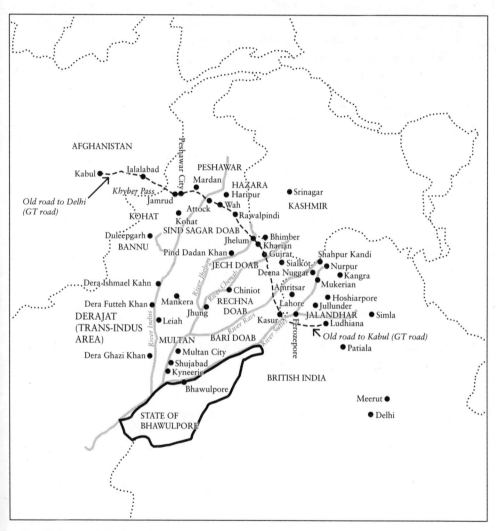

2. Detailed map of the Punjab

provinces as an independent prince,' argued Capt. Joseph Davey Cunningham, a veteran of the recent war and later author of the famous *History of the Sikhs*.

It was not just the financial arrangement but the morals of the transaction. 'Thus in the settlement the wicked had been exalted, the brave and simple debased. That a cunning opportunist like Gulab Singh should receive a kingdom, and cowards or traitors like the Rani and her friends the means of domineering over the patriotic Khalsa was due to the exigencies of the situation,' opined Septimus Thorburn, financial commissioner of the Punjab during the 1870s and himself a chronicler of the history of the Punjab.

While the treaties made Gulab Singh an independent sovereign, and left Lal Singh and Tej Singh with power and wealth at Lahore, the humble soldiers were to be paid off and faced an uncertain future, a situation not appealing to the more chivalrous-minded. Hardinge was not entirely happy with the award of Kashmir to Gulab Singh either, regarding it as the lesser of two evils. Nevertheless, on 16 March, a week after the original Treaty of Lahore was signed, Gulab Singh was made Maharajah of Kashmir at the city of Amritsar. His acceptance of the supremacy of the British government was to be shown, unusually, by the presentation of one horse, twelve shawl goats of approved breed (six male and six female) and three pairs of Cashmere shawls annually. Despite being given a large empire at trifling cost, it appears Gulab Singh was not satisfied and would enter into a correspondence later with Henry Lawrence, the political agent on tracts of territory which he thought should be his and which tended to test Lawrence's patience over the coming months. Gulab Singh had attempted to grab certain parts of Kohistan along with other estates as well as trying to obtain Jusrouta and the Hazara province. Lawrence would write to him on 11 April 1846 in the hope of extinguishing his ambition for more Lahore territory. 'I am grieved that such complaints as I have alluded to should have been uttered, for it seemed to me and to all India, and will doubtless appear to all in England, that your Highness had cause only of thankfulness; in that you had received much in return for very little; and I, in belief of your wisdom and forethought, was a party to the above arrangement.' Despite the grasping nature of Gulab Singh, however, there was no question of not installing him as Maharajah. He had voluntarily accepted British supremacy and had acted in the British interest during the recent war and would prove a good counter against the Lahore state in any future possible conflict. This transfer of a huge territory to a supposed vassal for a nominal sum, a sum he could easily have loaned to Lahore, naturally awoke deep envy among the Durbar members who were prone to petty jealousies – especially Lal Singh – with very serious repercussions later in the year.

***

In order to impress upon the people across India the victory gained over the Sikh army, Hardinge decided on a triumphant procession of the captured Sikh guns, to be taken slowly from the Punjab to Fort William in Calcutta, a journey of roughly 2,400 km. 'The sight will convey a much stronger moral lesson than the gates of Somnaut,' he wrote, referring to the sandalwood gates of the famous Hindu temple, ransacked by the Afghans in 1025 and returned to India by Lord Ellenborough in 1842 as an ostentatious show of British power. The 220 guns captured along with the 36 guns surrendered after Sabraon would make a lengthy train. By 30 March, Hardinge had mapped out the route the guns would take. The guns would be transported through the cities of Delhi and Agra before moving east to Cawnpore, Allahabad, Benares, Patna and Murshidabad before being put on display at Calcutta for several weeks. At each military station along the route, the guns would be shown to the assembled sepoys and ample time was to be allowed for the citizens of the cities en route to inspect the guns. The more decorated of the guns would be kept as trophies. The majority would be melted down to form the encasing of a new victory monument to the recent war at Fort William.

The guns finally reached Calcutta on 3 March 1847, over a year after leaving the Punjab and after wending their way through numerous villages, towns and cities across the north of India. A triumphal archway had been built on the plain to the south of Fort William in front of which the guns would be put on show. Huge throngs of people crowded the streets of Calcutta as the guns slowly entered the city early at 7 a.m. in the morning and headed for the meadow. The *Friend of India* estimated the cost of the procession to be 2.5 lakh rupees (approximately £2 million in 2016). One of the largest of the Sikh guns, the 'Futteh Jung' or Victor in War, drawn by three elephants, led the procession, the whole stream of guns and escorts taking around an hour to pass through the arch in stately fashion. A royal salute was fired as the first gun and last gun passed under the arch.

In the afternoon a grand celebration was held in the meadow, the guns being placed on the road leading from the fort to the Plassey gate, commemorating one of the earliest British victories in India. A spectacular military display was commenced with several regiments from Barrackpore marching up and down the meadow accompanied with much firing of cannons and muskets along with several salutes and a *feu de joie* while guns from the fort were fired at the same time in front of a crowd estimated to be around a 100,000 strong. All was done before the President of the Council, members of the government and all public functionaries of the government, and ten days' batta (bonus pay) announced for all troops present on the field. The guns would be left on display for several weeks under guard before most were sent to the furnaces of the gun foundry at Cossipore for destruction.

Back in the Punjab, the spirited resistance by the Sikh soldiers during the recent campaign had interested Hardinge. The coming reductions in the Sikh army would mean tens of thousands of Sikh regular soldiers would be made unemployed. Recruitment of these men into the East India Company forces would have a dual benefit. It would mean the best Sikh soldiers could be incorporated into the British military presence, simultaneously denying their service to the Lahore Durbar in any future war. An added benefit would be to give them employment and reduce the mutinous mood among these men. Disaffected bands of Sikh soldiers had already begun roaming round Lahore and beyond. Many had travelled north to seek employment in Gulab Singh's army. Others stayed near the Lahore area hoping something would turn up or that the Lahore Government may make some provisions for them. These men were conspicuous enough for Henry Lawrence to notice them everywhere he travelled. In the fields, ex-soldiers, many still wearing their red army jackets to keep warm, could now be seen tilling the land for money in desperation. He wrote to an already convinced Hardinge on the issue in March 1846. 'If you can do so we shall in the course of a month be able to raise two very fine regiments. I would suggest that fifteen or twenty men per company be Mussulmans or Hindoos of our own provinces. I can raise four or five hundred Sikhs here from the discharged men if your Excellency so desires. I have seen some very fine-looking fellows, and expect a large number to come to me this afternoon.' In the course of events, it was decided to initially raise two Sikh corps for the East India Company forces.

While Hardinge had left for Amritsar to sign the treaty with Gulab Singh, Gough had chosen to stay in Lahore and tour the country, examining the major fortresses and other strong points that existed in the state, reasoning as he put it that 'the time may arrive when a knowledge of these places may be useful'. In particular, careful examinations of the defences of Lahore and Amritsar and its fort were carried out. Gough toured Amritsar's Gobindgarh fortress in particular. The fortress was strong and could only be taken by sapping in his opinion, but Amritsar would be easier to capture than Lahore, the fortifications being old. On 23 March, after satisfying himself as to the internal defences of the state, he also left for British territories, visiting the battlefield of Ferozeshah on 27 March on his way. Meanwhile, Hardinge had already left the Punjab for Calcutta to oversee the triumphal progress and arrival of the Sikh cannons at Fort William.

***

The courtiers and high officials that the British Governor-General and his entourage had encountered at Lahore during his recent stay were very different from the bold and confident set that Lord Bentinck, Lord Auckland and Lord Ellenborough, the previous Governor-Generals, had encountered in past decades. During the past ten years and more, a whole crop of flamboyant and commanding personalities had left the scene at Lahore. Sikh Generals like Hari Singh Nalwa and Akali Phoola Singh who had assisted Ranjit Singh in establishing the empire had lost their lives in battle. Ranjit's sons had destroyed each other in fratricidal contests. Ranjit's grandson Nau Nihal Singh, who had inherited his genius and was slated to take over, had been killed in a freak accident, although some said it was murder. What Hardinge saw in Lahore instead was a collection of timorous and fissile bureaucrats with no clear and accepted leader. Lahore had none of the joy and confidence of the past. Lacking both royal blood and the necessary qualities of statesmanship to steer the ship of state, but not without ambition, those in the Lahore Government now spent their time in scheming against each other. On the surface all was decorum and friendship. That this was the thinnest of veneers was quite obvious to all who had cause to get to know the Durbar members. 'To see all the chiefs in Durbar one would say that he had never seen greater friends,' as Harry Lumsden, one of Henry Lawrence's assistants who had many dealings with the Durbar, would put it colourfully, 'but hear each man converse in private. There is not one of them who is not looking out anxiously for the time when, by our withdrawal from the scene, he may seize the opportunity of opening his neighbour's throat.'

Some of the Durbar members of the Sikh state were not Sikh and therefore shared little of the nationalism essential to binding the state and army together. Some were Hindus who had recently converted, hoping it would further their careers. Owing total loyalty to Ranjit Singh when he was alive, they were considerably more mercenary than the Sikh members when the state had begun veering towards the rocks. One of these nominal Sikhs held the highest and most visible position in the state now. This was Lal Singh, the Vizier, who was confirmed in his position by Hardinge. A Hindu Brahmin, Lal Singh was an undistinguished man in deeds and merit and his origins were humble. Henry Havelock, more well known for his role in the Mutiny of 1857, had occasion to get to know him during his stay in Lahore and described Lal Singh as a 'a man of low extraction'. 'He is marked with the small pox and rather what we should call in England an ugly dog but tall and graceful with a winning smile which shows constantly an indifferent set of teeth and insinuating manners.' Harry Lumsden would leave another memorable description of the Vizier:

> I have seldom seen a better-looking man than Lal Sing. He is, I should say, about thirty years of age, strongly built, tall, and very soldier-like, though as cunning as a fox; talks in

a bland, kind tone, which would lead anyone who did not know him to suppose he could not hurt a fly, though he would just as soon cut a man's windpipe as look at him. Every one of the sirdars hate him, and make no secret of their dislike, but say with the greatest coolness that Lal Sing's life is not worth two hours' purchase after the withdrawal of the British troops from Lahore, which, according to present understanding, we are bound to do in October.

Despite the ravages of smallpox, Lal Singh's good looks were his fortune, having attracted the attentions of the Maharani, Jind Kaur. She had raised him to the position of Vizier and he was now her paramour in a sometimes stormy relationship. As regards his insinuating manners, the unpopular Vizier clearly recognised he was fully dependant on the British for his status, and had determined on cooperation to the fullest degree with any and all British wishes. His obsequious manner would annoy Henry Lawrence in coming months, with letters full of excessive praise for the British political agent's advice, so much so Lawrence thought they were verging on sarcasm. As with others in the Lahore court, he led an indolent life before the war aside from the petty jockeying for position. He had a long-running rivalry with Gulab Singh, the ruler of Jammu. 'The Raja is more at home at such intrigues than other matters of public weal. No one in the Punjab will support him but the Maharani, and she against her better judgment,' John Lawrence, the brother of Henry, noted during his temporary stay at Lahore.

Tej Singh, Commander-in-Chief of the army, along with Lal Singh and Gulab Singh, was the second member of an undistinguished triumvirate. A Hindu Brahmin of small stature, he also carried the scars of smallpox from an early age, though his were much more unsightly than Lal Singh's. He was said to be a good soldier but like Lal Singh had decided the Sikh army janissaries were better off destroyed. Tej Singh would suggest to Henry Lawrence the disbanding of the whole Sikh army, arguing it would be easier to pick an entirely new stock of men. Jealous of Gulab Singh's reward of Kashmir after the first war, Tej Singh would approach the British later, offering 25 lakh rupees for a kingdom for himself carved out of what was left of the Lahore state. His offer was refused, the British preferring to keep him as a pliable Commander-in-Chief of the Sikh army. Tej Singh seemed to have a comical propensity for feigning illness when summoned by the later Lahore Residents for the discussion of difficult matters. He would spend a considerable part of his time on his jaghirs (small districts) and appears little in any correspondence and communication with either Lawrence or his brother and Frederick Currie over the coming years. On the rare occasions Lawrence wrote of his presence or feelings, he appears to have wholehearted concurrence with the Resident's view. 'Two more contemptible poltroons than the two generals of the Khalsa army – Lal Singh and Tej Singh, both Brahmans – never breathed,' wrote Alexander Gardner, an American adventurer serving in the Sikh army who knew the pair well for many years.

One of the youngest but easily the most intriguing and famous of the characters in high circles in Lahore at the time was the Maharani, Jind Kaur. The twenty-eight-year-old mother of the Maharajah would have stayed in the shadows of history but for the unfortunate circumstances after Ranjit Singh's death. She was his youngest wife. With Ranjit Singh's elder sons dying violent deaths, Duleep Singh, his youngest and last surviving, came to be regent and hence her current position as queen regent. Like others in Lahore high circles, she had been born of humble station. Her father had been the palace dog keeper but she caught the eye of Ranjit Singh with her extreme good looks, becoming one of his wives in 1828, eleven years before his demise. She perhaps first came to attention of the British eyes on her son becoming Maharajah in 1843. 'The mother of the boy Dhuleep Singh seems to be a woman of determined courage, and she is the only person, apparently at Lahore, who has courage,' Lord Ellenborough wrote when apprising the Duke of Wellington on 20 November 1843 of the situation in the Punjab.

No Maharani of India received so much attention as Jind Kaur from the British newspapers in India. Her famous beauty and the fact that she was ordinarily in purdah in public excited the curiosity of the English papers, and various reports figured in the newspaper columns of some person or another catching glimpses of her looks. Some of the officers escorting her during her exile out of the Punjab, seeing her without purdah, described her as 'pretty, and even more decidedly so, her nose being slightly imperfect which the officers blamed on being the bad feature in the Punjab'. Her hands and feet, they said, were perfection, and Jind Kaur was well aware of her captivating beauty. Her eyes were exceptionally beautiful, something that her son had apparently inherited. 'Those beautiful eyes, with which Duleep has taken captive the court, are his mother's eyes, those with which she captivated and controlled the old Lion of the Punjab. The officer who had charge of her from Lahore to Benares told me this. He said that hers were splendid orbs,' wrote an intrigued Dalhousie, the future Governor-General, in August 1854 on Duleep Singh's visit to the British court in London.

Perhaps because of her captivating looks, the most salacious news and rumours circulated in the British press in India and all vices and depravity under the sun were attributed to her and eagerly published. This modern Messalina, they said, had intimate relations with a poor Muslim water carrier called Gulloo in the palace and her son Duleep Singh therefore was not really sired by Ranjit Singh. It was suggested she developed loose morals from an early age, having several relationships by the time she was fourteen, and that she had many other relationships during and after Ranjit's death, all her pregnancies being terminated. She was profligate to the extreme, they said. She indulged in the grossest debauchery and was addicted to the hardest liquors. She loved intrigue. She was cruel and enjoyed watching servants being semi-drowned in the palace fountains. These reports continued to circulate before, during and after the war. According to Hardinge, there were reports in March 1846 that her life was in danger from a miscarriage from her relationship with Lal Singh.

More circumspect and sober reports of her strengths and character would replace this idle gossip and rumour in future months and years, although they portrayed her in no better fashion. 'She was known to be a woman fond of intrigue and her character to say the best of it was but "indifferent", *The Mofussilite* wrote in January 1849. 'Wherever the Rani has appeared, she has always shown considerable ability, and great power over those amongst whom she mingled. That to her voice, and to her appeals, the invasion of our territories in 1845 was owing, is a matter of notoriety. The Rani is very dangerous person.'

Less worthy of newspaper inches were her works of charity. She paid for the marriages of many of her servants and spent an inordinate amount feeding Brahmin priests and giving wealth to charitable institutions. For this she was loved by the common man in the Punjab.

Herbert Edwardes described her as having 'more wit and daring than any man of her nation' for her willingness to risk her fortune and high station in intriguing against the growing British power in the Punjab. She would also have the distinction of being the first Sikh woman to visit Britain. Unfortunately no daguerreotype exists of her in her youth. A portrait of her was completed by George Richmond in 1863 during her stay in England. Richmond perhaps paints a flattering picture but the portrait still may not do justice. Painted in the last few months of her existence, the image shows a prematurely aged woman bereft of her early sharp looks. She stares head on without expression or smile, perhaps a rather melancholic look. She happened to be half-blind at this stage and in fast declining health, the cost of a hard life in exile in Nepal and living on a pittance. She died shortly after the portrait was made at the young age of forty-six. That was all in the future, however. For now, she still had her youth and vigour.

Sitting on the throne at the time was the son of Jind Kaur, the young lad Duleep Singh, who naturally took a back seat due to his age. Few accounts survive of his early years as regent, simply because of his youth and lack of involvement. One of the more documented incidents of his life, and to which he was an eyewitness, was the death of his uncle, the drunkard Jawahar Singh, brutally murdered by the assembled army. All his brothers had met violent deaths during the power struggles of recent years. The continual danger to his life in the palace would traumatise him at a young age. These incidents, it was later said, alienated his young mind from his own people and, combined with the Christian zeal of the British in the European colony where he was brought up on orders of the Governor-General, turned him towards Christianity later in life. He was fond of falconry, a passion which stayed with him in later years. According to Lady Login, wife of Dr John Login, the British guardian imposed on him after annexation, he sometimes tried to draw and paint the hawks himself when not employing artists to do the work. Lady Login described him as 'unusually well-educated for an Indian Prince of those days, reading and writing Persian very well'. Later on he would be adept at picking up the English language as well. All who met him considered him a sharp and intelligent boy. His first prominent role as regent had been to pay obeisance to the Governor-General shortly after the cessation of the first war at Lullianee. Henry Lawrence was impressed with the young Maharajah, and during his stay as Resident at Lahore would remark 'that His Highness evinced more intelligence than most English children of equal age would do'. Like his mother, he too would die far from the palace of Lahore and in much reduced circumstances.

There were other figures in Lahore high society and the Durbar, perhaps not so visible. Dewan Deena Nath was a well-respected senior figure in the Lahore Government and looked after the finances. He had the look of a banker, moreover. Deena Nath was one of those averse to Britain's ever-increasing hold on the country in the coming months and years, something that made the British Residents in Lahore wary of him. Henry Lawrence attributed this to the fact that any increase in British power meant a reduction of his role in the treasury. He was also a supporter of the Maharani, unlike many of the others. 'He is a man both of courage and ability, and has his own notions of fidelity, however they may be opposed to ours,' wrote Henry Lawrence. Despite this, Deena Nath was careful to avoid any direct criticism of the British, keeping his position in the Durbar and later regency period.

To the north of Lahore, the substantial province of Kashmir was controlled by its Muslim governor Sheikh Imam-Ud-Deen. The Sheikh was a plain-speaking man and was in charge of elements of the Sikh army garrisoned in the province. It is unknown what his feelings were of the treaties that had been signed. However, his position was in danger of becoming redundant. The recent Treaty of Amritsar had awarded the entire province to Gulab Singh, and this would become a major issue in the coming months.

There were other members of the Durbar. Most of these were largely invisible, saying and doing little to merit any record of their presence in British records. On Sirdar Shumshere Sing Sindanwala, for example, one of the more reticent members of the government, Henry Lawrence would write during his term as official Resident, 'I am desirous of his voice being more frequently heard in Council.' On another less-than-prominent figure, Bhaee Nidhan Singh, high priest at Amritsar but ill fitted to the task of being in government administration, he wrote, '[He] continues a silent member of the Board.' On Fakeer Nur-Ud-Deen, he held a similar view: '[He] says little to anyone but myself and assistants.' Lehna Singh Majeethia was one of the more intelligent leading men but relatively timid: 'He is free enough in conversation with me but at Durbar he seldom speaks out,' noted Lawrence; and so on with the other members. These figures are infrequently mentioned in the accounts and correspondence of Henry Lawrence and later John Lawrence and Frederick Currie. When they appear, they invariably agree to any advice of the Resident or his assistants.

No doubt because of this, Henry Lawrence developed a low opinion of the Durbar members, although in public he kept good working relations with them. There was a certain amount of petty bickering and jostling for power that continued among the group. Lawrence, whose views of the Durbar members was akin to that of an amused bystander, provides interesting reading on the fractious nature of this group. 'I am very much troubled by family contentions between brother chiefs; almost every family has its feud and the matter of a well or a house affects individuals with a more lively anxiety than the most important affairs of the State.'

Only one person really stood out in the mediocrity of the Lahore ruling clique and possessed any sort of personal magnetism. This was Shere Singh Attariwala. It's safe to say he was a well-liked man by the British contingent at Lahore and by his peers and, perhaps most importantly, by the Sikh soldiers who looked up to him. 'Sirdar Shere Sing's frank and bold manner is strangely contrasted with the demeanour of that of almost every other chief in the Durbar,' wrote Henry Lawrence. He was seen as a dashing and energetic young military man with an amiable personality but who showed little political ambition. In fact, European accounts of him tend to be universally complimentary either to a greater or lesser extent, during and after the war.

Physically he was not impressive, being described as very common-looking by the various people who left descriptions of him. He was also of low stature and scarred by smallpox. 'Shere Singh is a good tempered, fat, chubby-faced looking chap – unlike a Sikh, or any pretensions to a great commander,' reported a newspaper correspondent on seeing him in Allahabad after the war. Another reporter described him as 'a villainous-looking black, with a settled black scowl, small pox mark, and sensual look besides being fat and unwieldy so that we cannot give him a very hero-like portraiture, and like Desdemona, must look for "Othello's visage in his mind"'. He had a mild voice, however, and the look of intelligence about him.

Looks aside, Shere Singh was generally liked and he in turn wasn't averse to European company either. He seemed to have developed a good, trusting friendship with Herbert Edwardes, the British agent stationed in Bannu province in the run-up to war. He was fond of hunting and frequently went on hunting trips with the various British officers during his time at Lahore. So much so, that one of his few requests in captivity after the war was that he be allowed once in a while to go hunting. 'I was much pleased with their fine open manly bearing, and enjoyed having long conversations with them, more particularly with Shere Singh, who was extremely intelligent,' recorded one of his jailors, Orfeur Cavenagh, who struck up many conversations with Shere Singh and his father during their incarceration around January 1854. He was also known to enjoy playing cards and therefore gave the impression of idle richness.

His father was Chutter Singh, the patriarch of one of the patrician families of Lahore, the Attariwalas. An ageing and bespectacled military man himself, he is probably one of the least understood of the Durbar members. Chutter Singh, according to the same reporter at Allahabad, looked every inch an aristocratic soldier unlike his son. Dalhousie, too, on seeing Chutter Singh was left with a positive impression. He found him having a proud and manly bearing 'without the least approach to supplication, far less to servility'. He talked little, however, during their meeting when he was prisoner in Lahore Fort. 'He is a fine looking old man with a good brow, aquiline features, and a mild dignified countenance. His voice was deep and loud, his expression deliberate yet animated, and his manner had all the measured grace which so marks the race,' recorded Dalhousie of his impressions of the ex-governor.

The last figure in Lahore state politics was Dewan Mulraj, the wealthy governor of the large province of Multan in the south of the state, who rarely ventured out of his province but who would come to dominate events shortly.

*** 

Aside from Shere Singh, this clique of men, largely unable to work together and patently unable to control or awe the Sikh army, would for the next two years be dealt with by Major Henry Lawrence, who was left behind to 'assist' the Lahore Durbar in bringing the ship of state back on an even keel. 'Broadfoot is killed and you are required forthwith' was the message received by Major Lawrence in Nepal on 6 January 1846, also confirming him as the new British political agent at Ferozepore on the border with the Punjab. George Broadfoot, the abrasive former political agent, had met his end at the Battle of Ferozeshah two weeks earlier. He had been in large part to blame for the downturn in relations between the states prior to the recent war. His replacement, however, was quite the opposite. A kindly man with a warm personality, he would build up good relations with the Durbar members in his future role. Just as Broadfoot, his predecessor, was in large part to blame for the war, many would blame the premature end of Lawrence's tenure as Resident for the breaking out of the second war.

Henry Lawrence had joined the Bengal Artillery in 1823 at Dum Dum and would experience hostilities in the First Burmese War. In 1829 he was appointed revenue surveyor before becoming assistant agent to George Clerk at Ferozepore. Both he and his brother George Lawrence's regiment were chosen as part of the grandly titled but ill-fated 'Army of the Indus' assembled to remove the supposed Russophile Dost Mohammad from the Afghan throne and replace him with the British puppet Shah Shujah. However, Henry Lawrence never got his chance to go – fortunately, as it would turn out for him, for the expedition ended disastrously, with George Lawrence being held captive by the Afghans. More recently he had been appointed Resident at Nepal, a job he regarded as a sinecure but which bored him terribly, there being few if any other Europeans in close proximity for companionship.

Lawrence therefore already had considerable contact with the Sikh state as assistant to George Clerk, and more so after the British retreat from Kabul when he was sent through the Punjab to Peshawar to push up support for the relief of the British garrison of Jalalabad. During this time, Lawrence developed a natural affinity for the Sikh nation, the last independent power in India, and the role provided him an ideal opportunity to liaise with them and learn more. Sadly, he had come too late for the role he really desired. Ranjit Singh, the ruler of the Punjab, would die within six months of Lawrence's arrival at Ferozepore. As the years went by, Anglo-Sikh relations became increasingly important. Lawrence became very well acquainted with the chiefs and foremost personalities of the land, its army, its politics and the intrigues that were tearing the country apart. His interest in the Punjab led him to write *Some Passages in the Life of an Adventurer*, which was published in portions in the *Delhi Gazette*. The book, a work of fiction, describes the adventures of Bellasis, a European colonel in the service of Ranjit Singh. Bellasis was generally accepted as a representation of the European officers who had sought employment with Ranjit Singh. During his time in Nepal, he had turned to writing on subjects that interested him for the *Calcutta Review*, including some on Sikhs like 'The Sikhs and Their Country'. One of the last entries in his journal regarding his stay in Nepal related to seeing a suttee (widow burning) in progress which led him to quote the Sikh holy book on the issue: 'They are not suttees who perish in the flames, O Nanuk! Suttees are those who die of a broken heart.'

The death of Major Broadfoot on the plains of Ferozeshah had left the post of the Governor-General's agent for the North-West Frontier vacant. Frederick Currie had written to Lawrence informing him of Hardinge's decision to give him the post. 'Come quickly. We have lost many valuable officers, and the Governor-General's staff has been much cut up … Your corps has its full share of killed … I have no time for more; lose no time in coming; you are a long way off.'

\*\*\*

Hardinge's instructions to Henry Lawrence were to assemble and assist a makeshift government which could continue the work of state but never be a threat to British power, and to begin the dismantlement of the only organisation that could: the Sikh army. This weakness of the Lahore Government became increasingly obvious as the British came to know more of its personalities, and contempt of the Durbar members was universal. 'There is not a chief in the Punjab worth his salt who has any influence or a thought but for his own personal benefit' was John Lawrence's view on the Lahore Government. 'They neither can nor will do anything. I have seen them in matters great and small and have not the slightest confidence in one of them.' This was echoed later by George Campbell, a deputy commissioner in the Sikh states of the Cis-Sutlej and later Lt Governor of Bengal after the war. 'The majority of the servants of the Durbar, and of the Durbar itself, are mere creatures of circumstance utterly without nationality. Tej Sing, the late Sikh Commander-in-Chief, is a Brahmin of Seharunpore, who served Ranjit and became a "Brahmin Sikh". From such people we have nothing to fear, nor need we go to any great expense in providing for them. In short, the Lahore monarchy is like any other native kingdom. If we do but dissolve it, in a few short years the place whereon it stood shall know it no more.'

Many others, including Hardinge, had similar doubts as to whether to continue the experiment of a Lahore Government and voiced this opinion just three weeks after the signing of the Treaty of Lahore in a letter to Henry Lawrence on 30 March 1846. Annexation, though, as discussed previously, would prove difficult and was not considered seriously at this point. Hardinge would warn Lawrence of the latent anger among the population as to the recent betrayal of the Sikh army by the Durbar. 'Rajah Goolab Sing may wish to see the Punjaub in a weak and disturbed state, and the cry of the country having been sold to the English might cause considerable excitement. It will therefore be necessary to be at all times in a state of military vigilance,' he advised the agent. Many Sikh ex-soldiers, apparent from the red uniforms they still wore, still roamed the countryside looking for employment. Others roamed round in groups, leaderless and unsure of what steps to take. While round Lahore the British took a firm grip, the rest of the country was unoccupied. There were several disturbances, particularly near the Jhelum to the west, by soldiers angry at the betrayal by their leaders during the recent war. There were promises that as soon as the British withdrew the Lahore Government members would pay for their treachery, threats that only made the Durbar more dependent on British support.

# 2

# The Downfall of Lal Singh

*He preferred the embraces of Venus at Lahore to the triumphs of Mars; and was, as all Brahmans are, held in the highest contempt by the Sikhs.*

Alexander Gardner, Col of Sikh Artillery

*I think he will be assassinated someday, and perhaps this would be the best thing that could happen for the Punjab...*

John Lawrence, Resident at Lahore, later Viceroy of India

After the signing of the recent treaties and the departure of the bulk of the British forces back into British territory, the Punjab would enter into a curious political limbo for the remainder of the year. It retained its own government and was independent, on paper at least, but British troops occupied the capital and Henry Lawrence, the British agent to the Governor-General, was left behind and, it would turn out, had much more influence than his title would suggest. This period of British occupation, as agreed, would continue for nine months. This was ostensibly to allow the Sikh army to be reduced and political stability to be increased, and to help the government re-establish itself free from the influence of the army praetorians. Less clear, despite the treaty, was whether British control would fill the vacuum and whether the political agent at Lahore and the British garrison would become a permanent feature through one means or another. States defeated by the East India Company rarely, if ever, returned to full independence. This wasn't helped by the rather listless Lahore Durbar and the dearth of men of quality to lead the government. This issue would only come to the fore at the end of the year, though, and the summer months were allowed to drift by without any concerted effort by the Lahore Government to reassert and strengthen itself in preparation for complete British departure.

The year of 1846 would not pass entirely peacefully in the Punjab, however, and a number of gestures of contempt and reaction towards the new British presence and influence would present themselves. One of the earliest, and most trivial, quickly labelled the 'cow row' by the news-sheets, came just two months after the occupation of the capital by British forces. On the morning of 21 April 1846, two months into the British occupation, a lone European artilleryman stood on sentry duty at the outer gates of an artillery barracks enclosure at Lahore that was used by the British garrison. The only exit and entrance to this place was through one of the city streets. These narrow backstreets of Lahore frequently posed a problem if a significant number of wagons or animals happened to be travelling in opposite directions at any one time. At 11 a.m. that day, a long train of camels carrying ammunition from the British station of Ferozepore was entering the street on its way to the barracks. It so happened that a herd of cattle entered the street from the opposite direction at the same time. Deciding to give the camels priority, the sentry attempted to ward the cows back in the direction from which they had come. Ordinarily a few strokes with the flat of the sword should have been enough to encourage the animals to turn, but such was the size and momentum of the herd he was unable to coax them to change direction. Without a thought for the consequences, the sentry decided on more violent means, slashing several of them with his sword, wounding four of them on the noses and face and drawing blood.

Cows being holy to Hindus, the news of the incident spread like wildfire, causing the Hindu population in the metropolis to congregate and commence loud protests on the streets. The shopkeepers of Lahore near the incident decided to close down their business in protest as well. A Major Brind, the officer in charge, went around the area explaining to the shopkeepers that the soldier had not meant to harm the cows but was merely attempting to change their direction of motion, albeit in much more rough fashion than was warranted. They appeared mollified by his explanation and reopened their shops, although by this time the news had spread further. As momentum for the protest increased, the shopkeepers again closed their premises and events portended a large riot by the Hindu population of the city.

On hearing of the tumult, Henry Lawrence sent a message to Lal Singh informing him the sentry would be punished in due course but that he must ensure the locals kept the shops open and allowed commerce to continue uninterrupted. In addition, all those who had gone around organising the shutdown and protests must be rounded up and punished. Brind, meanwhile, had seen the crowds quickly growing and increasing in aggression, with people gathering on rooftops with stones and brickbats by this stage. He had asked Lawrence to come to the scene personally. Lawrence arrived shortly with Major McGregor and Lt Herbert Edwardes and a bodyguard of a dozen armed sowars (cavalrymen) along with various servants and syces (horse grooms). Visiting the houses of two of the owners of the herd, he began explaining the overzealousness of the sentry but violence erupted outside. 'On going out, we found our attendants engaged in a scuffle with part of a crowd of Brahmins and Khatrees [Hindu priests and traders],' described Lawrence, 'who, it appears, had followed us; while, from the roofs of the adjoining houses, brickbats were being plentifully thrown. Scarcely a man or horse escaped untouched, and Lieutenant Edwardes was severely struck on the head.'

Lawrence, attempting to placate the mob, made an effort to address them but the locals were in no mood to listen and in any case it's doubtful his voice was heard over the shouting and jeers. The locals continued to bombard the group from the street and adjacent housetops, forcing them to retreat, Lawrence being hit himself. At this point he gave the order to secure the city, with all gates to be closed and guarded, and informed the British military force to be ready in case violence increased. The situation, if not countered swiftly, could easily develop into an expression of anti-British feelings and turn into an attack on the British garrison itself.

In a separate incident in the city, around the same time, a British sepoy of the 12th NI who happened to be walking through the neighbourhood to Brig. Eckford's office, a building that was formerly Prince Nau Nihal's house, was attacked and severely wounded in what must have looked ominously to British officers like the beginnings of something bigger. While heading back to his quarters, Lawrence sent summons to both Tej Singh and Lal Singh for a meeting on the affair. After a few hours, however, the 'cow row' petered out as the crowd's anger began dissipating and the people were seen to be returning to their homes. The incident was therefore not interpreted with hindsight as an anti-British riot, although British officers and soldiers had been wounded. Riots between Hindus and Muslims were not uncommon over the same issue,

Muslims protesting over the ban on eating beef while Hindus equally anxious to preserve the sanctity of kine. 'There was nothing pre-concerted in this affair, nor would I believe a single Sikh to have been concerned in it; on the contrary, many have since offered their services. Brahmins were the instigators,' mused Lawrence on the affair. 'It must not be supposed that we were attacked yesterday owing to ill will against us personally: we are daily to be found equally at disadvantage: and I believe that any other Europeans would, at the time, have been treated in the same manner.'

Despite this, retribution was to be exacted as British officers had been wounded. Lal Singh, Tej Singh and other members of the government, bringing along with them the young Maharajah, waited upon Lawrence to express their regret at the incident. An uncompromising Lawrence communicated to them that the houses from which the missiles were thrown must be seized and their owners arrested in readiness for a British force to raze them to the ground. In addition, any resident found armed was to be arrested and handed over to British authorities.

Religious sensibilities generally have a propensity to turn cowards into stronger people, and perhaps the attack on the cows by the British soldier sparked a hint of rebellion in Lal Singh. He would ordinarily never turn down a request by Henry Lawrence. He was also probably reticent on courting unpopularity among the Hindus of the city. After giving the request due consideration, the Vizier would send a message back to Lawrence explaining he was unwilling to arrest the culprits. His excuse was that they had threatened to kill themselves, an event which, if it occurred, he suggested, would only prolong a return to normalcy and instigate further incidents. Lawrence would brush aside his arguments, however, and was firm on exacting punishment. An investigation into the event was ordered and the persons who had been most active in throwing missiles and others whose rooftops had been used by the missile throwers were arrested and sent in irons to the British station at Ferozepore.

A flogging was the usual punishment for disorder, but Europeans had been wounded. Two of those arrested, a certain Dutt Brahmin, thought to be the ringleader, and Rullia Missar, one of the main instigators, had their faces blackened and were put in irons in a public place in Ferozepore to serve as an example to others while decisions were pending as to their punishment. On 24 April 1846, three days after the disturbance, Dutt Brahmin and Rullia Missar were hanged for their part as the main instigators of the riot. These capital punishments meted out to its citizens would elicit no protest from the Lahore Government.

\*\*\*

Shortly after the 'cow row', in the month of May, an altogether more serious incident would develop. By the Treaty of Lahore, the whole of the Sikh territory east of the Beas River (i.e. the Jalandhar doab) had been ceded to the British. Nestling in the foothills of the Himalayas in the far east of this ceded territory was the Kangra region. Here stood an isolated and formidable fortress by the same name. The commandant of the Kangra Fort, a Sunder Singh, alone among the other cities and strongholds in this country, was refusing to surrender the structure to British control. Lt Joseph Davey Cunningham had been sent to take charge of the fortress in April, several weeks after the recent treaties had been signed, but was forced to turn back on finding the fortress doors resolutely closed to him.

'Imagine Edinburgh Castle, on a rock much more precipitous, encircled by a rushing torrent and completely commanded from the hills above, and you can form an idea of that Eastern Gibraltar. Without siege guns the place was impregnable,' described Charles Hardinge, son of the Governor-General, who was touring the area of the fortress which formerly guarded Ranjit Singh's eastern borders. His assessment was correct. The fortress in olden times was virtually impregnable, being situated on top of an isolated rock 400 feet high. Its impressive walls were 8 km in circumference and the only connection (and therefore point of ingress or egress) with the surrounding area was a thin neck of land 20 yards wide. The neck of land was also fortified, with walls built with seven gates in succession, all overlooked from vantage points. If the fort was well manned and stocked with provisions, it was well-nigh impossible to take in earlier years (bar any treachery), and the commandant had enough provisions and ammunition to hold out for two years if necessary. In fact, in recent history it had withstood a siege by the advancing Gurkhas for three years without a hint of being captured.

The problem for the Sikh commandant was that he only had a garrison of between 300 and 400 men at the time, with seven large guns and three smaller guns, an insufficient strength to combat a determined foe. In addition, modern siege guns meant the fortress was no longer as immune to attack as before. Nevertheless Sunder Singh, a nationalist, was defiant and hoped his stand would garner support and become a rallying point for further resistance. He had no wish to hand the fortress under his charge over to the British without a fight despite orders from Lahore. 'I do not think that they will hold out; with the country against them and their own Durbar, it would be useless. However, no one can tell what fools may do,' pontificated John Lawrence, the new man in charge of the Jalandhar doab after its annexation and on whose territory the fortress stood.

For the British, the capture of the fort was a matter of prestige, for the garrison could not be allowed to hold out in what was now British territory. The commandant must be coaxed into surrender or the fort taken by arms. His scant resources meant he was limited to showing defiance only behind the safety of the fort walls. Hardinge was anxious, however, that this show of boldness should not be the seed for others of a similar mind, leading to a wider insurrection in the area. There were plenty of unemployed Sikh soldiers and others unhappy with British control in this annexed territory and who lacked only a satisfactory leader to rally them. There were other forts around the country that had not been yet handed over by their Sikh garrisons, and who might wish to emulate Kangra. In fact, the commander of the smaller nearby fortress of Kotla had already taken the cue and also decided to hold out against the British. Hardinge hoped for surrender without violence and would write his views to Henry Lawrence. 'I know you have done everything in your power to induce the surrender; but in this affair, where there may be many casualties, we must not only attend substantially to the means of avoiding them, but also to appearances. A gallant resistance by the Sikh garrison is a very undesirable result.'

There were other reasons for adhering to diplomacy. Capturing the fort presented various logistical problems as there was no road to the fort in this hilly area for the transportation of the required siege guns. A road would have to be laid for a large section of the journey, and in other parts the guns must be transported across a river and through territory highly unfavourable to laid roads. Due to these difficulties, it had been decided friendly approaches would be continued in the hope Sunder Singh would change his mind. The Lahore authorities had been told to do their utmost to coerce the commandant into surrendering, initiating a long series of fruitless attempts by the Durbar over the next few weeks. Lal Singh had duly written to Sunder Singh instructing him to give up the fortress, but to no avail. The governor's reply, as it was to the previous British officer, was that he would hold out 'until the Maharajah [Ranjit Singh] himself should come and bid them'.

The Lahore Durbar was then warned there would be serious consequences if their garrison were not persuaded into surrendering the fortress. Sirdar Ranjodh Singh, a Sikh general who had led the Sikh army against the British at the recent Battle of Aliwal, was sent with Cunningham early in April with orders to be more assertive. The garrison, however, blackened the face of the messenger bearing Ranjodh Singh's letter and replied in turn that 'they would obey no *parwana* [official order] but that of powder and shot (*Gole-barood ka parwana*)'. The *parwana* itself was torn up symbolically in front of the messenger before he was sent back. Another *parwana* was then sent in the name of Maharajah Duleep Singh. Although the messenger wasn't humiliated this time, he was sent back with a verbal response. Sunder Singh declared he despised 'Ranjodh Singh as a dog, held the Maharajah in contempt and defied the British'.

The gestures of defiance were not altogether peaceful, either. When Cunningham with a small party attempted to carry out some reconnaissance of the fort as a precursor to possible military measures, the party was fired on from the fortress guns and forced to retreat. On another occasion, when the garrison learned of a hut being used by British officers as a mess room, at the time dinner was usually served they fired a single shot with such precision that it passed through the walls and just over the dinner table as the officers sat waiting for food. The British force largely tended to stay away from the fort for the next month or so as the chance of a peaceful end became slimmer, and the wait began for reinforcements and the British guns. A few days later, however, another attempt was made to coax surrender. A Missr Rup Lal deputed a Doola Singh to deliver a *parwana* to the garrison to surrender. The commandant seemed to be tiring of the endless ultimatums, unbacked as they were by guns and armed men. They fired two shots at the messenger and shouted the message that this was the only answer he was getting and anyone else approaching would now be shot dead.

Henry Lawrence would reach Kangra Fort himself on 3 May 1846, ordering the Lahore Durbar emissaries back. He also wrote to the British Government complaining the Lahore authorities were not fully exerting themselves to the task of coaxing the garrison to surrender the fortress. This was quite correct, but then there was little else they could do short of sending troops across what was now British territory and laying siege to the fortress themselves. Dewan Deena Nath, who was mistrusted by Lawrence, at length offered the garrison 25,000 rupees as a bribe to surrender but Lawrence had ordered all negotiations to be at an end by this time. The decision had been taken to reduce the fortress as soon as British artillery could be transported to the area. Bribing the garrison to come out would send the wrong message about British resolution and strength.

On 13 and 14 May another reconnaissance of the fort was carried out by British engineers and it was thought around 500 rounds of shot would be required, double the previous estimate, to effect an entrance into the fort through the multiple gates. While negotiations had been taking place, 1,500 workers along with sappers and miners had been employed constructing a narrow road to the fort for the carriage of the heavy guns. Brig. Wheeler with John Lawrence now came up with heavy guns. They had been delayed around four days by the lack of boats across the Beas, there being only four boats available, although another twelve were procured from up- and downstream. By 16 May most of the guns and men had been brought across. The road was difficult, utilising the riverbed of the River Guj for much of the way, the water being around 2–4 feet in depth. There were also several hairpin bends in the mountain passes and two elephants were used in tandem to pull each of the heavy artillery pieces, including several 18-pounders, while a third elephant pushed each gun from behind.

On 19 May, Lawrence wrote back to the Governor-General warning that the fort would need to be reduced by military means and relatively quickly. The rains were due shortly, which would make passage to the fort all but impossible. The River Guj, normally a mild-mannered stream, typically becomes a raging torrent during the monsoon. Not capturing the fort in the near future would mean the governor of the fortress could continue to wave defiance for another two or three months as heavy rains inundated the area.

By 23 May, though, a considerable British presence had reached the fortress, comprising of three regiments of native infantry and a regiment of irregular cavalry along with a light field battery under Capt. Fitzgerald from the Phillour Fort, Capt. Christie's field battery from Jalandhar and a troop of horse artillery under Capt. Swinley. Meanwhile, two 8-inch howitzers, ten mortars and three 18-pounders were making their way up along with more troops on the newly made track to the fort and were expected to arrive soon.

Things changed rapidly with the appearance of British troops. While the British force had been accumulating, Sunder Singh had signally failed to raise any support bar the garrison at Kumlaghur. With the imminent arrival of the British heavy guns he had decided to end his stand, sending out a party to negotiate the night before the guns reached the British position. It was reported that a jaghir for the Sunder Singh, two months' pay for the garrison and the right to carry away their arms were the terms sought. The next day, 28 May 1846, as the guns reached the British camp in front of the fortress, the party went back with Lawrence, refusing to negotiate. With an overwhelming force of 6,000 men at his disposal and thirty-three guns, Henry Lawrence had no need to negotiate and now asked for unconditional surrender. There was no hope of succour from elsewhere and the commandant decided he was merely delaying the inevitable and surrendered at this point. The men of the garrison were each allowed to leave with a single bundle of possessions and taken to the fort of Phillour as prisoners while the British flag was hoisted on the fort ramparts. As far as retribution was concerned, Lawrence recommended to the Governor-General that they be handed back to the Lahore Durbar, who should be seen to be taking action against their insubordinate soldiers. For his part in the Kangra affair, Lawrence was promoted to the rank of lieutenant-colonel by Hardinge.

***

The cow row and the Kangra fortress incidents would be overshadowed by events at the close of the year, however. Lal Singh, reinstated by the British and confident of their continuing protection, had been busy consolidating his own position and accumulating ill-gotten wealth over the summer months. Sometimes this was at the expense of the state; at other times other Durbar members fell victim to his avarice. He had always had a grasping attitude; this much was known to all. But during the course of the year, freed now from the interference of the Sikh army, Lal Singh's greed had become much more unrestrained and overt. He had begun cutting state expenditure and extracting jaghirs from the rich and powerful families on the excuse that the state required money in order for reparations to be paid to the British. Henry Lawrence, thinking the jaghirs were going back to the state, did not interfere in any way. Much of this land ended up in his own holdings, however, or that of his relatives. The Maharani's brother, too, was awarded large jaghirs. The Vizier, already unpopular, became increasingly more so as the end of the year approached. His relations with the Maharani did little to endear him with the common population either. She was his main form of support, along with the several other cohorts that he enriched. The Sikh army, already detesting him for his treachery in the war, hated him all the more for the British puppet he had become. He in turn feared a return of their praetorian instincts once the British presence was gone. Taking pre-emptive action, he had begun making as many Sikh soldiers as possible redundant, replacing them with non-Sikh sepoys from British territory along with Muslim levies from Peshawar. Those that were retained in employment were not paid on time. These measures only served to further alienate the Sikh soldiery.

To ward off any assassination attempts from the many enemies he was making at this time, Lal Singh had recruited a Varangian guard for himself, a 2,000-strong bodyguard formed exclusively of Afghan Muslim recruits who were under his direct pay and could be implicitly trusted. These foreign soldiers and mercenaries, along with his equally foreign main support, the British troops, were disliked by the common population as well and only served to isolate him further.

Even the greed he presently displayed was said to be quite in moderation considering his character. Only the presence of the British at Lahore restrained his ambitions, and it was a general source of amusement and conjecture among the population in general as to what his future would be should his British supporters withdraw over the Sutlej River. That he would last less than an hour after British withdrawal was the general feeling. It was common knowledge he dreaded the departure of the British. Still others thought this dread may show itself as desperate and violent action. Self-preservation would lead him to destroy any rivals and enemies before they took their opportunities to destroy him. There was at this time, therefore, a certain climate of fear, the Vizier's worst excesses drawing no criticism from any quarter for fear of drawing his attention.

John Lawrence, with whom the Durbar members were more frank, concurred with general opinion of the Vizier's chances of survival. 'Every day I see more and more of the bitter feeling of the sirdars against Lal Sing,' he wrote on 28 August 1846, noting the fact that, conscious of his unpopularity, the Vizier now, following the example of Gulab Singh, always kept a loaded double-barrelled pistol with him in his belt while at the same time moving around with a strong guard even in British company. 'Nevertheless, I think he will be assassinated someday, and perhaps this would be the best thing that could happen for the Punjab, for the chiefs would then either set up Sirdar Lena Sing or Chutter Sing. He is a sad liar, and yet has ability; and if he could only be persuaded to act fairly, might weather the storm.' There was surprise among British circles that he refused to pay the soldiers' salaries on time, although his bodyguard and foreign clique round him were well paid. Towards Henry Lawrence and his coterie of assistants and political agents, he was sure to be courteous to the point of being obsequious. 'Your advice is as clear as the sun' was one of the phrases he used often in responding to Lawrence's correspondence. His grasping habits were causing doubts in the minds of his British allies, who preferred a weakened but stable Lahore state. As British perceptions of him became poorer by the day, Lal Singh's long-term suitability as the head of the Lahore Government began to be questioned. Henry Lawrence's impression was that he was deliberately building his ill-gotten gains as rapidly as he could with the full knowledge that he may have to flee shortly with the withdrawing British forces and was therefore already planning a wealthy retirement in British territory.

Despite his unpopularity, there never was any idea mooted by the British clique at Lahore, or any plan by Hardinge in Calcutta, to depose him. It's safe to say that if the Vizier had not dabbled in intrigue against his British overlords, he would have retained his position. The excuse to depose him, however, was not long in coming. It wasn't events in Lahore, but an unlikely attempted rebellion 300 km north of Lahore in the mountains of the province of Kashmir that would trigger his downfall.

\*\*\*

Sheikh Imam-Ud-Deen, the Governor of Kashmir, had seen his family's fortune rise dramatically since his childhood. His father had originally been a shoemaker, but, having joined Raja Gulab Singh's band and hung firmly on to his coat-tails, he had gradually climbed to prominence during the 1820s and 1830s. His father managed to accumulate huge wealth in this period until 1839, when he was made Governor of Kashmir, with his son, Imam-Ud-Deen, becoming the Governor of Jalandhar doab. Thus the family held a substantial portion of the Sikh empire under its grasp. The death of Ranjit Singh and the subsequent weak central Government had allowed father and son to avoid the payment of revenue into the Lahore treasury since then. This money, estimated to be more than a crore of rupees (10 million), was known to have been salted away for a rainy day in banks in British territory before the recent war.

The *Calcutta Review* of July 1847 paints a rather colourful description of the Imam-Ud-Deen's personality. 'The Sheik is, perhaps, the best mannered and best-dressed man in the Punjaub. He is rather under than above the middle height; but his figure is exquisite, "as far as it goes," and is usually set off with the most unrivalled fit which the unrivalled tailors of Cashmere could achieve for the governor of the province … his great natural intelligence and an unusually good education have endowed him with considerable conversational powers; and his Persian idiom would do no dishonour to a native of Shiraz.'

He also happened to be a literary person, later translating Herbert Edwardes' book *A Year on the Punjab Frontier* into Urdu in 1853. However, the *Calcutta Review*'s praise was offset by an equally colourful critique of his character. 'Beneath this smooth surface of accomplishment and courtesy,' continued the correspondent, 'lies an ill-sorted and incongruous disposition: ambition, pride, cruelty and intrigue, strangely mixed up with indolence, effeminacy, voluptuousness and timidity.'

Imam-Ud-Deen had stayed largely in the shadows during and after the late war, but events were about to involve him. The Treaty of Amritsar had awarded the Kashmir province to Gulab Singh, and the Lahore Durbar, to fulfil the agreement, duly asked Imam-Ud-Deen to begin organising the withdrawal of the Sikh army garrisons in the province and to make his way down to Lahore to hand over financial accounts. Similar to the commandant at Kangra Fort, the Sheikh would show reticence in complying with his orders. No one at this stage had any inkling that this demand would be refused, least of all Gulab Singh. He had good relations with the present the Sheikh's father, whom he had helped up the ranks, and relations with Imam-Ud-Deen were cordial.

Initially things went according to plan. Gulab Singh had sent some of his own troops north, and they reached the Kashmir capital, Srinagar, on 21 April. They had been duly given possession of the city fortress, the Hurree Purbut. However, there had been some argument between the two over expenses. Gulab Singh had then ordered up some of his forces to reinforce the Hurree Purbut garrison. Since then he had taken a rather leisurely approach to the issue of assuming control of Kashmir, perhaps waiting for the current governor to depart before he travelled up.

Four months after the Treaty of Amritsar had been signed, as August arrived, Imam-Ud-Deen still showed no sign of vacating Srinagar and had given no orders for the Sikh army garrisons to evacuate. Instead, on the pretext of collecting revenue, he delayed leaving week after week. There was the general impression that the governor was delaying in order to give himself time to move his substantial wealth out of the province and to sell the various properties he had. This was what Henry Lawrence thought as well, and little attention was paid at first, although during July Lawrence had asked the Durbar to be more forceful in its communiques with the governor to hurry him along so the Treaty of Amritsar could be fulfilled.

The reason for Imam-Ud-Deen's reticence in passing control of Kashmir to Gulab Singh was more serious and related to the jealousies endemic in the Lahore Durbar, principally Lal Singh's grudge against Gulab Singh. Gulab Singh, a former cavalryman, had risen by foul and fair means to high status. He was now being presented with a kingdom of his own by the British Government for merely staying neutral during the late Anglo-Sikh conflict. This had struck Lal Singh as unfair considering he had given active support to the British during the recent war, with all its attendant risks. In July, therefore, with little thought to how his decisions would affect him and his relations with the British, the Vizier sent covert correspondence to the Governor of Kashmir asking him to resist any attempts by Gulab Singh to acquire his new territory and therefore to avoid the Treaty of Amritsar being fulfilled.

My friend, you are not ignorant of the ingratitude and want of faith which Raja Gulab Singh has exhibited towards the Lahore Sarkar. It is indeed sufficiently glaring. I now write, therefore, to request you, my friend, that you will not set before your eyes the example of your late father's former relations with the aforesaid Raja, and consider both your duty and your interest to lie this way, and inflict such injury and chastisement upon the said Raja that he shall have reason to remember it. It is to be hoped that if the Raja takes but one false step, he will never be able to re-establish himself again. For your security and confidence, my friend, I have sent you a separate written guarantee, that you may have no misgivings as to the consequences. Let me hear often of your welfare.

P.S. – Tear up this paper when you have read it.

Dated 18th Sawan, 1903 (26 July 1846)

The separate letter was an *Ikarnama* or deed of promise carrying Lal Singh's signature, reassuring him of his support should the British intervene.

By the grace of God.

I hereby promise that if my friend Sheikh Imam-ud-din Khan Bahadur, with good-will and fidelity to his proper masters, duly performs the task imposed on him in a separate letter, my whole interest shall be exerted to secure him from being called to account by the British Government. Whatever allowance either he, or his jagirdari horsemen, or the Sheikh, his late father, received from the Lahore Government, the same jagirs, and something added to them, as a reward for service, shall be assigned to him in the Lahore territory. By the grace of God I will not fail to fulfill this that I have written.

Dated Lahore 12th Sawan 1903 (25 July 1846)

A third letter was an exhortation to the Sikh soldiers to stand by their governor with promises they would not suffer financially. Quite how the Vizier would prevent the governor being called to account by the British, who were resolved on separating Kashmir from the Punjab, wasn't elaborated. Imam-Ud-Deen, though, well aware of Lal Singh's duplicitous ways, would took care not to destroy the three letters he received.

The governor had had no real thoughts of rebellion prior to this correspondence, although he was none too happy at the loss of his governorship. The letters put him in somewhat of a quandary. He could follow the orders of the Vizier, his superior, and oppose the separation of the province from Lahore. This had the attendant risk of a dispute with the British, for eventually they would enforce the treaty. He had considerable wealth and jaghirs in the Jalandhar area now annexed by the British that were especially vulnerable to confiscation. However, Lal Singh had promised to forgive him the entire revenue of Kashmir due over the previous years, which he could now pocket with impunity for himself – more than enough compensation. A second option was to accept Gulab Singh's own offer of continuing in some capacity in the new administration. He had been offered a considerable salary of 1 lakh rupees per annum. However, the idea of working under Gulab Singh no doubt grated on the sensibilities of a man who had been subject to no superior for several years. He would also have to settle accounts with Lahore, losing much wealth. The third option was to attempt to make himself an independent ruler by making a counter-offer to the British over and above the sums offered by Gulab Singh. It was said he had his own ambitions ever since the decline of the Lahore court. Nevertheless, the treaty had been signed and it was unlikely the British would renege, especially so with Gulab Singh having determined to be their ally.

He chose the first option, having been, it was said, heavily influenced by one of his wives, a daughter of the Muslim Khan of Kohistan. She was apparently a bigoted woman. Kohistan was a feudatory to any ruler of Kashmir and she had no wish to have the Hindu Gulab Singh becoming the overlord to her father. When official requests began arriving from Lahore to hurry his departure for the handover, the governor now pointedly and openly refused to follow Lal Singh's request.

***

During the final weeks of August, noting the governor's refusal to cooperate, the British Government began to take an increasing interest in the issue of Kashmir. Under direction from Hardinge, on 31 August 1846, Henry Lawrence sent off a slew of letters to all parties concerned that the British Government had on no account forgotten the matter and that fulfilment of the Treaty of Amritsar must be observed. A letter to Lal Singh requested him to do everything in his power to force the governor to cooperate or, Lawrence warned, the consequences would be serious. On the same day he sent a letter to the Sheikh also, warning him of the grave consequences of a refusal to obey the Lahore and British governments. Nearly a week later, and still with no real movement, on 4 September Henry Lawrence reminded Lal Singh again that failure on his part to apply himself to this task would result in the Treaty of Lahore being considered null and void in a veiled implication that the Lahore state would suffer.

The Sheikh, however, continued to show defiance and with another week going by with no progress Lawrence finally decided on military action. Portions of the Sikh army at Lahore would be sent up with the British units in Jalandhar put on standby. On 12 September he formally instructed Lal Singh to supply significant portions of the Sikh army for an advance on Kashmir to bring the Governor and his soldiers to heel. All Sikh units and garrisons between the Ravi and the fortress of Attock were to give one-half to two-thirds of their number to form a separate army which would then march for Kashmir. A declaration was sent out that any person fighting against this force in Kashmir or on its border would have their property confiscated. Preparations were also being made to send in a British force in case the Lahore Army proved unenthusiastic in carrying out a role to give away its own territory. Brig. Wheeler, with his force of six regiments of native infantry and two regiments of irregular cavalry and twelve field guns, a total of around 11,000 men, was told to make preparations to move from Jalandhar to Jammu with artillery forming, if necessary, a two-pronged attack into Kashmir with the Sikh units.

As Lawrence began energetically looking into the Kashmir affair, it soon became apparent the British would for never countenance any deviation from the agreed treaty. Lal Singh therefore finally began to exert himself to the task of the transfer of the province, entirely abandoning the Kashmir governor despite his previous oaths he would support him to the hilt. The governor would have to make a stand on his own against both the Sikh and British forces marching north.

This base betrayal at the moment the governor most needed help would do him no favours with the Sheikh, while his previous tardiness on the issue had already aroused suspicions in the British camp as well. Hardinge realised there was little chance of the governor rebelling on his own against both the Lahore and British governments. He must be receiving a show of support from some, if not all, of the Durbar – and certainly Lal Singh. Added to that was the five months the Vizier had prevaricated on moving the Kashmir issue forward, making one excuse or another. Henry Lawrence, too, was conscious of possible foul play by the Vizier now things were coming to a head. He summoned Lal Singh's vakeel (representative) to his residence to tell him he would personally lead the Sikh force north. 'I was obliged to tell Lal Sing's vakeel that if anything happened to me, John Lawrence was told to put the Rajah [Lal Singh] in confinement. The fact was, I knew he was acting treacherously, but trusted to carrying the thing through by expedition, and by the conviction that the British army was in our rear to support and avenge us.'

Meanwhile as punishment for the Sheikh's truculence, all the considerable property and land the Governor of Kashmir held in the Jalandhar doab, now British territory, had already been confiscated by Henry Lawrence. An announcement was also prepared declaring that all Sikh soldiers were to obey the Lahore Durbar and that if they distanced themselves from the Sheikh their lives would be spared and all arrears paid before disbandment.

On 22 September Lt Edwardes, who had been specially deputed to oversee what progress was happening regarding Kashmir, wrote a final ultimatum to the Sheikh:

I now promise you that if within two days after the arrival of Vakil Puran Chand, Sardar Fateh Khan, Tiwana, and the other Sardars, you proceed to join me at once, and disperse those over whom you have any influence, your life shall be spared and orders will be issued for the release of your family, who are now in confinement, on the day that you give yourself up. With regard to your property, which has been confiscated, you must await the decision of the Governor-General.

From all this consideration on my part do not suppose for a moment that you have not incurred the resentment of the British Government, and that they do not intend making over Kashmir to the Maharajah [Gulab Singh], because arrangements for sending up an army have already been made and its march will not be delayed for your answer. Whether you come in or hold out, a force will be sent for the settlement of Kashmir and Kohistan. Don't therefore wantonly destroy yourself. There is but one hope left for you, and that is to come in and give yourself up.

Meanwhile the Sikh force from Lahore, comprising 7,000 men under Shere Singh Attariwala and accompanied by Henry Lawrence, finally set off on the road to Kashmir on 2 October. Progress was slow, the Sikh officers showing little enthusiasm for the task of carving off a significant chunk of the state for Gulab Singh's benefit. Tej Singh, the Commander-in-Chief, himself an enemy of Gulab Singh and Ranjodh Singh, who had led the Sikh army at Aliwal in the recent conflict, were to accompany the force. They continued to make colourful excuses that the astrologers did not recommend a march at this time. To this, John Lawrence, Henry Lawrence's brother, would send sowars back twice every day with the rather sarcastic question of whether the omens were fine or not yet.

When news reached him of this force eventually marching, Sheikh Imam-Ud-Deen realised all too soon he had been abandoned to his fate by the Vizier, any written guarantees to smooth matters over with the British being entirely worthless. His key supporters, too, realising the game was up, began abandoning ship. This included Mirza Fakir Ullah of Rajauri, a local chief and previously one of his staunchest supporters, who vanished and was soon seen carousing with Gulab Singh in his camp in Jammu. It didn't take the governor long to decide to accept Edwardes' offer, and he wasn't about to take the full blame for the whole incident either. Angry at the betrayal, the Sheikh sent his vakeel Puran Chand to meet with Herbert Edwardes at Riasi on the way south to Lahore and tell him the entire business had been instigated by the Vizier himself, that he had been merely following orders and that he had proof in the form of signed letters by the Vizier.

Edwardes quickly passed these revelations to Henry Lawrence, promising the Sheikh complete immunity and more for his cooperation.

I hereby promise that if you come in to me quickly and bring with you the written orders of the Lahore Durbar to act as you have done and create disturbance in Kashmir, not only your life shall be spared, but the British Government will not interfere with your Kashmir property, nor allow the Lahore Durbar to call you to account. It will not do, however, to say that you have them, or to produce certified copies; you must give up the originals. I will come as far as Thana, which is the boundary of Rajouri, to meet you. The kindness of the British Government depends on your coming quickly. Be under no anxiety for your family.

In addition, Edwardes promised the Sheikh he would be protected from any demands for financial accounts for the territory of Kashmir to the present time by the Lahore durbar, a hint that he could keep the ill-gotten gains he had salted away and for which he was later censured by the Governor-General for overstepping the mark. In response, on 1 November, in the middle of a fierce snowstorm, Imam-Ud-Deen travelled south and met up with Henry Lawrence at Thana near Rajauri. There he would hand over the three original letters sent by Lal Singh, which effectively sealed the fate of the Vizier.

So with the surrender of the Sheikh, and eight months after being awarded the beautiful valleys of Kashmir by the Treaty of Amritsar, the way was clear for Gulab Singh to travel to the capital, Srinagar, to be installed as the new and rather unwelcome ruler of the land. He entered the city at 8 a.m. on 9 November, the time being chosen by his astrologers as the most propitious for his new reign. His army had already been sent into the city prior to his entry to cajole the locals into lining the route to the palace to welcome him. There had been the rather delicate matter of whether the British, represented by Henry Lawrence, would ride with him in triumph into the city. The problem was that the presence of British agents and troops would show only too well to whom he owed his good fortune, and whose bayonets would be propping him up. Lawrence was diplomatic about his predicament: 'I thought that his Highness would prefer entering his capital by himself, and therefore gave him the opportunity of doing so, but the meeting at Pampur led me to imagine he was willing to sink his dignity in the increased opinion of British support that my formal accompaniment would afford him.' In the end, the

British political agent and soldiers would be seen escorting Gulab Singh and his train through the narrow streets of the city.

*** 

With the Kashmir impasse coming to a conclusion, Hardinge was determined to get to the bottom of the affair. The question was whether it was Lal Singh on his own or others in the Lahore Durbar who had been supporting the contumacious governor. If the Lahore Durbar was involved, punitive action would certainly be taken against the Lahore state. He sent Frederick Currie, who had a background in law, to conduct a so-called 'enquiry' into the Kashmir affair.

'It is apparent from the nature of the papers which he [Sheikh Imam-ud-Deen] has produced that the investigation will in reality be the trial of the Vizier Rajah Lal Sing and the Durbar,' Hardinge advised Currie (although the word trial was not to be used). But the British Government bringing to trial or questioning the Prime Minister of the Lahore state was an unprecedented step. For Lal Singh was not a subject of the British territories but the Prime Minister of a supposedly independent state. There was a way round it from a legal aspect, however, as Hardinge elaborated in a long letter to Currie on 23 November. Since he had surrendered himself to a British political agent after the revelations, this provided just the excuse for him to be 'questioned' by a British tribunal. As to what to do after the formalities, Hardinge was quite clear. If Sheikh Imam-ud-Deen could prove he was only following Lal Singh's orders, 'the Rajah's deposition from power and his immediate exile from the Punjab into the British territories will be demanded under such arrangements as may be determined upon after the whole case has been fully investigated'.

There were other opportunities as well now that changes would be forced on the Lahore Durbar. The Maharani, the only real supporter of the Vizier, could also be manoeuvred into a purely ceremonial role. Wrote Hardinge:

Facilities may be afforded arising out of this state of things to deprive Her Highness of power. The great scandal which Her Highness' intercourse with the Vizier has caused has rendered her government as Regent odious to the people and her deprivation of power would be justified on the ground that the notoriety of her profligacy has been carried to an extent which disqualifies her for the duty of acting as the Regent of the Lahore State during the minority of her son.

Removing both the Vizier and the Maharani at the same time would make the state headless, and Hardinge was anxious that it not be seen as a move to further dissolve Sikh power. He decided that the onus of this decision, if it was to be taken, must fall squarely on the Lahore Government, in other words the Lahore Durbar themselves must be coaxed into asking the British Government for the Maharani to be deprived of all power. That would be left for the future, though; the Vizier was to be dealt with first.

On 30 November, immediately on his return from Kashmir, Henry Lawrence began setting about organising the trial of the Vizier, the news of which caused much excitement among the Durbar and city population. Throughout the metropolis there was considerable satisfaction that Lal Singh's deposition, which was agreed to be a foregone conclusion, would be a good thing notwithstanding this further intrusion into the affairs of the Punjab by the British Government.

Lal Singh meanwhile was said to have been in great distress at the coming loss of power, holding meetings with well-wishers and supporters night and day.

***

Frederick Currie's entourage reached the small village of Bhyrowal on 1 December on their way to Lahore, where a large party of Durbar members including Tej Singh, anxious not to be implicated in the Kashmir issue, came to welcome and accompany him to his camp at Lahore. The day after Currie's arrival, a Grand Durbar was organised for his benefit. This event was far better attended than usual, with many more sirdars, Sikh army officers in Lahore and plenty of idle curious attending to hear what the Governor-General's secretary had to say. Arriving at the Durbar, after the usual pleasantries Currie moved on rapidly to business. He handed a *khureeta* in Persian from Hardinge to Duleep Singh demanding an enquiry into the recent behaviour of Sheikh Imam-Ud-Deen and any other persons involved in the recent Kashmir standoff. With Lal Singh already being held in Lahore and his accuser, Sheikh Imam-Ud-Deen, close by at the town of Shahdara, he informed them that the investigation would be starting the very next day, 3 December. There was a general murmuring of approval from the assembly, Currie noticed. There was, however, the issue of who was capable of judging the effective Prime Minister of the country. The Vizier, he informed the assembly, could only be tried by Europeans. Other members of the Durbar may be implicated as the investigation continued, and therefore it was unwise to include any of the Durbar members. And outside of the ruling circle, it would not be proper for people of lower rank to judge persons of higher station. In addition, it was his view that it would be impossible to find a person in high circles interested either in the Vizier's acquittal or conviction. In other words, no one in Lahore would give him a fair trial. The only impartial people, he explained, could be the British officers and agents in Lahore. He himself would head the tribunal as president, with the two Lawrence brothers along with Major-General Littler, the senior British officer at Lahore and now commander of the garrison at Lahore, and Lt-Col Goldie of the 12th NI forming the panel. The final question was who would defend Lal Singh at the enquiry. Currie glanced around the assembly, hoping a volunteer would step forward, but such was the Vizier's unpopularity that none offered to take the role. After an uncomfortable few minutes, Dewan Deena Nath would reluctantly agree.

***

The trial of Lal Singh, Currie had decided, would be an open one. He anticipated there would be much interest in the denouement, and this proved to be the case. The next day, his Durbar tent where the trial was to take place quickly filled to the brim. Sixty-five of the notables and officials of the Durbar were present also at the hearing, with their retinues and vakeels and other sundry curious people turning up. The proceedings themselves would last a bare two days. Currie kicked of the proceedings at 8 a.m. 'I was never present in a more orderly or attentive assembly,' described Currie in his report to the government later on the curious and hushed crowd gathered to watch their Prime Minister being questioned. Summarising the reasons for the trial taking place, that the Treaty of Amritsar had been threatened by the conduct of the Sheikh, Currie declared to the audience that the Sheikh had willingly agreed to submit to the British Government when promised the reasons for his refractory behaviour would be investigated. The panel had therefore been assembled to vindicate the Sheikh and to fully investigate the reasons behind his recent actions. Matters after that quickly turned to the role of the Vizier in the Sheikh's refusal to hand over Kashmir. Sheikh Imam-Ud-Deen was brought forward for questioning and summarised his position.

Puran Chand, my vakil, wrote twice to me from Lahore, to say, that if through my means Kashmir should still remain with the Lahore Durbar, and did not pass into the possession of Maharajah Gulab Singh, it would be well for me. I said that unless I received a written document to this effect, I could take no steps in the matter; it was not sufficient for Puran Chand to write; Raja Lal Singh or the Durbar must write. Accordingly I did receive written orders, through Puran Chand, and I have since given in the originals to Col Lawrence, Agent to the Governor-General.

He had also shown the *parwanas* to his officers, he said. The meaning of the letters being clear, a salute was fired in honour and he had accordingly made preparations to withstand Gulab Singh's army. The three surviving documents which Lal Singh had sent to the Sheikh and on which the whole case against the Vizier effectively rested were shown to the panel, read out aloud and the Sheikh asked to confirm the signature of the Vizier on the letters. One of the issues raised by the panel was why he had specifically ignored British requests to give up Kashmir, for he had received as many as five written requests from Henry Lawrence. 'I was the servant of the Lahore State and thought myself bound to obey its orders,' responded the Sheikh. As the proceedings came to a close for the day, Lal Singh was heard muttering that 'nothing was easier than to forge any man's signature'.

At 8 a.m. the following day the tent was even fuller than the previous day, with Sikh army military officers and others present as word filtered around that all were permitted to watch the enquiry. Deena Nath, realising the letters were the crux of the matter, would stand and argue that the signatures on the letters were forged. In order to prove this he would wave two recent forgeries of Lal Singh's signature on official documents. Separating genuine from false was very difficult, he declared. He also read out a statement written by Lal Singh, who had decided not to take the stand himself. In the statement, the Vizier too stressed that forgeries were extremely common and had caused much trouble recently. But his main defence was that having signed the recent treaties with the British, he would never dream of breaking them. It was the Sheikh himself who had decided to rebel for reasons of his own, he countered. Deena Nath concluded by suggesting this entire Kashmir affair had been a plot by Gulab Singh himself and the Sheikh to cause a rupture between the British and the Lahore state. He declared how 'considerate and merciful the British Government had been to the young Maharajah Dhuleep Singh, to the Lahore state and to the members of the Darbar and that it would was highly implausible that anybody taking this into account would not only endanger the future of the state and the Maharajah but also his own life and material prospects'.

Lal Singh and Deena Nath's explanations of plots and forgeries made no serious impression on Currie and the tribunal. When the proceedings came to a close on the second day, a unanimous verdict of guilty was quickly made. Currie did not deem it right to discuss the verdict in public, however. So while Lal Singh, Sheikh Imam-Ud-Deen and lesser attendees waited with Lt Edwardes, all the leading sirdars and ministers of the Durbar, twenty-two in number, were taken aside to hear the verdict of the panel. Addressing them, Currie explained the evidence was overwhelming. He said that they had found no evidence of other persons of the Durbar guilty of aiding Lal Singh in any way. If they had, the Governor-General would have considered this a gross violation of the recent treaty and a termination of friendly relations. However, he was satisfied that what had happened was purely the Vizier's doing and therefore friendly relations would continue. The Vizier still had to be deposed, and held under surveillance pending the Governor-General's decision as to his fate. 'It was manifestly impossible that the Government of the Maharajah could be carried on with any prospect of success by one who had proved so faithless to His Highness' interests, or that the British Government could continue to act in concert with one who had so grievously offended against them,' Currie declared to those assembled. As expected, the response from the sirdars was unanimously in favour of Currie's decision, such was the hatred for the Vizier. Discussions immediately began on the need to strip the Vizier of all his jaghirs and wealth he had accumulated during his tenure. Even Dewan Deena Nath, his recent defender, it was noted, turned his attention to arranging the arrest of Lal Singh's relatives who had also been appropriating jaghirs and were in tax arrears. A letter was tabled later that day by the members of the Durbar thanking the Governor-General for his generosity in letting matters rest at this point. 'The guilt of the Vizier and the justice of his deposition are admitted by the members of the Durbar and they notice in strong terms of gratitude the equity and mercy shown by the British Government in absolving the State from the consequences of the Vizier's crime,' Hardinge would inform the Secret Committee later.

Meanwhile, an ashen-faced Lal Singh was brought before the British tribunal after the Durbar members had all been dismissed and told of the verdict by Currie before being led back by regular units under Tej Singh to his own house. Seated on his own elephant, his own hand-picked former bodyguards now became his jailors, preventing his escape. He was to be kept incarcerated in his residence until the Governor-General decided on his place of exile in British territories or other suitable punishment. All that remained now, before a public declaration of the guilty verdict, was to inform the Maharani that her favourite was more than likely to be exiled and Lawrence would go along with the rest of the Durbar to the palace to inform her in person.

No disturbances or demonstrations by the Lahore population would take place following the public announcement of the deposition of Lal Singh. 'Everything is to-day as quiet in the town [Lahore] as if nothing of interest to the people had happened, and the deposition of the Wazir is said to have given universal satisfaction,' reported Currie to the Governor-General. In order for the work of government to continue uninterrupted, a temporary council of four to govern the state comprising of Tej Singh, Shere Singh Attariwala, Dewan Deena Nath and Fakeer Nur-Ud-Deen was immediately selected by Lawrence and Currie. Only orders and *parwanas* with the seals of all four members of the council should be obeyed from now, all officials were informed. Somewhat symbolically, the Seal of the Maharajah was presented to Henry Lawrence at the specific request of the council of four.

On 9 December, five days after being found guilty, Lahore received the news from the Governor-General as to the Vizier's fate. Lal Singh was to be exiled in British territory. He would be taken to Ferozepore while thought was given as to his eventual destination. Four days later, under a heavy guard comprising the 12th and 27th NI, a company of Sikh infantry, 200 Sikh sowars headed by Lt Wroughton and two 9-pounder guns, Lal Singh, along with a huge retinue comprising several thousand servants, various camp followers and his family, left Lahore in a lengthy convoy towards Ferozepore across the Sutlej River.

The decision to depose him had apparently hit the Vizier hard, and he is said to have been deeply upset at his loss of power and wealth, having been given no opportunity to organise his financial affairs and ill-gotten wealth. His family, too, were placed under house arrest. His hurried departure meant he would leave an unexpected windfall for the British. A huge cache of money, jewels and gold mohurs valued at 23 lakh rupees was later found hidden in the Vizier's wardrobe in his apartments in the palace the following year. Guards had been placed over his property since his exile, the properties having been sealed. An inventory of his entire wealth and property would be ordered and the apartments minutely searched.

As the Vizier's long convoy of elephants and camels made its way out of the streets of Lahore and took the road to Ferozepore, he was watched with indifference by the people and with most barely showing a passing interest. 'The momentous events I have above recorded were enacted in perfect peace; perfect quiet reigned in the city and the country,' noted Henry Lawrence. 'Not a shop was closed or plough laid aside during the trial, deposition, or removal of the Vuzeer.' His ultimate destination would be exile in Agra, where he would stay under house arrest until after the end of the Second Anglo-Sikh War, when he was allowed to leave for Dehra Dun. There he would end his life in relative obscurity.

# 3

# 'If the English Stay, We Will Be Ciphers'

Should no chief of eminence or vigour enough to control contending parties or
maintain without our aid the tranquility of the country arise we may probably be
compelled to take possession of it for ourselves.

*Bombay Times*, October 1846

… in any agreement made for continuing the occupation of Lahore, her [Maharani Jind
Kaur] deprivation of power is an indispensable condition.

Hardinge to Henry Lawrence, 7 December 1846

The deposition of the Vizier Lal Singh, whatever his failings, in early December 1846 effectively
left the Lahore state headless and with less direction than before. A council of state comprising
four individuals was now responsible for steering the country, any decisions requiring all
their signatures before any action could be taken. Nevertheless, all four individuals, of similar
political stature, were content to defer to the British political agent Henry Lawrence. Lawrence,
in turn, held only an advisory role at the time, his job as a political agent being to help bring
stability to the country prior to the British force leaving Lahore. This made any great decisions
all but impossible, with the assembly only stirred into action when cajoled to do so by Henry
Lawrence or Frederick Currie. This interregnum would last little more than two weeks before
the council was swept aside in favour of direct British control of the state.

Months before the trial of the Vizier, the issue of continuing or increasing British influence
in the Punjab or the alternative of withdrawing the British garrison from the capital had been
taxing Hardinge's mind. The Treaty of Lahore specified a British presence in the Sikh capital
no further than the end of the year. During the short time since his exile, and in fact many
months prior to that, there had been few serious moves by the Durbar to establish a secure
government requiring no support from a British force at Lahore. Now, as the months ticked
by, the question of the return of the British troops across the Sutlej loomed large. The Durbar
members, weak and lacking in authority themselves, were undoubtedly happy with the status
quo. The British troops brought stability and that was one of the issues on which they could all
agree. There had already been some vague attempts to extend the British stay in Lahore prior to
the Vizier's trial. On 10 September 1846, Lal Singh himself, being asked by Henry Lawrence as to
preparations relating to the British departure, replied in a frank manner that he had little chance
of surviving unless British troops remained at Lahore. He had also asked Henry Lawrence to
canvas the Maharani as well on the question. She, too, voiced the same opinion the same day.
Her opinion would not change despite his subsequent trial. 'No one has expressed a more
anxious desire for our stay than the Maharanee; and, even on the day following that on which

Rajah Lal Sing was deposed from the Vizarut, and her grief was at the worst, she declared to me, when I called on her, that she would leave the Punjaub when we did,' Lawrence would report of their conversation on the issue. She had suffered much grief from the Khalsa (the army), she explained to the Resident, and her life and Duleep Singh's depended on the British presence. Following these meetings, Lawrence had asked Lal Singh to write to the Governor-General expressing his wishes. The letter was duly sent off, requesting British troops to be stationed in Lahore for a further six months on the same conditions. This would, the Vizier explained in the communique, give more time to organise the state and the army.

His trial would overshadow these moves, however, and no progress on this front would occur. Hardinge's opinion on the Punjab, though, unbeknown to the Lahore Government, would completely change by the end of September. Earlier in the year, he seemed to have had less interest in continuing the occupation of the capital. His correspondence and personal letters of the time indicated a desire to pull out of the Punjab in December as stipulated in the treaty, going as far as to inform Henry Lawrence to advise the Durbar that on no condition would British troops continue their stay in Lahore. Durbar members pleading for British troops to remain at Lahore, he argued, would weaken further the regard the ordinary population had for their government. There were other issues as well. 'Such a course, notwithstanding the good terms on which the British troops have remained with the people and the Sikh soldiery, would cause discontent to the troops as well as the Chiefs and excite great mistrust of the ultimate intentions of the British Government,' he briefed the Secret Committee as late as 3 September. There had also been the issue of propping up an unpopular Vizier. Backing someone as corrupt as Lal Singh was seen in retrospect as a mistake, something that Hardinge was anxious not to repeat. The obvious and continuing weakness of the Lahore Government, however, swayed his decision as the year came to a close. Certainly the ease with which the Prime Minister of the state was toppled could only have strengthened his beliefs that nothing substantial stood in the way of an extension of control should he desire it. Therefore, as the autumn of 1846 arrived he would decide to exact many more concessions from the Durbar in return for the stability the occupying British force offered. The country would have to pay a substantial sum for the maintenance of a British force in the capital, but, far more drastically, the reins of government should be transferred entirely to a British representative or Resident. Arguing that withdrawal of the British garrison from Lahore would only mean instability and a resumption of war, he now began advocating British control of the Punjab was necessary for the foreseeable future. 'The other course – which it may be open to the British Government to take,' he wrote in a despatch to the Secret Committee on 10 September 1846, 'and which has constantly occupied my attention since the 3rd of September – would be, to carry on the Government of Lahore in the name of the Maharajah during his minority [a period of about eight years], or for a more limited time, placing a British minister at the head of the Government, assisted by a native council, composed of the ablest and most influential Chiefs.'

This proposal would maintain the façade of a Sikh government for the time being, with British control ending when the Maharajah came of age in 1854. Whether any future Governor-General would deign to give back the independence of the country in any fashion after the Lahore Government had been reduced to rubber-stamping the Resident's commands for so long was entirely moot. This would be for later Governor-Generals to decide. As these plans developed in his mind, Hardinge planned also to reduce the role of the Maharani. If British troops were to stay, she must be shorn of all power; he would press this point to Frederick Currie. In other words, all power must be unequivocally in the hands of a future British political agent with the

Maharani reduced to a purely ceremonial role. The Governor-General was cognisant, however, that it would not do to force these steps on the Sikh government. The request for the permanent stay of British troops and the transfer of power must come from the Durbar itself lest it be seen as an exercise in aggrandisement by the British Government. There was also be less internal dissension and opposition inside the Punjab as well, for the British Government had been requested to govern by the Durbar itself, and had not forced itself on the country. Whether the Lahore Government could stomach a complete handover of power was another issue entirely. To encourage them to do so, a stark choice would be offered to the Durbar. Either the Lahore Government must fend for itself against its own mutinous army or accept British control of the state. The imminent departure of some of the British troops from Lahore over the Sutlej as per the treaty would be declared as a precursor to a complete evacuation. 'My object is to give the Lahore Durbar a hint that the garrison is on the move,' Hardinge reprised Currie. 'These announcements will be made to accelerate the Durbar decision.' At the appropriate time, with British troops visibly departing, the ultimatum would be given. If the Lahore state opted for a British withdrawal but could not control its army in future, then the British Government would hold the Durbar itself responsible, with the possibility of a state of war being renewed. The Governor-General was aware their fear of the army praetorians and the return of anarchy would ensure conduciveness to any alternative British proposals, however damaging they may be to the independence of the state.

On 9 December, the same day that the exile of Lal Singh was declared, Frederick Currie invited the Durbar members to a meeting and presented a letter informing them that British troops would be withdrawn shortly as per the recent treaty. 'The receipt of this letter caused the greatest excitement at the Court, the majority of the sirdars being filled with alarm at the prospect before them, in the event of our withdrawal,' Henry Lawrence would report to Hardinge, confirming his prediction. There was the expected response. Deena Nath, among others, enquired as to whether the British Government would consent to continue maintaining a nominal force at Lahore to preserve order for a few more months. This was the cue for Currie to push forward Hardinge's ultimatum. He informed them the Governor-General did not believe maintaining the British force at Lahore was possible as it was not in keeping with the recent treaty, and that therefore a new agreement must be made. He then told all the Durbar members to assemble for a meeting so that he might tell them the one and only condition upon which the Governor-General would assent to maintaining British troops at Lahore. If this was unacceptable, British troops would leave immediately. The meeting was scheduled for a week later on 15 December.

The intervening days would involve hints of Hardinge's conditions being voiced in informal fashion to the government members. Hardinge had reminded Currie that the Durbar members must be manoeuvred into acceptance in the appropriate way. You must, he insisted to Currie, 'persevere in your line of making the Sikh durbar propose the condition or rather their readiness to assent to any conditions imposed as the price of the continuance of our support. In the preamble of the supplementary articles this solicitation must clearly be their act.' Meanwhile, Currie let it be known that one of the British native regiments and two guns that were escorting Lal Singh to exile were not to return to Lahore. The news was designed to spread. A further native infantry regiment was also to be moved away. Hardinge recommended encamping them as close to the citadel as possible prior to departure to make it more obvious. HM 80th were to be given orders to be ready for a move to Meerut, while HM 10th, which was meant to relieve them, would be retained at Ferozepore to further underline the move back across the border.

The hustle and bustle of hundreds of wagons and the thousands of soldiers, camp followers and animals clogging up the narrow Lahore roads being readied for the move to Ferozepore could hardly be missed by the eyes by the Durbar members.

Not all went smoothly for the British plan. From the palace walls, Jind Kaur could also see the British preparations for departure. Beyond the initial surprise at the sudden British withdrawal, the Maharani had begun thinking about the formation of a new government under her own auspices. As the mother of the Maharajah and the wife of Ranjit Singh, she had the necessary gravitas that none of the Durbar members possessed to become the head of government. Summoning the Durbar members to a number of lengthy and stormy meetings over the next few days, she would attempt to win support for an arrangement whereby she would be head of state until the young Maharajah came of age. It proved too late. Used to the safety of British rule, they proved unsupportive. The only member who offered support for her plan was Dewan Deena Nath. Leading the opposition to the Maharani's suggestions in these meetings were Tej Singh and Shere Singh Attariwala, who stubbornly resisted her plans. According to Lawrence, the sirdars would walk out of their meetings with her, frequently declaring the Maharani would bring ruin on the country and that they would prefer crossing the Sutlej along with the British force if she had her way. Finally they agreed not to interfere in a letter tabled by Deena Nath to the Governor-General regarding the Maharani assuming the reins of the state. However, they would later pen a second letter themselves to Lawrence stating they had no say in Dewan Deena Nath's correspondence with the Governor-General and disowned any part in its composition. Shere Singh was particularly averse to the Maharani having power, even though he was the Maharajah's brother-in-law. Writing privately to Lawrence, he asked for a meeting to explain his point of view that the British must stay in the Punjab regardless of conditions. Lawrence would decline his requests for a private interview, preferring to deal with the Durbar as a group. The opposition of the Durbar had the effect of scuppering the Maharani's plans permanently.

The day before the Durbar meeting scheduled by Currie, Deena Nath would make a final attempt to have British troops stay in Lahore without strings. He wrote to Currie to suggest that only a token British force was required to ensure tranquillity.

> As the Governor-General is desirous of maintaining this state, it is not proper that the whole of the British force stationed here should be put to further inconvenience and annoyance. Nevertheless with regard to the necessity for establishing the Government of the country and the fact of the time for the withdrawal of troops having arrived, it is hoped, that the agent, with two battalions, and one regiment of cavalry and one battery may be allowed to continue from some months during which what remains to be done to complete the organisation of the Government in an efficient manner may be effected, and there is no doubt that Col Lawrence will according to the provisions of the Treaty, give every aid and assistance in establishing the Government.

Currie, who had communicated this letter to Hardinge, was given an answer the very same day. Hardinge now regarded it as 'so absurd, that I considered it as equivalent to a desire to undertake the management of their own affairs, without our intervention'. There would be no half measures, he stressed to Currie again. They must accept his proposal or fend for themselves. He also refused to countenance a British force of less than nine battalions of infantry and the present complement of artillery and cavalry still at Lahore. The size of the British force stationed at Lahore would not be less than 10,000 men unless he decided otherwise at some point. There was also the matter of paying for the occupying force. 24 lakh rupees would be demanded for the permanent stationing of British troops at Lahore – to be paid at a rate of 2 lakh rupees monthly. If the sirdars did not agree to this, the threat to leave Lahore would be carried out. Hardinge finished off his letter with some more veiled sabre-rattling to be communicated to the Lahore Government during the coming meeting regarding any future anarchy in the Punjab if the British troops departed and its consequences. 'The Governor-General is bound by his duty to the Indian subjects of the British Crown to maintain order on the frontier by such means as may best secure that essential object and without the intention of expressing any threat you will declare my determination to hold the Lahore State responsible that the public tranquillity shall not be interrupted.'

The following day, 15 December, the meeting was held in Currie's tent. A huge number of Durbar members and officials along with other influential people, many more than expected, turned up for a gathering that was to effectively decide the independence of the state. Currie rose and addressed the assembly. After a brief preamble and general expressions of friendship between the British Government and Lahore, he reiterated the Governor-General's views aloud and the terms Hardinge had specified to him. If the Durbar members had ideas on self-government they must declare these now, he said. If, however, they preferred the British presence, then the British army would continue its occupation of the country and no units would leave the state – but the Governor-General could not consent to a half solution. He would not give the aid of British soldiers to a state over which the British Government had no control. If the sirdars wished for the British presence to stay then it would be of a different nature than the previous months since the end of the war. 'They must understand that his interference would be complete, i.e., he would occupy Lahore, or any other part of the Punjaub, with what force he thought advisable; a stipulated sum of money being paid monthly into the British treasury for the expenses of the same; and, further, that the whole civil and military administration of the Punjaub would be subject to the supervision of a British Resident, though conducted by the Durbar and executive officers appointed by them.'

Henry Lawrence would be the Resident and would therefore have unlimited powers lasting till 4 September 1854, when the Maharajah would reach the age of sixteen and take over the reins of power. Hardinge did sweeten the pill, though; the Durbar members were reassured of their positions in the new regime and their jaghirs would be guaranteed to them. Several of the senior people would be given honorary titles in addition. Copies in Persian of the conditions set out by the Governor-General were then distributed to all to peruse. Neither Currie nor Lawrence, who was also present, detail the reaction of the assembly and it's unclear whether most of those assembled really understood the implications of the new arrangement being offered, although some did. In conversation with Henry Lawrence a few days earlier, Fakeer Nur-Ud-Deen had drawn attention to the entire eclipse of the Sikh government in this new agreement. 'If the English stay, we will be ciphers,' he had protested to Henry Lawrence. 'There is some truth in the observation, such is the case whoever is in power; that he or they rule and the others obey,' Lawrence would admit bluntly, unwilling to gloss over the implications of this new agreement.

In the meeting, though, little opposition was voiced. Or maybe the sounds of British troops busy packing directly outside the fort had already had the intended effect as they entered the palace. For there was a general murmuring of approval after Currie had finished his address, most if not all showing their immediate willingness for the new agreement. Only Dewan Deena

Nath showed any visible disinclination. He demurred over Hardinge's offer, asking Currie for an adjournment whereby the Maharani Jind Kaur's wishes could also be taken into account. No doubt the extra time would allow discussion with the other sirdars on the implications of the offer. Currie replied the Governor-General only wished for the opinion of the sirdars and not the Maharani. She was not to be consulted.

The other issue Deena Nath raised to stall the agreement was that the amount to be paid to the British Government should be stated in any agreement. The agreement could not be made if the state could not bear the cost or it should prove too onerous. 'Upon that amount would depend their ability to avail themselves of the Governor-General's kindness,' he added rather sarcastically. Currie replied that, bearing in mind the financial embarrassment of the state, 24 lakh rupees would be requested. The Governor-General would on no condition accept a smaller force at smaller cost. With no other questions from the assembly, both Currie and Lawrence agreed to leave the room for an hour to allow the large gathering to confer.

Surprisingly, the only issue raised after its resumption was the compensation to be paid. Currie was asked to reduce the 24 lakh rupees demanded as that would put too crippling a strain on the country's resources and a counter proposal of 20 lakh rupees was put forward. After some discussion Currie compromised on 22 lakh rupees, which was quickly accepted. This being the only source of concern, Currie then asked each of the leading sirdars, fifty-one in number, to add their signature to the new agreement, overseen by the meer moonshee (chief secretary) in the presence of himself, Lawrence and Lt Edwardes. 'Though there were not a few in that Durbar who were foremost among the war-party at this time last year,' Lawrence recalled later, 'it is gratifying to know that, on this occasion, there was not one dissentient voice – not one who did not prefer British protection to a short-lived, anarchical independence.'

The meeting concluded, many of the Durbar members came to Currie to show their gratitude towards the Governor-General for continuing to extend his protection to the Maharajah's government. It had been decided to finalise the Articles of Agreement for a new treaty the following day when Currie, Lawrence and the various leading sirdars would discuss and formalise the new British-led government. Among the usual professions of eternal friendship and respect, four of the articles would carry the substance of the treaty. Article two would give the resident, Henry Lawrence, 'full authority to direct and control all matters in every Department of the State'. Article seven allowed the occupation of the capital, Lahore, by a British force, the size of which would be decided by the Governor-General. Further to this, article eight allowed the British to occupy any fort or defensive work in the state as wished. Article nine specified the sum of 22 lakh rupees, agreed the previous day, to be paid for the expenses of the British in occupying the country. Finally article ten provided a pension of 150,000 rupees to the Maharani, who was still unaware of the new treaty being crafted.

Further to the Resident having full authority, the Lahore Government would essentially be dissolved, with the creation of a 'Council of Regency', essentially a collection of deputies working under the Resident. The council would be composed of Sirdar Tej Singh (Commander of the Sikh army), Sirdar Shere Singh Attariwala, Dewan Deena Nath (the Chancellor), Fakeer Nur-Ud-Deen (Secretary of State), Sirdar Ranjodh Singh Majithea (the Sikh commander at Bhudowal and Aliwal), Bhaee Nidhan Singh (the High Priest at Lahore), Sirdar Utter Sing Kaleewala (Commander of the Sikh cavalry) and Sirdar Shumshere Singh Sindhanwala, a member of the leading family of the Sindhanwalas. The new treaty, it was agreed, would be signed in ten days' time, on 26 December 1847. News of the agreement and acquiescence of the sirdars to all British demands reached Hardinge later the same day and provoked mixed feelings within the Governor-General, who perhaps at this stage may have harboured desires for full annexation and a Union Jack flying at Lahore during his tenure:

> The moral effect of the Sikh Chiefs entreating the British Government to become the Guardian of their Prince, by the continuation of a British garrison at Lahore and our consent to undertake the responsible charge must be felt throughout Asia in raising the reputation and extending the influence of the British character. Personally I may regret that it has not been my fate to plant the British standard on the Banks of the Indus. I have taken the less ambitious course, and I am consoled by the reflection that I have acted right in the interests of England and of India.

The issue of the Maharani being pensioned off was a contentious one and Hardinge no doubt hoped she would cause no fuss or voice indignation in public. Giving the nod to Currie on the reduction of the annual payment to 22 lakh rupees, he wrote to Currie suggesting her exile if necessary, although at this stage would be too draconian a step.

> I am of the opinion that she will be harmless at Lahore than in any other part of the Punjab. If she should become troublesome and her expatriation be justified, she must be sent across the Sutlege, in which case she might perhaps be domiciled in the Raja of Ladwa's house and occasionally see her son. As Ranjit's wife and the mother of the Prince of all the Sikhs! I am disposed to act with caution, although the notoriety of her profligacy by itself would be a strong case of justification.

Word would soon reach the Maharani of the new treaty, and she was livid. A delegation of sirdars led by Tej Singh would visit her, giving her a veiled threat that if she opposed the treaty they would have nothing further to say to her and she would lose what little influence she had remaining. Powerless to do anything, she calmed down and swallowed her pride. However, she would not forget the negotiations completed behind her back. By the time Henry Lawrence went to see her in person on 21 December, five days after the drawing up of the new treaty, she had recovered her poise. Seated behind a veil, she thanked the British Government for the arrangements that had been made, which she said would save the throne and protect her and her son's life from danger. She reminded Lawrence she had always believed that if the British were to leave Lahore she would go with them as they alone guaranteed her safety. Lawrence was not convinced of her feelings. 'It must not be considered,' he surmised, 'that the Maharanee's words altogether expressed her feelings. I am aware that she is rather submitting to what she perceives is inevitable than that she is really pleased with present arrangements. I do not mean that she is dissatisfied at our remaining at Lahore; on the contrary, I have a sort of doubt that she could have given anything – even to half the kingdom, except the supreme authority – to have induced us to stand fast; and I even believe that she prefers her present condition with us to supremacy without our protection.'

***

Early in the morning of 26 December, the day agreed for the signing of the new treaty, a large cavalcade of Durbar members headed by the young Duleep Singh left Lahore and headed for the Governor-General's camp at Bhyrowal village. A large British gathering awaited them in an impressive and grand tent over 200 feet long. Hardinge, Gough, Sir Charles Napier and Waldemaar, Prince of Prussia, plus around 300 British officers were present, all waiting on one side of the tent with the other side reserved for the Sikh party. After pleasantries, at 10 a.m., the Treaty of Bhyrowal was signed with much fanfare and pomp followed by the roar of British guns effectively marking the passing of power to the East India Company. The Governor-General then delivered a long speech while sitting on the vice-royal throne, translated sentence by sentence by Currie into Persian in what was a sombre affair for the Sikhs present as the implications of the new treaty seemingly had been absorbed by this time: 'The Chiefs appeared perfectly listless and apathetic; but I understand they are dissatisfied and disappointed, and that they repented immediately after they had given assent to the terms of this treaty, which had been proposed to them at Lahore as the only alternative, if we were not at once and altogether to abandon their country, noted James Coley, the army chaplain watching the proceedings. The grand ceremony was polished off with an exchange of nuzzurs and a large amount of presents, among them guns, jewels and Kashmir shawls and other rich gifts.

With the serious business over, the period immediately after the signing of the treaty was one filled with parties and parades. The new treaty was signed just five days after the first anniversary of the Battle of Ferozeshah in the late war, and that evening the Governor-General had held a large dinner party for the occasion, making another one of his lengthy speeches. Hardinge also made arrangements for travelling to Lahore. There, on the eve of the New Year, a large garden party was held at the famed Shalimar Gardens, illuminated that night and where a brilliant firework display brought in the New Year. The next day a grand parade of British troops was held under the walls of the palace where Duleep Singh and Jind Kaur, in a closed palanquin and accompanied by Hardinge, inspected the British force, now to be a permanent garrison of the city. Four days later, on 6 January, a Durbar was held in the palace in the hall of audience by Duleep Singh with the ceremonial presentation of nuzzurs between Durbar members and the British party followed the next day as per custom, with the Governor-General returning the complement by holding a large dinner party in his camp outside the city. Tej Singh, Shere Singh and the other members of the Durbar were there, with large hurrahs following toasts to Duleep Singh and the Durbar. Two days later, another reception was held for Duleep Singh before Hardinge finally left the capital and the Punjab settled down to accustom itself to its new ruler, Henry Lawrence.

# 4

# The Prema Plot

A Raj is not to be procured without troops and treasure.

Astrologer to Prema

It is wise to keep before our eyes the fact that the animus of unrest and insurrection
slumbers but is not yet dead in the Punjaub.

Henry Lawrence to Government of India, 2 June 1847

As the new year of 1847 began, owing to the weakness of the Lahore Government and Hardinge's
ultimatum to remove all British support unless his demands were met, the East India Company
agent Henry Lawrence found himself to all intents and purposes the successor to Ranjit Singh
while the Durbar accepted a subservient role. This role would be reduced further still in the
coming months after Bhyrowal. Lawrence, now with power concentrated in his own hands, had
his own vision and plans for the Punjab, the more visible of which was the usage of a coterie of
European assistants to help him at Lahore instead of the Durbar members, while other agents
were chosen to effectively govern the provinces of the state.

These men, labelled Lawrence's young men on account of their youth, would fan out over
the state in the coming months, acting as advisors to the local governors but in reality being
deputies of Lawrence, through whom all decisions by the Sikh authorities had to be passed.
They reported directly and solely to the Resident in Lahore, with the Sikh governors reporting
to them in turn. Thus a new thin layer of British officers and political agents now managed
the country in the aftermath of Bhyrowal. Provinces would retain their Sikh governors and
administration, but these would work under what frequently amounted to the lone European in
the province. The Sikh army units, too, were expected to take their orders from these political
agents. Nevertheless, on paper at least, these men were still governing in the name of the
Maharajah of Lahore.

Some of these men made names for themselves in the Punjab during this time and the
coming war, while others became better known during the Great Mutiny in 1857 and beyond.
The province of Hazara, over 300 km to the north-west of Lahore, would be assigned to James
Abbott, a forty-year-old officer of the Bengal Artillery, with Chutter Singh as the nominal Sikh
governor. Hazara had initially been awarded to Gulab Singh in the aftermath of the recent war
but he had failed to establish control over the province and the territory had been given back
to Lahore in January 1847. To the west of Hazara, across the Indus River, lay the province of
Peshawar. Here George Lawrence would hold sway, which with Henry Lawrence as Resident and
John Lawrence in Jalandhar formed a family triumvirate in the Punjab. Below George Lawrence
a selection of other British political officers would work at various times: Reynell Taylor, who had

previously been in Kashmir, plus Lt Lumsden and John Nicholson. The nominal Sikh governor of Peshawar was Gulab Singh. Around 160 km south-west of Peshawar lay the border area and valley of Bannu, another rich and fertile area but wilder and more lawless than Peshawar. Here Herbert Edwardes would be assigned as political agent. Van Courtlandt, a mixed-race general in the employ of the Sikh army, was in charge in the Derajat, the area south of Bannu between the Indus and the mountains, but subservient to Herbert Edwardes. Meanwhile, to the east, across the Beas in the Jalandhar doab John Lawrence, the commissioner in the new British territory annexed recently, would be assisted by Henry Vansittart, Robert Cust, Lt Lake and Mr H. Scott. In Lahore, Henry Lawrence himself would be joined by Mr A. H. Cocks along with Major G. Macgregor of the artillery.

Changes were swift, with different policies applied as necessary by the British agents. The issues in the eastern provinces were quite different from the wild west of the trans-Indus provinces and the experiences and levels of difficulty varied depending on where the political agents were stationed. In Jalandhar, for example, one of the richest and most productive areas, there were no refractory tribes to deal with and the area was adjacent to British territory, allowing for closer control. Here, John Lawrence, having lowered taxes, had decided to dispossess much of the landholdings of the feudatories of the previous Sikh regime. These were people who gave military assistance to the Sikh army when required in return for their jaghirs. With the British having no need for their military services, action was taken to dispossess these often powerful people. 'We want neither your soldiers nor your prayers, and cannot afford to pay you for them' was the invariable and brusque reply John Lawrence gave on hearing the petitions and pleas of these people. Instead it was agreed they would pay money instead of the previous services and their jaghirs were reduced accordingly. These men having fought in the Sikh army in the recent campaign, the feeling in British circles was that they must bear the consequences and there was little sympathy from John Lawrence. In consequence there was a disaffected section of the population who, though incapable of insurrection by themselves, were open to rising up as part of any larger movement.

In the far west, where fanatical Muslim tribesmen, generally immune to the lure of organised government, formed the bulk of the population, there were different problems. Herbert Edwardes was generally pessimistic as to whether the establishment of law and order by British officers could ever succeed any better than during Ranjit Singh's period.

> It may, perhaps, be urged that the administration of just laws should conciliate the good opinion of the people, and reconcile them to the loss of their former barbarous liberty. But this theory is at variance with all the experience which we have gained of the Affghan character; and perhaps must not be too confidently applied to our oldest possessions in Hindostan. The hope that a Sikh Government, even with all the supervision that British officers can give it, will ever succeed in securing the affections of an ignorant, and, therefore, most intolerant, Mussulman population, is, I am afraid, delusive. What has it to offer them, in return for one fourth or one third of the produce of their fields? – Nothing but laws. And it has been very fairly doubted whether the want of laws was ever felt by any society which had never known them; though once enjoyed, their loss is a severe infliction.

Edwardes' impression was that these unwilling subjects would always be ready to rise at an opportune moment, and always remain the secret enemies of any administration, be it Sikh or British. His role and the role for the other British political agents turned out to be a sinecure for most of the time, however. They were welcomed to varying degrees by the local Muslim population in the Indus area and beyond. These tribesmen typically would fight against any ruling power that levied taxes on them, which at this time happened to be the Lahore Government. These British agents represented allies against a more immediate enemy, therefore. Edwardes and the other political agents could also offer and court public popularity, with two policies which the Sikh governors could not. One policy was a return to some sort of law and order. During the anarchic period after Ranjit's death, corruption had increased massively and many ruthless officials and kardars had taken to extortion and bribery. These officials were no longer trusted by locals. The other was tax reductions, which Lawrence had ordered from Lahore. If these reductions succeeded and tax revenues in total went up, this was a measure of the success of the new British administration. If tax revenues fell, then the Lahore treasury would take the hit rather than East India Company coffers and therefore this policy held no loss for the British administration. This allowed good relations to develop between the agents and the Muslim populations during the year, to the extent that Edwardes and Abbott in Hazara would become Cortés-like figures during the coming war, recruiting Muslim tribesmen with ease for their own 'armies' to fight the Sikh armed forces.

They had plenty of independence in action as well, largely dictated by their distance from Lahore. A letter from Peshawar, nearly 500 km from Lahore or from further south from the Derajat, could take a week or longer, and more if these areas were in a disturbed state. This delay meant these men effectively had much freedom in everyday affairs. By the end of 1847, only Multan, the large, southernmost province bordering the recently conquered British province of Sind, had a local Sikh governor, Dewan Mulraj, untrammelled by a British political agent.

Lawrence himself was impressed by these men and held them in high regard, and there seems little doubt that many had the expertise and skills required. But there were problems associated with letting the political agents loose in the Punjab. They were usually alone, or few in number, in their newly established fiefdoms and far from any supporting British military force. Most of these figures were flamboyant and outspoken men, as well as being young. Taking orders from these fresh-faced youths, frequently in their twenties, no doubt grated heavily on the sensibilities of the Sikh establishment and army in the provinces where no conquering British army had been seen. Many of them also seem to have had an eye on publicising their achievements and success in the British press, irking the locals, as George Campbell, the commissioner of some of the Cis-Sutlej states, noticed.

> They were sometimes young men without any civil training, yet too much inclined to interfere with native methods, and to assume to themselves the role of rulers behind a screen of native form. I think too a good many of them were rather too much connected with the Indian press, and too apt to get their heroic deeds rather over-puffed by that medium. In the management of the Punjaub under the Residency system from 1846 to 1849 I rather think that there was a good deal of that sort of thing. It is quite startling the way in which hitherto unheard-of Politicals start up in every corner, to be chronicled in the pages of the *Delhi Gazette* and, in truth, one way and another getting up conspiracies or suppressing them, taking forts or keeping them, fighting battles and wigging kardars they have hugely illustrated themselves.

More importantly, the policy of sending lone political agents to rule over these distant areas with only British prestige to protect them was a dangerous one. Others, too, albeit in hindsight, were critical of this policy of allowing the agents in the provinces to override the Sikh governors in such visible fashion and noticed danger surfacing. 'As reforming Englishmen, ignorant of Punjabis but aware of their own powers toured throughout the land, redressing abuses and treating as servants men who had been lords of hundreds of villagers, the Khalsa, from sirdar to peasant felt that their raj was over, and that even when the Maharajah came of age and was proclaimed the independent sovereign of the Punjab, he would still be a king in leading-strings,' wrote British chronicler Septimus Thorburn, later Financial Commissioner of the Punjab. These policies of Henry Lawrence made the installed Sikh governors largely redundant although they were retained in their positions. Lawrence's assistants at Lahore also meant the use of Lahore Durbar members was largely dispensed with for more prominent decision-making, and their presence was increasingly required only for the more ceremonial occasions. Relations between himself and the timorous Durbar remained good, however, and the Durbar members quickly became used to Henry Lawrence as their superior. Certainly there was never any disagreement with the Resident, the members recognising they and their fortunes were dependant on British largesse and goodwill, and they assisted as and when they were asked.

'On the whole the Durbar and the chiefs give me as much support as I can reasonably expect,' he would report to the government. 'There has been a quiet struggle for mastery but as although I am polite to all I allow nothing that appears to me wrong to pass unnoticed; the members of the Council are gradually falling into the proper train and refer most questions to me and in words at least allow more fully even than I wish that they are only executive officers to do as they are bid.'

***

Discontent at this new order and the voluntary surrender of power by the Lahore Government was most noticeable in the barracks of the Sikh soldiers, although there were plenty of nationalist groups sprouting up around Lahore and beyond as well. The soldiers' scorn for the Durbar members had never been latent. The Sikh army had over the last year already lost many men due to enforced cuts as specified in the Treaty of Lahore. Many unemployed Sikh soldiers could now be seen milling around Lahore and the country, a telltale sign to any passer-by of the changing state of things. George Campbell, passing through the Jalandhar doab after the signing of the Treaty of Bhyrowal, noted the discontent among these men. 'They could not be expected to be very amiable after their defeat, and when their country was being surrendered to a sort of British tutelage,' he noted. 'I saw groups of them standing about near the villages; they seemed rather sulky and took no notice of me, but neither did they molest me, and I got through all right.'

These men were open to suggestions of insurrection and lacked only a leader who could give them direction and arms. What was also required for insurrection was access to money, and this became available from a new source: the Maharani, who had been deprived of all influence in government by the recent treaty. Angered at her British 'allies' usurping power, Jind Kaur quickly became the focus of attention for nationalist elements who required her wealth and connections to fund their plans.

The first plot surfaced in the capital around six weeks after the Treaty of Bhyrowal. Nationalist elements in Lahore, led by a Brahmin Hindu called Prema, had formulated an audacious plot to dispose of the Resident along with Tej Singh and Shere Singh, the more pro-British of the Durbar members. The plan would become known as the 'Prema Plot' after its main instigator.

Formerly a soldier in Gulab Singh's army in Kashmir, Prema had left his employment for reasons not clear. Unhappy with the state of things, he came to Lahore where he rapidly set about making contact with other disaffected elements as well as like-minded Sikh soldiers and officers. Plots required money and the right contacts, and Prema ensured he met with Bhai Maharaj, a famous Sikh preacher and vociferous opponent of British control, then at Amritsar and of whom more will be heard later. Bhai Maharaj, realising Prema had the necessary qualities, would write a letter of introduction for him to give to Boota Singh, the Maharani's moonshee. Prema would make acquaintance and hold meetings with the moonshee and others over the coming weeks. With plentiful money being received from Jind Kaur via her moonshee, more men began to be recruited to the cause. This included British sepoys, essential to any success as the European elements of the British garrison would have to be overpowered and done away with along with ingress to fortifications and other occupied buildings managed.

The plan essentially was to dispose of the Resident and the Durbar members at a suitable opportunity. This would then be a trigger for a general uprising led by the Sikh army contingents near the city, who would then seize the fort and palace. An opportunity to dispose of said persons, however, wasn't easy to find. The British residences and the fort were too well guarded and there was no guarantee all the intended victims would be present together in any case. The only realistic opportunity for an assassination would be when these persons ventured outside of the fort and residence buildings on some occasion, and these were few and far between.

The chance, quite by coincidence, would come sooner than thought. It became known there would be a garden party organised on 12 February 1847 at the Shalimar Gardens, a 40-acre pleasure ground for the nobility around 7 km east of the palace. Most of the members of the Durbar would be attending and the Resident and various British officers too had been invited. The event would be attended by the usual limited escort, which could be overwhelmed if a large group of several hundred well-armed men could be recruited for an attack. Part of the plan, later revealed, was to shoot Tej Singh separately as he made his way to the gardens as it was known he would not have a large bodyguard. So even if the main plan failed, the most pro-British of the Durbar members would have been disposed of as a consolation.

The detail of the attack on the Shalimar Gardens would be that Prema, with his several hundred armed men, would attack the main entrance to occupy the guard. A separate, smaller assassination team led by Prema's nephew Nihal Chand would enter the gardens from the opposite direction to dispose of the Resident and Durbar members retreating from the shots.

With so many people involved, trustworthy recruits were essential. However, as more and more people were recruited, news began leaking out; Prema himself was less than discreet. Believing the plot must be carried out at an auspicious time to guarantee success, he had apparently begun visiting various astrologers in the city to acquire their suspect knowledge of the future. A certain Brahmin called Khosiyal Pundit had been approached by Prema and quickly turned informant. 'He had been promised the Raj of the Punjab, and intended to cause a disturbance, attack the British and kill Sirdar Tej Singh,' Pundit later recalled Prema saying at their meeting. 'A Raj is not to be procured without troops and treasure,' the pundit had countered, trying to dissuade him but without success. Prema in their conversations had divulged he had the backing of the Maharani, had the necessary funds and had already recruited a sufficient number of men. That he had been promised the Raj suggested delusions of grandeur, although the plan that Prema had come up with was essentially sound.

Meanwhile, Khosiyal Pundit gossiped about the plot to another astrologer colleague, Ruttun Chund. One of the Brahmins already in the conspiracy had also taken an influential man called

Shahzad Singh Bundelkhundiya to see Prema. Prema tried to recruit him but Shahzad Singh had shown no interest and instead tried to discourage Prema himself. Prema, not one to give up easily, offered him 3 lakh rupees if he joined the plot. He also indicated he was recruiting other British sepoys through a sepoy called Purusram Bog in the British garrison. Purusram Bog was targeting the sepoys who manned the gates of the city as it was essential to capture these places during the coup.

Prema's nephew, meanwhile, had also been liberal with information. He had spilled the beans to a sepoy officer, a certain Hayat Khan who had been curious as to why so many soldiers had suddenly begun visiting Prema's living quarters. All this information would be reported by the astrologers to Tej Singh, no doubt gaining large financial rewards in the process.

Lawrence, when he was informed by Tej Singh, ordered the garden party preparations to continue as before with a mind to catch the plotters in the act. Much tighter security was ordered in the garden and along the road and secret measures taken to surround and arrest the armed conspirators at the gardens. On the day, the various dignitaries and the Resident gathered at the Shalimar Gardens as previously arranged.

Lawrence's counter-preparations may have been a mistake, however. At midday, as Prema and his 200-strong party approached the Shalimar Gardens, they developed an inkling that all was not right and aborted the mission. A disappointed Lawrence waited at the gardens for an attack that never came, but nevertheless orders were quickly issued for arrests. Eleven of the ring members were almost immediately apprehended, including Prema himself. At the enquiry the next day, as the conspiracy unravelled and information began to be volunteered by the more mercenary-minded of the recruits, more arrests were made until more than twenty-five men were in hand.

The questioning proved much more difficult than the arrests, however, each man having a different story and naming different ringleaders, and a rather byzantine plot was uncovered. Many of the plotters accused most of the Durbar members and other chiefs, falsely or otherwise. In fact there was no shortage of accused, so much so that many of those arrested rapidly lost credibility. One of the ringleaders, Man Singh, an Akali, said that the Maharani was financing the plot and wanted Tej Singh and the Resident killed but had stated to them she would not give any written instructions in case any correspondence was later used as evidence. The fact that Boota Singh, the Maharani's moonshee, was mentioned by many seemed to firmly implicate Jind Kaur. But Boota Singh denied he had ever met Prema and protested he was being falsely implicated. 'There is abundant evidence on the face of the proceedings as well as from the admissions of the parties concerned to show that dangerous schemes were under contemplation. It is difficult however clearly to determine what were the actual designs of the conspirators and still more so who were the influential movers of it. The names of the Maharanee, Mean Jowahir Sing, nephew of Maharajah Golab Sing and indeed of every sirdar except Tej Sing, Dewan Deena Nath and Noorooddeen are more or less used by the different actors,' remarked a confused John Lawrence, then present at Lahore, in his notes on the case.

It would take another seven months, until September, for the long-winded investigations into the conspiracy to reach their conclusion, with little hard evidence uncovered in the meantime. Prema and three other ringleaders – Boota Singh, Man Singh and Dewan Ali – were sentenced to life imprisonment in British territories. Purusram Bog, the British sepoy active in recruiting other sepoys, and two others were sentenced to fourteen, seven and five years respectively for being accessories in the conspiracy. Two others, a Gurmukh Singh and Thakoor Das, were found guilty of concealing knowledge related to the plot and given three years. Another three – Budh Singh, Sheofyal and Goodur Das – were released due to lack of evidence, while for many others there was simply no evidence at all beyond accusations.

***

With accusations of financial help by the Maharani having been bandied around by the conspirators, British suspicions fell heavily on Jind Kaur over the next few weeks. Henry Lawrence tried hard to obtain any evidence of her involvement to no avail, but his animosity had been aroused. The Maharani had been expected to quietly retire from public affairs with good grace after Bhyrowal, despite being shunted out of power. Instead she was funding plots to oust British control. She had developed other enemies as well. Tej Singh, already at loggerheads with her, had been apparently greatly alarmed at the plot and had fits of fear afterwards of further attempts at assassination. Meanwhile, other timid members of the Durbar, anxious at being implicated in the plot by the conspirators, were distancing themselves from the Maharani as well. The result was that she had lost the support of the entire Durbar.

Henry Lawrence could do nothing without more proof, but he had determined on restricting the Maharani's access to her supporters and well-wishers and the outside world to prevent further attempts to fund conspirators. For this he would bring into play the excuse of social restrictions and customs prevalent round India at the time. It would be four months after the Prema Plot that Lawrence set these ideas in motion. A letter was drawn up addressed to the Durbar members with a copy sent to Jind Kaur as well. In this letter he spelled out that she had no political authority left and that she was not abiding by the spirit of the Treaty of Bhyrowal.

> Her Highness the Maharanee mother of Maharajah Duleep Sing has no share whatever in the Government of this kingdom. A lakh and a half of rupees per annum are assigned to her that she may pass her days in honourable retirement. But I hear that Her Highness is in the habit of holding levees of fifteen or twenty sirdars at a time and also of giving private interviews to individual sirdars and officials.

He also went on to say she had been admitting fifty Brahmins daily into the palace in order to wash their feet and to feed them. This was all a pretence, he suspected, and the priests were merely messengers communicating to her sympathisers and other conspirators. 'I now therefore write to say that the conduct of Her Highness in the above respects is quite without precedent and altogether unnecessary and out of place. It is moreover a breach of female decorum and royal etiquette.' He asked her to refrain from inviting followers into the palace. The only people who should have access to her must be her servants and other employees only. In regard to religious observations, the Maharani should only carry out any religious observances like feeding the poor on the first of each month or on holy days, when presumably her visitors could be monitored more effectively. Further, essential visits by visitors should be carried out in groups at certain specified times rather than individuals entering the palace as and when, presumably also as a way of easily monitoring proceedings.

Another point was the custom of women staying in purdah, or behind the veil. It was common for Hindu and Muslim begums and Maharanis round India to not be seen in the open, to be transported behind curtained palanquins and to conduct any business from behind a screen. The veil was not the Sikh custom, however, and Jind Kaur was famed for watching the parades of the Sikh army on her elephant with her face uncovered in earlier years. But the old custom would now be enforced. 'Her Highness should sit behind the screen as do the Princesses of other Courts such as Jodhpore Jyepore and Nepal,' Lawrence advised forcefully.

Her reply would anger Lawrence. She thanked the Resident in sarcastic manner for his advice.

> You say that I have no share whatever in the Government! Remembering ancient friendship that existed between the two Governments, I invited a force and British officers to stay at Lahore solely for the sake of punishing the faithless servants of the State defending the Maharajah and myself and protecting the people and now you set me on one side and consult my servants only in conducting the affairs of the kingdom ... So long as the Maharajah is sovereign of his own kingdom it is the same as if I was sovereign myself. But if the new treaty has devised some better plan for securing the State's welfare, why, I am content.

Her reason, she explained, why so many persons visited her, was because her ministers were now hostile towards her and could not be trusted. Nevertheless she would acquiesce, she said, to all Lawrence's restrictions and demands and curtail her communication.

Despite these new restrictions, relations between her and Lawrence suffered further shortly afterwards. The letter Jind Kaur had sent to Lawrence had been meant for his eyes only but he had shown it to the Durbar members, who were incensed at her implication that they could not be trusted or were not well intentioned towards her. Learning of the letter being made public, the Maharani took this as a breach of confidence and an attempt by him to ensure a widening gap between her and the Durbar ministers.

As relations between Lawrence and Jind Kaur soured, the Resident's suspicions of her behaviour increased too and trivial actions by her or her servants began to be given greater significance. A somewhat amusing instance of this was when Lawrence notified the Government of India that the Maharani had sent a slave girl to Mulraj at Multan on a mission. Her task was to ostensibly collect leaves of the white Ak tree (Swallow wort) for medicinal purposes, but since her object was not, as the Resident thought, publicly declared and her arrival disclosed only in the Multan newspapers, he was sure it was a secret embassy to the Multan governor. Another incident two months later was also misconstrued by Henry Lawrence as more interference in Government affairs. The slave girl Mungla, the closest confidant of Jind Kaur, asked the Maharani to lobby for a jaghir for her. Calling the Durbar members to the palace, Jind Kaur had asked them to urge Lawrence to award her slave girl the land. Although a minor issue, Lawrence was irritated by her meetings with the sirdars. 'As Her Highness will thus interfere, I see no reason why she should have any communication at all with the sirdars more than any of the other Ranees,' he recorded.

The most obvious repercussion of the recent Prema Plot was the increased security and precautions taken by Lawrence and his assistants from then on. On 3 March 1847, another breakfast was organised for Lawrence at the Shalimar Gardens by the Lahore Durbar and all the British officers at Lahore were invited. Thinking a similar plot may be in the offing, Brig. Gen. Colin Campbell, now commanding the Lahore garrison, left half the British officers in the fort, allowing only the other half to attend. Sikh units were still located close by and in the fort, and Campbell had written detailed instructions for all British units in Lahore should an attack occur during the event.

Nothing materialised, but news of another plot did in fact surface shortly. In late April, Lawrence had heard from one of the hill chiefs of plans by some leading sirdars to rise against the British. Colin Campbell decided at this point to make the position of HM 10th, the only European regiment in the capital, more permanently secure. HM 10th were not being quartered in the fort itself but in the garden section outside, a large quadrangle between the fort itself and the Badshahi Masjid opposite, while a Sikh garrison of around a thousand men still manned the fort which overlooked the British position. Campbell was uncomfortable with this, and considered the regiment vulnerable to being massacred during a surprise night attack. Asking for the ejection of the entire Sikh garrison with the British garrison taking its place would be impolitic, however, and Lawrence advised sentries to be placed on top of the gateway of the fort to raise the alarm if required. The gateway had already been converted into a mess room for the regiment. The only problem was a nearby building of recent construction adjacent to the gateway that was higher than the gateway itself and therefore commanded it, giving the Sikh soldiers in the fort an advantage. An engineer was sent to inspect the building, and he reported if occupied and strengthened it would give a strong defensive position to the regiment. The following day, Lawrence and Major Macgregor came down to inspect the building and it was decided to ask the Durbar to destroy the building while the gateway was occupied as normal. The occupation of the gateway, a high vantage point, also meant the regiment had full control of who entered and left the fort.

These precautions and a more vigilant eye on suspected nationalist groups meant little else of importance would happen during the summer months except for more minor issues. In July 1847, for example, attention was drawn to another cow riot, this time in Jalandhar. Ranjit Singh had long before banned the slaughter of cows in the Punjab in deference to the wishes of the Hindu citizens. With the passing of Jalandhar to the British came the decision to overturn this law under pressure from the Muslim residents, who had a taste for beef. A large number of Hindus assembled to protest before the courthouse where Hercules Scott, the assistant commissioner of the area, had arrived. Scott refused to sympathise and John Lawrence, also at the scene, told them the law could not be rescinded, the decision having been made by the Governor-General. At this point violence broke out, and several of the Indian servants of John Lawrence were assaulted. In addition, fifteen sowars who had been ordered to disperse the crowd proved unequal to the task and were instead dragged off their horses by the rioters. John Lawrence, on appearing, was then the target of brickbats and stones thrown by the crowd. At this stage, he ordered a company of sepoys from the nearby civil treasury to assist and the subedar (officer), on seeing the sowars being roughly treated, quickly ordered his men to fix bayonets. On observing the naked bayonets, the crowd dispersed and there was no further violence. The local Hindu shopkeepers and business would keep the issue alive for several weeks by organising a *bund* (strike), however.

There was also a minor incident in Peshawar in July indicative of the frustration of the Sikh soldiery at the new order. An ex-colonel of the Sikh army called Ram Das was removed from his position. He had been reduced in rank to commandant earlier. On trial for financial irregularities, he had been found guilty by George Lawrence, the British viceroy in Peshawar. Ram Das openly lamented the current situation in which he and his fellow soldiers found themselves: 'It was reported to me that he had been heard talking to his orderlies of the state the Sikhs had come to when they allowed two Feringhees to rule them,' reported George Lawrence to his brother Henry on 20 July 1847. Ram Das was arrested and placed in confinement. He was later transferred to Lahore and imprisoned by the Lahore Durbar authorities for his behaviour.

***

With news of plots and the sullen faces of soldiers all too visible around Lahore and further afield, Lawrence needed no further cautioning and was well aware of the unrest among the

Sikh army and population in general to the new order. A sample of his letters and reports to the Government of India during the middle of 1847 provide a long catalogue of warnings as to the general dissatisfaction apparent amongst the Punjab population. In his report of the state of affairs in a letter to the Government of India on 29 April, for instance, he mentions rumours of many plots. Many of these were exaggerated, he believed, others had little chance of success and still others were false:

> That there are many who, like Sirdar Shere Sing, have not found all the advantage they expected from the recent arrangement, is most true; that there are others who accustomed to revolution and excitement, are ready for any move that, by turning out those in power, may, by possibility, bring in themselves, or friends, is also true; and that there are ten or twenty thousand disbanded soldiers, still on the surface of society, ready to take part in any disturbance, is also correct; but I much doubt if, in any man's mind, there has yet risen the thought of serious, overt opposition to British authority. No; the time has not yet come for anything beyond private schemes of treachery.

He heard of many people grumbling, he said. Others he said consulted priests for any prophecies on when Sikh power would be ascendant again. Stories abounded of former officers, colonels and generals of the Sikh army who had been made redundant and were struggling to survive and who were open to suggestions as to how to get rid of the British presence.

> If opportunity be given, the natural independence of the Sikh character may dictate the attempt to escape from under a foreign yoke; for, however benevolent be our motives, and conciliating our demeanour, a British army cannot garrison Lahore, and the fiat of a British functionary cannot supersede that of the Durbar, throughout the land, without our presence being considered a burden and a yoke, not only by those who have nothing to lose, and all to gain, by revolution, but by many of the bolder spirits among the better classes, who are ready to venture their lives, and property, in the cause of the Khalsa, and in the chances of a revolution that may make Generals, Sirdars, and even a Vizier, or a Maharajah.

Hardinge, while acknowledging the bitterness and resentment, had the opinion that the complete annexation of the state in his opinion would have increased other dangers for the British Government. If the British sepoys had to garrison the forts of the Indus and beyond with the population inimical to British rule their loyalty would be lessened, while the European troops available would be even more thinly stretched by having to man the entire Punjab in addition to existing British territory, increasing their vulnerability. 'These dangers, which, in my opinion, are remote, will be eventually the cause of our loss of this Empire, and would be aggravated by annexation,' he responded to Henry Lawrence's thoughts. His preference would always be a single, large force kept in readiness for war and with a large garrison kept only in Lahore to hold the capital.

Again, though, on 2 June 1847, Lawrence would warn of a strong underlying resentment against the British presence and the chances of rebellion:

> With the experience of fourteen months, I can certify to this people having settled down in a manner that could never have been hoped or believed of them; but yet they have

not lost their spirit. To this fact I frequently testified last year, and commented on their bold and manly bearing. A large majority of the disbanded soldiers have returned to the plough, or to trade; but there are still very many floating on the surface of society; and, such is the fickleness of the national character, and so easily are they led by their priests and pundits, and so great is their known pride of race, and of a long unchecked career of victory, that if every Sirdar, and Sikh in the Punjaub were to avow himself satisfied with the humbled position of his country, it would be the extreme of infatuation to believe him; or to doubt for a moment that, among the crowd who are loudest in our praise, there are many who cannot forgive our victory, or even our forbearance, and who chafe at their own loss of power, in exact proportion as they submit to ours.

The recent British disaster at Kabul, Lawrence pointed out, was much discussed in the towns and villages of the Punjab, and not without meaning, with the common man hoping the same disaster may befall the British garrison now stationed at Lahore.

# 5

# 'She Should Not Have the Means of Offering Large Bribes'

The Maharanee is the only effective enemy to our policy that I know of in the country.
Henry Lawrence to Government of India, 9 August 1847

Her Highness must be warned that on the first occasion of her entering into intrigues other and more serious steps must be taken.
Hardinge to Henry Lawrence, 14 August 1847

As the hot days of the summer of 1847 slipped by, Henry Lawrence made himself more comfortable in his new position as head of the Lahore Government. Few problems would surface in his dealings with the Durbar or the Sikh army, but it was not so with the Maharani, Jind Kaur. Relations with her, already cold after her pensioning off and her suspected subsequent involvement in the Prema Plot would get colder still till a full rupture in August.

The cause would be Lawrence's usurping of royal prerogatives now that she had been removed from power. He had decided during the latter weeks of July to award honours and titles to various members of the Durbar and others for their service and loyalty to the state. This was ordinarily something the senior royal would ponder on, but with the Maharani forced into seclusion and her role in government entirely reduced, Lawrence had assumed the role of deciding who would receive which honour. The young Maharajah himself, however, would still perform the annual ceremonial bestowing of the titles.

The titles distributed generally involved no cost to the state, but as in the present day were much sought after and valued. So much so that Lawrence had been inundated with nominations for titles for that year. The chief beneficiary this time would be Tej Singh, Commander of the Sikh army and committed enemy of the Maharani. Tej Singh had been largely anonymous over the previous year but his friendship with the British had cemented his high position. He was to be given the honorific title 'Raja of Sialkot', the Resident had decided. Shere Singh Attariwala, son of Chutter Singh, the Governor of Hazara, would also be given the title of Raja. Chutter Singh had initially been offered the title but had refused the honour (which would have been non-hereditary), giving the reason that he had few years left to live and requesting his son instead should be honoured. Another nine people in all, including Lehna Singh Majithia, Fakeer Nur-Ud-Deen and Dewan Deena Nath, would be given titles of honour 'for good service during the past six months' as Henry Lawrence put it. Others on this list included Heera Singh, the Maharani's brother and hence the Maharajah's uncle. He was a dissolute young man according to Lawrence but had mended his ways during recent weeks.

Jind Kaur, when the news reached her, was furious at Lawrence for usurping her role. Lawrence, meanwhile, compounded the problem further by not formally informing the Maharani at all of the honours ceremony, choosing instead to write directly to the young Maharajah. More provocatively, he was honouring her enemies, like Tej Singh, who had agreed to divest her of power during the signing of the Treaty of Bhyrowal. There wasn't much she could do on Lawrence assuming her role, but in retaliation she decided to tutor her son not to cooperate during the proceedings. Since the Maharajah would be the figure bestowing the honours, his non-cooperation would effectively make a mockery of the ceremony and embarrass both the Durbar members and Lawrence in front of a large audience on the day.

Lawrence kicked off proceedings by requesting the Maharajah's advisors for a suitable date from the court astrologer for the occasion. The astrologer, after careful reflection, duly advised 2 August, two days hence, which Lawrence suggested was too imminent for the lavish preparations and decorum demanded for such an occasion. The astrologer, with no great difficulty, found another propitious time, and chose the exact time of 8.17 a.m. on the morning of 7 August, a time more agreeable to all, and a grand ceremony, to be held in the palace, was duly organised for that date. After the formalities, a memorable firework display in the evening for the general amusement of the guests was also planned along with a banquet to conclude proceedings. Invitations were sent out to the great and good along with all the British notables and their wives in Lahore in what was to be one of the major social events of the year.

On the day, the large assembly of invited guests along with the Durbar members receiving honours streamed into the palace, which was beautifully decked out for the celebration. The courtyard and throne area of the fort, where the Mughal emperors in olden days used to hold court when in Lahore, the Tuklitgah, had been chosen for the occasion. The festivities went according to plan, with all having a gay time until formalities began at around 3 p.m. in the afternoon. Prior to the ceremony the eight-year-old Duleep Singh had been in a pleasant mood and gave no indication that something was amiss. For the ceremony, he had been escorted back into his apartments to change into the appropriate attire for the ceremony. An hour would pass while the assembled host waited uncomfortably for his reappearance. News would eventually reach Lawrence that the Maharani was refusing to allow the Maharajah to change in readiness for the occasion. She was heard by informants in her quarters to be in a dark mood and complaining of Lawrence's interference. 'Rajas of the Kingdom are created, and she is not consulted!' they reported her saying to her confidantes. Several requests were sent, to which she finally relented, and Duleep Singh joined the party. However, in a calculated snub, it was found she had not clothed the Maharajah in the appropriate fashion for the occasion.

Nevertheless, the ceremony was begun and Tej Singh was the first to step forward to be honoured. The ceremony involved the customary smearing of the tilak (saffron) paste on the forehead of the recipient as he bowed down before the Maharajah. Duleep's demeanour had changed considerably since his time with his mother, who had instructed him in the intervening hour to refuse all directions. When the commander-in-chief bowed down in front of the Maharajah, Duleep Singh sat back on his throne and pointedly crossed his arms in defiance, refusing to comply with the ritual. The Durbar members would try coaxing him into cooperation. Tej Singh was seen begging him to apply the mark while still in the bowing pose, all to no avail.

Lawrence's first impression was that the Maharajah shrank from performing the formalities because of bashfulness or a dislike of getting his hands wet with the saffron paste. His prompts were also in vain, and the Maharajah continued to refuse to comply. What followed was a few uncomfortable minutes as the guests filling the hall watched on, during which Tej Singh continued to bow, expecting the Maharajah to cooperate. Lawrence, realising the Maharajah wouldn't cooperate, decided to keep the show moving by asking Bhai Nidhan Singh, the head priest, to do the formalities instead. The *khillat* that was to be given as part of the honouring had also not been touched by the Maharajah and Lawrence, suspicious that the Maharajah would observe the proper formalities for other persons receiving honours, a greater slight to Tej Singh, decided not to hand him the other *khillats*, allowing the priest instead to complete all formalities.

Jind Kaur schooling the Maharajah in non-cooperation turned out to be a badly judged move, gaining her only a temporary embarrassment for Tej Singh and the Resident. Tej Singh was seen to be too angry to take part in conversation after the ceremony. Other Durbar members were also annoyed, including Shere Singh and Lehna Singh. It also gave Lawrence a mandate to take further punitive action against the Maharani. What form this would take would be discussed the following day.

Nevertheless, the day's entertainment continued after this incident. The fireworks display and banquet went on with no further embarrassing incidents aside from a cryptic comment by the Maharani's brother. 'Your Highness is out of spirits! I'll bring a company or two soon and show you some much finer sport,' he was heard to say to Duleep Singh, who was looking a trifle bored with the adult company as the evening progressed. What his meaning was is unclear, but it was taken in a most suspicious manner by Lawrence. Most of the European officers and agents were present at the palace, and there was no better time to dispose of them all in one scoop. Further doubt would be raised in his mind some days after the ceremony when the Maharani's brother unexpectedly rode out of Lahore to Duleepgarh in the Bannu doab. The council and other persons of distinction in Lahore normally had to give notice of any departure from the capital to the Resident. What would have been ordinarily regarded as impertinence on his part by Lawrence was treated as much more.

The day after the banquet, Raja Tej Singh (as he was now) and Dewan Deena Nath informed Lawrence they had discussed the events of the day with the other members of the Durbar, and it was agreed this sort of incident must never happen again. What they would hint at was a separation of the Maharani from her son or even her removal from the palace to prevent her ever schooling him against the Resident and Durbar again. 'There can be little doubt what they wish; but, whether they will have the courage to come forward with a distinct proposition, before they know whether it will be sanctioned, is another question. I do not think they are so bold,' reported Lawrence to the Governor-General, although concurring entirely with them on the eviction of the Maharani from the palace. 'I have before reported that I look for no contentment from the Maharanee. Money is not enough for her; she must have power; and to be happy must have free scope to satisfy her lusts and to avenge her supposed wrongs,' continued Lawrence, arguing action against the Maharani was a necessity and going so far as to suggest 'her expulsion from the Punjab for ever' was quite necessary: 'I do not disguise for myself, nor do I wish the Governor-General to be ignorant of the fact, that the Maharanee is the only effective enemy to our policy that I know of in the country.'

Hardinge, then in Simla, was in full agreement and entirely approved the separation of mother and son. He would go further as well. Harking back to her involvement in the Prema Plot and her ability to fund other plots against the British presence he asked Lawrence to consider reducing her pension at the same time. 'She should not have the means of offering large bribes,' he made clear to Lawrence, although she was not to be deprived of the comforts and luxuries of life. In correspondence with the Secret Committee on 16 August, Hardinge detailed his own view and reasons for recommending her eviction from the palace, arguing a heavy animosity to the present administration had begun to be manifested by the Maharani.

> Since Her Highness's loss of power in December 1846 the most hostile spirit of enmity has been evinced by the Ranee against the members of the Durbar ... On political grounds a strong case of necessity exists for removing Her Highness from Lahore and of separating her from the Prince. Her Highness's whole conduct shows her determination to thwart the Government and to train up her son as the instrument of her hatred against the Durbar and to instil into his mind sentiments of aversion to the Resident and to the chiefs who are engaged in administering the affairs of the Punjab.

Perhaps more importantly, people similarly discontented with the new Resident-led government were being drawn to her. To add further to the argument, he would accuse her of low character and of therefore being unfit to bring up her son.

> The Ranee's personal conduct since her separation from her paramour Raja Lal Sing in December 1846 has been marked by the same habitual indulgence in low debauchery as that which has been so frequently recorded in the official papers dated in 1845 and which have been laid before Parliament ... To allow the Prince a child of eight years of age to be trained up under the baneful influence of so unprincipled a mother would not only be contrary to prudence but would be a departure from the spirit of the treaty of Bhyrowal and in effect would neutralize and obstruct the power expressly given to the British Government for administering the affairs of the Punjab during the Prince's minority. There is therefore in the Governor-General's opinion a sufficient justification on political grounds for separating the Prince from his mother at the present moment.

Both Hardinge and Lawrence agreed that sending her into exile outside of the Punjab would be damaging for both the British Government and the Durbar at the moment due to her popularity, but that keeping her under lock and key at the palace was also insufficient. Nothing was easier than her servants passing messages between her, her son and her supporters and sympathisers. Internal exile was therefore decided upon, with various destinations mooted for her new residence. Hardinge would suggest Shikarpore, Nurpur, Chamba or Kangra, all locations within the Punjab but at such distances as to make her involvement in any conspiracy difficult. Lawrence would suggest Kasur and Sheikhupura, both much nearer the capital. Kasur fort had the advantage of being close to the British Ferozepore cantonment, from where a British guard for her could be drawn. Sheikhupura, a provincial town around 35 km north of the capital, was finally agreed on. The town was off the beaten track and had a heavily Muslim population. It was thought that this would make it more difficult for any Sikh plotters to covertly take up residence nearby in any attempt to communicate with the Maharani. She would also have her residence within the town fort, where she could be better kept in seclusion with the garrison, ensuring no conspirators or sympathisers could meet or pass messages to her.

Hardinge's endorsement was welcomed by the Durbar members in a meeting with Henry and John Lawrence. They were asked to keep the plan confidential as Lawrence planned to have her out of the palace within an hour's notice the same day. She was to be separated from the Maharajah by the pretence of a pleasure trip for the lad to the Shalimar Gardens that morning.

She could then be evicted from the fort with ease and without the embarrassment of having to force the young Maharajah from her arms. Precautionary measures were taken against the Maharani becoming aware of the eviction, and Shere Singh was asked to lock the outer doors of her apartments in the palace. Strangely enough, after Lawrence returned to the Residency following the meeting a letter from the Maharani was waiting for him asking for an interview. Perhaps she was aware something was afoot with the doors being locked. Whatever the reason, Lawrence would decline the request.

During the next day, 19 August, two companies of infantry, 200 sowars and two guns were readied as an escort for the Maharani while Duleep Singh was taken to the Shalimar Gardens for a picnic organised by Gulab Singh. Arrangements had already been made for elephants and palanquins and other carriages to carry the Maharani and the reduced retinue of servants allowed her to Sheikhupura.

She had to be informed of her move and allowed to pack what she could but none of the Durbar members seemed at all willing to volunteer to inform her and so Lawrence finally chose Heera Singh, her brother, to break the news to her. The message from the Resident and Durbar, he was told to tell her, was that the Governor-General had agreed to her removal from Lahore and that she could leave voluntarily with decorum or face being removed more unceremoniously if necessary. Jind Kaur, powerless to do otherwise, would accept the decision. She did, however, request to be sent to a place of pilgrimage like Benares or Hardwar perhaps. Matters had been arranged, her brother informed her, and the fort at Sheikhupura was already being made ready for her.

Lawrence was anxious that the Maharani's party leave as soon as possible. To facilitate this, she was told to leave two trusted servants behind to organise the transport of all her clothes, jewels, money and other possessions that could not be immediately carried away on the elephants. Shortly before 9 p.m., her convoy was readied, and in the darkness of the night and without fanfare, the Maharani left the palace for what would be the last time. Mr Bowring, Lawrence's assistant, staying behind after Lawrence left for the Residency to manage affairs, reported that she left without any tears or angry words, although she had emotion in her demeanour. The only response to this action was shown as she left the gates of the fort. Two armed Sikh guards at the gate approached her palanquin, Bowring would report to Lawrence later, and said 'our power was gone' and that they would assist her if she needed. On the way to Sheikhupura, she recovered most of her composure and was heard in conversation saying she would 'appeal to London' for the rough treatment being meted out to her by the Resident and Governor-General. Her property, meanwhile, would be moved out of the palace over the following days.

Lawrence had determined on a stricter regime than previously for the Maharani at her new residence to reduce still further any chance of her communicating or funding nationalists. She would be closely watched. She would have no contact with her son. She was to be allowed few if any visitors in her new dwelling. Few if any confidantes would be allowed to go with her as well. This meant excluding most of the remaining Maharani's maid servants. Many of these women and servant girls would be ejected from the palace, their employment terminated. The Maharani's eventual exile outside of the Punjab was not dismissed entirely: 'I can only regard therefore this removal to Sheikhoopoor (and I am not alone in the Council of this opinion) as the first step to the final banishment of Ranee Jhunda from the country which she has so long disturbed,' wrote Henry Lawrence ominously.

Meanwhile the young Maharajah had been kept amused at the Shalimar Gardens for several days while the Maharani's possessions were being moved out. Shere Singh, on being chosen as the emissary, asked Lawrence for the best way to approach the issue of her mother's disappearance. Tell him in plain but kind language, replied Lawrence, that 'the Maharanee's reputation was so notorious, her vices so incorrigible and her example so pernicious that the Governor-General thought it wrong to leave him with her any longer'.

The public proclamation was issued by Henry Lawrence the very next day before rumours began circulating, with copies distributed round the Punjab. The notice declared Hardinge felt the interests of a father to Duleep Singh, and this meant a necessary separation from his mother who was not only intriguing against the British Government and the Lahore Durbar but leading the young Maharajah astray by fostering a hatred of the British and the Durbar. The Governor-General could not take the risk of this hatred continuing to be instilled in his young mind and neither could the Lahore Government. 'So long as her Highness the Maharanee occupied the Lahore Palace strangers visited her without restriction; and every seditious intriguer who was displeased with the present order of things looked up to the Queen-Mother as the head of the State; some of them even went so far as to plan the subversion of the restored Khalsa government.'

Therefore it was necessary to remove her entirely not only from the palace and to remove her son from her but to put great restrictions on her freedom. Jind Kaur would protest at these draconian restrictions. Her appeals, though, would fall on deaf ears as Henry Lawrence had other things on his mind – namely, a return to England. The expulsion of the Maharani from Lahore would in fact be the last act of Henry Lawrence's seven-month stint as Resident. Suffering from failing health for several months, he was replaced by John Lawrence, his brother, before Frederick Currie, a member of the Supreme Council, replaced him as a more permanent Resident seven months later. Two days after her departure from Lahore, both the Lawrence brothers travelled to the Shalimar Gardens where the young Maharajah was still being kept. Henry Lawrence was there to bid his farewells to the Durbar members and the Maharajah before travelling back to Calcutta and England, while John Lawrence was there to present his documents from the British Government announcing his Residency at Lahore. All the Durbar members had travelled to the gardens to wish Henry Lawrence farewell and he was given a surprisingly friendly send-off as he departed the Punjab. Durbar members accompanied him to his waiting carriage, repeatedly shaking his hand and hoping they would see his return soon. His departure would coincide with the end of Hardinge's tenure as Governor-General. Henry Lawrence would return to England on the same ship as Hardinge, who himself was making way for the Earl of Dalhousie. Thus the New Year of 1848 would not only see a new Governor-General but a new Resident at Lahore.

# 6

# 'The Necessity of Full Interference'

No Governor-General has ever taken charge of the Government of India under such
peculiar and advantageous circumstances.

*Friend of India*, 20 January 1848

... in the exercise of a wise and sound policy is bound not to put aside or neglect such
rightful opportunities of acquiring territory or revenue as may from time to time
present themselves.

Earl of Dalhousie, 30 August 1848

By the end of the first month of 1848, and less than three months before events at Multan would
lead to war, Henry Lawrence and Hardinge had both departed, to be replaced by John Lawrence
and Dalhousie respectively. John Lawrence had taken over from his ailing brother as Resident
on 21 August 1847, with Dalhousie assuming his new role of Governor-General in Calcutta on
12 January 1848. Both men had differing views and methods from their predecessors and it's
quite probable that without John Lawrence and Dalhousie taking over their respective posts
the coming war and the annexation of the Lahore state would never have taken place. Many
chroniclers and participants like Dewan Mulraj and Shere Singh would lay the blame of the
war solely on John Lawrence's new and more heavy-handed reign during his six months in
the role, while the future of the state and the question of annexation lay squarely in the lap of
the expansionist-minded Dalhousie.

That John Lawrence and his brother Henry's views on how to govern the state of Lahore
were starkly different became obvious at an early stage. Henry Lawrence, despite his treatment
of the Maharani, tended in general to be more cautious in his approach to the Durbar. Careful
to keep up the formality of getting the Durbar to rubber-stamp his decisions, he bore in mind
that the British presence in the Punjab was, on paper at least, temporary and that the country
could become independent of British control when the young Maharajah came of age. His
general bearing towards the Durbar members and other officials of the state was also generally
acknowledged to be warmer and more conciliatory, although he left no doubt in their minds
that he was in charge.

John Lawrence, in contrast, tended to be much colder, more businesslike and authoritative.
Sweeping away all pretence, John Lawrence had no qualms about reigning over Lahore as a
virtual ruler. He tended to care little for the opinions of the Durbar and showed little time for
Lahore institutions and customs, preferring to override them with British rules and regulations.
Because of this, John Lawrence would never build the same relationship with the Durbar
members that Henry had. Not that there was any overt friction apparent during his relatively

short stay – the Durbar members were too timorous to raise objections – but a general feeling pervaded Lahore and beyond that the more autocratic nature of John Lawrence's rule signalled the quiet dismissal of Sikh government forever.

The chronicler Septimus Thorburn, future Commissioner of the Punjab, was one of those critical of his tenure and the brusque manner in which he went about his plans. Thorburn compared Henry Lawrence to a hand which was firm but 'warm and softly gloved' compared to his brother's hand which was 'iron and never gloved'. 'He rushed his reforms with indiscreet haste, and treated many of the proud sensitive chiefs of the country with contumely, and thus transgressed his instructions both in spirit and letter. These facts are undeniable, hence on his head rests the chief responsibility for the universal odium in which Sikhs of all classes regarded the English dominion through-out 1848.'

It's fair to say John Lawrence treated the Lahore state as if it was already part of British possessions and he took his decisions accordingly. 'The country is tranquil and the people apparently day by day learning to appreciate the benefits of British interference,' he wrote on 25 September 1847, early in his tenure in the new role. It wasn't just the Lahore Durbar but other high officials who met with the same irreverent attitude. The Sikh kardars, who were semi-rulers in the provinces, were also called into account. These men during the time of confusion had extracted huge amounts of money and had abused their positions. Rather than going through the Lahore Durbar, the new Resident would summon and deal with them personally. This rough treatment on people answerable to nobody for so long no doubt grated on their senses. 'To treat dignitaries, who for years had exercised despotic powers within their principalities, like common defaulters and malefactors may have been justice but was not wisdom,' continued Thorburn.

Much of the Punjab was still a feudal system whereby jaghirdars (feudal levies) and landlords would keep their own men-in-arms, but John Lawrence would regard these men as little more than enemies to the working classes and as nuisance. The reforms he would order had a direct bearing on their finances, and they would complain to John Lawrence. He in turn countered by telling them to dismiss their armed contingents if they wanted to save money – half of which, however, must be given to the government. 'To this, they all demurred, but it had the effect of silencing all complaints,' he reported to the Governor-General somewhat triumphantly.

John Lawrence would stay in Lahore till the end of March, although his Residency ended on the 8th of the month. Its speculated that John Lawrence never really detected the growing undercurrent of dissent either in the army or the population in general. He preferred to keep his eye on the books, changing the financial management of the country and reducing powerful people, oblivious to the effect it was having. One of his last reports to government before making way for Frederick Currie, true to form, commented on the southern province of Multan and raising its tax revenues. If headed by a British political agent, he said, it could quite easily raise another 5 lakh rupees a year in revenue, mentioning in dismissive fashion that 'one of the junior assistants' at Lahore would suffice for the management of Multan. 'To the last day of his retention of the post of Acting Resident, his reports show that politically he was blind, seeing things only from the standpoint of the energetic district and settlement officer, posted to a backward tract in a British province, and not as British Resident holding extraordinary powers for a few years in a warlike kingdom, which would shortly be absolutely autonomous, if not independent,' summed up Septimus Thorburn.

John Lawrence's tenure, although key to adding significantly to the underlying resentment of British interference, would be relatively quiet itself. John Lawrence's first major engagement was one of the major social occasions of the Punjab calendar, the Hindu festival of Dussehra celebrating the Hindu legend of the destruction of the demon Ravana by the god Rama. That year, the event fell on 19 October. The festival was always celebrated in the palace with great pomp, and 1848 was no exception, with a magnificent public Durbar arranged. Joining the crowds in the palace were John Lawrence and Sir John Littler, along with all the British political agents in Lahore at the time. All went as normal and it was a memorable scene by all accounts, with courtiers dressed in brilliant yellow. Duleep Singh seemed to be enjoying himself, and the scene was one of jollity and high spirits. Meanwhile, in an open space a mile outside the city, a huge crowd had gathered for the public celebrations and waited for the Maharajah to appear and for the fireworks display to begin. The Sikh army band now played 'God Save the Queen' for the first time as Lawrence and Littler reached the plain outside the city where the festivities were arranged. Troops, both Sikh and British, presented arms and guns were fired. At the raised platform for the Maharajah, Lawrence and Littler were given seats to either side of him with everyone presenting nuzzurs. Then the three mounted an elephant to watch the play of Rama and Rawana being performed. There were dancing girls aplenty for the festive occasion. John Lawrence had imposed a much bigger guard than normal around the Maharajah, himself and the other British political and officers in order to ward off any conspirators thinking of disposing of the Durbar and the British clique in Lahore. The festivities finished without incident, however.

It was during December of 1847 that many of John Lawrence's plans began to be implemented. In early December, one of John Lawrence's more controversial wishes was the lifting of the ban on the five-times-daily Muslim call to prayer in the cities of the Punjab. This had been treated as undesirable by Ranjit Singh, by and large a secularist. John Lawrence wished it back despite the obvious dismay of the submissive Lahore Durbar. The loud Muslim calls to prayer in the heart of the capital and elsewhere would be incongruous in what was the Sikh empire, they argued. 'I never saw them so averse to any measure we have proposed as to this one so reasonable and just,' the Resident recorded. There were warnings by the Durbar this would lead to trouble but John Lawrence refused to change his mind, realising this would garner much approval from the Muslim population at no cost. On 9 December 1847, the Durbar bowed to the Resident's wishes and the Muezzin's call to prayer was heard again in the capital and cities across the state.

Other changes to the administrative and legal running of the state also came into play around this time as well. John Lawrence would begin changing the customs and excise system and other matters of revenue collection, along with modifying the land tax and its collection. In addition a new criminal code and procedures were drawn up for the Punjab courts and kardars with new judges selected by John Lawrence personally. A new civil code had also been drawn up. 'The assessment of the land-tax is progressing admirably,' he wrote in a despatch to government on 16 December 1847. 'The Durbar have resigned all control over it ... I am sanguine that in another three months the whole assessment of the Punjab will be determined and recorded; a change to the benefit of the agriculturists, which no one, not conversant with the enormous evils of the former system, can fully appreciate.'

A Postmaster General was selected and the Penny Post introduced into the Punjab. Each letter cost just 1 anna (one-sixteenth of a rupee) and 150 letters had been posted from Lahore to Peshawar within six days of its introduction, something John Lawrence showed much pride in. All these changes were made without any significant involvement of the Durbar and were areas in which Henry Lawrence had not deemed it necessary to interfere.

John Lawrence also took a deeper role than his brother in managing the day-to-day life of the Maharajah. His relations with him were friendly but cool. It was noted he had been tutored to show much courteousness and civility to the Resident so as not to seem annoyed about his separation from his mother. He would greet the Resident in English, saying, 'Good Morning', and John Lawrence determined on further changes to the way he would be brought up.

I now seldom hear the Maharanee's name mentioned. The Maharajah seems happy. I propose that one of the junior assistants should daily visit His Highness for an hour, hear him read, see him write, and read and explain a few pages of English or Indian history to him. A little at a time may gradually induce a liking for literary and scientific pursuits. He has a mechanical turn, is fond of drawing, and very much enjoys little pictures that Lieutenant Edwardes sometimes draws for him. He rides daily, and is encouraged in manly pursuits, but will not be tempted to play the soldier.

Reductions in the Sikh army were continued as well. John Lawrence had decided on a further reduction of 2,000 irregular cavalry, bringing the cavalry side of the Sikh army to 10,000 men. The surplus would be pensioned off. This was expected to reduce the Lahore Durbar expenditure by upwards of 5 lakh rupees per annum. Two committees of British officers were set up to deal efficiently with the process as fast as possible and the 1,300 cavalrymen stationed at Lahore were the first to be released. The plan was to keep only the older soldiers who had been in service the longest. 'These old soldiers the companions and partners of Ranjit Sing in all his conquests presented a noble spectacle the majority varied from 50 to 70 years of age and many preserved the remains of stalwart frames many were covered with wounds and as they pointed to each they recounted the place and time they received', John Lawrence noted, although this policy meant an ageing army. John Lawrence would also manage to make savings by making redundant some of the regimental accountants, writing that his action had caused much sensation, which he said tended only to encourage him in making changes. 'Nothing in my mind shows more clearly the necessity of full interference and thorough scrutiny into every charge than this reduction.' The cuts meant a drastically reduced Sikh army from that of earlier years. In 1844, the Sikh army had amounted to 85,000 men with 350 guns stationed at Lahore or near the Sutlej border. Its strength had been reduced after the war to 32,000 men (around 22,000 regulars and 10,000 cavalry). The continuing cuts by the British Residents meant that by February 1848, only around 17,000 regulars remained. Specifically there were 16,972 infantry and 1,568 artillerymen. The cavalry had been reduced to a total of only 11,891 cavalry of all sorts, composed of 3,263 regular cavalry, 5,128 Gorcharas (horsemen) and 3,500 jaghirdars.

Records into the demographics of the army showed that after these cuts, two-thirds of the force that remained was Sikh while the remainder was either Muslim or what were called poorbeas – Hindu sepoys recruited from British territory. This was supplemented by what was thought be around fifty guns only, most of them horse artillery and hardly any large or siege guns. This did not include, though, many guns diligently buried by Sikh soldiers in various forts away from British eyes after the first war. As per Hardinge's policy, this reduced army had been split into small garrisons across the border with Afghanistan specifically to reduce the possibility of these units acting in concert easily in any new insurrection. Units were stationed mainly in Hazara, Peshawar and Bannu, with various smaller garrisons dotted around in forts on the border with Afghanistan to keep order among the tribes.

A Lahore Durbar report of early February provides a more detailed analysis. Around 4,300 regulars at this time, with 1,600 irregulars and 850 Gorcharas, making a total of 6,750 Sikh troops, were stationed in Peshawar. Another 5,000 or so were in Hazara, with smaller contingents at Bannu, Hassan Abdul and Kurri Kahorta. At the capital of Lahore, only three regiments (around 2,000 Sikh troops) now remained while around 600 men manned the fort of Gobindgarh.

The only violence that would surface during John Lawrence's period was on 31 January 1848. An Akali soldier, Gunda Singh, with eight followers had taken control of one of the *bhungas* or buildings adjoining the Harmandir Sahib or Golden Temple. John Lawrence declined to mention the reason for the stand by the Akalis in his report of affairs in the Punjab. Gunda Singh and his men killed a subedar and wounded an officer along with several other men before eventually surrendering. He was hanged along with two others on 14 February, the rest being sent to prison for hard labour for seven years in British territory.

For the Maharani, the new Resident's arrival signalled no better prospects. John held similarly dim views of her as his brother Henry, and declined to visit her at Sheikhupura. Shortly after arriving he commented on the Maharani in his report of 28 August 1847 to the government. 'Such is her spirit, energy, and intriguing habit, that I am persuaded she will leave no stone unturned to revenge herself on her enemies, and recover her independence. Admonition and warning for her are all in vain.' She was chafing at the restrictions that had now been placed on her, he wrote. In line with his brother's views, a close eye would be maintained on the Maharani. On 18 September, it was reported to the Resident that she had been giving necklaces in the form of bribes for assistance to a Jemadar and Havildar of the garrison. John Lawrence ordered the guard to be changed and the new guards explained any such offers should be refused or they would face severe penalties. The necklaces (made up of pearls costing 60 rupees each) were confiscated and put in the public treasury. 'It is evident from this circumstance that the Maharanee was attempting to tamper with the guard and I have no doubt that so long as she possesses the means she will continue to act in a similar manner,' John Lawrence reported to the Governor-General, hinting at the removal of her wealth and jewellery. In the meantime, Jind Kaur had made a request to be sent to Benares instead, perhaps hoping the British leash on her would be relaxed at such a distance from the Punjab. But John Lawrence in his response made it clear to her she would face the same restrictions on her freedom there as in the Punjab, also warning her to cease communicating with persons interested in insurrection in future.

Taking cue from the new Resident's harsher attitude, the Durbar members had also taken opportunity to vent their animosities and grudges against Jind Kaur. Soon after the beginning of his Residency, they concurred in a reduction of her allowance to just 4,000 rupees, which would reduce her means to little more than paying for her staff and general subsistence. The Governor-General replied giving his consent to this change. The new lower sum would be sufficient for her comfort, he said, and 'if a larger amount of funds were placed at the disposal of either [the Maharani or her brother], it is probable that such would be employed for purposes inimical to the public interests'.

Her brother, although recognised as no danger, was to be stripped of his jaghirs, these replaced by a monthly allowance of 1,000 rupees. In addition he would be made to live in Deena Nuggar in virtual exile from the capital. Issues would also be raised regarding the property Jind Kaur had taken to Sheikhupura during her eviction in September which the Durbar members argued was state rather than personal property. Other petty issues raised included the payment of the cost of a proposed monument to her dead brother, the former Vizier, Jawahar Singh. He had been murdered by the army in the convulsions prior to the First Anglo-Sikh War. They argued that the cost should not be borne by the state. John Lawrence, agreeing, would transfer it to her own account. She clearly had no finances for this new monument, and it was never built.

It was also suggested to John Lawrence that Shere Singh Attariwala rather than the current 'untrustworthy' commander should have control of the Sheikhupura fortress to keep an eye on the Maharani. Shere Singh would in fact decline the offer, fearing the odium he would receive from the public should he take the role of jailor of the future mother-in-law of his own sister.

Jind Kaur, meanwhile, despite the vigilant British watch on her, had determined to continue to help nationalist groups as well as nurturing her own plans. On 31 September 1847, for example, John Lawrence received word from informants in Kashmir that a Fakeer sent by the Maharani or her sympathisers had come to Srinagar to plead with Gulab Singh to assist the Maharani, proposals which Gulab Singh had refused to contemplate. A day or two later, word reached John Lawrence that the pensioned-off ex-Maharajah of Bhimber was approached by one of her emissaries to raise an armed force. This force was to rescue her from Sheikhupura and then to capture the fort of Bhimber. It was hoped this would be the trigger for a general insurrection in the Punjab. The ex-Maharajah was hardly the sort to attempt something so dangerous, however, and promptly informed the Resident. John Lawrence, as a precaution, would order the removal of all the sixteen guns in the Bhimber fort in case the garrison of the fort had sympathy for her plight.

John Lawrence's own view was that there would be more attempts, and not just from inside the Sheikhupura fortress. 'It is therefore quite apparent that the Maharanee has friends however humble who are exerting themselves in her favor and that she herself is endeavouring to add to their number,' he added in his report to the government on 4 October 1847. His response would be to further increase security at the Sheikhupura fortress. A new guard would be put round the fort every fifteen days so that the Maharani or her servants could not get acquainted with them sufficiently well to offer bribes. Jind Kaur was also refused permission to meet with visitors of her choice. She would write several times to the Resident during the months of March and April 1848 complaining of being removed from Lahore, of confinement and surveillance more rigid then necessary. The food was not food that she wished but food chosen for her and which she said was of poor quality and unpalatable. The Resident countered that she had abused her liberty by meeting with people inimical to British power, although agreeing he would pass any message to the Government of India.

Determined to use legal means to the full on the issue of the constraints she had been placed under without proof of any seditious activity, the Maharani would write to her vakeel Jeebun Singh in Calcutta. On 2 January, in turn, her vakeel would write a strong letter to the Government of India complaining of the harshness of the regime she had been placed in at Sheikhupura. She had not been charged with any crime, nor was there any evidence of any misdeeds or conspiracy against the British. She wished, he said, a full and impartial investigation of any charges, if there be any. In the meantime, she wished to be treated with the respect due to the widow of a Maharajah and the mother of another. The deprivation of communication with her friends and sympathisers was unjust and should be reviewed. He asked for an audience with the Governor-General on the matter. The answer, however, was not promising. A terse reply was sent that the government 'declines to recognise you as a vakeel of the Ranee Junda Khore, except through the representative of the government, the Resident at Lahore'. In other words, all correspondence must be done through the Resident at Lahore. Jeebun Singh countered that if he went to the Punjab to meet his client or to have an audience with the Resident, his life would be in danger from the enemies the Maharani had made in the Durbar and reiterated the difficult condition in which she found herself.

> The confinement in which the Ranee is now kept, is of the most close and rigid description. She is shut up in the fort of Sheikhoopoor, formerly used as a gaol for common felons, under the custody of those Sirdars from whose dangerous machinations against her own life, and that of her son, she, first, solicited the protection of a British force stationed at Lahore – all intercourse with her friends and advisers, or even with the ministers of her religion, is strictly prohibited, and the only attendants allowed her are a few female servants, not of her own selection, but appointed by her keepers. So penal is the nature of the treatment she undergoes, that she is not allowed even the privilege of choosing her own diet.

The friends she had, he continued, were now intimidated at the power that her enemies in the Lahore Durbar and elsewhere wielded and were afraid to visit her in case of vendettas. She must be placed under a British officer, he said, to ensure her safety from scheming Durbar members and the restrictions on meeting her friends and advisors must be lifted. Nothing would come of these exertions on his part.

John Lawrence would be replaced as Resident by Frederick Currie, who had vacated his position as member of the Supreme Council of India for the role. Currie had already spent much time in the Punjab accompanying the British force during the first war and then touring the Punjab with Hardinge as the new treaties were signed after the war. Once he had time to settle into his new role, he would voice his discomfort with the deep changes John Lawrence had made into Lahore affairs. In his report to Dalhousie on 5 April 1848, he warned that the administration of the country was now much more in the hands of the British than perhaps had been envisaged, and that 'the conduct of all details even the most minute in all departments except that of account devolves now on the Resident and his subordinates ... I could wish that our interference with these details [financial matters] had been less, but it is impossible now to recede ... In the judicial department, also, our interference with details has gone further than was at first intended.' At least some of the responsibility, he said, could be handed back to the Durbar; however, this advice would come much too late.

***

One person who had never visited the Punjab but had watched and monitored the late war and subsequent events from afar with interest had been the Earl of Dalhousie. Dalhousie, the third and youngest son of the 9th Earl of Dalhousie, had a distinguished track record. He had studied at Christ Church, Oxford before becoming a Member of Parliament at the young age of twenty-five. With the death of both his elder brothers, he had inherited his father's title on his death in 1838. He would serve successively as vice-president and president of the Board of Trade in Sir Robert Peel's government in 1843 and then in 1845–6 respectively, during which time he pushed through much progress in the construction of the railways. When Peel's government fell, he was offered the Governor-Generalship of India by his political opponent Lord John Russell in 1847, which Dalhousie accepted. At thirty-five, he would become the youngest to occupy that role.

On 11 November, Dalhousie set sail for Alexandria with his wife on the frigate *Sidon* before boarding the *Moozuffer* for the trip through the Red Sea and Indian Ocean. He arrived at the port of Madras on 5 January 1848. A three-day stint of meetings and greetings followed at Government House before he sailed again, reaching Calcutta on 12 January. The landing proved somewhat of an ill omen for Dalhousie. The *Moozuffer* travelled so rapidly towards Calcutta that it succeeded in nearly swamping the state barge on which Dalhousie was to have been transported to land. A common country boat instead had to be used as the darkness of evening gathered pace, allowing Dalhousie to set foot on Chandpal Ghat on the Hooghly River.

The ceremony was simple for someone assuming the role of ruler of 200 million people. He was driven to Government House, where he met the outgoing Governor-General Hardinge before being led to the council room. His commission was read to the members of the council, followed by Dalhousie taking the oath and signing his name on the appropriate documents, which allowed him to walk out the Governor-General of India shortly after.

Much lengthier were the formalities that followed and which took up much time for Dalhousie. For what followed was a seemingly interminable set of dinners and formal occasions. 'On the same night,' Dalhousie would record, 'there was a dinner; on the next a greater; and on the third Lord Hardinge gave a ball to Lady Dalhousie. Then my entertainments began. For the first three days the outgoing Governor-General feasts the incoming man; for the next three days, or as long as he stays, the Governor-General in the present tense is host to him who has reached the praeter pluperfect. So on the next day I gave the same great dinner to Lord Hardinge that he had given to me: all the same people, whisker for whisker among the gentlemen, pin for pin among the ladies. Then came Sunday, and we sat together in the Cathedral under the same canopy. Never was such a sight seen since the sweet-smelling days of the dynasty of Brentford!'

Dalhousie had a pleasant first few months in the job. Following the numerous balls and banquets, he spent time sailing up the Ganges in late February on a yacht towed by steamer to Barrackpore and then to Hooghly in high temperatures. A mission from Nepal welcoming Dalhousie was entertained among the usual bureaucratic issues in India. 'Everything is quiet, and the only discontent I have heard of in the Punjab is that of the little Maharajah, who complains that they have given him too many lessons' was one of his first comments on a subject that would consume a large amount of his attention for the next year and a half. The British newspapers in India had given him a warm welcome, although it would be fair to say the general impression of the Governor-Generalship at the time Dalhousie took over was that it was a relative sinecure. Dalhousie would be picking up the fruits of pacification of the country by previous occupants, especially in the Punjab. The *Friend of India* forecast a quiet period for the new Governor-General on 20 January.

> No Governor-General has ever taken charge of the Government of India under such peculiar and advantageous circumstances. The youngest ruler who has assumed the responsibilities of this empire he receives it from his predecessor in a state of tranquillity which has hitherto no parallel in our Indian annals. He arrives at a time when the last obstacle to the complete and apparently the final pacification of India has been removed when the only remaining army [Sikh army] which could create alarm has been dissolved and the peace of the country rests upon the firmest and most permanent basis. The chiefs whose ambition or hostility have been the source of disquietude to his predecessors have one and all been disarmed. Not a shot is fired from the Indus to Cape Comorin against our will.

Peace there was, but Dalhousie's attitude to the Punjab and the issue of British expansion in India would dominate matters in the first year of his rule. Dalhousie's opinion, formed from the years of anarchy before the First Anglo-Sikh War to the more pacified present, was that the time of a strong Lahore Government were gone forever. 'There never has been a Punjab nation for centuries. It has been congeries of independent and battling tribes, until the strong mind and strong arm of Ranjit Singh reduced the whole into obedience to himself, the head of the dominant sect, the Sikhs. Since he passed away there has not been even a pretender to the position of either the strong mind or the strong arm. The army has ruled supreme. I see no prospect in the future of finding materials for a government strong enough to control them, any more than there has been in the years since Ranjit Singh's death,' he mused on the weakness of the Lahore Government and the lack of a strong successor to the founder of the Sikh Empire.

Dalhousie's natural inclination was one of expanding British control throughout the Indian subcontinent, and although not expressed publicly he was of the firm opinion that British control of the Punjab was a good thing. For Dalhousie was a firm believer in the general superiority of European rule and administration and therefore manifest destiny to rule over the subcontinent. Generally dismissive of the Indian rulers and states of the time, very much like John Lawrence he viewed them as anachronistic and inefficient. The population of India would do best under direct British control, and he viewed it as his task to bring this about as time and circumstances allowed.

Dalhousie would be famous for pushing forward the Doctrine of Lapse, whereby the annexation of any Indian state could proceed where the ruler was 'manifestly incompetent or died without a direct heir'. Articulating on his new policy, Dalhousie declared, 'I hold that on all occasions where heirs natural shall fail, the territory should be made to lapse and adoption should not be permitted, excepting in those case in which some strong political reason may render it expedient to depart from the general rule.' The other, lesser reason was to make travel and administration of British territories more easily manageable. At the time, the numerous minor and petty principalities dividing the various British territories were seen as an annoyance to direct travel and communication. At the local ruler's expense, the British Empire would become a more manageable entity.

In order to do this, the local monarchs needed to be deposed albeit with suitable pensions, allowing for their territories to be subsumed into the East India Company's holdings. Although annexation by war was nothing new, a hard-line policy of escheat had never been pursued during the previous half-century of British rule. In the twelve years prior to Dalhousie's arrival, for instance, fifteen rulers had died without heir but only one state had been annexed. Local rulers with no natural heir had used adoption as a matter of course to continue the royal line, the necessary permission from the British being seen as a matter of formality. Dalhousie's controversial proclamation meant this option would no longer be available.

It was said of Dalhousie that he abolished titles when there were no heirs apparent and that when there were heirs plentiful, in the interminable squabbles between rival claimants he would make the abolition of the title a condition of recognition of family headship for the chosen candidate. Pensions too were dependant on cooperation. During the eight years of his rule leading up to the Mutiny, therefore, a sea change would occur in the way the Indian rulers and the general populace would view the British. Dalhousie's eight years as Governor-General would thus turn into a litany of acquisitions. The states of Satara (1849), Karauli (1849), Jaitpur (1849), Sambulpur (1849), Jhansi (1853) and Nagpur (1853) would all fall to the new policy of Doctrine of Lapse, although the decisions on Karauli and Udaipur would be reversed. Meanwhile portions of Sikkim (1850), Baghat (1851), Chota Udaipur (1852), Jhansi (1853) and Nagur (1853) and the

Burmese province of Pegu (1853) would be annexed outright, although Baghat and Udaipur would be restored to their ruler.

Dalhousie would also be remembered for his policy on what was left of the Mughal Empire. The Mughal emperor Bahadhur Shah Zafar, a relic of the previous century and still titular ruler over Delhi, would have the distinction of being the unwilling leader of the sepoys during their mutiny as well as being the last in the line of the Mughal dynasty. Nine years earlier, however, as Dalhousie settled into his new role, Zafar lived in comfortable but much-reduced circumstances on a British pension in the Red Fort in Delhi. Dalhousie had made up his mind soon after his arrival that the dynasty, irrelevant as it was, would be extinguished. To reduce its importance prior to this, he would decide Zafar must cease the usage of the imperial title of Padishah or Emperor and instead used the lesser title of Shehzadah or Prince. In addition, the royal family should move out of the Red Fort in Delhi, the historic seat of the emperors, and move to more modest accommodation within the city somewhere. The displacement from the imperial palace and fort would much diminish any remaining status and mystique surrounding the Great Mughal and leave the abolition of the Mughal line following Zafar's death an easier step. The act of stripping a sitting emperor of his title, however nominal the title that may have been, was seen as a step too far by the East India Court of Directors and Dalhousie was overruled. The directors, although they agreed to the changes, thought it best these should be quietly brought about in the interregnum between the expected death of the ageing Zafar and the crowning of a new monarch.

The two most famous of Dalhousie's acquisitions, however, would be his first and last major ones. He would end his career of expansion with Oudh in 1856. The state of Lahore would form his first major acquisition, and the first justification for this move would originate in events beginning not at Lahore at all, nor from the various main Sikh barracks to the west of the country, but from the provincial southern city of Multan far to the south, the only province not yet ruled by a British political agent.

# 7

# 'A Fish Caught in a Strong Current'

My desire is that my honor may remain untouched.
Dewan Mulraj to Frederick Currie, Lahore Resident, April 1848

Moolraj would seem by nature and habit to possess more of a mercantile than a martial character.
C. G. Mansel, court president, trial of Mulraj, June 1849

One of the more significant areas of the Punjab, but which had figured little in the dealings of the Residents or in fact any of the British political agents to this time, had been the southern city and province of Multan. The city of Multan, a large and prosperous metropolis, lay around 10 km to the east of the Chenab River, and marked the southern periphery of Lahore. The name Multan was generally believed to be a corruption of the original Mali-us-than or Mūlasthān, a name derived from the Mallians, the tribe resident in the vicinity 2,500 years ago. Multan was in fact one of the oldest cities in the world. Located on the trade routes between Delhi and the east and the markets of Afghanistan, Persia, central Asia and beyond to the west made the city inherently wealthy. All trade to these destinations passed by necessity through the province and provided good revenue. The city was perhaps best known throughout central Asia as a centre of excellence for the silk trade, much material being transported to Kabul before disappearing towards the numerous trade routes through to the republics round the Black Sea and further north. A reporter for the *Bombay Times* would comment on its riches after the coming siege of Multan as he ambled though the wreckage of the adjoining fort.

The Fortress was filled with stores to profusion. I think Multan is the beau ideal of a Buneaa's Fort, or rather fortified shop: Never perhaps in India have such depots existed of merchandise and arms, amalgamated as they with avarice. Here opium, indigo, salt, sulphur, and every known drug, are heaped in endless profusion-there apparently ancient in the bowels of the earth disclose their huge hoards of wheat and rice; here stacks of leathern ghee vessels, brimming with the grease, fill the pucka receptacles below ground. The silk and shawls reveal in darkness, bales rise on bales, here some mammoth chest discovering glittering scabbards of gold and gems-there reveals tiers of copper canisters crammed with gold Mohurs: My pen cannot describe the variety of wealth displayed to the inquisitive eyes.

The city's wealth had attracted unwelcome attention through the ages, and Multan had a long and chequered military history. Sometimes its inhabitants were fortunate enough to repel the invader, other times less so. Darius had captured and incorporated the city into the Persian Empire in the sixth century BCE. It was from the ramparts of an earlier incarnation of the city's fortress 300 years later that Alexander the Great had been famously wounded by a Mallian archer as he rode outside the city inspecting its defences in preparation for a siege in 324 BCE. The archer had wounded the Macedonian in the sternum. For his temerity, the Greeks had killed all the defenders during their sack of the city. Timur the Lame, or Timurlane, had captured the city as well in 1398 CE. In more recent times it had fallen into Mughal hands but during the mid-eighteenth century the city changed hands again and into the possession of the Persian invader Nadir Shah. The city later fell under the sway of the Afghan adventurer Ahmed Shah Abdali by the middle of the century. The grip of his successors had become successively weaker, however, and by the turn of the nineteenth century the city and the general area had descended into a patchwork of small principalities controlled by Pathan chieftains. The last in the long line of famous conquerors was Ranjit Singh. It was in 1817 that the Maharajah, having consolidated his rule over the Sikh nation to the north, first cast his attention southwards towards the Multan district. That year an exploratory siege was laid on the city by the Sikh general Diwan Bhiwani Das. The following year the capture of the city began in earnest under his son Kharak Singh and General Akali Phula Singh, the city and its strong fortress falling under a most determined attack.

What the few Europeans who had visited Multan to this time had tended to notice the most was the intense heat that pervaded the area during the summer months. Multan was said to be the hottest area in India, the temperature rising inexorably towards 50 °C and frequently passing this point in the summer months. In May 1869, for example, a temperature 51 °C was recorded in the city.

A famous ancient Persian couplet described the qualities of the city: 'These four gifts has Multan, dust, beggars, heat and mosques'. This seemed to have gone into common circulation around India, including among the European population who were familiar with the place. The reason why there were so many mosques and beggars, the locals countered, was because the city was so prosperous and the locals so generous to unfortunates. As far as the extreme heat during the summer, this was explained by a local legend. A Muslim saint, Shams-i-Tabrizi, had been flayed alive centuries before by the local people. In his death throes, he had cursed the city, asking the sun to move closer to torture its inhabitants for eternity. Sometimes the city got a respite from the heat in unexpected fashion, though. The area was known for its heavy rains, which were infrequent but had the habit of inundating the city, and there had been several severe floods decades or more apart.

The city had a correspondingly large population. Estimates ran to between 30,000 and 40,000, with Lahore, the capital, having a population of 80,000 at the time; Multan thus vied with Amritsar and Peshawar as second city. The bulk of the inhabitants were Muslim, many being Afghans, although well settled under the rule of the previous governor Sawan Mull. According to the British census of 1881, the province had a population that was 80 per cent Muslim, with the rest being Sikh and Hindu. 'Multan, lying as it does half-way between the fanaticism of the frontier and the listlessness of the down-country, shows Mohamedanism perhaps at its best,' pontificated the *Multan Gazetteer* of 1901–2, noting little animosity between the various communities. That was much later, however. In 1849, many of these Afghans and high-status Muslims recalled their lofty positions as rulers before the Sikh conquest and therefore harboured a latent dislike of rule from Lahore. Thus there was a hidden fault line among the population of the city and province.

The city of Multan had always had a propensity to expand, and the city suburbs had been inching out for several hundred years. The old city walls still enveloped the heart and much of the city. Rebuilt just a century earlier in 1756, they had quickly been breached by the growth of the city of recent years and by 1848 considerable sections of the city suburbs had sprawled out to the west of the walls, with pockets in the south and east as well. Today, the westernmost suburbs of present-day Multan lie little more than a mile from the easternmost channels of the Chenab River. Back in 1848, the limits were somewhat further back, around 6.5 km from the river.

Cutting through the middle of the old city within the walls and its warren of small streets was the Chowk Bazaar, the commercial heart. This large road ran from the Haram gate in the south to the fort in the north. Many of the streets were narrow, as in other cities, with humbler dwellings. However, there were prosperous people as well, as Corporal Ryder of the 32nd Foot would note: 'The houses are high and some of them well built and very tastefully laid out, the wood work and doors being beautifully carved and the walls of the rooms in the higher class houses covered with splendid paper. What a thousand shames that such splendour should be destroyed.'

John Dunlop, assistant surgeon of HM's 32nd Regiment and a veteran of the coming siege, also left a colourful description of the heart of the city:

> The houses within the city are built of burnt bricks, are surmounted with flat roofs, and sometimes rise to the height of six or seven storey. They are ranged in lanes close together, to exclude as much light, and therefore as much heat, as possible; for Mooltan has the character of being in summer the hottest place in India. The streets therefore are even more gloomy than the numerous ornamented and highly-venerated tombs, to worship at which multitudes of pilgrims were formerly attracted.

Within and without the walls plenty of commerce occupied the inhabitants, with commodities traded including shawls, cottons, silks and brocades. The city and its fortress to the north were adjacent but had separate walls. The circumference of the old walled city itself was just under 5 km. Six fortified gates gave access to the old walled city, two each on the east, south and west sections of the wall, with the fort occupying the area to the immediate north. At the north-eastern end of the city was the Daulat gate, named after a local Muslim saint, Pir Doulat Shah, whose tomb was situated close to the former location of the gate and still proves a magnet for devotees to this day. Around 700 metres to its south was located the Delhi gate, opening to the east and named for the direct road to the aforementioned city, through which the Mughal emperors and state guests entered the city in days of old. Some 600 metres to the south of the Delhi gate lay the Khooni Burj, the bastion built in the extreme south-east of the city walls. Literally meaning 'Bloody tower', it was here the Greeks of Alexander managed to finally effect a breach during their siege. On the southern stretch of the walls, and around 300 metres west of the Khooni Burj, stood the Pak gate, named after another Muslim saint, Hazrat Musa Pak Shaheed, whose tomb lay near the gate. Another 400 metres west of the Pak gate was the Haram gate, connecting the main thoroughfare and commercial Chowk Bazaar road with the outside world. At the south-western corner of the city walls stood the Bohar gate, named after the profusion of Bohar or Banyan trees that formerly occupied the area between the city and the river. In previous centuries, when the river was closer, this gate was the main entry for food supplies coming to the city by the stream. In the north-west of the city was the Lohari gate, or the Metalworkers gate, named after the profusion of small metalworking shops that populated the area at the time. The walls of the city itself, enclosing the old quarter, varied between 20–30 feet to around 40–50 feet high in places and were loopholed for the benefit of defenders. They were well built, with semi-circular bastions at appropriate distances.

Anyone approaching the city could not miss the city fortress looming large to the north of the city. Separated from the city proper by an ancient bed of the Ravi River, the city fortress stood on a large area of natural high ground which made for an excellent defensive structure. In medieval times, two old riverbeds of the Chenab, to the south and north, being wet, gave excellent protection to the fortress by acting as a natural moat. However, apart from the occasional flooding of the area, the riverbeds now increasingly tended to be dry. In fact, there had been no rains in the city for four years. The year 1848 was very dry for the province. Not that the province suffered, as the Chenab and relatively close Indus and Sutlej rivers provided sufficient water for the province of irrigation. The space between the fort and city, now dry, was used as a parade ground for the garrison as well as holding stables for their horses and cattle.

Many fortresses had stood at the same spot in the previous three millennia. The fort that occupied the position in 1848 was an impressive, well-built structure with a circumference of around 2 km, complete with forty-six bastions. Alexander Burnes, passing through Multan in 1831, described the fortress as an 'irregular hexagon', the longest side being around 600 yards. The medieval chronicler Al-Idrisi in the twelfth century wrote of the fortress having four gates at the time and this was the way it had stayed ever since. The Sikki gate led to the east, the De or Delhi gate to the west. The Khizri (or Khidri) gate, named after Khidar Khan, who was the city's governor during the invasion of Timur, led to the north and to the Chenab River. The Rehri (or Hareri) gate to the south gave access to the city. Each of the gates of the fort were of similar style, being guarded by two flanking towers.

John Dunlop was one of those who left a detailed description of the structure:

> The Fort stands on the highest part of the mound on which the town is built. It is an anciente formed by a hexagonal wall from forty to seventy feet high, the longest side of which faces the north-west and extends for 600 yards, and which isolates it from the town. A ditch twenty-five feet deep and forty feet wide is on the fort side of the wall, behind which is a glacis exhibiting a face of some eighteen feet high, and so thick as to present an almost impregnable rocky mound. Within the fort, and on a very considerable elevation, stands the citadel, in itself of very great strength. The walls are flanked by thirty towers, and enclose numerous houses, mosques, a Hindu temple of high antiquity, and a Khan's palace, the beauty of which was severely damaged by the battering it got from the guns of Ranjeet Singh in 1818. This fortification is said to be more regular in construction than any other laid down by native engineers.

What Dunlop failed to mention was the fort had a double set of walls, the lower wall enclosing a higher one. John Jones Cole, another assistant surgeon to the British Army during the coming siege, reckoned the fortress to be perhaps the strongest native fortification in India. Giving further description of the ditch, he adds,

> There are three narrow bridges passing over it, slightly built, without parapets, and capable of being destroyed; two of these were blocked up during the siege. The counterscarp is for the most part built of mud rendered solid and very durable by the admixture of chopped straw. The walls are wholly of massive brick-work of great thickness and neatly

put together. They are raised against a high and extensive mound of earth or little hill and supported and defended at equal distances by well-constructed bastions pierces with three or more embrasures for cannon. The scarp wall is considered too low, in some places the guns placed on it scarcely overlook the crest of the glacis and the curtain wall is said to be somewhat too high. The third, or mine wall, which encloses the citadel is of lesser importance and adds but little to the strength of the place.

There were towers within the fortress which had 14-pounder guns stationed on them. 'These cannons are capable of propelling shot to great distances; and they command a greater part of the town and fort,' he added. The height of the ground along with the lofty walls allowed for most impressive views from the battlements. Visitors recorded they could see as much as 20 km away. On the ramparts bristled eighty guns, the normal complement for a fortress of this size.

According to Herbert Edwardes, who had opportunity after the coming siege to speak to many officers and staff of Sawan Mull, the previous Governor of Multan, the fortress had been much improved and its defences enhanced and a large amount of munitions stored with a view to throwing off the yoke of Ranjit Singh or his successors when an opportunity arose. The improvement of the defences had been done in careful fashion without raising suspicions at Lahore. Sawan Mull had promised the then ruler, Nau Nihal Singh, that if ever he had need of support from enemies, he would always find a strong fortress in Multan and Sawan Mull and his army by his side. But that the fortress needed maintenance. Nau Nihal Singh suspecting nothing and having more immediate issues than faraway Multan gave him the order to strengthen it sparing no money. The vast improvements had taken two years and a large new fosse lined with masonry and a glacis were added to the fortress along with a *fausse-braye*. The ditch around the fortress varied from 20 feet to nearly 50 feet wide with a depth of 14 to 20 feet deep depending on the location.

Two large structures dominated the inside of the fortress and the skyline from the exterior. One was the Tomb of Shah Rookn-e-Alam, situated to the west near the De gate, named after Rukn-ud-Din Abul Fatah, a thirteenth-century Muslim saint adopted as the patron saint of the city. Two octagonal lower storeys supported a dome 20 metres in diameter. The whole structure, at 30 metres in height, could easily be seen from the suburbs outside the fortress walls and invited perhaps the attention of guns during a siege. In the courtyard of this large structure was built the garrison barracks with bombproof roofs. The Muslim shrine, being tall, also afforded good views of the environs. A *Delhi Gazette* correspondent climbing to the top after the siege described the view: 'It is a most massive structure and from its great height commands a beautiful view of the surrounding country. On ascending two winding staircases the parapet is reached thence may be seen the snowy range, the winding course of the Chenab, the numerous canals gardens and fields which dot the far spreading jungle even Jhung on a very clear day is said to be visible.'

The other structure was the tomb of Bahauddin Zakaria to the eastern walls of the fortress. Bahauddin Zakaria was the father of Rookn-e-Alam. The tomb looked somewhat similar to his son's apart from the square base. Being heavily built, the tombs could both be used as makeshift bombproof magazines as well.

Magazines and stables were built alongside the citadel walls, being marked with domed roofs of considerable thickness. In the middle of the fort stood the governor's own residence with garden, the magazines and storehouses along with a few other lesser buildings. Few descriptions of the structure or the inside survive. 'Moolraj's house appears to have been once a good substantial one,' noted a *Delhi Gazette* correspondent. This was after the coming siege, however, when the structure was entirely in ruins, although a large garden with raised walkways was still apparent. 'Between this [the garden] and the before mentioned tomb there is an enormous domed magazine surrounded by a dry ditch several feet deep a trench has been cut to communicate with it underground and the surface being closely packed with logs of timber.' Beside the residence there was the treasury, which was a substantial underground chamber within which was stored the city treasure. There were various other buildings used as storehouses along with two large brick furnaces for the casting of new cannon. After the capture of the fort, moulds of large new cannon were seen lying close by being readied for manufacture. Contemporary maps of the fortress show a road leading through the middle of the fort from the De gate on the west to the Sikki gate in the east, linking the buildings on each side.

The more devout or superstitious of the Muslim population seemed to think the fortress impregnable due to the presence of the tomb of Shah Rookn-e-Alam. There were more practical justifications for thinking the fortress invulnerable, too. Patrick Vans Agnew, a British political agent, of whom in due course more will be heard, would describe the fortress as the strongest he had seen in India, noting that he had seen many in this travels round the country. In fact, all visitors in war and peace could not fail to be impressed with its nature. Brig. Cheape, who later took part in the second siege of the city, mirrored the feelings of other visitors. 'I have been round Multan, and the fort is a very strong place with great command, height of terreplein being at least 75 feet above the glacis. The fort is certainly a place of great strength, and will, if defended, require all our means both here and that is coming, and we cannot risk such a loss of men as we should probably sustain by alone attacking the city.' But warfare had changed over the previous several hundred years, and the descriptions of its strength did not take into account the strength of modern siege weapons. Ranjit Singh had pummelled his way into the city and fortress using his artillery train despite the difficulties.

\*\*\*

Several other landmarks dotted the cityscape and its environs. Any visitor approaching from the capital of Lahore could not fail to notice the Eidgah, a towering mosque built in 1735 CE that had seen better days. The structure, decorated with glazed blue tiles on the outside and mosaics on the inside, although strong, was crumbling somewhat through neglect. A local landmark, it occupied a substantial 5-acre site. By some quirk of fate, the mosque lay just inside the range of the guns on the ramparts of the fort, just over a kilometre to the south, but as it proved later it was built strongly enough to withstand bombardment for some time. Various other temples and mosques were scattered around the vicinity.

A kilometre east of the fortress stood the mausoleum of Sawan Mull, the previous governor and father of the present incumbent. The structure was sound, although some of its ornamental work had been damaged in the previous years. A few hundred metres to the east of the fortress was the residence of the governor, by all accounts a luxurious place although of modest size. It was surrounded by a high wall, with buildings all round and a central square yard. The buildings were beautifully decorated with images of animals and trees, intricate carved woodwork in the mix also. The central yard contained a water tank and baths. 'It was the finest place I saw in this part of the country. I was informed that it was where the Dewan Moolraj kept his wives and his concubines,' remarked Corporal John Ryder of HM 32nd Foot on visiting the structure during the siege. It happened to be within range of the fort guns as well. Further out were the occasional mud dwellings of the humbler inhabitants, along with more impressive dwellings called havelis. There were also various historic buildings and stately ruins scattered around. The mausoleum for Shams-i-Tabrizi, for example, was a hollow shell, having suffered from bombardment in previous battles.

The Mundee Ava was a large, hilly landmark occupying the area 400 yards east of the city walls and on which an old brick kiln stood. In fact, apart from temples and mosques, the skyline of Multan was dominated by an unusually high number of brick kiln chimneys, both working ones and remains of old ones, a sure sign of the industry related to the city.

The city was situated in well-cultivated land, the Indus, Chenab and Sutlej rivers passing close by and providing more than sufficient water. Feeding the gardens and groves was an extensive set of canals and waterways crisscrossing the area outside the walls. The frequency of nullahs, canals and irrigation channels in the vicinity, along with the numerous groves of trees and walled areas and gardens, though, made the environs of the city entirely unsuitable for the movement of cavalry.

One of the other distinctive marks of the area was the Wollee Mahomed's Canal or Grand Canal, a large and majestic irrigation channel 20 feet deep that split off from the Chenab to the north and passed by the east of the city before heading towards the village of Suraj Khund and then moving south. This canal, along with the many others in the city, were deep cuts through the earth with the excavated earth piled of up each side to make high embankments.

Because of the well-watered nature of the ground, the environs of the city were heavily laden with mango trees, sheesham trees and dates as well. 'The country all round this part of the town was beautiful. There were a number of splendid gardens full of all kinds of fruit trees and native noblemen's mansions and very fine temples and all round was scattered with hundreds of date trees presenting a grand and truly Indian picture,' added Ryder on the landscape north-west of the city. This was true enough, for beyond the city walls Multan was surrounded by a number of large gardens and havelis and a substantial number of groves of date trees. The origin of these groves was said by locals to be the Persian invaders of Nadir Shah in the previous century, who had littered the grounds of the suburbs of the city with countless date stones while laying siege to the city. The city was known for its oranges, peaches and pomegranates as well. Further out, there were fields of wheat, grain, corn and tobacco along with poppy fields for the production of opium.

Multan province was bounded 90 km to the east by the Sutlej River. To the south the province ran to the junction of the Chenab and Sutlej rivers. Beyond Multan, the territory held another important and commercial city, Leia, 100 km to the north-west by the left bank of the Indus. A map of the Multan province shows the effect of the major rivers on the topography of the area. The province could be essentially divided into three segments. To the west, the great Indus River separated the capital from the Derajat, the long thin section of fertile land stretching from the right bank of the river to the mountains and tribal areas that formed the border with Afghanistan. This trans-Indus territory had been conquered by Ranjit Singh in 1820–21. The middle section fell between the Indus and the Chenab, called the Sindh Sagur doab, a more desert and less well-developed area. A smaller section followed to its east, the area between the Chenab and Ravi, called the Rechna doab. To the east of that was the considerable area of the Bari doab, the strip of land between the Ravi and Sutlej. Beyond the Sutlej was the territory of Bhawulpore, a Muslim state whose ruler was pro-British beyond question and an enemy of the Multan governor.

***

On the surface, at least, Multan gave off a calm and prosperous impression, belying the uncertain nature of things in the city of late. The present governor happened to be a young man called Dewan Mulraj. He was far from content, and the same was true of the soldiers of the city garrison. An image of Mulraj by the early photographer John McCosh, taken during his period of captivity after the war in 1849, survives. It shows the governor shorn of all the usual finery becoming his status. The jewels and rings and a large necklace of pearls he had a penchant for wearing are missing, having been confiscated, and only the superior clothes he was allowed to retain give some indication of his former status. Mulraj is seated towards the photographer and looks sideways and downwards in a grave and contemplative posture. At the time the photograph was taken his future was uncertain, with the possibility of a death penalty or a lengthy incarceration hanging over him. The mood of the image perhaps reflects this.

Probably the best contemporary description was recorded by a correspondent of *The Englishman* at Multan as he saw Mulraj riding out of the fortress after the siege.

> I should imagine Moolraj is about thirty-three years old if not more and he stands about 5 feet 7 inches. He has small limbs, light colour, tolerable countenance, high forehead, small deep eyes, a good nose and mouth, thoughtful expression in which despair and dignity seem deeply blended which made him look grave and melancholy though stern so now you can work up your imagination and fancy 'the valiant assassin of Mooltan'.

Others described him as middle height with a longish black beard, with his speech having a mildness and humility to it. He was said to look to be in his mid-forties, a product of the responsibilities he was burdened with although he was a decade younger. The governor by all accounts always had a thoughtful persona and conciliatory habits which tended to give anyone who met him a good impression. Although not a great statesman like his father Sawan Mull, Mulraj seemed to be well liked by the people of his province. This also seemed to extend to the Europeans who met and conversed with him. According to John Lawrence, who would have dealings with him during his stay in Lahore during the end of 1847, he was a popular governor, perhaps the most popular in the Punjab excluding Lehna Singh Majithia, who had been in charge of the Manjha district. Lawrence did not have the perception that Mulraj was cruel in any way. Some British prisoners whom he treated with kindness before releasing during the coming months also described him as 'a man of very engaging manners'. This extended to the day of his capture. John Ryder was one of those who saw the governor and seemed to develop an instant empathy for him. 'He was a good looking man of the middle stature,' he wrote, 'having fine features and a mild countenance yet a keen piercing eye and a determined expression. He was altogether a fine, pleasant, good humoured looking man. I could not help but feel for him, indeed I felt very sorry for him.' It was rare, even during the war, for the naturally partisan British press in India to portray him in a strongly negative manner either; there seemed to be a strange respect for the bureaucrat who would find himself the head of a rebellion by circumstance.

That he was not a military man or a budding general could be instantly judged on seeing the governor, a slight, weak body and his gentle mannerisms instantly betraying a non-martial character. He possessed a somewhat timid character, which also quickly became apparent. Mulraj had no experience of warfare or soldierly qualities and so his part in coming events would be of much surprise to those who knew him well.

He did, however, have other strengths and a way of attaching men to his cause. He also seems to have been well respected judging by the way his principal officers and garrison seemed to have a strong affinity for him. 'Moolraj seems to have been actually adored by the people and no stronger evidence of this attachment and fidelity can be given than that supplied by the fact that though for a fortnight his defence was known to be desperate, though hundreds were being slaughtered daily and no result whatever could be looked for but death or captivity, no one ever threatened to abandon him or thought of betraying him,' commented the *Bombay Times* correspondent.

Despite his youth, Mulraj had developed a strong world-weariness as 1848 came to a close. Along with the strain of governing a province for which he was perhaps ill-fitted, he was having problems with his ambitious brother along with a myriad other family troubles. There was considerable discontent as to how the family wealth had been divided after the death of his father. However, it would be problems caused by the strengthening British authority in Lahore and its impact on his province and his relative independence that would cause both him and his troops much anxiety and discontent.

The fact was that recent months and years had proved to be exceptionally frustrating for Mulraj, who had harboured aspirations of the highest degree – becoming an entirely independent ruler. Mulraj and his father had always had a colourful relationship with the authorities at Lahore. Sawan Mull had been one of the most accomplished of Ranjit Singh's governors, turning the prosperous city and province into a significant revenue earner for the state. During the period of uncertainty after Ranjit Singh's death till the recent war, Sawan Mull's authority had increased as central authority waned. This had gone on for several years, hardening the sense of independence – or the longing for it, at least, as neither Sawan Mull, nor latterly his son, overtly challenged Lahore's authority at any time. During these years, the governor had at the same time salted away through good management a total of 90 lakh rupees, all of which Mulraj and his brother would inherit. Sawan Mull's ideas of a separate state had seemingly begun to materialise as anarchy continued at Lahore. There were suggestions he had even approached the British hoping to move out of the orbit of Lahore.

Sawan Mull's assassination by a disgruntled soldier on 16 September 1844 left his hopes unfulfilled, but Mulraj inherited his aspirations. On being confirmed as governor, he gave the promise of a nuzzur of 30 lakh rupees annually to Lahore demanded by the then Prime Minister Heera Singh, with any revenue over and above this to be his own. This would never be paid due to the disorganised state of the Lahore Government and was later reduced to a request for 18 lakh rupees by Jawahar Singh, the next incumbent. The money owed by Mulraj became a small matter at the tail end of 1845 as the First Anglo-Sikh War broke out. Mulraj, sensing an opportunity, offered help to the British through their agent at Ferozepore, George Broadfoot, hoping the British would recognise Multan as an independent state in return. His offer was perhaps not taken seriously at the time, as nothing came of it. Mulraj would instead end up sending a contingent of troops which would fight at Ferozeshah on the Sikh army's side, although he had kept most of his force at Multan.

After the war with the British ended, the issue of the money owed to Lahore was once again raised by Lal Singh as the treasury was empty. There was no love lost between the Vizier and Mulraj and the Vizier, in somewhat ham-fisted fashion, had decided to send a small army southwards to enforce the collection of the unpaid dues. The force was defeated by Mulraj's forces near the city of Jhung. Mulraj, realising the British Resident would no doubt side with the Vizier and the Lahore Government against a recalcitrant governor, then pre-empted Lal Singh's appeal by appealing himself to Henry Lawrence to arbitrate on the issue of the tribute to Lahore. Lawrence's decision went against Mulraj, not surprisingly perhaps, as he had blatantly not paid what was owed to Lahore for many years. In order to make up the shortfall, the Resident had decided Mulraj must give up the area of Jhung, approximately one-third of the province of Multan. He must also pay 20 lakh rupees, still to be received for his succession to governor and for other arrears. Also the money he paid annually to Lahore would go up by a third. So from now instead of 1.5 million he would pay just under 2 million rupees. These decisions almost smacked of punitive action. In contrast, he was estimated to collect revenue of between 27 and 28 lakh rupees, leaving him around 8 lakh rupees only.

On 30 October 1848, Mulraj publicly expressed his satisfaction at Lawrence's decision in that it guaranteed him the governorship for three more years and British protection from his enemy Lal Singh at Lahore. Privately, he was much more reticent as the tax burden on the province had now increased substantially – and now it would actually have to be paid, with the British pulling strings in Lahore. Gone were the days of a weak central Lahore Government, when he could put off the matter indefinitely.

Another contentious issue weighing on his mind at this time along with the increase in payment was an expected fall in tax revenue for his province. The Resident had in his infinite wisdom dropped all octroi duties within the Punjab while making various other articles of trade duty-free. This drop in taxation no doubt earned plaudits from the trading community and the ordinary man on the street. Whether this was good or injurious to the state's finances was quite another thing. Multan, so far not under direct British control, had been excluded from these new arrangements, but this did not mean the province was not affected. Businesses and traders with their eye on other provinces began complaining of undue financial pressure and were threatening to move out of the province to the lower-taxed adjacent areas if matters did not change. Consequently Multan's revenues were already decreasing and Mulraj found himself having to dream up more ingenious ways of raising money. He began extracting tax in instalments as goods made their way through ferries and towns. This meant the initial tax was lower when entering Multan territory whereas the rest of Lahore territories were higher since there were no further internal duties. Mulraj began advertising the fact that merchants could enter Multan and then pass into other Lahore territories and thus decrease their tax liabilities. For this he was censured by the Lahore Government.

With the recent fall in revenues, Mulraj had also been forced to make corresponding cuts in expenditure and one of the more visible and painful decisions he had had to make was the size of his armed forces. His troops, fortunately for him, were different from those at Lahore in their attitudes. While the level of insolence displayed by the troops at Multan never approached the levels seen at Lahore after Ranjit Singh's death, there was a quiet understanding that they could not be messed around. They had seen how the Lahore troops managed to extort big pay rises and other pecuniary rewards and presents for their support or their acquiescence. On one occasion already, the Multan contingent, seeing the profitability of mutiny, had asked for Mulraj for two months' pay and a necklace each (gold being a common form of payment), which he was forced to provide. Alongside this there were persistent rumours of further proposed redundancies, and the soldiers had ominously begun showing increasing symptoms of disaffection and mutiny.

It is known the province had 12,000 men under arms during the First Anglo-Sikh War. However, his reduced means during the course of 1847 had forced Mulraj to cut this to 6,000 men. By the end of 1847 he had to make further reductions according to John Lawrence, who had heard of various complaints from the Multan soldiery reaching Lahore. Mulraj also had garrisons at other places in the province as well. It was estimated by the British authorities that at the beginning of 1848 Mulraj had a force of only around 2,000 men remaining at Multan, although local sources mentioned less. In addition he was supposed to have only five or six field guns, no money having been spent on manufacture of more. Redundant soldiers milling around the fortress or city speaking to employed soldiers of future cuts, and of mutiny or violent solutions to their predicament, became a common sight.

Cuts in revenue and spending aside, perhaps more importantly Mulraj now found his overlord and master to be the British Resident rather than the nonentities of the Lahore Durbar, so the governor found himself more restricted than previously. Multan was no longer a de facto independent state. This grated heavily on a man used to relative independence for so many years. Nevertheless, he held his tongue as he wished no quarrel with the British.

*\*\**

Few British officers had passed through Multan province before the war, but this would change in 1846. After the Treaty of Bhyrowal, as the British inroads into Lahore Government increased, and with tutelage to the central authority again growing, visits became more frequent to the dismay of Mulraj. Multan had been already been visited by a British officer, Lt John Nicholson in April 1847, a visit during which the governor perhaps betrayed his feelings, although he had acquiesced and cooperated with the British agent. Lawrence would pass on Nicholson's comments on Mulraj to the Government of India, noting Mulraj's disappointment in his new, subservient role. 'He has evidently been in the practice of acting as if he were the sovereign of the country and was in the first instance inclined to resent Lieutenant Nicholson's visit.'

It was this loss of authority and independence that frustrated Mulraj the most, and this showed up in other happenings. In a legal case earlier in the year he had imprisoned a group of bankers possibly engaged in some white-collar crime. Unsatisfied by Mulraj's ruling, the plaintiffs had appealed to Lahore and Lawrence's assistants, Lt Nicholson and Mr Bowring, had looked into the matter. Unsatisfied by this judgement too, the bankers then appealed to the Governor-General, who ordered a fresh hearing at Lahore presided over by John Lawrence. John Lawrence was unfamiliar with the case, which involved looking into a myriad of accounts, receipts and documents among other things. So he in turn handed over the case to a group of bankers more familiar with dealing with accounts. This group decided against Mulraj. The decision was expensive, Mulraj losing 5 lakh rupees of revenue and being ordered to release the prisoners.

Another case involved some Muslim soldiers who claimed they had not been paid and who resorted to appealing to Lahore as well. This issue had also gone against Mulraj. There were several other appeals to Lahore also in the pipeline. Cases such as these were ordinarily the jurisdiction and responsibility of the governor of the state and not something that the authorities in Lahore would have interfered with. With the arrival of the British this had changed. The British Resident was now the ultimate authority and seemed to welcome any complaints against Mulraj. Seeing the success of these two cases going against Mulraj prompted an increasing number of people to begin filing complaints against the governor's decisions, further undermining his authority in the process. The future looked uncertain for Mulraj as his actions and decisions, never under any control before from higher authority, faced increased scrutiny.

Tiring of his position and with revenue ebbing away, Mulraj had decided to retire by the middle of 1847 unless he could soften the policy of the British Resident. His ambition was to obtain a jaghir and then go on a long pilgrimage to the Hindu holy places, followed by a comfortable and wealthy retirement. He had a large mansion at Akalgurh near Ramnuggar where he planned to while away the rest of his years. Sometime in August, news reached Mulraj on the imminent departure of Henry Lawrence due to illness. Mulraj had enquired as to a meeting with him where he could air his grievances, and Lawrence had agreed to this. However, Mulraj arrived three days too late; Henry Lawrence had already departed for Calcutta. John Lawrence had filled his place and would receive Mulraj instead.

Several meetings, formal and cold, took place between John Lawrence and Mulraj during the next few weeks as Mulraj prolonged his stay in the capital. In the initial meeting, the governor enquired whether the tax revenue now demanded could possibly be reduced – something the new Resident ruled out entirely and without further thought. Realising quickly that John Lawrence would not budge, Mulraj expressed his desire to resign if the Resident would show no leeway. John Lawrence, never as diplomatic as his brother, was civil but quite terse with him. 'I explained,' wrote John Lawrence, 'that the Durbar had in no way interfered with his charge in the late reform and would not interfere during his lease, that he would get no reduction and might if he pleased resign his charge which I would accept.' However, John Lawrence softened his stance in later meetings, perhaps realising he was being somewhat harsh with the governor. He advised him to take time thinking over a possible resignation and to consult his friend Dewan Deena Nath and others in the Lahore Durbar before coming to a final decision. Mulraj also enquired as to whether a jaghir might be offered to him if he resigned. John Lawrence replied this was not possible. He had a good reputation and was thought of as a candidate for joining the Regency Council in due course, and if he became a member, would receive a jaghir as a matter of course, but it could not be given to him on retirement. John Lawrence was also reluctant to promise him a council seat or raise his expectations as the offer was a matter for the British Government and yet to be decided. However, he hinted a jaghir may be given if the province's accounts were handed over in complete and up-to-date fashion. Despite the threat, John Lawrence did not think he would resign and he noted Mulraj went away reasonably content. 'The fact is,' he mused, 'that Dewan Moolraj has so long enjoyed sovereign power in Mooltan that he forgets the duties of a subject and where he dares not openly refuse obedience, delays and hesitates to comply.'

According to the Resident, Mulraj would try several times to try and reduce the amount of revenue requested, including asking his friend Deena Nath to intercede on his behalf – all in vain, however, as John Lawrence refused to budge. In these conversations with John Lawrence, he also stated his second and more important issue – that the growing trend for Multan inhabitants to appeal to Lahore against his judgements was eroding his authority. If something could be done on this issue, the problem of the level of taxation could be dealt with amicably and easily. John Lawrence proved just as uncompromising on this issue also.

'To this I would not consent, saying that I did not wish to interfere with his jurisdiction in petty matters but that no authority could be permitted to exist in the Punjab independent of appeal and unaccountable to the law,' the Resident recalled later. 'With amusing frankness he told me that his *izzut* [honour] was involved in the matter and as I considered our national reputation was equally so it ended in the Dewan resigning his charge.'

Mulraj therefore seems to have determined on resigning and finally wrote a resignation letter, asking Deena Nath to take it to the Durbar to be handed over to John Lawrence. Deena Nath did so a few days later, on 18 December. This was without the Resident's knowledge and consent, and when Deena Nath brought the letter John Lawrence asked him to read it out loudly for all to hear. After the usual greetings, the letter requested permission to resign 'from the commencement of the last harvest'. In other words, Mulraj would give accounts from several months previously and not have to pay revenue taken during the last few months – this would need to be collected by the new governor. This was unsatisfactory to John Lawrence. As Deena Nath read out the letter Lawrence ordered him to halt, declining to hear the rest of the letter. Mulraj leaving at such a time would involve a loss of revenue.

> I added that the Dewan had behaved unusually in asking for such terms from the Durbar more especially as I had clearly given him to understand at our private interview two days before those on which alone I would recommend the acceptance of his resignation. I therefore requested that the Durbar would state to the Dewan in writing that he had accepted a lease for three years and any modification of it must be by mutual consent and for mutual benefit; that he must now proceed at once to Mooltan and carry on its management; that if he wished in reality to give up the province he must give reasonable warning beforehand and resign the charge at such a season as would admit of others taking charge without danger to the revenue.

Mulraj would stay in Lahore for a few more days mulling over things and last saw John Lawrence on the 21st of the month. He had given the whole matter more thought, he told the Resident, and the object of the visit was to tender his resignation as governor at a date the Resident was happy with. This would be at the end of April 1849, incidentally when all records including the new harvest could be included. This was the date John Lawrence had previously agreed could be the earliest date Mulraj could resign. In a more informal and friendlier meeting than the previous ones, Mulraj opened his heart out on the other various problems bedevilling him, citing ill health and internal family issues that were weighing on his mind, especially a quarrel with his brother over their inheritance. But although this had been sorted and reconciliation taken place, there were still contentious issues. 'I remember his dwelling on the dissensions of his own family; and, baring his arm (which was very thin) he asked me, if that was the arm wherewith to control a province.' He was most worried, though, about Multan residents dragging him into legal cases after his resignation. According to John Lawrence, Mulraj also attempted to bribe him into having a more sympathetic view using his vakeel for correspondence. But whatever failings John Lawrence had, corruption wasn't one of them.

> I told him that Sahibs never took bribes or presents. This appeared to surprise him; and he asked me rather pointedly if none of us did so. I said, 'Not one in a hundred, and that one is not worth bribing; for, depend on it, he has neither influence nor character.' He seemed puzzled a good deal, and told me that he had hitherto had little to do with us, and that for the future he was our best friend, and ready to do our bidding.

There was one request, quite important as it turned out, on which John Lawrence did agree with Mulraj. This was that Mulraj's resignation would be kept confidential from other members of the Durbar. There were several reasons for this. If news got about that he was resigning it would be difficult to extract the winter revenue at Multan as the population would naturally see him as yesterday's man. The main reason, though, was that it would undoubtedly cause consternation among his troops if they found out prematurely about his departure. It was considered axiomatic that when a British political agent took over at Multan, which would undoubtedly be the case after Mulraj's resignation, cuts in the garrison would inevitably occur, just as they were occurring round the rest of the country where British political agents had been sent. Hence the soldiers had no particular desire for Mulraj to resign and a British political agent take his place.

John Lawrence consented to keep this news from the Durbar members, with the proviso that the news would be communicated to other British officers and the British Government. The other arrangement was that two British officers would be sent down to familiarise themselves with the province and its revenues and accounts before the handover. He was anxious, however, that British political agents trudging around the province would betray the fact that Mulraj was resigning. Mulraj had no worry on this issue. Since the Resident's assistants were looking into the affairs of other provinces this would not be seen as anything other than normal procedure, he countered. There was also the question of full accounts from previous years. 'I recollect telling him that to settle the revenue we should require the accounts of some previous years; and though I do not remember his precise answer, he certainly consented,' John Lawrence mentioned at Mulraj's trial. 'This indeed was one of the conditions the fulfilment of which would entitle him to a jageer; and I purposely mentioned it to Moolraj, because I was aware that rendering accounts is a thing to which all natives have the greatest objection, while demanding them is both just and expedient.' This was a grey area because as far as Mulraj was concerned he had paid all his dues up to 1846 as specified by Henry Lawrence and the matter was closed. John Lawrence now requesting full accounts for several years previous was unreasonable. Nevertheless, Mulraj left Lahore seemingly quite satisfied, although privately none of his demands had been met.

***

Mulraj's desire for secrecy was not honoured. Frederick Currie was slated to take over the position of Resident on 6 March 1848. John Lawrence, briefing the new Resident, had asked Currie to keep Mulraj's resignation confidential from the Durbar, explaining there was 'a difference between the publicity of a rumour, and that of an authorized announcement'. Currie, John Lawrence stated at Mulraj's trial, 'was, however, of opinion, that the Durbar ought to be consulted; and that doing so on a matter so generally bruited abroad could do no harm'. In fact, even before he took the post, the news had passed through the British grapevine, reaching his ears at Agra, 700 km from Lahore. Currie felt no need to treat it as confidential since the news was what he considered open knowledge. The news of Mulraj's retirement would no doubt have reached the soldiers and garrison at Multan relatively quickly as well, he would argue later.

News of his resignation now being public knowledge put Mulraj in an awkward position. The few soldiers he still had in employment would not take it well. There was little he could do about it, though. 'He either thought the garrison would acquiesce, or cared not if they resisted and maintained him. It is not improbable that, like a weak swimmer, he threw himself on his back, and determined to let the stream of fate decide his course,' Herbert Edwardes offered later as an explanation on the news being made public.

He was quite right in this. In fact, due to financial constraints Mulraj was forced to make further cuts upon his arrival back at Multan, stoking more resentment at British revenue demands. Exact figures of the reductions are not available. However, it's known the corps commanded by Ram Rung, his brother, formerly 500 strong, was reduced to 175 men, showing the seriousness of the situation. Whether this had been planned before or after his trip to Lahore is unclear.

Although no violence had broken out on the news of his resignation, what was apparent to the remaining garrison now was that their jobs too were under immediate danger. Discontent among the soldiers reached boiling point, fuelling open plotting in the barracks and among their unemployed former comrades around the city. Mulraj ignored his troops' concerns, making active preparation for retirement, immediately selling off much accumulated material at low prices to the local merchants to realise a quick profit. All the stores in the fort bar the grain and gunpowder were sold, and the wood and iron and building material was sent to his village for the construction of a new residence. This went as far as selling a trifling five maunds of cannonball (137 kilograms), which was converted into chains and staples for use in construction in Multan. Instructions to refrain from fixing the carriages of the various horse artillery guns that required maintenance to save money were sent out, this being work that could be carried out by the next governor.

Curiously, a letter from Mulraj to the new Resident arrived at Lahore on 6 March, the same day as the arrival of Frederick Currie in the capital. It was in answer to a letter by John Lawrence asking him if he had anything he wished to communicate to the new Resident. Mulraj's response was that he had nothing to add to what had been discussed but that his 'honour and dignity should be guaranteed', that no charges should be heard against him after his resignation, that he would only supply accounts for the last year and that a sufficient jaghir should be given him for future maintenance. This hardly tallied with what he had talked about and agreed with John Lawrence, and perhaps he was hoping Currie would show a more sympathetic ear. In this he was mistaken too, for Currie was just as specific on all these issues, having being tutored by John Lawrence on where matters stood with Mulraj. The new Resident would write back somewhat coldly that the state reserved 'to itself the right to see that he committed no oppression or wrong in his government but that if he really desired to resign his Nizamut he must do so unconditionally as the Durbar would make no stipulations with him regarding indemnity for past misdeeds or for future provision'.

Currie was not prepared to make any guarantees that people who felt that they had been wronged would not be allowed to chase him through the courts. Neither was the issue of accounts running back several years cleared up either. Mulraj replied on 16 March assuring him it would be impossible to show records simply because they no longer existed.

> With regard to the order which was given for the production of the papers of the last nine or ten years, I replied that I trusted I might only be called on for those concerning my one year of Government. For through my incessant application to matters of business, the papers connected with my father's Government had been neglected and been eaten by ants. Some few which still exist in a box are utterly spoiled and nothing can be made of them and all those pertaining to the eastern districts were lost during the disturbances. My life is at your disposal. After once sending in my resignation of what use could these papers be to me. Moreover my happiness consists in doing good service to the State and in obedience to your wishes. At all times I am anxious for the care of the province and the people both in obedience to your orders and out of regard for my own good name ...
> In everything I trust to your friendship and am only solicitous for the preservation of my honor and for future provision. If there should be any balance of revenue for the two last harvests or any outlay for the army &c after March 11 1848 these sums should be deducted.

In such anomalous circumstances, with confusion over what period of accounts needed to be handed over, with uncertainty as to whether Mulraj's previous dictums could be questioned or not, and with an irate soldiery at the Multan fortress fearful of their livelihoods, two British political agents were sent by the Resident to take over the running of Multan province.

# INSURRECTION

I have surrendered to you my country: do not ask me for an explanation of all my acts.

Dewan Mulraj to Patrick Vans Agnew, 18 April 1848

If you want to die like a man, declare at once your independence; throw yourself into the fort; and we will only yield with our last breath.

Multan soldier to Dewan Mulraj, 19 April 1848

# 8

# Did You Find It So Easy to Take the Fort?

Frederick Currie would choose Patrick Alexander Vans Agnew of the Bengal Civil Service as the European to effectively replace Mulraj at Multan. With him would go another European assistant. Mr Cocks, the Assistant Resident at Lahore, had originally been considered for the role of Agnew's assistant by John Lawrence when Mulraj's intentions to resign became clear, but as he was senior in status to Agnew this was deemed inappropriate. Fortunately, as it turned out for Cocks, when Currie became Resident he decided to keep him at the capital in any case. William Hodson, who would later make his name during the Great Mutiny of 1857, was then for a time considered. 'It is an important mission, and one that, I think, you will like to be employed in,' Currie informed Hodson, asking him to come to Lahore immediately. However, he changed his mind later for some reason, with Hodson then remaining as assistant at Lahore. Instead Lt William Andrew Anderson of the 1st regiment of the Bombay European Fusiliers was eventually chosen for this role.

Both Agnew and Anderson were well thought of. On the subject of sending Agnew to Multan, John Lawrence had advised, 'It requires an officer of experience in revenue and judicial matters and he is the best man who is actually available.' Currie, too, evidently thought much of Agnew, describing him as 'the oldest political officer on this frontier, and a man of much ability, energy, and judgment, with considerable experience in administrative duties', a description that perhaps gives the impression of an older man than he was. In fact Agnew was relatively young, being twenty-five years of age, joining the Bengal Civil Service in March 1841 and having spent much of the time up to December 1845 as the assistant to the Commissioner of the Delhi division. With the outbreak of the First Anglo-Sikh War in that month he accepted the post of assistant to Major Broadfoot, the political agent in charge of the Cis-Sutlej states. His time after the war was spent in settling the boundaries of the newly independent state of Kashmir. Used to unquestioning obedience in long-conquered and pacified areas where his weaknesses and experience were less apparent, Agnew would be dealing with an area that had never known British rule and where his brusque and imperious method of going about things would illicit a more vigorous response.

Anderson comes across as a more enigmatic figure and, apart from his presence being noted by eyewitnesses at vital times during the coming days, he appeared to stay in the background and say or contribute little, perhaps as to be expected of an assistant. Twenty-eight years old, he had experience already of Multan, one of the reasons for his selection. Currie described him as 'an excellent Oriental scholar'. Herbert Edwardes thought of him as 'an officer of unusual acquirements, and of peculiarly conciliating manners'. He had been in the Punjab assisting Major Napier in surveying the country. Prior to this he had been in Sind province, employed as a deputy collector under Charles Napier, which had given him the opportunity to travel around the Multan province and thus gain experience of the area. Currie noted Agnew considered himself quite fortunate to have Anderson with him as an assistant.

Another European, a Dr Wilkinson, whose role apart from that suggested by his medical expertise is unclear, was also selected for the party. Wilkinson would not travel with the main party, however, travelling separately and lagging behind Agnew's retinue, to his good fortune. Also travelling with Agnew and Anderson would be Kahn Singh, chosen as the new and nominal Sikh Governor of Multan, who would take the place of Mulraj. Kahn Singh, too, largely comes across as an enigma. Little is known about him although as it turned out later he had a hand in an earlier plot against the British. He was in fact, like Anderson, a second choice for the role, a senior Durbar member named Sirdar Shumshere Singh Sindanwallia being the preferred man, but he was reticent on leaving Lahore for so long. Currie describes Kahn Singh as 'a man who bears a very high character as a brave soldier and intelligent man'. He would be no vice-regent like Mulraj, however, but would instead be on a fixed salary of 30,000 rupees per annum. Currie had also made it quite clear both to him and the British officers that his role would be largely ceremonial. 'The Sirdar will in the administration of the province be guided by your advice on all occasions and in the conduct of the duties of every department' were the clear instructions to Agnew. In a revealing letter to Kahn Singh that indicated the confusion prevailing on the agreement for accounts made with Mulraj for the handover of the province, Currie informed him and Agnew clearly that Mulraj must hand over records for the past ten years.

Dismayed at John Lawrence's tenure, where too much intrusion had taken place into Lahore Government practices and customs, Currie also warned Agnew not to follow John Lawrence's example at Multan. He was to treat the officials there with respect and avoid major changes in the system of taxation applied in the province. But there would be no compromise on the matter of expenditure; cuts in the garrison force and military expenditure were to be the priority. All irregular troops not entirely necessary were to be made redundant, with all recent recruits also being reduced. From the remaining regulars, the pick of the troops were to be sent to Lahore while Agnew's escort were to form part of the new garrison of the city. Therefore very few of the soldiers currently stationed at Multan were expected to remain at their posts once Agnew had settled into his role.

Meanwhile, quite unaware of the hostile mood of the Multan soldiery, and new to the job himself, Currie was confident of an uneventful start to his period as Resident as preparations were made for the takeover of Multan. 'Perfect tranquillity prevails, at present, throughout all the territories under the Lahore Government; and I have no reason to think that the apparent contentment of the people is other than real,' he advised the Government on 6 April. But he also delivered a note of caution as to the curious rumours that had been circulating of late. 'We have now, or have had during the cold months, British officers, in all parts of the country; and the impression seems general that all classes are satisfied at the present state of things; in those villages, chiefly in the Manjha, to which numbers of the disbanded soldiery have returned, we sometimes hear of prophetic rumours being circulated, of a day coming when the Sikhs are again to be brought into collision with the British, and with a different result from the last; but beyond this idle and infrequent talk, there is nothing to indicate that the return of the Khalsa independence is either expected, or desired.'

Currie was confident, with the redundancies of the soldiers plus other adjustments and cuts in expenditure to be organised by Agnew, that Multan province would yield even more revenue than in Mulraj's time, predicting the take would rise to 24 lakh rupees from the present 19 lakh rupees. This increased revenue was not necessarily destined to go into the Lahore treasury, though. The entire revenues from Multan, John Lawrence had advised the government on 27 December the previous year, should be directed straight to East India Company coffers.

> While on this subject, I may add that it would appear to be advisable that the net income of Mooltan should be paid directly into the British treasury; it will, no doubt, exceed the annual sum the Durbar is bound by treaty to pay; and thus we shall, gradually, and insensibly, reduce the arrears now due, which, inclusive of the current harvest, exceed forty lakhs of rupees. Some such arrangement would be more grateful to their feelings, and certainly more secure to us. So long as little comes into their exchequer, the Durbar will have less excuse, or temptation, to expend in superfluities; and we shall be relieved from the unpleasant position of constant importunity, without which, I feel certain, we shall not be paid.

***

Agnew's party was the usual large and unwieldy group seen accompanying British officers and political agents across the length and breadth of India. It would include a large clique of moonshees, syces, cooks, punkhawallahs (fan operators) and assorted other servants along with camp followers in total over a hundred strong. Among the group of moonshees were principally Kootub Shah, Ussud Ali and Wuzeer Allah Khan. Kootub Shah was a moonshee of Kahn Singh and had formerly been in the service of Sheikh Imam-Ud-Deen in Kashmir. However, he had come along with the party on the promise of employment by Kahn Singh at Multan. Among the servants were Bunsee Dhur, a Brahmin accompanying the party, while the military escort included Elahee Buksh, an officer. Accompanying him were Salabut Kahn and Jemadar Kesra Singh, two other officers. Much of the story of the altercation at the Multan fortress and the violence that followed in its wake in the following days would come from these and other eyewitnesses in the party.

Along with this party was organised a military contingent which would accompany the British officers and comprised of a force of around 1,400 men. Specifically this consisted of a Gurkha regiment 600 strong, cavalry 700 strong led by Gulab Singh, and a hundred artillery men for six guns. All the men were of the Sikh army and there was no British or European contingent. Some of the military force, as Currie had ordered, would serve not only as an escort but were to replace the garrison, who were destined for redundancy, and these soldiers had been briefed accordingly.

One of what would be a whole litany of mistakes during the attempted installation of Agnew as viceroy at Multan was the size of the force accompanying the party, something that would be criticised in many quarters later, albeit in hindsight. 'Another error, now easily perceptible, was a sending of so small force with your officers. Either no troops at all or a large force should have been moved down to Mooltan. The numbers actually sent were just sufficient to invite attack, but not to ensure a successful resistance. If 6000 or 7000 were sent to Benares, it seems strange that only 500 were moved to Multan, a country which never since its conquest by Ranjit Singh had been accustomed to a Sikh Garrison or to the sight of Sikh troops,' wrote Sir John Hobhouse (President of the Board of Control and responsible for overseeing East India Company affairs) to Dalhousie on 24 June as they later pondered on the happenings at Multan. Criticism also extended to the manner of the transition of power at Multan decided upon by Currie. Ordinarily a resigning governor should have returned to Lahore bringing his accounts with him, his replacement as governor being sent out subsequent to that. Instead Currie, for his own reasons and oblivious of the unsettled nature of the Multan garrison, had decided the two British officers would be sent to the city and would receive the final accounts from Mulraj at Multan, which would then be forwarded back to Lahore. This was an unusual way of going about things and something Shere Singh, the Commander of the Sikh army during the coming war, would point out too, claiming the crisis would never had arisen had the normal procedure been followed.

The irregularities on the handover of the province and the weakness of the escort aside, on 4 April Agnew's party left Lahore for the long journey to Multan. They would not march in unison, however. Already the warmth of the new season was making itself felt, each week hotter than the last. Agnew decided with Anderson and Kahn Singh to travel down by boat instead, sailing down the Ravi on 5 April. This would, he declared, in the gathering heat, be a far more comfortable alternative to riding down the roughly 350 km to Multan. Their escort and most of their servants, meanwhile, would travel on foot and horse. This meant the British officers and their military escort would meet for the first time at Multan, giving no time for familiarity and a friendly relationship to develop, a move the political agent Herbert Edwardes would later comment on as a great error.

The officers' boats slowly drifted downstream, entering Multan province and passing the town of Toulumba near the junction of the Ravi and Chenab rivers on 13 April, stopping at a place called Khalik Wullee, around 100 km north of Multan city. It was here that Agnew, till now entirely oblivious of the mood of the Multan garrison, first heard rumours of the mutinous feeling of the soldiers in the city from the servants who had alighted to gain supplies. 'The villagers of the place mentioned to us, that a refractory spirit had shown itself at Mooltan, and that Sahib Deen, their Jaghirdar, was their authority for the report. I informed the British officers of this and remarked that it was strange that none of the Dewan's officials had appeared to welcome them. To this, they replied that the report was without foundation,' Kootub Shah, the moonshee of Kahn Singh, would later relate. British officials visiting a town or city were normally greeted as they neared the place and escorted in with the appropriate ceremony.

Continuing to travel down the Chenab, the small convoy of boats finally reached the Raj Ghat, the landing place opposite Multan at around 11 a.m. on 17 April. Here, as the party got off their boats, no welcoming party from the city stood on the riverbank. Mulraj would have been expected to be here himself, along with plenty of his officials, to present a nuzzur and to escort the officers into the city. Despite this Agnew ordered his servants to offload the baggage from the boats in preparations for travel to the city. Eventually, several hours later, a lone horseman, Toolsee Ram, a high official of Mulraj, appeared on the road from the city. Anderson questioned him on what provisions had been made for their arrival and he informed them arrangements had been made for their camp at the Hazuri Bagh and Begee Bagh, two gardens to the north of the city fortress, while Kahn Singh's retinue would camp at the adjacent Eidgah Mosque, but that they could stay where they wished. Agnew after the disembarkation had already decided to rest and encamp at the Raj Ghat for the rest of the evening and night in any case, deciding to travel the 15 km to the city the next day fully refreshed. But the majority of the servants were ordered to head off with most of the supplies and baggage to prepare the British camp in advance of Agnew reaching the city the next day.

As it happened, just prior to reaching the Raj Ghat both Agnew and Kahn Singh had received worrying letters from Kootub Shah, one of Agnew's moonshees. He was travelling in the main party bringing the officers' horses and other supplies and which was lagging behind Agnew's group, who had made quicker progress sailing down the river. Kootub Shah had just reached

Toulumba, around 80 km north of Multan, and reported that things were nowhere near as settled as they should be at the town. Disaffection and hostility towards their armed contingent was quite apparent, Kootub Shah wrote. The local kardar, seemingly in sympathy with the Multan soldiery, had refused to supply wood for their campfires. He had, while at Toulumba, also heard rumours that an insurrection by the garrison, fearful of their jobs, had either begun or was about to begin in Multan. The locals in the town who were friendly towards him urged him not to go south in case he should put himself in danger. Agnew would dismiss the warning, replying back he had noticed no disaffection himself of any significance, and that there was no need for worry as Mulraj was, in any case, a friend of the British and would stand for no such behaviour by his soldiers.

The next day, before setting off to the city, Agnew would report his status and arrival at Multan in a letter to Currie. His strength was, he said, much less than it should have been for his units were still on their way, marching south to join him. Only 350 infantrymen were available at this time. Some of the artillerymen were missing, just eighty being present and only 100 of the cavalrymen too. Thus he had less than half the fighting force that set out from Lahore. However, he was loath to wait as this would cause unnecessary delay in the handover. After finishing his letter and sending a sowar to carry it back to Lahore, both British officers promptly mounted their horses and along with the remnants of their party at the riverbank set off to their prospective camp at the city.

Events in the Multan fortress while Agnew had been resting at the riverbank during that night are a little more confused. According to some witnesses, including Rung Ram, Mulraj's brother, the governor had summoned his leading officers and high officials for a meeting during the night to prepare for the handover to the British officers the next day. This seems to have been interpreted by his soldiers outside as a 'council of war', for the news of his failure to get concessions at all at Lahore was common news. Word of the meeting spread the next day, and, interestingly, the citizens by and large interpreted it as a council of war as well. What was the need for a meeting at such a late hour? Why had Mulraj not waited till the next day? What was the reason for such urgent conversation with his officials? Surely there must have been some plans that needed to be agreed on during the opaqueness of the night.

The local people knew the mood of their soldiers well enough and this was soon amply understood by Agnew's servants as well, who had made their way up to the city the day before and who now entered the city on the morning of the 18th to replenish their supplies and food. One of these was Ussud Ali, one of Agnew's moonshees, who went to a shop in Multan to purchase some new shoes near the Lohari gate. The shopkeeper, on finding he was one of Agnew's moonshees, became intensely interested and posed many questions about the military force attached to the British officers, whether it was the whole force or whether more reinforcements were coming, and if so when. On Ussud Ali replying more would come, suggesting the present force was not strong, the shopkeeper had replied, 'This is unfortunate', which struck Ussud Ali as very odd. Later he was told in the camp at the Eidgah by a barber of the hostile nature of the garrison towards the transfer of the city to British hands. Agnew's small escort would scarcely cause any anxiety among these soldiers, he was warned; the soldiers could easily brush this escort aside.

A similar story emerged from Wuzeer Allah Khan, the other moonshee. He too, the same morning, had taken the opportunity to travel into the city to purchase some provisions. In the passageway of the Lohari gate he saw some seated men quietly smoking a hookah. He had joined them for a while during which time the conversation had gravitated toward the token strength of the force that the British officers had brought with them. The locals had asked Wuzeer Allah

Khan for details but he replied this was no business of theirs. They also then mentioned that Mulraj had assembled all his leading men and sirdars together for a nocturnal meeting, a sure sign that trouble was brewing as far as they were concerned.

***

While this gossip and conjecture was being shared by the locals with Agnew's retinue, the British officers had ridden up to the city, having been met halfway by Rung Ram who escorted them to the Hazuri Bagh where the British camp had already been prepared by the camp followers. Even here, though, Mulraj had declined to appear himself and had sent no welcoming party, a slight which Kootub Shah impressed on Agnew's mind as they settled into the camp. Anderson mentioned in turn he had visited Multan once before travelling from Bhawulpore. That time he had been hailed by a salute from the fort's guns with Mulraj coming several miles out of the city to warmly greet him. These comments made no impression on Agnew, whose attention at the time perhaps was more on his surroundings. The crumbling Eidgah nearby and the Hazuri Bagh were picturesque local landmarks. A kilometre to the south, the city fortress loomed large and high, hiding most of the city beyond and presenting an impressive view. 'The fort is by far the most imposing I have seen in India and is, I dare say, one of the strongest,' he declared in his report that night to Currie. He was not happy with the camp arrangements, though. The bagh was too small for his personal retinue and he had complained to the city officials present. Kahn Singh, on hearing of this, had offered to make room for them in the Eidgah, a larger place; Agnew accepted and so orders went out for the baggage to be repacked and moved to the Eidgah instead.

By this time, advance units of Agnew's escort that had progressed by road had begun arriving at the outskirts of Multan and there was considerable fraternisation between the townsfolk and the soldiers in Agnew's party, beginning a few kilometres outside the city. Many of the Gurkha soldiers of the Sikh army had relatives who had settled in the city and who now came to visit them, and the area around the Eidgah was full of hawkers and other tradesmen making money selling supplies to the recent arrivals and turning the whole area into a makeshift bazaar. The bulk of the troops, including the Gurkhas, proceeded to make their tents in the open spaces between the mosque and the fort.

As Agnew settled down in his tent, he busied himself writing orders in preparation for his new reign. Letters to Mulraj asking which persons were enabled to collect taxes in the province were drawn up as well as enquiries about articles currently taxed in Multan. A second letter officially informing the soon-to-be ex-Governor of Kahn Singh's new governorship was also drawn up. Mulraj, Agnew wrote, was expected to assemble the city garrison for inspection when he visited the fortress with the veterans separated from the more recently raised recruits. This was to make it easier for Agnew to announce to the recent recruits they would be made redundant immediately. These letters were sent in the hands of the moonshee Wuzeer Allah Khan to Kahn Singh for his comments. Kahn Singh bluntly replied that he did not agree with his wish for a parade of the garrison troops. This would be asking for trouble, he opined, bearing in mind the stories emanating from the city of the angry mood among the local troops. Gathering them all in one place would only make the probability of a gesture of defiance more likely as group bravado came into play. In addition, he was suspicious of the governor's motives. 'I do not think it politic to enter the fort of Mooltan to-morrow; Moolraj is but a boy, mischief-making and deceitful; he has paid to you none of the honours or compliments customary to such occasions as the present, and one knows not what may happen.'

Agnew, firm in his conviction there was nothing to fear, would treat the new governor's comments lightly, replying that if he was so worried an incident may arise he need not accompany him the next day to the fort but could remain at the Eidgah during the handover. Seeing this as an appropriate point to voice his own concerns, Wuzeer Allah Khan, standing nearby, related his own stories of what he had heard from the locals at the Lohari gate. Again, Agnew paid little heed.

It was at this point, with the British party settling into their camp, that a small advance party sent by Mulraj arrived with sweetmeats and other food. Mulraj himself arrived at the Eidgah a short while later with 200 men, going on to present a nuzzur of 250 rupees to Agnew. The governor, according to Sadik Mahommed, was apparently kept waiting half an hour by the British officer, who was apparently dressing. Whether this was a calculated snub, a response to Mulraj's own muted welcome or something entirely innocent was never understood but Mulraj was eventually led to the tent of Kahn Singh where he found the British officers also seated and waiting for him. Invited to sit between them, with Kahn Singh on their left, it was noted Mulraj seemed to dislike Kahn Singh, never acknowledging or addressing the new governor despite Agnew signalling Kahn Singh's presence several times.

The first meeting between the governor and the British officer would be pleasant enough. 'My rulers do me a great kindness in taking off my hands so great a charge as this army and fort are to me,' Mulraj addressed the officer. Agnew congratulated him on his attitude in turn and remarked he would take possession of the fort the next day. After the usual compliments and pleasantries, it was all over in less than half an hour, with another meeting being arranged for later that afternoon after Agnew had rested to discuss the matter of the handover of the fort and other business.

Afternoon arrived, and between 3 p.m. and 4 p.m. Mulraj's party reappeared at the Eidgah, this time being promptly led to a large tent which had been made for the meeting. Ten chairs had been arranged in the tent, two of them in front of the rest. Agnew led Mulraj by the hand to a chair situated between his own on the right and Kahn Singh's to the left. According to Toolsee Ram, Mulraj had asked him to stand close by his side. Mulraj was having problems hearing with one ear of late and needed assistance: 'Remain near me; much of what the Sahebs say I do not perfectly understand; you will explain their words to me,' Toolsee Ram recalled Mulraj ordering him.

The meeting started amicably enough and with the usual salutations. 'I shall ever be a faithful servant to the Lahore Sirkar; your arrival fills me with gladness as the fort and army and district are a great charge to me; the management of them I was unequal to. They are now yours. Whatever order you give I shall obey,' Mulraj declared. 'The British Government unwillingly deprive you of your authority but you should not be angry for that; you will still be respected and have authority,' the British officer told Mulraj in turn. After agreeing to aid Kahn Singh in his installation as the new governor the next day, the conversation quickly turned to other matters and Mulraj now requested his Rooksut and Razeenameh (deed of acquaintance and satisfaction) from Agnew, thus allowing him to leave straight away, but Agnew would decline to issue one. The matter of the financial records, he insisted, must be dealt with first before Mulraj could leave. Things now took a more serious turn.

Agnew turned discussions to the matter of the accounts for the preceding ten years, as requested by Currie. The receipts and records for the revenues received by the different districts must be handed over as a guide for future taxation, he declared. This was something that Mulraj seems not to have been expecting, and he seemed perturbed by this request. 'My papers have been eaten by the ants or otherwise destroyed; but I can show you the receipts [for all money expended] which I have received from Lahore and others,' he responded. Sheikh Ghoolam Mustapha, a regimental moonshee, recalled Agnew appearing to be quite annoyed at this response, expecting all records to have been readied for him to peruse. Perhaps he thought Mulraj was attempting to make a fool of him. He leaned over to Kahn Singh. 'Bring forward your chair and listen to what Mulraj says.' Kahn Singh moved closer and said to Mulraj, 'Give to sahib the papers he requires.' Mulraj simply reiterated his answer, adding he could bring the boxes that contained the destroyed documents if that would satisfy Agnew. 'How is it possible for me to produce papers for ten years? I have been Dewan but two years.' Agnew explained he wasn't asking for papers to call him into account but for his own satisfaction and better understanding. 'In asking for your papers, I only wish to ascertain from them the state of the country, and what has been the custom for the last ten years.' Uncompromisingly, he continued, 'In instances such as the present, it is customary for papers to be delivered up.'

Nevertheless an agreement seems to have been reached after a while that Mulraj needed to provide documents only for the last six years. 'Tomorrow having sought for the papers of Sawan mull, I will give them to you,' he replied. Toolsee Ram, Mulraj's aide, recalled the governor replying that the papers were with the Patwaree (keeper of state papers) and that he would order him to get them readied to send to Agnew.

The conversation then turned to something more serious still. Agnew brought up the matter of complaints being registered by the locals against the governor at Lahore. 'I shall listen to all complaints made by those who deem themselves to have been injured by you,' he informed Mulraj, who was a little taken aback. The governor would protest. 'This is my custom, when anyone over whom I have authority behaves improperly or acts unjustly towards another, a fine is inflicted on him. Now you wish to give redress to all those who have complaints to bring against me. That is not right. I have surrendered to you my country: do not ask me for an explanation of all my acts.'

Perhaps Agnew felt he had been too harsh, for after listening to Mulraj's remonstrations he would soften his position somewhat. 'I shall take no notice of aught that happened during the first two years of your nizamut,' he would finally pass judgement, 'but the complaints of the last year, I shall listen to you, and those complainants whose cases are worthy of consideration or redress, I shall send to you, that you may make them happy.'

The conversation would end on the paying off and dismissal of half of the garrison troops immediately. Agnew would turn down a request by Mulraj for another ten days in order to complete these arrangements, insisting the governorship must be given to Kahn Singh the next day and redundancies made promptly on the morrow. The meeting therefore ended abruptly and in cold fashion. Mulraj, visibly stung by Agnew's authoritarian attitude throughout, addressed him as he stood up to leave. 'In the morning I shall visit you, and show you the army and the fort, previous to surrendering them to you; but I have done nothing to deserve such harsh treatment from you.'

He left by all accounts with an angry expression on his face. Back at the fortress, Sadik Mahommed was told by an angry Mulraj that he had been treated contemptuously by the sahibs, touching on Agnew's demand for full accounts. As far as Mulraj had been concerned, the issue of accounts had been settled in Lahore the previous December and with Currie more recently. Now Agnew was again asking for a full ten years or at least six years of accounts. So annoyed was he, Sadik Mahommed recalled later, that in a fit of anger the governor declared if he had just 500 loyal men ready to die for him he would defy any orders to surrender the fortress to these Europeans. That this was said in the heat of the moment by the timorous governor there was no doubt, but it was clearly heard by members of the garrison, who also heard Agnew had insisted on immediate redundancies. Word immediately spread around the garrison that Mulraj had been slighted by the British officers and was in belligerent mood himself.

Back at the Eidgah, Kootub Shah, reflecting on the frosty end to the conversation and judging that some disturbance by the local soldiery was likely, had advised Agnew to take possession of the fort immediately the same day. The issue of accounts could always be dealt with on a later day, he advised. Agnew insisted on sticking with his plan. 'It matters not; Moolraj is my friend,' he replied to the moonshee. On Kahn Singh suggesting a force of at least 200 men should accompany Mulraj's party to take immediate possession of the fort, Agnew reiterated his curt reply of before: 'If you are afraid, do not go; I will go alone.' Both Kootub Shah and Kahn Singh left the matter at that. The British officer had patently listened to no word of caution from any of his party since they had approached Multan and seemed to be immune to advice. In his private letter written in the evening of the 18th to Frederick Currie, though, Agnew mentions the words of caution by Kahn Singh which seemed privately to have had some effect. 'I don't know what has put into Sirdar Kahn Sing's head some imagination that we had better get the fort into our hands as soon as we can but in any case it is right to lose no time in the transfer,' he communicated, before iterating his view on the governor: 'Everything seems to bear out the character Moolraj has always borne for peace and quietness.'

Thus it was decided the very next day the fort would be occupied by his escort and much of the garrison ejected. Plainly the safest and most straightforward course for Agnew would have been to order the present garrison out of the fort before he marched in to take possession, thus avoiding contact between the two contingents. Instead, though, continuing to largely disregard the possibility of any disturbance, the British agent decided all would be well if he took two companies of his own into the fortress while Mulraj's soldiery watched. The garrison soldiers would then be asked to transfer charge of each gate of the fortress one at a time, handing over the corresponding keys to his own men as he marched through the citadel with his retinue. This procedure, in retrospect, seems almost designed to humiliate and illicit an angry response. Moreover, the parade of the garrison was to follow directly afterwards, when Agnew would dismiss large portions of these men immediately from service. 'It would be perhaps going into the extreme and alarm the rest of the sepoys to change the garrison at once altogether,' he added in his letter to the Resident, possibly hinting a complete dismissal of Mulraj's soldiers at a later stage but certainly not that morning. That night, therefore, as per Agnew's orders, Kahn Singh organised an escort of two Gurkha companies of infantry with three officers and around sixteen to twenty-five sowars for the trip to the fort the next day. The force would be led by a Kuldeep Singh, with the cavalry officer Gulab Singh accompanying also.

By sunrise the next day, the party that was to enter the fort was readied and waiting only for Mulraj to reappear to escort them personally into the fort. The Dewan did not appear, though, in what was perhaps another snub after the difficult end to the meeting the previous day, and neither were any messages as to his non-appearance sent. Eventually Agnew and Anderson decided to leave for the fort regardless. As they were leaving the Eidgah, Ussud Ali appeared and approached them with the story of what his barber had mentioned of Mulraj's meetings two nights ago. Agnew, increasingly annoyed at the constant words of caution from all, was seen to get quite visibly angry with the moonshee, whom he ordered back to his tent while he moved out on his elephant. This was the last warning the officer would receive.

\*\*\*

The elephant convoy, with Agnew, Kahn Singh and Anderson all on their own elephants, moved in slow and stately fashion out of the Eidgah and down the straight road to the fortress, accompanied by their escort who marched behind them. As they passed Mulraj's residence, the Aam Khas, Mulraj, who had been informed of their departure, finally appeared with his entourage. Riding on horseback, he dismounted and mounted an accompanying elephant. The joint party then slowly moved to the gate of the fortress where all dismounted and proceeded on foot. All the servants and moonshees and junior officers were asked to wait at the gate while Agnew, Anderson and a few servants followed, including a Mohkum Furrash, holding a carpet and fan.

Agnew's first direct experience of the ugly mood of the garrison soldiers came early. As the British party prepared to enter the fort by the Sikhi gate, they found several surly soldiers loitering around the gates, ready for a confrontation with the Europeans. Mulraj, heading the party, had already entered through the gate but as the British officers trailing a few feet attempted the same, one of the guards in a fit of pique insisted on formalities. He declared the British officers could not enter till orders from his master Mulraj were received. 'The Sahib is Master,' Mulraj replied from a few feet away. Agnew apparently said something to the guard, and in the ensuing charged conversation the guard angrily declared 'he [Agnew] had better not turn him off'. According to other eyewitnesses, Mulraj further addressed the soldier after the British officers had passed the gate: 'You were formerly my servant; you will now serve the Sahib who will treat you as well as I have done.' To this the soldier responded rather cryptically, 'I am now your servant but when I have been removed from your service we shall see.' Agnew may have infuriated the soldier further with a show of his authority. 'Don't fear; the Dewan's servants shall be as mine, and mine as his,' he was heard saying, insinuating the garrison would soon be taking his orders from him.

This wasn't the end of the matter. As the party progressed into the fort, the guards, determined to be difficult, then shut the gates on the Gurkha escort bringing up the rear. According to Kootub Shah, some of them were struck by the members of the garrison. The guards would again only take orders to let them in from Mulraj, and Agnew on turning round and seeing the issue then asked Mulraj to give the necessary command to the soldiers. The gate was then reopened and the British escort allowed to stream in.

It was while they commenced going into the fort that Mulraj, noticing the charged atmosphere prevailing among his men, advised Agnew it would be both hazardous and provocative to bring in all of his troops into the fortress, advice Agnew readily accepted. A message was sent back ordering one of his companies and the sowars to stay out of the fort and that only one company of troops should continue into the fort, marching behind the leading party. Many of the servants, orderlies and the usual rabble of attendants were also told to wait outside the fort gate, although a few, like the moonshee Wuzeer Allah Khan, continued to accompany the party. Looking around as he followed the British officers, what struck Khan was that the soldiers all around the interior of the fort were fully armed and moving about with a strong air of belligerence. Kootub Shah, also with the party, mentions artillerymen in the fort in a rather disturbed state, some shedding tears as the British party sauntered round the citadel, expecting this to be the last day in their posts. 'I said to Mr Agnew if the Dewan intends to give up the fort why does he not allow our troops to enter and why do you go in thus unattended,' he recalled later on the subject of the Gurkha companies being told to stay outside the fort.

Things seemed to calm down once they were inside the fortress, but there was little warmth apparent as Mulraj personally showed the party around its defences. The tour included his living quarters, after which he proudly led the officers to a strongly fortified structure built specifically to be bombproof by his late father. Agnew, though, showing little diplomacy, bluntly retorted that it could be destroyed quite easily. To the west of the fort, the officers were shown one of the largest guns in the citadel along with the magazine, ammunition and grain stores and the prison. As they moved around the fort visiting the various buildings, Agnew ordered a Gurkha sentry and moonshee from his own party to remain behind at each building to take control. As they passed each of the fortress gates the keys were transferred to his Gurkhas, although the old garrison soldiers continued to stay sentries as well. The result of all this was that Agnew's retinue gradually became smaller as the tour progressed as men were peeled off and assigned their new jobs. The contents of each building, Agnew informed Mulraj, would be calculated and a receipt given to him later.

Curious garrison soldiers could be seen shadowing the party around at this stage, casting angry looks and ready to trade insults given any excuse. Sadik Mahommed, Mulraj's Commander of Cavalry, escorting the party, would relate later he could plainly hear various soldiers murmuring about creating an emeute or skirmish in which the British officers could be taught a lesson and shorn of their imperious bearing.

Towards the end of the tour, there was a general muster of the fort's garrison for review by Agnew. 'The bearing of the whole garrison during Mr Agnew's inspection,' wrote Herbert Edwardes, 'was indeed much of the same kind; and if ever clouds foretold a thunderstorm, the fate of the British officers was assuredly foreshadowed in the dark looks and angry mutterings of Moolraj's soldiers. They needed but a word, a nod, from the master they were losing, to break out, and fall upon the intruders.'

Agnew, still impervious to the general mood of the soldiers, addressed the assembled men, informing them any new or recent recruits would be disbanded immediately. They would receive their pay from Mulraj that they were owed up to this day. They were to leave their arms behind in the fortress but were to carry all their personal possessions out of the citadel. Deciding to address the obvious signs of disaffection, the British officer later approached some of the men, telling them they would be sure to find employment elsewhere; this must have been of little solace to them. To Mulraj, too, he gave the order to remove all his possessions now he was no longer the governor, but warned him to leave behind all state property. With the formalities of the handover complete, the party slowly moved back towards the Sikhi gate to return to the Eidgah.

\*\*\*

By this time, Agnew's retinue had thinned considerably. There was no escort or guard left for Agnew and Anderson, all the Gurkha troops having been given their new stations in the fort. The Sikh officers who had accompanied the party had remained behind too, busy arranging things for the takeover. With Agnew and Mulraj was a party around ten strong comprising Anderson, Kahn Singh, Rung Ram and a few servants and moonshees of Agnew.

It was quite different on the other side of the Sikhi gate where a large, curious crowd had developed. The servants that had been ordered to wait had been joined by a legation of local merchants around 150 strong. These merchants had come to meet their new masters, bringing sweetmeats with them, and were in the hope of arranging a meeting with Agnew. Their original destination had been the Eidgah, but as they passed the Dowlut gate news had reached them that the British officers and Kahn Singh were in the fortress instead, arranging the transfer of the fortress. Entry had not been allowed by the guards and so they waited near the outer edge of the fosse for the chance to perhaps introduce themselves to Agnew. Along with them were the attendants of Mulraj. Adding greatly to the crowd were plenty of locals attracted by the spectacle of the fort handover, watching the Gurkha company left outside the fort by Agnew. The crowd was several hundred strong by now, with more interested parties arriving, meaning the area became congested. Many locals were seen sitting on the side of the ditch with their legs hanging into the fosse to watch the scene in what was an informal and lively atmosphere full of conversation.

Several guards manned the Sikhi gate at this time, among them one named Ameer Chund, a local braggart and roughneck of dark complexion who happened to be on duty at this time. A proclamation on the incident later by Sikh officers leading the rebellion describe Chund as a *benaukur* – an irregular who was already out of service having been paid off, but who appeared in any case at the gate, perhaps hoping for pay. Chund lived near the Lohari gate on the other side of the fort and was known by the locals to have an unstable character, to be frequently erratic and bad-tempered in his behaviour, a condition not helped by his addiction to bhang, a cannabis-based narcotic. His weakness for the drug was also well known throughout the area and it was quite apparent he was in a drug-induced stupor at this time. 'I saw Ameer Chund often before this. I have seen him since. He used to drink bhang and was crazy,' recalled Jesoo, a merchant's agent at the trial of Mulraj who was with the crowd outside the fort gate that day. Nobody was attempting to talk to him and he was seen to attempt no conversation that day, his mind perhaps focussing on what he was about to do. Mustapha Kahn, one of Mulraj's right-hand men, in his talks with Edwardes later mentioned Ameer Chund had claimed he had some sort of vision which drove him to do what he did. 'The man himself could only account for it by the miraculous appearance of Gooroo Gobind who stood before him in black garments and bade him kill the enemies of his religion.'

Beyond the gate of the fort, a small, narrow, temporary wooden bridge served to allow access to the fort over the glacis. As they approached the bridge, Agnew and Anderson's horses were in the lead with Mulraj, Kahn Singh and Rung Ram slipping behind as the narrow bridge would only allow the horses to traverse in single file. There are differences in the various testimonies of the witnesses to the incident at this point. Wuzeer Allah Khan says Ameer Chund had concealed himself behind a small door to the right of the party as they approached the gate and that Mulraj was seen making some sort of sign to him presumably as signal to attack. His account was considered suspect, however, as he bore grudges against Mulraj. Bhunsee Dhur, one of Agnew's Brahmin servants, recalled Mulraj beginning to ride away in the opposite direction, which was presumably, he suggested, a signal for the attack. Sheikh Goolam Mustapha, the regimental moonshee, who was walking just ten paces behind Agnew's horse, one of the closest to the incident, did not think Mulraj was in any way involved or that Ameer Chund was receiving orders either from Mulraj or other parties. At any rate, the Brahmin recalled Ameer Chund sitting on the ground at this point with his back resting on the fort gate. As he saw the party approaching the bridge, Chund got up and ambled towards the unsuspecting Agnew. Keshow Ram, a servant of Agnew who was following behind his master, recalled someone goading Ameer Chund while he had been seated. 'Why do you not get up and make a salute when a Sardar is passing,' the man had said, which had angered Chund further.

Without so much a word, as he reached Agnew, Chund struck out with his spear in a desultory fashion which had the effect of knocking Agnew off his horse and wounding him under the right armpit. The action was to humiliate rather than kill, the attack being neither carried out with sufficient energy nor followed up by a further attack as a stunned Agnew lay on the ground recovering. Finding one of his feet caught in the stirrup as he fell, he would take some moments to recover while extricating his foot before standing up and regaining his composure. Chund, meanwhile, had stood over him and watched the officer struggle to release his leg. The unexpectedness of the attack had caught everyone by surprise, including Agnew. It didn't last long, and on standing up, and with his blood up, the officer hit Chund with his riding stick in response. Chund, angered by this, now threw his spear away and, drawing his sword, wounded Agnew twice, once on the left arm and once on his shoulder.

All the witnesses, both Agnew's party and the guards at the gate, had been too stunned by the sudden attack to make any immediate moves. But after the momentary confusion and chaos several people brandished naked swords. Elahee Buksh himself got involved straight away and pulled out his sword. He struck at Ameer Chund but managed only to wound him slightly on the cheek, although it had the effect of making Chund lose his balance and he fell into the fosse. Buksh then picked up Agnew's hat, which had been knocked off during the altercation, and gave it back to the injured officer. Meanwhile, another of Agnew's servants began to descend the ditch to despatch Ameer Chund but was called back by Agnew, who did not want a death resulting from the exchange. The other sentries nearby, though, comrades of Chund, had decided now was the time to humiliate the European intruders. Without any hesitation, following Chund's example they closed on Anderson and attacked him too. He was wounded on the forehead and on the back. Some other soldiers walked up and wounded him in the thigh and under the arm before he was left alone. No wound was given to the vital parts, however, and they failed to press on with the attack while he lay on the ground, suggesting taking of life wasn't the objective.

Many of the curious bystanders quickly began fleeing from the scene, fearing shooting would take place, while others curious to see the outcome stayed. The noise and shouting came to the notice of several of the soldiers in the fort, who had begun running out towards the gate. While all this had been happening, Mulraj, riding a few metres behind Agnew and Anderson, had shown no inclination at all to take command of the situation. Rather than attempting to assert his authority, he fled, turning his horse around and riding off in the opposite direction. Some later suggested he had the impression this was a general revolt against authority and that the object of Ameer Chund and the other soldiers was to dispose of him as well as the British officers. Whatever the reason, he rode rapidly to the safety of his garden house, the Aam Khas, outside the fort and would take no further part in events for the next few hours. Several of the witnesses saw Kahn Singh pointing at Mulraj in an accusing fashion and ordering his sowars to kill Mulraj as he rode away, suspecting the governor was behind the attack.

While Mulraj rode off, a wounded Anderson took the opportunity to remount his horse and, fearing another attack, fled on the road towards the Eidgah himself. He would be pursued by some of the garrison sowars, who seem to have impulsively decided they should finish what they had started. Being wounded, he made slow progress and was quickly intercepted a few hundred metres outside the fort, attacked again in a more deliberate manner and left for dead. He would be found on the roadside later by the Gurkha escort who had been led into the fortress by Agnew but who would be ejected by the garrison soldiers as the situation developed. They would take him back to the Eidgah, heavily wounded but still alive. This left a wounded Agnew still at the fort gate along with Kahn Singh. Fortunately for both they were protected from harm by Rung Ram who, unlike his brother Mulraj, was not afraid to show his authority, and the two between them hoisted the stricken British officer onto Kahn Singh's personal elephant ready to take him back to the Eidgah. Kahn Singh and Agnew's elephants then slowly made their way back towards the Eidgah, followed by the rest of Agnew's servants and moonshees. With no more violence having taken place, the crowd of onlookers gained courage. Curious as to the outcome, they followed the elephants as they were ridden back. So on to the road to the Eidgah on which he had ceremoniously arrived with an escort of soldiers several hours earlier, a wounded Agnew now returned but with an equally long escort of servants and curious locals.

The road in fact passed within a few hundred metres of the Aam Khas, where Mulraj had retired with his escort, and there were garrison troops present there as well. As soon as Kahn Singh's elephant cleared the houses situated immediately outside the gate and passed close enough to the Aam Khas, they were greeted by a desultory discharge of musketry from the soldiers situated outside the Aam Khas's gates. These men apparently already knew what had gone on in the fort and had decided to side with their comrades as well. Guns were also seen being brought up to the gates of the Aam Khas and Kahn Singh purposely veered the elephants he was leading as much to the left as possible to keep a big a distance between them and the Aam Khas, although one of the elephants was still wounded by fire.

***

Fleeing from the altercation at the Sikhi gate did little good for Mulraj's authority, and as news of the incident spread like wildfire over the next hour what little mastery he had over the situation would disappear. Curiously, the same would be the case at the Eidgah, although Agnew, who had reached sanctuary there, probably little suspected it at the time. Inside the Aam Khas, an indecisive Mulraj mulled over whether to remain faithful to his soldiers or to assist the stricken British officers. As he had ridden of from the fortress gate he had been heard to say 'that it [the altercation] had brought the very heavens upon his head'. He knew unreserved and swift assistance of the wounded British officers would absolve him of all blame for the attack, although Agnew would no doubt ask for the unruly soldiers to be handed over for British retribution. This was quite impossible, as the whole garrison was in a mood for fight and would not countenance surrendering their comrades into British hands. So strong was the anger against the British officers that to try and compel them would be to risk his own life. Siding with his own soldiers, though, would make him a rebel against both Lahore and the British Government of India, although it guaranteed the support of his men and his life for the time being at least. In the short period he had to himself, he continued dithering between the two options.

The ability to make his own decision became harder as a steady stream of soldiers and officers from the fortress poured in to the Aam Khas eager to have their say on events. Rung Ram, Mulraj's brother, arrived too after having transported Agnew back to the Eidgah and was one of the few who tried persuading Mulraj to assist the British officers. 'Never mind; it's not your fault. Now, come along with me to the Sahib, and assure him that this is none of your doing. As for this rascal [Ameer Chund], we'll hang him!' Rung Ram suggested to Mulraj. One of the soldiers present angrily reproached Rung Ram for his timidity. 'You're pretty *nimuk-huram* [faithless to salt, i.e. disloyal] to hang our comrade for trying to keep our Dewan [Mulraj] in Mooltan!' he countered. On Rung Ram scolding him for insubordination, the soldier struck out with his sword, wounding Rung Ram three times, a plain indication if it were needed that nothing could be decided without the consent of the soldiers.

Heated and confused discussions as to what had happened and who was to blame broke out. Sadik Mahommed, one of Mulraj's senior officers, recalled some officers who had recently arrived addressing Mulraj. 'What have you done?' Mulraj explained the situation and how the soldiers were now assuming command. 'They have wounded Rung Ram; they would have wounded me too. I remained away against my wish; God's design in doing this I do not know.'

Mulraj would ask Sadik Mahommed his advice privately, to which Mahommed had answered the best course would be give himself up to Agnew. 'Dost Mahomed gave himself up, and was treated badly,' an unsure Mulraj would reply, referring to the treatment of the Afghan ruler after he had given himself up to the British after the First Anglo-Afghan War. Toolsee Ram had also turned up at the Aam Khas by now as news spread round the city of the altercation. Mulraj had indicated to him he was no longer being allowed to leave by the guards. 'Wicked men have wounded the sahebs; it was not my fault,' he explained.

It was quite obvious the bulk of the common soldiers, dismissed already from service by Agnew that morning and therefore harbouring a large grudge, were for punishing the British officers whatever the consequences. Mulraj's officers, though, with more to lose, were calmer and took a more considered approach but by and large supported their troops, advising Mulraj to plunge boldly into the unknown with his head held up high. He mustn't betray his soldiers, they advised, and in any case the British would hold him responsible later for not controlling his soldiery. 'You see what a mess you are in. If you want to be hanged, go off to Lahore. If you want to die like a man, declare at once your independence; throw yourself into the fort; and we will only yield with our last breath,' one officer was heard to say.

When he asked if the Sikh soldiers and officers present would swear on the Guru Granth Sahib, the Sikh holy book, that they would stand by him, they all readily agreed as did the Muslim soldiers with the Quran. Sadik Mahommed reminded Mulraj that he did not have the strength to oppose the Lahore authorities or the British. Only around 1,500 soldiers could be mustered at most in the city and neighbourhood. 'God has a design in what has happened,' Mulraj had said in response, anxious not to face the wrath of his soldiers 'This is the hot weather, and the Europeans cannot move before the cold weather; I shall then have collected an army, and I hope there will be a rising in the Punjab.' The governor was referring to the well-known British dread of marching in the hot season, during which time mortality among European troops tended to increase. Therefore the opportunity to prepare for conflict would exist for several months. In that short hour or so, therefore, browbeaten by his soldiers, Mulraj now unexpectedly found himself a somewhat reluctant leader of an insurrection with few resources at his command instead of looking forward to a comfortable and wealthy retirement.

\*\*\*

While discussions were in full flow at the Aam Khas, Mulraj's soldiers, beside firing the odd shots at Rung Ram and Kahn Singh's elephants as they took Agnew back to the Eidgah, had taken no great interest in pursuing the convoy to finish the job. So with Agnew's Gurkha units bringing back Anderson as well, both officers ended up back at the Eidgah a short while later. Kadi Buksh, an Indian doctor of the Gurkha regiment who had accompanied the party, would sew up the wounds that Anderson had received, Agnew being in better shape and requiring much less attention. The lull that followed meant both officers could rest for a while and some sowars were sent off to hasten the arrival of Mr Wilkinson, the apothecary. His party was still a couple days' march from the city. No further violence would happen that day. The night, too, passed without incident, the city soldiers unsure of their next step.

What did materialise during this time was an exchange of correspondence between Mulraj and Agnew. As the governor expected, Agnew wrote to him saying he did not attribute any blame to him for the incident at the fortress gate but expected him to cooperate unreservedly and hand over the soldiers who had taken part in the attack. In addition Mulraj must come personally to the Eidgah as a matter of urgency and bring the guilty with him to prove his innocence. He also asked him to reprimand his troops for the attack and their indiscipline pending further investigation. His appearance was awaited all evening and night by Agnew, the officer firmly believing Mulraj would distance himself from the culprits. As the evening wore on and no response arrived, though, he prepared for the worst. Sentries were posted all around the mosque quadrangle. The Eidgah happened to be just in range of the fort guns, so initially Agnew prepared orders to retreat further north from the fort. The Sikh officers in his party, however, suggested staying at the mosque. The structure was solidly built and could withstand much punishment, they argued. Water was also available along with provisions. Another place, while safer, may not afford the same defensive qualities and amenities. Agnew concurred and the decision to stay was made but defensive preparations were stepped up during the night and a defensive ditch would be ordered to be constructed round the complex the next day.

At 11 a.m. the following day, after waiting in vain for Mulraj's arrival, Agnew sent a much more authoritarian message to Mulraj at the Aam Khas.

> I know you are not the guilty party in this affair; seize those persons who have wounded Anderson and myself and send them to me and do not fail to come also yourself. People will then see and know that you were not a party to this affair and that you are still my friend. If you will not come, then will I also entertain doubts of your friendship.

He was also, he said, cognisant of the spontaneity of the incident and exonerated him of any involvement in the altercation if he would come immediately. The letter was given to Kootub Shah to take the short distance to the Aam Khas. The moonshee would meet a hostile reception as he neared Mulraj's residence, the crowd of soldiers having lost none of their aggression. Eventually the letter was allowed in, serving only to increase Mulraj's indecision. Elahee Buksh, who was present with Mulraj at the time of the arrival of the letter, asked to have a private word with him. Mulraj confided to him that the soldiers were beyond his control and that he would have to go along with their wishes regardless. The soldiers had harangued him that the British could not be trusted. 'These Sahebs never fulfil their promises, no faith can be kept with them. When Lal Singh voluntarily gave himself up, see how he was treated by the Sirkar company, and look what they have done to the Maharanee.' What Mulraj confided to Buksh was his worry of a possible exile even if he gave himself up to Agnew, assuming his soldiers allowed him. 'If I do so [surrender to Agnew], also I shall be transported. I am childless. I shall fight.' He was also conscious that his reply, if he sent one, would commit him one way or the other. It would be a full five hours before he responded with a letter back to Agnew.

Back at the Eidgah, meanwhile, Agnew had decided to report the incident and his situation to Frederick Currie. Around 2 p.m. he dictated a letter to one of his moonshees.

Multan, 19th April, 1848.

My Dear Sir Frederick, – You will be sorry to hear that, as Anderson and I were coming out of the fort gate, after having received charge of the fort by Dewan Mulraj, we were attacked by a couple of soldiers, who, taking us unawares, succeeded in wounding us both pretty sharply.

Anderson is worst off, poor fellow. He has a severe wound on the thigh, another on the shoulder, one on the back of the neck, and one in the face.

I think it most necessary that a doctor should be sent down, though I hope not to need him myself.

I have a smart gash in the left shoulder, and another in the same arm. The whole of the Multan troops have mutinied, but we hope to get them round. They have turned our two companies out of the fort.

Yours, in haste,

P. A. Vans Agnew.

A copy was sent to Peer Ibrahim, the British agent in the neighbouring state of Bhawulpore, around 100 km away to the east, the ruler or Nawab of the state a firm friend of the British and therefore the closest source of help. Agnew was ignorant of Herbert Edwardes' relative close proximity in the Derajat and a second copy was therefore made out to Van Courtlandt, who was holding court in Bannu province. The following was added as a postscript.

My Dear Sir, – You have been ordered to send one regiment here. Pray let it march instantly, or, if gone, hasten it to top speed. If you can spare another, pray send it also. I am responsible for the measure. I am cut up a little, and on my back. Lieutenant Anderson is much worse. He has five sword wounds. I have two in my left arm from warding sabre cuts, and a poke in the ribs with a spear. I don't think Mulraj has anything to do with it. I was riding with him when we were attacked. He rode off, but is now said to be in the hands of the soldiery. Kahn Singh and his people are all right.

Yours, in haste,

P. A. Vans Agnew.

19th, two P. M.

The air of optimism of the first letter had vanished and there was an increase in urgency in the postscript as it became increasingly clear Mulraj had no control of events and that further hostilities were imminent. Mulraj's response eventually reached the Eidgah at around 4 p.m. as well. He could not come himself to the Eidgah, he wrote, for his soldiers would not countenance it: 'In my heart I wish to visit you but my army (both Hindoo and Musulman) is averse to it and would be greatly dissatisfied if I did so. Moreover my brother Rung Ram has been wounded for having spoken in your favour; take care of yourself.'

In short, he could do nothing to help and they must fend for themselves. Things would move quickly after this. During the evening and night of the 19th, soldiers from the fortress gathered the cavalry horses, and all bullocks and camels used for baggage by the British party's escort which had been put out for grazing around the Eidgah thus making flight impossible for Agnew's party. Only the few horses stationed in the Eidgah remained to them. But Agnew had not been idle either and by 4 p.m. of that day had recalled all his men into the grounds of the compound. The six guns he had brought were organised into three batteries and further preparations made for an entrenched camp. Agnew was confident he could hold out for a few days, at least till succour arrived, his letters for help already on their way.

Kahn Singh, meanwhile, firmly tied his fortune to the British officers and spent the night helping to organise the defences. This was despite a letter supposedly from Mulraj urging him to join them and desert the British officers. 'I am tukra [firm] in this spot, and won't move,' was the answer he sent back to the Aam Khas on the morning of the 20th. A curious story was told by Kootub Shah later. He mentioned a 'fakeer' coming into the British camp and making his way to Kahn Singh where he had a private word with him, urging him to reconsider. It was generally understood in the camp that he was no fakeer but one of Mulraj's soldiers who had come to spy and to judge the attitudes of the soldiers.

Meanwhile Agnew sent off his last communication, this time directed at Mulraj's officers, asking them to disassociate themselves from Mulraj and the common soldiers if they wished to avoid retribution. They were now officially under Kahn Singh's command, Agnew wrote, and were disobeying the Lahore Durbar's orders, but all would be fine even now if they stepped back from the brink and obeyed their new superiors. Along with the letter was sent what he thought would change their minds and give his letter more gravitas, the parwana of Maharajah Duleep Singh from the Lahore Durbar ordering Mulraj to relinquish control of the city to the British officers. This was too little too late, and Agnew's messenger found Mulraj and his officers in the middle of preparations for battle. Mulraj had, the messenger heard, already begun sending letters to the various districts asking the population and garrisons for assistance to join him and all was in motion for an insurrection. The officers sent back an uncompromising message – that Mulraj was their governor and they would obey only him.

No fire had been exchanged till this point but hostilities finally broke out between 9 and 10 a.m., the four fort guns that happened to be pointing north opening up initially with the eight guns in the Aam Khas quickly following suit. They had been moved closer to the Eidgah, on to an area of hard ground with a clear line of sight to the mosque. In the Eidgah, the biggest problem was found to be the amount of ammunition available. Agnew had asked Kahn Singh how much ammunition he had. Enough only for three or four days was the reply, as no one had expected a pitched battle. Agnew then suggested not firing back to save ammunition at this time, the guns only to be fired if the Multan soldiers came closer. However, this issue became moot a few minutes later. The first shots of the fortress guns landing near the Eidgah was the catalyst for the almost immediate desertion of large elements of Agnew's own troops, who baulked at fighting against their comrades in the city garrison. One shot was reportedly fired in response before the gunners ceased any vigilance and casually walked out to join the garrison soldiers at the Aam Khas, leaving the guns entirely unmanned.

Despite this setback, Agnew was confident the sheer strength of the building meant the party were safe for a while although eight or nine horses out in the courtyard had already been killed or wounded by the cannonade. As the hours slipped by more and more of Agnew's escort began drifting off to join their comrades towards the fort. The gunners that had defected earlier had meanwhile reprised the garrison troops about the feelings of the rest of the troops in the Eidgah and that they were wavering in their loyalty as well. The cannonade then immediately ceased to allow for friendly overtures. A small party of troops headed by one of Mulraj's senior officers, Hur Bhugwan, was sent to the compound to invite the remaining troops to change sides, an increase in pay to all troops defecting being offered. The commander of the Gorcharas, the irregular horse, Gulab Singh, left the mosque first and was given gold necklaces and bracelets, a common form of payment, as presents and then sent back to encourage others to leave. The men would be given two months' pay for defecting, he was told. This was enough for most of the sowars, especially since their commander had already decided to switch sides.

Agnew, on learning of these manoeuvres, made a feeble counter-attempt, announcing his men only need hold out for three days before reinforcements from Bhawulpore arrived. He also offered the soldiers a sum of 1,000 rupees to be shared among the troops plus compensation for lost baggage and possession. This was insufficient, and the drift of the troops out of the Eidgah continued. Within a matter of an hour or so, he had already lost the bulk of his troops. The remaining troops were too principled to take the 1,000 rupees and desert at the same time – they simply declared they would fight and did not require bribes. However, they too melted away during the next few hours. By the evening of the 20th, therefore the only members of the previously 1,400-strong party still remaining to Agnew were eight to ten horsemen, a few servants of the British officers, the moonshees and Kahn Singh – around thirty-five men in total, with twenty-five of them armed. No resistance was possible now, and Agnew sent a vakeel to Mulraj to sue for peace and ask for transport to allow him and Anderson to depart Multan. This Mulraj would permit, sending a messenger back assuring them they should have no fear of attack and that he would order a ceasefire from his troops.

***

Whatever promise Mulraj made, the garrison troops weren't about to lose the chance to punish the British officers who had confidently ridden into their fortress to dismiss them from service. As evening turned into twilight, a mob of angry soldiers, along with a motley mixture of curious townsfolk several hundred strong, led by some Muzabee (low-caste) Sikhs, made their way down the road towards the virtually deserted Eidgah compound. Wuzeer Allah Khan, the moonshee with the officers, mentioned 100 Chukr wallahs (Akali soldiers) leading the gathering. He also claimed he saw various well-known officers in Mulraj's army among the crowd as well. A few minutes before the mob arrived at the gate, Kahn Singh had been readying himself to go to the Aam Khas for direct talks with Mulraj when he saw the angry crowd advancing. One of the soldiers in the crowd, on seeing him, fired a pistol at him and Kahn Singh fired his own pistol in return before retreating back into the Eidgah and into the room where the British officers were resting. From what he had seen it was obvious the crowd were in a murderous mood, and as they entered the mosque compound Kahn Singh was heard saying, 'There is nothing left now but to die.' Many of the mob fanned out and set about looting the unguarded baggage in the compound while the main group headed for the room to which the small party had retreated. The few remaining armed men in the Eidgah had already fled from the mob by this time, leaving just the two British officers, Kahn Singh and a few moonshees in the room. Kahn Singh would suggest preventing the mob from any excesses by raising a white sheet of surrender. Agnew, conscious nothing would stop the mob, is reported to have replied, 'The time for mercy is gone; let none be asked for. They can kill us two if they like; but we are not the last of the English; thousands of Englishmen will come down here when we are gone, and annihilate Moolraj, and his soldiers, and his fort.'

As the mob entered the room the few remaining servants were pushed aside and they faced Agnew who was sitting, holding the hand of the more heavily wounded and unconscious Anderson, lying on a cot. He had become delirious earlier and slipped out of consciousness. Accounts vary as to what happened next. Some eyewitnesses later reported Agnew firing his pistol at the crowd but the weapon appeared to have jammed and refused to fire. Perhaps trying to calm the crowd and initiate a dialogue, Kahn Singh had addressed the crowd. 'I am the guilty party,' he said 'take me before Mulraj and you remain here as guards over the Sahebs who are wounded.' This declaration appeared to have no effect on the soldiers, however, as they gazed at the wounded British officers. The Brahmin Bunsee Dhur, also watching, had a slightly different story. 'I will not fight,' said Kahn Singh to the crowd. 'Take me and my son and the two Sahebs to Moolraj. In coming here I have only acted in obedience to the orders of the Maharaj Duleep Singh.' The crowd's attention, though, was on Agnew and Anderson, and he was held by members of the crowd and taken to the side.

A certain Goojur (or Goodhur) Singh, a Muzabee Sikh, said to be heavily deformed, now stepped forward from the crowd, drew his sword and offered a few choice insults and taunts at the man who was to have been the new ruler of Multan. 'Did you find it so easy to take the fort? What right did you have to come to Mooltan?' Agnew replied he had come under the orders of the Lahore Government and that he should be taken to Mulraj, who could kill him or let him go as he pleased. The chance for further conversation was cut short by Goojur Singh stepping forward and decapitating Agnew with three sabre strikes while another soldier fired into the body. The unconscious Anderson was then despatched and the bodies dragged out into the courtyard of the mosque for the rest of the angry mob to vent their fury. Some of the mob cut at the bodies with swords before moving on to the looting. They would be left there till the next day. Goojur Singh meanwhile took Agnew's head with him back to the city as a trophy wrapped in a cloth. As the crowd's fury dissipated the people gradually dispersed to their homes, leaving the Eidgah silent and deserted, with the baggage of the party looted and strewn over the grounds. Only Agnew's moonshees remained, with some Gurkha soldiers who would camp there that night.

Early the next day, the 21st, at 8 a.m., Mulraj would hold a durbar at the gate of the Aam Khas, Goojur Singh being the centre of attention as he brought Agnew's head to present to Mulraj. The governor would order the elephant of Kahn Singh to be given to him as a gift for his actions. This Goojur Singh was reluctant to accept. 'What can a poor man like me do with an elephant?' he was heard to say, and Mulraj, accepting his argument, offered to let him keep Agnew's horse along with 350 rupees as a further reward for his action. Kahn Singh, who had been taken prisoner the previous day, had his life spared and was given the chance to leave the city and return to Lahore. Mulraj ordered the head of Agnew to be passed to the would-be governor. 'Take the head of the youth you had brought down to govern at Mooltan,' he declared. Kahn Singh refused, and Agnew's head was taken back from him and he was ordered to be imprisoned instead. The head was thrown back to Goojur Singh, who for the general amusement of the assembled and to add further insult filled the nostrils and mouth with gunpowder. The moustache and beard were wetted and plastered also with gunpowder and set on fire. Other indignities were carried out with the head before it would be finally disposed of. The bodies of both Agnew and Anderson had already been buried. It appears some Kabul merchants had informed Mulraj that the bodies were still lying in the Eidgah and that they should be given a decent burial. Some of the local ruffians of the city managed to dig them up twice, robbing them of any possessions and clothes they had been buried with. They were buried for a third time, Mulraj resorting to placing sentries by the graves.

***

With Agnew and Anderson dead, the remnants of the British party that had come to Multan would find themselves facing different fates. Kahn Singh, imprisoned inside the fortress by Mulraj, would die from a shell that fell on the citadel during the siege of the city. He was found bound with chains so heavy it would have been difficult for him to stand. The rest of the British party, the diverse group of servants, syces, cooks, moonshees, punkhawallahs and other servants, had differing fortunes, some escaping and others becoming reluctant witnesses to the siege of the city. Most would resurface, being questioned at the trial of Mulraj a year later. Of the Sikh officers, nothing is known about the fate of Eesar Singh, the commander of the artillery. His adjutant Hari Singh, who also defected, was known to have died at the Battle of Suraj Khund seven months later. One officer who continued to show open loyalty to the British was Guldeep Singh, the colonel of the Gurkha regiment of the party. He declared he would rather be blown away by a gun than transfer allegiance. He was put in irons, but, disgusted and embarrassed at his men's conduct, threw himself into a well while being taken to the fortress for imprisonment.

The erratic Ameer Chund, who had initiated all that had happened over the last few days, would survive. He was seen with a wound on his face and with his ankle bound up, indicating the altercation at the fort and his subsequent fall into the fosse was not without effect. Twenty-five days after the attack on Agnew, Chund went to Mulraj in expectation of a reward for his actions. The governor, now busy organising for an entirely unexpected war, had instead turned him out. Three months after the incident, he was confined in fetters for having attacked a dhobee (washerman) in one of his drug-fuelled fits of anger. He was well treated, Mulraj giving him four rupees a month for food and maintenance, and he served as a soldier during the siege of the city. He managed to effect an escape from the fortress before its surrender and disappeared into obscurity, never being heard of again.

With the British officers dead, the die was cast. Entirely in the hands of his soldiers, Mulraj made the best of the situation, seeming to show much initiative – at the beginning, at least. He brought his family and property into the fort shortly and set about the task of organising his defences for the British retribution that was now certain to come. Recruitment of ex-soldiers, irregulars, mercenaries and malcontents was quickly organised. Recruits were offered good pay – higher than they would receive as British irregulars. Stocks and supplies were brought into the city over the next few weeks. Crops were cut and brought into Multan in preparation for a siege. The fort itself had been strengthened quite recently under his father's rule and required little work. An enormous amount of gunpowder and shot was already stored in the fort's cavernous spaces below ground and there were cannon foundry facilities if need be for the manufacture of new guns. It appears some guns had also been buried to escape British eyes, similar to other places. These were extracted from the ground. Very soon, intelligence reports would put the complement of guns in the fort at around sixty. Taxes too were being collected urgently for payment of troops. The Multan kardars were given orders to ask for the first instalment of the spring crop in advance.

In addition, all communication links and dak (postal service) with Lahore were now cut and the Lahore news writers present at Multan would be forbidden to report or send news on what was happening in the city in the days after the British officers' deaths. Mulraj would also do his best to spread the insurrection further north and west. Proclamations would be readied and sent throughout the Multan province urging recruits with the promise of good pay. The governor would also write to the various officials of the other provinces, to Gulab Singh in Kashmir and to Dost Mohammad in Kabul. He also published an open proclamation calling on all Lahore troops to join his force. According to Ussud Ali, Agnew's moonshee, who had stayed on in the city for around fifteen days after the events of the 20th, men for hire, and of vastly varying quality, had already begun flocking to Mulraj's standard.

## 9

# A Grand Shikar in the Cold Season

You will, however, not fail to make it clearly understood that the Government which you represent is neither indifferent nor inactive; but that, fully prepared for every event, and deeply resenting all that has occurred, they will assuredly inflict severe punishment, and exact a heavy reparation.

Government of India to Frederick Currie, 19 May 1848

My expectation is that the rebel Moolraj will either destroy himself or be destroyed by his troops before the next mail goes out.

Frederick Currie to Government of India, 22 June 1848

At the same time as Agnew and Anderson were meeting their untimely ends at Multan, Frederick Currie was still settling himself into his new role of Resident at Lahore. He had busied himself with the reduction of the state's expenditure in order that reparations demanded could continue to be paid into British coffers in timely fashion. The recent cuts in the Sikh army had formed the bulk of his work during the first few days and weeks, many thousands of soldiers being paid off and pensioned at the capital. On 21 April, therefore, there was much hustle and bustle in the Lahore fort as soldiers milled around patiently waiting for their final settlements before heading off home. Currie had also been busy assessing the state of the country and was readying a report on the country's finances documenting a recent payment of just over 13 lakh rupees into East India coffers by the Lahore Government as agreed by the new treaty. This left only 8 lakh rupees in the Lahore treasury at this time, the bulk to be used to pension off the Sikh troops as part of the ongoing reductions. Essentially the state was bankrupt, and more so with the annual payment to the British treasury.

'The Durbar in making this payment have now exhausted all the gold that was found in Raja Lal Sing's toshakhana [treasure house] as well as all that they had in the Motee Munder or Great Treasury with the exception of a few vessels of this metal which they have retained as relics of Maharajah Ranjit Sing's time,' he informed the British Government on the parlous state of the finances of the country. 'This gold was of little use to them and in the course of time would have been gradually wasted away,' he added a little flippantly, 'whereas by this payment they have reduced their debt to the British Government from upwards of 40 lakhs of rupees to less than twenty seven.'

It was as he busied himself on the soldiers' pensions that the messenger Agnew had sent from Multan with his letter describing the altercation at the fortress gate galloped through the palace gates and asked for an audience with Currie. The messenger, having left Multan before the deaths of the officers, was ignorant of the way the matter had ended in his absence. This was two days since the day of the incident at the fortress, but the news had been preceded by the grapevine and there had already been murmurings of some sort of trouble brewing at Multan around the city.

The attacks on the British officers took Currie by surprise, but the Resident wasted no time in summoning the various Durbar members present in the capital. Within the hour, they had appeared at Currie's Residence promising their support for any decision he might arrive at in punishing the Multan garrison. The general consensus among the Durbar members, hardly any of whom were friends of Mulraj, was that what had happened was a deliberate plan by the Dewan himself. Quite by coincidence, a letter from Mulraj had arrived in Lahore on the same day as the express letter from Agnew although it had been written two days before the incident. Couched in diplomatic language, Mulraj voiced his annoyance at not being allowed to leave his post immediately and having to stay to explain his accounts to Agnew. He also articulated again his complaints at the absence of any immunity from past alleged demeanours. Apparently a flood of complaints were suddenly being made against him, the locals realising he was pro-consul for but a short time longer, the time being at hand to press any claims. He described intrigues within his own family as well, his brother having written to the Resident offering to take Mulraj's place as governor. All in all, it was a letter from an unhappy man, venting his frustrations before his departure.

The letter only reinforced suspicions that Mulraj had orchestrated the attack himself. He was a sullen and discontented man, members of the Durbar rushed to tell Currie. With no sons or family that he cared for, the governor obviously preferred to die in a desperate plan of some sort than be accountable for past errors in his accounts and judgement. Soon after this, a letter by Kahn Singh to Currie also arrived detailing the angry exchange between Mulraj and Agnew during their meeting at the Eidgah, further hardening suspicions against Mulraj.

Currie quickly penned a report on the incident to the Government of India, unsure of whether this incident was a portent of something bigger or an isolated incident by unruly soldiers. There were things that were hard to understand from the information he had received so far. The fact that Agnew in his letter had assigned no blame to Mulraj was significant, he thought. 'If the attack was preconcerted and ordered why was it not more effectual,' he wrote, voicing his doubt on the extended manner of the proceedings that had taken place at Multan. 'It does not appear in any account how the wounded officers were brought off. If Moolraj fired a gun in attack on the small returning party, why did he only fire one and did not as he might have done annihilate them.' The petty animosities in the Durbar towards the governor he dismissed entirely at this stage. 'He has only one friend in the Durbar and none in his own family,' he explained in his letter, indicating Dewan Deena Nath as his only supporter. What was more significant, he rightly surmised from what he had gleaned so far, was the unsettled nature of the garrison due to the by now well-known redundancies Agnew had been ordered to carry out.

***

Besides conjecture, Currie took immediate military action to ensure local malcontents did not emulate the Multan incident and commence assaults on Europeans in the capital itself. The British garrison was put on full alert at Lahore. The defences and gates of the city were secured by garrison contingents. The British political agents in nearby locations were ordered to withdraw to Lahore in case of assassination attempts and all officers on leave ordered to return. What intelligence and information there was on Multan city and its fortresses' defences was gathered over the next few days. Along with other documents, one curious item that turned up was a previous letter by Lt Anderson himself during a visit in September the previous year which contained a detailed map of the Multan fortress.

The British position was strong in the Punjab and Currie had no anxieties at this time. Large numbers of British troops had been kept close to the Punjab in readiness for any rebellion by the Sikh army or any disturbance of any sort. Northwards of Meerut sat 54,000 East India troops, 10,000 of them being Europeans with 120 guns and over 100 siege guns. South of Multan in Sind there were an additional 17,000 troops with additional artillery. Three moveable brigades, 3,000–4,000 men strong with 36 guns, equipped with baggage and carriage and therefore with the ability to march at short notice, had been kept as a matter of policy for just such a contingency, allowing multiple revolts to be addressed in the Punjab (in theory, at least). Each consisted of a European corps with three native regiments with one cavalry regiment and twelve guns. These were stationed at Lahore, Jalandhar and Ferozepore. The Treaty of Bhyrowal also allowed the commandeering of any fort or defensive place in the country.

The pressing problem was that the officers had asked for help and some military force had to be sent immediately for their succour. The topography of the Punjab being what it was, this force could easily be sent down the Sutlej or Ravi rivers, both being eminently navigable. So while troops were easily available, the question was whether sufficient boats could be collected at such a short notice. As for the type of troops, whether they be Sikh or British, he had no doubt. 'Dewan Moolraj is an officer of the Sikh Government. He is in rebellion, if in rebellion at all, to the Sikh Durbar and the orders of that Government. The coercion must come from the Sikh Government unaided by British troops if possible,' he advised the Government of India.

These words, innocuous as they seemed at the time, summed up the legal aspect of the rebellion – that it was an internal matter of the Lahore state. Neither Agnew's letter nor any of the earlier correspondences of Mulraj or conversations with Currie or earlier Residents indicated any anti-British motives. More news of the happenings in Multan filtered in later on the 22nd with a second letter from Kahn Singh. He had written after the altercation at the fort but prior to the killings at the Eidgah. From what was written it was quite obvious the incident wasn't premeditated, with Kahn Singh describing the wounds received by Agnew and Anderson as not fatal. This served to confirm Currie's own thoughts on the matter. The incident at Multan was not planned, he believed; however, Mulraj may be using it to his advantage. 'It may be that, not wishing to give up, and yet not willing to hold on our terms of dependency, he allowed what he thought might be a petty imeute to be got up, in order to show us how troublesome it would be to manage the province.'

By noon of 23 April, though, the trickle of information from Multan turned into a flood as travellers, messengers and copies of newssheets began reaching Lahore along with the usual rumours and more lurid versions of the events. The Multan news writers, since they had not been allowed into the Eidgah, used their full imagination to describe the events of the 20th. Newspaper deadlines meant the stories did not include the killings of the officers later in the Eidgah. These would appear in the next day's papers. On the 24th, a highly sensationalised account of the happenings was also received from Peer Ibrahim Kahn, the British agent at Bhawulpore, which did little to dampen the rumour mill at Lahore. This account reported the manner of the deaths of the officers and that Mulraj had distributed a pair of gold bracelets to Hurdas Singh, one of the jemadars of the garrison, as reward. A hundred rupees to various soldiers who had been conspicuous in the altercation and events later at the Eidgah were also given out by the governor. 'All the rest will receive similar rewards,' Mulraj is reported to have openly declared. Messengers were at this very time flying to all points of the compass, to governors and to high officials in the province, instructing them to begin enlisting troops in preparation for a rebellion and to collect taxes early. Further, all news writers had been banned under threat of severe punishment for communicating news to Lahore, with any messengers bringing news to the various cities being chased by cavalry patrols intent on stopping news from being disseminated. It was obvious Mulraj was doing his utmost to fan the flames of rebellion.

'Such utterly unprovoked and apparently objectless treachery is unheard of, even among this treacherous people. The immediate punishment of this outrage is imperative; but the consequences to be apprehended, throughout the whole Punjab, from this outbreak, and rebellion of Moolraj, unless instantly put down, are most serious. Measures the most prompt and decisive must be taken,' Currie wrote to the Governor-General on 24 April, informing him of the deaths of the two officers. Others had to be stopped from emulating the governor's stand or joining Mulraj's standard. He had already taken the precaution of sending a Sikh force by land under the command of Shere Singh after Agnew's letter had arrived asking for assistance but both Agnew and Anderson were now dead. It would be only right, Currie thought, that retribution for the deaths of two British officers should be carried out solely by a British force, not the Sikh army.

However, the matter of raising a sufficiently large force and the logistics involved quickly became obvious even to his non-military mind and he plumped for a joint Anglo-Sikh force which would involve a smaller amount of British troops who could be readied in a few days. The Sikh army contingent already sent south would continue but would be followed by a British column as soon as it could be organised at Ferozepore and Lahore and boats readied or manufactured. Along the way the Sikh column would be met and reinforced by a field battery stationed at Ramnuggar and other troops under Sirdar Utter Singh Kaleewala, who commanded the irregular Sikh troops. Dewan Deena Nath would also accompany the force along with Tej Singh as senior Durbar members. To further supplement this force, Currie sent off a letter to Van Courtlandt at Dera Ishmael Khan in the Derajat to advance towards Multan with two battalions and a regiment of cavalry and a troop of horse artillery. Thus a total combined force of seven infantry battalions, two regular cavalry contingents along with 1,200 irregular horse and three troops of horse artillery, a total of around 6,000 men with 18 guns, would coalesce into a force along the way towards Multan. This along with the allied British column joining later would be more than enough to awe and unnerve the Multan garrison into submission without any resort to violence. 'I trust the demonstration will be sufficient,' he explained in his correspondence with the Government of India. But in case Mulraj should not submit, the city would have to be taken. The fortress of Multan was formidable and had large guns, but Mulraj was known to be short on soldiers. And apart from the big guns in the fortress, Mulraj was thought only to have five or six field guns at this point. Currie had a low opinion of the governor's abilities in any case, and suspected disloyalty among his officials. 'He is very unpopular both with the army and the people,' he incorrectly observed, 'and it is generally thought, by the natives, that he has been urged to what he has done by the machinations of unfriends, who desire to make him compromise himself with us, to effect his ruin.' Any siege, therefore, was unlikely to be a lengthy affair and the culprits who had murdered the British officers could be brought to justice within a matter of a several weeks.

This scheme would hardly get off the ground before it was aborted. Brig.-General Colin Campbell, who was commanding the British troops stationed in Lahore at the time, remonstrated against sending what he thought would be an inadequate force with no means to capture a large fortress. 'A force without the means [artillery] of taking the place would be laughed at by the garrison,' he replied to the Resident's enquiries, and would lead to disaster. If the column was forced to retreat or give up for this reason it would not only reduce British prestige but encourage the garrison and further the rebellion. There were other compelling reasons for not marching down immediately. It was known that the Chenab River tended to rise at the end of June, inundating several miles of land either side of its banks and covering tracts of country all round Multan. This would make siege operations, if the garrison did not immediately surrender at their approach, difficult if not impossible. And while there was little doubt Mulraj's force, small as it was at this stage, could easily be defeated on open ground, capturing the fort was another thing if the garrison elected to ensconce themselves firmly on the defensive. It could be a long affair even with siege guns. This extended operation so far from Lahore and British cantonments and magazines meant effective resupply of the troops would be problematic. In addition the excessive heat of the coming months would play havoc with operations. Perhaps most important was the issue of the loyalty of the Sikh column sent from Lahore. That they were heavily nationalist was obvious. If they were to cross over to Mulraj's side as effortlessly as Agnew's escort had done a few days earlier, the British column could be overwhelmed and massacred. It was only safe to send a British force strong enough to sweep aside any and all opposition, even supposed allies.

As if Campbell's reservations weren't enough, there was a complete disagreement from the British Commander-in-Chief, then at Simla. Gough concurred entirely with Campbell: 'There can be no doubt that operations against Mooltan at the present advanced period of the year, would be uncertain, if not altogether impracticable; whilst a delay in attaining the object, would entail a fearful loss of life to the troops engaged, most injurious in its moral effects, and highly detrimental to those future operations which must, I apprehend, be undertaken.'

He went further than Campbell as to the size of the force required. Only a British force sizeable enough to deal with a war against the whole of the Sikh army should it rise up and join Mulraj must be considered for reasons of safety. His recommendations to the Governor-General would be an army of 24,000 men (8,000 European) with fifty siege guns and the necessary number of guns to be readied by November. But it all depended on the Sikh army. If the likelihood was that it would stay neutral, he reckoned, less than half that number perhaps would be required to reduce Multan and any other sympathetic insurrections that may arise in the Punjab. But even gathering such a force would take time.

'In consequence of furlough granted, a very considerable time would elapse before I could assemble 10,000 men of all arms on this side of the Satluj,' he responded virtually throwing up his hands at his inability to wage war 'There is no carriage whatever, the whole having been discharged. To move without camp equipage, doolies, and ample commissariat at this season of the year would be certain annihilation.' And now that the deaths of the two British officers had been confirmed, there was no need to respond immediately in any case, he argued. From a military perspective, maintaining a strong hold on the Sikh capital was far more important than spreading thin a small British force in the Punjab. Mulraj was no general and his troops were undisciplined, a matter Currie quite agreed on. In addition, the unity among the very diverse garrison at Multan, consisting as it did of Sikh and Muslim soldiers along with Bengali sepoys, was ephemeral at best and could not continue. Mulraj had no ability to attack beyond the confines of Multan province. He could be allowed to expend his financial resources hiring unreliable recruits and levies. Disorganisation and headstrong soldiery could well mean the insurrection imploding with this motley force wrangling among themselves over the coming months. But if necessary, Gough replied, a British force could march in the cold season in October. Till then there was no harm in leaving Mulraj to his own devices, even if it meant a growing insurrection.

Many would see the reasons Gough had put forward as entirely spurious. The heat had never stopped a British campaign before, and there was a general suspicion, as Herbert Edwardes and others like Henry Lawrence would later point out, that a 'grand shikar' of the rebels in the cold season was much more preferable to the ageing Commander-in-Chief, who wanted to end his career with a large campaign. Thus the insurrection could be allowed to grow till it reached the right stature for titles, rewards and medals to be handed out. The newspapers in India would scoff at such reasoning too, and at Gough's reticence to dole out retribution immediately for the British officers' deaths. His view that Europeans could not handle the heat was an insult to the British troops, they would opine.

This criticism from the press would only materialise in the coming weeks, though, and with so much opposition by Campbell and Gough to his plans, Currie changed tack again. 'That condign punishment must be visited on those who have committed this perfidious outrage and insult to the British Government is indispensable but at this season of the year, operations of the magnitude which will now be required, and at such a distance as Mooltan from our reserves and magazines, cannot, I fear, be thought of,' he wrote, informing the government of his volte-face. As many as one in five of any Europeans would fall victim to the stifling heat of the Multan summer, with half the remainder unable to do any service again, he wrote, echoing Gough's feelings. Now the Sikh force he had sent under Shere Singh must attempt to bring Mulraj to heel by themselves.

Currie immediately recalled Shere Singh and his Sikh officers and in a meeting on the morning of the 26th, he explained to them that no British column would join them now. They must reduce Multan and defeat Mulraj and his garrison themselves. They listened and showed scepticism at this decision. In another meeting late into the evening with Currie they explained that such was the sympathy among their Sikh troops for their Multan counterparts that the chance of success was negligible. In fact, taking the troops close to Multan only made it easier for them to defect, as did Agnew's contingent. It would be better, they advised, to keep the Sikh column as far away from the city as possible and to send an entirely British force instead.

Currie was not about to change his opinion again, however. Rejecting their suggestions, he warned them that the future of the Sikh state was at stake. They must cooperate in halting this rebellion or the British Government would take action when a sufficient force was organised. But if the latter occurred, he said, the repercussions on the country would be severe, hinting at annexation or heavy reparations. Failing to change the Resident's mind, Shere Singh and his officers would reluctantly return to their force and resume their march towards Multan.

Their advice had been quite sound and wasn't entirely dismissed by Currie, however. Acknowledging the difficulties of taking the fortress and the nationalist sympathies of the Sikh soldiers, the plan was modified and made less ambitious. Now the plan would be simply to confine Mulraj and his influence to the confines of the city and a radius of around 100 km. No attempt would be made to take the city by assault or siege. To achieve this, additional units of the Sikh army would march down and a total of five columns would converge on Multan province. Keeping a distance from Multan had the dual benefit of making it difficult for these Sikh troops to defect to Mulraj while preventing Mulraj from gathering taxes and recruiting more soldiers from farther afield. The final capture of the city and fort was to be left to an overwhelming British force with siege guns in October, when the temperatures dropped sufficiently, as suggested by Gough himself.

To achieve this, Shere Singh was to continue southwards with what would now effectively be the first column. He had 5,000 men who would march down the Bari doab by the side of the Ravi River and halt at Toulumba. This force consisted of one infantry regiment, the rest being cavalry and accompanied by ten horse artillery guns along with two mortars. A new second column, 3,000 men strong, headed by Dewan Jowahir Mull Dutt would march down the Sindh Sagur doab, halting at and occupying Mankhera and its fortress. This also had an infantry regiment along with the Churunjeet Regiment of cavalry, comprising 1,000 men. The other 2,000 the Dewan was given sanction to recruit from the areas he passed through. A troop of horse artillery would accompany them.

Sheikh Imam-Ud-Deen, the ex-Governor of Kashmir, would march from Lahore with a third column. This force, 2,000 strong, would march along the right bank of the Sutlej up to Loodhen. This column was the weakest, 2,000 new levies or levies to be recruited on the way. The column would march with two horse artillery guns. The fourth column would come from an entirely different direction – from the south. This was the army of the Nawab of Bhawulpore, a Muslim state on the left bank of the Sutlej opposite Multan. He was friendly towards the British and had responded positively to Currie's request for assistance against Mulraj, having also received Agnew's call for help. The Nawab and his troops could be relied on implicitly. Lastly Herbert Edwardes, the British political agent in the Derajat, would head a fifth column recruiting local tribesmen along with the force he had. He would consolidate a hold over the entire Derajat, denying Mulraj tax revenue and recruits from this area. Together these columns from north, west and the south, Currie thought, would easily confine any rebellion till the cold season. There remained one issue, and that was of the attitude of the Muslim tribes in that area, always ready for tumult, who might find the prevailing confusion an attractive opportunity to raise their own rebellion. If they decided to rebel against authority themselves, this may even work to British advantage. 'If the Khalsa army can be kept from joining Moolraj, the atrocious misconduct of the Dewan and his troops may be easily punished. I have great hopes that this may be effected. There remains doubtless the probability of revolt and insurrection of the Mahomedan tribes on the frontier but though the Khalsa army will not act against Moolraj, they will, I think, against their almost natural enemies in their own districts.' By fighting the Muslim tribesmen, the Sikh troops would be denying both their own and the tribesmen's services to Mulraj.

At Lahore, meanwhile, Currie ordered immediate punitive financial action against the truculent governor. Expenses for the entire operations listed above would be kept and the cost of this exercise, as a penalty, would come out of Mulraj's personal wealth, which was said to be around 70 lakh rupees at this time, if not more. As he had been recently planning to retire to Amritsar after the handover of Multan and had been busy transferring his assets northwards, a lot of his personal wealth was already at Lahore and Amritsar. The sum of 640,000 rupees was found to be in the possession of his lawyer in Lahore, presumably waiting to be deposited into a bank account, with further sums of 31,000 and 2,000 of gold rupees already in various bank accounts in Amritsar. His gomastha (agent) was found to have another 7,750 rupees deposited in Amritsar. Elsewhere he had 4,500 rupees deposited in Lahore but had also invested a large sum in a large quantity of lead. His properties in Lahore and Amritsar and Akalgurh near Ramnuggar were confiscated too, and ordered to be auctioned off and his vakeel at Lahore and gomastha in Amritsar both arrested and put in prison pending investigation.

One of the consequences of the Multan uprising was that, for a few weeks at least, the general air of acquiescence and deference to British rule and its agents vanished to some extent, with some Durbar members and the population in general perhaps feeling the Multan uprising might portend the beginnings of a bigger rebellion against British power. Currie, recognising this, ordered the Durbar members and other high officials to be put under much greater scrutiny. Anyone showing anything less than the usual deferential behaviour towards British authority was suspect with even the words of the young Duleep Singh being analysed. In a story published in *The Englishman*, Currie allegedly was perturbed at some of his no doubt innocent comments. 'A story is told of this youth,' reported the newspaper, 'which if true shows him to be infected with the insolent spirit of those about him. Sir F. Currie is said to have observed that it was a long time since the Maharajah had paid him a visit. He replied, "What is it necessary that I should visit my own servant?"'

Alongside this greater spirit was a visible reluctance to energetically aid in organising against Mulraj or disciplining the Sikh army forces. This would begin to change markedly over the month of July as it became more and more certain that a British force would enter the Punjab and as each member looked to maintain his own future and position. During the first few days of July, for instance, 30 elephants, 2,000 camels, 650 gun bullocks, 200 carts of 4 bullocks each and 8,000 baggage bullocks had been collected to help the Sikh columns closing in on Multan. By 14 July Currie would confidently inform the government on the change in cooperation from the Durbar, members energetically helping the Resident in confiscating the jaghirs and wealth of those officers and men in the garrison at Multan and those trekking down to join the rebellion.

***

News of the Multan incident and the British officers' deaths would reach Calcutta on 4 May and was immediately communicated to Dalhousie. Currie in his reports stressed he had the matter in hand although little could be expected in redress from the Durbar members or action from the Sikh army. 'The chiefs are, collectively and individually, utterly without resource or energy: in a crisis like the present, they are quite useless, and to all appearance, Durbar and all, as far as their actions go, quite indifferent as to what may be the result of the present state of things,' he would relate. 'I have warned them, distinctly, openly in Durbar, and each member individually and personally, that upon their conduct now, and the result of their exertions, depends the only chance that remains for the preservation of the Khalsa state.'

The exact reason and the precise details of the insurrection were a mystery as yet but Dalhousie, as Currie had rightly surmised as well, was also of the opinion the rebellious soldiers were at fault and that Mulraj had simply been swept along by the current. But British officers had been murdered and the Governor-General was unequivocally for strong punitive measures against the Lahore Durbar for its inability to control its governor. 'Of one thing be sure – that I will hold the state of Lahore responsible for the blood of these poor fellows and for the insult shown to the British power,' he wrote back. 'I will have a signal reparation from it. If the Sikh power is tardy or impotent to right us, then I shall feel it to be my duty as a servant of the company and crown to exact a national reparation from the state of Lahore. Unfortunately, at this season of the year, the day of reckoning must be postponed; but it will come assuredly and the reckoning shall be a heavy one.' The postponing of the reckoning was due to Gough's reservations, which had also reached him, and which the Governor-General wholly agreed with, regardless of whether the insurrection grew in the meantime. For now, as Currie had pointed out, the issue was technically an internal problem of the Lahore state and since the Resident was heading the government Dalhousie was quite content to have Currie handle the situation as he saw fit.

News of the Multan insurrection spread rapidly in what was an exceptionally quiet month in India, provoking lively discussion both in the Punjab, in British India and in the bordering states as to British reaction to the death of two of its officers. The general feeling was quite correctly that Mulraj was not entirely in command of the situation and that the insurrection could and would be snuffed out quite easily and quickly. John Lawrence, who now ruled in Jalandhar, immediately wrote a letter of support to Currie as the news was brought to him. Multan could be easily taken, he suggested. Only a force of two European corps and six native regiments would be sufficient. Regarding the Multan governor, he like everyone else entirely discounted the idea that Mulraj had anything to do with the attack on the two British officers at the bridge. 'Depend on it he has been forced into it by circumstances. He was notoriously a timid man, and one of the chief points on which he originally so much insisted with me was, that he might be allowed to get away before it could be publicly known that he had given up the country.'

There was talk, too, on the opportunities the deaths of the officers and the rebellion may give the British Government in self-aggrandisement. Perhaps Dalhousie, known for his expansionist ideals, would use these events as *casus belli* for outright annexation of the Multan province if not the entire Punjab. Major Hodson was one of those for annexation while Herbert Edwardes, the political agent in the Derajat, was decidedly against any attempt to seize the country, and their lively debate mirrored what was being discussed in British circles around the country. 'You express a hope in your letter that the British government will act for itself, and not prop up a fallen dynasty,' Edwardes wrote to Major Hodson on 24 May. 'In other words you hope we shall seize the opportunity to annex the Punjab. In this I cannot agree with you, for I think, for all that has happened, it would be unjust and expedient. The treaty we made with the Sikh government and people cannot be forfeit by the treachery of a Gorkha regiment in Multan, the rebellion of a discharged kardar or the treasonable intrigues of the Queen-mother, who has no connection with the Sikh government of her son.' Would it be justice to seize a state voluntarily put under British protection by its own feeble government? The state was under British protection during the minority of the Maharajah and paying a handsome amount of money for the stationing of British troops in Lahore. If a state under this position could be annexed, then it was far better to annex all the independent Indian states immediately. British protection otherwise had little meaning.

By early May, news of the happenings at Multan had travelled across the Khyber Pass and reached the ears of Dost Mohammad, the ruler of Kabul in Afghanistan, followed promptly by letters from Mulraj himself enquiring about an alliance and military or financial assistance. The current incumbent on the Afghan throne, curious as he was of this insurrection, gave it little chance of success. The struggle, he said, was a minor one and not beyond the abilities of the British to put down. He saw no reason to quarrel with the British by assisting Mulraj. 'There was no war, nor any chance of war,' he was heard to declare in his court. So certain was the Afghan that the Multan insurrection would be crushed that the latest news reaching Lahore during the following weeks was that he was busy reducing his forces to cut costs. Added to that he had his own interminable problems in his intrigue-ridden court. The Dost was wily enough, however, to monitor events, having little love for either the British or the Sikh power. He had been toppled from power in 1839 by a previous Governor-General, Lord Auckland, who had preferred the more malleable Shah Shuja as a puppet ruler, a desire that had led to the recent First Anglo-Afghan War. Equally Ranjit Singh had systematically ended all control east of the natural boundary of the Khyber Pass, relieving the Afghans of Kashmir, Peshawar, Multan and the entire trans-Indus region. The loss of the rich vale of Peshawar, the summer playground of Kabul rulers, had particularly stung the Afghans. If the insurrection grew, his opinion was there may be opportunities by backing either the British or the Sikh state in return for territory lost. For the time being, Dost Mohammad decided to do nothing but watch and wait.

News of the insurrection reached London by steamer in mid-June and the views held there were similar to the Kabul ruler's. Taking advice from the previous Governor-General, Hobhouse would write a calm letter to Dalhousie on 24 June expressing confidence in all decisions that had been taken by Currie. 'I have consulted Lord Hardinge and Sir Henry Lawrence on this business and find that neither of them entertains any apprehensions of a general outbreak in the Punjab or adjacent provinces, nor has the transaction produced the slightest sensation here. Moolraj is a very rich man, not a soldier and as you know sincerely wished to resign his authority. In all probability, he was forced to take part in the catastrophe, preferring like weak men, to acquiesce in violence rather than to be a victim of it.' He hoped by the time his letter reached Dalhousie the matter would be entirely at an end, with the insurrection either imploding or Mulraj apprehended by forces from Lahore. Sir Charles Napier, the future Commander-in-Chief of the British Army in India, concurred although he was more cautious than Hardinge on the matter and declared the figures Gough had suggested for a cold-season campaign too large and that only a fraction of those were needed to end a potential rebellion.

The death of the British officers would also provoke much speculation among the Indian newspapers looking for turmoil to report. Curiously, a general sympathy was apparent for the unwarlike Governor of Multan caught up in his men's personal vendetta against British authority. He was merely a 'victim of circumstance', as one paper described him. 'A fish in a strong current' was what another publication declared. At the mercy of his soldiers and with a British noose waiting for him in any case, he preferred riding the tiger. A death valiantly defending a breach in his fortress was the more honourable and heroic way out of his predicament and was expected when a British force eventually arrived at the city.

When made public, Currie's initial decision to send the column of British troops had been quickly lampooned by the newspapers. *The Mofussilite* decided to print Campbell's anecdote on being chosen to lead the force. He had asked the Resident what he was supposed to do without siege guns once Mulraj's men were driven into the fortress, which the newspaper described as one of 'stupendous strength'. The order had been absurd, they declared. Rumours were also rife that the uprising was an attempt to fragment the British force in Lahore and the Punjab in readiness for other uprisings, each British column then to be picked off at leisure. General consensus was that any British force in the Punjab must remain as one irresistible force.

While talk and conversation swirled around on the real implications of the revolt, the soldiers of the three Sikh columns heading towards Multan from the north would march around two-thirds of the way to Multan before halting as Currie had ordered. Here these columns would stay doing little but sitting round their campfires, not trusted enough to approach any closer to the city. It would be the other two columns – those of the political agent Herbert Edwardes and his Muslim irregulars, and the Nawab of Bhawulpore from across the Sutlej – that would between them attempt to snuff out the nascent rebellion. In fact, unbeknown to Currie, as he prevaricated at Lahore on the composition of the force to deal with Mulraj and the appropriate time for retribution, Herbert Edwardes, sitting on the right bank of the Indus, had already taken the initiative and had begun marching towards Multan with what men he could accumulate.

# 10

# Opening Moves

Orders are issued and letters written just as the soldiers please and by their desire all the materials of war are now being prepared. In short nothing can be done without their consent and the Dewan is afraid to oppose them.

Mustapha Khan Khagwanee to Herbert Edwardes, May 1848

He [Herbert Edwardes] will co-operate with Bhawul Khan, and will, I think very probably drive Moolraj into his fort, there to remain, if not murdered by his own troops, till the British army can take the field.

Frederick Currie to Government, 5 June 1848

While Frederick Currie dithered over the composition of the force that was to contain the rebellion and Dalhousie mulled over the reparations that would be demanded of the Lahore state for the deaths of the two officers, Mulraj, the reluctant rebel, would signally fail to make the best of his situation. Confident he had the best part of a month or more before any force of a respectable size could be organised and sent down to oppose him, Mulraj had begun recruiting as many guns for hire as he could to supplement his current meagre force as well as re-enlisting all his ex-soldiers that had been made redundant in previous months. He had success drawing in irregulars and tribesmen in the Multan province and in the Derajat across the Indus. What quickly became apparent, however, was the complete unwillingness of the professional Sikh soldiers in the garrisons to the north in Peshawar, Hazara and Bannu to come to his aid, although they naturally watched proceedings with interest. Prophesies of villagers aside, and despite their eagerness to eject the British presence from the Punjab, they recognised the Governor of Multan as being no general. The vast bulk would show a complete reluctance to chance their livelihoods fighting for the bureaucrat. Over the course of the first few weeks, after the deaths of Agnew and Anderson and beyond the initial haul of recruits, it therefore became clear to Mulraj that he could expect little help from the Sikh regulars.

In turn, Mulraj did little in terms of military strategy and initiative to alter their low opinion of him. Little was attempted beyond recruitment and no military manoeuvres were taken to increase the area under his control. The governor preferred keeping his slowly growing force on the defensive at Multan rather than seizing the initiative. Rather unexpectedly, however, he found he was facing competition for local mercenaries and conscripts from a source across the Indus. This was from Herbert Edwardes, stationed at Dera Futteh Khan, 150 km due north-west of the city of Multan, and the lion's share of activity and initiative taken over the following weeks would come from Edwardes rather than Mulraj.

\*\*\*

Of the three messengers Agnew had sent with letters on 19 April, the two sent north and east had duly found their way to their separate destinations of Lahore and Bhawulpore, alerting the authorities of the altercation at the city. The third messenger had headed initially north-west to the Bannu valley, 300 km north of Multan and one of the westerly outposts of the Sikh Empire. This was a province which General Courtlandt, a mixed-race officer in the Sikh service, commanded. The messenger never went there, however. Noting Herbert Edwardes, Courtlandt's superior, was holding court at Dera Futteh Khan in the Derajat, the strip of land west of the Indus, less than half the distance to Bannu, he veered towards this camp instead.

Three days after having been despatched by Agnew from Multan, the messenger entered Edwardes' camp where he happened to be deliberating over the trial of a local. 'It was towards evening of April 22nd 1848 at Dera Futteh Khan on the Indus that I was sitting in a tent full of Beluchi zemindars [landowners], who were either robbers, robbed, or witnesses to the robberies of their neighbours, taking evidence in the trial of Bhowani Singh,' Edwardes related later as part of his colourful narrative of the war and how he learned of the emeute at Multan. A red bag signifying mail of urgency was handed to him by the messenger, who intimated the letter was for Courtlandt but that he may as well look at it. On the front of the letter was written in Persian, 'To General Cortlandt, in Bunnoo, or wherever else he may be.' Edwardes decided to open it. Courtlandt, although with the Sikh service, was answerable to Edwardes and the urgency of the message was justification enough. Conscious of not showing any alarm at the contents of the letter to the accumulated tribesmen, Edwardes feigned a sense of calm and continued with the matter of hand. Around an hour later, he wrote a letter in response to the now dead Agnew, informing him he would come to his assistance with all possible speed. British officers had been assaulted with impunity and it was obvious Mulraj was powerless to intervene. Action was therefore required by him as the nearest British political agent to the scene, and sooner rather than later. Edwardes decided on moving what force he had with him closer towards the city and without waiting or consulting with the Resident.

The messenger was sent back with the message that help would be forthcoming but that it may not be as rapid as hoped. Only three ferry boats were in close proximity to effect a crossing of the Indus and time may be required to collect more; he nevertheless expected to reach Multan by the 27th, five days away, a realistic target for a distance of 150 km. This was far too long, of course. Further questioning by Edwardes of the messenger, a witness to the recent goings-on around the Eidgah, showed that the situation for the British officers was quite hopeless. The messenger while leaving Multan had distinctly heard the beginnings of a cannonade and much firing, suggesting things were already coming to a head as he left.

Edwardes would write a letter to Currie the same day explaining his unilateral decision to march and informing him when he expected to reach Multan. In addition a third letter was penned for the attention of Lt Taylor, the British agent in Bannu province, asking him to send his Muslim levies along with four guns to the Leia ferry on the other side of the Indus, which Edwardes expected to hold soon after crossing the river. Letters were also sent to many of the trans-Indus chiefs, officers and government officials in the Multan province to transfer their loyalties to the Lahore Government rather than Mulraj, whose position was either uncertain at best or at worst that of a rebel against the Lahore Government.

Edwardes wasn't a well man at this time. He had been wounded in an altercation with some Muslim tribesmen of the area on 16 March and was being carried around in a palanquin, unable to either walk or ride. His actions in organising a force to march towards Multan were beyond the bounds of a political agent but, as he quickly realised, provided a chance to make

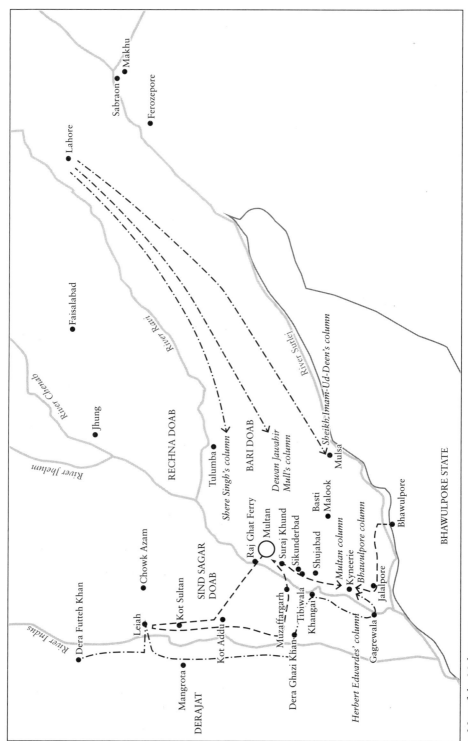

3. Map of the Multan area

a name for himself and he grasped the opportunity with both hands. 'I am aware,' he wrote, 'that it has been said (and strangely enough by many who desired nothing so much as a like opportunity of being useful; and who, had it fallen to their lot, would I gladly believe have used it honourably), that I interfered where I had no call of duty, levied soldiers to carry on a war for my own ambitious ends, and with all the rash presumption of a subaltern – "rushed in where Generals feared to tread".

To not move forward, though, would have been cowardice, he declared, and in consequence he set about organising his force as quickly as possible and made preparations for crossing the Indus, the first step on the road to Multan. Edwardes at this time had with him twelve infantry companies and 300–350 sowars with two guns and twenty zambarooks (camel-mounted guns). In total this constituted a force of around 700 men. This was a rather motley force consisting of three very different kinds of men. A portion of the infantry, four companies to be precise, was composed of Poorbeahs or easterners, meaning Bengal sepoys recruited into the Sikh army. The second portion, the bulk of the sowars, consisted of Muslim Pathan levies and tribesmen. These men, fiercely conservative in outlook, had no particular love for the developing British yoke in the Punjab but were at this time more preoccupied with the opportunity of overthrowing the more visible Sikh rule. The third portion of the force was the Futteh Paltan, the Sikh regiment, professional soldiers and easily the most disciplined and sturdy of Edwardes' force but whose sympathies were strongly nationalist and who thus had little appetite to fight Mulraj. Many of these men had spent many years in campaigns against the refractory Muslim tribesmen across the Indus. These men of the Sikh army served Edwardes reluctantly and only because they had orders from Lahore to do so. In the short term, though, the antagonism and suspicions among these units would allow Edwardes to direct affairs with little difficulty despite being the only European for 160 km or so.

There were other military contingents nearby in Bannu province under Col Courtlandt which Edwardes could use as well. Specifically these totalled around 2,800 men and around fifteen guns. Even these were still around a week's march from Edwardes' current position. If a junction could be effected, however, Edwardes realised he could muster a respectable force of around 3,500 men. He therefore promptly wrote to Courtlandt for assistance as well.

By noon on 23 April, the day after hearing of Agnew's predicament, he had moved the force he had at his disposal to the banks of the Indus. The crossing of the river or rather the several branches which it broke into in the immediate area were always difficult at any time of the year but the river had swollen considerably in the last few days in consequence of rains upstream and a storm had kicked up later in the evening that day. The crossing subsequently took most of the night, with the Sikh regiment walking across a known ford with water reaching their chins. Each round trip of the boats lasted two to three hours and thus the crossing continued slowly during the evening and night until thirteen boats, seized 40 km further upstream, were brought in and quickened the pace, although one boat sank, taking eight of its fifty occupants down with it; a storm slowed the progress still further.

The crossing completed, Edwardes advanced on the city of Leia on the morning of 25 April and entered it without a struggle. By this time, the deaths of Agnew and Anderson had been confirmed and so any urgent march towards Multan to assist the officers was unnecessary. The decision to stop at Leia was made. Edwardes warned the Resident that Mulraj was already busy recruiting soldiers, messengers from Multan being everywhere in the area, and that urgent action needed to be taken to stop the rebellion spreading. Meanwhile he would hold on to Leia and assume a defensive position. His view, from what he had gleaned from various sources from the city, was quite correct. Mulraj was entirely in the hands of his soldiers, but a settlement was easily possible if it secured the garrison's jobs and no loss of face was encountered by the governor and his men.

> I think Moolraj has been involved in rebellion against his will, and, being a weak man, is now persuaded by his officers that there is no hope for him but in going all lengths; that the origin of the rebellion was the natural dislike of the Puthans, Beloochees, and Mooltanees (men of high family, courage, and false pride) to be turned adrift, after a life spent in military service well rewarded; and that these men will fight desperately, and die hard, unless a provision is held out to them just before the siege (before the last moment they would not accept it, and only then will they do so with dexterous vikalut [diplomacy], carried on by one of their own blood, who knows their points of honour).

Meanwhile, waiting for Currie's response, he busied himself recruiting the plentiful local tribesmen both to increase his own force and to deny their services to Mulraj. This led to an amusing situation, with all the villages in the district having posters plastered in prominent places by men of both Edwardes and Mulraj, encouraging people to enlist for good pay. The offer of pay from both sides also meant a constant stream of men, particularly from across the Indus, could be seen heading either to Multan or to Edwardes camp depending on who they thought would pay more. Some of the men collected by Edwardes amusingly turned out to be tribesmen who had been ferociously opposing him a few days previously across the Indus but who had been swayed by the reliable pay on offer.

\*\*\*

Back at Multan, Mulraj, surprised at having an opponent earlier than expected and learning he had already crossed the Indus, made plans to oppose Edwardes. Attempting to smash Edwardes' smaller force before he received assistance from both Lahore and Bhawulpore, he organised what turned out to be a half-hearted advance toward Leia. The hope, apart from destroying Edwardes' force, was that moving his men forward would precipitate the Sikh units in Edwardes' force defecting. A force of around 5,000 men from the conscripts he had accumulated and eight heavy guns was assembled around 28 April and sent north.

Edwardes, though, would prove elusive. Learning of this move, the British officer decided to fall back across the Indus to his original position on the right bank which would allow him to join up with Courtlandt's detachment, already marching down from Bannu to reinforce him. Only once he had these troops available, Edwardes decided, would he recross the Indus and chance a battle with Mulraj's contingent with a force strong enough to win. 2 May therefore found Edwardes' force retreating back to the left bank of the Indus, where it had been over a week earlier, with preparations being made to cross back to the right bank. All baggage was ordered to be sent across with the force maintained on the left bank but ready to cross as well at a moment's notice.

Mulraj's force would never arrive in sufficient numbers at Leia, however. Learning that the Nawab of Bhawulpore, the friend of the British, was gathering his force to attack Multan from the east, Mulraj as a precaution ordered his force back closer to the city losing any chance of destroying either Edwardes or of marching against the Nawab. With Mulraj showing an entirely defensive strategy over the coming weeks, the route for Edwardes to circle round Multan to join up with the Nawab's forces would be largely clear in the coming weeks.

On 4 May, Courtlandt's reinforcements arrived in a 'fleet' of twenty-six boats carrying Muslim infantry and six horse artillery guns, markedly increasing the strength at the British agent's disposal. Edwardes would send some of these men down the Derajat under Courtlandt as a vanguard to occupy as much of the territory as possible, thereby denying the tax revenue to Mulraj while he reoccupied Leia on 8 May.

A surprising turn of events happened on the same day, indicating the vacillating nature of Mulraj even at this stage. Mustapha Khan Khagwanee, one of the governor's confidantes, would send a letter to Edwardes asking to meet Foujdar Khan, Edwardes' right-hand man. Edwardes, correctly surmising Mulraj wished to surrender, was content to have his man in negotiations. Mustapha Khan's message was that Mulraj himself could not send a letter or come himself, being a virtual prisoner of his soldiers, so he had asked Mustapha Khan to slip out and negotiate on his behalf with Edwardes. He further explained Mulraj would be only too happy for all previous arrangements to continue – that he would continue as governor and continue to remit the tax revenues to Lahore as before but that the soldiers must be given a full pardon and their honour spared. Only these conditions would bring the rebellion to an end. What Mulraj wanted was reassurance, firstly that Edwardes had the authority to negotiate and act on behalf of the Resident and British Government. If he did, his second question was what assurances Edwardes could give Mulraj for his future and whether his life and honour would be respected. Edwardes replied that on the first issue – incorrectly, as it turned out – he had authority to negotiate.

'To the latter, I replied, that neither I, nor the Resident at Lahore, nor anyone else, had authority to stand between the murderer of the two British officers, and the retributive justice which their countrymen would demand,' Edwardes recalled, indicating Mulraj would have to stand trial. His only promise was that his life and honour would be safe. The third issue was that many of the Pathans and recent Muslim recruits had no heart in a war. The war, said the emissary, was 'the work of Hindoos' and the Sikh and the Hindu sepoys had been the prime movers in the assault on the Eidgah, the Muslim troops being swept along by the tide. The killing of the officers too had been done by Sikh troops of the regiment of Deedar Singh along with those who had defected. The Pathan soldiers would probably leave Mulraj and fight with the British given the chance. 'They had lately been estranged from him [Mulraj] by his ceasing to intrust them with the chief management of his affairs and choosing for his favourites and counsellors men of vulgar birth whose airs and slights had become insufferable,' Mustapha Khan related to Edwardes, revealing some of the petty intrigues and jealousies that had already become prevalent in Mulraj's ranks. The Muslim Pathans and Sikhs were not getting along and Mulraj had broken up the Sikh units to placate the levies, which had only served to annoy the Sikh soldiers. On this issue Edwardes was more than happy to answer that any of Mulraj's men who wished to defect would be offered employment in his force, bar any that may have had a hand in Agnew and Anderson's deaths, who would stand trial.

Dalhousie, when news reached him of Edwardes' negotiations with Mulraj, would take grave exception to the political agent electing himself plenipotentiary and offering terms without so much as asking the Resident. 'I altogether disapprove of army officers, such as Lt Edwardes taking upon himself to volunteer negotiations on a subject of such magnitude, absolutely and utterly without authority even from his immediate superior and to the possible embarrassment of the Government of India,' he wrote to the Resident on 28 May, for he had been mulling over much more punitive action against Mulraj and the Lahore Durbar. The talks were too conciliatory and had too much the odour of an overture unfit for the British Government in India. 'The Dewan Moolraj has offered a flagrant insult to the British Government; he has participated in, and approved, the murder of two valued servants of that Government; and he is now a rebel in arms against British authority and power. To such an offender as this, the Governor-General in Council conceives that no terms should have been offered; and that no overtures should have been entertained, which did not convey the Dewan's unconditional surrender of himself to the British Power, and his unconditional submission to that justice, which it never fails strictly to observe.'

Dalhousie's anger was beyond the ears of Edwardes at this point, though, and the emissary would return to Multan with a guarantee of a fair trial for Mulraj and the more covert guarantee to the Muslim troops that they would be welcomed and employed in Edwardes' camp. However, the offer of gambling his future in a trial would do nothing to persuade the unsure Mulraj to surrender, and these early negotiations never came to anything.

*\*\*\**

On 8 May, Edwardes would receive a letter from Currie at Leia commanding him to stay on the right bank of the Indus whatever the situation may be. The Resident informed him of his grand plan for five columns to act in concert with each other. Edwardes was to control the trans-Indus Derajat area only with the additional three columns of the Sikh army marching down from Lahore stopping at around Toulumba and thereabouts to prevent the rebellion spreading northwards. A fifth column headed by the Nawab of Bhawulpore's army was to cross the Sutlej and approach Multan from the east. The columns were not to attack Multan at all but simply to hem in Mulraj from north, west and east to deny him the benefit of recruits and to decrease his tax revenue to fund his force. Then when the hot spell finally broke, in October, a British force complete with siege guns could travel down from Ferozepore and settle affairs with an assault on the city and fortress itself. Edwardes had strong personal reservations about this strategy, which would allow a large number of Sikh soldiers to coalesce into a single force north of and near Multan, and he sent a plain warning on the issue.

> I feel it a duty to express earnestly my conviction founded on observation that a more dangerous risk could not be run at the present moment than to give a Sikh army the opportunity of collecting before Mooltan. The Sikh soldiers have neither forgotten, nor forgiven, their humiliation on the banks of the Sutlej and incapable of gratitude to us as they have ever been of fidelity to their own rulers, it is only a very small and reflecting portion of them on whom our extraordinary moderation has made any impression. The large majority would hail any feasible opportunity of rising, as a God-send.

Nevertheless, with the plan already in motion he followed orders and crossed back to the right bank of the Indus. A march south was proposed, allowing any Multan outposts to be captured and also allowing more recruits to be gained. Meanwhile, the chiefs of the cities in this strip of land were ordered by the Lahore Durbar to pay their taxes to Edwardes instead of Mulraj. The bulk of the Derajat would fall quite easily to Edwardes, Mulraj failing to send any reinforcements or assistance to his outposts. This included Sungurh, the district closest to Leia, and the fortress of Mangrota, 35 km further south, on 11 May. From there, Edwardes used the small fleet of boats that had been collected to move his force further downstream on the Indus. On 19 May he joined up with Courtlandt's force again, reaching the recently fallen Dera Ghazi Khan on 26 May.

With complete success so far, and Mulraj showing little military competence, a confident Edwardes would write to Currie asking for permission to cross the Indus to achieve a junction with the Bhawulpore army. This Currie would readily agree to, now seeing his success. Bhawul Khan, the Nawab of Bhawulpore, reluctant to cross the Sutlej and approach Multan on his own, had also asked Currie to allow Edwardes to cross the Indus to join up with him in fact. Along with this, the Resident had also sent Lt Lake to take command of the Bhawulpore army on 9 June, to ensure the force had some semblance of discipline as their current commander was well into his dotage. All Bhawul Khan's force, around 6,000 men and nine guns, were expected to be on the right bank of the Sutlej by 2 June and to reach Jalalpore on 3 June. From here an advance on Shujabad would take place and the Nawab hoped to achieve a junction with Edwardes prior to this, before Mulraj had the chance to march his force down and prevent the two columns joining. By 6 June the Bhawulpore army was encamped at Jalalpore, close to Shujabad. Edwardes' force in response crossed the Indus between 10 and 11 June, marching rapidly towards the Chenab, a mere 40 km further eastwards. His force, through continued recruitment, had now ballooned to around 9,000 men and 12 field guns by this stage. By 15 June, he would reach Khangurh, a mile from the Sutlej River, with his vanguard of mounted troops; Courtlandt joined him the next day with the rest of the force.

While Edwardes and the Bhawulpore force were effecting a junction, Mulraj, ensconced in his fortress, continued to waver between defiance and surrender if it could be engineered without loss of face. Gholam Moostapha Khan Khaghwanee, in a letter sent to Edwardes on 6 June, informed him he had urged the governor to surrender and to accept the terms the officer had offered earlier but that Mulraj had become angry at the suggestion in between bouts of despondency at the way the rebellion was flagging. Although Mulraj's army was increasing, the rate was far less than it should have been and gave no cause for confidence. The capture of the Derajat by Edwardes had denied him the Baluchi and Pathan mercenaries and many had joined the British officer instead. His officers, too, were showing signs of frustration and urged him to show initiative. He must destroy the force of Edwardes and his Bhawulpore allies before British reinforcements with heavy guns were sent from Lahore and the balance tilted entirely against him, they urged him. He must fight a battle soon.

11

# The Gulaba Plot

It is true many of the officers employed under the Resident have expressed forebodings
of such an event but we trust there does not prevail any such general feeling of
animosity against the British influence at Lahore as should unite all classes of the
population in an attempt to subvert it.

Dalhousie to Secret Committee, 3 June 1848

Let him be hung quickly.

Frederick Currie, 11 May 1848

Back at Lahore, just a little over two weeks after the first inklings of trouble at Multan had
reached the capital, a major conspiracy was uncovered. Whether the plot was hatched after news
of the Multan outbreak reached Lahore or whether it was being considered prior to that – or,
indeed, whether the plotter had any connection or communication with those at Multan – would
never really become clear, despite extensive investigations by Frederick Currie. The object of the
ringleaders, it was discovered by the British authorities, was to dispose of the Resident and his
assistants and leading British officers in the city along with collaborating Durbar members in
one swoop. One of these ringleaders was highly placed. Col Kahn Singh was a well-known Sikh
officer of some standing in the Sikh army. The colonel had in fact led units of Sikh artillery in the
recent war and had been made redundant during the recent reductions imposed after the Treaty
of Lahore. Also involved and highly placed was a certain Gunga Ram, one of the moonshees of
the Maharani, Jind Kaur.

Early in May, a native officer, Gholam Nubbee Khan, in one of Major Wheeler's regiments, the
7th Irregular Cavalry stationed at Lahore, was approached by a man who tried recruiting him
into working against the British for good pay. The trooper feigned interest but later informed his
officer, who in turn informed the Resident. Currie interviewed the man and suggested he join
the conspirators so more about their plans could be discovered and its ringleaders apprehended.
The recently arrived Lt Lumsden was given charge of investigations. Lumsden decided on a
scheme whereby Gholam Nubbee Khan would encourage a meeting where all the conspirators
would be invited so all could be easily arrested in one swoop. The plotters in fact had been
meeting every night for several weeks prior to Gholam Nubbee Khan being approached in any
case, and so this was deemed easy to arrange. But the sowar failed to wear the mask successfully
and the conspirators became more suspicious of the new recruit and consequently more
cautious. In fact one of Kahn Singh's retainers had told Gholam that Kahn Singh suspected
the British knew something was up and had already decided on flight soon. The retainer was
immediately arrested to prevent Kahn Singh fleeing the capital.

Early on 7 May, Mr Cocks, the assistant to the Resident, was informed by the spy that most of the conspirators would be meeting in Col Kahn Singh's house that night. Deciding the moment had arrived, Currie gave out orders for the arrest of all those known at the time to be ringleaders with further instructions to seize as many papers and other documents as possible at the house. As darkness fell, Lumsden marched down with a company of Guide Corps, quietly surrounding the house. By 11 p.m., all those attending the meeting had arrived and the raid began. The house had strong barricades and so the windows were forced open. Kahn Singh was arrested, along with his moonshee and a confidential agent. In all fifteen arrests were made at the house and elsewhere that night. In parallel to this, houses of other conspirators who had not attended the meeting were raided before they were alerted to the earlier British swoop.

Interrogation of those arrested began the same night and reminders of waiting nooses encouraged the weaker-willed to talk and so the details of the plot were quickly revealed. The plan had been for ten select men to kill the leading British officers of the Lahore garrison as they slept in their bungalows on the early morning of 13 May. This would deprive the British force in the capital of its organisational strength for a time, leaving it unable to respond effectively to the insurrection that was to follow. It was known that a British force might leave for Multan soon to reinforce Edwardes' force, diminishing the British strength at the capital. Rumours among the conspirators had been that half of the British force, comprising around 10,000 men at Lahore, 3,000 of them being European, would depart the capital. Other rumours suggested 2,500 of the total 10,000 would be despatched to Multan. Whatever the case, it would leave a much weaker British force of around 7,500 at the most to be dealt with, including around 2,000 European troops. A letter was to be sent out to Mulraj encouraging him to hold out for as long as possible, thus keeping the units sent to Multan busy and unable to reinforce or aid the Lahore garrison. Once the British officers had been disposed of, Sikh troops stationed nearby would quickly begin dealing with the British garrison, who it was supposed, lacking officers, would be much less effective. It was important to effect entry to the officers' bungalows and capture important and strategic places in the city currently held by the British, hence the importance of recruiting a substantial number of sepoys whose responsibilities involved guard duty at these places. The city gates and the fort were the primary points that needed to be seized. Once these had been captured, Sikh soldiers who were currently barred from the city could enter. It was hoped that the ejection of the British from the city would trigger other sympathetic insurrections elsewhere.

It was an audacious plot. There were plentiful risks – principally that it required a considerable number of sepoy recruits – and informers tended to be well rewarded for news of conspiracies. The man heading the recruitment of sepoys was a man named Gulab Singh, or Gulaba as he was commonly known around town. He was one of those arrested on the 7th and who now quickly volunteered information. Owing to his position in the group, he had considerable knowledge of the ringleaders and sepoy recruits who had been bribed. Twenty-two sepoys had already joined the conspiracy, divulged Gulab, and others were being currently persuaded. He also explained the main means for their recruitment, which was through the many fakirs or Hindu holy men of the city.

These men preferred to have their abodes near the city gates (through which the thoroughfares into and out of the city ran), which were strategically good positions for the begging of alms. These fakirs had good opportunity to converse and befriend the sepoys stationed at these places and hence influence them by bribery or otherwise. British sepoys were being offered sixty rupees a month in cash for joining the plot, far above their normal six-rupee monthly salary.

Currie wasn't interested in rounding up the numerous fakirs of the city but he was most anxious to capture and punish any sepoys who had joined the conspiracy. The next day the entire sepoy force in the city was put on parade and Gulaba was escorted up and down the columns of men and asked to point out those who had been recruited. It appeared the men were mainly from three regiments – the 8th, 18th and 50th NI. Some of the men of the 50th regiment accused attempted to run but there was little chance of escape. Nine desertions quickly followed, presumably by conspirators yet to be exposed.

The uncovering of the plot only confirmed in Currie the dangers in the capital. British engineers were promptly ordered to raise parapets at appropriate locations around the city and to further strengthen the garrison camp. The conspirators were summarily tried on 9 May and guilty verdicts duly delivered. 'It was next necessary at the present moment that decisive measures should be taken and a prompt and severe example made,' Currie reported to the government on 11 May. A death sentence was decided against four of the captives, Col Kahn Singh, Bhaee Gunga Ram, Toolsee Ram, a Brahmin, and Gulaba himself, despite his aid in pointing out the sepoy recruits. Other lesser members of the ring were given exile for life overseas or long life sentences in British territory, while one man's execution was suspended because he offered to give further information in exchange for life.

With the noose ever closer, two of those condemned to capital punishment began volunteering more information hoping their sentences would be reduced. The night before his execution Toolsee Ram asked to speak to Lt Hodson, assigned charge of the captives. He could point out yet more sepoys in the British force, he declared, who had joined the plot. He also made substantial other accusations – that the Maharani was the instigator and financier of the plot and that she had appealed to all the sirdars of the Durbar (excluding those who had tied themselves to British fortunes) to help expel the British. Maharajah Gulab Singh had also been contacted. Gunga Ram, one of the prisoners and moonshee of the Maharani, also volunteered information in exchange for a pardon. He too said the letters came from the Maharani. He told of messengers hiding letters in armlets and jewellery. He corroborated Toolsee Ram's story about letters being sent out to all but the most pro-British Durbar members. In addition the Sikh columns being sent down to Multan were merely being obedient in so far as it gave them an opportunity to rebel or join Mulraj's army on reaching Multan, he claimed. A premature show of insurrection at Lahore would mean they would be disarmed. Specifically mentioned in the plot were Raja Shere Singh, Ranjodh Singh Majithia and Sheikh Imam-Ud-Deen. The events at Multan, he said, were entirely instigated by the Maharani. The prisoners seemed to be naming anyone and everyone of importance out of desperation and Currie realised much of the information being volunteered was probably suspect. Cooperation did not save Gunga Ram's life. At sunrise on 11 May, in front of a large assembled crowd, both he and Kahn Singh were brought to the public gallows adjacent to the Delhi gate to be executed. Two sepoy companies from each of the sepoy regiments present in the capital had been drawn up in the open ground in front of the gallows, numbering around 2,000 troops. The executions were a demonstration of British power and resolution for the locals as well as any sepoys with uncertain loyalties.

Kahn Singh's wife was present at the hanging. She had asked to have the bracelet of her husband before he hanged. Upon being given the object, she extracted a small piece of paper from it by pressing a concealed spring and tore it into a myriad of small pieces, some of which she swallowed. 'Ah, you would have given half the Punjab to have read that paper,' she exclaimed to the British officers present, proof that her husband had not revealed anything to the British before he was executed.

Gunga Ram, before being hanged, had asked for the British guard on his house to be removed as his family had caused no offence. As the hanging was carried out, Gunga Ram did not die quickly but struggled. 'Let him be hung quickly,' Currie ordered on seeing his extended death throes. Some of the guards then pulled at his legs to hurry on the process. Gunga Ram's brother and sister would later be arrested and interrogated while their belongings were searched and an amulet containing an incriminating letter discovered.

Toolsee Ram, the Brahmin, was given a reprieve for his help. The fourth man who was to be hanged, Gulaba, was also reprieved as he stepped up to the gallows on him saying he would provide yet more information and point out more conspirators. Subsequent to this, several more sepoys would be arrested while others were discovered to have slipped away successfully. More news and details were surfacing during this time. It appeared the plot was of long standing but the recent happenings at Multan had given it new urgency and the conspirators thought action in unison with Multan gave the best chance of success. Some of the information given by those apprehended centred on the obtaining of arms and gunpowder. The conspirators mentioned an old Sikh army magazine on the plain of Mean Meer near the city which had not been discovered by the British and had consequently not been emptied of its weapons and powder. Currie ordered the magazine to be destroyed. A lot of the gunpowder in the magazine had already been spirited away along with other arms and muskets. The remainder of the powder, still a huge amount, rather than being blown up *in situ* since it would have destroyed a large area besides the magazine was instead thrown into some unused but flooded wells by British troops, where it was assumed it would be harmless. A few weeks later, however, a huge underground explosion akin to a minor earthquake was felt in the city. The summer heat had apparently dried up the water and the powder by some means caught fire. Residences nearby were damaged and three or four people were killed.

Investigations by the British authorities into the plot rumbled on till September of that year, the Resident determined to capture all participants. Eight more British sepoys in Lahore would desert for fear of being arrested over the summer but three of these were subsequently arrested. The issue of who in high circles was helping or financing the plot was much less clear. Letters were discovered to various sirdars and high-placed individuals containing veiled messages asking where their loyalties lay but this did not necessarily implicate them as no favourable responses from them in return were captured. Currie's own opinion was that most were too timorous to involve themselves in such matters. But there was a common factor. All the conspirators who had decided to speak up had said the Maharani was involved and had letters from her in proof. Currie would now give his full attention to these allegations and to organising further punitive action against Jind Kaur.

12

# Exile to Benares

As a woman of great resolution and great ability and the widow of Ranjit Singh, she had most influence with the army. Had she escaped, her name would have been a tower of strength to Mulraj.

Dalhousie to Sir John Hobhouse, 12 June 1848

I look with some interest to the effect that the removal of the Maharanee from the Punjab will have on the Sikh soldiery.

Frederick Currie to Government of India, 19 May 1848

The hanging of the main conspirators in the late plot to kill the Resident and British officers was by no means the end of the matter. Its discovery, so soon after news of events at Multan, caused quite a sensation in the capital during the months of May and June. Frederick Currie was much less apprehensive with the ringleaders apprehended, but he was preoccupied with the fact that many of those involved in the late plot had accused the Maharani of financing the operation. Not only that, but her personal moonshee Gunga Ram had been intimately involved in the conspiracy. It was naturally supposed that he must have been taking orders from her and managing the day-to-day planning on her behalf. Still, there was no real proof of her involvement beyond accusations by desperate men with nooses round their necks.

The sheer number of accounts, frequently conflicting, seemed to overpower Currie for a while, leaving him wondering how deep the roots of the intrigue ran. Gunga Ram had confirmed the plot had been developing for some time along with making other assertions. One was that the Maharani had been garnering support from all members of the Durbar apart from those too supine, like Tej Singh, and had gone as far as canvassing for support from Maharajah Gulab Singh of Kashmir. This implied the Lahore Durbar members, if not behind the plot, certainly had knowledge that something was afoot before the event. This fitted in with Currie's suspicions that at least some of the Durbar members, disillusioned by the British supremacy in Lahore, were, if not brave enough to plot themselves, passive enough to ignore others plotting. Gunga Ram had also asserted that the Durbar members knew that the elements of the Sikh army sent to Multan might join Mulraj as soon as they reached the city and therefore supported their move to the city. One of the more startling allegations made was that Kahn Singh had been one of the ringleaders. But if this was true then there was little reason for him to oppose Mulraj's actions in Multan. Currie never believed the allegations against Kahn Singh, especially as news filtered in of him being held in heavy irons in the Multan fortress prison. Kahn being part of the plot seemed too incredible. The importance of all other suspects faded, however, before the suspicions and accusations about the Maharani.

Currie already suspected Jind Kaur, some incriminating letters of hers to Mulraj having been intercepted prior to the plot.

Quite what to do with the Maharani, the figurehead and inspiration for nationalists around the capital, was the issue. Bringing the Maharani to trial for conspiracy was out of the question as far as he was concerned. With events at Multan ongoing, dragging the widow of Ranjit Singh, the friend of the British, through the courts would be highly inflammatory and bring her more sympathy. 'Legal proof of the delinquency of the Maharanee would not perhaps be obtainable,' he admitted in his correspondence with the government. She was also already in British hands and held in conditions of high security. If she was plotting against the British while in incarceration, it was a failure in the measures taken to preventing her communicating with her supporters, something that could be rectified by a change of guards and increased vigilance.

The retribution he finally settled on was more draconian than a trial. He would recommend to government that she be banished to British territories. She would reside in comfortable but well-guarded surroundings in Benares in eastern India, far away from the Punjab and her supporters. This would also minimise the chance of her being rescued from Sheikhupura by nationalist elements of the Sikh army aided by sympathetic guards, something widely speculated on in Lahore circles. 'There is no proof, though there is some ground for suspicion, that the Maharanee was the instigator of the late violence and outrage in Mooltan; but it is certain that, at this moment, the eyes of Dewan Moolraj, and of the whole Sikh army and military population are directed to the Maharanee as the rallying point of their rebellion or disaffection,' he wrote to the government explaining his decision on 16 May. 'Her removal from the Punjab is called for by justice, and policy; and this is no time for us to hesitate about doing what may appear necessary to punish State offenders, whatever may be their rank and station, and to vindicate the honor and position of the British Government.' From his records the decision appears to have been taken unilaterally and without the concurrence of the Council of Regency. 'Her summary banishment from the Punjaub and residence at Benares under the surveillance of the Governor-General's Agent subject to such custody as will prevent all intrigue and correspondence for the future seems to me the best course which we could adopt,' Currie continued.

Dalhousie in Calcutta didn't believe in any particular connection between the plot and the events at Multan either. The fact the conspiracy had been hatching before the Multan uprising he thought was conclusive proof of this. On the matter of the expulsion of Jind Kaur from the Punjab, though, he entirely concurred with the Lahore Resident, going as far as to dismiss any opinion the Durbar members might have on the subject. 'In the event of the Durbar showing any reluctance to do this you are authorized to take your own measures and unless reasons very urgent indeed lead you to a different conclusion to remove the Ranee accordingly without waiting for the consent of the Durbar,' he replied.

Currie nevertheless thought it wise to make the decision look less like a British edict and to give it a semblance of a Lahore Durbar decision. Three members of the Council of Regency who happened to be in Lahore at the time were rounded up and asked for their assent to her exile, Tej Singh, her sworn enemy, being one. A fourth signature was obtained on behalf of Shere Singh (absent at Multan) from Golab Singh, his teenage brother, although he wasn't a member of government. This Currie decided was sufficient backing for the move. With the Durbar rubber-stamping the decision, Currie moved quickly. Although the Durbar members were told to keep the news of her impending exile confidential, he knew the decision would be quickly leaked. He was wary of any remonstrations against the move by the Lahore public as well, Jind Kaur being remarkably popular with the common population. But the main reason was his anxiety that the Maharani herself would certainly refuse to cooperate. This would make her eviction embarrassing in that force would be required to make the royal lady comply. Therefore it was advisable she be transported to her new destination in British India with the minimum of fuss and as soon as possible.

In order to ensure her cooperation and avoid any manhandling, a certain amount of subterfuge was decided upon. 'Lumsden and myself were deputed by the Resident to call on her, and intimate that her presence was urgently required,' Hodson recalled later, giving Jind Kaur the impression that she was being taken back to Lahore. Travelling with purdah by elephant, the Maharani would be unaware of her true destination, in the first case Ferozepore across the Sutlej in British territory. As a further measure, Currie, always suspicious of the fort garrison, had taken the precaution a week before the event to change the entire guard from Sikh soldiers to a company of Rohillas, Muslim irregulars from the east who it was supposed would have no sympathy with her cause and would be unlikely to aid her in any way should the news of her impending exile leak.

On the night of 13 May, then, a small party composed of Capt. Lumsden, Lt Hodson and some agents of the Durbar set off from Lahore to Sheikhupura. Along with them was a company of the 7th Irregulars. An armed unit under Major Napier was also readied consisting of the two squadrons of HM 14th Light Dragoons and two 9-pounder guns in case of any resistance at the fort. A plan of the fort and its exits had been made by Napier on a previous visit and so all exits could be watched. Travelling through the night, the party reached Sheikhupura before daybreak on the 14th, unsure of its reception. Despite the guard change, 'I was prepared if opposition was offered to enforce the execution of my orders,' Currie recorded. 'Happily there was not the slightest opposition; all was acquiescence and civility from the Maharani downwards, very probably induced by the execution which took place a few days ago.' The execution he referred to was that of Gunga Ram, the Maharani's moonshee. One of the maid servants of Jind Kaur was heard to exclaim on seeing them enter the fort that if they had only come just two hours later, things might have been different, suggesting plans may have been afoot to spirit Jind Kaur away from British custody. The British officers were shown into the apartments of the Maharani where in addition to the order from the Durbar they presented the letter from Currie. 'Whatever instructions they give you about your removal from Sheikhoopoor,' the Resident had written, 'you should immediately attend to. They will conduct you with all due respect and consideration; no personal injury or indignity towards you is intended'. When she asked where she was to be taken no information was volunteered, Hodson and Lumsden deciding to be economical with the truth rather than using open deceit. The orders were for her to leave immediately for Lahore, the British officers told her, and she therefore began making preparations. There were insufficient baggage animals and elephants for her possessions, however, and she was reassured these would follow soon. She was allowed to take her jewellery and her servants and as many clothes as could be packed in short time.

The party would set off for Ferozepore before daybreak and while it was still dark, barely an hour after Hodson and Lumsden had arrived as per Currie's instructions to move her as rapidly as possible. Sheikhupura lay only 35 km to the north-west of Lahore across the Ravi River. However, the entourage after crossing the river continued to the south of the city, a journey of fourteen hours without stop before resting temporarily at the village of Kanna Kutch. It was only when Jind Kaur alighted from her palanquin on a journey longer than it should have been that she was told of her exile to Benares. She gave full vent to her feelings against Fakeer Nur-Ud-Deen accompanying the party for the deception. Complaints had little effect, however.

On recovering her composure she made the best of things and asked to see Lumsden. 'I know now that you are taking me to the British provinces. This is the road to Ferozepore. I have requested your attendance to beg that you will inform Sir F. Currie the Resident that I am under a deep obligation to him for sending me into the Company's territories. I have long wished to leave the Punjab where I am surrounded by enemies bent on misrepresenting me and working my ruin. I am now happy and satisfied.'

The heat was intense that day and the journey still long with Ferozepore over 70 km away. Lumsden therefore made plans to rest at Kanna Kutch for a few more hours and then proceed during the afternoon when temperatures dropped. Travelling through the night, they would reach the city early the next day. Her possessions, beds and bedding, he informed the Maharani, were already being transported to Lahore ready for her move to Benares. The party crossed the Sutlej into British territory during the dark of the early hours of 15 May, the last time the Maharani would see Punjabi soil. Later that day, she was ensconced in a house at Ferozepore under the authority of Capt. Maitland of the 72nd NI.

'A correspondent from Ferozepore says that the Ranee is most strictly watched in the house in which she is located near the Artillery bazaar having sentries at every corner,' the *Delhi Gazette* noted as word quickly spread of her exile in the city. Her stay was expected to be for three days while provisions for her escort were made and her baggage train caught up. Currie, meanwhile, had decided to separate her from her closest servant, the slave girl Mungela, who was ordered to come back to Lahore for further questioning relating to the recent plot.

At Ferozepore, a Capt. Browne now took over responsibility for escorting her for the rest of her journey to Benares. The Maharani's retinue would reach Ludhiana on 31 May. She was noted to be very downcast, although she had put on a brave face after the unsettling news of her exile but had begun to recover her composure by this time. In public at least she was in high spirits, although on being questioned close servants mentioned she was devastated at leaving the Punjab. On her way to Meerut, orders were received by Capt. Browne that Jind Kaur should be told she would not in any circumstances be allowed to hold correspondence either verbally or by letter with anyone from the Punjab. If she was found to be breaking these rules, she was warned she would instead be transferred to the fortress of Chunar, 35 km upstream of Benares and used as a prison for political prisoners.

Back at Lahore, Currie was still as determined as ever to find proof against her, and energetically continued investigations into the recent plot. The case against the Maharani was being strengthened by allegations by other persons recently arrested. Some of these had decided to turn informers on the offer of lighter sentences. Incriminating letters were given up, allegedly written in the handwriting of Jind Kaur. Other letters given up included those written to her of the plot but not delivered as she had been banished to Sheikhupura by this time, the close guard having prevented delivery the week before her exile.

The Resident, energetically continuing his investigations into the Maharani's conduct, had the effect of encouraging her enemies in the Lahore Durbar as well. They began to raise issues regarding the personal wealth she had been allowed to take with her. It so happened that one of her elephants, during her move to Ferozepore, had come to Lahore instead of Kanna Kutch. The Maharani, when at Kanna Kutch, had been anxious as to its location and had asked Lumsden to ascertain its whereabouts. On its arrival, the Maharani showed much relief. The elephant was apparently carrying much jewellery and gold bullion. This prompted complaints from Lahore Durbar members that she had taken significant amounts of state property with her from the Toshakhana before she had been exiled to Sheikhupura, words which were listened to with receptive ears by the Resident. There were accusations of her taking jewels, expensive horse and elephant trappings, shawls and cash among other things as well. Among objects taken were a necklace of 105 pearls; another of 131 pearls and emeralds with Jawahar Singh's name on it; a bracelet made of 732 pearls; and a pair of earrings with a large emerald and 7 pearls each of 'English manufacture'. Some of her property, to the value of 1 lakh and 10,000 rupees, was still in Sheikhupura awaiting transportation to Benares. Currie intended showing these items to the Durbar members. Any items they deemed state property would be kept, the rest sent on. He also promised the Durbar members all her property would be removed from her at Benares subject to a full examination in search of state property. Anything identified as such would be returned to Lahore. With this in mind he wrote an express letter to the British authorities in Benares on the matter, to reach them before her retinue arrived, asking for all wealth to be removed from her. He was also desirous of uncovering any incriminating letters or correspondence in her baggage either in her or her servants' person possession. In addition Currie also suggested to the Benares authorities that her confinement at the city should be considerably more stringent and that 'as a state prisoner, she should not be allowed to have the command of wealth, of which she has, hitherto, not scrupled to make use to accomplish purposes the most treasonable, and to procure open violence and murder, and secret assassination'. In his suggestion that a further reduction of her pension allowance should be made as a punitive measure Dalhousie would entirely concur.

> The position she now holds is materially different. She has been guilty of plotting against the British interests at Lahore, and, for this offence, the mere removal of her to British territory, cannot be called a punishment, while she is treated in the same liberal manner as before. His Lordship in Council is, therefore, of opinion, that you should consider, in communication with the Council of Regency, the propriety of a further reduction of the allowance, such as would still leave it ample, considering that the Ranee is taking with her a very large amount of private property and jewels.

So from her original allowance of 1.5 lakh rupees or around £15,000 per annum as specified during the signing of the Treaty of Bhyrowal, and which had been reduced to 48,000 rupees per annum on her expulsion to Sheikhupura, it was decided she would be reduced to just 12,000 rupees a year. This was understood to be roughly equivalent to her monthly outgoings, leaving her little wealth to finance any schemes by malcontents.

Jind Kaur's entourage eventually reached Benares on 2 August, where she was received and placed under the custody of the Governor-General's agent, a certain Mr Macgregor. A residence had already been assigned for her but first, as per instructions from Currie, she and her baggage and servants were searched and an inventory made of all her possessions with Mr Reade, the commissioner of the Benares division, and Mr D. F. McLeod, the city magistrate, along with Macgregor and an assistant carefully going through the property. Her collection of jewellery apparently generated much interest and excitement among the prominent jewellers of the city, who were called in to value the collection – the whole being estimated to be worth 8–10 lakh rupees and consisting of 'gems of the most costly description, jewels and vessels of gold' and upwards of 5,000 Lahore gold mohurs.

Her jewellery and wealth, as ordered by Currie, was taken away and deposited in the vault of the British treasury in the city. The Maharani was herself bodily searched by two European matrons but nothing was found. The search of the Maharani's papers and correspondence revealed no incriminating evidence. Most of them were written in Goormukhi (Punjabi) between her and her sympathisers and contained no information related to any plot. Others were of letters between her and the Resident and vice versa. The search, reported Macgregor to Currie, had caught the Maharani genuinely by surprise and if indeed she had had any documents they would have been found. The only discovery of note was one of the pieces of jewellery in her possession, a necklace which matched the description of a set demanded by the Lahore Durbar members, and this was to be sent back to Lahore. Stripped of all her wealth, the Maharani was now given strictly guarded accommodation in the city. Although it wasn't a formal incarceration, she was not to be given permission to venture out, her servants bringing her all provisions and any visitors strictly vetted and searched.

***

On 16 May, two days after her departure from Lahore, Currie would release the official declaration of her exile bearing the seal of the Lahore Government for the general public's consumption. The Durbar, Currie had written, bearing in mind her predilection for plots and intrigue, were entirely at one with him in the need to banish the Maharani from the Punjab. Her dabbling in such matters had occasioned her removal from Lahore to Sheikhupura. But she had declined to change her ways: 'Her Highness has not desisted from her intrigues; and, at this time, some of the immediate and confidential dependants of the Maharanee have been convicted of evil practices, and designs, of the most serious character – such as, had they been accomplished, and the intentions of the conspirators fulfilled, would, inevitably, have caused the ruin of the Khalsa State.'

These conspirators had been punished but as the instigator and financier of these crimes, she must bear the consequences. The declaration included the warning that had been given her as she was being transported east: 'If Her Highness shall not, at Benares, abstain from practices and designs of a tendency to subvert the administration of the Punjab, and injurious to the Maharajah, or the British Government, it will, in such case, be necessary for the Government of India to cause the Maharanee to be confined in the fortress of Chunar.'

Dalhousie would approve of the brusque and speedy manner in which Currie accomplished her removal. 'Nothing could have been better planned, more speedily and more secretly or better executed than the removal of the maharani with the sanction of the Durbar … You have got rid of very serious danger by that act,' he complemented the Resident on 28 May.

The Resident, however, had engineered the exile of Jind Kaur largely oblivious or indifferent to the effect it would have on the population round the country. The news was much less welcome around the Punjab and the disclosure of her exile created much shock among the residents of Lahore the day after her eviction, the correspondent of *The Mofussilite* newspaper at Lahore reporting there was general disbelief among the city locals that she had been exiled to British territories. A week after her exile had been announced, Currie would report Lahore and its neighbourhood were in a much more unsatisfactory and agitated state than before. The general feeling among the populace was that, trial aside, the accusations against her should have been communicated to the Maharani and that she should have been allowed a fair chance to answer all questions. The subsequent news of the confiscation of her wealth, the warnings not to communicate with her supporters and the manner in which the Maharani was bodily searched by European women and kept under strict guard raised further fears of the acute level of British interference in her affairs.

A criticism of this manoeuvre would come from Dost Mohammad, the Afghan ruler, later in the year. 'Such treatment is considered objectionable by all creeds, and both high and low prefer death,' he would write in a letter to Capt. Abbott in Hazara as he made his entry in the war later in the year. News of her exile travelled rapidly to the Sikh cantonments in Peshawar, Bannu and Hazara and was the stimulus for much new bitterness on top of the recent redundancies. The Maharani was now far away in British territory, much to their chagrin. Such were feelings among the troops that an uprising had been planned for the 22nd or 24th of the month, according to the Resident in writing to the Government, although in the event nothing would materialise.

Currie himself gained little by the exile of the Maharani. The deception used to gain Jind Kaur's cooperation in her move to British territory was criticised by some of the British newspapers. More used to showing her as a modern scheming Messalina, she received some rare sympathy from this quarter at this time. The feeling was that the deception used was below the dignity of the British Government. Currie ignored the criticism for a while but was eventually stung into a response, a month after the event. Currie's version of her eviction, sent to the Government of India, was that members of the Durbar themselves had suggested telling the Maharani she would be going back to Lahore and that he himself had counselled otherwise.

Meanwhile, investigations into the May plot would continue; two months after its discovery, Currie reported his feelings that the plan was far more extensive than first thought. 'I do not yet know all that was, or the extent to which hopes are still entertained of success to the scheme for expelling us from this part of India. Every day brings new revelations, some of which seem to elucidate, and some to mystify the whole affair,' he wrote on 31 July. 'It is quite certain that, all last autumn and cold weather, plans were forming, combinations were being made, and various interests were being enlisted, with a view to a grand struggle for our expulsion from the Punjab, and all the territories west of Delhi.' He suspected the intrigues began soon after the Maharani was ejected from the palace and that many Lahore Durbar members were secretly in favour or at least passive to designs against the British and that support from as far afield as was possible both within British India and outside was being gained.

> Emissaries were sent to Cabool, Candahar, Cashmere and Jummoo, and the Hill States; the protected chiefs on the other side of the Sutlej were consulted, as were the chiefs of Rajpootana, and the Nawabs of Jujjur and Rampoor. It is positively asserted, that effectual co-operation was promised by all that I have mentioned, with the exception of the Rajpootana States and Putteeala, the former of which sent no positive replies, and the latter a direct refusal. The great hopes of the conspirators lay in the promised aid from Cabool and Cashmere. Whether either Dost Mahomed, or Maharajah Golab Sing, intended to keep their promises, I cannot tell, but there is no doubt that the former has collected a large army in the neighbourhood of Cabool, ostensibly for operations to the north west.

It was known that Maharajah Gulab Singh of Kashmir, too, was secretly strengthening his position and it was beyond doubt he had been in secret communication with Jind Kaur at Sheikhupura. Currie's investigations would continue remorselessly but without further success. In any event, this was soon overshadowed by events close to Lahore, instigated by a person whose anti-British persuasions were already known to all.

# 13

# Bhai Maharaj

It is well known in certain circles that the influence of this man is unbounded amongst the Sikh chieftains and the whole population of the Punjab; and there is little doubt but that he has generally been the prime mover in all the conspiracies and revolts which have lately caused so much of the Punjab expense and led to so much bloodshed.

*The Times*

I send a brief narrative of the rise, progress, and, as I trust, the termination, of the career of a person who has caused a great sensation in the Punjab, during the last few weeks.

Frederick Currie to the Government of India, 13 June 1848

During the weeks after the uprising at Multan, Frederick Currie would not only be distracted by the Gulaba Plot but also found himself having to deal with a famed and popular itinerant preacher by the name of Bhai Maharaj. The Bhai had decided the time was right to raise the standard of rebellion against the British.

The rise of this preacher forms one of the more colourful strands in the narrative of the war. Bhai Maharaj's origins were humble in the extreme. Born as Nihal Singh in the village of Rabbon near Ludhiana in what was British territory, Bhai Maharaj quickly turned to spiritual pursuits at an early age, joining the preacher Bhai Bheer Singh's camp. This preacher was an ex-soldier who had turned to religion and was now a well-known saintly man. Unnoticed at first, Nihal Singh would spend his formative years offering free service and charitable work at the camp. He was baptised as a true Sikh and given the name Bhagwan Singh by his mentor, who made him his cook.

It was the political convulsions of the time before the First Anglo-Sikh War that would propel the cook into the public spotlight. In 1844, factions fighting for control in the Lahore Durbar inadvertently arrived at the camp he had made his permanent home. Prince Kashmira Singh, a son of Ranjit Singh and a legitimate heir to the throne, had been attempting to wrest power from Heera Singh, a usurper unconnected to the royal family who had briefly risen at that time to the summit of power. The prince had failed and had come to take refuge in the camp of Bhai Bheer Singh, who was a well-wisher of the royal family and himself opposed the Heera Singh faction. His pursuers, too, arrived at the camp with a large army bent on murdering the prince and demanded he be handed over. Bhai Bheer Singh courageously refused to cooperate. This prompted an attack on the camp. Heera Singh, with 20,000 soldiers and fifty guns at his disposal, launched an assault during which the prince was killed and Bhai Bheer Singh fatally wounded. Before expiring, Bhai Bheer Singh passed leadership of his clan to Bhagwan Singh. Then, rather than passing away on his deathbed, he asked his followers to cast him into the river to end his life sooner. The leadership thus passed to the charismatic Bhagwan Singh. His preaching, powers of leadership and persuasion earned him much fame and supporters and he soon became known by the sobriquet Bhai Maharaj around the country.

Unlike Mulraj and the various other personalities of the Durbar at that time, Bhai Maharaj was what could be termed a true nationalist. Not swayed by monetary gain or promises of jaghirs, he was frustrated by the internecine Lahore Durbar conflicts after the death of Ranjit Singh and the surrender of power to the East India Company. He reserved most of his ire, though, for those content to work under the British. The Punjab lay in thrall to the Europeans, he preached, and those in the Lahore Durbar and other high positions were content with this situation and thought only of their own personal gain. The empire of Ranjit Singh was crumbling before their eyes. He openly espoused war against the British and their overthrow became his *raison d'etre*. This gained him much support from the Sikh population in the Punjab who saw in him an incorruptible figure to rally round. But his criticism of the timid Durbar members and other leading collaborators made him many powerful enemies, not to mention the British. Tej Singh, the Commander-in-Chief of the Sikh army and the most enthusiastic ally of the British, had a particular dislike of him.

Henry Lawrence during his tenure as Resident had done little initially to stem his progress, seeing him as an eccentric preacher with no armed following. Arrest and incarceration of this popular figure would do more harm than good, he thought. A careful eye was kept on his movements, however. Informers were maintained in his camp – a general policy used for persons thought to be inimical to the British presence – to report on his whereabouts, his followers and his preaching. This period didn't last long. Bhai Maharaj was one of those implicated in the Prema Plot, and this meant he rose permanently to the attentions of the Lahore Resident. Henry Lawrence decided to act. Bhai Maharaj was ordered to stay at Naurangabad under detention while his role in the plot was investigated. He managed to effect an escape, though, the first of what would prove to be many in subsequent years. Thereafter he kept a low profile, moving around the Lahore area in disguise, never staying in one place more than a night to frustrate British attempts to locate him. Henry Lawrence had ordered his possessions and property to be confiscated and a reward of 1,000 rupees was declared for any information leading to his capture. During the next year, he would stay largely underground silently raising support, finance and gaining followers.

During the beginnings of April 1848, shortly before the Multan insurrection, newspaper reports appeared of his presence round the Amritsar area and that he had set his standard at the Golden Temple. Orders for his arrest were issued and parties sent out to capture him and his followers but he escaped the dragnet.

It was the Multan uprising, though, that provided the opportunity for a campaign against the British. The attention of the British authorities at this time was firmly directed southwards and on keeping a firm hold on Lahore. This gave Bhai Maharaj the leeway to begin an open insurrection in the Jalandhar area, east of Lahore, and he wasted little time. Reducing his retinue to around four horsemen to travel light, Bhai Maharaj travelled rapidly throughout the Amritsar area raising support for insurrection. Such was his standing and influence that supplies and money were given to him by villagers wherever he passed. Local police officers and officials alike were sympathetic to his cause. In their official capacity, they would feign obeying British orders to arrest or give chase to his party. Orders were discretely leaked, however, and any pursuit carried out in tardy fashion, allowing him to evade the various British operations against him.

Bhai Maharaj's command of oratory was impressive and as he tirelessly moved from village to village, preaching war, he quickly won over those who heard or conversed with him. The British authorities, too, realised the danger of the moment and a party of spies were organised to infiltrate his group. Currie gave Lt Lumsden the job of choosing a select group of six Sikhs from his men who could be relied on implicitly to provide information leading to his capture. It was hoped there would be enough intelligence from these infiltrators to capture Bhai Maharaj and his closest associates. Lumsden had chosen three cavalrymen and three jemadars from the Guide Corps who then proceeded to join the preacher's camp. However, it's probable they were already sympathetic or were won over by the preacher as well as they never reported information vital enough to lead to his arrest.

A week after the news of the killings of Agnew and Anderson had reached Lahore, Bhai Maharaj had recruited hundreds of irregulars from the local population. He was able to comfortably finance supplies and weapons as well. He moved further north and east towards the foothills of the Himalayas near Deena Nuggar, about 160 km from Lahore. This bigger distance between him and Lahore meant a surprise move against him was no longer possible. His increasing recruits meant he had a small army several thousand strong with camp followers running into the tens of thousands. Too large an assembly for the relatively small British military outposts and police stations, they quickly ceased challenging him, preferring instead to wait for a sufficiently strong field force. 'He had evidently the command of large funds for he fed the poor wherever he went and distributed money to those who came for service,' wrote Currie in his report on the preacher. 'Here the number of his armed followers increased considerably; he no longer pretended to elude the authorities but he paraded the villages with drums and with an immense retinue.'

His smaller force had been ideal for guerrilla raids and for attacking British outposts and police stations. But while his numerical strength increased, the supporters flocking to his standard weakened him in other ways and Bhai Maharaj was aware of this. His force was becoming cumbersome and the largely raw recruits and irregulars lacked the necessary discipline to face British or Durbar regulars. He also had no guns; the British authorities, when they finally gave chase, would do so rapidly with sufficient men and artillery to destroy his force in a single action. Currie, in Lahore, was aware of this situation as he planned to capture the elusive preacher. 'When his followers became so many,' he wrote, 'he was unable to move from place to place as quickly and as unobserved as before and I was in hopes that by a sudden raid upon him from the nearest military post he might be taken and his followers punished and dispersed.'

It was while Bhai Maharaj's camp was situated near Deena Nuggar that Currie asked the Lahore Durbar to proclaim a 5,000-rupee reward to anyone who could help capture him. Lt Hodson would head the 14th Irregulars with two guns in the chase against Bhai Maharaj, he had decided. There was some suspicion by the British authorities in Jalandhar that the preacher would recommence raiding quite soon and orders were given to strengthen all military points in the vicinity. Currie, despite the precautions and plans, was somewhat pessimistic on the chance of forcing Bhai Maharaj into an encounter disadvantageous to him. 'I had no hope that the Bhaee would let the force I had sent from this get near him. I knew that, whatever might be the number of his adherents, directly he heard that a British force had moved against him, he would go off with all speed.'

Nevertheless, some action had to be taken to show British authority, and the Resident on 21 May sent orders to the British military outpost and police stations nearest to Deena Nuggar to stock supplies sufficient for a force being sent up from Lahore, and the local officials were ordered to assist Hodson. At this stage, Bhai Maharaj was known to be travelling with around

500 armed men in the area. Hodson therefore travelled towards Amritsar and then on to the Beas near Bhyrowal before moving up to Mokerian in Jalandhar, the plan being to cross the river with a smaller party and catch Bhai Maharaj in a surprise attack. The local officials, sympathetic to Bhai Maharaj, however, leaked the plans to his party and so the orders only served to inform him of the British advance. The day after the British force moved out of Lahore, Bhai Maharaj had already decided his next step. He would move west to cross the Ravi River before turning south in the doab to travel to Multan and join forces with Mulraj. 'I have scoured this part of the country (which my late surveys enabled me to traverse with perfect ease), got possession of every boat on the Ravee from Lahore to the Hills, placed horsemen at every ferry, and been bullying the people who supplied the Saint with provisions and arms,' reported Hodson, whose main aim now was to ensure Bhai Maharaj could not easily cross back into the Jalandhar territory. Hodson made plans to cross the river himself as well and move towards Wazirabad to chase the Bhai. With Currie planning a second column from Lahore, there was the possibility of catching Bhai Maharaj's party in the Bari doab in a pincer movement.

With the Resident about to organise another force against him and with Hodson hot on his tail, Bhai Maharaj deemed it the right time to proclaim war openly and he now declared all those with wished to eject the British should join him immediately. The area he was going through at the time was the Sikh heartland and he continued to quickly gain a lot of support here. 'Whole villages went out to meet the Bhaee and his retinue. They fed his army [for he had now some thousands of armed followers, perhaps at one time between 5,000 and 6,000] gratis and brought offerings of sweetmeats fruit &c and from every village numbers of recruits joined his train; while the Kardars with their police and soldiers pretending to be following him for the purpose of arresting his progress encamped quietly within a mile or two of him on the best terms possible,' recorded a somewhat frustrated Currie.

However, Bhai Maharaj had problems to come. The topography of the Punjab being what it was, reaching Multan would mean marching down the Rechna doab, bounded by the Ravi and Chenab rivers and hence passing close to Lahore. He realised Currie may well try and block his passage here. The alternative was for him to travel further west and cross the Chenab before marching south on the right bank, a much longer albeit safer course. There was another issue as well. 160 km south of Lahore, south of Jhung, the population changed to one that was almost exclusively Muslim. These people had no interest in rallying round the Sikh preacher and, along with the Governor of Jhung, a Misr Sahib Dyal, were happy to assist the British. The Jhung territory could not be bypassed en route to Multan.

Currie, recognising the opportunity at Jhung, drew up plans accordingly. Orders were sent to Misr Sahib Dyal to do all he could against the preacher. All boats on the Chenab were withdrawn to the right bank to prevent the rebel party leaving the doab easily. The governor meanwhile collected as many Muslims as he could recruit in Jhung and a militia of 150 men was formed to attack Bhai Maharaj's party when they arrived nearby. The preacher would pass the village of Jhundalla on his march down the doab, only around 50 km from Lahore and an ideal distance for a surprise attack, and he would make the most of the opportunity. A taskforce comprised of the 7th Irregulars, the cavalry section of the Guide Corps along with a squadron of the 14th Light Dragoons, would cross the Ravi River at night from Lahore, marching rapidly across the doab to attack the preacher's camp at daybreak. No word was given beforehand to the troops, European or native, lest the news leak out to the enemy camp. If complete surprise was achieved, the entire rebel force would be destroyed the next day, leaving the Jhung governor to only mop up any escapees to the south. Currie knew this would be the last chance to intercept the preacher. Multan was only 160 km further south from Jhung and Mulraj was known to be sending troops northwards to help his ally.

The Resident's plan was perfect on paper but not, as it turned out, easy to accomplish. The taskforce left on the night of 31 May. Fortunately for Bhai Maharaj, the weather had changed drastically the day before. Rainstorms had caused the Ravi River's levels to swell significantly. The crossing by the British troops, ordinarily a matter of an hour or so, took all night and was still continuing when day broke. Only the Irregulars had crossed by this time, the Dragoons still being on the left bank. All were exposed to the intemperate weather during the night and, being tired and bedraggled, were obviously in no fighting condition. Attempting to make the best of it and with the element of surprise lost in any case, Currie ordered a halt till the evening and added another regiment of native infantry along with four more guns to strengthen the force before an advance.

The situation had its comical aspects. Little could be kept secret in Lahore and news of British troops leaving the capital generally leaked out well before time. It was similarly so for Bhai Maharaj. With so many new recruits joining his party as he travelled through the country, it was impossible to differentiate spies from true followers. So with both camps riddled with informers, little about each side's strength or location was ever secret.

News of the abortive British crossing of the Ravi reached Bhai Maharaj at midday and he broke up camp and rapidly moved 32 km south to make full use of the time gained. So by the time the British force reached Jhundalla, there was little sign of his party but extinguished campfires. This was a temporary respite. With a large following and camp followers it would have been impossible to outrun the British force, so Bhai Maharaj ordered his followers to disperse and to make their way to Multan as best they could. With a core force of around 1,000 fighting men, the preacher continued southwards, marching, it was said, three days and nights without sleep to keep a distance from the British units chasing him. The exhausted party reached Jhung weakened by lack of sleep only to find the city's makeshift militia opposing their path and ready to fight.

Although smaller in number, the militia was fresh and took full advantage of Bhai Maharaj's men's weakness. In the contest that followed many of Bhai Maharaj's men were killed and the few that survived found the only option was to cross the river under fire or be annihilated. However, the rainstorms that had slowed the British force several days earlier now proved just as much a disadvantage for his party. Crossing the swollen and fast-flowing river without boats was hazardous in the extreme and nearly half the force that had cut through the Jhung militia, around 500–600 men, fell victim to the waters or to the muskets of the Jhung force firing from the riverbanks, according to intelligence reaching Currie later. The Governor of Jhung had also stationed men on the other bank who fired on any that attempted to reach the right bank, while fifty-six men were made prisoner on the left bank. It was an almost perfect ambush.

300 men had managed to swim across to an island midstream. They were kept there, pinned down by fire from both banks for three days without food and water and exposed to the elements until they surrendered. These men, including four of Bhai Maharaj's officers and close associates, were imprisoned in Jhung and later sent to Lahore in irons.

Bhai Maharaj had in fact been close to succour. Mulraj had, as Currie had known, sent a force northwards with three guns that happened to be only 40 km south of Jhung on the right bank when the fighting had been taking place. British informers at Multan reported only twenty-five of Bhai Maharaj's men reaching Multan over the next few days, although others would come in during the following weeks from the force dispersed at Jhundalla.

This was thought to be the end of Bhai Maharaj himself, the fast-flowing water of the Chenab laying claim to the preacher. 'I was for some days sceptical as to the death of Bhaee Maharaj Sing,' reported Currie on what he thought was a conclusive end to the story. 'I thought he had been hidden somewhere, perhaps by his followers; for the respect and veneration with which he was regarded is most extraordinary; but there seems no reason to doubt that he is drowned. Two of the prisoners, taken on the other side of the river, say that they saw him nearly half across the Chenab, swimming with hold of his celebrated black mare's tail; that they saw him lose his hold, and disappear; after which they saw him no more. The mare got safe to land, alone, on the other side.'

Despite the treacherous current and suffering from severe exhaustion, the preacher managed to survive the ordeal of the water. He would appear at Multan a few days later, with up to around 500 followers drifting in over the following weeks. The first inkling the British had of his re-emergence was through intelligence reports reaching Herbert Edwardes at Dera Ghazi Khan by 10 June. He had lost or abandoned all his baggage in the crossing of the river. Bhai Maharaj had, it turned out, taken refuge with sympathetic villagers in a village called Ooch from where he was transported to Multan despite the reward on his head. 'I did not believe this report at first, and can scarcely do so now, but it has reached me from so many quarters, that it cannot be doubted that either the Bhaee has reappeared, or else some impostor, who has assumed his name and character, which comes to much the same thing, for it is the name of a Gooroo which constitutes so powerful an appeal to the Sikh soldiers,' wrote Herbert Edwardes in his report to Currie. He had received news of his arrival from the city, also with the news that the morale of the garrison had been much increased by the event. Mulraj, who had much respect for the preacher, promptly ordered a salute fired in his honour and would give him living quarters in his own residence. He was said to go and consult Bhai Maharaj every day for the next few weeks. During the period he stayed, he urged Mulraj to take a more determined stance against the British force of Edwardes. The coming Battle of Sadoosam would be a direct consequence of this.

'There seems no reason to doubt that Bhaee Maharaj Sing really perished,' a confused Currie was writing in his reports to the government as late as 18 July. What was evident from this episode was the strength of nationalist feeling in the Sikh and Hindu-dominated areas of the Punjab, something that would be a frustration and hindrance to the Resident later as well. Not only this, but the local officials and others in positions of authority had colluded, openly or not, with the preacher. Few of the local kardars and village headmen bar the ones at Jhung had cooperated with the British authorities despite the offer of a large bounty. This would be a problem later on as well, and one which Currie would continue to raise. Any Sikh soldiers who headed off to Multan from the Lahore districts to join Mulraj found little difficulty on the way despite orders to the local police forces and authorities to apprehend them. No Sikh soldier or civilian was known to have been arrested for joining Mulraj.

In Calcutta, the supposed death of Bhai Maharaj (for news of his reappearance had not reached the city yet) was welcomed by Dalhousie. 'The destruction of the outlaw Bhaee Maharaj and the utter discomfiture of his followers is an event which has greatly tended to the support of British authority,' Dalhousie would inform the Secret Committee.

14

# The Battle of Kyneerie

The Dewan is collecting a disorderly mob, and it is not improbable that they may quarrel among themselves and cut his throat, and then one another's. The disaffection may not spread, and the affair may be comparatively small.

Frederick Currie to Government of India, 10 May 1848

The Sirdars are true I believe, the soldiers are all false, I know. The Sikh army in Peshawur, Bunnoo, and Hazara were watching this force to take their cue from its conduct.

Herbert Edwardes to Frederick Currie, 22 June 1848

While the news of the Gulaba Plot, the subsequent exile of Jind Kaur and the destruction of Bhai Maharaj's force had been taking attention at Lahore, events in Multan province were leading to the first major hostilities between the mercenary armies of Mulraj and Herbert Edwardes. For Herbert Edwardes had, within a few weeks of learning of the Multan insurrection, gained control of the entire Derajat with little opposition from Mulraj. He had also crossed the Indus, making his way to the right bank of the Chenab to join up with the Nawab of Bhawulpore's force, which had crossed the Sutlej from the east. Both of these columns were now little more than 80 km south of the city.

Mulraj had been kept fully aware of the movements of these two columns, but, staying true to his nature, had continued to dither on a response. This was despite Rung Ram and his other principal officers advising him the Bhawulpore army were largely undisciplined irregulars and headed by the geriatric Commander Futteh Mohammad Khan Ghoree. This force could be disposed of before Edwardes managed to cross the Chenab, they argued. Edwardes could then be tackled separately shortly afterwards and destroyed. A junction between these two forces, on the other hand, would tilt the balance comfortably in Edwardes' favour, both numerically and in the matter of guns. The combined force would total around 18,000 men and twenty-one guns with fifty zambarooks, much too strong for Mulraj to contemplate a battle in the open.

It was only on 15 June after much pleading by his officers that Mulraj finally resolved on action. He ordered almost his entire force to be readied, with Rung Ram given command. The plan formulated, as recommended by his officers, was to engage and destroy the Bhawulpore force on 17 June, a day before Edwardes was expected to cross the Chenab and effect a junction. This plan had hardly been decided on before it reached the ears of Edwardes. Mustapha Khan, the Pathan chief at Multan, who was still undecided on which side held most advantage for him, had sent off a messenger to Edwardes' camp with news of Mulraj's plans. Mustapha Khan was of the opinion that Rung Ram himself could be recruited to the British cause. His enthusiasm was only a mask, he wrote to the political agent, recalling he had been wounded by his own soldiers in the aftermath of Agnew and Anderson's murders and was known to be still suffering from the effects of the wounding. Edwardes agreed wholeheartedly and sent off a diplomatic approach to the Multan commander.

> To Rung Ram, also the commander of the rebel force, I have written to say that I presume he accepted the command to give him an opportunity of coming over to us with his nephew Hur Bugwan Doss as it is no secret that his loyalty got him the wounds from which he is still suffering … Should he come over I have assured him of every kindness. Either one or the other of these desertions would damp the ardor of the rebels considerably.

He also wrote back to Mustapha Khan on the same day. Rung Ram's army was composed partly of the Khan's men and the approach of the Multan army would be an ideal time therefore for the Khan's soldiers to defect as well. They could simply leave their fellow soldiers and join his force after leaving the city or prior to the battle. With Rung Ram possibly joining Edwardes as well, much of the leaderless Multan force would simply melt away, ending the insurrection in one stroke. These potential defections were not at all certain, however, and with the knowledge Rung Ram was to press for battle on the 17th he also made plans to join up with the Bhawulpore force as soon as possible, advising Futteh Mohammad Khan Ghoree to avoid a fight under all circumstances till the junction was achieved. If necessary he should adopt a defensive position behind entrenchments.

***

Rung Ram's southward advance with the Multan force when it eventually began was slow, hampered by the numerous nullahs that criss-crossed the area and the few bridges available south of Multan. He would only reach the village of Buggarah, a few miles north of where the Bhawulpore force was camping, on the night of the 17th rather than in the morning – a fatal delay, as it would turn out. Showing less urgency than he should have, he elected to delay battle for the morning of the next day to give his troops some rest.

Edwardes, meanwhile, on that same evening had reached the right bank of the Chenab at Khangurh. If there had been boats in the vicinity he could have crossed the same night. However, local units of the Multan garrison had already destroyed these. Anxious to cross in the knowledge the battle would certainly be fought the next morning, he turned south and by the night of the 17th had marched the 25 km or so to the Gaggianwallah ferry, where forty-seven boats were found for a crossing. This number wasn't enough for a rapid transfer of his entire force – that would take three days including horses and baggage with the few boats at his disposal. Therefore, given the urgency of the situation, he decided on pouring as many troops as he could across to the left bank during the night, the remainder of the men, baggage and guns crossing during the following day as time allowed. No horses would be transported across the river and therefore all the cavalrymen ferried across would fight on foot if need be.

By 7 a.m. on the new day, 18 June, as Rung Ram resumed his advance south and reached the Bhawulpore force with the guns of both sides commencing fire, Edwardes had managed to ferry around 3,000 men on to the left bank of the Chenab and was only around 7 km from the battlefield. The fact that the day was 18 June he took to be a good omen, for this was the anniversary of Waterloo (although labelling the battle as he did, the 'Waterloo of India', was perhaps stretching the analogy a little far). Advancing with his vanguard and ordering the troops and gunners still crossing to join up as soon as possible, he quickly travelled north, reaching the Bhawulpore line at 8 a.m. near the village of Kyneerie. No defection had taken place either from Rung Ram or the Pathan leader, though, dashing Edwardes' hopes of confusion in the Multan ranks.

The battlefield on which the opposing sides found themselves was a sort of 'jungled plain' as Edwardes would later describe it, with areas of dense trees obstructing vision interspersed with clear areas. It wasn't at all level, either. The Multan line in the distance was clearly on higher ground, strung out behind a nullah. Mulraj had sent out what was later estimated to be four regiments with 2,000 cavalry, around 8,000–12,000 men in total depending on sources, along with ten guns and forty zambarooks. Rung Ram's men had thrown up breastworks along the nullah in what was a more defensive position than it should have been given the urgency of destroying the Nawab's force before Edwardes' army could join up in substantial numbers. From the Multan line, the land sloped down gently towards a low point where the Bhawulpore commander had positioned his line. Behind the Bhawulpore line the ground began rising again gently. Because of the jungled section between the two lines, however, this wasn't totally apparent to anyone.

Edwardes quickly organised the Nawab's forces so that they held the middle and right while his own force formed the left, which was set to gradually strengthen as more of his troops arrived from crossing the river. The Nawab's force turned out to be ten regiments strong with cavalry, a total of 9,000 men with eleven guns, although their discipline and training was highly questionable. The main problem, however, as expected, was the commander of the Bhawulpore forces. The aged man was patently confused, his memory having declined to the point where he was frequently changing his mind having forgotten his own earlier opinion. At other times, Edwardes claimed later, Futteh Mohammad Khan Ghoree lied openly to mask his inability to remember what he had said earlier. This was a view others shared. Peer Ibrahim Khan, the British agent at Bhawulpore, for example, openly called the Nawab's commander a 'moorkh' or fool. When he arrived on the battlefield Edwardes had found Futteh Mohammad Khan Ghoree busy finishing his prayers rather than actively managing his force, who were under fire at the time.

What there wasn't any worry about for this new combined force was ammunition. Nine bullock-loads of powder had been received by the force organised by Peer Ibrahim Khan with plenty more powder and shot coming in supplied by the Nawab of Bhawulpore in the days prior to the battle. The disadvantage was the position. Being situated on the higher ground looking down, the Multan gunners had a slightly better view of what was happening in the Bhawulpore ranks and therefore had better fortune with their firing. The Bhawulpore gunners, meanwhile, were finding it awkward to fire up the slope accurately.

Edwardes had decided to wait till his guns and the rest of his troops had arrived before attempting anything ambitious and therefore, with Rung Ram also remaining cautious behind the nullah, the game of ball would continue for six hours, with neither side making much of an impression or any hint of a movement. To escape the worst of the fire, Edwardes had ordered all his men to lie down flat or take cover in any case. They were also ordered not to fire till the opposing line was within musket range.

At around 3 p.m., Rung Ram, finally deciding to show more urgency, ordered the whole of the Multan line to begin advancing. Interspersed with this advance was grapeshot from his advancing guns and musketry from his infantry. This began to have a telling effect on the Bhawulpore men, forcing them to fall steadily back up the slope behind them. After a while, as the Multan line continued advancing, though, the nature and difficulty of their movement was reversed. Having reached the bottom of the incline and the former enemy position, they found themselves moving up the slope on the other side now while Edwardes' line, having already fallen back, had reached or was close to reaching the summit behind them and now had the advantage of the higher ground. Moving uphill slowed the Multan infantry and made things difficult for the Multan gunners as well.

Determined to force the issue despite this difficulty, Rung Ram turned his main attention to Edwardes' force on his right, correctly assuming that if his troops could be defeated the Bhawulpore force would probably make a headlong retreat. He readied his cavalry on his flanks for a charge. Edwardes, seeing the move, ordered grape and round shot to be fired while his infantry also now opened up, which had the effect of forcing the Multan line to retire in places. While he was holding his ground, it turned out that the Bhawulpore troops on his right, who were receiving less attention from the Multan guns, had actually been pushed back much further than Edwardes' troops, their fighting spirit and organisation not being up to the mark.

'The Nawab's officers were in such a state of trouble and confusion that I cannot write a proper description of. They were constantly boasting of their prowess, and what they could do, but you will soon hear from others of the state they were in. The Daudputras also, who were constantly bragging, did not join in the battle, but remained in their own places like so many rats. We were in this state, with no peace or quietness from the balls of the enemy, when Edwardes sahib, with the Nuwab's officers, made an attack on the enemy's forces, with whom they fought sword-to-sword and hand-to-hand for nearly an hour,' Peer Ibrahim Khan, the British agent from Bhawulpore, would record in a letter. Realising his entire middle and right would collapse if the Nawab's forces continued to be pushed back, Edwardes quickly penned a message to Courtlandt, his deputy, who was crossing with the rest of Edwardes forces, advising him the situation was tenuous at best and that assistance was required urgently; however, help was closer at hand than he thought. A considerable body of Edwardes' men and guns had already crossed the river and arrived at just this time to join the fray. The Multan line was known to charge three times hoping for a breakthrough, the casualties examined after the battle showing many died from sword cuts rather than musketball. Edwardes men managed to hold on to their position despite the severe pressure.

'I feel unable to do justice to the gallantry with which this order was obeyed,' wrote Edwardes later. 'Men whom I had only enlisted a month ago shook their swords with a will and rushed upon the rebel cavalry with the most desperate and irresistible valour. The fight was hand to hand in five minutes and the opposing guns were pouring grape into each other almost within speaking distance. For half an hour fighting could not have been harder and we were left entirely to ourselves, the Daoodpotras being either engaged on their own account or thinking they had done enough.' He would also attempt a cavalry charge of around 100 men which surprised the Multan line, although the numbers were too few to make a lasting impact and turn the contest.

Time was against Rung Ram. As the minutes ticked by, more and more of Edwardes and Courtlandt's men and guns arrived to reinforce his line from the river crossing. Six guns had been transported across along with two regular regiments, the Suraj Mookhee of Courtlandt as well as the Muslim troops of Shoban Khan, an ally. When these reinforcements finally arrived, the contest swayed entirely in Edwardes' favour. The newly arrived guns immediately began pouring grape into the Multan line, which had expected decreasing rather than increasing resistance. Edwardes ordered a general advance with his reinforcements as the confused Multan line began turning and retreating down the slope, a retreat that became general. 'Bravely, I must allow, did they labor to carry off their guns but one by one they all fell to either the sword or the bayonet,' the British agent wrote later. 'In the morning, they commenced the action with ten guns and in the afternoon advanced with six across a nullah which was between them and us leaving four guns behind. All six are now in our possession but they managed to carry off the more distant four though we followed them up for two coss after they broke.'

The Pathans on the Multan side, whom Edwardes had hoped would switch sides before the battle, showed their more mercenary instincts now, bolting quickly as the tide turned against their side. These troops fleeing changed what would have been an organised retreat into general flight, with all baggage and stores having to be left behind despite a spirited rearguard action. 'They showed none of that hot headed gallantry for which their race is distinguished and having no heart in the cause left the brunt of the fighting to the Sikhs who suffered in consequence out of all proportion,' Edwardes continued. The Gurkhas, the third contingent in Rung Ram's force, also reluctant to yield, suffered heavily too.

The last shots were fired around 4.30 p.m., by which time Rung Ram had retreated to around 8 km south of Shujabad. The Sikh and Gurkha troops retreated with their commander while other remnants of the force went back to Multan. Those less enthusiastic for more fight, like the Pathans, left for home at this stage.

Edwardes' losses overall would end up relatively small, estimated to be around 100 men killed and wounded, with the Nawab's troops suffering around the same in casualties. Capt. Macferris' regiment had twenty-four killed and wounded, Capt. Jadar Ram's regiment had twelve killed and the troops of Muiyez-Ud-Deen, the Kardar of Khanpur, another local ally, suffered eight killed and forty wounded. A fair number of horses and camels were victim to the fire. During the battle one of the magazines on Edwardes' side had caught fire, blowing six men into the air in the ensuing explosion.

It's difficult to say how many men Rung Ram lost. There were inflated casualty figures running into several thousand being bandied around in the British newspapers later. Edwardes himself estimated 200 killed and 300 wounded. Later estimates put Multan casualties at around 300 to 380 killed, although there may have been more wounded taken back. On the battlefield around 200 corpses from all sides were recovered later, suggesting many were taken away or that estimates for casualties had simply been too high. What was equally important for Mulraj was the loss of eight out of ten guns he had sent into battle. Although Rung Ram had managed to pull back with four guns, two had to be abandoned on the way back, being thrown into wells to avoid capture by Edwardes. Equally discouraging was the news that all the baggage and stores had been abandoned.

There would be major celebrations of this first major victory against the 'rebel force' in the joint allied camp, and a salute was fired to mark the victory that evening. Not all would go smoothly, though. Some of the problems associated with having such a diverse and disparate irregular force, problems which were currently bedevilling Mulraj, were now becoming all too apparent to Edwardes now as well. One of these was the delicate matter of who would keep the captured guns. Edwardes' troops had only captured the last two of the Multan guns, having been occupied in the pursuit. The Nawab's troops, having lagged behind, found themselves in possession of all the others. The Bhawulpore officers naturally thought the guns were theirs by rights, with their commander already planning on parades through Bhawulpore before an impressed Nawab. Edwardes had to remonstrate with him the day after the battle, asking him to give them up. Technically this was a rebellion against the Lahore state, and the captured guns therefore belonged to the Lahore Government. There followed a rather tense period, with the slow-thinking Bhawulpore commander and his men eventually and reluctantly agreeing to give up the guns.

There was also the issue of looting of the Multan camp and neighbouring villages which had begun shortly after the battle. The Bhawulpore troops, being on what they saw as foreign soil, thought it entirely in their right to commence plunder. To their credit, Edwardes and the Nawab's officers both issued a declaration forbidding all looting, with severe punishments to any man found partaking in such activities.

Having realised the Bhawulpore commander would be a major handicap in future battles, Edwardes would pen a diplomatic letter to the Nawab asking to have him replaced with a new nominal commander, the Nawab's eldest son. This the Nawab would agree to and Edwardes would later reward the Nawab in turn by giving him five of the captured ten guns, all obligations to the Lahore Government seemingly forgotten. The former Bhawulpore commander, meanwhile, would be despatched from the battlefield with a *khillat* as reward for his 'services' during the battle.

Apart from these minor disagreements spirits were naturally high in the camp. The following day, on hearing the news of the victory, the Nawab would send fifteen maunds of sugar candy to be distributed to the army with 500 rupees to be given to each of the artillerymen. In addition 100 horses, 200 camels and forty tents were sent for distribution to those most deserving.

Edwardes wrote a most optimistic letter to the Resident reprising him of the victory and stating confidently that the rebellion would no doubt be snuffed out shortly. He was, he said, quite capable of marching further north and laying siege to Multan himself. 'My expectation is that the rebel Moolraj will either destroy himself or be destroyed by his troops before the next mail goes out,' Currie in turn confidently reported to the Governor-General. Currie would also begin thinking about ordering the three Sikh columns still hovering to the north of Multan southwards to reinforce Edwardes and push the rebellion into extinction, although he would wait a while longer before giving the order.

At Multan, meanwhile, the setback at Kyneerie and the loss of the entire Derajat territory in the previous weeks had apparently pushed Mulraj into much despondency and despair. 'The season of peace has long since passed; and even if such were to be the case, what hope is there of it's being any good or benefit to me now?', Mulraj is reported to have replied on hearing of the defeat and on an officer suggesting renewing peace overtures or surrendering himself to British clemency. He would decide to continue the fight after spending the next few days pondering over the matter.

# 15

# The Battle of Sadoosam

The present plight of Dewan Moolraj does not offer so decided an encouragement; and I hear that he, yesterday, informed his officers that his resources were exhausted, that he could neither lavish on them rewards, or even give them their pay; that those who were not prepared to fight for their mere religion, had better leave him; many are said to have taken him at his word.

Herbert Edwardes to Frederick Currie, 3 July 1848

The neck of the Multan rebellion may be considered broken. The fort of Multan is all that remains to the Diwan.

Frederick Currie to Government of India

There was nothing to stop Edwardes advancing after Kyneerie, and no resistance offered by a discouraged and hesitant Mulraj, so he duly obliged by continuing the march northwards towards Multan. The day after the battle he ordered the Nawab's officers to advance and take up a suitable position around 5 km from Shujabad, a city around 30 km to their north. Edwardes own baggage and cattle and rearguard had still not crossed the river due to insufficient boats and he delayed his own advance for three days to allow for the crossing. His own force therefore effectively formed the rearguard for the time being, marching a few days behind the Nawab's force.

There would be no hostilities at Shujabad. Mulraj pulled out its fortress garrison of 3,000 men on 20 June to strengthen his own force at Multan, allowing the Nawab's troops to take the town along with the village of Kote nearby on the same day. The local killadars (fort commanders) of Shujabad and Kote would come out and hand over the town keys to the occupying force. A salute was fired to celebrate their capture but the Bhawulpore irregulars found little to please them in the fort. Although banned from looting, they searched the fort diligently but the garrison had taken care to leave little in the form of plunder apart from some camels and horses past their prime. This lack of treasure at Shujabad happened to be unfortunate for Edwardes too, as he was running out of funds for the payment of his burgeoning force. More and more irregulars and local mercenaries were drifting in to join his force. He had been forced to write to the Nawab of Bhawulpore asking for a loan 50,000 rupees until more money arrived from Lahore. Shujabad had therefore been looked on with opportunity for the notable residents of the city had been known to be Mulraj's strongest supporters and some of his heaviest backers in terms of financing a war. 'One Shroff alone of Shoojabad, a mean looking little fellow, undertook to furnish Dewan Moolraj with two months' pay for his army if he would only send them against the Nawab's troops, a circumstance which I shall not forget whenever we are hard pressed for cash,' Edwardes commented. 'Such monied men are invaluable in these times.'

At Shujabad his force increased further still, a number of the local Muslim chieftains of the area and their armed contingent also opting to join the side on the ascendant. Some 12 km north of Shujabad on the road to Multan was the town of Secunderabad and its small fort. This was reached on the 26th with its capture as bloodless as at Shujabad. Some of the nominal garrison voluntarily surrendered upon seeing six guns being drawn up in front of the fort gate while others escaped out of the rear gate. Edwardes would treat those who surrendered warmly, returning their swords, thinking this would help to reduce the resolution of Mulraj's men still further. Spies at Multan, meanwhile, brought news that the casualties at Kyneerie along with desertions since the battle had reduced Mulraj's muster roll by over 1,200 men. This was buoyed by further intelligence of the Mulraj's indecision and suspicion of his own troops. 'The breach between the Puthans and Moolraj has been much widened by the Kineyree disaster which the Dewan persists in attributing to their treachery,' Edwardes relayed to the Resident. 'It is said that Moolraj indeed distrusts the whole force which fought on the 18th and is not inclined to let them into the fort but means to encamp them under its walls. So treated they will probably melt rapidly away.'

Many of these Pathans had already been drifting in to Edwardes camp where they were, like the Secunderabad garrison, warmly welcomed and hired. The news he was receiving from the city was quite correct, for Mulraj had lapsed back into despair at his recent setbacks. Displaying his characteristic indecision and now veering towards giving up the contest entirely, Mulraj would pen a letter through his emissary Mustapha Khan Khagwanee which reached the British agent on 24 June. He protested his innocence in the killings of Agnew and Anderson and declared he had been entirely in the hands of his soldiers after the incident. He was willing to surrender even now if his life and rank would be respected, his only condition being he did not wish to be put on trial. If this could be agreed, he would voluntarily give himself in – assuming he could escape his own troops. Edwardes had had his fingers burnt previously offering Mulraj immunity and would decline to reply to this overture, although he forwarded the letter to Currie. What he did do, however, was tell Mustafa Khan confidentially that the Dewan's life would not be spared in his opinion now that lives had been lost at Kyneerie and earlier. After hearing no response from Edwardes, a dejected Mulraj was reported to have changed his mind again on surrender and held what turned out to be a bad-tempered conference on the 26th with his principal officers on continuing the fight with increased vigour. 'Moolraj said that nothing now remained but to fight, and that he did not wish to retire with the troops into the fort before he was obliged to do so; fearing that from being shut up in the fortress, the troops might become discontented, and desirous of leaving his service,' Noorullah Shah, a high-placed informer in the fort, reported in a revealing letter to a Capt. Neale at Shikarpur later. The governor had also launched another strong verbal attack against his Pathan soldiers for their performance at Kyneerie. Their fleeing from the battlefield had lost the battle, he complained, and in a fit of anger, he even went as far as saying it was lawful to kill them wherever they were found, although this statement was retracted later when his anger subsided.

Many of his Sikh officers, already tiring of their poor performance, suggested getting rid of most of the Muslim recruits and levies. These men, they argued, tended to fight with little enthusiasm, having friends and families in Bhawulpore and among Edwardes' Pathan contingent. They also happened to be riddled with informers and spies. The arguments went as far as a prominent officer, Dhonda Singh, laying down an ultimatum that he and the Sikh contingent would desert Mulraj if the Afghan and Muslim soldiers were not ejected from the force. Mulraj needed little convincing and shortly afterwards summoned his senior Afghan soldiers, informing them they and their men's services were no longer required. This action simply meant this contingent promptly joined Edwardes' camp, where they received employment and in turn gave plentiful intelligence on the situation within the city. This policy also lost him some of his experienced Muslim officers, like Sadik Mahommed who, though wavering in respect to the rebellion had nevertheless stuck by him till then.

With large parties of Pathan soldiers walking off and Edwardes' force now only a day or two's march to his south, prospects looked the dimmest they ever had for Mulraj. However, events would conspire to give the embattled governor fresh hope and confidence over the next week or so. Undoubtedly the pivotal event near the end of June would be the arrival of the charismatic preacher Bhai Maharaj at Multan. Arriving less than two weeks after Kyneerie, he brought with him, according to Nurullah Shah, a fresh infusion of around 500 of his men who had survived the disaster at Jhung. Over the coming days, as Bhai Maharaj's supporters drifted in, morale at Multan rose.

The second factor that helped buoy Mulraj's confidence was, somewhat perversely, the news of further impending reinforcements for Edwardes. Confident the rebellion was on its last legs and therefore sure that the fidelity of the Sikh soldiers could be relied on now, Currie began ordering Shere Singh and his Sikh force camped to the north of Multan to advance from Toulumba to Sardurpur, only 30 km from Multan. With Edwardes' success at Kyneerie, both Sheik Imam-Ud-Deen and Jowahir Mull Dutt, the commanders of the other two columns, were eager to earn some credit in ending the fading insurrection and had asked to join Edwardes as well. Edwardes would assent as more men would be required in any siege or assault on the city. Sheikh Imam-Ud-Deen would reach Multan on 28 June, adding another 4,000 men to Edwardes' army, although ignoring his order to leave all his Sikh soldiers behind at Mulsee and to bring only the Muslim contingent.

Mulraj knew well the Sikh units approaching Multan had no appetite to fight against their comrades in the city and their imminent arrival gave hope of large-scale defections of Sikh regulars to his cause now that they were in such close proximity. There were rumours that Bhai Maharaj was personally going out to meet Shere Singh's men as they marched down, attempting to persuade them to shed their inhibitions and anxieties about Mulraj's leadership and join the city garrison.

These events would lead to Mulraj assenting to Bhai Maharaj's pleas for another battle outside the city. The day picked was 1 July, which Mulraj's astrologer informed the governor would be a propitious day for a battle. The location chosen was the village of Suraj Khund, a small village lying on the plain 8 km south-west of the city that Edwardes' force would have to pass to reach Multan. The village's salient feature was that it lay on the west bank of the very wide and substantial Wollee Mahomed's Canal, which both dominated the local area round Suraj Khund and the terrain towards Multan. The nullah, around 40 feet wide and around 10 feet deep, ran from near Toulumba, taking waters from the Ravi River before its junction with the Chenab for the purposes of irrigation and flowing to the east of Multan city before turning south-east and flowing by the west of the village before resuming its journey southwards. As was usual with nullahs, the earth excavated to make the channel was piled up on each side of the channel to make high banks. These were sometimes, as in this case, flattened to make for a thoroughfare along the banks, inadvertently making a strong defensive line as well. The canal was full with water at this time, the current being rapid enough to prevent wading across even had the depth not been so substantial. Three bridges connected its east bank with its west from the village of Suraj Khund up to Multan. The two nearest bridges to the village, narrow defiles at best, Mulraj had already taken the precaution of defending with around 1,000 troops and four guns. The third bridge, a well-built brick construction, lay close to the city itself and thus did not need monitoring.

This point near Suraj Khund would be the ideal location to stop Edwardes' army, Mulraj speculated. True to his cautious nature, he would decide to choose a defensive position on the east bank of the nullah, hoping Edwardes would be tempted into a rash attack across the canal. It was an eminently good position – almost too good, for to try and cross a deep canal under heavy fire would be suicidal. Unusually, and perhaps because of the strong position, Mulraj confidently declared he would lead his army personally, the first and last time he would do so in the field. His decision to choose this as the battleground perfectly betrayed his lack of military ability; the ground Edwardes was crossing as he made his way to Suraj Khund was the same difficult ground Rung Ram had crossed on his way to Kyneerie. Criss-crossed with deep nullahs, the area north of Shujabad formed an equally good defensive position while preventing Edwardes' march north at the same time.

News of Mulraj's plans leaked into Edwardes camp with the usual speed. 'The most highly disciplined army could scarcely fail to be thrown by them into confusion; and I could not but marvel during the march at the folly of Moolraj in not turning his local knowledge to account and attacking us among these dykes,' Edwardes mused. Edwardes himself was quite happy with a contest at Suraj Khund. The nullah would be an obstacle but it was much less hazardous than scaling the city and fort walls if the garrison chose to lock themselves up in the city, and the casualties hopefully smaller. If he could overcome the obstacle, destruction of the remnants of Mulraj's force would largely conclude matters. He immediately recommenced his march on the road from Secunderabad northwards on 27 June to Adee Walla Bagh and towards Suraj Khund.

***

On the morning of 1 July, Mulraj could be seen exiting the city on his elephant and leading almost his entire garrison out personally. Proceeding south, he and his force reached the bridge at Suraj Khund as planned where he set up his line along the east bank of the nullah a few hours before Edwardes was expected to arrive at the village. That same morning, Edwardes continued his march north and approached Suraj Khund on the opposite west bank. As he marched closer, the Multan force lined up on the other side of the nullah became quite visible. While not averse to taking chances, Edwardes was sane enough, on now seeing the nullah, to realise an attack across it would be madness. Instead he simply decided to bypass Mulraj's force, continuing to march north-westwards towards the city with plans to set up camp at the village of Tibbee, where the city could be attacked on its south-west and western suburbs.

What he didn't figure on was Mulraj deciding to cross the nullah himself. As Edwardes' force continued marching north somewhat parallel to the nullah, his move was replicated by Mulraj on the opposite bank, with the Multan troops marching back towards the city in order to continue facing Edwardes' force to their west. Realising by now Edwardes wasn't about to attack across the nullah, Mulraj, in a further show of initiative, ordered his force to cross to the west bank themselves by the brick bridge nearer the city. Opposite the bridge was situated the small village of Sadoosam along with several other hamlets through which Mulraj moved his line before forming up opposite Edwardes. It was around twelve noon at this time, and preparations were being made to encamp when news was brought to Edwardes of Mulraj's approach and his Bhawulpore pickets being forced back. The call to arms was sounded and a line immediately formed.

The two sides, roughly 2 km apart at this stage, weren't quite visible to each other. The whole area was dotted with small mud hamlets along with a reasonable amount of jungle and groves of date trees interspersed here and there, making it impossible to see beyond a few hundred metres. One thing that did stick out, however, was a high area or sandy mound in front of the right wing of Edwardes' force.

'The highest estimate of the rebel numbers does not make them above 12,000 and I scarcely think they were 11,000 though they left hardly any men in the fort,' reported Edwardes later, although even this may have been exaggerated and contained a many irregulars recently arrived. He estimated the numbers to be around two-thirds Sikh and Hindus, with the remaining being Muslim troops. These men were still sticking by their governor for the pay and despite suspicions about their loyalty. Other estimates put Mulraj's force at around seven thousand men. There was confusion as to how many guns Mulraj had brought. Some accounts declared as low as seven, while other estimated as high as twelve.

On the British side, Edwardes could now muster comfortably over 18,000 men and twenty-two guns (not including the eight captured at Kyneerie), both outnumbering and outgunning the Multan force. As well as his own irregulars this included the Bhawulpore force, Courtlandt's men and the Kashmir force under Sheikh Imam-Ud-Deen who had recently joined him, but not Shere Singh's column, which was still making its way down. Two more Europeans had appeared on the scene by this time as well. Lt Lake had arrived on 29 June to take over formal command of the Bhawulpore troops as requested by the Nawab. Another European, going by the name of Mr Quinn, an Englishman who had been residing in the Derajat, had brought eighty camels for carriage the day after the Battle of Kyneerie, an asset Edwardes sorely needed.

It was obvious that a battle would be fought and Edwardes quickly divided his command. Lake would command the Bhawulpore troops on the right. Courtlandt held the centre right along with the Muslim troops of Sultan Khan, another ally. Quinn, working under Courtlandt, was given the command of the Suraj Mookhee regiment in this section. Edwardes would manage the centre left himself with his Pathan cavalry, while on the extreme British left were placed the troops of Sheikh Imam-Ud-Deen. Ten of the guns would be placed in the centre, with the rest spread out on both wings. Seeking to gain an advantage as the Multan army approached, Lake was first to make a move.

'I directed the Nawab's troops to occupy some high ground on the right of our line which not only afforded them the advantage of cover but enabled their guns to fire from a considerable elevation down into the plain. This was a matter of no small importance in a country abounding with brushwood behind which the enemy were seen with difficulty,' he related in his report of 2 July. The plan that had been decided was for Courtlandt and Lake to challenge and keep the Multan centre and right occupied while Edwardes, using the superior numbers he now had, would wheel around clockwise to the north and attack the Multan line in the rear, at the same time preventing them from retreating back into the city.

Lake's men would open the firing first with Mulraj's gunners returning the favour and this would stay the situation for around fifteen minutes, by which time Edwardes and the British centre had advanced too and the cannonade became general along both lines. On the extreme left Sheikh Imam-Ud-Deen, who had two guns, also opened fire. This cannonade would continue for six long hours but it made little impact on the infantry of either side. Utilising ditches and the various nullahs and drainage canals for cover, the men on both sides were entirely safe. It was different for the artillery, though. The Multan guns made little impact on Lake's men on the British right, with the mound largely protecting them, but their superior fire in return had good effect. 'It was impossible therefore for them long to sustain the superior fire of 22, which were brought into action on our side; though justice requires me to pay the tribute of admiration to the obstinacy with which Moolraj's Sikh artillerymen stood their ground,' Edwardes commented in his report the following day to the Resident. After the battle it was seen that the Sikh gunners, more exposed to the punishment, had suffered the bulk of the casualties, their corpses lying close to their guns along with seventeen horses strewn close by who had also been hit. Mulraj had some small success on his right, managing to put Sheikh Imam-Ud-Deen's two guns out of action quite early on, but was forced to pull back slowly as Edwardes finally ordered an advance at around 4 p.m. Utilising the agreed plan to circle clockwise on the north, Edwardes began moving round to threaten the Multan rear while Courtlandt, in command of two regiments of regular infantry and seventeen guns, continued to fire on the rest of the Multan line.

The trigger for a collapse of the Multan line came from a nervous Mulraj himself. While the exchange of shots had been going on, the governor on his elephant had stationed himself in the centre of his line, where most of his guns were positioned. Here, under a grove of date trees with a nullah in front of him, he had observed the battle during the day. This portion of the line was said to be a little in advance of the flanks and was the first to be forced back as Courtlandt led the advance in the centre. A chance shot from a gun hit Mulraj's elephant's howdah (seat) at this time. Some sources say the governor was wounded slightly. The Dewan, in panic, dismounted his elephant and switched to his horse and proceeded to flee back to the city, ordering all his guns back except for two to form a rearguard. His line, although outgunned, had held on well to this point but the order to retreat for no clear reason sent confusion down the ranks, more so when he himself was seen bolting back to the city. Although the fighting continued heavily at points, much of the Multan line began disintegrating with many quickly making their way back to the city following their governor's example. The two guns that had been ordered to serve as a rearguard by Mulraj were by all accounts desperately served and helped to prevent a disorderly retreat in parts turning into a complete disaster. These guns were captured later by a charge of the Suraj Mookhee regiment led by Mr Quinn, followed by a general advance which pushed the last sections of Mulraj's army back towards the city pursued by Edwardes' force.

Edwardes' own contingent's losses in this encounter were slight. Eighteen men had been killed with seventy wounded. One of the more noticeable losses was a Capt. Macpherson who was employed in the Bhawulpore force and who was buried on 2 July with military honours. One of the Nawab's principal officers, a Shah Mohammad Khan, was also killed. Both of these were casualties to cannon shot. The casualties on the British left were more significant. Sheikh Imam-Ud-Deen's troops suffered eighty-one killed and wounded. The total killed and wounded in the whole force including allies came to 281.

It's difficult to assess Mulraj's losses at Sadoosam. Many of the deaths and casualties were entirely avoidable but for Mulraj's panic and the ensuing disorder. Along with the Sikh contingent, the Gurkhas, who had put up a stiff fight and had stayed their ground, also suffered heavily. Only 150 of the 400 Gurkhas who had deserted Agnew were said to remain for Mulraj, the others being *hors de combat* or dead. The only good piece of news for the governor was that only the two guns left to act as a rearguard were captured, the rest having been recovered and taken back into the city.

Many of Mulraj's irregulars, disheartened by this second loss and Mulraj's own cowardice, were seen to desert him after the contest and leave for home, openly throwing their uniforms to the ground. Others again blamed the Muslim contingent for not showing enough vigour and took their wrath out on the Muslim officers still serving with Mulraj. One of these was Peer Buksh Adawlutee. 'Peer Buksh Adawlutee the worst and most influential adviser of Moolraj received a severe sword cut across the back while flying from Suddoosain from the hand of one of his own men, a Sikh who declared that Peer Buksh had sold the day to the Sahib log,' described Edwardes later. 'This incident and Moolraj's firing on his own troops at the bridge gives a very fair idea of the dissension and distrust which pervades the rebel army.' The firing at his own troops related to an order by Mulraj for his gunners to prevent some of his own troops retreating back across the bridge while he himself fled, which only led to increased casualties. Another casualty, discovered later, was Mulraj's trust in his astrologer, who had signally failed to predict a successful day.

Following the battle Edwardes moved back to make camp at the village of Tibba, allowing for the disposal of the dead. An informal truce had been agreed the day after the hostilities, with both sides recovering their comrades' corpses from the plain. In the evening of that day, funeral pyres could be seen burning brightly outside the city walls from the British camp. Suttee, the ancient Hindu practice of the widow voluntarily immolating herself alongside her husband on his funeral pyre, was witnessed. Foremost among these was the wife of the adjutant of the Gurkha regiment which had accompanied Agnew and who had defected at the very start of the conflict. He had been killed fighting courageously in the battle during the retreat.

\*\*\*

Sadoosam along with the victory at Kyneerie had the effect of making Edwardes supremely confident he could defeat Mulraj and capture the city all by himself, given a few heavy guns and with only the most nominal help from a British column. Without having set eyes on the city or fortress, he speculated in his stream of despatches to Currie that a few siege pieces and some sappers were all that was required to gain ingress into the city. So depleted and discouraged was the city garrison now, he argued, that the siege pieces would only require forty-eight hours to batter breaches in the walls at worst and the city would immediately fall into his hands. The weather was clement, displaying none of the devastating heat for which the area was famous. The guns, if sent downstream on the Ravi and Chenab from Lahore and Ferozepore, would only take a week to arrive. Therefore the city could quite easily be in British hands in around ten days, bringing the rebellion to a definitive conclusion.

Currie, though, continued to be much more circumspect and sober about the scale of the task and his response was that the sending of British guns was a much more complicated affair than Edwardes made out. 'It would be useless sending you heavy guns and a mortar battery from Ferozepore without artillerymen to work them and an abundant supply of our ammunition. If our breaching artillery and sappers and miners are employed, the British army will become to a certain extent identified with the operations you are conducting, and any check or reverse which you might sustain would to the same extent reflect upon the character of British prowess,' he cautioned Edwardes, also reminding him that the rains were still to come and could turn the city environs into a quagmire and paralyse the besieging force. He would, he informed Edwardes, stick to the agreed policy of a large force during the cold season. 'After what has happened, if the British arm is raised at all, it must be with power to strike a blow that shall at once vindicate its insulted honour and crush the insulters.'

This did not prevent Edwardes from trying to change Currie's mind over the following weeks, with letter after letter presenting a far rosier image of a quick end to the conflict than was warranted. 'The present plight of Dewan Moolraj does not offer so decided an encouragement,' he wrote in his report to the Resident on 3 July, 'and I hear that he, yesterday, informed his officers that his resources were exhausted, that he could neither lavish on them rewards, or even give them their pay; that those who were not prepared to fight for their mere religion, had better leave him; many are said to have taken him at his word.' Delay or tardiness only meant more canons would be cast inside the city to replace those captured, which would make things more difficult later.

> I trust that it will not be thought presumptuous on my part to moot again the settled question of immediate action, or delay till the cold weather; but the enemy is now reduced to so humble a position; is so hemmed in, disheartened by defeats, and weakened by desertions, since the last battle, that we all here feel it would be matter for great regret, if you should not bring to bear on the rebellion, at once, the very little extra impulse which is required to end it. Such is the state of feeling now in the rebel army, that I am quite confident the announcement of a British brigade and heavy train leaving Lahore or Ferozepore for Mooltan, would be the signal for so great a desertion, as would leave the fort in a hopeless state of indefensibility.

Only the heavy guns, sappers and miners along with two European regiments and two native regiments were needed to tip the balance now and close proceedings.

Edwardes was strongly supported in his view by Lt Lake, whose reports also made out the city would fall with only the slightest of effort. 'The battle of Suddoosam will doubtless confirm you in those views,' wrote Lt Lake on 6 July, 'for it has reduced the rebel Moolraj to so abject a condition and made his followers so dispirited that no combination of circumstances would render him less formidable than he is now. His cause is now wholly despaired of; large numbers of his adherents are daily deserting him even the so called Bhaee Maharaj Sing has thought it prudent to decamp and the news of a British force being on its way to Mooltan will be enough to disperse those who are still wavering.'

Bhai Maharaj had in in fact had left Multan already. Tiring of Mulraj's indecision and military incompetence himself, he had decided to strike north and continue his own insurrection in the hills.

Two weeks after the battle, Edwardes continued to send in confident report after report to Lahore, still hoping to change Currie's mind. Mulraj was strengthening his fort but in an entirely disheartened manner, he reported. The swings in his moods from desperation to confidence and back again left his soldiers undecided on their future and consequently his relations with them fluctuated wildly day by day. Colourful and comical reports on the governor were relayed to Lahore. 'Moolraj himself as well as his troops is at his wit's end,' reported Edwardes to the Resident from Tibbee on 13 July, 'sometimes he talks of a night attack and sits up all night in a Hindoo temple near the bridge cased in chain armour from head to foot like Don Quixote watching for his knighthood in the cathedral aisle. But nothing comes of it. Another time he talks of cutting the canal but is restrained from doing so by fear of destroying the fort ditch. One day he fortifies the city, another day he fortifies the fort. Today he tells all his soldiers to leave him because he has got no money to pay them and tomorrow keeps up their spirits by assuring them that when iron shot fail he will fire silver on the besiegers.'

Whether these stories were true or mere hearsay was never substantiated but other evidence suggested Mulraj was by no means as weak and desperate as portrayed by Edwardes. It was quite true that many deserters from the city, disheartened by seeing Mulraj lose twice, were making their way to Edwardes camp or simply walking off home, but there was a continuous stream of new recruits arriving at the city lured both by nationality and/or the good wages on offer by Mulraj. These men were trekking down from the north and the Manjha area. Edwardes would complain to Currie that the local Sikh authorities were doing little to stop these men from travelling down south. They could easily be intercepted by local officials and police along the way. Moreover, with the city not being besieged as yet it was easy for them to enter. Currie replied that he knew this all too well from the Bhai Maharaj incident but could do little.

For other men, generally mercenaries, it seemed beneficial from a pecuniary point of view not to see Mulraj defeated too rapidly. Despite Mulraj being on the defensive, many irregulars were eager to join him simply to keep the contest going. That Mulraj still had plenty of money was obvious. A promise of a shilling a day plus a pension along with a leave of absence every three years was dangled in front of the levies of the British and saw a small but steady stream taking up the offer and moving the opposite way to the deserters from the city. On 3 July, just two days after the battle at Sadoosam, for example, intelligence had been received by Edwardes that around 200 men had deserted his own ranks and joined Mulraj. On 5 July, 400 men from Sheikh Imam-Ud-Deen's force suddenly deserted to Mulraj. These were in addition to the raw recruits that were drifting by tens and twelves into the city every day. Due to these additions, Mulraj's overall strength was now increasing, albeit slowly, much of it of questionable quality apart from the 3,000 to 4,000-strong core of Sikh and Gurkha troops he could draw upon.

There were other potential recruits as well nearby. Shere Singh's force had by now advanced from Toulumba to Gogran, just 25 km from Multan, at the wishes of the Resident. His closer proximity allowed Mulraj's agents to make extra efforts to woo the Sikh soldiers, something Edwardes in his correspondence had always warned Currie about, and already some Sikh regulars from Shere Singh's contingent were seen and heard making their way to the city. These Sikh troops, Edwardes pointed out, were the only force that could effectively and decisively swing things the way of Mulraj and therefore there was good reason for keeping them well away from Multan if possible.

Curiously, and despite Mulraj's defeat, it was noted most of the inhabitants of Multan appeared quite unconcerned about the arrival of Edwardes' army outside the city and continued to stay in the metropolis conducting their business; Edwardes' weakness in siege guns and therefore his inability to conduct a siege was obvious to all at this stage.

While he urged a change in policy by the Lahore Resident, Edwardes made plans to keep his force intact. Assuming a British force and siege guns would only come in the cold season meant a wait of several months outside the city till temperatures cooled. This meant his men doing little but sitting in camp, for a full encirclement was impossible with the means at his disposal. Allowing the nearly 20,000 irregulars he had now accumulated plus around five times as many camp followers to idle around Multan for this lengthy period was to court disaster. Many of these men were hardly fit to be called soldiers and were only present for the steady salary. Others were plain opportunists ready to profit from looting and robbery and general disorder if not kept busy in some fashion. Best, it was, to keep them busy in preparations for the arrival of the British column. Large amounts of cotton were ordered to be collected from the surrounding area. This he ordered to be stuffed into a large number of specially made bags by the men to act as protection from the city guns for the working parties, who now began preparing the ground close to the city. The Nawab of Bhawulpore was also asked to send 3,000 pioneers and other workers to build positions for batteries and guns as and when they arrived. Meanwhile, other men were ordered to prepare defensive works for the camp, set up around 6.5 km from the city in case of surprise sallies by the garrison, with entrenchments and defences to be dug around the circumference. To discourage the Multan garrison and conversely to keep morale high among his irregular force during the long wait till the cold months, news was also spread that a British siege train along with a powerful force was already being readied to assist in the reduction of the city.

# 16

# The First Siege of Multan

We have but to march and send by water a British force with siege guns about 220 miles
to effect our object at once.

Frederick Currie to Government of India, 10 July 1848

I adhere to the belief I have always entertained that the Dewan will die hard, and I
doubt we may suffer loss. He has under 5,000 men with him but these Sikhs fight, as we
know, well and long behind walls and guns.

Dalhousie to Duke of Wellington, 7 September 1848

The most important effect of the victories at Kyneerie and Sadoosam and Herbert Edwardes'
confident appeals for siege guns was Frederick Currie's decision to reverse his policy on waiting
till the cold season before a British column was despatched to Multan. Convinced by Edwardes'
analysis being reinforced by Lt Lake, Currie would now jettison any ideas of assembling a large
army and instead would sanction a smaller British force as per the original plan. One division,
around 5,000 men, complete with sixty guns including siege guns, would be quite sufficient,
he thought, to push the insurrection into oblivion. He did this with the confidence of a man
who believed all anti-British plots and nationalist forces in and around Lahore had either been
crushed or could be managed, allowing for a high proportion of the British troops from Lahore
to be sent down to Multan. With this in mind he wrote informing the Government of India on
10 July of the reversal of his previous policy and the imminent march of a British column into
the south of the Punjab.

Instead of the state of things in which the rebellion commenced, there is comparative
re-assurance throughout the Punjab districts, and we have a faithful army in our interest
of above 20,000 Mahomedans with 30 guns, investing Mooltan, and merely requiring the
aid of British skill, and British siege materiel, to enable them to reduce the fort, which
may, as further investigation and better information have established, be approached, and
attacked, at any season of the year. An overwhelming force, such as was not available, is
no longer necessary.

Sufficient carriage was available almost immediately, he argued, for a smaller British force. In
addition, with the climate unexpectedly moderate, the European troops were unlikely to be
taxed as much as had been expected. 'We have but to march, and send by water, a British force,
with siege guns, about 220 miles, to effect our object at once; and that object is the important one
of vindicating our power, by punishing the insulter of our authority, and the murderer of our

British officers, and of putting an end to a dangerous rebellion,' Currie continued. The Resident would further justify his volte-face, mentioning he had canvassed the opinion of the only two Europeans who had stayed in Multan for any length of time. These were Major Mackeson and Capt. Cunningham, and they both suggested operations could be done in comfort in July and August. He didn't explain why consultation with the above hadn't taken place earlier.

Orders for the assembly of this force would be given the very same day at Lahore, and the commander Currie chose to head this column would be Major-General William S. Whish, with Major Napier (later Lord Napier of Magdala) as the chief engineer. Whish's force would consist of brigades from both Lahore and Ferozepore so as not to leave the British hold on Lahore overly weakened. The first brigade formed at Lahore, to be led by Lt-Col Hervey, would consist of HM 10th along with the 8th and 82nd NI. With them would be one troop of native artillery and two squadrons of the 11th Native Cavalry and two squadrons of irregular native cavalry of the 14th Regiment. The supplies for this column were to sail down the Ravi River on boats while the troops marched down beside it. The second brigade, to be formed from the Ferozepore units, would consist of HM 32nd Foot with the 49th, 51st and 72nd NI accompanied by the 11th (regular) Light Cavalry and 11th Irregular Horse, all under the command of Col Markham of the 32nd Foot.

Similar to the Ravi column, the supplies for this column would sail down the Sutlej River with the troops marching beside it rendezvousing with the first column in front of Multan. Along with these columns would go the artillery of varying descriptions, including the thirty-two siege and heavy guns, of which six were 24-pounders and six 18-pounders along with twelve large and small mortars and six howitzers as well as sappers and miners collected at Ferozepore, totalling around 7,500 men. The siege train, slower to transport, was expected to reach Multan around ten days after the two columns of troops arrived, when operations against the city if required could immediately commence. The general consensus, however, was that any firing in anger would be entirely unnecessary as there was a good chance Mulraj would have surrender by then, or certainly would as soon as the British troops and formidable array of guns appeared before the city and an ultimatum given.

With the sanctioning of this force to Multan, and their march expected to be begin around two weeks later, a vast network of logistics quickly slipped into motion and all manner of supplies began to be gathered on the banks of the Sutlej. By 18 July, shot and shell along with food supplies from further afield began reaching Ferozepore on the backs of hundreds of camels every day. On 19 July the siege guns at Ferozepore were moved down to the riverbank and ammunition began to be loaded onto the boats by the artillerymen. Twenty-nine large boats had been collected with more being added. Along with this plenty of other carriage, carts and tumbrils had been gathered along with 22,800 cattle as well as elephants to facilitate its movement.

Currie had asked the Lahore Government for assistance as well and the Lahore Durbar provided forty boats on the Ravi with more being readied. Along with this nineteen large elephants (with eighteen more being brought in) and 600 oxen and 1,600 camels for the guns and carriage had been collected and handed over to British authorities. Over and above this, 6,000 more bullocks were being requisitioned for the carriage with special strong bags being made for carrying cannon shot along with 2,000 carts and hackeries. This was excluding the carriage, around 1,000 bullocks and 600 camels collected by Shere Singh and the Nawab at Bhawulpore. Both Whish and Currie were confident this would be more than sufficient for a mission that was not expected to last more than a few days in front of Multan.

One thing of concern, though, was the heat that had suddenly begun to arise in the days directly after Currie's decision and much to his chagrin. On 21 July, several European artillerymen would die, it was said, from heat exhaustion and overexertion during the preparations at the Sutlej. Perhaps because of this, it was decided all the European troops would now sail down to Multan on the boats while the sepoys would march by land. This would cause some complications, as the boats gathered were only sufficient for supplies as had been planned.

Meanwhile orders were sent to Edwardes to begin work to block the canals bringing water to Multan from the Chenab River. This would have the double benefit of reducing the water supply for the city and allowing successful siege operations as the nullahs frequently flooded over a wide area during the monsoon. He was also to send a complete report on the terrain and the features of the surrounding countryside round Multan in order to enable plans to be formulated in case Mulraj declined to surrender. This was to include information on the nature of the country between Bhawulpore Ghat and Multan in preparation for the transport of the siege guns which would be deposited at the ghat after being brought downstream.

\*\*\*

Dalhousie, when news reached him of the Resident reversing his decision, was not a little bemused. For the Resident had been only a few days earlier steadfastly in alliance with the Commander-in-Chief against marching any British troops early. Still siding with Gough himself on the issue of a grand campaign in the cold season, Dalhousie nevertheless was averse to stop the British force from advancing now the order had been given.

'When I received the Resident's despatch announcing he had ordered off a force and commenced his preparations, I had no option but to confirm his order,' he informed the Duke of Wellington. 'To hold the troops fast from the commencement was safe; to countermand the movement once commenced would have shown vacillation, and betrayed want of unity between the Resident and his Government; it would have disgusted our own men, and would have been attributed to fear, and to fear only, by the natives. Consequently it would have encouraged rebellion and have done more mischief than letting them go.' He was also cognisant of the need to allow Currie to make the ultimate decision. Sitting in Calcutta 1,900 km from the Punjab and Multan, it was essential to allow Currie the leeway to make the decisions himself. So Currie's decision would stand despite his reservations, a rather cold letter being written back promising support for his action: 'Since you have considered it necessary, in exercise of the powers conferred upon you, to assume this responsibility, and in pursuance of it, have issued publicly the orders for carrying your resolution into effect, the Government, being anxious to maintain your authority, do not withhold their confirmation of the orders you have issued.' With the decision having been taken, Dalhousie wished for as much vigour to be shown by the Resident as possible, with disregard to all hazards and issues that may crop up. Unlike Currie, he firmly believed this would be no quick operation. 'I adhere to the belief I have always entertained that the Dewan will die hard, and I doubt we may suffer loss,' he continued in his letter to the Duke of Wellington. 'He has under 5,000 men with him but these Sikhs fight, as we know, well and long behind walls and guns.'

\*\*\*

Back at Ferozepore and Lahore, meanwhile, preparations had been completed for travel down to Multan. At Ferozepore, on 24 July, with the confidence of the British troops high, a light and cheerful atmosphere prevailed at the departure of the Sutlej column with a British band playing at the riverbank as the men of the HM 32nd and the accompanying flotilla of boats drifted off. In addition to the boats, makeshift barges had been hastily assembled since the decision to transport all the European troops by river. The reason for choosing barges rather than boats had been that they could negotiate the shallowest sections of the river more easily, requiring just a few inches of draft. The barges proved both leaky and uncomfortable, however, and locals were employed in continually chucking out water over the side. Even with the quickly manufactured barges there turned out to be insufficient water transport, with some of the Ferozepore force having to wait a week before making their way down. Some of these barges carried thirty men while others only had a capacity of sixteen men and were crowded enough that there was no place to sit. Due to this discomfort, the troops were to draw the convoy of boats and rafts to the riverbank during evenings and nights, allowing them to stretch their legs and to sleep more easily on land during their journey down.

On 10 August, a Capt. Christopher with one of the British steamers on the Sutlej arrived upriver to assist. His steamer was one of five now taking an active part in the proceedings. The steamers *Comet*, *Meanee* and *Conqueror* were stationed on the Chenab while the *Planet* and *Nimrod* were plying the Sutlej to help transfer the troops and artillery stores to Multan. The boats and barges were connected to the steamer in a long chain to speed their passage downstream. At this time, because of the excessive twists and turns of the river in this area, the sepoys on foot had actually made more progress to Multan than the boats drifting down with the current but with the steamer the position was reversed and the boats took the lead.

By 12 August the Ferozepore columns had reached Kurrumpore near Bhawulpore and then took the route direct on foot to Multan, five marches to the west. The heat had in fact continued to rise to very high level for a while, prompting more fears during the voyage downstream. The temperature in a hospital tent despite being cooled by wet blankets was found to be 127 degrees Fahrenheit and on tents in hilly windy surroundings no less than 119 degrees, suggesting normal ambient temperatures may have been close to 60 degrees centigrade at this time, although temperatures dropped to much more tolerable levels shortly. HM 32nd on arrival at Bhawulpore were found to have lost eighteen men with ninety-six sick during the voyage, much of this being attributed to this burst of high temperature.

The Lahore column, meanwhile, had begun moving off downstream on the Ravi by 21 July. Similar to the Ferozepore column, the Europeans (HM 10th) and artillery moved by boat, the sepoys (8th and 52nd NI) along with the three companies of foot artillery and a troop of horse artillery and cavalry marched down the left bank of the river at the same time. The boats on the Ravi formed an impressive fleet nearly 5 km long. The force here had also moved off with a carefree attitude and much jollity on what was evidently thought to be a short trip rather than a campaign. 'The accounts from the land columns are most satisfactory, all are in high spirits at the trip, the only dissatisfied parties being those that are left behind while from the number of applications for permission to go with the force merely as amateurs, several of which have been granted by the General, one would think that the expedition was looked upon as one of pleasure rather than to be accompanied danger and distress,' mused the Resident on the news returning from the convoy on 31 July.

Meanwhile, vast amounts of ammunition and other supplies would continue to be sent down for the next two weeks or so to Bhawulpore. Major-General Whish himself left Lahore on 24 July, three days after the Ravi column departed. The journey down to Multan for both columns proved largely uneventful. Mulraj had barely enough resources to contest Edwardes'

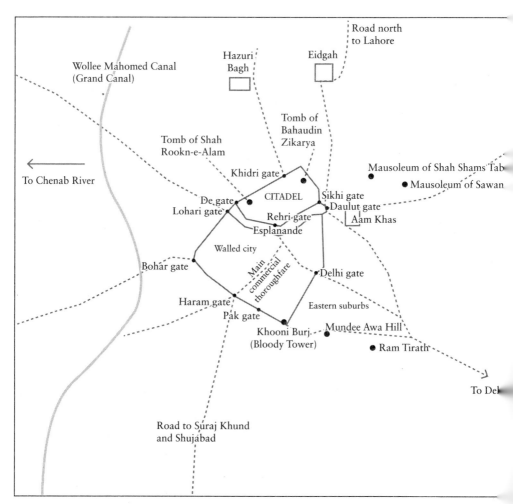

4. Close-up of Multan city

force, let alone the Whish's columns. The only incident occurred on 16 August when Whish's Ravi force was still around 24 km from the city. A small force, possibly on a reconnaissance mission outside the city, approached Whish's camp at around 2 p.m. The British general had ordered his column to be ready to turn out at the shortest notice. There appears to have been some skirmishing lasting around one and a half hours before the Multan force retired. Mulraj according to the prisoners taken had sent out 1,500 infantry and 350 horse in total. None were killed on the British side but eight wounded. The Multan force suffered eighteen dead and some were captured. The Lahore and Ferozepore columns would meet at Multan between 18 and 19 August, the citadel of the city being easily visible in the distance for several days prior to arrival.

\*\*\*

With the arrival of Whish's force, the large and now very motley force comprising the British force and its many allies took up position in a wide arc round the eastern end of the city to show its resolution to take the city. Whish's columns would set up camp at Sital-ki-Mari (Mareeseethul), an open plain around 4 km north-east of the city fortress and well outside the range of its guns. Edwardes', Van Courtlandt's and the Nawab of Bhawulpore's men meanwhile, still camped at Suraj Khund, around 10 km south of the city, were now ordered to join up and take up positions at the city alongside Whish's units. To the immediate left of Whish (i.e. to his south) were positioned Courtlandt's and Edwardes' contingents. Arcing round the south of the city and to the left of Edwardes' force would sit the army of the Nawab of Bhawulpore. Extending the arc round to the south of the city were the troops of Sheikh Imam-Ud-Deen from Lahore. Completing the arc round the city and to its west were the Sikh troops of Shere Singh, a force of around 3,000 men, who had also reached Multan by now. Meanwhile Sirdar Utter Singh, a Sikh commander, had also joined on 14 July with 6,000 men, ten guns and two mortars.

All in all this composite and extremely diverse force totalled over 32,000 men with seventy-five guns of both heavy and smaller calibre, although surprisingly only 2,000 of this total (HM 10th and HM 32nd along with other assorted units) were European. Opposing them at this time, give or take the continuous defections and new recruits, was a garrison estimated at 7,000–12,000 men with between fifty-two and fifty-six guns. This was comprised of the nucleus of Sikh and Gurkha professional soldiers of 4,000 to 5,000 men with the rest of the men being irregulars, recent recruits and mercenaries of varying levels of loyalty and discipline.

\*\*\*

Despite the enormous strength in numbers, there was little Whish, who now took over formal command of the allied force from Edwardes, could do prior to the big siege guns arriving. What was equally obvious was that the garrison wasn't about to surrender merely on sight of British soldiers. Therefore the two-and-a-half-week interval before the guns finally arrived was spent in reconnaissance and preparations for siege with little in the way of fighting and with most of the troops of both sides having an opportunity for rest and repose.

Not that this time was entirely uneventful. A poisoning incident was discovered a week after the arrival of British columns. On 26 August, a local man who was initially thought to be a camp follower was seen selling milk in the British camp. Many of the men from HM 32nd were seen eagerly buying large quantities and consuming it promptly. Half an hour after drinking the milk, many of the men were seen to be foaming from their mouths and complained of feeling quite ill, with many vomiting and experiencing severe pain. It was apparent the milk had been poisoned. The men recovered later, with the doctors being called.

Three days after the poisoning incident, on 29 August, the whole of the British force moved a mile closer to the city, prompting some skirmishing; the firing of guns and muskets was heard all the following night, although Whish had no inclination to escalate things at this point. With the arrival of the siege guns imminent, plans for cutting off the water supply to the city by closing the nullahs bringing water from the Chenab, already commenced by Edwardes, were completed. This also had the added advantage of making life easier for the British force in case of flooding, for there was a fear that the Chenab, heavily swollen at this time, would inundate the nullahs perhaps to the point of overflowing and cause much disruption for the besieging army round the city. The nullahs irrigating the area did not run from the nearest point to the city but acted as almost minor streams, diverging from the river as far as 27 km north and running southwards parallel to the river before reaching Multan. A hundred workmen supplied with entrenching tools were sent on board the steamer *Conqueror* upriver to where the big nullahs drawing water departed from the Chenab. They were to cut the water supply by damming the junction of the nullahs with the river. To protect the workmen, a party of a thousand Sikh soldiers with two guns were sent north under the Sikh officer Mallee Singh. Here they dug in along an entrenchment around 4,000 yards from one nullah to another, providing a good defence and with the 26-pounders placed in battery. A British steamer stayed too, the water being a depth of 5 feet, with its guns aimed at the bank giving further protection.

There was little initial success in damming the waters. The river was in flood and the mud-and-stone dams constructed could not withstand the pressure of the swollen waters. Twice the dams were constructed and twice they were washed away. The third time the dams held as the river waters finally began subsiding. How much impact the damming of the nullahs had is unknown. Though it harmed the gardens and nearby crops, the city had an ample supply of wells and none of the stories of the conditions in the city leaked out by deserters or informers later indicate at any time a shortage of water. Nevertheless, once the dams were made these men were set to cutting the local trees for making fascines and gabions for the besieging army. Ten of the boats in British hands were then used to transport the material downstream to the British camp over the following days.

The 1,000 men, all Sikhs, along with the steamboats were now stationed permanently at this place despite little chance of an enemy attack. This gave rise to the perception among these men and their Commander Mallee Singh that they had been quietly moved away from the battlefield, something that would annoy them greatly. The conclusion they had come to was correct, for Whish and Edwardes, who heavily distrusted the Sikh soldiers, had used the damming as a pretext, the fear being these men may defect en masse to Mulraj. This policy would have severe repercussions a fortnight later.

***

Regarding the siege of the city, Whish also began organising a more thorough reconnaissance of the approaches to Multan and its fortress. On 1 September, strong diversionary attacks were carried out by the forces of Edwardes, Courtlandt and Sheikh Imam-Ud-Deen against the south of the city, allowing the general to do an exploratory tour of the northern approaches to the fort with Col Franks (HM 10th), Col Markham (HM 32nd) and Major Napier of the Engineers and several other Engineers under the guise of an attack using HM 10th, two companies of HM

32nd, elements of the 8th and 52nd NI, six guns and a troop of the 11th Cavalry and elements of Wheeler's horse. The advance was carried out as far south as the Eidgah, using the mosque minarets as observation posts. The mosque being barely within range of the fort guns, a lively cannonade was initiated by the garrison once they were spotted. Whish and his coterie were fortunate, one of the shots passing just over his head and under a certain Dr Thorp of the Irregular Horse. Another passed through a group of accompanying sappers without causing any fatalities. As the gunners in the fort began finding their distance more accurately, the Eidgah was abandoned and the British line withdrawn 1,100 yards to the north before a return to the camp was ordered. Some of the garrison had sallied out to fight Edwardes' force and there had been some heavy skirmishing in the gardens to the south of the city, with the fort guns opening up. The heavy cannonade lasted several hours. After some time the garrison troops were forced to move back towards the walls and the protection of the fort guns.

These reconnaissance missions revealed to Whish that Edwardes had been far too confident in his appraisal of the situation. The fort was generally reckoned to be the strongest in India for good reason and even though the bulk of the garrison were irregulars and numerically insufficient to hold the city and fortress together in good fashion, taking both would be no simple feat. Adding to the difficulties posed by the fortress was the terrain. The extensive suburbs which spilled out past the city walls made a general advance difficult and provided good hiding places for snipers as well as makeshift defensive areas. Each house could easily be turned into a defensive compound protected by the fort guns on the city walls behind. Then there was the matter of the huge number of irrigation channels and nullahs crisscrossing the whole area round the walled city. 'The number of water cuts is surprising and you cannot take a gallop of a hundred yards without coming across one', commented the *Delhi Gazette* correspondent who had arrived recently to cover the siege of the city. This made the use of cavalry next to impossible in the suburbs and the transport of men, material and supplies slow unless the area was entirely drained of water – hence the blocking of the nullahs upstream had been essential. Nevertheless, traversing dry water channels with the few bridges available was still an obstacle for guns and supplies. Adding to the problem were the numerous gardens and groves of trees and walled areas that during peace made the city pleasant to live in but during war impaired vision of the whole area for anyone on ground level. There were also an exceptional number of brick kilns with chimney stacks and other high buildings dotted around the suburbs which helped to obscure the lay of the land still further.

While Whish and Edwardes decided on the best course of action, skirmishing continued. The area of the Sheedee mound was fought over. This was an area of high ground situated halfway between the city walls and the British camp that offered a good strategic view over the city walls on the east of the city and surrounding area. Reconnaissance continued also close to the walls, sappers and miners going close as possible to examine the weak points of the city's defences, although the city guns were quick to open up on any activity below. The first trenches were also being dug, albeit relatively far from the city. Over the next days they would be moved closer to the city and batteries also began to be erected.

***

The siege train accompanied by its escort, the 11th Irregular Horse and the 49th NI, finally wound its way into the camp on 4 September. The convoy that came in on this day consisted of 280 bullock carts and 3,500 camels carrying baggage and munitions and other stores and was so lengthy that the rear of the train had not left its previous night's camp 13 km away by the time the head reached Multan. Hundreds of camels had also been arriving each day for several days prior to this with all manner of supplies. Before Whish's arrival, Edwardes had already been told to warn the inhabitants of Multan in no uncertain terms to evacuate the city if they wished to save their lives and property. Therefore a proclamation had been drawn on 22 July and widely circulated in the city urging all to leave before Whish's arrival. This though seemed to have had little impact with few departures being seen from the city gates. Having the required material and men for an assault on the city, Whish had high hopes that the array of firepower, resources and a large fighting force, eminently noticeable from the city walls, would now awe not just the citizens of the city but the garrison into deserting their governor, thus negating the prospects of real and destructive hostilities. Therefore a second proclamation was drawn up that evening. Whish's initial draft made no mention of the Sikh government or the Maharajah of Lahore in whose territory the siege was being conducted. However, the general had taken the precaution of passing the draft to Edwardes, who on scanning the proclamation noticed the glaring error. Multan was Sikh territory and it would be imprudent to not mention that the operation was being carried out in the Maharajah's name. 'It would seem as if we had already determined to confiscate the State,' he pointed out to the general. Including Duleep Singh's name would both counter the rampant rumours that the Punjab would be annexed if the British operation was successful and discourage any Sikh soldiers from joining Mulraj. Whish concurred entirely and would change the proclamation, inserting 'and her ally Maharajah Dulleep Sing' into the line mentioning the Queen of Great Britain. Copies of the final draft of the proclamation which read as follows were produced in quantity to be distributed liberally inside the city and its suburbs.

Proclamation

By Major-General Whish CB commanding the army before Mooltan addressed to the inhabitants and garrison thereof.

I invite both to an unconditional surrender, within twenty four hours after the firing of a royal salute, at sunrise to-morrow (5 September) in honour of HM the Queen of Great Britain and her ally Maharajah Dulleep Sing.

I shall, otherwise in obedience to orders of the Supreme Government of India, commence hostilities, on a scale that must ensure early destruction to the rebel traitor and his adherents, who, having begun their resistance to authority with a most cowardly act of treachery and murder seek to uphold their unrighteous cause, by an appeal to religion, which everyone must know to be sheer hypocrisy.

If the town be surrendered to me, as above suggested, private property will be respected; and the garrison of the fort will be permitted to withdraw unmolested, on giving up Dewan Moolraj and his immediate associates, and laying down their arms at one of the eastern gates of the town and fort respectively.

Given under my hand and seal this 4th day of September 1848
(Signed) WJ Whish
Major-Gen. Comg.

The proclamation sent into the city by messengers coincided with the last of the siege train guns arriving. At sunrise on the morning of 5 September, as a further demonstration of the military strength at his disposal, Whish ordered a grand parade of his entire force within viewing distance of the city walls and a royal salute of twenty-one guns to be fired. The proclamation had no real immediate effect. None of the spies inside the city reported any disaffection. Rather the royal salute prompted the fortress gunners to open up as well. Six 12-pound shots were fired at British lines and the British gunners fired back in response, bringing a premature end to the lull and the start of an artillery exchange that lasted the rest of the day.

It was later discovered the amnesty had an effect on at least one high-placed official who nevertheless had no opportunity to desert. That was Rung Ram, Mulraj's brother and commander at Kyneerie. Informers apparently brought out news that, after Whish's arrival, he had been trying to establish communication between himself and the British force outside and the Lahore authorities. He was evidently of the belief further resistance was futile. For this action, Mulraj had his brother arrested and Rung Ram would be kept in prison for the rest of the siege.

Seeing that his proclamation had triggered no mass exodus or displays of white flags on the city walls and therefore no peaceful conclusion was likely, preparations for the siege were immediately put into operation by Whish. Prize agents were appointed to attend to the considerable booty expected to fall into the hands of the force and plans made to capture all the garrison defensive works and key points outside the city walls. All assaults it was decided would be on the garrison defences on the eastern side of the city before attention could be given to the city walls by the siege guns. There were several points in particular that needed to be captured prior to an attack on the walled city. The first was the Sheedee mound, the piece of high ground on which stood the Ram Tirath, a Hindu temple complex. Mulraj had placed some infantry with one gun at this structure, which had been constantly troubling the British pickets and advanced posts in the last few days. The second was the Hummund Ghurree, a well-defended outwork closer to the city walls.

While plans to deal with these garrison outposts were being formulated, the British mortars began to fire in earnest into the city for the first time on the evening of 6 September, signalling the start of a more brutal chapter in the proceedings. Edwardes' force, also provided with two howitzers from the siege train, opened up as well on the city from the south in what would be a prelude to formal operations the next day. The large number of shells fired on this day had the effect of finally driving out some of the inhabitants.

During the night six 18-pounders and four 8-inch mortars were also moved 1,200 yards from the city walls in the south-east of the city to clear out the suburbs of defenders. The plan was to eventually move the 18-pounders within 400–500 yards of the walls and commence effecting a breach in the city walls. A storming party consisting of the HM 32nd, the 49th and 51st NI along with McKenzie's horse artillery was readied in case a breach was made quite rapidly with the possibility of a *coup de main*. A closer inspection and initial fighting found that the interval between the British lines and the city walls was defended in organised fashion with good entrenchments by a stubborn foe, and there was little chance of an early breakthrough.

The attack on the Ram Tirath structure on the hill took place early on 7 September. At 3 a.m., before daybreak, Capt. Anderson led a party consisting of the 72nd NI and most of the 11th Irregular Cavalry along with three guns. To support them, a battery of two 8-inch howitzers and three 8-inch mortars were placed to the left of the Ram Tirath while four 18-pounders and a rocket were placed to the right, the guns being placed so they were not apparent from the city walls or the fort. The defenders were driven back easily into a village closer to the city walls. Here they were under some protection from the fort guns but a determined push sent them into the fort. The British force had six men killed in this operation. At the same time Edwardes' force in the south continued to fire upon the fort with its howitzers to keep the garrison distracted.

The same day of the capture of the Ram Tirath, Whish called his principal officers and engineers to a meeting to assess the best way forward for an assault on the walled city itself. Major Napier, the chief engineer, had drawn up two plans. The first plan was a *coup de main*, a surprise attack on the Khooni Burj in the southeast of the city. An ambitious attempt to capture the city on one day, all the siege guns would target that section of the city walls prior to a general assault later in the day. Many of the officers warned however there would be substantial casualties even if success was achieved, the chance of which was slight and that an early repulse would harm British prestige.

The second option was to attack the fort itself from the north by regular approaches. This would take time but would result in much fewer casualties. Once the fort fell, the capture of the city would be relatively easy, it was argued. Edwardes however would have to keep the road to Bhawulpore to the south open for supplies from that quarter and he voiced concerns over whether this was possible or not at the same time. This plan would also mean Whish's force moving from the east of the city where camp had been established to the north. This led to its rejection, it being felt by many officers this would be taken as a sign of inability by the British to take the city from the east, a perception that would also have an unfavourable effect on the British allies and buoy up the garrison's morale.

It was finally decided to essentially keep the present position and to run trench and defensive works from the north-east of the fort in a line to the Ram Tirath, a distance of about a mile. The siege batteries instead would be allowed to do much destructive work to minimise British casualties as far as possible. On the morning of the 7th the parallel trenches to the fort had already been commenced by the sappers and miners. Eight hundred British troops during the night and the same number of sepoys during the day set to work on the new trenches and making approaches to the city. It had also been noticed that all the buildings or defendable points between the city walls and British lines had been occupied or strengthened to some degree and were manned by men of the garrison and that these needed to cleared first.

Fighting for the Ram Tirath would continue the next day, the garrison sallying out to try and recapture the position but being repulsed. The day after the capture of the Ram Tirath, a heavy battery was placed within 600 yards of the Khooni Burj, the tower on the south-east of the city. The only thing that worried the confident Whish during these days was the heat, which had again risen to a high of 114 degrees Fahrenheit in the British tents, outside being yet higher, although it fell significantly after a few days, lessening his concerns.

The only significant place remaining to the garrison east of the city walls by 9 September was the Hummund Ghurree, the strengthened position close to the walls, and this would cause Whish considerable problems. This consisted of two clusters of houses. The cluster closer to the British lines had a large Hindu temple in it while the further cluster was close to another large sand mound on which a battery of guns had been placed by the defenders. A house in addition had been turned into a stronghold by a portion of the garrison with the windows filled in with loopholes for the muskets and hence making it difficult to capture. Inside this house and the surrounding area 400 defenders were dug in, marshalled by Jhube Singh, a relative of Mulraj and a very able commander, as it proved.

An initial attack was done late on the 9th around 9 p.m. in the darkness by portions of the HM 10th, 49th and 72nd NI led by Lt-Col Pattoun. An attack was launched against the fortified house itself with the door being forced open but so great was the resistance that capturing it proved impossible.

'Three times they rushed to the walls and three times were driven back shattered. Once the door was burst open by an officer of the 69th (Richardson) and a man of the 10th; the former was no sooner in than his face and body were covered with sword cuts; severe wounds he received as he was dragged away. Death's hand was so heavy that the place could not be held, and the party was obliged to retire, taking possession of an old building and demi-fort-looking house about 300 yards in rear. Thus perished many a gallant fellow,' described eyewitness Henry Daly of the 60th Rifles, who had made his way up to the city before his regiment would arrive.

A retreat was ordered. As the British troops withdrew, they were pursued by the defenders buoyed by their success. The British attack had ended up suffering a fair number of casualties, four officers being wounded and HM 10th suffering six killed with two officers and thirty-six men wounded (thirty severely) out of ninety that took part, the 49th having twenty-eight wounded. Two men of the 10th and one of 72nd NI were also taken prisoner with overall casualties running to 150 men in the attack.

After the abortive attack, there was also some heavy firing from both sides elsewhere on the 9th along with musket volleys with some of the fort guns managing to fire shells into the British camp. Flush with success, the defenders with their lone gun had also continued to fire into the advance British positions all night. Meanwhile Mulraj had sent some troops out elsewhere with the attention of disrupting the British working parties, although with no success. In order to pummel the defenders, a British battery was set up overnight consisting of four guns which the defenders attempted to stop being erected but were repelled. 'I saw our colonel in the morning; he looked very pale and in great trouble of mind. He did not like being defeated but he was in good spirits and joked with the men,' recalled Corporal John Ryder of HM 32nd on the morning of the 10th as plans were made to launch another attack on the garrison position. However, this never materialised as it was decided to soften up the garrison position for a further day before another attempt on the 11th. That day, the garrison outpost was continuously bombarded by four 5.5-inch mortars and three 8-inch mortars to the south.

However, the planned attack on the 11th was also cancelled because a fierce wind blew up huge amounts of dust all day, making an attack awkward, although the steady barrage on the compound was maintained. By this time, it had been noticed by the men of the outpost that during the night British lines were more vulnerable, the pickets being less vigilant than required and British guns frequently silent. On the night of the 11th, they therefore made a counter-attack which had moderate success and which allowed then to set up a battery in a garden in a more advance position.

Although the British camp round the city had been set up at such a distance to be safe from gunfire from the fortress and city, it was quickly found this was not so as balls appeared, causing confusion. These were almost exclusively the fire of a single gun, the only gun with sufficient range to reach the British camp having been placed on the portion of the city wall closest to the British camp. By necessity it became a target for the British artillery, which attempted to silence it over the next week although without any fortune; it continued to fire till the end of the siege of the city. The gun developed a sort of fame in the British camp, as Henry Daly would describe.

There I stood under my first fire of heavy shot. Brown and I had walked out in front to look at a battery the Sikhs were busy erecting, a sound indescribable was heard just over our head, and about 10 feet in our rear, a ball, a cross between an 18 and 24-pounder, fell slap between the horses of an artillery waggon; the shock floored one, but killed none. The distance from which this came could not have been less than 1 and 3/4 miles. It is a gun which, from his constant visits since, has obtained great celebrity in camp under the title of 'Long Tom', 'John Long'; his voice and range are alike peculiar: after the Sikh artillerymen had succeeded in obtaining the range of the 'Ramtirat' during the whole day he fell about in a manner most unpleasing to gents who love their ease and comfort, some two or three sepoys being cut to pieces by him; yet 100 shot from him must have fallen within a space of 50 square yards.

Whish, meanwhile, dismayed by the failure to take the outpost for several days, determined on making a much more significant attack on the 13th. At 7 a.m. of that day, twelve companies of European and two regiments of native infantry – above 2,500 men in all, some claiming 3,000 troops (1,000 of which were European) – accompanied by a troop of horse artillery under Capt. Mackenzie and a squadron of cavalry from each of the three regiments were readied under Brig. Hervey while batteries continued to bombard the garrison stronghold. The attack would be commanded by Col Pattoun (Brig. Markham having been wounded on the 10th) and Major Montizambert while 1,000 troops were kept back to protect the baggage. The windy, dusty conditions prevailed until 4 p.m., when the wind subsided and the attack was ordered. The fighting wasn't easy. 'The enemy's fire was so dreadful that we were ordered to lie down when the balls skimmed over us by thousands,' wrote John Ryder, part of the attack force. 'The musket balls came shower after shower, cutting the grass off close to our heads or burying themselves in the sand close by whilst the cannon shot was ploughing the earth up all round.'

Eventually the British line moved forward, coming across a deep nullah around 12 feet deep and 5 yards wide after around 200 yards of advance. This was crossed, one man being killed while crossing. The cavalry and artillery brought with the column could not cross and the infantry therefore continued on its own.

'The reception given at the building was most desperate. The place was full of loopholes and swings for camel-guns; but so gallant was the foe that on our approach they rushed outside to charge us. The 32nd on seeing this, doubled in with a cheer. Now the struggle began: the enemy got back, and every loophole was raging death,' Henry Daly wrote of the contest. Ladders allowed for scaling of the building, which had a square roof the soldiers of HM 32nd managed to clamber onto, although Col Pattoun died in the attempt. He had called for ladders to escalade other buildings in the village which could not be seen earlier because of the foliage in the village. Daly continues:

While we were on the top of the first place, which was built of mud, the fire which had been ignited at the bottom by some of the men, flamed forth, and the centre, weakened by the loopholes which we had made to command those inside, came down with a great shudder. The flame caught their ammunition, of which we knew not, and the interior trembled fearfully, and the cry was raised, 'Mine!' A fearful sight ensued, the dying and wounded so thickly packed, friends and foes, though comparatively few of the former at this place, were engulfed in the flame, which burst out with renewed vigour, having caught some of the dried grass which had been their beds: poor wretches, their clothes were on fire, the little they had! I got almost accustomed to this during the day, for many, many did I see burning alive, their skin baked. Their matchlock lights, burning when they were shot, set their clothes in a flame, and their burnt skins were crackling as the miserable creatures were weltering in the grilling sun.

The walls of the village were scaled and the fighting became general and intense. The sheer weight of numbers of the attackers now told, although there was determined resistance. 'We soon made ourselves masters of the first village but the encounter was terrible as the enemy were no cowards nor were they afraid of cold steel,' related Ryder. 'They defended every inch of ground most bravely but we drove them from house to house, leaving numbers of dead behind them. They fought desperately for the temple, for it was full of men. One of their chief officers had taken up his quarters here. He and all the men inside were killed I believe; not one escaped; they did not ask for quarter and none was given.'

At length, the loopholed house was broken into with rifle butts. Near the end of the fight, one of the defenders set off a mine which killed both the remnants of the defenders and the attackers close by. The fighting here had been the fiercest and most uncompromising seen yet. The commander of the outpost, Jhube Singh, died defending his position with his men as well.

The first village having been captured, attention now switched to the second where the remnants of the defenders had retreated, a garden pleasure house beautifully built and guarded by fifty defenders, found dead later. 'In this some spoil was found, and many carried away much who were not there when we entered. Swords, percussion pistols, were in a hole in the wall – silks etc. In a little cool place separate from the building, as we ran through, I espied a bed which had not been long quitted, evidently from its appearance belonging to one of their chiefs. Peacock's plumes for brushing away the flies from the sleeper lay at the head. I seized one of these: all my plunder! The sepoys plundered much, and there was none to stay them,' wrote Henry Daly on the entry into the second village.

Since the garrison defenders had been pushed out, the advance continued. However, it was a confused and disorganised move. Col Pattoun was thought to have died and the men were in no semblance of order and scattered round the vicinity. Few men knew for sure of his death and the next-in-command feared ordering a retreat in case Pattoun was alive. Some casualties resulted from a desultory attack on the city walls and retreat followed shortly, helped along by determined firing from the defenders. This retreat encouraged the few of the garrison troops still outside the walls and they rushed forward to harry the retreating British line but were too few in number to make it count. Whish gave orders to maintain the advance positions captured while the houses and buildings in the area were razed to the ground bar several strong structures which would be used by the British for shelter. Sappers moved in, blowing up the various houses and setting others on fire; containing powder and ammunition, they blew up with much more energy than expected.

That evening an informal ceasefire took place on both sides, with Whish ordering funeral pyres for the burning of the dead of the garrison in the captured positions. The British dead were recovered for burial as well, unmolested by the city defenders, and the whole presented a very melancholy picture, with a considerable stench hanging in the air as the cremations and burials took place. 'The field all round presented a most awful sight of the wreck of the action. Broken arms of all description lay strewed all round with dead men and horses. The village was but a heap of ruins,' wrote Ryder.

With the stronghold captured, in the evening the trenches began to be advanced again in the direction of the city and British batteries advanced into the village. Fighting continued well into the night. The capture of this outpost and surroundings was significant, for all garrison outposts east of the walled city had now been captured and this allowed the British guns to all be moved to within 600 yards of the eastern walls of the city and to finally turn their attention to the city and fortress walls themselves.

The close-quarters combat during the last few days had taken its toll, however. On the British side, there had been thirty-nine killed, 216 wounded and four missing. However, thirteen of the wounded were officers. The more notable among the British dead were Col R. T. R. Pattoun (32nd Foot), Major T. S. Montizambert (10th Foot), Quartermaster G. Taylor (32nd Foot) and Lt T. Cubitt (49th NI). Lt Bunny of the horse artillery was also wounded. Whish, gazing at the action from too close, also had a horse shot under him during the attack on the Hummund Ghurree. The defenders of the Multan outposts suffered much more in comparison. Of the estimated 400 defenders, it was noted only five survived to make their way back to the city. Around 100, if not more, were thought to have been killed by the intense British artillery fire on the village during the several days before the capture of the outpost. The rest of the men fought bravely to the death; their bodies were found heaped in various places. Many of the bodies were found scorched by the landmine that had been detonated.

*** 

With the British and allied troops situated so close to the city, one of the issues noted during this early fighting was how easily the garrison irregulars, spies and saboteurs could move within the separate British camps round the city. This was largely caused by the allied force being so diverse, with both the Multan irregulars and the Bhawulpore men along with Edwardes' recruits from the Derajat not wearing any sort of uniform. Several men had been challenged in the British camps over the last few weeks by suspicious officers and asked for their identity. The answer would invariably be that they were with Edwardes or Courtlandt's men if they happened to be in Whish's encampment or with Bhawul Khan's sepoys if they were within Edwardes' area, and so on, at which point they were allowed to proceed as checking the men's credentials was too time-consuming and the camps too open in any case to stop locals or spies from venturing in. During the battles, too, many of the Bhawulpore men had said they had been shot at by the other allies, being easily mistaken for defenders due to the lack of uniform.

One of the more serious consequences of mistaken identity for the British happened on 9 September. A section of the garrison who had sallied out was cut off and had quietly sauntered into Whish's camp. A British officer, Lt Lloyd of the 8th NI, had refused to allow his men to fire on them as they had told the British pickets they were Bhawul Khan's men. Once in the camp they struck a conversation with Lt Lloyd after which one of them drew his tulwar on seeing an opportune moment and instantly killed him, nearly decapitating him in the process. They then walked out of the British camp as calmly as they had come in and made their way back to the city, with the dead officer discovered much later. On their way out they had conversations with British sepoys. 'We have no quarrel with you, it's only the Sahib-log: leave them and come along, every man shall have a gold necklace,' they were reported to have urged, but without success. No action was taken and in a sense there was little that could be done bearing in mind the lack of uniform and with the tribesman allies carrying no identification. One result of this incident was that any men from the city caught distributing letters in the British camps urging men to defect were henceforth bayonetted as policy.

So by the evening of 13 September, with all garrison outposts on the eastern side of the city captured and with British guns now trained firmly on the city walls in readiness for breaching and a final assault on the city, confidence was as high as it would get in the British camp. It was thought the city would fall within a matter of days once a breach was apparent.

However, events were to take an entirely unexpected turn the next day, upsetting Whish's plans completely. Despite the successes during the last few days, there had been puzzling whispers and rumours swirling around and through the allied camps that something major was about to occur. 'The enemy was gaining courage and something very strange was going on but our General kept everything very secret,' Corporal Ryder recorded. 'Still he could not help seeing that his handful of men was worn out with fatigue and hardship and the siege not yet commenced.'

These rumours were caused by events that were happening in parallel to the siege of Multan in the hilly province of Hazara, over 500 km to the north. The events there would cause the entire Sikh contingent of Whish's army to defect en masse, putting the general's position in grave peril and ending the siege of the city. A rebellion that appeared to be in its last stages was about to turn into a full-scale war.

# 17

# Chutter Singh and the Hazara Rebellion

Reports have been industriously circulated in Hazara that British influence has but a
month more to run.

James Abbott, 5 June 1848

I have commenced the fight at your call and you leave me to perish unaided.

Mulraj intercepted letter to Hazara soldiers, May 1848

The hilly northern province of Hazara, far away from the heat and commerce of Multan,
was generally seen as one of the backwaters of the Sikh Empire. Neither as picturesque as
neighbouring Peshawar across the Indus nor as rich and populous as the plains of the Punjab to
the south, this area on the left bank of the Indus had few points to recommend it. It had been
parcelled off recently to the newly promoted Maharajah Gulab Singh as part of his independent
domain with the signing of the Treaty of Amritsar. However, he had little interest in it. Tax
revenues were small, and the Muslim tribes resident in these parts were troublesome enough to
require a bigger garrison than he could afford. Finding he had not the wherewithal to enforce
his hold on this territory, Gulab Singh had quickly handed it back to Lahore before gaining
other, more attractive land elsewhere in exchange.

By the spring of 1848, as in other provinces around the Punjab after the Treaty of Bhyrowal,
there were two rulers in the province. One, the British political agent assigned to the area, Capt.
James Abbott, held real power; the other, Chutter Singh, the Sikh governor of the province,
had a more nominal power. The cool and unsettled relationship between these two men and its
subsequent breakdown would bring matters to a head in this part of the country and make a
direct impact on the siege of Multan.

Chutter Singh, an ageing and sickly man, was generally seen as a safe pair of hands by the
British prior to the insurrection at Multan. The governor came from the patrician family of the
Attariwalas, a wealthy clan with extensive jaghirs along the road from Rhotas to Attock close
to Hazara and at Rawalpindi. Several descriptions of what Chutter Singh physically looked
like survive. One of these was left by Dalhousie, who visited him after the war during his
incarceration at Lahore in November 1849. He described him as possessing a manly bearing,
something others would also remark on, and 'without the least approach to supplication, far
less to servility ... He is a fine looking old man with a good brow, aquiline features, and a mild
dignified countenance. His voice was deep and loud, his expression deliberate yet animated, and
his manner had all the measured grace which so marks the race.'

Other accounts also portray him in similar fashion and as being a military man of the time
of Ranjit Singh, one of the few along with his son Shere Singh who could garner considerable

respect from the Sikh soldiers. '[He] is looked up to by the Khalsas as the last of their old Sirdars,' George Lawrence, the British agent in Peshawar, had noted of Chutter Singh. Herbert Edwardes, who knew Chutter Singh, also had a high opinion, calling him 'one of the most sagacious persons in the Punjab' even after hostilities broke out.

Curiously, others had diametrically opposite views. John Lawrence was one of these as was Frederick Currie, who reported the following to the Government of India:

> Lieutenant Edwardes has, also, I consider, entirely overrated the talent of Sirdar Chuttur Sing in calling him one of the most sagacious persons in the Punjab. I know him but little, personally, but my impression, when I used to meet him, at the time of negotiating the treaty, was that he was a very stupid old man; and this I find is the general impression among those who are well acquainted with him. Mr John Lawrence in a private letter received yesterday, writing of him, says 'I cannot, in any way account for Chuttur Sing's conduct; I always looked on him as a harmless old fool.' He is, moreover, now very infirm, and suffers much from chronic disease. His conduct is unaccountable except on the belief that he is acting under the advice and with the secret support of others.

What struck most observers on seeing the bespectacled governor face to face was his rapidly declining physical condition in what were his twilight years. He had a chronic but unknown illness. George Lawrence, passing by Hazara on his way to Peshawar to take up his new post, had gone to meet the elderly man. The governor, he noted on 1 February 1847, had been and was still very ill. He would ask his own apothecary, Mr Thompson, to prescribe some medicine for the governor. He continued declining, and by 10 April 1847 his health had deteriorated to such an extent that he could no longer attend a meeting with George Lawrence on another one of his visits, being quite unable to mount a horse. This ill health would continue to dog him through the year and into 1848, although there were better periods mixed with worse. A year later, for example, Chutter Singh was planning to travel the province on a tax-collecting trip but had to abort his journey. 'Sirdar Chutter Singh's health will scarcely admit of such an exposure,' noted James Abbott in his diary on 30 April 1848.

His illness belied an active and politicking mind, however. Chutter Singh had dabbled in the Lahore power struggles in earlier years after the death of Ranjit Singh. He had been instrumental in the murder of Peshora Singh, one of the sons of Ranjit Singh and a legitimate heir to the throne. The prince was a favourite of the army, however, and Jowahir Singh, who was Vizier at the time and sanctioned the murder, was quickly killed by troops in Lahore. Chutter Singh had been luckier and had escaped death by finding refuge with his old friend Gulab Singh in Jammu. Taking no part in the First Anglo-Sikh War, he resurfaced to sign the treaty with the British following the war in 1846.

'Chutter Singh was much dissatisfied at the loss of power and influence he and other old leading sirdars had suffered by the assumption of the supreme administration of the Punjaub by the British Government, and he was willing to join in any attempt to restore a pure Sikh sovereignty to the country,' commented George Lawrence on the governor's feeling towards the Treaty of Bhyrowal.

This much was true, but it's unclear whether Chutter Singh ever had any real intentions of heading a rebellion in Hazara province in his present situation. One source that suggested he was willing was another Durbar member, Sheikh Imam-Ud-Deen, who would later mention Shere Singh, Chutter's son, receiving messages in early June from his father that he would rise against the British and that he should do the same. Shere Singh had refused and had advised his father against these measures as well. The Sheikh, however, was a known enemy of the family and may have chosen his words carefully to implicate them further.

Chutter Singh had, like others in the Lahore Durbar during the last year, shown a quiet acquiescence to the drift of power away from the Durbar towards the British Resident, an attitude that was explained for many by the fact that he had too much to lose in being vocal. He had been given his present position as governor by the British. He was also to be the father-in-law of the Maharajah soon, his daughter having been engaged to Duleep Singh, which would raise the status of the family still further. He was wealthy, having much land and many jaghirs. Altogether this was too much to gamble away in a desperate rebellion. In any case, due to severe ill health and being largely bedridden, it's unlikely he could apply himself to a role that would have required energy and a healthy constitution. So in recent months he had enthusiastically plumped for assisting the Resident and his assistants, giving no grounds for suspicion. A test of this acquiescence came in May 1848 when the Maharani had been exiled into British territory by the Resident. It was well known he harboured anger at this decision, having a strong loyalty towards Jind Kaur, but he would register no protest. His silence at this time irked those who looked for a focal point for their frustrations on the question of the new British ascendancy.

'The family is unpopular with the Chiefs and the old adherents of Ranjit Sing, as being upstarts, and the creatures of the British Government. They are unpopular with the army, and they have no weight with the people,' Frederick Currie would sum up. Although he entirely misjudged the loyalty of the Sikh troops to the family, as events shortly showed, his analysis of their new association with the British was true.

\*\*\*

The man who held real power in Hazara was Capt. James Abbott of the Bengal Artillery. Abbott had a good reputation in British circles and was generally thought to be a fine administrator. He would strike up a good relationship with the Muslim tribesmen in the area, who generally chafed at Sikh rule. A portrait of James Abbott by B. Baldwin resides in the National Portrait Gallery. Painted in 1841, he poses as an Indian aristocrat, complete with beard, turban and eastern dress. Abbott is shown as a thin, athletic young man with wide eyes. He was not new to India and the east and had staked his claim to fame two years previously at the age of thirty-two, embarking on an eventful trip to Khiva, one of the exploratory journeys into central Asia labelled later as 'the Great Game' in which both Britain and Russia sought to establish diplomatic relations and extend their influence in the area.

Like other explorers he had a propensity to somewhat exaggerate his achievements, and this was sometimes noticed. His reports of his adventures always tended to be colourful and 'alarmist', as one commentator put it, and he had a tendency to show himself in a more heroic light than was perhaps necessary, thus inadvertently calling into question his accounts of events. His publication of the book *Narrative of a Journey from Heraut to Khiva, Moscow, and St. Petersburgh, During the Late Russian Invasion of Khiva* described his journey and adventures in central Asia and brought him further public attention. His close brushes with death, the ever-present danger and the general brutality experienced in the time he spent in central Asia may, some speculated, have been instrumental in developing his instincts for distrust and suspicion against natives wherever he went.

Henry Lawrence, during his tenure as Resident, noticed the downbeat outlook typically displayed by Abbott and although describing him as an excellent officer mentioned that he was 'too apt sometimes to take gloomy views of questions'. Frederick Currie also commended his qualities and his administrative prowess to the Governor-General after becoming Resident. 'He has many excellent qualifications as a public officer,' he wrote on 15 August 1848, praising the way he had won over the Muslim tribesmen before going on to describe his more negative traits as issues came to a head in Hazara. 'His Lordship will have observed a very ready disposition on the part of Captain Abbott to believe the reports that are brought to him of conspiracies, plots and treasons – a suspicion of everybody, far or near, even of his own servants, and a conviction of the infallibility of his conclusions, which is not shaken by finding, time after time, that they are not verified.'

Abbott's continual suspicions and therefore cold treatment of Chutter Singh and the Sikh officers in Hazara and his pre-emptive actions in response to what he believed was an imminent insurrection in the province would become somewhat of a self-fulfilling prophecy shortly.

The British political agent initially mentions little about his relationship with Chutter Singh in his diaries or correspondence with the Resident at Lahore. What comments exist are invariably terse and short with few anecdotes. His impression on reaching Hazara to take his post and meeting the governor for the first time on 15 July 1847 was that 'the former is less old and emaciated than I had been given to suppose', suggesting he had been fully briefed as to Chutter Singh's ailing health. Few mentions of the governor follow in his diary or correspondence over the following weeks after his appointment at Hazara. A further note in Abbott's diary for 28 August records that 'sirdar Chutter singh, with his usual politeness, called upon me' without going into details of conversation. In fact little warmth would develop between the two men, Abbott having a largely dismissive attitude towards the Sikh governor, and from this time on he mentions almost nothing of Chutter Singh in his correspondence or his diaries. Having no interest in the pretence of Sikh government, he would consult or communicate with Chutter Singh as little as possible in what he believed to be effectively his own fiefdom now.

'[Chutter Singh] complains of your want of confidence in him, of your having set him aside in the Government, till he had become a mere cypher, of your suspicion and misconstruction of his conduct on all occasions, during the last two or three months, and of his feelings of distress and humiliation on the subject,' Currie would write on 16 August 1848, relaying Chutter Singh's complaints on the difficulties of their working relationship after the rupture.

No doubt Chutter Singh, like everybody else in the Punjab at the time, was keeping a close eye on events at Multan as well as on the mood of his soldiers. It's entirely likely, however, that the bedridden governor had discounted assisting the fading Mulraj in any fashion and he certainly never contemplated leading an insurrection in his present state. He was making preparations to retire, and his thoughts were largely on arranging the impending royal wedding of his daughter, the preparations of which would take time. The governor, for his part, therefore seemed to accept the much younger European as his superior, although he was not entirely content at being a mere figurehead.

This quiet if uneasy relationship would no doubt have continued. But as news arrived in Hazara of the killings at Multan of the two British political agents on 26 April and pleas for help from Mulraj to the Sikh garrison began drifting in during the following weeks, relations between the two quickly worsened as rumours of plots and insurrections in sympathy with the Multan soldiery by the local Sikh garrison fed Abbott's natural instinct for suspicion.

\*\*\*

Hazara, much like the other parts of the Punjab and Lahore, was awash with a heady cocktail of rumours, plots and half-truths about the Multan uprising, and another officer would perhaps have kept a vigilant eye on matters without unduly suspecting his underlings. Abbott, however, began openly declaring his suspicions and these extended to Chutter Singh, whom Abbott knew harboured latent nationalist feelings. He was sure Chutter was the mastermind behind intrigues and plots being hatched in the province. In his diary, Abbott would go on to record an extraordinary number of these stories, rumours, supposed events and machinations, too many to mention, almost on a daily basis during the months of May, June and July. Some were entirely false, some true and others no doubt had at least a grain of truth.

One of the rumours circulating around Hazara was that Duleep Singh had been spirited away from British hands and had been taken to Multan where he would be the inspiration for a general uprising against the British. Others reported news from Kashmir, where Gulab Singh was busy casting a large number of guns in preparation for supporting a Sikh army insurrection against the British in Hazara. Yet other stories mentioned he had already moved 3,000 men towards the border to help the Hazara Sikh garrison. Stories from Kabul suggested Dost Mohammad, who was in communication with Gulab Singh, was following suit in Afghanistan and preparing his forces for entry into the Punjab.

Of the rumours based on correct information, one was that Bhai Maharaj, thought to have drowned, had actually survived and was now in Multan helping in the defence of Multan. Other stories had Bhai Maharaj appearing elsewhere round the country with suggestions he might appear in Hazara to instigate rebellion. There were also rumours of dates agreed upon when all the Sikh army in Peshawar was to rise up as well. The biggest story by far, however, and a true one, reached Hazara on 19 May. This was news of the exile of Maharani Jind Kaur into British territory, which had caused much disgust in the Sikh barracks around the province.

In addition to these, many men from outside the area, some from Multan, others from Lahore and beyond, were reported entering into Hazara province with the aim of encouraging the soldiers to rise up and support their comrades at Multan. In late May, a man called Urbail Singh, an adjutant of the Sikh army and a known nationalist, appeared in Hazara. According to Canora, an American in service with the Sikh army who was also stationed in Hazara, he was 'the most mutinous man in the Sikh army' and his sole ambition for being transferred to the province was to instigate rebellion in support of Mulraj.

There was no lack of emissaries of Mulraj crisscrossing through Hazara, as well as at nearby Rhotas, and Rawalpindi and Attock, wooing the soldiers. They carried letters from Mulraj addressed to the Sikh soldiery. 'I have commenced the fight at your call and you leave me to perish unaided,' Mulraj pleaded in the message. Other letters, without signatures or with any marks showing their origin and with incendiary declarations, were being distributed to the Sikh soldiers. These captured letters pleaded with the soldiers to rise immediately. 'Are you Sikhs? If so, what do you hear when your Guru is calling you at Multan?' the unknown writer pleaded.

The priests and chaplains of the Sikh units were known to be the most passionate and were the most active in persuading the soldiers to rebel. Some of these, like the other emissaries, came from outside the province. In early June, for example, a Sikh preacher by the name of Bhai Achara Singh arrived and his presence was quickly made known to Abbott. 'A sikh gooroo has arrived at Hurripoor and has been received by the sirdar and troops with extraordinary honour. I have not yet learnt who he is, from whence he came, or wither bound,' Abbott recorded on 6 June. Achara Singh would stay for over a week at Chutter Singh's residence and they would have deep talks on the state of the Punjab.

'Great mystery is preserved respecting him, the Nazim [Chutter Singh] affecting to know nothing of him, and his name being ascertained with the utmost difficulty. He is in a few days to proceed to Peshawur and doubtless is not without his mission. I presume he is one of the priestly jaghirdars who were deprived of their lands for treason.'

***

After Herbert Edwardes' victories at Kyneerie and Sadoosam and with British units from Lahore and Ferozepore sailing down to help lay siege to the city of Multan, the chance of a sympathetic rebellion in Hazara, if the Sikh troops ever considered rebellion seriously, decreased markedly as the opportunity was generally considered to have passed. Abbott's suspicions should have decreased correspondingly but this was not the case. Instead he began openly blaming the nationalist leanings of the Sikh garrison entirely on the governor, whom he declared secretly supported them and was only waiting for the right moment to throw off the mask. He also accused him of allowing emissaries from Mulraj and other intriguers free and unchallenged passage across the province without the least hindrance by the Sikh authorities. The local Sikh officials, he complained, were following the lead of their governor and with full sympathy for the rebellion arrested few if any of these individuals. Any odd defections from the garrison to Mulraj Abbott also blamed on the governor, arguing that he should have exerted himself and his men to prevent his troops absenting themselves without leave. Instead hardly anyone was being apprehended in their journey south. Chutter Singh and his officers, he wrote in his diary, was going as far as covertly aiding their journey south. In practice there was little Chutter Singh could do if a soldier decided to go absent without leave, and the same trickle of defections were also taking places in Bannu and Peshawar and elsewhere across the Punjab at the same time. There was also the matter of his authority being nominal, with all decisions being largely Abbott's to take in practice.

Communication between Abbott and Chutter Singh, never particularly frequent, gradually tailed off during July. Abbott had by August stationed himself in Shirwaun. This was around 30 km north as the crow flies from Haripur, the main city of Hazara and where Chutter Singh had his camp, but was further in terms of travel due to the hilly and broken terrain. The two rarely if ever met during the weeks of July and August, the governor never receiving a summons from the British political agent for a meeting. This was a situation which allowed suspicions to grow unchecked, making Abbott dependant on the many spies and informers eager to make money from news and happenings, either genuine or fictitious.

One of Abbott's chief informants was the American Col Canora. Canora was an American by birth and in the service of the Sikh army as an artilleryman commanding a horse battery of four guns at the time. Resident at Haripur in the Sikh cantonments, he became Abbott's eyes and ears in the Sikh camp and was quick to relay the idle chat of insurrection round the Sikh campfires. The impression the American had was that Mulraj must be in league with the troops at Hazara to even contemplate such an insurrection as had taken place, and he therefore strongly suspected the Sikh garrison would rebel soon as well. Abbott's suspicion based on Canora's feelings was therefore that Shere Singh, Chutter Singh's son, in charge of the Sikh contingent at Multan, had purposely put himself in this position so that when the time was ripe both father and son would be head up considerable portions of the Sikh army.

'Intrigues are in operation, but are conducted with the most extraordinary circumspection,' Abbott had communicated to the Resident on 21 June. 'I can learn nothing of the movements of Raja Shere Singh's brigade. The sirdar Chutter Singh, his father, assures me that he never hears of or from him. I replied that the eyes of every Sikh in the Punjaub, with one exception, are watching his movements; it was marvellous that the exception should be the Raja's father'. Abbott warned the Resident that an insurrection headed by the governor himself was imminent and he accused Chutter Singh of faking his illness.

> He shuts himself up in his house all day and pretends of sickness, whilst letters and emissaries are being dismissed in all quarters – to Kabul, Peshawar, Bunnoo, Kashmir and throughout Hazara and qatur. Such at least is the information brought me by my spies, and it agrees with general rumour and with my own observation. At the same time, a degree of caution, quite uncommon, is preserved in consequence of two of his sons being in our power, and to the very last moment he will preserve the veil.

The Sikh garrison in Hazara, meanwhile were sympathetic to their counterparts in Multan and the effect of rumours and emissaries over the last few months encouraging insurrection was that a few of the braver individuals had begun defecting and make the long trek to Multan to join Mulraj's force. Over the previous weeks there had been a steady trickle of soldiers disappearing from the barracks. The vast majority of the soldiers, though, while nationalist, quite rightly had no wish to chance their luck with Mulraj. While talk of insurrection to throw off the British yoke around the campfires was cheap and plentiful, the bulk of the soldiers waited for their officers and governor, without whom no effective uprising could take place, to show the lead. This was particularly so after news reached Hazara of the defeats for Mulraj at Kyneerie and Sadoosam. For his part Abbott made as much of these clashes as possible. On 25 June he had a salute fired at Haripore and Pukli both to mark the victory at Kyneerie and to impress on the soldiers which way the tide was going at Multan. Again on 8 July, Abbott ordered salutes of twenty-one guns at Haripur and Pakli and Hassan Abdul to mark the victory at Sadoosam.

*** 

This was the way the situation continued during the heat of the summer months and into the beginning of August when the estrangement between Chutter Singh and Abbott suddenly turned to violence on 6 August. It was on the evening before, that Chutter Singh, to clarify any misunderstandings, sent a confidential vakeel to Abbott's residence. He was there, he said, to reassure Abbott of Chutter Singh's loyalty. The governor had sent a letter with the vakeel detailing how he had been favoured so much by the British that he could not understand how Abbott would think of him as a traitor. He was, he wrote, content to send his son as a hostage to Abbott if that would put the agent's mind at rest. Abbott immediately sent a response back with the vakeel that having his son as hostage would be little security and his presence in his camp would be more of one as a spy than a prisoner. He then referred to the talk of insurrection, or mutiny as he put it, in the Sikh cantonments and his belief that some regiments were in readiness for an uprising, being out of their barracks already.

> I replied to his vaqeel that I hoped he was as true as he wished me to believe, but that it was most difficult for me to comprehend how a mutiny of his forces could be carried on for two months and the Gahndia brigade be actually prepared for a March to Lahore without his cognisance … that it would soon become evident who were innocent and who

guilty, and that I suspended judgement until full evidence should be afforded me: that he must march back the companies aforesaid and order all troops to keep their cantonments, otherwise I should consider any movement of troops as a signal of rebellion.

Abbott had been specifically warned by the Resident in July not to take any aggressive action that would precipitate a revolt by the Sikh soldiers. With the Multan rebellion being smothered by Edwardes, all would be well if warm and cordial relations were kept between him and Chutter Singh. But Abbott decided on pre-emptive action. To counter the supposed mutiny by the Sikh garrison in the province, the agent would urge the local Muslim tribesmen, with whom he had cultivated good relations, to rise up against the Sikh units. This, he communicated to the tribesmen, was an opportune moment to settle old scores with the Sikh army. Their assistance, moreover, would stand them in good stead with the British government. The local tribesmen were directed against the Sikh garrison at Hurripore, where Chutter Singh had his headquarters and elsewhere at Pukli, further north, where another contingent was stationed. The legitimate peacekeepers of the province were now therefore pitched against the local armed Muslim peasantry, who were normally on the receiving end of police action.

On the morning of 6 August, thousands of tribesmen could be seen massing high up in the hills round Haripur. Chutter Singh, unaware the tribesmen had been encouraged to attack his force by Abbott, concluded this was a general uprising against authority – a not uncommon occurrence – and began making preparations to defend his position. The garrison being too small to defend both the town and the fort together, orders were sent for all troops in the town to retreat back into the fort. Only five guns were outside the safety of the fort, their crews in the town under the command of the American Canora, and messengers were quickly sent ordering him and his guns to move back into the fort as well.

Canora, however, pointedly refused to obey the order, replying that no troop or gun movements could take place without Abbott's consent; Abbott was at Shirwan and beyond easy reach. Chutter Singh replied he would give Canora a written certificate assuming responsibility for the removal of the guns. To this the American continued to demur. With the armed villagers moving down the hills, the governor asked some of his men in the fort to go and seize the guns as a matter of urgency. As the troops turned up at the position, rather than submitting, Canora promptly ordered his own golundauze to open fire on their advancing comrades. This his men refused to do, saying they would only follow their governor's orders. Canora in anger then cut down one of his own men and lit a port fire, stood defiantly between two loaded guns pointed at the troops and threatened to fire if the troops came any closer. With the amicable atmosphere gone, the troops replied with their muskets, the American being disposed of by a shot by one of his own gunners to end the standoff. Whether the order to shoot Canora, if necessary, came from Chutter Singh or whether it was a decision by his own gunners was never clarified.

After this incident the guns were moved into the fort and the emergency dealt with, the tribesmen being repulsed. The governor quickly moved to clarify the issue of Canora's death, offering to come and see Abbott personally to ask for a free pardon for his men for the incident. The agent when news reached him the next day had no hesitation in thinking this was the long-awaited proof of Chutter Singh's duplicity and wrote warning Currie that the Sikh insurrection in Hazara had already begun. What Abbott suggested was that a large number of troops had been readied by Chutter Singh to free the Pukli garrison to the north which had been surrounded by Abbott's villagers also, and that a march to Lahore with his troops was being mooted by the governor.

By the time this letter travelled to Lahore and Currie's response was received, relations between the two men had broken down entirely. Abbott accused the governor of awarding the killer of Canora 1,000 rupees and wrote further to the Resident that he would countenance no further communication, also declining any meeting till, as he wrote, he knew the sentiments of the government on his conduct. 'His last letter is so insolent that all correspondence henceforth is impossible,' he summed up. An ultimatum was sent demanding the surrender of the troops involved in the death of Canora, who must appear before Abbott by the morning of 14 August and who would be subject to British justice. Further, Chutter Singh must restore order among the Sikh troops in Hazara, though many were not in their cantonments. If he didn't receive an acceptance of the above he would assume the worst – that a rebellion by the Sikh garrison was now in full swing. While he waited for a response, Abbott invited all the tribal chiefs of the area to a meeting and at the same time moved his camp from Shirwan to the foot of the Gundgurk hills to be closer to Haripur. Here he further encouraged the latent instincts of the tribesmen, telling the chiefs this was the moment that they could take revenge on the Sikh army.

'I assembled the Chiefs of Hazara, explained what had happened, and called upon them by the memory of their murdered parents, friends and relatives to rise and aid me in destroying the Sikh forces in detail,' he would describe later. 'I issued purwannas to this effect throughout the land and marched to a strong position. I have placed a force in the Margulla Pass to destroy Pertaub Sing's Regiment should it refuse to turn back at my reiterated orders. I have ordered out the armed peasantry and will do my best to destroy the Sikh army.'

Similar to Herbert Edwardes' call for recruits in the Derajat to oppose Mulraj, the lure of plunder, especially with official sanction, meant Abbott found himself with a rapidly increasing but makeshift army of local tribesmen eager for battle. Back at Haripur, Chutter Singh found himself in a predicament similar to Mulraj after the deaths of Agnew and Anderson. With news reaching him of Abbott's ultimatum to hand over the men who had killed Canora, Chutter Singh prevaricated on what action to take. He was not short of advice from his men, who were quite opposed to their comrades being meekly handed over to the British officer, no doubt for capital punishment. Sensing the time and moment had arrived for joining the struggle against British control, they began urging him to lead them in an uprising.

***

At Lahore, meanwhile, the news of Canora's death had been received on 12 August and a supposed insurrection by the governor quite bemused Frederick Currie. He held to the belief Chutter Singh had neither the energy in his physical condition nor the inclination to lead an insurrection. Informing the government of events in Hazara immediately, he would side entirely with Chutter Singh, disbelieving Abbott's account of recent events. Currie wrote back remonstrating with Abbott on his poor views of the governor and the aggressive recent measures taken in inciting the local tribes, which had only heightened the urge among the Sikh troops to rebel. He ridiculed Abbott's suggestion that the small Hazara garrison had any capacity to march towards Lahore in the near future. Instead, he made it plain Abbott's well-known rocky relations with his Sikh counterpart were at fault in what had happened.

The death of Commedan Canora is stated, both by the Sirdar and yourself, to have been occasioned in consequence of his disobedience of the reiterated orders of the Nazim, and his having offered violent opposition to those whom the Governor, after many remonstrances with the Commedan, sent to enforce his orders ... I cannot at all agree with you as to the character you assign to this transaction. Sirdar Chuttur Sing was the Governor of the province, military and civil, and the officers of the Sikh army were bound to obey him, the responsibility for his orders resting with him. Taking the worst possible view of the case, I know not how you can characterise it as 'a cold blooded murder, as base and cowardly as that of Peshora Sing'.

Currie was also anxious on the matter of Abbott appealing to the Muslim tribesmen's religious inclinations to wage war against the Sikh units. Peace must be maintained, only to be broken if the Sikh garrison fired the first shots. A pardon by Abbott with a promise of an impartial and full investigation into the matter of Canora's death later would have soothed matters, he suggested. There was general disbelief elsewhere on the possibilities of the Hazara governor managing a rebellion as well. John Nicholson and George Lawrence at Peshawar held similar views – that a pardon for the troops who had shot Canora would swiftly end the matter. Herbert Edwardes, too, found it difficult to countenance. Why, if it was true that the governor was secretly aligned with Mulraj, would Mulraj be continually sending emissaries to him pleading for him to change his allegiance? And why was his son, Shere Singh, so enthusiastically aiding the British at Multan to the dismay of his troops?

To defuse the situation, Currie would advise Abbott no further military action must be taken by the British agent unless the governor and the Sikh garrison made an aggressive move first and it was clear to all that open revolt was taking place. No action must be taken based on hearsay and rumours. The military situation was of no concern. Chutter had only 1,500 men with him, at the moment at least, although he was strong in artillery. Extreme caution must be taken at this time. Currie wrote back a strong and critical letter to Abbott on his conduct over the previous months on 24 August.

I have told you, when you assured me that a part of the Hazara field force was about to rise against the Government, in aid of the rebellion in Mooltan, that, if they did rise, I hoped you would use your influence with the Mahomedans around you, whose hatred of the Sikhs is notorious, to prevent their leaving Hazara scatheless; but, at the same time, I cautioned you that there must be no doubt in the case; the insurrectionary movement must have been made, before you took active measures for its suppression.

I have given you no authority to raise levies, and organise paid bands of soldiers, to meet an emergency, of the occurrence of which I have always been somewhat sceptical.

I cannot approve of your having abstained from communication with the Nazim on the state of his administration, for the purpose of making his silence, or otherwise, on the subject, a test whereby his guilt, or innocence, was to be determined by you. You had, already, withdrawn your office to a distance from the seat of Government, and had ceased all personal communication with the Nazim; and you had told the Nazim's vakeel that you had no confidence in his master. It is not to be wondered at that, under such circumstances, a weak, proud chief should feel offended, and become sullen, and be silent as to the disaffected state of the troops under his Government, if he was really aware of the fact.

It is much, I think to be lamented that you have kept the Nazim at a distance from you; have resisted his offers and suggestions to be allowed himself to reside near you, or to have his son, Ootar Sing, to represent him at Shirwan; and that you have judged of the purposes, and feelings and fidelity, of the Nazim and the troops, from the reports of spies and informers, very probably interested in misrepresenting the real state of affairs.

I think, under the circumstances, the making the communication you describe, on the 13th, in the mode you mention, was far from judicious; it would assuredly, have the effect of outraging the Nazim's feelings, if innocent, and of exasperating him, if guilty.

None of the accounts that have yet been made, justifies you in calling the death of Commedan Canora a murder, nor in asserting that it was premeditated by Sirdar Chuttur Sing. That matter has yet to be investigated.

The Resident was also sceptical on whether the local tribesmen would be as servile as before after having been raised against the Sikh army and having tasted plunder.

The distance from Hazara to Lahore being what it was, and with many mailbags simply being intercepted by Sikh units eager for war, Currie's recommendations were largely inconsequential as things moved rapidly towards a confrontation between the Sikh troops and Abbott's irregulars. By the time Currie sent his letter chastising Abbott, Chutter Singh, much like Mulraj, had decided the honourable route would be to throw in his lot with his troops rather than submitting to the British agent's whims. For days after Canora's death Chutter Singh had busied himself with arrangements for a struggle despite his ailing health.

In any insurrection, drawing the Peshawar contingent's support was absolutely imperative for the Hazara contingent could do little by itself. Other allies were important as well. During late August Chutter Singh actively sent off letters in all directions asking for assistance. He wrote to Shere Singh, his son at Multan, informing him of what had happened and urging him to join him as soon as possible. One of the letters advised his son to be '*tukra*' (to be strong) in view of the way events were moving. His other son, in Lahore, he asked to join him as soon as possible. Letters requesting assistance were also written to Dost Mohammad and Sultan Mahomad Khan, the governor of Kohat and the brother of Dost Mohammad. After the war and during Dalhousie's second trip to the Punjab, Maharajah Gulab Singh would admit he received a huge number of letters from both Hazara and Multan pleading with him to send troops into the Punjab. Chutter Singh also made preparation to march towards the Indus and Attock hoping a march in that direction would spur the Peshawar garrison to rise up in sympathy. Letters were sent to other Sikh garrisons at Hassan Abdul, Rawalpindi and Kurara.

Most of these entreaties would be in vain, certainly for the time being, with little help forthcoming from either local rulers or the Sikh troops who like at Hazara looked to their officers and officials to make the leap first. Ill of health and hamstrung by the uprisings of the local Muslim villagers, Chutter Singh would spend the bulk of the next four months criss-crossing his way in vain through Hazara battling Abbott's force in a series of skirmishes, laying siege to Attock fortress, which was in British hands, and pleading again and again for help to the same sources. His main hope, however, was Shere Singh, commanding the Sikh troops at Multan. If only he could persuade his son to join him in the struggle, there was a good chance the rest of the Sikh troops stationed round the country would join the national cause as well. Shere Singh, however, as everyone knew, had tied his fortunes strongly with the British.

# 18

# Shere Singh, 'The Mussulman'

If you do not listen to my words, the opportunity will not come again. The religion and
the government of the Khalsa are yet still extant.

Mulraj to Sikh officers at Multan, July 1848

With respect to the Sirdars I believe them to be heart and soul on our side which is
the side of Jaghirs titles employments and whole throats. But their force with equal
confidence I report to be against us to a man.

Herbert Edwardes to Frederick Currie, 13 July 1848

The greatest impact of Chutter Singh beginning his rebellion in Hazara would be felt at Multan.
The Sikh units that had earlier been moved down to Multan under Shere Singh numbered
between 3,000 and 5,000 men and twelve guns. These had arrived at Multan in early July after
Currie had sanctioned their move forward. The welcome these troops would receive from
Whish and Herbert Edwardes was distinctly cool, both being well aware of their nationalist
leanings. Even before they had reached the city, Edwardes had made plans to station them well
away from his other troops, across the nullah to the west of the city, isolated from the rest of
the allied force by the city and suburbs. This was to keep any fraternisation between these men
and his largely Muslim irregulars to a minimum. Neither did he want to involve them in any
fighting, as they would show little heart in fighting their Multan colleagues. So these units had
been conspicuously absent in any of the skirmishing and clashes of late. Instead they were given
the nominal and what was considered rather menial job of blockading the city from the west.
Because of these orders, the Sikh contingent after their arrival would remain largely idle round
their own campfires, with little to do except to discuss the events going on round them and at
Hazara and elsewhere.

By contrast, the reception the Sikh soldiers had received from the city, despite being enemy
troops, had been quite different. Mulraj and his garrison had welcomed the arrival of the Sikh
troops, seeing in them their last hope of success. Overtures to the soldiers by Mulraj's agents had
already begun even before these troops neared Multan, and these agents were welcomed by the
soldiers in turn. Mulraj, knowing their feelings, would continue to woo them during the next
few weeks. 'Moolraj has issued proclamations in Mooltan that the Sikh army are his friends and
that the Khalsa soldiery are to have free access to the city and bazaars unmolested and to buy
whatever they may want at favorable rates. I feel every day the increasing evil of allowing this
rebellion to continue unsuppressed and Moolraj unpunished,' Frederick Currie informed the
government on hearing of their reception at Multan, perhaps regretting giving the order to these
troops to advance towards the city. But to pull the Sikh troops back towards Lahore would show

indecision, and he concluded the less dangerous solution was, as Edwardes had already decided, to keep them separate from the other British allied troops and uninvolved in the day-to-day fighting till the city fell and their opportunity to tilt the balance disappeared.

Most of the Sikh troops, as at Hazara, certainly never considered defecting individually to Mulraj and this attitude didn't change during the first few weeks of their arrival. The general feeling in Shere Singh's camp was that the whole force should go over en masse, along with Shere Singh and his officers, for the force could not be led without officers. The Sikh troops waited for their commander and officers to join them but Shere Singh was unwilling, having a similar attitude to his father, no doubt reinforced by letters between the two during this time, and was determined to keep a friendly relationship with the British. As time went by, however, keeping a lid on dissatisfaction in his camp became an increasingly difficult job for the Sikh commander.

Things had already been difficult on his march down to Multan. The camp had been rife with discussions on fighting the British and he had had to order flogging for any soldier voicing his opinion openly on this subject. One soldier he had gone so far as to blow away from a gun for preaching war against the British. After reaching the city there had been an attempt to murder Shere Singh by some frustrated soldiers, who no doubt hoped his replacement would be more sympathetic to the national cause. A Sikh cavalryman called Shujan Singh Mull, along with two others, Durbara Singh and Chunda Mull, were involved in the plot. A man had been picked to mix poison in Shere Singh's milk. The plot was uncovered, and Shere Singh had allowed the plan to mature while gathering evidence before arresting Shujan Singh and his fellow plotters. These men were charged and found guilty of attempted murder and for carrying on treasonous correspondence with Mulraj's men. The Sikh commander had Shujan Singh's face blackened and he was paraded round the camp on an ass. His arrest was reported to the British camp and news passed to Lahore for the Resident to decide suitable punishment.

In another incident, two men caught disguised as fakirs in the Sikh camp and suspected as being agents from the city were arrested and taken to Shere Singh. He threatened to blow them away from a gun also, unless they gave up information. They admitted they were delivering friendly letters from Mulraj to two of Shere Singh's senior officers, Sirdar Shumshere Singh and Kehur Singh of the Sindanwala family, before being flogged and expelled from the camp.

It was not only the Sikh units in his force that showed increasing frustration as they sat around week after week in front of the city with little to do. The Purbeah regiment (Hindu sepoys in the Sikh army) as well as some officers showed increasing discontent. That they were being kept apart from the other units till the city fell was obvious. The commander of the Purbeah regiment was known to be sympathetic to Mulraj as well. So difficult was the situation, as time went on, that Shere Singh was forced to post a permanent guard on his guns for fear they would be snatched and taken to the city by parties within his force.

Despite these difficulties, the Sikh commander figured he would only have to keep a lid on discontent till the British column with siege guns arrived and all would be over. But on 10 August, around six weeks after his force's arrival at the city, a messenger suddenly appeared at Multan carrying dramatic news that his own father Chutter Singh had raised the standard of rebellion, making his position considerably more difficult. Shortly after the messenger, letters from Chutter Singh began arriving asking for assistance from his son and his troops. News of this correspondence between father and son spread like wildfire round the Sikh camp, his soldiers redoubling their efforts to win him over. Soldiers could be seen openly haranguing Shere Singh for his faithlessness to the national cause as he toured his camp. Mulraj had revolted, and now his father. Surely he should desert the British, who in any case had no wish for his assistance, they urged him.

Currie notified the government monitoring the situation at Multan:

I agree with Lieutenant Edwardes in thinking, that Raja Shere Sing, after all that he has done, will not commit himself, unless his father's rebellion is more successful than I hope it will be; but, if the rebellion assumes the national character which the Sirdar desires to attach to it, and becomes more general, I cannot expect that Raja Shere Sing will continue faithful. As yet, no chief has openly joined Sirdar Chuttur Sing; not because they are generally better affected to us, but rather because they have all separate and conflicting interests, and feuds; and a combination between them is very difficult.

Edwardes and Whish both fully recognised the Sikh commander's predicament as well. During late August, after his evening meals Shere Singh came daily into the British camp for frank discussions with Edwardes. The Sikh commander's own feelings were that if no real collision took place between British and Sikh forces in Hazara then tempers would cool shortly and all would be well again and his father would give himself up. Conciliation therefore was not only possible but probable if James Abbott handled matters properly. He only wished his father, who at his advanced age had wished to resign and manage his daughter's wedding, was treated well and honourably after matters were settled. The strain on the Sikh commander at this time was plainly visible. 'It is I who have to bear on one side all the suspicion of betraying the English and on the other all the odium of betraying the Khalsa,' he would confide in conversation with Edwardes. In order to reduce the discontent in his camp, he advised Edwardes, his men should be given an honourable position in the fighting at Multan as a way of cementing them to the British side. Allowing them to languish to the west of the city with no purpose around their campfires only increased their resentment.

Edwardes in turn was sympathetic and reassured the Sikh commander that both father and son had given the British service over the last year which would stand them in good stead and that he was unlikely to lose out in any way because of his father's conduct.

'The Raja's position is evidently a difficult one,' he informed Currie. Certainly he felt Shere Singh would stay on the British side – for the time being, at least – and could be trusted. 'His manner was earnest and convincing and I feel assured that if the Raja is unable to make the Sikh force very active allies in the approaching siege he will at least prevent them from being enemies.' Still, he and Whish were quite averse to the Sikh force joining the rest of the allied army on the west of the city and being involved in any fighting. They must stay isolated from the other troops, they told Shere Singh, in case these men spread their nationalist fervour to the other troops.

\*\*\*

Several events would nevertheless bring matters to a head by mid-September in Shere Singh's camp. Early in the month, a messenger brought news that a death sentence had been handed out by Frederick Currie to the prisoner Shujan Singh, who had earlier plotted to poison Shere Singh. Reticent about executing more of his own men, Shere Singh asked Edwardes to have the prisoner blown away by a British gun and troops instead, a request Edwardes refused, saying it was the Sikh commander's responsibility since the man was one of his soldiers. This execution was then reluctantly carried out from a gun in the Sikh camp in the face of bitter hostility from the Sikh troops and the possibility of instant mutiny.

The effect of all this was that Shere Singh faced open mockery and sarcasm round the Sikh camp, many of his men by this time losing all inhibition. He was openly referred to as 'the Mussalman' (the Muslim) round the camp for mimicking the Muslim soldiers' loyalty towards the British. Other nicknames also went into circulation, 'Raja Sheikh Singh' being a popular one with its Muslim connotations. Many Sikhs round the campfires sat round joking or taking part in mock arguments as to whether he was really a Muslim.

On 9 September, a man was seen loudly and openly proclaiming war on the British around the Sikh camp. Labelled the 'Sadh' or the saint, he addressed large crowds of Sikh soldiers, urging them to free the country from the British yoke. 'Listen, O Khalsa! This war is not a war between Moolraj and the Durbar, but a strife of religions; and he who wishes to go to heaven, will die a martyr in defence of his faith!' he told the men. The soldiers had loudly acknowledged him and spoke openly in sympathy. The man had been put in confinement by Ootar Singh, one of Shere Singh's lieutenants. Edwardes recommended capital punishment but Shere Singh had had his fill of executing his own men by this time. In any case, another execution, he responded, especially of such a popular man, would in his opinion cause an immediate rupture with his Sikh troops.

Despairing of their commander ever deserting the British, small contingents of Sikh soldiers had begun defecting to Mulraj during early September. On 8 September, for example, fifty to sixty sowars were reported to have left Ootar Singh's regiment and ventured into the city. On the 9th another twenty to thirty joined them. The defections were not limited to Sikh soldiers. On 10 September, three entire companies of the Hindu Purbeah regiment had attempted to desert but news had got about and one of their officers had managed to discourage them from doing so. These defections were fuelled by rumours, not altogether accurate, that Chutter Singh had succeeded in gaining support from Dost Mohammad in Kabul and Gulab Singh in Kashmir, thus making a war against the British in India a much more general affair.

Defections were spreading to Sheikh Imam-Ud-Deen's troops as well by this time. The Sheikh would report to Edwardes of his officers receiving letters from Chutter Singh and that several of his officers and many soldiers had become much more vocal on assisting Mulraj. The same day Sirdar Shumshere Singh, another Sikh commander, reported rumours that his troops were about to defect, the excuse to be the lack of payment of wages – the soldiers being eight to nine months behind in arrears. The troops had decided they would demand the arrears be paid immediately or they be allowed to leave the service. If no money was forthcoming they would ask permission to leave and then look for employment with Mulraj. If payment was forthcoming they would still leave but with full pockets.

Whish and Edwardes, on the other side of the city, had differing views on these happenings in the Sikh camp. Whish, while lamenting the possible loss of the Sikh force, considered it better than having untrustworthy allies. Edwardes, in turn, was for disarming Shere Singh's contingent entirely if it could be done, to stop them taking their arms and guns to Mulraj. 'Unfortunately,' he explained to the Resident in one of his letters, 'they are in such a position that it is impossible to turn their flank either right or left and if I was to move straight down on their rear they would in self defence be driven into Mooltan.' This last point, that it would precipitate their going over to Mulraj, was considered crucial and it had been decided to let things lie in the hopes a quick capture of the city would make the Sikh soldiers feelings immaterial.

***

A point that would be discussed at length both during and after the war was when exactly the Sikh commander finally relented and joined the nationalist cause. Some would point to the correspondence he received from his father on 10 September revealing the punitive actions the British Government would now direct against him and the family. Almost certainly an entire loss of fortune and property would be involved. Edwardes believed it was later. Two years after the event he would write, 'The question with which I am concerned in this event is "When did Shere Sing resolve to join his father?" I have no hesitation whatever in stating that it is now as certain as anything in this world can be, that it was on the 12th or 13th of September – certainly within forty-eight hours of the fatal step being taken.'

Others would argue the decision may have been taken a week or so earlier. Some of the papers seized after the capture of the Hummund Ghurree outpost, for instance, were letters written by the Sikh commander to the garrison officers indicating some sort of friendly discourse had already begun. Whatever the case, all that is certain is that it was Edwardes himself who lit the fuse with a rash action on the evening of 13 September.

Increasingly anxious to dispossess the Sikh force of its guns in case they were spirited into the city, he decided on ordering away the Sikh units entirely from the Multan vicinity. This was something Currie had been loath to order over the previous weeks but something Whish desired. The pretext would be that patrolling the highways further north was required to prevent recruits and guns for hire joining Mulraj. One of the Sikh regiments would be sent to Toulumba. The other one would be sent to Kurrumpore with the same reason while the rest of the troops would be marched to the river to 'protect' the ferry where the British steamers docked. Since these patrol duties required no guns, the Sikh unit could be relieved of them with good reason, the excuse being they were required for the fighting at the city.

The division of the Sikh force into three contingents, quite apart from moving them away from Multan, would also make any defection in concert difficult due to the distance between them, Edwardes reasoned. This operation was to be carried out at the earliest opportunity, essentially early the next day. The Sikh officers were summoned by Whish and told their new orders. The guard and patrol duties fooled no one. None of the Sikh officers liked it and they treated the order as an insult. Patrol duties such as these were considered even more menial than the blockade work currently given, and the officers knew their men would be outraged. Whish, however, refused to change his mind and the officers quietly went back to the Sikh camp to communicate the order to their men.

Sheikh Imam-Ud-Deen, who happened to be present in the Sikh camp, would later relate what happened that night. As the Sikh officers gave out the orders for the next day, they were surrounded by hundreds of angry soldiers remonstrating with them for accepting unsoldierly work from the British. Passions ran high and in the heat of the moment most of the officers, equally disturbed at the orders, decided to join their soldiers. A large group of soldiers and officers combined now surrounded Shere Singh's tent demanding he lead them. They pleaded that this was the one opportunity before the British, using the Multan rebellion as a pretext, swept away the Khalsa Raj forever and annexed the country.

Shere Singh, already no doubt considering his father's pleas for assistance, quickly gave in and declared he was with his men amid loud cheering. He asked his officers if they would stand by him and they took oaths to do so. In the early morning of 14 September, the decision was made public throughout the camp that Shere Singh would support his father and Mulraj. The letter to his brother Golab Singh telling him of his decision, most probably written the morning of the 14th and seized by the Resident after his arrest in Lahore, sheds further light on the meetings in the Sikh camp during that night. Shere Singh blamed James Abbott's behaviour towards Chutter Singh as bringing the issue to a head.

'The Sing Sahib [Chutter Sing] has several times written to me, stating that he constantly obeyed Captain Abbott's directions, but that officer, acting according to the suggestions of the people of Hazara, has treated him most unjustly, and caused him much grief and trouble; and that he has also exerted himself to destroy and disperse the Khalsa troops,' he wrote of events in the north of the country. 'I resolved therefore yesterday to join the Sing Sahib and devote myself to the cause of our religion.'

Not all would join him. Some of his officers, perhaps fearing for their livelihoods and property, slipped off towards the British camp. These included Sirdar Ootar Singh, who walked out with 200 sowars. His son Lal Singh was made a prisoner by the Sikh troops in revenge. Kirpal Singh Mulwaree and Kiber Singh Sindanwala, along with some of the lesser officers who showed reticence, were arrested. The Sindanwala clan had a dislike for the Attariwalas and were not expected to side with Shere Singh in any case. Shumshere Singh Sindanwala was also arrested after showing his unwillingness to join. He escaped on foot to Courtlandt's camp with a follower the next day, shooting a picket along the way, but losing his baggage, tents, elephants and other property, which was later retrieved by followers. Kehur Singh, the nephew of Shumshere Singh, also escaped along with and Shere Daol Singh, son of Futteh Singh Mann. Sheikh Imam-Ud-Deen was another who didn't join and would be the one who brought the news to the British camp.

Shere Singh's original instinct, as specified in his letter to his brother, had been to immediately head off with his troops to Hazara to join his father. But he was cautioned against this. Although some of his officers supported marching north, the majority advised on staying at Multan. The River Chenab would have to be crossed and all boats in the near vicinity were held by the British, they argued. A crossing could then only take place further up the doab, and this would mean crossing the Ravi, the Chenab and the Jhelum. The distance to Hazara was also great, and with all the collection of revenue between in British hands. The treasure he had with him was modest, while Mulraj had wealth at his disposal. So it made sense to stay at the city and ally himself with Mulraj instead. Shere Singh could see the sense in this and messengers were accordingly sent to the city with the good tidings that Mulraj now had a new ally. A meeting between the two was requested.

Any illusions of a strong alliance with Mulraj, though, were shattered fairly quickly at the meeting. What happened at the talks between the governor and the Sikh commander was later related by reluctant rebel Shumshere Singh to Herbert Edwardes. The meeting had been arranged at the Shivallah, a structure outside of the Bohar gate in the west of the city. Mulraj came out with a large retinue of soldiers suspecting a ruse and showed great distrust throughout, for Shere Singh's reputation as an ardent supporter of the British was well known. Mulraj refused to believe his conversion was genuine and coldly declared to Shere Singh that he had already fought for a long time on his own, that he welcomed Shere Singh's assistance if he had indeed deserted the British and had come to protect the cause of his religion but that he should remain outside the fort for the time being till Mulraj was assured of his fidelity. He and his men would have to man the defensive positions outside of the city, encamping in the Hazuri Bagh within range of the fort guns till then. No amount of convincing would change Mulraj's mind and Shere Singh had to swallow his pride and agree to Mulraj's suggestions with the hope he would gain his trust later. Notwithstanding the cold reception from Mulraj, Shere Singh's troops paraded outside the city that day and within sight of the British camp. His men were treated differently, it being well known where their sympathies lay. They were made to swear loyalty on the Guru Granth Sahib, the holy book, and warmly welcomed into the city to procure food and supplies.

***

In the British camp, meanwhile, on the opposite side of the city, the news of Shere Singh going over to Mulraj was brought to a sleeping Edwardes in the early hours of 14 September with Sikh kettle drums being clearly heard in the distance. Edwardes wasted no time in his tent, rushing out to converse with Whish on the course of action.

'I hastened to lay the same before Major-General Whish and begged him to consider us as no longer engaged with a rebel Kardar alone but with the whole Sikh army in another struggle for independence,' wrote Herbert Edwardes later. What was clear was that since almost the whole Sikh force under Shere Singh had defected, the British force was nowhere near strong enough against any potential action by Mulraj and Shere Singh acting in concert. With only two European regiments present there was the distinct possibility many of the Muslim irregulars would either join Mulraj or simply melt away in the present state of things. Therefore the British regiments could be overwhelmed. Meanwhile murmurings that something big was happening quickly spread through the British camp. Officers were seen accumulating in various tents, before all being ushered into Major Napier's tent to hear the news and Whish's response.

'The Major-General adjourned to the tent of the chief engineer, where several senior officers were, also, called together; and an unanimous opinion come to, that the siege was no longer practicable. Col Franks even said that he had come to that conclusion, two days ago. It was, therefore, decided to concentrate the troops, and assume a defensive, yet dignified, position, until the Government can organise its measures for the Punjab war, into which we are thus launched,' Edwardes reported to the Resident the same day.

The defensive but dignified camp would, it was decided, be towards Suraj Khund, 8 km to the south-west of the city rather than the current exposed position. British lines of communication and supplies with Bhawulpore would be under threat and this move would protect the road going south. Whish was anxious to protect the siege guns as well. Major Napier had recommended during the meeting moving the siege guns into the fortress of Shujabad further south along with a suitable garrison for safekeeping from where they could be brought forward again as and when required. The move would have to be done sooner rather than later, on that much Whish and all his officers were agreed; there was complete uncertainty on what Shere Singh and Mulraj would do. At this time they had little inkling of the frosty reception Shere Singh would be receiving from Mulraj later in the morning but nevertheless between them, they could now muster nearly 20,000 troops. Not only that, but news shortly arrived that Sheikh Imam-Ud-Deen's force was also wavering amid calls to join Shere Singh.

The British troops were shortly after the meeting told of the defection of Shere Singh and his troops at around 9 a.m. along with the decision to retreat from Multan, although many had already heard of the news. Immediate action to protect the big guns was taken. All were withdrawn from the advance positions during the day along with baggage and other siege equipment. By early on the 15th, all the working parties and guns had been pulled back, followed later by the horse artillery and then by the infantry although two engineers were found to be missing, having been taken prisoner in the hasty move back. During the night of the 15th, Whish passed orders that there should be no campfires and as little sound made as possible. All energy was to be directed at packing the baggage as quickly and as silently as possible so that the army could retreat at the shortest notice. Meanwhile a rearguard of sorts was sent close to the town in case of surprise attack.

As soon as dusk had arrived, the tents were also struck. All British outposts were finally abandoned on the morning of the 16th. The greatest problem over the last day and a half of packing had been found to be logistics. A retreat had not even been contemplated and there were found to be insufficient beasts of burden available for the move. The prime reason for this was that many of the hackeries and carts along with camels and bullocks of the siege train that had arrived several weeks previously had been sent back as it had not been anticipated they would be required again. Many other animals had died or had been carried away by the Multan garrison. Nevertheless, as much as could be carried away was organised.

'Some 3,000 sand bags and numerous cotton bags, gabions and facines, being left in an advance post, these we were prevented from destroying. It was with great difficulty that even the working tools, &c., could be brought in, so suddenly were the troops withdrawn,' recalled M. McMurdo of the Bengal Engineers. In order not to leave ammunition behind, all the infantrymen were ordered to carry either shot or sandbags with the Bhawulpore sowars ordered to carry the heavier 18-pounder and heavier shots on their saddle bows.

Since all baggage animals were to be used for carrying essential items and ammunition, many of the men quickly put on clean shirts, realising they would need to leave behind their personal baggage. Despite all these preparations, it was estimated around thirty days' supply of grain and forage along with a large amount of ammunition, around 250 camel loads and other supplies had to be subsequently abandoned. Over the following days, there would be much private grumbling over the retreat and the general state of things in the British camp with most of the troops having sacrificed their prized possessions and clothes. 'A 1st class siege, a 2nd class train, a 3rd class army' was the saying quickly coined in jest and which spread around the camp at this time referring to the strength of the fortress and the lack of sufficient guns and European troops that had been made available.

The time was 4 a.m. on the morning of the 17th and the sky was still dark as the retreat towards Suraj Khund began. 'Something like a deathlike silence pervaded us – not the sound of a shot was to be heard, nor the loud booming of cannon. It was an awful moment of time! God knows what each mind was thinking of! – for the very word "retreat", to a British army is like poison: it is hurtful to the soldier's mind,' wrote Corporal John Ryder of the melancholic atmosphere among the soldiers as they marched south in the gloom. The Ram Tirath was the last stronghold to be given up by the rearguard. Luckily for the British force the march wasn't harassed, Mulraj being too busy keeping an anxious eye on his new ally. Some of Mulraj's men rode up occasionally to the British rear and there was some desultory firing, but no casualties ensued in the retreat and in any case Whish had given out orders for skirmishers to avoid firing unless hard pressed. The British columns streamed southwards through the camp of Edwardes' irregulars, where guns and batteries were still positioned protecting the columns. The grand nullah was re-crossed and a camp near Suraj Khund established.

This new location would turn out to be a far from satisfactory, being heavily sandy and with few natural defensive qualities. Jungle surrounded the position, allowing for enemy soldiers to advance unannounced. The position also required much clearing of the land and it was found there was no supply of water either and what was available was bad. No air or wind seemed to make it through the surrounding jungle either, and by all accounts it was stifling hot. The area also seemed to have some unfriendly residents in the form of a large population of scorpions, snakes and jackals at night, though this would be discovered only in the following days. So the

British force busied itself immediately in clearing the ground round the camp to leave a clear field of fire for defensive purposes.

Since waiting for reinforcements was to take time, to keep the troops busy, preparations were already begun in anticipation of the renewal of the siege. The town of Shujabad, 40 km south-west of Multan itself, had largely emptied itself due to the war, the only occupants remaining being the moneychangers, shopkeepers and merchants hoping to make a profit from the British presence. On 30 September, four companies of pioneers and sappers were sent under a Capt. Siddons to take command of the place for the storage of fascines and gabions that were being collected.

At Calcutta, meanwhile, Dalhousie was furious when news reached him of the retreat of Whish, reflecting badly as it did on British prestige. On 8 October he wrote to the Duke of Wellington:

> The Officer commanding at Mooltan has accordingly raised the siege. On his own showing, I think he was not justified in this act; and I am vexed and angered by it extremely; but I wait for his explanation before anything public is said. If his explanations are not satisfactory to the Commander-in-chief, I have begged him to supersede him without hesitation or delay. There is no time to stand on ceremony.

The British papers, too, generally dismissive of Mulraj and the strength of the fort, criticised what they thought was Whish's premature lifting of the siege. *The Englishman* wrote, 'All the letters which we have seen agree that the greatest despondency prevails in the enemy's camp and that their sufferings from the bombardment had been such that they could not have held out many days longer. A less cautious man than General Whish would have weighed the moral effect of taking Mooltan against that of a retreat and would have held on to the last confident that at all events he would be reinforced in a short time.'

There was a quiet acceptance by Gough, however, that Whish had little choice in the matter and that a stay in the current position risked the annihilation of not just the British regiments Whish had with him but capture of the sizeable collection of heavy guns assembled for the siege, and this would have been a disaster. The matter of the retreat was therefore questioned no further.

***

Back at the city, Shere Singh, now committed to the nationalist cause, began making energetic attempts to garner as much support both from the Sikh and other troops still with Edwardes and wider afield in and outside of the Punjab. The day after switching sides, 15 September, a proclamation signed by both Shere Singh and Mulraj would be sent out to all the non-European officers and men in the British camp inviting them to join his camp.

### Proclamation

To all the officers of the Sepoys and Sikhs and Mussulmans and regiments, all others that eat the salt of the Sovereign of the Khalsa, Maharajah Duleep Sing Bahadoor; such for instance as Sheik Emamooddeen and Jowahir Mull Dutt and General Cortlandt Sahib Bahadoor and Col Budri Nath and Soobhan Khan and Commandant Lahora Sing &c &c.

A religious war being now afoot, it becomes every public servant whether he be Sikh or Moslem, at sight of this document to march without delay and join the camp of the Khalsa along with Raja Shere Sing Bahadoor and Dewan Moolraj in the work of eradicating the Feringees from this country of the Punjab.

1st For their own religion's sake.

2nd For the salt they have eaten.

3rd For the sake of fair fame in this world.

4th For promotion's sake.

5th For love of the Jaghirs and dignities which are to be obtained.

And whoever shall not join in this religious war,

1st He is unfaithful to the salt of the Sirkar.

2nd An outcast from religion.

3rd Worthy of any punishment that may be inflicted on him.

Sealed by Raja Shere Sing, Dewan Moolraj, Sirdar Khooshal Sing Morareea and others

The declaration was already being spread throughout Edwardes' force as they departed Multan and had the effect of heightening British suspicions of their native allies. Several of the artillerymen in Courtlandt's units suspected of planning to join Mulraj with their guns were arrested and the two guns they possessed seized in anticipation. Due to these overtures, Whish was by now extremely suspicious of any Sikh officers left in the British camp. He would over the course of a few days inform the few that were left, namely Utter Singh, Shumshere Singh and Kehar Singh, who had fled the Sikh camp on the night of the 14th, that they were required back at Lahore, a pretext to remove them from the scene. He also dismissed Sheikh Imam-Ud-Deen's Lahore force and Dewan Jawahar Mull's contingent as being too untrustworthy and liable to defect. So apart from the British regiments, only the Muslim and Afghan irregulars from the Derajat under Edwardes and Courtlandt and the Bhawulpore force deemed to be sufficiently loyal would be retained. No officer or Sikh units of the Lahore army would be retained by Whish at Suraj Khund.

Shere Singh, meanwhile, hoping for support, had penned letters to the members of the Lahore Government, others to the Sikh officers in Bannu and Peshawar, and still others to high officials and kardars as well. Some of these, like the one to Raja Deena Nath in Lahore, who had no plans to join the rebellion, were quickly handed over to the Resident. A separate and more general proclamation would also be penned by Shere Singh encouraging the population of the Punjab to rise up against the British. Copies were made and distributed around the country and posted in prominent places in the cities by sympathisers during October.

### Proclamation

These orders are circulated for all people under the government of Lahore: both small and great well know what oppressions have been practised by the English on Ranjit Singh; that is, the Khalsa and inhabitants of the Punjab.

1st That they have imprisoned the Queen and sent her to Hindostan and thereby violated their promise and agreement.

2nd The Sikhs, who are children of Gooroo Khalsa Jee, are weary of the English, because they commit acts contrary to the Sikh religion.

3rd That the authority of the Khalsa people has been diminished to such a degree, that they are powerless; therefore according to the decrees of Shree Akal Poorush Jee and Shree Wa Gooroo Jee, Rajah Shere Singh Bahadoor and the other rulers and princes, together with a large force on behalf of Maharajah Dhulleep Singh, are appointed to root out this tribe of oppressors; and the loyal Dewan Moolraj is concocting a plan for driving out those deceitful oppressors, and striving to do so with heart and soul. Thus it behoves the subjects of the Sirkar Khalsa Jee to strive to join the army of Moolraj, to kill the English wherever they may meet them and stop the dak. In return for such fidelity they will ensure for themselves the goodwill of the Gooroo, the happiness of all men, and their exaltation. Whoever acts according to this proclamation, and gives his life as a sacrifice, will reap the reward of his fidelity in this world and in the next; and whoever refuses acquiescence to this mandate, is not a true Sikh.

Shere Singh and Mulraj would also both write to the rulers of the Cis-Sutlej states as well for assistance. In response to these efforts, some of the Durbar members, headed by Dewan Deena Nath, anxious at being implicated as nationalists, would duly release counter-proclamations a few days later in support of the British, fiercely criticising the Attariwala family for what they termed as treachery toward the state.

Despite these joint letters, which gave the impression of a good accord between the two leaders, Shere Singh would never manage to instil enough trust in Mulraj. No advantage had been taken of the British retreat and none would be taken in the following days either as the new British camp and its defences materialised near Suraj Khund. This failure of Mulraj to work well with their commander was apparent to Shere Singh's men as well after the first few days and many were already declaring it folly to have stayed at Multan when a march against Lahore could have been organised. The troops openly began canvassing for a move north but Shere Singh kept his patience for the time being, hoping Mulraj would develop a greater trust. Time was not on his side, however, for Whish's reinforcements had been ordered from Bombay and these were expected the second week of December.

With the two Sikh leaders unable to work together and with Whish firmly on the defensive, there would be an almost complete lack of activity over the following few weeks. What relative peace didn't do was prevent the bi-directional stream of defections endemic among the auxiliaries and irregulars on both sides. On 19 September a large body of Mulraj's Muslim troops defected from the city, or at least attempted to, despite the new accord between Mulraj and Shere Singh. They arrived at the British camp only to find Edwardes refusing to give them employment, suspecting they were spies or informants. The balance of defections at this time undoubtedly remained in the other direction as Pathan irregulars in the British camp continued drifting off to the city in large numbers on seeing Shere Singh's invitations. This worried Edwardes. 'A further defection of three regular infantry regiments and seventeen guns would perhaps compel him [Whish] to retreat altogether which could only be considered as a disaster,' he wrote, warning the Resident on 22 September, a week after Shere Singh had left the British camp. The general belief among the men, according to Edwardes, was that if the British won they would be made redundant again; the longer the war went on, the longer they could gain employment with Mulraj. In order to allay these fears and reduce the high rate of deserters, Edwardes would suggest to the Resident that these troops should be offered permanent employment of some sort or another in the army after the war. Currie quite agreed, and the announcement was made that no man recruited would suffer financially after hostilities had ended.

Aside from the troops with Whish, there would be other high-profile defections to Shere Singh as well. One was that of Mallee Singh, the Sikh officer who had earlier been sent by

Whish to build and guard the nullah dams 20 km north of the city at the Chenab. Also switching sides would be a Sikh unit headed by Bhoor Singh, travelling south to Multan as reinforcements for Shere Singh (prior to his defection). All in all, these totalled 1,000 men. The dams previously built were destroyed by the same men and the city nullahs filled up again, reducing any shortfall of water in the city if there ever had been any. Mallee Singh was deputed by Shere Singh to stay at the river and attempt to board if possible the British steamer *Conqueror*, which itself was preventing supplies by river reaching Multan from Hazara. Informers relayed the news to the British camp, and Whish advised the steamer captain to stay midstream to prevent any surprise attempt to board. Mallee Singh, meanwhile, prevented locals in the area supplying fuel and supplies to the crew, resulting in somewhat of a stalemate in this little mini-theatre of war.

Both sides were in possession of a cache of prisoners by this time. The British had captured a certain Oomra Singh during the fighting. He was known to have been one of the conspirators in the Prema Plot to kill the Resident. He had been a member of the 12th NI and had asked for discharge, which was given. Of a nationalistic leaning, he had then joined the conspirators and proved a useful ally because of his knowledge and acquaintance with most of the sepoys stationed at Lahore. It was Oomra Singh who had recruited most of the sepoys in the plot. He was sent to Lahore to be sentenced.

Good use was made of the other prisoners. Those taken by the British were made to burn or dig up the jungled area around the camp at Suraj Khund. Meanwhile, Shere Singh had captured some European prisoners, including some engineers. A certain Irishman had also been captured. He was being treated well and given a house and a servant in the city. Mulraj had him interpret British mail between Whish's camp and Lahore intercepted in recent weeks. He was also used to translate British newssheets, the governor being curious as to how the hostilities were being reported around India.

Cognizant that that the continuing defections along with his retreat from Multan had reduced morale among his allies, early on 23 September Whish ordered a parade in the British camp, after which a strong force was marched with eight guns towards the Multan city walls to show he was ready to offer battle. According to one of the newspaper reporters present, the 'operation was conducted in a very ostentatious manner in sight of the fort and city'. The appearance of the force prompted Shere Singh to pepper the British line for several hours as they advanced, although no great hostilities broke out. Whish ordered all men to remain under arms lest Shere Singh advance to an attack. After noon Shere Singh led his force back. Only one sepoy and a horse were killed in a rather desultory and pointless encounter.

On the next day, the 24th, finally tiring of the breezeless location of the camp he had initially settled on, Whish ordered a move further back a couple of miles. The natural lay of the land here meant a good breeze was always present compared to the stifling heat of the previous location. The decision was popular since the stay was expected to be till December. This position was much stronger as well, with a string of sand hills protecting the camp towards Multan which were made into advance posts. Beyond the cleared area there was jungle but to the west was more open ground, with small clumps of palm trees and small villages scattered here and there. These villages were where the allied troops of Edwardes were stationed. Trees and undergrowth were again cleared and wells were sunk over the next few days as one thing the area also lacked was a good water supply. Even with the wells, however, there proved to be a severe shortage of water in the British camp over the next few weeks. The rations were restricted for around a week till supplies from Bhawulpore became more frequent.

In the city, Mulraj's trust of Shere Singh would never really develop during the weeks after his defection, despite the Sikh commander's efforts and letters from Chutter Singh encouraging an alliance between the two. However, two weeks after Shere Singh's defection Herbert Edwardes succeeded in orchestrating a grand deception that largely destroyed what little warmth had been developing. Edwardes wrote a letter on 27 September designed to be captured. It was addressed to Shere Singh and talked of a plan, the letter 'thanking him for his scheme and congratulating him on its approaching fruition'. The letter was duly intercepted by Mulraj's pickets, who passed it on to the governor. The ruse had the expected effect, with Mulraj in a public Durbar accusing Shere Singh of duplicity. Shere Singh protested his friendship and pointed out it was an obvious deception by the British, but to no avail. The Sikh commander and his troops were refused all entry to the fort after this time, prompting several hundred troops, annoyed by the inability of the two commanders to work in concert, to publicly threaten to rejoin the British.

With both sides staying resolutely away from each other, the only real activity during this period of lull, which would last till December, was to protect convoys, treasure and supplies arriving at Multan, mostly from Lahore but also from Bhawulpore and Ferozepore. Some of the treasure had been destined for Shere Singh and Imam-Ud-Deen's troops and was already in transit by the time Shere Singh had defected. Other treasure was destined for the British troops. Some 400 camels with grain supplies that were destined for Shere Singh, possibly from Chutter Singh, were captured by Edwardes' levies on 24 September. The British steamers plying the Chenab were also having an effect, quantities of ammunition being intercepted heading for Multan that week.

On 26 September, Shere Singh despatched troops to intercept 2 lakh rupees being sent by the Lahore Durbar for the payment of his troops but which was now destined for the British camp. In this he was unsuccessful. This was fortunate for Whish, who was as desperate for funds as Shere Singh and had recently written to the Nawab of Bhawulpore for more loans over and above the money already loaned to Edwardes.

In the city, meanwhile, on the 27th, Shere Singh's men pleaded with Mulraj for a month's salary to sustain themselves. Mulraj, however, retorted that they must fight the British first in a pitched battle to prove their allegiance to him before he would part with funds. Fortunately for them some supplies and money were forthcoming from Hazara, where Shere Singh's father was doing his utmost to supply his son.

Sometimes British supplies were intercepted too. Mulraj's men managed to carry away around 200 camels laden with supplies on one raid. On 30 September Shere Singh's troops intercepted treasure worth 18 lakh rupees coming from Lahore.

Not all supplies coming down the river were from Chutter Singh, strangely enough. A boat floating down the river from Lahore with supplies for the messes in the British camp had, it was discovered, been sent by a British merchant in Peshawar. This had been intercepted by Mallee Singh. Some of the treasure for the British camp was transported on the steamboats plying the Chenab, which was considered a safer method. On 30 September, for example, 50,000 rupees and a large cache of ammunition reached Whish on the steamer *Meanee*.

\*\*\*

The only time that hostilities would ever be threatened by Mulraj in concert with Shere Singh would be prior to the major Hindu festival of Dussehra. The festival fell on 7 October that year and marked the destruction of the demon Ravana in Hindu mythology. Recognising that the martial aspect of the event would provide good motivation for his force, especially the Hindu and Gurkha elements, Mulraj made plans for battle. Combined with Shere Singh's men along with other recent arrivals, a force as much as 24,000 strong could be fielded. The gossip was that if they won Mulraj would bathe in the holy Hindu tank at Suraj Khund, which lay close to the British camp, as was his habit since childhood as part of celebrating the festival. On the day of the festival no attack materialised, and it was thought his reticence was due to a rising fear of a ruse by Shere Singh or plain vacillation.

This failure to show initiative on Dussehra against the weakened British force did have an important consequence; it finally convinced Shere Singh that his interests were best served leaving Multan and joining up with his father. Relations were if anything getting worse between him and the governor in any case, and this had been apparent for some time. Both had been resorting increasingly to communication by letter than by direct talks. His other complaint against Mulraj was the issue of finance. Shere Singh's funds were minimal and the main reason for staying at Multan had been Mulraj's wealth, which could be utilised in paying the troops, but the governor had released little money in the last three weeks. On top of this, the cost of basic foodstuffs within the city and around had been rising rapidly due to the conflict, leading to discontent among Shere Singh's troops.

Early on 9 October, therefore, Shere Singh left Mulraj to his own devices and struck northwards to join up with his father. With him went around 5,000 men (some sources suggest as many as 7,000 men) and the twelve guns he had at his disposal, including two mortars. The news reaching him was that the Bannu troops, around 5,000 men, were also expected to join him shortly if he marched north. Chutter Singh was thought to have collected around 9,000 men. Shere Singh's brother Aotar Singh had an additional 1,500 and was already waiting for him at Jalalpore on the Jhelum River. Another 3,500 irregular cavalry and new levies were also heard to be ready to join him. This made an approximate force of well over 20,000 men under the direct control of the family, with twenty-six to twenty-eight guns. The immediate objective, though, was to reach Wazirabad, where these separate units could combine before a potential march on Lahore.

Marching along the line of the Chenab towards the salt range, by the end of the day he reached Gaggera, 19 km north of Multan, and the next day he reached Sirdarpore, 50 km from Multan, where he was joined by Mallee Singh's contingent. The Ravi River was crossed between the 11th and 12th, after which he travelled to Jhung. The people of Jhung, largely Muslim, had little sympathy for the Sikh struggle and had earlier been enthusiastic in blocking Bhai Maharaj's passage to Multan. In revenge, Shere Singh would commit several excesses in the city. Two Muslim priests were killed and a businessman ransomed for 10,000 rupees, with several mosques defiled and several nearby villages looted to pay his troops. Meanwhile Surat Singh Majithia, one of his lieutenants, carried out similar actions at Chuniot, 80 km upstream, with the advance guard. This was a grave error at a time when he needed all the support he could garner.

'The excesses committed by the troops under Raja Shere Sing upon the Mahomedans of Jhung, may, on the other hand, serve to exasperate the feelings of the Mahomedan population against the Sikhs, and altogether neutralize the attempts to maintain the incompatible alliance which has sprung up between them at Peshawur,' wrote a satisfied Dalhousie to the Secret Committee hoping his actions would permanently scupper Chutter Singh's attempts to get the assistance of Dost Mohammad, the Afghan ruler.

After extracting as much money as possible from the city, Shere Singh continued his march north, leading his force up the left bank of the Chenab to Jalalpore, reaching Ramnuggar, only

100 km from Lahore. Along the way, a treasure boat carrying 184,000 rupees for the payment of Whish's troops was captured. This was sufficient funds for two months' pay, alleviating his more immediate financial worries. At Ramnuggar, the Sikh commander called a halt to the march. Here he would await the forces of his father and the arrival of the Bannu troops, something that disappointed many of his soldiers. A good number of them had houses and property near Lahore and to the east and wanted to continue the rapid march and seize the capital, which was held only by a nominal British force. Letters from Chutter Singh to Shere Singh intercepted by the British seem to indicate this was Chutter Singh's advice as well. This was sound reasoning, and there was no doubt he could have taken Lahore. However, the Sikh commander decided on a more cautious policy and the chance was lost.

Shere Singh had planned his move north from Multan meticulously, and nothing had been noticed by the British pickets on the day. It was only late on the 10th, as he made preparations to cross the Chenab, that the disappearance of his force was noticed in the British camp. Whish, initially surprised at Shere Singh's move, had originally contemplated pursuing him northwards but was advised against it by Edwardes. Edwardes believed it to be a ruse to draw the British force away from the city and thus lay the British camp and siege guns open to capture by Mulraj.

***

Mulraj famously regretted not having formed a working partnership with Shere Singh almost immediately after his departure. It is known that he wrote to the Sikh commander repeatedly to turn back and return to Multan. The withdrawal of Shere Singh left a rump of only around 10,000 men under Mulraj, while many thousands of men would drift away, despondent at the discord between the governor and Shere Singh. Around 300 Muslim troops, not wishing to march with Shere Singh, immediately surrendered to Edwardes and were offered employment on the same day. These men, many of whom had been stationed in the fort, would be of great help later on. They would offer to make a large model of the fort and its defences in mud for the benefit of the British gunners targeting the city, which would be happily accepted.

The rumours emanating from the city were that Mulraj had once again fallen into despair, primarily over his folly at not trusting Shere Singh, and was readying himself for surrender. He had decided to set free some prisoners, which was thought to be a goodwill gesture in preparation for coming to the British camp. A sepoy of the 72nd NI, captured on 9 September, was among this batch. He had been treated well and brought back news that the other British prisoners were also comfortable, although they could not return due to injuries from which they were immobile. Other rumours circulating around the British camp suggested Mulraj was contemplating leaving the fortress altogether and would take his troops northwards to join Shere Singh and Chutter Singh's forces. Still others mentioned he was planning to flee across the Chenab into the Derajat region. Once the Bombay troops that were being readied to reinforce Whish reached Multan, it would be impossible to vacate the fortress.

Whatever the case, once Shere Singh had left with his force and struck north, the fighting at Multan would be very much overshadowed by bigger and more momentous events closer to Lahore. 'The Sikhs, generally,' informed the Resident to the British Commander-in-Chief on 18 October, 'have ceased to consider Mooltan as the place where the battle for their faith is to be fought, and with the fickleness, and faithlessness, peculiar to their character, are now, apparently, abandoning Dewan Moolraj, without scruple, to his own resources ... Unless the accounts received, by the last four dawks, are much exaggerated, the greater part of his Sikh followers have left him, to join, as they say, the national standard, under which a vital struggle is to be made, for the restoration of Khalsa supremacy in the Punjab.'

Shere Singh's move north, as Currie rightly surmised, meant the fate of the Lahore state would be decided in the heart of the Punjab rather than in the far south.

# WAR

When the news of Raja Shere Sing's open defection reached me, I considered the time
for negotiation entirely at an end.

Frederick Currie to Government of India, 30 September 1848

Such an army is enough to conquer India *de novo* – much more to put down an
insurrection in the Punjaub, though it should extend from the Sutlej to Peshawur.

*The Mofussilite*, September 1848

# 19

# War with a Vengeance

At Lahore, meanwhile, the news of Shere Singh's defection, only five weeks after Chutter Singh had raised the standard of rebellion in Hazara, would have an immediate impact. British suspicions were immediately heightened as to the possibility of a general uprising in the city once news of the event spread. Currie took immediate action. The day the news arrived he replaced the Sikh guard round the young Maharajah with British troops. It was rumoured nationalists would attempt to extract him from British control and transport him to Shere Singh's camp at Multan where the Maharajah's presence would provide the inspiration for the rest of the country to rise up against the British. In fact, under his new British guard the young Maharajah would never know during the entire year there was a war being fought, Currie keeping him in the dark as to events outside the Lahore palace. The only change Duleep Singh would notice was that his companion Golab Singh, brother of Shere Singh, was no longer with him and that European sentries of the HM 53rd now stood around the fort and its gates in place of more familiar faces.

On the night of 16 September, at around 10 p.m., HM 53rd Regiment had been put on general alert and moved into the Hazuri Bagh, the garden area directly in front of the palace and fort gates. They were told to stay in readiness for any gunfire in the capital. In addition, all Lahore state jewels and property were ordered by Currie to be secreted away for safekeeping. The regiment was moved into the fort the next day and all people not immediately required in the fort were ejected. In addition, with the fort secured, all the commanders of the various British regiments present in Lahore were summoned to receive instructions to counter any uprising in the city. Currie also ordered the members of the Durbar to the fort, ostensibly for a meeting but in fact to put them effectively under detention during this critical period. They were kept there from four to nine on the morning of the 17th to more closely monitor their behaviour and to assess if any had covert feelings towards the rebellions.

Over the course of the day and subsequent days most of the leading sirdars would be questioned and arrests were made. Those detained included Ranjodh Singh, the general who had commanded the Sikh army at Aliwal. Of the members of the Durbar, Golab Singh and another relative of Shere Singh, Nar Singh Attariwala, were taken into confinement along with two other prominent chiefs. European guards were placed with them to eliminate the risk of bribery in any escape attempts. Currie went personally to arrest and question Golab Singh. All his papers and documents were seized for inspection. As a future brother-in-law of the Maharajah, his sister being engaged to Duleep Singh, he had been given an influential post in the Durbar and palace. It was suspected by Currie that he was in fact one of the ringleaders in the plan to spirit the young Maharajah away. Currie, in a frank discussion, informed him that although he had not done anything personally against British interests as yet, the fact was that he was the son of Chutter Singh and the brother of Shere Singh, both leading rebellions against British authority. Therefore it was hardly possible for him to keep his present position, and the Resident had no option but to place him under arrest. He was asked for any letters from Shere Singh or his father he had received lately. He replied he had received two during the previous night and these he handed over. A search of his apartment in the fort was conducted and it was found that Golab Singh had been moving his property and valuables out of the fort and Lahore in preparation for joining his father in Hazara, confirming Currie's suspicions of some collusion.

Currie also hurriedly recalled Raja Deena Nath along with any other Durbar members not at Lahore at that time. Deena Nath's allegiance to the British seemed sure, Currie thought, as he had already very zealously applied himself as soon as the news from Multan had come in to confiscate the property and jaghirs of the principal rebelling sirdars, Sikh army officers and the Attariwala family. He had also rounded up other persons sympathetic to the rebellion.

'There is no doubt whatever his views and feelings may be regarding this conspiracy that he is disaffected towards the British government as I have constantly reported. Still in this rebellion set up by the Attareewallas, I have no reason to believe him to be in any way concerned,' he informed the government. However, in the tense and uncertain atmosphere of those days informers proved invaluable and Currie's suspicions of Deena Nath would increase as reports of his conversations with other Durbar members were communicated to him. 'It was reported to me, two days ago, and I consider the authority quite trustworthy, that Deena Nath remarked, in the Durbar at the palace, to Raja Tej Sing, that the Sikhs were uniting and combining so generally, that it appeared they were determined to try to make this another Cabool [Kabul] business, and that there was this in their favour, that they had a powerful artillery, whereas the Affghans had no guns. The remark was, of course, not without a purpose,' he mused in further correspondence with Calcutta. It may have been that Deena Nath had been sounding out other leading members of the Lahore Government as to joining the insurrection, or it may have been an innocent remark on proceedings. Whatever the case, Currie took no chances with either him or any of the Durbar members. Over the next few days more were questioned and surveilled and all asked to give up any and all letters they had received from Shere Singh asking for assistance.

Meanwhile, false rumours that the Maharajah had been spirited away from British control to join Shere Singh's army had already spread round the city. To counter this, Currie summoned Duleep Singh and a small royal cavalcade through the city during the evening of the 18th was organised to show the Lahore locals he was still in British hands. The same day Currie wrote to the Governor-General of the urgency of the situation and his resolution for firm action. 'When the news of Raja Shere Sing's open defection reached me, I considered the time for negotiation entirely at an end,' Currie wrote at the time, personally marking this as the first chapter of a new war. Publicly, however, orders were issued by Currie that business would carry on in Lahore as quietly as before in order to defuse any excitement among the population. He had a proclamation put out for public consumption declaring Shere Singh's force as rebels against the Lahore Durbar and said British forces would now enter Lahore territories – as friends, not enemies – in order to restore order and not to invade. No one would have anything to fear from the British force.

***

A day after news of Shere Singh's defection came the dramatic news that Whish had raised the siege and had retreated from Multan, which, despite Currie's attempts to keep the city calm, served only to increase the tension for the British community in Lahore. Discussions everywhere centred on whether this was still a rebellion or if it could now be termed a war between the Sikh army and the East India Company. What were typically small matters were analysed to a far greater degree, and less obsequious statements by Durbar officials were treated as impudence or signs of untrammelled behaviour. An incident at Lahore involving Duleep Singh and the Resident was one such case. Frederick Currie had, in conversation with the Maharajah, casually mentioned that Duleep had not paid him a visit for some time. The Maharajah had innocently replied, 'What, is it necessary that I should visit my own servant?' This was noted in some newspapers as more independent an attitude than was warranted. '[This story] if true shows him to be infected with the insolent spirit of those about him,' wrote the correspondent of *The Englishman*. Hodson, one of the Resident's assistants in Lahore, harboured more suspicions than most after recent events in Multan and Hazara and speculated on a much larger conspiracy quashed only by Currie's brisk security measures at Lahore and beyond.

> It is now morally certain that we have only escaped, by what men call chance and accidents, the effects of a general and well-organised conspiracy against British supremacy in Upper India. Our 'ally' Gholab Singh, the creature of the treaty of 1848, the hill tribes, the whole Punjab, the chiefs of Rajpootana, and the states round Umbala and Kurnal, and even the King of Cabul, I believe, have been for months and months securely plotting, without our having more than the merest hints of local disturbances, against the supremacy of the British Government. They were to unite for one vast effort, and drive us back upon the Jumna. This was to be again the boundary of British India. The rising in Mooltan was to be the signal.

The proof for such a large and complex conspiracy he did not present, but it was an example of the wariness prevailing at the time. The failure of the plan to work, he wrote, was due to pettiness only; Gulab Singh, a proud Rajput, did not want to follow in the wake of a 'Mooltan merchant', as Hodson labelled Mulraj.

\*\*\*

Suspicion at Lahore and Delhi also fell on a well-known European visitor making his way through northern India during this time. This was the French general Ventura, who had travelled north towards the Punjab during the Multan outbreak. Ventura had formerly served in the Sikh army under Ranjit Singh and gave the reason for his sojourn towards the Punjab, complete with his former adjutant, as the disposal of some jaghirs that he still possessed. He also wished with his adjutant to establish contacts for the trade of Kashmir shawls to Europe, with horses and fine champagne to be transported the other way. His reason was not entirely believed, as his landholdings were small in relation to the cost of travel to India from Europe and he did not need to travel in person to settle his affairs. However, he moved through the country, not incognito but in a quiet, unpublicised fashion, which in itself excited interest and suspicion from the British Indian society and press, who ventured to suggest that he was on the verge of rejoining the Sikh army.

'We do not intend to accuse General Ventura of participating in the present plots, insurrections and rebellion which are observable in every direction of the Punjab,' *The Mofussilite* declared on 2 October 1848, 'but at this juncture we deem it our duty at all hazards to bring him most prominently before the public and to dwell on the impropriety of our Government having allowed Frenchmen to walk about Lahore and other parts of the country. According to recent reports they are doing so still.'

Ventura had arrived at Bussean and then moved on to Ludhiana, in British territory but only a short hop to Sikh territory, the Sutlej River being a few miles to the north. He was genuinely in an unsound financial position at this time, hence the trip to sell off his assets, and he ridiculed these assertions in the British papers, going as far as to visit Major Mackeson, the British agent at Ferozepore, in November 1848 to reassure him of his neutrality. Ventura's own belief was that the insurrection had only come to this point through British inaction and that the Multan rebellion could easily have been snuffed out at an earlier stage had the authorities wished. Whatever his reasons for his trip to northern India, he would never travel in Shere Singh's direction or towards Multan. Either the suspicion of his intention was misplaced, or perhaps the attention he had begun receiving may have changed his mind.

Several other morsels of information and intelligence had made their way to the Resident's ears. Currie received 'most authentic information' during this time that a rebellion was planned at Kaithal and that all Europeans in that region were to be massacred while British attention was focused on the Punjab. No specific details were gleaned and no names were mentioned in the plot. The Rani of Kaithal, however, was not present in the state and was living at Saraswati. The Raja of Ladwa, who had sided with the Sikh army in the previous conflict, escaped from his confinement at the fort of Allahabad and British forces were ordered to be on the alert to apprehend him as he made his way, it was suspected, to the Punjab to join Shere Singh's army. He was never caught.

One of the more unlikely events associated with the general paranoia at the time was a genuine plot far away in Calcutta. The leader of this plot was a certain well-known local man, Pertab Chund, and it seems his ambition was to take advantage of British attention on the Punjab to effect a mutiny among the sepoys in Bengal. Sepoys at Barrackpore and Dum Dum were to be involved and a day chosen for the revolt when the sepoys would march on Calcutta, precipitating, it was hoped, more sepoys joining other allies recruited and stationed in the Burra Bazaar market section of the city. The plot was found to have been developing for two months, sepoys being gradually recruited. Pertab Chund was known to have pretensions to power, and was generally felt by many to be the genuine heir to the Burdwan Raj. As such he had sufficient gravitas and had therefore been selected as leader.

As ever, recruitment for the plot was a dangerous activity. An officer, a Havildar Major belonging to the 16th Grenadiers, who was asked to join feigned interest but immediately reported the approach to his superior officer. He was asked to continue showing interest. The plot seemed well financed. The officer had been offered 1 lakh rupees if he could persuade all the men under his command in the 16th Grenadiers to join. The seven sepoy regiments would also get 1 lakh rupees each to be split among the men with an opportunity to loot Calcutta for two days once the city was theirs. Other sources suggested 10,000 rupees were being readied for each sepoy who joined. There were also suggestions from Pertab Chund that the Nepalese were involved and that two regiments of the Nepalese army would immediately proceed down to assist and that many of the local rajas would join in too with their armed contingents. Nationalist representatives from Lahore had also been contacted and involved in the conspiracy. Orders were issued by Sir Herbert Maddock, Deputy Governor of Bengal and President of the Council of India, for the arrest of Jeebun Singh, the agent of Maharani Jind Kaur, suggesting a real link to the Punjab. However, he was released later after he had applied for habeas corpus, no proof appearing of his involvement. The plotters, including Pertab Chund, were arrested in a house in Mirzapur later and a further twenty men in total arrested as ringleaders.

\*\*\*

Plots aside, quiet preparations for war had swung into action at Lahore under orders from Currie. One of the foremost things on the Resident's mind after news of Shere Singh's defection was the occupation of the important fortress of Gobindgarh in Amritsar, 64 km north-east of Lahore. The fortress was a strategic structure commanding the route to Jalandhar and therefore its capture, along with the installation of a British garrison, was vital. The Sikh garrison there was known to be in sympathetic to Shere Singh, although they had not organised themselves sufficiently to declare their allegiance.

'I know that the Governor-General in Council is fully impressed with the expediency of our occupying Govindgurh, but with a jealous Sikh garrison, who had only to keep their gates shut to defy us, and who care not the slightest for the Durbar orders, getting possession was a delicate operation, while an unsuccessful attempt would be disastrous,' wrote Currie. The structure was a powerful piece of work, guarded by eighteen guns at the time. It had served as a treasury in the past, along with being a prison as well as a temporary palace for Ranjit Singh during his stays at Amritsar. Because of this, its control was considered paramount. Unknown to the British at the time, the Sikh garrison had buried another fifty-two guns inside the fort as well, firstly to ensure they didn't fall into British hands and secondly to use as and when war appeared.

Currie realised an advance by a British force would tip the garrison into open support for Shere Singh. Therefore, a more subtle plan was devised. Four men, acting as state prisoners, would be escorted to the fort to be incarcerated in its prison. Along with the escort, Currie sent a regiment of infantry and Skinner's irregular horse. The distance to Amritsar was covered in a day and a night. They arrived at the fort early at dawn the next day. The four men were taken up to the gates of the fortress and the sentries were told these were prisoners that the Lahore Durbar had ordered to be imprisoned in the fortress. The unsuspecting guards let them in and 150 of the Guide Corps marched into the fort as well. With the doors open, the cavalry followed and the unprepared garrison was disarmed and told its services were no longer required. The fortress was placed under Col McSheery's control, and he marched up the next day.

\*\*\*

Currie's precautions and extra security would extend to the annual celebrations of the Hindu festival day of Dussehra on 7 October that year. The festival meant large crowds could accumulate in the open grounds outside the city, ostensibly to celebrate the event. It would also allow them to vent their anger or partake in riots or worse. There was also strong intelligence reaching the Resident of an armed revolt planned for the holiday. The rumour was that a British officer or a member of the court allied to the British would be attacked as they witnessed the festival, the shots fired being a signal for the uprising. There was in addition a report reaching the Resident that up to 4,000 armed men were already hiding in the city ready to take advantage as and when. Letters had been seized from Shere Singh to the Lahore Government members encouraging them to take a stand and join him on this holy Hindu day, which confirmed Currie's suspicions. Raja Tej Singh on receiving the letter had immediately sent it to the Resident. Currie was loathe to stop the annual festival as this would suggest anxiety in British minds but extra precautions would be taken. Only people vouched for by the Durbar sirdars were to be allowed to enter the fort and palace on this holiday. Two companies of HM 53rd occupied the fort along with a squadron of the HM 14th Light Dragoons. Three regiments of native infantry were divided up and guarded all the city gates.

The population normally celebrated Dussehra on the plains beyond the parade ground of Meean Meer. A large assembly had developed on the ground. Currie escorted the Maharajah to the ground with two regiments of infantry, a squadron of HM 14th, one irregular cavalry and a troops of horse artillery along with twenty-one guns to provide a salute for the Maharajah but which could easily be turned against the crowd, nearly 100,000 strong if necessary. In the face of such a force, no violence was attempted and Duleep Singh, escorted by the British Resident stayed for a while to enjoy the celebrations and accompanying fireworks before returning to the palace.

Currie need not have feared any outpouring of nationalist rhetoric by the Durbar members themselves. Despite the strident talk of war against the Sikh nation and annexation of the state by much of the British newspapers and society, there was a curious sense of calm amongst the Lahore Government members as if events of no importance were happening. The Durbar member stayed largely mute, whatever their inner feelings, giving Currie little reason in the coming weeks and months to write of their behaviour or attitudes. The Lahore bureaucracy would continue to function and cooperate with Currie. After the arrival of the British force and Commander-in-Chief at Lahore, the Lahore Durbar would go as far as to depute some senior administrators, Boodh Singh and Kishen Lal, to his staff in order to supply grain and other supplies to the British force in the Punjab. Beyond this nothing would be heard of them, all remaining passive to the events going on round them and on the battlefield.

***

It was in Calcutta that the ultimate decision on war would be decided. Dalhousie's outpourings on the Punjab over the previous months, in private at least, had become more and more strident and he had already been weighing up the advantages of annexation of the Lahore state. But when news reached him on Shere Singh's defection and the raising of the British siege at the end of September, he was entirely in agreement with the Lahore Resident's sentiments on war. A brief communique was sent on the matter by the Secretary to the Government of India advising Currie as to the stance he should be taking publicly and privately.

'I am desired to intimate to you, that the Governor-General in Council considers the State of Lahore to be, to all intents and purposes, directly at war with the British Government; and he expects that those who may be, directly or indirectly, concerned in these proceedings, will be treated, accordingly, by yourself and your officers.' But there would be no overt declaration of war to prevent the conflict being seen as a national one against the British in the Punjab. For this would only benefit Shere Singh. The official British policy, Currie would be advised, would remain one of supporting the Lahore government to 'restore law and order' and the backing of the Government of the Maharajah against 'rebels'. 'Our ulterior policy need not be promulgated till Mooltan has been taken and the Sikh rising has been met and crushed; but I confess I see no halting-place midway any longer,' Dalhousie wrote declaring the continuation of a weak Sikh government as entirely unfeasible. In line with this, Currie was also advised to steer clear of giving any guarantees of the future of the Lahore state in future conversations with the Durbar members. To give public guarantees that the state would survive in some fashion would mean that a declaration of annexation later would be seen as disingenuous in both the Punjab and in the British public's eyes. On 8 October, Dalhousie communicated his decision on hostilities to the Secret Committee: 'The Government of India after anxious and grave deliberation have without hesitation resolved, that the Punjab can no longer be allowed to exist as a power and must be destroyed. The war, I believe, will be like the last one. Many a head will go down before it is done.'

As far as Dalhousie was concerned, by far the biggest and most immediate threat was Shere Singh and his force, with Multan to be treated very much as a secondary theatre. There was also little to fear from Chutter Singh, who had done little beyond collecting men. The danger was of his overtures to Dost Mohammad of Kabul and Gulab Singh of Kashmir being received more sympathetically in the future. Although not possessing great military strength himself, Dost Mohammad's entry on the Sikh side would mean the whole Muslim population in the north-west could very well transfer their loyalty to Shere Singh if Jihad against the Firangis was declared. Gulab Singh, also weak militarily, could offer treasure and provisions to the Sikh army prolonging the war and making it easier for Shere Singh to wage war and pay his troops. But if Shere Singh's army could be crushed, all other issues would matter little.

\*\*\*

Despite his own strong warnings to Currie advising against talk of this coming conflict as a war between the two states, the Governor-General found it difficult to contain his own enthusiasm in the following days. On 5 October for instance, at a ball at Barrackpore given in his honour by Sir Dudley St Leger Hill, he gave one of his most aggressive speeches on the Punjab and an open declaration of war against the whole Sikh nation.

> I came to this country a friend to peace. I wished for peace, I hoped for peace, I strove for peace; and the whole of mind and the efforts of my Government were for peace and its happy results. I have been disappointed: war has come upon us and that people and that country, unwarned by precedent and uninfluenced by example, have called for war; and on my word, Sirs, war they shall have, and with a vengeance.

This was a speech whose invocation of patriotism was reported to have reduced a Col Gardner of the 16th Grenadiers to tears, with another officer reportedly declaring openly in the proceedings he was ready to fight a regiment all by himself. Sir Dudley Hill was also carried away by the fervour in the room for war, adding his own warlike declaration.

> I will only add a very few words, which, coming from a soldier and addressed to you, my Lord, the son of a soldier, may not be considered ill-timed. The great preponderance of power we possess in British India has been gained by the sword, has been maintained by the sword, and must, as long as we possess a foot of ground in the country, be still preserved by the sword.

The speech the Governor-General had delivered would come in for some criticism later. The war 'with a vengeance' was seen as far too aggressive for a state that was effectively ruled by a British Resident and with what nominal government it had left cooperating and assisting the Resident. Dalhousie too perhaps realised the mistake later. 'If I had known that what I said at a supper after a ball would be reported and commented on as a State phrase, I would not have spoken, and it will be a lesson to me,' he wrote in his private letters. 'An after-dinner speech such as this may not stand strict criticism, but if it produces what the speaker aims at that is enough, and trust me, this one to which you have alluded did so.' The nature of his speech quickly filtered through to the Punjab, however, and was said to have been instrumental in making up the undecided minds of many a Sikh soldier in Peshawar, Hazara and elsewhere in joining Shere Singh's army.

\*\*\*

War had been chosen. Dalhousie now determined on moving closer to the Punjab for communication purposes, stationing himself at Ferozepore on the borders of the Punjab. Preparations had already been in full swing for around a week but he would fall ill and his departure would be delayed. It was only on 11 October that he finally left Calcutta for Allahabad in a small fleet of three steamers towing flats travelling up the Ganges. Patna, Dinapur, Ghazipur and Benares were passed, where he met the local rajas along with various Mughal princes from Delhi. Allahabad was reached on 10 November, a city which had recently witnessed riots between the Hindu and Muslim residents, although these had died down by the time the Governor-General passed by as he moved up through Cawnpore, Agra and then on to Delhi.

From Delhi, Dalhousie would continue on to Meerut and Saharunpur where evidence of the preparations for war was now becoming more evident. His journey was much slower as the carriages were dragged by bearers, all horses having been diverted for the war in the Punjab. Dalhousie reached Ambala on 25 November and by early December had made the move to Ludhiana, taking a tour of the battlefield of Aliwal before moving west towards Ferozepore. However, finding all sorts of scarcities of supplies in Ferozepore due to the preparations for war, he moved northwards. He would eventually make his final camp on 1 January 1849 at a place called Makhu, 40 km northeast of Ferozepore and scarcely a mile from the battlefield of Sabraon on the banks of the Sutlej. This gave the advantage of being close to both Lahore and the British force under the Commander-in-Chief (which had already by this stage moved into the Punjab) and yet was still on British territory. Here he would stay and make camp till the conclusion of the war. He was adamant about not crossing into Lahore territory or joining Gough, who had reached the Chenab River by this time. Firstly his presence would require extra protection, which would rob Gough of part of his force, he argued, for he happened to be travelling with a large party almost 8,000 strong with only a nominal escort. The other reason was more subtle and related to having a civilian superior with the army and the complications that would entail.

'Because I should not *viva voce* have produced as much effect as by letter. Letters he read conned over, broke out, cooled, read again and perhaps acted upon. A *viva voce* remonstrance by a civilian half his age on a military matter would have had no effect whatever on him, and would only have produced altercations more violent, and greater scandal, than those which occurred when remonstrance was made by Lord Hardinge as G.-G.; a General, and an experienced one, and as experienced nearly as himself,' he explained later. He was alluding to the problems the previous Governor-General had at the Battle of Ferozeshah, a mere three years earlier, where Hardinge disputed Gough's methods and decisions before the battle. The distance, in any case, from his camp to Lahore was only around 80 km, with the Chenab, where fighting had already taken place, barely double this distance. This he felt was close enough for communications to be carried out relatively quickly while sufficiently far enough to allow Gough to make his own decisions.

One of the stranger and more anomalous things that became apparent during Dalhousie's time at Makhu was the composition of his bodyguard: 'It is odd enough to add that this moment a Sikh Regiment furnishes my guard, and a Sikh is walking sentry at my door!' he wrote in his private letters one day.

\*\*\*

The month of October, then, would see military preparations in full swing in British India, with two British armies being readied for the Punjab, both with different destinations. The plan was for the smaller one, from the Bombay presidency, to be sent to reinforce Whish so that the siege of Multan could be recommenced; the second (and main) force, under the personal command of the British Commander-in-Chief, would advance and destroy Shere Singh's force, which was currently stationed at Ramnuggar, 100 km from Lahore.

The plan initially formulated was to move the Bombay troops to Multan by sea but the dangerous surge and currents in the water near the Indus River's junction with the Indian Ocean at this season and the problems this would cause in landing men and boats put paid to the idea. Even if landing could have been done easily, they simply lacked sufficient boats to transport the troops and it was felt that waiting until there were enough would delay things until after the monsoon. The land route to Multan was thus chosen.

This force was to be led by Major-General Auchmuty who at the time commanded the Poona division with Brig. Dundas, second in command. Orders for the gathering of this force which would consist of troops from Bombay and from Scinde (Roree) were declared on 11 October. This force would be around 9,000 strong, consisting of 2,050 European infantry, 3,648 native, 1,292 cavalry plus accompanying sappers and miners, horse and foot artillery. In addition to this, a siege train consisting of sixty guns, thirty being heavy, would be sent to supplement the guns Whish already had. It was scheduled to march between 21 and 26 November from Roree, reaching Multan by 21 December, when an advance on the city could immediately be made.

However, it wasn't long before it was realised Auchmuty outranked Whish and that therefore Whish would need to relinquish command once the Bombay force reached Multan. This was seen as undesirable by Dalhousie himself, as replacing a commanding officer who had already assumed operations would have suggested a want of confidence in Whish's abilities; the decision to give command to Auchmuty was therefore withdrawn. Other officers who would outrank those already at the scene of conflict were withdrawn as well. This was much to the dismay of Auchmuty, who had ambitions of leading a victorious siege of the city himself, and he would show a certain pettiness at this loss of command, preparing and leading this force as slowly as he could. He halted the Roree-bound troops at every place, providing sundry excuses for the lack of progress. At one stage the troops were halted a week, the excuse being lack of carriage and cattle. At other times he claimed many of the men or the cattle were too sick to continue. This behaviour, and the resulting delays, raised the ire of Dalhousie.

'I fear there is too much reason to believe that the troops have been purposely delayed. And the nearer portion of them, at all events withheld from General Whish, and none whatever have joined him, although some have been lying for several weeks comparatively near him. I shall do nothing without full proof, but if what is alleged is made out, I shall come down very heavily on General Auchmuty and I shall look with confidence for your Grace's support in so doing,' Dalhousie informed the Duke of Wellington on 7 December as news reached him of the column's slow progress. These delays would end with Auchmuty being placed under arrest. He was not tried, but he would be reprimanded for his actions in delaying reinforcements and provisions for Whish's force.

This Bombay force itself had been readied by 20 November, the march to Multan commencing in three columns leaving on 25, 28 and 30 November. The column would eventually reach Ahmedpore on the border with the Punjab between 15 and 18 December before advance columns began reaching Multan by 21 December. The siege train was transported on the Chenab on boats and flats pulled by the British steamers. *Comet* and *Conqueror* were being utilised nearer to Multan while the *Meanee, Assyria, Napier, Satellite, Meteor* and *Nimrod* were also used to ferry the troops and stores upstream to the city.

*** 

While the Bombay units were being assembled and marched north to Multan, 700 km upstream from Roree, the main British force, to be led by the Commander-in-Chief himself, was assembling at Ferozepore and Lahore. This force was initially intended to have seven brigades of infantry and four of cavalry, plus artillery, sappers and miners. There were currently 4,000 men at Ferozepore and 8,000 at Lahore. As reinforcements came up these would increase to 7,000 and 12,000 respectively. This army would be comprised of 21,204 infantry (6,164 being European, 15,040 native) and 6,414 cavalry (1,414 European, 2,500 native and another 2,500 irregulars). Along with sappers, pioneers, horse artillery and bigger guns and other irregulars this would, it was planned, make up a force 30,360 strong.

Gough's strength at this stage comprised of four regiments of British infantry and eleven native regiments. Along with this force was three regiments of British cavalry and five regiments of native cavalry. Compared to the first war, however, it was the artillery where most of the changes would take place. British artillery had suffered against Sikh guns at Ferozeshah and lessons had been learnt. The army was equipped with sixty-four field pieces. But it was the addition of a battery of 18-pounders and large howitzers that was thought would give Gough the decisive advantage in the campaign for the Sikh army had been deprived of all its heavy pieces after the end of the first war.

As to the tactics to be deployed against Shere Singh's army, Gough had been instructed in no uncertain terms by Dalhousie that none of the failures of the previous war would be countenanced and that the campaign should be short, sharp and decisive campaign unlike the first war.

'Lord Gough has already come down into the plains. I have told him this job must be done clean this time, and within the next cold weather. Gobindgarh is in our possession – also the citadel of Lahore and the Maharajah,' informed the Governor-General in his correspondence with the Duke of Wellington on 8 October and the overwhelming force and guns with which he was being supplied. He was confident the job could be done without complications. 'The Sikh strength was in their guns, and the most of them are reposing placidly at my elbow in the arsenal of Ft. William. In short, there is no fear of anything except the lives of the officers detached, and I am sanguine even as to them.'

The major talking point at Ferozepore as the force accumulated was not only the extreme scarcity of food and grass for the animals but the scarcity of carriage for the army. In consequence, the Lahore Government was being cajoled for assistance on this front. With the Governor-General's instructions in mind, Gough's plan therefore was to wait till the problems of carriage were addressed sufficiently. Meanwhile an advance guard commanded by Cureton proceeding with the units already available was to shadow Shere Singh's force without attempting to contest any ground and to guard the approaches to Lahore, thus denying him the capital. This would give Gough the time to assemble the main army at Ferozepore and Lahore before advancing to meet Shere Singh near, it was expected, the Chenab.

It was customary to label the British forces of that time with somewhat grandiose names. The 'Army of the Indus' had invaded Afghanistan a few years earlier. In the previous war, the British army had been given the title 'Army of the Sutlej' in reference to the river border between the two states during the First Anglo-Sikh War. Gough had unilaterally decided to name the assembling force 'the Army of the Punjab'. Dalhousie was irked by this. Whatever his feelings on annexation after the war, making British aims obvious by naming the army as such would only fan nationalism and drive more Sikh soldiers into Shere Singh's camp. 'I perceive that he has christened it "army of the Punjab". I regret that he has done this. He had neither instructions nor any authority to do so. I dislike the fashion in itself, and political significance may be attached to the name sooner than I write. But it is done and there is no use in saying anything about it.'

Meanwhile reaction from the British newspapers on Shere Singh's defection and the coming war was swift and clear. Almost all welcomed the clarity of the situation now despite Dalhousie's attempts to still treat the issue as one of rebellion against the Lahore Durbar.

'The perpetual apprehension of war is as costly as war itself perhaps more so and is an excuse for putting off the consideration of every suggestion for the improvement of the country,' *The Englishman* wrote on 18 October, 'a treacherous foe will now be met as he ought to be with a crushing force. His means of future resistance must be removed and then indeed we may hope for a long and uninterrupted peace.' The *Bombay Times* welcomed the decision to send troops but criticised the delay in sending troops previously, which would have ended the nascent rebellion at Multan. The *Friend of India* was of the same opinion. 'All disasters in the Punjab, during the present year, the first excepted, have arisen from unnecessary and most culpable delays,' it declared. Regardless of what had happened, though, all were in agreement that the war would be brief and decisive. With such a grand army as that assembling at Ferozepore, little difficulty was expected in brushing aside the remnants of the Sikh army and irregulars that Shere Singh could weld together. 'Such an army is enough to conquer India *de novo*,' declared *The Mofussilite*, confidently prophesying one large battle in the Punjab would end the insurrection with a crushing British victory. There would be a delay in the reckoning, to be sure. Shere Singh would no doubt collect more troops till confident of marching on Lahore. Meanwhile, the British force was also being prepared. But one violent collision, it predicted, somewhere in the middle of the Rechna doab, would settle matters conclusively in British favour. So confident were they of a crushing victory that there was an impression that Gough would advance slower than necessary into the Punjab, thereby allowing Chutter Singh's and Shere Singh's forces to combine to be destroyed in one swoop. The only fear, it was speculated, was that Shere Singh might elect to retreat into the hilly country across the Jhelum. There the British cavalry would be hampered, manoeuvring would prove difficult and British supply lines from Ferozepore would stretch, complicating matters. The result, though, a crushing British victory, was not in doubt.

The Indian press was also broadly behind the expected annexation of the state after the expected victory. 'Politicians are already speculating on the fate of the Punjab, and annexation is confidently talked of' was the attitude of one of the Calcutta newspapers as to recent events.

'That it would be the best course for the country itself, is not doubted by any person here whose opinion deserves consideration; in fact the wretched condition of what are called "protected states" is so apparent that nothing could induce a continuation of the system, but the prudery of the Home Government, which dreads the accusation of ambition.' *The Messenger* was equally strident. 'It is positively puerile to discuss the honesty or dishonesty of the act of annexation. If we have made treaties with the Sikhs they have been made on the understanding that would govern their country peaceably and leave us unmolested. They have had a fair trial and now deserve no quarter,' it declared, comparing the Punjab to other annexed territories and arguing an annexed Punjab was an infinitely better solution than a propped-up dynasty: 'Since we have annexed Scinde to the empire not the slightest effort has been made to throw off our yoke.'

Meanwhile, back in the Punjab, whatever the ruminations and reflections of the public and the newspapers, Frederick Currie would stand steadfastly although unconvincingly by official policy, that the army currently assembling on the border of the Punjab was not entering as an enemy of the Lahore Government, but to assist it against rebels. Declarations were issued out at Lahore and other cities that nobody need have any fear but the rebels and those who were enemies of the accord between the Sikh and British governments.

# 20

# Ram Singh and the Hill Insurrections

I hear from all sides that Bedee Bikrama Sing has been the prime mover in the present insurrection and has seduced these foolish Rajas who are a primitive unsophisticated race to seize the present opportunity for asserting their independence.

John Lawrence to Frederick Currie, 30 November 1848

He [Ram Singh] is described as a man of a most villainous countenance and appeared rather proud of the notice he attracted.

Newspaper correspondent after Ram Singh's arrest, April 1849

While British preparations for a large force to advance into the Punjab to tackle Shere Singh's army were still being planned, Frederick Currie found his attention being diverted by further insurrection towards the east of the Punjab – to the newly annexed British hill territories of Kangra and the adjacent Jalandhar. These areas till now had had displayed a peaceful appearance and were thought to be entirely passive, leading the British authorities to reduce the military force in the foothills during 1847 and early 1848. However, there were grudges held by many against the new British administration. The deposition by the British of some of the hill chiefs who had helped the Sikh army during the late war hadn't been forgotten by those men. On top of these, other changes John Lawrence had made recently while managing the province had harmed many other influential persons.

This area had stayed quiet till the beginning of September when news of Chutter Singh's rebellion in Hazara filtered through, receiving a positive response from certain quarters. The feeling was greatly strengthened on the news of Shere Singh's defection and his letters asking for support along with promises that any deposed chieftains would be given their privileges back. The lack of British garrisons in the area no doubt helped as well. Only one European regiment and four native regiments were stationed in the area, along with irregular cavalry and a battery of artillery. In addition to these were two local corps of military police (one Sikh and one of Hill Rajputs). The main British garrisons were stationed in the Kangra fort, Hoshiarpore city, Mukerian and Nurpur to the north. In addition there were much smaller garrisons dotted around in the hill country and in the various police stations. The Kangra fort contingent in the hills had actually been reduced recently, with the Hill Corps now manning the walls. The fort garrison at Nurpur in the north had also been reduced. Only three companies that had formerly been at Hajeepore were now stationed there. When news of the Multan uprising broke, as a precaution, three companies of the 28th NI were ordered to Hoshiarpore to be stationed at Kangra fort while the Hill Corps were sent back to their usual cantonments in the valley.

John Lawrence would warn of the dangers of keeping this area garrisoned so lightly as insurrection in Multan and Hazara grew but believed there was no great animosity to the British in these parts and that financial inducements and offers of employment would be sufficient.

'These hills are full of disbanded soldiers, not inimical to us, but wanting service and bread,' he wrote to Brig. Wheeler, stationed in Jalandhar, on 25 September, 'and more danger is to be apprehended here than in the plains of the Jullundur doab ... In the Jullundur Doab there are few disbanded soldiers, an open campaign country, and no forts. Two infantry corps, or a couple of irregular cavalry corps and a battery, would, I think, render all safe. In the hills we have an area of three thousand square miles, full of soldiery, with but three companies at Nurpore, and the Sikh local corps locked up at Kangra.'

While the British had manpower problems, the prospective rebels also had their issues. Far away from the Sikh cantonments and the support of regular Sikh soldiers, they never had the wherewithal in terms of arms, ammunition and artillery to make an effective challenge. On top of this, John Lawrence never gave them the respite to either increase their numbers or acquire substantial arms.

***

One of the more energetic persons involved in the fighting against the British here was an official by the name of Ram Singh Pathania. He was the son of the Vizier of Raja Bir Singh, the chief of the petty state of Nurpur in the foothills of the Himalayas. He also happened to be a devotee of Bhai Maharaj. Impressed with the preacher and sharing his uncompromising views on the ejection of the British from the Punjab, he had initially joined Bhai Maharaj's following. However, after Currie's interception of the Bhai's army at Jhung and the scattering of his force, he had made his way back to his home area to continue the struggle there. Bhai Maharaj had given him funds to recruit more men. It would take him time to recruit a sufficient force without being detected, the area being full of informers. Men from as far as Jammu were recruited, it was later found.

His first guerrilla attacks began in late August 1848. With the men he had collected so far, he launched an attack on the nearest British presence at Pathankot, 25 km downstream, looting and relieving a British customs house of its money and killing two persons and wounding two others while three men were captured and taken prisoner. Other exploits included attacking the small fort of Shahpur Kandi, 30 km east of Nurpur, with around 200 men, expelling its small garrison and making it his own base instead. As news of these attacks spread, sympathisers from around the area streamed in to his camp and support and money began to be offered to Ram Singh.

He clearly had considerable funds at this stage, or was managing to raise them either from sympathisers or through looting British customs posts and the like. He was known to be offering 8 rupees a month to recruits. For comparison, British sepoys at the time were paid 6 rupees. At around the time of his attack on Shahpur Kandi, intelligence was also received that 300 men on the right bank of the Ravi were waiting to join him. These were ex-soldiers from Gulab Singh's army in Kashmir, looking for employment and attracted by the salary and the chance for a fight. There was suspicion Gulab Singh was secretly aiding Ram Singh, in any case, and John Lawrence would send Gulab Singh's vakeel back to Kashmir with a stark reminder to the Maharajah that he was a British ally and must do his utmost to stop his ex-soldiers and other rebels on his territory from crossing the border to join Ram Singh's party. This reminder was in vain, the hilly border being so porous and difficult to police.

Hearing of the Shahpur incident, Mr Charles B. Saunders organised a force to march and recapture the fort. Saunders was the deputy commissioner of Jalandhar, based 100 km south of Pathankot at Hoshiarpore, and was described as 'a cool judicious officer, one of the best I have got' by John Lawrence. The news had also reached the ears of Mr Barnes, the deputy commissioner of Kangra, who organised a force independent of Saunders. Further reinforcements were sent by John Lawrence, who had by now learned of these infractions by Ram Singh. The various columns heading towards Shahpur comprised a company of the 29th NI, Fisher's 15th Irregular Horse, Capt. Davidson's 16th Irregular Horse, 100 men of Major Ferris' corps, a company of the 1st Sikh Regiment of Infantry, 150 men of the 2nd Sikh Regiment and a detachment of the 30th NI. Further units at Hajeepore and Nurpur were also asked to assist by John Lawrence, who personally took control at Nurpur.

The columns began reaching Shahpur around the 10th, and Major Fisher, heading the 15th Irregular Horse, had already ordered ladders to be constructed for storming the place. The fort was strong but the number of rebels small, and Ram Singh knew guerrilla warfare was his best hope. On the British columns reaching the fort, both sides opened fire for the entire day. During the night, however, the defenders made off by a back entrance unnoticed, crossing the Ravi into Gulab Singh's territory before recrossing the river and the Beas and disappearing back into familiar hill country. The next day the British force found the fort empty and entered without a struggle.

The very next day, John Lawrence received intelligence that Ram Singh and his party, now reinforced to a strength of 400, had established a new camp 30 km southwest of Shahpur Kandi on a hilltop near the town of Nurpur. From there he had begun writing letters to all the local village heads asking for assistance and urging them to join him in the struggle. Determined to give him no respite, John Lawrence also arrived at Nurpur with his force early on 13 September with 150 men of the 2nd Regiment of Sikh Local Infantry, preceded by the columns of Fisher and Davidson, and set up camp at the foot of the hilly area overlooking the town where Ram Singh and his followers sat, a mere 2.5 km to the south.

Ram Singh had chosen his position well. His camp was on a village at the top of a jungled backbone of hills that stretched 3 km from south-east to north-west, and was admirable from a defensive point of view. He also had water close by, several streams running down the incline of hills. Supplies were procurable, local villagers being sympathetic to his cause. From the heights, more importantly, Ram Singh could easily see any British columns being sent against him well in advance of their arrival at the summit. 'The whole surface consists of rugged hills, more or less covered with trees and brushwood, intersected with strong valleys, cut up in all directions by mountain torrents; on this side of the hill, which the insurgents occupy, is the native village of Ram Sing, some of the people of which, have joined him. He might take up much stronger positions at no great distance, and the object, therefore, is to prevent his escape, until sufficient force can arrive to enable us to attack him,' explained John Lawrence.

Four roads, or rather dirt paths, led out of the area and each could be used as an escape route; therefore all had to be watched. This meant the British force would have to be large enough to be split up into four columns, each covering a path. According to local informers, Ram Singh was estimated to have only 200 to 250 men, armed only with matchlocks and swords at the time. Whatever the numbers, Lawrence was adamant about not letting Ram Singh escape again and therefore for the next week or so he took little action while reconnaissance and preparations for an attack were formulated and more troops arrived. The general impression was that if the operation was not properly carried out, Ram Singh and his band would simply melt away only to assemble again somewhere else. 'Ram Sing has been very cautious in his movements since my arrival, and now that Major Fisher, with his force, has joined, will I am afraid, attempt to escape,' wrote John Lawrence. 'The country round this town, and the vicinity, which he will, probably, not leave, except he decamps altogether across the Ravee, for it is here where his influence alone lies, is extremely strong.'

Spies were sent out to Ram Singh's camp and the supplier villages nearby to ascertain his strength. Reconnaissance of the hilly area proved difficult due to the awkward nature of the terrain and the danger of being shot at. Lawrence, in addition to his force, had around 800 men drummed up from local villages to help in the dragnet around the hilly area.

While John Lawrence waited, Ram Singh chose to take the initiative by advancing some men to the town in preparation for an ambush. Lawrence's habit of taking a daily morning ride doubling up as reconnaissance round the foot of the hills with only a few men as an escort had been recognised. On 16 September, on their way back to camp after the ride, Lawrence's party was ambushed by a group of around forty of Ram Singh's men. Both Lawrence and Major Fisher were fired on but both escaped without wounds. The tumult would alert the British camp and reinforcements drove off the assailants.

Both sides following this incident moved their attention to the nearby villagers. Lawrence declared a reward of 1,000 rupees for the capture of Ram Singh and 100 rupees for each of his principal men, hoping to entice the local villagers into betraying the rebels. Ram Singh would in turn respond by keeping himself busy attacking suspected collaborators and informers. He had his men torture the locals of several villages who had been suspected of passing information to the British and several houses of suspected collaborators were burnt down as much as 15 km away in the village of Ghuntul.

Lawrence had fixed the morning of 19 September as the day of the attack in the British camp, and at 3 a.m. on that day four separate parties advanced to their respective positions in readiness to attack the rebel position. The first column under Major Hodgson comprised 360 men from 1st Sikh Regiment Local Infantry. A second column was composed of two companies of the 29th NI under Lt Johnston. A third column, four companies of the 71st NI, around 240 men, was commanded by Captain Rind with the fourth column, principally the Kangra regiment and numbering around 150, men fighting under Lt Wallace. The remainder of the British force was stationed outside of the hilly area. Major Fisher commanded the 15th Irregular Cavalry and the 16th to the south and south-west at the villages of Bassa and Jach, while east of the hills John Lawrence and Mr Barnes watched the action unfolding with 400 Rajputs. Some 200 of these men had been supplied by the local Rajas of Mundee and Chamba, supplemented by others drummed up from the local villages to assist. These two forces were to intercept and mop up any of the rebels who had managed to elude the four attacking columns and were attempting to escape the area.

By dawn all the columns were at the foot of the hilly area, the village situated on top of the hill where Ram Singh had positioned himself being easily visible. Firing soon commenced after the advance and the columns gradually made their way to the top and reached the village dispersing the rebels.

'The village I directed to be fired, and thereby destroyed a considerable quantity of supplies, two magazines, and various other property collected by the rebels. Two native British subjects, confined by the enemy, were released, and some mules, formerly captured, belonging to Government, were recovered, and made over to the Commissariat Agent. The dislodged enemy amounting to, I should say, about 100 men, then retired firing further up the mountain, closely pursued. Having reached the crest, they were joined by others, and attempted to make a fresh stand but were quickly routed, and chased down both sides of the hill, dispersing singly in all directions,' Major Hodgson would report of the fighting to Mr Lawrence.

The loss was small for the British columns with one sepoy killed, nine sepoys of the 29th NI and 1st Sikh Infantry wounded, three critically. Fisher was confident that the capture of the camp and the dispersal of the rebels had effectively ended the insurrection:

> The hill in the possession of the rebel Ram Sing, was attacked, this morning, by the troops in four separate parties; the villages were burnt; Ram Sing and his followers were driven from the different heights, and dispersed with slaughter; their tents and drums were destroyed; and the character of Ram Sing, as a successful soldier, is I think, totally annihilated, in the eyes of the predatory soldiery who have, hitherto been his support.

The word slaughter was perhaps a bit optimistic, for fifteen bodies of Ram Singh's men were recovered from the hill, the total number being thought to be around thirty men killed but with the jungle making the task of finding the corpses difficult. Several hundred men did manage to get away, including a wounded Ram Singh himself; however, papers and letters, which he had to leave behind in the village, were captured and during the day and subsequent days upwards of 200 suspected rebels were arrested by the British in the vicinity as villages nearby were searched. These arrests made John Lawrence confident that a successful conclusion had been reached in the operation.

> The dispersion of Ram Sing and his followers appears to be complete. The day before yesterday I went over the hill on which they had taken up their position and found it in many cases not accessible to troops except by narrow footpaths. In the evening I received information that Ram Sing with five men had been seen in a wood some eight or nine miles off. I at once sent off a party after him who were out all night. It appeared that he had only left the place an hour before their arrival. I have now reason to believe that he has crossed the Beas and gone towards Seeba, north of Hoshiarpore where there are extensive jungles though others seem to think that he has taken refuge in Hurripore. I have sent off a party of the hill rangers in the hope of seizing him.

Meanwhile posters of the dispersal of Ram Singh's force were sent to all the heads of the local villages in the area, also reminding the villagers of the bounty on his head. Ram Singh himself, having evaded capture, would decide to lay low for a while to shake off the trailing British columns. For the rest of September and October, no intelligence was received as to his whereabouts. The informers in the area could glean no information on him either and it was rumoured he had either left the area for good, died or withdrawn to recover his strength. There were even rumours he had gone to Shere Singh to ask for financial and other assistance. With no intelligence at all on his whereabouts, the British force which had been assembled now began to be dispersed.

John Lawrence's recommendations after this particular episode was that more pressure must be applied on Maharajah Gulab Singh of Kashmir by the Resident and British Government. Ex-soldiers and other guns for hire from Kashmir still continued to be recruited by Ram Singh, and this movement of men along a long, porous and hilly border could only be closed by the full and earnest cooperation of the Maharajah. 'If Maharajah Golab Sing could be prevailed on to discontinue the disbandment of his surplus soldiery at the present crisis it would conduce to the public tranquillity. At any rate it would not appear unreasonable that His Highness should in some measure be responsible for such characters not collecting in bodies within the Maharajah's territories and joining malcontents in arms against the British power,' he suggested to the Resident on 22 September.

Ram Singh's disappearance would not last long. Exactly two months after escaping at Nurpur, he surfaced again. 300 of Ram Singh's men appeared in the town of Deena Nuggar, recruiting more men while plundering and killing British collaborators. Meanwhile, on 19 November he signalled his own presence by advancing the bulk of his men and laying siege to the fort and police station of Pathankot, 20 km west of his previous hilltop redoubt. This time he had a much bigger force of 700–1,000 men with between two to five guns. In addition to this there was news he was about to receive large reinforcements of around 2,000–3,000 men from across the Ravi.

Opposing them was a British garrison consisting of only fifty men of the 2nd Sikh Local Infantry and some police, along with a certain Mr Bowles, the custom officer, and his chuprassies (helpers) with supplies that would not last more than a couple of days. The garrison was safe behind the walls but short of supplies; in addition, Ram Singh didn't have time on his hands, knowing succour for the garrison would arrive within a matter of days. Orders from John Lawrence were received by Major Ferris at Kangra on 21 November to move to relieve the garrison at Pathankot and he duly did so, his 2nd Hill Regiment reaching there on the 23rd. He was beaten to it by Major Simpson from Hajeepore, who had moved up with five companies of the 29th NI. The combined force would stay there till the 25th. Lawrence himself moved up to Mukerian with Major Hodgson and his Sikh corps, 30 km south of Pathankot with four guns and 300 of Major Hodgson's Sikh corps. A squadron of the 10th Cavalry was also ordered up from Kartarpore.

Due to this energetic response, Ram Singh had no option but to abort the attempt to capture the fort and he retired towards Deena Nuggar. Lawrence followed and attempted to surprise his party with a night march but his force only reached the rebels at around 8 a.m. A short skirmish took place and as expected Ram Singh's party dispersed as the British artillery opened up. Several rebels were killed and wounded and some captured, including one of Ram Singh's chief lieutenants, prompting the group to melt away again into the hills. They would stay quiet for another two months.

Ram Singh's third appearance would be in the new year of 1849. In January, information was received that he had set up his rebel camp in the Dulla hills near Shahpur with a strong party of around 1,000 men. Upon receiving intelligence of this, Brig.-Gen. H. M. Wheeler, who had previously been putting down insurrections closer to Lahore, was put in charge of the operation to destroy the rebels. On 8 January Wheeler left Pathankot for Shahpur, taking with him on the expedition Harry Lumsden and William Hodson, with John Lawrence also appearing later with reinforcements. The new rebel camp Wheeler found on top of the Dullah heights was just as hard to attack as the Nurpur position.

'On reaching the valley, the positions of the enemy were found to be admirably chosen, and I at once saw that a direct attack was out of the question, more particularly as they showed in great strength,' Wheeler related. Instead the general used the next three days (12th to 14th) for reconnaissance while more troops reached the scene. 'So bad was the nature of the country over which Lumsden followed them,' wrote Hodson of his colleague, 'that at one time more than half of the horses of the troop were down, pursuers and pursued rolling together in desperate strife in the middle of the deep marshes.'

On the evening of 14 January, Wheeler made his plans. Hodson would move up the right bank of the Ravi River with 400 men of the 3rd Regiment NI early the next morning before crossing towards the hill and attacking the rebels from the north. Meanwhile Lt-Col Downing with the 4th Regiment NI and a risallah (100 men) of irregular cavalry was to move up the Chakki River and attack from the east on hearing the British guns going off, which was to be the signal. If the guns were not heard, there being many hills between the two forces, he was to attack at 8 a.m. on the 16th at the latest in any case. Meanwhile the rest of the troops formed a third column comprising the rest of the 3rd Regiment NI and 2nd Irregular Cavalry under Major Butler. By this time John Lawrence had again joined the force, bringing reinforcements, the 16th Irregular Cavalry and 1st Sikh Local Command under Capt. Davidson. These were formed into a fourth column to join in with Butler when he began ascending the high ground from the south-west of the hill. It was thought that these columns, attacking from all principal angles, would be able to dispose of most of the rebels.

Things didn't go quite according to plan due to the difficult terrain. Hodson left at noon on the 15th; rain had already begun, and increased in ferocity all day and night. This made his progress very difficult, especially having to cross the swollen Ravi River and various chasms in the terrain. He was supposed to get into his allotted position by 6 p.m. on the same day. Due to the delays, however, he only reached his position at 6 p.m. the next day.

'Of this he could give me no intimation in consequence of the weather preventing any one from coming round and the occupation of the mountain by the enemy equally preventing any one from coming across,' described Wheeler later. 'All were ready in my camp at 8 am and although it poured, moved off in capital spirits to be ready to ascend at the signal.'

Meanwhile, the British 24-pound howitzers and mortars were dragged up the hills to play on Ram Singh's position, an awkward manoeuvre itself in this hilly territory. Only the two columns from the south-west made it to the top under Major Butler, 250 men in total of his own men, the 3rd NI, and about 200 cavalrymen of the 2nd Irregulars who had dismounted. Ram Singh had a brisk interchange with the British columns before disappearing, his men dispersing in all directions with the usual plans to meet up later. The next day, the 16th, as they fled the area around 500 of Ram Singh's men attacked an outpost of the 4th NI under Lt Aikman, who was protecting the road to Nurpur, and killed two more men and wounded four; this brought British casualties to four killed and twenty wounded in the operation. 'The enemy has lost severely, 35 bodies were counted and many more must have fallen on different parts of the hill which have not been seen. Of their wounded I know nothing,' reported Wheeler. 'Ram Sing's party is utterly broken up for the present, and he has recrossed the Ravee with two followers'.

By skill, luck and pluck, he had escaped the British columns for the last few months but Ram Singh's rebel career would be cut short by treachery. On 12 February, Ram Singh was praying in a temple, alone and unarmed near the fortress of Shahpur Kandi. The priest, on noticing his presence, and swayed by the substantial reward on Ram Singh's head, gave information as to his whereabouts at the local police station. He was promptly arrested and incarcerated at Lahore, there to await sentencing at the same time as the other Sikh protagonists after the war.

*\*\*\**

Ram Singh wasn't the only one to attempt an uprising in this hilly and difficult region. His exploits, along with news coming in of the inconclusive Battle of Ramnuggar at the end of November, convinced others during late November to try their hand at liberating themselves.

These included a string of minor rulers further south dissatisfied with the new British regime. In mid-November, Bikram Singh Bedi, a Sikh priest and a wealthy, influential man, decided to revolt. Gathering several hundred armed men, he turned the Nurpur and Oonah police officers out of their station. Messages were also being sent out to all the other nearby villages to rise up. His example was followed by others. On 24 November, Raja Omed Singh of Juswan declared his independence, followed by Raja Chund of Mahal Mori (Kutoch), who captured a string of lightly defended forts of Riyah and Abwanpur as well as his ancestral palace of Teera, a good stronghold. In these forts some ammunition and guns of the Sikh army remained and these were captured and distributed among his force. From the fortress of Riyah, the raja fired a royal salute of twenty-one guns to signal the new order and the end of British rule in the region. He had a small army of around 1,100 men. The local British district officer gave him plenty of inducements to return to British allegiance, going as far as offering him his jaghir back and full pardon if he disbanded his following and returned to Mahal Mori, but to no avail. Another who joined the uprising was the Raja of Duttarpore. These were not formidable insurrections by any means, but petty rulers rebelling with several hundred irregulars at their disposal.

'I hear from all sides that Bedee Bikrama Sing has been the prime mover in the present insurrection and has seduced these foolish Rajas who are a primitive unsophisticated race to seize the present opportunity for asserting their independence,' reported John Lawrence to Frederick Currie, informing him the whole area from Rupar to Hajeepore was now revolting. John Lawrence at this time was free as Ram Singh had disappeared back into the hills and he immediately turned his attention to putting down these revolts. 'The circumstance of the Bedee having joined the insurrection will have an immense effect no doubt on all the Sikhs in the Doab; they are not numerous compared to the whole population but are no doubt the most warlike portion of it.' He continued in his correspondence on 29 November, 'I heard this morning that a number of them have met and sworn to drive us out of the Doab. Nearly all the Rajas in the hills seem to be raising men and are doubtless more or less implicated and watching events in the hope of benefiting by them.'

In order to deal with these Rajas in the shortest period of time, he divided the force he had used against Ram Singh into two columns which would march south by two different routes, mopping up any opposition as they went along. Deputy Commissioner Mr G. Barnes was given one column to arrest the Raja of Kutoch. Meanwhile Lawrence, with 500 men and four guns, moved against the other insurgents down the Juswan valley to Dumgoo initially, where another local raja had declared independence. As the British force under Lawrence arrived he gave himself up and his fort was blown up.

By 1 December, Lawrence had made his way to Umbotah from where he proceeded to Umb Ka Bagh while Hodgson's 2nd Sikh Corps moved towards Aknot, where Raja Umaid Singh (the Jaswan Raja) of Umbotah resided. The following day the Raja's residence at Aknot was attacked at two different points by the 2nd Sikh Corps under Major Hodgson and his other residence at Umb by the wing of the 29th NI, with the residence and village burnt. Knowing the hills intimately, most of the raja's men got away, although thirty-eight men were captured and arrested. Raja Umaid Singh, who had fled after the attack of Umb, was arrested on the same day.

From here, the march south was continued to Chooloo and then to Oonah by two companies of the 29th NI and two of the Sikh corps. This was to capture Bikram Singh Bedi of Oonah himself. But he had realised the game was up and wisely decided to retire from the Jalandhar area, rapidly heading off to join Shere Singh with around 150 horsemen. Crossing the Beas River, he was for a short time pursued by Brig.-Gen. Wheeler, who was then at Mukerian, but he had too much of a lead and successfully joined the main Sikh army. Later, he would take part in the battles of Chillianwala and Gujrat, surrendering along with Shere Singh.

On 4 December Lawrence advanced from Umbotah to Oonah, confiscated Bikram Singh's jaghirs and had his fort at Oonah blown up and his houses razed to the ground. Several guns were also captured. The priest had considerable wealth and all his property was put up for auction, including a menagerie containing rhinoceros and lions. His departure ended all conflict in the Jalandhar doab and adjoining hills – a conflict that had lasted only thirteen days due to the vigorous response of Lawrence, with three local rajas made captive.

Meanwhile Mr Barnes with the other columns was having similar success. On 1 December the Raja of Mahal Mori was overwhelmed by a wing of the 2nd Sikh Local Infantry Hill Corps with help from Major Ferris's column from Nurpur. The raja lost twenty-five men killed, including some senior men. He surrendered himself and his forts. Mr Barnes marched next day to the right bank of the Beas, receiving his surrender. The only raja to put up much resistance was the Raja of Katoch. He moved his force of around 800 men from Teerah to attack the British column. His irregulars were beaten back quite swiftly, with the raja himself wounded. Retreating back to Teerah, he found his followers quickly deserting his standard and later gave himself up and was taken prisoner. The British columns destroyed his fort, confiscating his guns, including two 11-pounders. The Datarpur raja was taken prisoner without violence.

By 3 December, John Lawrence could declare all was peaceful in the Jalandhar doab: 'Had we not thus promptly acted, I am convinced that the rebellion would have assumed a formidable aspect and have cost blood and treasure to suppress. Many who had every intention of joining against us were paralyzed by our movements and the good intentions of the well disposed were confirmed,' John Lawrence summed up in his correspondence with Currie. But this wasn't quite the end of the insurgency in the hill area, although things would stay quiet for a period of a month or so. In January, Harry Lumsden was employed in an excursion by several hundred rebels led by a Gunda Singh from north of the Chenab who were possibly trying to join up with like-minded people at Nurpur in Jalandhar. By a process of rapid marches, despite heavy rain he caught up with the group on 3 January during the afternoon. Catching them by surprise, he destroyed the party.

\*\*\*

The first and only outbreak of violence closer to Lahore would occur in early October. This was the raising of an armed force by Arjun Singh, a wealthy and nationalist notable in the city of Gujranwala, a city just 70 km to the north-west of Lahore. Arjun Singh openly declared his support for Shere Singh and welcomed all who would fight with him. He also owned several forts in the Amritsar area and his influence made him dangerous. Collecting around 100 armed men of similar views in a few days and recruiting more, he openly showed defiance to the British-led government. 'It is necessary that an immediate example should be made of any who may bring their rebellious proceedings so close to Lahore,' Currie noted to Colin Campbell on 7 October. 'If this man is not promptly punished we shall have his example extensively followed.' Determined to stamp down hard, he promptly ordered the Lahore Durbar to organise a force against Arjun Singh. Two companies of Lahore troops had been previously sent to punish the rebels but being in sympathy with the rebels they had showed little enthusiasm for action, preferring to remain outside the town. Currie, on seeing no obvious progress, then decided to send a British column instead to force the issue. All rebels were to be killed or taken prisoner, he ordered. For this mission, Currie's main assistant Mr Cocks would accompany the force. 'There is no probability of their fraternizing with the garrison but the party should for precaution sake be of strength sufficient to annihilate them if they do,' added Currie regarding the fidelity of the Sikh units that had been sent earlier and which were still camped outside the town. Since they had been given no guns, the British force with guns could overwhelm both. The British force consisted of some of the 2nd Irregular Cavalry, two guns, the 46th NI and portions of Skinner's horse. They set off on the same day.

Arjun Singh, however, on hearing news of the British force with guns approaching, promptly vacated the fort. Therefore, when the British column appeared at Gujranwala on 9 October they found his premises empty. Currie had declared any rebels would have their property destroyed and possessions auctioned. In line with this policy, the structure was destroyed and possessions and valuables seized for auction, with the column returning on 11 October. Arjun Singh was believed to have joined up with Shere Singh's army as well.

Arjun Singh was also owner of a fort about 60 km in the direction of Amritsar. In the same direction was another fort at belonging to Lal Singh Moraria, another person known to have strong connections with Chutter Singh. In order to eliminate these two rebel outposts, Currie would send a strong force under Brig. Wheeler consisting of the 61st Foot, 7th Cavalry, 2nd Irregular Horse, 3rd Troop 1st Brigade Horse and 4th Company 6th Battalion Foot Artillery with No. 19 Light Field Battery and the 3rd NI. This force left Lahore on 12 October. Wheeler would pass Amritsar and reach the right bank of Beas the same day. The next day, on reaching the village of Mehta, they found they were only a few kilometres away from the fort of Rungur Nungal.

The fort had already been invested on the 9th by William Hodson's advance units, arriving before Wheeler with the artillery. The usual greetings were exchanged, with the garrison firing their matchlocks and Hodson giving them an ultimatum to surrender within the hour or face annihilation from British guns or the gallows afterwards if caught. With the garrison refusing to surrender, Hodson sent off a map of the fort to Wheeler before retreating a mile from the village for the night. He waited another day, by which time his Guides had made their way up, giving him around 200 men. A brisk fire was now kept up by both sides. 'The fort, though very small, was immensely strong, and well garrisoned with desperadoes, and we had sharp work of it during the two nights and day which elapsed before the brigadier appeared with his troops,' remarked Hodson. Once Wheeler arrived with the guns, the cause of the garrison was lost. Wheeler immediately began pummelling the walls with the two 24-pounder howitzers, one 12-pounder and a battery of 9-pounders. This bombardment carried on for most of the day and into the night, by which time the walls had begun crumbling. Realising it was only a matter of time before a good-sized breach was made, the garrison effected an escape during the night.

Bombardment resumed the next day till it was discovered the garrison had disappeared. On entry, a considerable amount of grain inside the fort was found but no guns. The British loss in the operation was one man killed and several wounded. This fort was destroyed, 'a work which consumed a week of incessant labour, and forty-one mines loaded with an aggregate of 8000 pounds of powder' as a bemused Hodson noted. Meanwhile, several chiefs were bidding defiance across the Beas River in the Baree doab and Wheeler was ordered to deal with them as well. 'Their representatives have garrisoned their dwelling houses and have replied to the Government order that their castles stand or fall with Mooltan,' the Resident had written to Brig. Campbell on 1 October. 'An example is necessary.' Some of these forts were found to be deserted while in others resistance was shown. In one, a fight did take place with a garrison of around 200 men. They had no guns but asked for no quarter and met with none, Wheeler's force killing all the men. All the forts were blown up. Wheeler then turned his attention to the rebel outpost at the village of Moraree, 40 km further north from Rungur Nungul, lying a few miles northwest of the city of Deena Nuggar and near the Beas River. The man who owned the fort was wealthy and influential.

'The owner Lal Sing Morareea was the second in command to Sirdar Runjore Sing at Aliwal and the spoils of Buddowal are believed to be for the most part in Moraree with other property also to the amount of many lakhs of rupees,' Currie noted. Bhudowal was a battle that took place in the First Anglo-Sikh War and in which the Sikh force under Ranjodh Singh had captured much of the British baggage. This was a chance to even the score. His property and possessions, estimated to the value of many lakh rupees, were to be confiscated. The fort had a garrison of around 3,000 men, albeit irregulars, but by the time Wheeler had received reinforcements on the 13th and hauled the necessary guns and four 8-inch mortars to reduce the fort by 25 October, the garrison had dispersed. The fort was subsequently blown up.

These actions served to permanently destroy any opposition to British control in the vicinity of Lahore and to the east, although the British authorities now found that almost the entire Sikh army stationed in Peshawar and Bannu provinces had risen and joined Shere Singh's army.

# 21

# The Bannu and Peshawar Insurrections

I could not but perceive a growing spirit of disaffection among the troops, shown by
their insolent bearing towards myself and my assistants.

George Lawrence to Frederick Currie, August 1848

I felt confident that the force at Lahore and in the Jalandhar, with the support we had on
this side of the Satluj, might defy the Devil, much more the Khalsa.

Dalhousie to the Duke of Wellington

The only two large contingents of Sikh troops that had not joined the uprising by the end of
September were those stationed in the provinces of Bannu and Peshawar. Realising the support
of these troops was a *sine qua non* for war, Shere Singh had begun requesting help from them
immediately after joining Mulraj. The soldiers at Peshawar, although sympathetic to the national
cause, were reticent on committing themselves. The reaction of the troops at Bannu was
enthusiastic, however. The news of Shere Singh's defection, along with his letters asking for their
allegiance, reached Bannu province on 19 September and provoked a rapid response.

The main Sikh garrison in Bannu, stationed at the fort of Duleepgarh, consisted of four
regiments of infantry and five hundred sowars and along with other units totalled around 5,000
men with four heavy guns and a troop of horse artillery (six guns). These men were currently
under the command of a Col John Holmes, a European employed in the Sikh army. Meetings
between the soldiers would start immediately and the following day, the garrison declared
themselves openly for Shere Singh. They were led by Sirdar Ram Singh Chapawala, the most
senior Sikh officer present. What was obvious to the soldiers was that the heavily pro-British
Muslim governor of the province, Futteh Khan Tawana, had to be disposed of and the fort
possessed before any assistance to Shere Singh could be provided, for all ammunition and
supplies were stored inside the structure. Tawana was not a popular man among the Sikh troops,
perhaps one of the reasons he had been placed in his position of authority by the Resident,
being as he was a natural counterweight. He had been one of those instrumental in the murder
of Prince Peshaura Singh, a son of Ranjit Singh and heir to the throne years earlier, something
not forgotten by the Sikh troops. This was perhaps seen by the troops as a convenient time to
pursue the vendetta against the man.

Holmes, in a carbon copy of the situation in Hazara with Canora, refused to take orders from
anyone but British officers and agents. After his refusal to countenance any support for Shere
Singh, he unwisely decided to stay and sleep in the Sikh cantonments that night. Thinking that
six sentries around his tent situated in the middle of the camp would be sufficient, he went to
sleep in a carefree manner. During the night, a large party of Sikh soldiers, too large for his

sentries to dare challenge, marched to the tent. The conversations outside and in the tent are not known but it ended with Holmes being shot and decapitated, his head being paraded around the camp.

Tawana, a more cautious man than Holmes, had quickly shut himself up in the inner section of Duleepgarh fort with his Muslim levies when told of the soldiers' decision to rise up. These levies would open fire on the Sikh troops as they approached to take control of the fort. Two soldiers in the fortress had refused to fire on their comrades in a show of support; one was personally killed by Futteh Khan and the other's hands were cut off, a severe punishment to serve as an example to the others. Tawana did manage also to send word out to the local Muslim tribes asking for help. This provoked a mixed response. Some offered help while others, his personal enemies, preferred helping the Sikh force. So a confused situation developed outside the fort and in the area round the city after a few days, with many thousands of tribesmen heeding his call to lay siege to the Sikh camp while they in turn continued to lay siege to the fort. Many hundreds of these tribesmen, ill equipped and undisciplined, would be killed during this time.

In normal circumstances the Sikh regulars would have been unfazed by the tribesmen, easily putting them to flight. What was hampering their performance was a shortage of ammunition and supplies, most of which were stored in the fort itself. Nevertheless, they persisted in the siege for it was common knowledge there was an insufficient reserve of water in the fort and sooner or later Tawana would be forced to surrender. This process took a leisurely ten days. Inside the fort, finding his water running short, Tawana had attempted to finish off an already half-constructed well without success. He was then forced to make a desperate sally with six of his most loyal adherents, in which he was killed. Other accounts mention him attempting to escape via a rope from the walls but being captured and beheaded by the Sikh troops. News of Tawana's death pretty much ended hostilities in Bannu, the Muslim tribesmen's counter-siege melting away as the Sikh troops obtained new ammunition from the fort. With these supplies, they now organised themselves to cross the Indus as soon as possible, a separate contingent being sent to collect the boats in the area in and around Esakhail, essential for crossing the river.

For a time, the Sikh troops would remain undecided on whether to assist Chutter Singh in Hazara or travel down to Multan to aid his son. However, news arrived that Shere Singh was striking north and Chutter Singh had in any case written letters to them that their services would be required for a push on Lahore. It was therefore decided to march east and join up with Shere Singh as he moved north. On 17 October camp was struck and the move commenced. The boats captured earlier at Esakhail were utilised to cross the Indus on 21 October, with the troops all over on the left bank the next day. From here the troops moved to Mianwali, a few miles inland from the left bank. Ram Singh, their commander, then marched along the bottom of the Salt Range towards Pind Dudun Khan to link up with Shere Singh. On 24 October Capt. Nicholson, stationed at Ramnuggar, sent intelligence to Lahore that the Bannu troops had already reached Jalalpore on the Jhelum. Here they were met by advance units of Shere Singh's cavalry, which had advanced up the Chenab to effect a junction.

*** 

The story of the uprising at Peshawar was considerably more tortuous than at Bannu. The nominal Sikh governor of the province was Gulab Singh Povindia but George Lawrence, brother of Henry Lawrence, effectively held sway over the province. He had in fact been governing

Peshawar for well over a year, having entered Peshawar city with much pomp and fanfare on 20 February 1847. He also had a number of European assistants aiding him. He had been formerly helped by Lt Harry Lumsden, but by May 1848 he had been replaced by John Nicholson as chief assistant, Lumsden having been recalled to Lahore to assemble a corps of Guides. Two other officers, Lt Herbert and Lt Bowie of the Bengal Artillery, were also present. Bowie was given charge of organising the artillery while Herbert took over as the drill instructor for the infantry regiments stationed in Peshawar. There were a few other Europeans in the province. One was a Mr Thompson, with his wife, while a Major Lawrence had his family with him.

A colourful figure also residing in the valley was Sultan Mohammad Khan Barakzai, the former governor of the province during its days as an Afghan possession. After his deposition he had been residing in Lahore but his estates were restored to him. Although he lived a comfortable, indolent life in Peshawar, with a large harem running into the hundreds, Mohammad Khan was well known as an opportunist. As brother of Dost Mohammad, the ruler of Afghanistan, he still harboured aspirations for power, either in Afghanistan or in the province he formerly governed. He had therefore been looking on with lively interest at events at Multan and closer to home in Hazara and Peshawar and the fortune this might bring him. He was generally held in low opinion by all and sundry, although his natural animosity as an Afghan towards the Sikhs meant he was a natural ally for the British. 'The most treacherous and intriguing of a race and family notorious for treachery and intrigues' was Frederick Currie's view of the sultan, for he had dabbled in machinations of one sort or another ever since coming of age, thereby making no sure friends either in Afghan, Sikh or British circles. He was said to be hated by his brother Dost Mohammad, who, being no fool, rightly saw in his own brother an ambitious rival for the Kabul throne.

The Sikh military presence in the province at this time amounted to six regiments of infantry, four of cavalry and thirty-six guns, in total about 6,000 men of which 2,000 were Muslim, the rest being Sikh or Hindu, but the population in Peshawar province itself was a mixture of Afghans of various description, Pathans and other tribesmen. They were, as perhaps to the present day, an unruly and difficult population, required to be held in check by a strong military force present at all times. They were allowed to practice their beliefs and tribal culture as they wished as long as taxes were paid and they accepted the supremacy of Lahore. The view of the British political agents and government on this difficult area generally coincided with those of Ranjit Singh both during the war and after annexation. Shortly after the war, Sir Richard Temple, private secretary to John Lawrence in the Punjab and later governor of the Bombay presidency in 1855, wrote a damming indictment of the population in Peshawar and adjacent mountains in an official report.

> These tribes are savages – noble savages perhaps – and not without some tincture of virtue and generosity, but still absolutely barbarians. They have nothing approaching to government or civil institutions. In their eyes the one great commandment is blood for blood, and fire and sword for all people not Mahomedans. They are superstitious and priest-ridden. But the priests are as ignorant as they are bigoted, and use their influence simply for preaching crusades against unbelievers, and inculcate the doctrine of rapine and bloodshed against the defenceless people of the plains.

That this propensity for Jihad could be turned against the Sikh government and its forces hadn't gone unnoticed, as in Hazara by Abbott, and it was generally reckoned, and rightly so, by the

British political agents that the Muslim population in the event of a general war against the Sikh army would enthusiastically side with the British against their current rulers and tax gatherers.

There was a sizeable Hindu minority in the province as well and at times there tended to be friction between the Hindu and Muslim populations, invariably over killing of cows. The killing of kine was illegal in the Punjab in deference to Hindu sensibilities. George Lawrence during his short tenure had already had to mete out various punishments to Muslims for slaughtering cows. Various houses belonging to perpetrators in the province had been razed to the ground for this 'crime'. As late as 27 February 1848, for instance, seven men were found guilty of cow killing and each sentenced to seven years in prison.

***

Prior to the events at Multan during April 1848, George Lawrence had been entirely dismissive of any portents of war as he travelled the breadth of the Punjab to visit Henry Lawrence, his brother, who was temporarily leaving his post as Resident at the end of 1847. 'So profound,' he wrote, 'was the tranquillity prevailing there, and throughout the entire Punjab, and so, complete the absence of all causes of alarm, that I was accompanied by my wife and children.' Even after 27 April 1848, when news of the Multan incident would reach Peshawar, George Lawrence would continue to be supremely confident that no mutiny was likely at Peshawar despite the intense scrutiny the news received from the Sikh soldiers. He was right to a large extent, for little would happen as all sides and parties at Peshawar waited to see how events panned out. With Herbert Edwardes successes in the Derajat, any news emanating from Multan tended to be advantageous to the British, bolstering Lawrence's confidence further.

From the beginning of May through to near the end of October, a period of nearly six months, a huge litany of messengers and emissaries, letters and entreaties would arrive at the Sikh cantonments in Peshawar, all with the singular aim of urging the troops to rebel but all failing in their objectives. These came firstly from Mulraj during the months of May and August, then in parallel from Chutter Singh during the summer months and then latterly from Shere Singh during mid-September and beyond. The very first emissaries from Multan began arriving in secret during the early weeks of May, urging Sikh soldiers to support their comrades in the city. Lawrence was advised at this stage to send his family away to Lahore but his own feeling was that this would only suggest weakness on his part and a want of confidence in the Sikh soldiers. Where Frederick Currie and George Lawrence agreed was in the need to take similar steps to Herbert Edwardes in the Derajat in regard to the use of the local Muslim tribesmen as and when the need arose.

'Sikh fanatics had been heard abusing the Feringhees, and urging the soldiery to wipe out the disgrace they were under from their late defeats on the Sutlej by our troops, which I well knew they were burning to do. I was glad therefore to receive the Resident's instructions to raise a corps of Mahomedan Puthans as a counterpoise to the Sikh element, and I accordingly enlisted at once 600 of these men,' George Lawrence recorded.

This alternative force, he had determined, would be given command of the Sikh guns, making it more difficult for the Sikh soldiers to consider rebellion. He also began stockpiling ammunition and supplies in the British residency at this stage in case events took a more serious turn. Around 15 June the dramatic news of the death of the preacher Bhai Maharaj, suspected drowned in the Chenab, had reached Peshawar but there was considerable doubt amongst the Sikh soldiers that he had died. 'We are all quiet here, though the Sikhs still looked longingly towards Mooltan, and say that British rule in the Punjab will only last two months,' George Lawrence mused in his report of 17 June.

There were many Sikh preachers visiting the Peshawar soldiers and encouraging them to rise against the British. A preacher by the name of Bhai Achara Singh was arrested on the orders of Lawrence on 4 July. This was the same preacher who had been visited by Chutter Singh and treated as an important guest. He had not come to his notice earlier and thus had had been in the city and environs for eleven days, during which time he had spoken to the Sikh troops to bring news and encouragement for an uprising. While travelling round the city Lt Nicholson had seen gatherings of people including other priests near some caves near the city and had immediately alerted Lawrence. George Lawrence had the preacher incarcerated. On being questioned he would admit he had left Hazara two weeks earlier, having met Chutter Singh and various soldiers on his way to Peshawar. He denied any nationalist motives, however, and argued that he was merely visiting the province for personal reasons. Both Achara Singh and another preacher Ram Singh were ordered to be taken to Lahore guarded by Nujeeb (Muslim) soldiers via Ramnuggar rather than to the north to prevent any communication with the Sikh soldiers in Hazara.

On 20 July, a series of letters arrived from Amritsar asking for the senior Sikh officials and army officers to contribute towards the upkeep of Harminder Sahib, or the Golden Temple. These George Lawrence interpreted as a way of raising money for the insurrection, since no letters such as these had been received before. The priest who had brought these letters, Bhai Gunga Singh, was refused permission to stay in Peshawar and ordered to return to Amritsar immediately.

Among the more prominent emissaries crisscrossing the province near the end of July was a man called Wuzeer Singh. He was a fakir, or more likely dressed as a fakir as disguise. He was making the dangerous mission to encourage the Muslim Yusafzai tribesmen to rise up in coordination with the Sikh soldiers. He had also been offering Khader Khan, the headman of Esakhail town, a large jaghir of 25,000 rupees, if he encouraged the hill men and tribesmen of the area to stop payment of their taxes in order to encourage instability and encourage an uprising mentioning that the Sikh army troops would rise up in early September and they should do the same. Attempting this unholy alliance was dangerous and the tribal chief, more at odds with the Sikh government than the British, had handed him over to the British authorities at Peshawar. The fakir had also earlier visited Dost Mohammad in Kabul, soliciting assistance for Mulraj but without success. 'The Dost had, however, dismissed the messenger, declaring himself to be an ally of the British, and declining to have any further communications with Moolraj,' reported George Lawrence to the Resident on the information extracted from the emissary. This time the British officer took a far harsher stance and decided to make an example. With the sanction of Currie in Lahore, capital punishment was decided on to discourage other parties with similar motives. On the morning of 8 August in Peshawar city, the example was made.

'The sentence of death was carried out this morning on Wuzeer Singh, the Fakeer emissary of Mulraj; the ground was kept by a company, Mahomedans of Meer Jung Ali's Regiment, and a strong body of police, but beyond the assembly of a great crowd, no sympathy was displayed for the culprit, whose body, after hanging till the evening, I had burnt by the police,' he wrote.

\*\*\*

As the summer progressed, urgent letters and emissaries began to come in from Hazara and Chutter Singh. Chutter Singh had a different tactic, appealing to the Sikh officers to join him. He equally wrote to the Muslim officers asking for assistance. Many of these letters were simply handed over to Lawrence. Elahee Buksh, the Muslim commander of the Sikh artillery, was one of those who displayed little sympathy and the messengers were apprehended.

An attempt by Chutter Singh to gain Gulab Singh Povindia's support and other officers was revealed on 16 August. A *motber* (confidential servant) had arrived at Peshawar with letters requesting troops to put down the uprising of the Muslim tribesmen. The *motber* asked for three regiments of infantry along with cavalry to be sent. This was unlikely to have been granted, however, as its doubtful if George Lawrence would send troops without the say-so of James Abbott. However, whether this worked or not, the other motive was for the messenger to meet up with the senior Sikh officers, which these letters gave him the excuse to do without suspicion.

By the middle of October, Chutter Singh's desperation would increase. It's known he had gone as far as sending his personal sword and turban to Khan Singh Majithia, a senior Sikh officer at Peshawar, begging him to join the rebellion before the British could move in force against him. About a week after this incident, on 20 October, a letter carried by a disciple of Bhai Maharaj also turned up at Peshawar. He called on all Sikhs to join the cause and claimed Bhai Maharaj was in alliance with Chutter Singh. The messenger was arrested and thrown into the prison although, like Currie, George Lawrence believed Bhai Maharaj was dead and that the letter was a forgery.

\*\*\*

Because of these almost continual overtures, over the summer the Sikh troops, although not having the consensus as yet to openly rebel, became noticeably less and less deferential towards their officers and the British political agents to the point of abuse. Realising doing nothing would show weakness, Lawrence generally tried to address these issues head on. Anyone insulting European officers or being reported to have done so would be punished, he declared. Some soldiers were sentenced to six months' imprisonment with hard labour in irons for voicing their inner feelings.

'I could not but perceive a growing spirit of disaffection among the troops, shown by their insolent bearing towards myself and my assistants. While passing on one occasion with Lt. Bowie, I drove to Raja's Cheyt Singh's cantonment, on passing close to the lines of Utter Singh's Regiment, a subedar and seven or eight sepoys were seated on their cots, from which they neither rose nor saluted me. I ordered all forthwith into confinement. It would not do at any time to pass over so gross a mark of want of discipline, much less at the present period, when all my acts are watched and weighed,' he would write on 15 August.

The men were arrested and brought to him the next day, but Lawrence, having recovered his composure, decided it was better to release them than to create a cause célèbre for the Sikh regiments by handing out severe punishment.

All, of course, depended on the success or failure of operations round Multan, and the spirits of the Sikh soldiers rose and fell accordingly as news arrived. News of the Battle of Kyneerie would reach Peshawar on 25 June and that of Sadoosam on 9 July. Word of Herbert Edwardes' successes in driving Mulraj's force back into Multan seemed to portend a quick ending to the insurrection sometime in August, as soon as the large British siege guns could be brought down to the city. Royal salutes were ordered by George Lawrence to be fired for both victories when the news came in both as celebration and also as proof that the insurrection was being slowly strangled.

\*\*\*

Various words of caution were given to George Lawrence despite his confidence. A former servant of Alexander Burnes, for example, seeing him on 9 August, recommended he move into the fort of Peshawar as a precaution, using the example of what happened to Alexander Burnes and the British troops in Kabul in 1841, an event still fresh in everyone's minds. Lawrence continued to be unwilling to take such overly defensive measures as he was of the opinion this would precipitate an uprising rather than decrease its chances. Keeping a calm, confident appearance was the key.

On the evening of 21 September, a messenger brought the sensational news of Shere Singh's defection to the nationalist cause. Along with this came news of the raising of the siege at Multan and the retreat of Whish's troops. Realising this may be the event that could finally trigger a revolt, and that he only had a day or two at the most before news by more normal means reached the Sikh troops, Lawrence began to take much more preventative measures. The guns were the important thing, and he sent some Muslim soldiers to man some of them while the rest were secured. This action stopped an outright revolt as the news drifted into the cantonments a day or two later. With the guns under his control, he had the confidence to declare Dalhousie's proclamation that all Sikh officers and soldiers who opted to join Shere Singh would have their estates and property seized. This was news that apparently caused much talk among the troops and provoked much anger.

***

Taking the risk himself was one thing, but keeping his family at Peshawar during this time of declining stability was quite another. George Lawrence now made the decision to send them back to Lahore. The capital, though, could only be reached via Kohat as Chutter Singh's force was blocking the direct route via Attock. So the plan was for them to be transported to Kohat and then pass south of the Attock road towards Ramnuggar and then on to Lahore. The family would be escorted by troops of Sultan Mohammad Khan, present at Peshawar at the time and who promised he would do all he could to facilitate their journey. George Lawrence, like others, had little faith in the ex-governor. With Chutter Singh now offering Peshawar to Dost Mohammad in return for military assistance, Sultan Mohammad Khan would be in line to become the governor of the province again and it was thought this would be sufficient reward for him to side with a Sikh insurrection. Already on 6 September he had acted suspiciously, deciding to send 300 women of his harem to Kohat, where he had his stronghold. 'Although I entertained grave suspicions myself of the sirdar's fidelity, I could not but trust him on this occasion, especially as he took the most solemn oaths on the Koran to protect my family, and see them himself safe across the Indus,' wrote an uncertain Lawrence.

His family left Peshawar with a strong escort of 500 Afghans the next day (22 September) and reached Kohat before turning east to Lahore, the party being headed by the sultan's son, Buksh. It was at Chuckowal in the Sind Sagur doab, around 80 km south of Rawalpindi, where news arrived that Chutter Singh had sent a cavalry force to intercept them before they crossed the Jhelum. The party then moved around aimlessly for a while depending on where food was available till Buksh decided to move back to Kohat, around 120 km back in the direction from which they had come. It's quite probable the sultan had actively joined Chutter Singh by this time and therefore the holding of this party as hostages became desirable. According to Mrs Lawrence, Buksh had not brought any fresh clothes with him for the long journey from

Kohat, something a man of rank would never do, perhaps an indication that the sultan had already decided to detain them before they had left Kohat.

The sultan had no wish to harm the family and would give assurances to Mrs Lawrence as such when they returned, treating them as guests and going as far as give her his rings. 'So long as you keep these, no one can prevent you doing anything you choose,' he assured her. Some of the women of his harem also showed friendliness. 'If a pig took refuge with us, we should be bound to protect it!' they declared in conversation. Relationships soured quickly after a few days, and Mrs Lawrence's suspicions increased in equal measure as she attempted to leave Kohat. On questioning the sultan on his motives and plans to hand them over to Chutter Singh, the sultan replied angrily, 'Do you think we are dogs, that we should do such a thing?' A guard was then put on them. Meanwhile George Lawrence, quite unaware he would be joining them shortly and unsure as to how things would turn out in Peshawar, wrote to his wife. The family would stay prisoners till the end of the war.

\*\*\*

Life went on without major incident for a few weeks after news of Shere Singh's defection, although the Sikh commander would continue urging the troops for their support. But it was only when he left Multan and marched northwards that the uncertainty ended. On the morning of 23 October, a sufficient number of voices in the Sikh cantonments began speaking in support for Shere Singh and the consensus was that now was the time to rise up and join the Sikh commander. Preparations began to be made in the barracks.

Lt Bowie happened to be riding into the city from the Residency for his daily ride and bath that same morning. George Lawrence was about to follow him when the Governor Gulab Singh Povindia warned him not to proceed as he had heard that something was up. Word was immediately sent to Bowie, who instantly fled back while halfway to the town. The rapid retreat meant he avoided capture, for as he was riding back he reached the summit of some high ground from where he could see some Sikh Dragoons approaching from the city. These men saw him in turn and gave chase, but the vital few minutes' lead allowed him to reach the Residency, although the Sikh troopers took a few shots at him. Once near the Residency he was aided by the Muslim garrison, who fired on the chasing Dragoons, forcing them back.

Lawrence promptly ordered the Muslim Pathan and Hindustani troops, whom he thought could be relied on, to come to the Residency along with the guns they had in their possession to prevent them falling into the hands of the Sikh soldiers. The gates of the Residency were promptly closed forthwith. A general insurrection was confirmed by various informers and messengers who filtered in over the next few hours and by the sight of Sikh troops gathered outside the Residency. 'From the house-top, we could see that the two Sikh cavalry corps, and three infantry ones, had assembled on the grand parade, and were, evidently, in a state of revolt. Messengers came shortly after, and confirmed this,' he quickly wrote, informing the Resident at Lahore the same day.

Within the Residency there was a strong group of defenders, mainly Afghans on whom George Lawrence thought he could rely. The Afghans, though, proved mercenary as ever; having received overtures from Chutter Singh in recent days promising good pay and carriage for their baggage if they would hand over the guns Lawrence had entrusted to them, they soon declared for Shere Singh. With the Sikh units outside waiting for the few guns at their disposal to turn on the gates, it was plainly obvious to Lawrence it was only a matter of time before a breach was made and he and his fellow Europeans taken prisoner.

He wasn't alone in having problems, however. The problem for the Sikh soldiers was the reluctance of many of their officers to join at this time. During the day many messages flitted to and fro asking for their support but to no effect. Several of the Muslim officers, including General Elahee Buksh, Commander of the Sikh artillery, plus Col Meer Junglie and Col Ameer Khan, were refusing to join, along with the Sikh officer Khan Singh Majithia, commanding 300 Gorcharas. The Muslim colonels were in charge of the guns and went as far as to say they would fire on any men approaching to acquire the guns they had in their possession in the cantonments.

Meanwhile, the soldiers outside the Residency, having no great wish to harm Lawrence and his party, had sent messengers asking for pay due to them and for sufficient carriage so they could move out from Peshawar and join Shere Singh. This Lawrence agreed to on the condition they moved 11 km away from the city. To this the Sikh units assented, moving the appropriate distance to the east. This is where matters continued to stand till the evening, when it seemed the soldiers began tiring of being fobbed off and returned.

Inside the Residency, after a meeting with Sirdar Khan Singh Majithia, Col Boodh Singh and Ruttan Singh Mann and three other colonels, George Lawrence decided to remain on the defensive as there was little chance of competing with the troops in the open. In any case the rest of the Sikh units who had not yet risen were expected to join the rebels soon, tilting the balance even further. Chutter Singh was also expected to make his way up in a matter of days on hearing of matters.

No violence occurred during the evening or that night. Lawrence's garrison stayed on the defensive while the Sikh troops, in the hope that the Muslim troops would join them, refrained from firing. As the morning of the 24th broke, however, events moved rapidly. Lawrence issued pay for the Muslim soldiers inside and outside the compound holding the guns in the city to bind them to his cause, but this seemed to have an opposite effect: 'No sooner had I issued pay on the 24th instant, to Col Meer Junglie's Mahomedan regiment, than I heard that many desertions were taking place, and, towards evening, the Col and Commandant, with the Governor and Deputy-Governor, reported that, such was its state, they could not answer for the safety of the guns, during the night.'

The troops inside the compound, while changing allegiance, were sporting enough not to turn their guns on Lawrence himself and quietly left out of the gates. The only men remaining with Lawrence were around 3,000 Muslim Pathan levies, but since there was every chance these would defect as well he sent them out ostensibly to face the Sikh troops but in reality to remove them from the compound. These troops promptly joined their comrades outside.

At 8 p.m., the first fire from the Sikh guns commenced against the Residency, the soldiers having had enough of waiting. Lawrence, realising his authority was fast vanishing, had already made plans for escape. Initially he had decided on escaping to Shahmeer Ghur or the fort at Attock, but the sight of a bedraggled European party being chased by the Peshawar soldiers would only push the Attock garrison into joining the rebellion, he surmised. In any case, some of the Sikh troops, it was discovered, had earlier gone and captured the ferry at the Indus, making escape in that direction impossible. So Lawrence summoned Sultan Mohammad Khan again and asked him for protection at Kohat, where with his family he could make his way south to Whish's force at Multan. According to Lawrence he 'received from him the most sacred promises of protection at Kohat and to be escorted by him at any time in perfect safety to Bahawulpore, Mooltan or Sinde', Sultan Mohammad Khan going as far as to promise in writing his protection. This was enough for Lawrence, and sufficient horse and carriage were organised for an escape.

Taking advantage of the gathering dark, Lawrence gathered the few Afghan horsemen still prepared to take orders from him and with Lt Bowie and Mr and Mrs Thompson made preparations to leave through the southern gate of the compound, opposite to the north where Sikh and Afghan units outside had commenced their fire.

Inside the residency compound, the most loyal servants and other staff had also decided to join the uprising. They attempted to block the escape route, but the party fled just in time, with only the clothes on their back and a few possessions hastily assembled. Fortunately for them, the Sikh units decided not to pursue and the party eventually made it to Kohat around 10 a.m. in the morning of 25 October.

Three days after their arrival, George Lawrence's group would find they were effectively prisoners. All thoughts of joining the British force at Multan vanished. For the second time in his life, Lawrence found he had become a hostage of the Afghans, the first being several years earlier as a prisoner in the aftermath of the First Anglo-Afghan War. Sultan Mohammad Khan had originally agreed to transport Lawrence and his party down to Esakhail on the Indus, around 100 km due south of Kohat. There, on the river, a British steamer had already arrived to pick them up and transport them downstream. At eight in the evening of the 28th, however, a messenger sent by Chutter Singh, who had by now heard of the Peshawar troops declaring for the nationalist cause, appeared at Kohat asking for the Europeans. The messenger informed the sultan what he had by now already heard: Dost Mohammad, his brother in Kabul, had agreed to an accord between the Afghans and the Sikhs. The Afghan army would shortly be entering Peshawar to resume control of the territory. He in turn was to give assistance to Chutter Singh and his son. The deal Chutter Singh had struck with the Afghan ruler was a payment of 60,000 rupees, 30,000 rupees to be paid in cash with 15,000 paid in Kashmir shawls, a common form of currency at the time. The remaining 15,000 rupees was to be given to him at Rawalpindi once his force arrived to join up with the Sikh army. Dost Mohammad was to supply 1,000 horsemen (although only 800 men eventually turned up with his son, Akram Khan, at Rawalpindi). In return Chutter Singh promised the sultan 1 lakh rupees a year along with the tantalising prospect of again being governor of Peshawar as it retuned to Afghan control.

It was a poor bargain for Chutter Singh, but aside from any doubtful military assistance by the Afghans, the prospect of obtaining British prisoners for negotiations later in return for his son Golab Singh and the Maharani was too good to miss. 'Sultan Mahomed, notwithstanding his solemn promises to me, acquiesced at once, with the usual treachery of his race, in this arrangement, and directed that I should be sent back to Peshawur,' wrote a rather annoyed Lawrence.

The party would be kept in comfortable circumstances, being allowed to send and receive letters pending their transfer back to Peshawar. The few servants that had accompanied them were told to return to Peshawar, however. According to the sultan, Major Lawrence would try to bribe the sultan's moonshee to effect an escape before they were transferred but the moonshee had refused. Chutter Singh had written to Mrs Lawrence meanwhile, suggesting she could sit out the war in comfortable conditions in Kohat if she wished although her husband would accompany his force, but that for negotiations it would be best if all the Europeans were in one place rather than being held separately. To this she agreed and the whole European party were then escorted back to Peshawar.

'He must really believe that the Sikhs are likely to be shortly more powerful in the Punjab than the British,' a rather disbelieving Currie informed the Governor-General on the new status of George Lawrence as prisoner and on the developing accord between Chutter Singh and Dost

Mohammad on 23 November. Dalhousie, although showing concern, was more anxious with the wider implications of this agreement and its effects on the local tribes, hitherto friendly towards the British. 'The mere treachery of this intriguing chief will be of no consequence, provided the European officers escape free from his hands; but it is to be feared that his open declaration of the re-establishment of an Affghan dynasty, on the other side of the Indus, may affect the feelings of the Mahomedan population, and, by thus raising up a new combination against us, which has hitherto promised to be one of our main sources of success, add considerable embarrassment at this difficult crisis.' The Governor-General was right to a large extent; with Dost Mohammad and his brother supporting the Sikh cause, the divide between Muslim contingents in the Sikh army and population and the Sikh regulars could vanish, making the job of Gough, who was advancing into the Punjab at this time, much more difficult. At Multan, too, most of the Afghan and Pathan irregulars collected by Herbert Edwardes might have second thoughts about continuing in the employment of the British. A general Muslim uprising from Hazara down to Multan would be most difficult to put down.

*\*\*\**

Meanwhile, back on the left bank of the Indus, Chutter Singh had quickly made plans to reach Peshawar and take control of his new prisoners. The boats on the Indus had been under the management of the Afghan Peer Mohammad Khan, another of Dost Mohammad's brothers, and had previously been denied him. Now Peer Mohammad Khan openly joined Chutter Singh as well due to the new accord. Crossing on 31 October, Chutter Singh made a grand entry into Peshawar on 3 November, the receiving party headed by Sultan Mohammad Khan and his brother, with all the Afghan nobility paying him a visit as his cavalcade moved closer to the city. A royal salute was fired. In a grand Durbar that evening, Chutter Singh formally handed over the province to the Afghan brothers, Dost Mohammad having not made his way through the Khyber Pass yet, with George Lawrence's horse being given to the brothers to be sent to Dost Mohammad as a present. The new titular governor, Dost Mohammad had decided, would be Peer Mohammad Khan, much to Sultan Mohammad Khan's chagrin, although he would apparently hold the strings. New Afghan taxation on the province was immediate and Peer Mohammad Khan on the same day set about bringing in Afghan laws and the organisation of collection of revenue. Major celebrations were ordered in the city for the brightest jewel of the former Afghan Empire was back in Afghan control. A large fireworks display was organised that night in the city. The Afghans in the city, according to intelligence reaching Currie, were 'openly and insolently declaring that like as we gave up Cabool so shall we Peshawur', alluding to the British expulsion from Kabul in 1842.

Chutter Singh would stay on in Peshawar, awaiting collection of the British prisoners. They would be escorted back, reaching the city on 11 November. They were met by him personally several miles outside of Peshawar with some of his senior officers and treated with kindness, with a nuzzur presented and a salute of nineteen guns. Chutter Singh had also arranged a guard of honour for George Lawrence, which saluted him as he arrived at the tents provisioned for the party. 'I expostulated with the sirdar on this display in my honour, as absurd and quite out of place, considering that I was a helpless prisoner. "Why is it absurd?" replied the sirdar, "we have no quarrel with you; on the contrary we feel highly indebted to you, as we never received anything but kindness and consideration from your two brothers and yourself. Although it is for our interest that you should be with us, and we must therefore detain you, we desire to treat you in all respects as if you were still Governor of Peshawur."'

Chutter Singh would give the British party the option of residing where they wished. Jammu, Rawalpindi and several other places were suggested for their comfort with Sukhoo eventually agreed upon. On 5 December, they were given comfortable quarters at the town but were strictly guarded, the party excluding George Lawrence and Lt Bowie, who would be used as emissaries by Chutter Singh. They would spend the rest of the war there, only being given up several days before the surrender of the Sikh army in mid-March 1849.

The durbar at Peshawar, making formal the accord between the Afghans and Chutter Singh, would be the cue for most of the Sikh and Muslim officers still undecided to come over to the nationalist side. These included the experienced Elahee Buksh, the Muslim commander of the artillery, who would command the Sikh guns at Chillianwala. Few officers now declined to join the Sikh army accumulating under Shere Singh.

At Lahore, news of Dost Mohammad's agreement with Chutter Singh had already been suspected by the Lahore Resident even before news reached of the official accord. Stories had been carried through the mountain passes by merchants entering India from Afghanistan that Dost Mohammad had commenced recruiting soldiers in November, the excuse being that soldiers were required to collect the taxation in the Jalalabad vicinity.

'There seems very little doubt that the Ameer Dost Mahomed Khan is in communication with the Sikh sirdar and that the province of Peshawur has been made over to the Barukzyes but it remains to be seen whether Dost Mahomed will give the aid of his troops in the coming operation,' Currie would inform Dalhousie on 25 November. This was confirmed by captured correspondence from the Kabul ruler to Multan advising Mulraj that he would send assistance to him as well as in the form of diversionary attacks across the Indus in the Derajat. Letters were also received by the Muslim garrison at the fortress of Attock from Mohammad Shurree Khan, another son of Dost Mohammad, 'inciting them to desert and to join for the sake of their religion in a war against the British' according to Lt Herbert, who was commanding the fortress.

The tentative British hold on Peshawar had vanished, although Frederick Currie didn't give up on the area entirely. A plan to thwart Dost Mohammad's attempts to assist the Sikh army was formulated in the coming weeks. This would take advantage of the petty jealousies and rivalries in the region, and the fact that many chiefs, especially the Afridi and Orakzai tribes, still held an allegiance to Shah Shujah's family (the British puppet installed during the First Anglo-Afghan War) and were therefore sworn enemies of Dost Mohammad. The plan was to send an advance payment of 30,000 rupees with Prince Shahpur, a son of Shah Shujah, along with a small force to these chiefs who were to instigate an uprising against the Barakzai clan to which Dost Mohammad and his brothers belonged. Prince Shahpur would then be declared for the Afghan throne, with the chiefs of these tribes as his viziers. This, it was speculated, would entirely neutralise Dost Mohammad's plan to advance into Peshawar for fear of losing his throne at Kabul.

Another scheme was the declaration of a reward of 4–5 lakh rupees for the capture of Dost Mohammad and his family for the tribesmen around the Khyber. It was thought this would at the very least be a distraction for Dost Mohammad, with his family vulnerable to capture in Kabul while his army was in Peshawar. Henry Lawrence was in complete agreement with these plans, although in practice they would never come to fruition, attention being firmly fixed on meeting the growing force under Shere Singh and on the resumption of the siege of Multan.

# 22

# The Battle of Suraj Khund

An immediate victory was deemed so indispensable as to require a single attack by the
British column which was finally arranged to come off at 10 am.

Herbert Edwardes, 8 November 1848

If it is God's pleasure the insignificant ant may overcome the furious elephant.

Mulraj to Whish, 8 November 1848

The strengthening of Shere Singh's force with the Peshawar and Bannu contingents of the Sikh army now meant there were two major theatres of war, although events and conflict would progress in each theatre almost entirely independently of each other. The British force at Ferozepore would begin crossing the Sutlej and heading due west into the Punjab during November to grapple with Shere Singh's army, now situated on the banks of the Chenab River. Meanwhile, reinforcements from Bombay began marching towards Multan to supplement Whish's force before the renewal of the siege of Multan, expected in late December.

After Shere Singh had left Multan, there had been relative quiet between the opposing sides at Multan. Mulraj's newly weakened state, though, meant Whish could afford to be more adventurous and there was a corresponding increase in frequency of British reconnaissance parties capturing supplies and grain coming into the city. This tightening of the noose would increase gradually over the weeks, leading to acute shortages in the city. The duress this caused along with the Multan soldiers reproaching their governor over his failure to coordinate with Shere Singh before his departure northwards and his inaction since then would culminate in Mulraj trying his fortune on the battlefield for the last time. The result would be the Battle of Suraj Khund on 7 November.

Five days after Shere Singh's departure, on 14 October, a large reconnaissance mission was organised by Whish to ascertain the status of the city's defences. The entire cavalry and half of each regiment, backed by all the horse artillery available, was organised with the rest of the force staying as a camp guard. The force was to go towards the city and to its north-west and then head north of the fortress, moving to within 400 yards of the walls. Here one of the bastions of the fort was to be inspected. Early in the day, then, before daybreak, this force marched silently towards the city to inspect these defensive works and entrenchments, the dark protecting their movements. They reached the city at daybreak and were spotted when 500 yards from the city walls, at which point the alarm was raised and the Multan cavalry came out, with the guns of both sides firing away merrily and some skirmishing resulting. The British force arrived back in camp at 11 a.m.

There happened to be several close escapes for British officers during these weeks, including an attempt on the life of Whish himself. Some of the Multan soldiers had noticed the British general had unchanging habits as to his morning routine. Whish would without fail take a morning ride everyday along the outer line of pickets accompanied by just a few of his staff. This presented opportunities for a sniper. Five men from Multan silently crept towards the British lines of pickets on 21 October, and one managed to fire a musket shot at Whish; however, it failed to find its mark. Two were captured by the irregular cavalry escort with Whish, one being badly wounded, and the other three escaped.

On 29 October another advance was ordered, with British engineers trying rockets but doing little damage. Two British officers had a close encounter during this manoeuvre while riding very close to the city walls. They were suddenly charged by Mulraj's cavalry and barely escaped capture. Apart from these tentative moves by Whish nothing of note would occur, the general still being reluctant to advance and recommence hostilities in earnest till the reinforcements arrived from Bombay. Week after week would pass with little or no hostile action.

The situation in the British camp in terms of supplies was still tenuous. Whish had ordered rationing of food ever since the abrupt retreat from Multan, where the vast bulk of his supplies had been left behind. Uncertain as he was of his allies and the practicalities of supplies reaching him from Lahore or Bhawulpore in consistent fashion, the rationing had been maintained ever since. And while supplies headed for Multan were being intercepted, many of the supplies destined for the British camp were in turn being intercepted by the garrison at this point as well. On 14 October, British contingents captured two large convoys of supplies being transported to the city and these were instantly put to use in the British camp. Despite this, by mid-October the shortage of supplies was becoming acute, with all local forage for the animals approaching exhaustion. 'Our men looked very bad for want of proper food,' recorded Corporal John Ryder of this time. 'Our living was dreadful. The hospital was getting full, and men were dying every day, from nothing but want; our living consisting of very bad mutton and boiled rice. The sheep at the best of times are bad, and what could they be then, when it took six of them to weigh 90 lbs. They were but skin and bone. Our men said that we often ate dead dogs for sheep, which I was inclined to believe; for they were about our camp by hundreds.'

By the end of October, however, the situation would begin to gradually improve in the British camp. Fresh new supplies, along with more consistent supply lines from Bhawulpore, meant all rationing was ended and full rations were again being distributed shortly thereafter. Despite this, flour would stay rare well into late November. A large supply convoy would arrive in the British camp on 22 November which included bedding as well. This convoy was especially welcome for most of the men had been sleeping on the bare sand for the previous two months, all bedding also having been left behind during the retreat. Their uniforms were also falling apart, with trousers being patched. The good news for Whish was that the treasure for payment of troops was no longer being disrupted and salaries could be paid promptly.

\*\*\*

While things improved in the British camp as November approached, there was news from inside the city that the situation was getting correspondingly worse, fuelling rumours that Mulraj was again mulling surrender. At the end of October, he had surprisingly released all the British prisoners he had taken thus far. The prisoners commented on the exceptionally kind treatment during their captivity. This was thought to be a token of good gesture before giving himself up. This never happened, however, and his dilatory method of conducting war and then pondering over surrendering were not impressing his soldiers. They were frustrated with

Mulraj for not taking energetic action despite being fully aware reinforcements for Whish from Bombay were being readied by the British Government. The time to take advantage was now, they harangued him, before the British strength increased and the scales moved too heavily in the British favour. During the last few days of October, Mulraj had thought it sufficient to send out parties of cavalry to harass the British pickets but this level of activity was hardly sufficient, declared his soldiers. These discussions had culminated in an argument between his soldiers and officers when an officer, Ruttun Singh, had been accused of cowardice by an Akali soldier and killed for not conducting the war with more vigour. Equally apprehensive of his own soldiers' wrath and the British force sitting at Suraj Khund, Mulraj expelled all thoughts of surrender for the time being and would decide to make a more spirited approach. Still too cautious to gamble all, from the beginning of November onwards he began sending larger parties of cavalry to harass the British line and supply columns and plans were drawn up for a substantial force with artillery to move towards the grand canal to bombard the British camp. According to the general gossip and rumour among the camps at this time, this operation was due entirely to a dream that Mulraj recently had. He supposedly dreamt that he was an elephant rapidly crushing the British troops under his feet and that he was unstoppable. 'This is a good sample of the sort of gup [gossip] that just now gains currency and credit in reference to Mooltan affairs,' the *Kurrrachee Advertiser* wrote.

***

On the morning of 1 November, six guns – some sources say as many as twelve – were advanced with substantial troops up to the eastern bank of the grand canal, directly opposite the irregular force of Edwardes stationed on the west bank. These commenced firing on the same day at 11 a.m. The canal was by now mostly dry and hence not as formidable an obstacle as previously but its sheer depth and width formed a respectable defence. Some guns were stationed opposite Whish's force as well, to the left of Edwardes' camp, but Whish's heavy guns had overpowered them, forcing the Multan gunners to retreat beyond range. The gunfire on the British right was more telling, with no British batteries here among Edwardes' irregulars. The cannonade continued into the night of 2 November.

It was at this time that several of the men of HM 32nd and a Capt. Maitland were killed after mistaking Multan soldiers for British irregulars and joining in with them during a skirmish, a sign of the continuing confusion as to identifying irregulars; this confusion would cause much greater losses later in the week.

The Multan guns would in fact fire for the next five to six days, with Whish finally ordering the movement of fifteen to twenty guns in his camp into positions to respond in kind on 4 November. Six of these were placed in a battery 400 yards away from the nullah banks. Another three heavy guns and various mortars were transported to the east bank of the nullah to the south of the garrison's guns to commence an enfilade while another four guns were placed to the north-west, around 1,800 yards from the other British guns. Despite these efforts the Multan guns could not be dislodged, the batteries having been dug so that the guns could not be seen and the nullah proving a good defensive position. 'The enemy now redoubled his fire and having got the range of our tents rendered it exceedingly dangerous to remain in them; our little party was more than once startled by the shot passing within a few feet and men were being killed whilst cooking their bread,' a combatant wrote. The skirmishing and firing continued without intermission into 5 November, and the continual precautions necessary as shot passed through the camp began to have an effect on the more mercenary of the irregulars. 'We were getting the worst of it now. Our allies too were becoming dissatisfied; for we learned that 150 of them had deserted during the night and joined the enemy; and no wonder, as the enemy's balls killed numbers in their camp. They could pitch them where they liked, killing the men in their tents; and our men were as much dissatisfied, from want of rest and food. The general feeling among the men was to fight; they might as well die fighting as be picked off by odd ones, as they were, and getting no forwarder. There was a general murmur through the whole camp. For want of sleep we were so overpowered sometimes, that we dropped off as we manned the entrenchments, when salvo after salvo from our batteries roused us up again.'

The skirmishing and aggressiveness of the fire from the battery increased markedly on 6 November as the Multan force realised the British force had no effective solution to the cannonade. Mulraj too was gaining in confidence and pushed out all his cavalry, which began advancing towards the most exposed of British batteries early on that day. To counter this, Whish pushed forward the 72nd NI and two companies of the HM 32nd to protect the batteries. Again there was some confusion as the British guard mistakenly thought the Multan cavalry were Bhawulpore sowars coming back from skirmishing. 'Our men were rather taken by surprise. They saw a European at the head of a number of native troops and supposing them to be a portion of our allies under Edwardes allowed them to approach quite close before they found out their mistake. Our men said he had white trousers and a red jacket and uniform cap on but he was a Frenchman and had played his part well,' recorded Ryder. The ruse, if it was meant to be one, or whether he was a French officer was never discovered. It fooled the British officers, who ordered their guns to cease firing. They only realised their mistake when the charge continued towards them and the Multan troops advanced right up to the British line, with hand-to-hand fighting breaking out; however, the numbers of attackers was too small to allow them to make a breakthrough, although the outcome was uncertain for a while.

'This unhappy affair threw a damp over our spirits and both we and allies began to fancy the Sikhs too strong for us,' summed up the correspondent of the *Agra Messenger* at the battlefield. This error in identity had proved costly. The British contingent had been pushed back with the loss of twenty-two men killed and around an equal number wounded. HM 32nd alone lost fifteen killed and the same wounded in this encounter, with 72nd NI suffering six killed and seven wounded. Meanwhile, the Multan battery on the east bank continued pounding the camp all day with impunity.

The hostilities since Mulraj had adopted a more aggressive approach up to 6 November had cost thirty-seven killed and 144 wounded in total in the British and allied camp, perturbing both Edwardes and Whish, who came to the conclusion that something must be done. A powerful attack designed to eliminate the Multan battery on the east bank was decided. At 4 p.m. that day, the general organised a council of war and the decision therein was taken to attack the battery the very next day, 7 November, with as much force as possible, overwhelming the Multan contingent.

A full-frontal attack across the Grand Canal, which, though dry, was 20 feet deep, was rightly considered suicidal. Therefore it was decided the entire force would be split in three. Edwardes' Bhawulpore irregulars would swing clockwise, crossing the nullah a few kilometres northwards and attack the Multan force on their right flank and rear. Meantime a British force would cross the nullah a few kilometres to the south and then perform a semi-circular, anti-clockwise motion to attack their left flank and rear. Once these two forces were engaged with the garrison, the rest of the allied force and British troops still stationed on the west bank would cross the nullah and also engage with the enemy, the Multan troops being expected to be too fully occupied protecting their rear and flanks by this time to contest the crossing. Firm orders were given for this force not to cross the nullah till the two forces outflanking the Multan force had circled round and engaged the force for fear of unnecessary losses crossing the canal under heavy fire.

The British force crossing the nullah to the south would consist of two brigades of infantry, 1,400 men each, making a total infantry force of 2,800 men. Each brigade would be accompanied by 600 cavalry each, making a grand total of 4,000 men. Lt-Col Franks would lead one brigade comprised of six companies of HM 10th Foot, eight companies from the 8th, eight from the 52nd NI. The other brigade would be made up of six companies of HM 32nd Foot and eight companies each from the 45th and 51st NI under Lt-Col Brooke of HM 32nd. They would be accompanied by three squadrons of cavalry from the 11th Light Cavalry and the 7th and 11th Irregular Cavalry and a troop of the 3rd Brigade of Horse Artillery under Major Wheeler. The command of this entire force was given to Brig. Markham. Both outflanking forces were slated to move an hour before daylight to take advantage of the darkness.

Things didn't quite go according to plan, however. In order to execute the scheme, Whish had ordered some of the advanced heavy guns to be withdrawn for the defence of the camp along with some of the advance troops since these were required for the circling manoeuvres. Only two horse artillery guns were to remain in the advance position.

On the evening of the 6th, Lt Pollock was assigned the task of taking control of this advance British position. Replacing the withdrawn troops would be the Kuthar Mookhee regiment (Hindu Purbeah sepoys in Lahore Durbar service) under Courtlandt and around 1,000 Daudputras (being commanded by Lt Lake) and 500 of Edwardes' irregulars. It was heavily dark, around 10 p.m., as he approached the advanced battery with the replacement troops and they were mistaken for the enemy with ten to twelve men killed before the mistake was realised by the advance guard. The firing alerted the Multan troops manning the battery opposite as well, who also began firing, increasing the discomfort in the British position. 'It was midnight before this party was properly posted and as the enemy were then perfectly quiet, I returned to camp in order that I might be present with the main body of my troops during the contemplated attack of the 7th,' recorded an apparently satisfied Lt Lake as he prepared for the attack the next day. These replacement troops had their own plans, however. In the early hours of the day, after having been put in this advance position, six companies of the regiment, virtually all the force, gradually defected to the Multan position in small detachments. This left the officers present, Lt Pollock, Lt Paton (of the engineers) and Lt Bunny of the artillery, with hardly any troops. The defection in general didn't seem to have been particularly well planned as the British officers could quite easily have been taken prisoners. Instead, small groups drifted off over the hours as they saw other comrades crossing the nullah. As these groups reached the Multan position, they could be heard shouting friendly and encouraging words to the rest to join them. The defection was believed to have been triggered by the news arriving that evening of the Peshawar troops joining Shere Singh's army.

With only 300 Rohillas and assorted Bhawulpore troops remaining with him, Bunny, who had command of the two guns, sent immediate notice of the defection to Whish, also asking for horses to take away the guns and reinforcements in case the Multan troops advanced to capture the equipment. 'The defection of the Kuthar Mookhee soldiers became generally known by daylight of the 7th and produced a very disheartening effect upon the whole of the Nawab's army. Some of his officers counselled an immediate retreat and separation from the rest of the

Irregular force at this juncture,' Lt Lake would later report in his despatch to Whish on the 9th as news of the Peshawar and Bannu garrisons rising up spread round the camp.

Whish would begin learning of these defections at around 2 a.m. Early in the morning of the next day, it was found another 300 of the irregulars occupying an advance position had defected too, only their officer remaining. This created much confusion and suspicion of the irregulars in the British camp later that day. Edwardes set off for Whish's tent at 3 a.m. to advise him he was confident more of his troops would leave. Certainly it seemed many more wished to go over to Mulraj. Between 4 a.m. and 6 a.m. on the 7th, a hurried meeting took place between Whish and all his officers. The general consensus was, therefore, not to entrust to Edwardes' troops an important arm of the attack lest more should switch sides. Rather these troops would stay on the defensive and man the camp with other troops while the British troops would form the bulk of those attacking the Multan position. 'There is no doubt that the defection of the men of the Kuthar Mookhee was premeditated as those who went had packed up and taken with them their most valuable property to the battery which they would not have done had they meant to return,' Edwardes would later record in his report to Whish. Whish, on hearing of the news of the defection of the Peshawar troops, also feared this would lead to more large-scale defections that day. He was reluctant to abort the attack on the Multan battery, though, fearing a change to more defensive plans would only show anxiety and precipitate more defections. The attack would still go ahead, but there would be a change to the original plan for a double pincer movement. 'It was quite impossible for me to conjecture to what extent the force of the Allies might prove faithless and Lieutenant Edwardes could not at that time give me any encouragement to indulge in auspicious forebodings,' Whish would write later. Therefore Edwardes with his troops would stay in camp where further defections among his irregulars could do less damage than if done prior to or in midst of battle. Now only the southern pincer movement would go ahead, wheeling around to attack the Multan position from the rear while the rest of the troops, whether faithful or not, would stay on the west bank of the nullah. The British troops would pass through Edwardes' camp and be ready to march by 6 a.m.

But as these troops marched off south early in the morning, the Multan troops, sensing the uncertainty in the British camp, had decided to seize the initiative themselves. They advanced across the nullah at 8 a.m. to attack what was left of Edwardes' irregulars. The guns, however, were left on the east bank of the nullah with a small guard. This move took the British camp by surprise. Edwardes and other officers were making their ways back to their own positions at this time after the meeting when they heard hostilities commence. 'I left your tent at about half-past six, and had scarcely reached my own, before a sharp musketry fire opened, at our advanced battery on the nullah; and, growing hotter and hotter, soon proved to be an open attack upon that post by the rebels, in such force as, at one time, to drive completely back the 500 pathans who held it, and turn the inner flank of the 8-gun battery at the well, 400 yards in front of our camp,' Edwardes would record in his despatch to Whish on 8 November.

While they were successful in this move, the Multan troops were so busy attacking Edwardes' line that they failed to notice the British troops that had departed the camp to attack their original position in the rear. The most desperate hand-to-hand fighting took place along the west bank, the British advance post being in real danger. Edwardes would immediately request of Whish a diversion to relieve the pressure and succour soon arrived, with Courtlandt's guns opening up on the Multan line having been brought out of their embrasures from further south. Two irregular regiments who had not defected with additional parties of Bhawulpore troops also joined the defenders at this stage and threatened to outflank the attackers. This and a charge by some of Edwardes' Rohillas was sufficient to force the Multan troops back towards their position, and half an hour after the counterattack the Multan men could be seen clambering back across the nullah with others retreating back to the city.

While this had been happening, Brig. Markham had crossed the bridges on the nullah on the right-hand side of the British camp and proceeded to execute his anti-clockwise movement, reaching the rear of the Multan line by 10 a.m. Here they found much of the Multan position and batteries undefended. The force had been obscured by jungle while they had been executing this circular manoeuvre, but as they closed in on the east bank of the nullah the terrain was quite clear and the remaining Multan soldiers could be clearly seen along with various villages in the distance towards the city. These soldiers, with cavalry, had also spotted the British line behind them and, realising their position was compromised, began making general moves to head back to the city.

Markham decided there was ample chance of preventing this retreat and of capturing the guns and he immediately organised his force. Three guns were brought about on the British left and three on the British right with the cavalry placed on both flanks, by far the larger group on the right to cut off the Multan soldiers retreating back into the city. The advance was ordered with the guns firing. The Multan gunners had managed to wheel their guns around and commence firing by this stage. The fire was not accurate, though, and although some of the horses were wounded no impact was made on the riders. The British line closed too rapidly in any case, and much of the grape was seen whistling over the heads of the advancing line. When the British line was 20–30 yards from the position, the gunners fired a last discharge. One of these guns would be pulled out of position to attempt to enfilade the advancing British, but they moved too fast for this to be effective; however, the other was captured. 'At this moment I ordered the Cavalry to attack a large body of the enemy who were moving to our right and to prevent their removing their guns. Major Wheeler, in command of the Cavalry, advanced in the most brilliant manner, charged the enemy, cutting up numbers of them, taking a standard, and preventing the removal of the guns, swept the whole of our front, and re-forming speedily, and in good order, on our left, moved off to cover the right,' Brig. Markham would record in his report to Whish later. 'As the Cavalry cleared our front, the horse artillery opened their fire, the line charged, and took the position with the whole of the guns, on the bank of the nullah, driving the enemy across and up it, with considerable loss.'

The guns were spiked and the Multan force was driven into the canal, with British troops lining up on the banks. 'We stood upon the bank and shot them like ducks; for they had got into such confusion, in trying to make their escape, that they could not move along – they were in one another's road; and the best of it was they could neither return us a shot, nor could they escape out of the canal, the banks on both sides being so steep. It was fairly choked up with dead,' described Corporal John Ryder.

The cavalry (and horse artillery) under Major Wheeler and Capt Anderson charged and were completely successful in discomfiting the Multan cavalry. A standard was captured here. Three men were killed, and twelve to fourteen wounded, in a short, sharp exchange that was completed with success.

With the Multan guns and position on the east bank overrun, Edwardes' loyal troops along with the Bhawulpore troops now advanced, pushing back the remaining Multan troops into the canal on the west bank. Other Rohilla irregulars crossed over, managing to capture a gun. However, they were mistaken for Multan soldiers by the British troops owing to no uniform and two were shot dead. Firing at these irregulars continued till a soldier of HM 32nd ran up towards the Rohillas and put his shako on the end of his bayonet, waving it around to show his comrades they were allies.

The Multan batteries were destroyed before the British columns recrossed the nullahs and returned to the camp. The battle had effectively finished by 3 p.m. The casualties on the British side including allies were light. Two Europeans were killed and eighteen wounded in all, with four sepoys killed with fourteen wounded. Major Wheeler, commanding the cavalry on the east bank, had a horse shot under him and had fallen heavily, although not badly hurt. In total the British side including allies suffered thirty-nine killed with 172 wounded. The Bhawulpore allies suffered five killed with thirty-eight wounded, many being in the early part of the day when the Multan force was attacking Edwardes' camp.

Wild estimates of up to 1,000 wounded and killed for Mulraj's force were speculated. One of the more high-profile casualties was Hurree Singh, the commander of cavalry. He had been with Mulraj ever since defecting from Agnew on the day of his murder. Whish generously wrote a letter to Mulraj after the battle enquiring whether the governor wished for the body of Hurree Singh back and offered to liberate several prisoners that had been taken in the battle for the purpose of carrying his body back to the city. The commander of the troops who had deserted the previous night from Courtlandt's force was also wounded.

Seven out of the eight guns Mulraj had sent were captured, including two 6-pounders. It was noted several of the guns captured were the Lahore Durbar guns that had accompanied Agnew on his trip to Multan. Much stock and supplies along with horses, camels and bullocks were also captured. The only gun to escape capture was the one pushed north to enfilade the advancing British line.

News of this defeat reached Mulraj while he was in a temple for the funeral rites of his nephew, killed in the skirmishing on 6 November. He took it badly. 'You gave them the guns, eh? I thought you promised me that by this the whole camp should be moved to Soojabad. Go and break your heads with your devices,' he replied to his officers in frustration and dismay. The loss of this last batch of field guns meant he had now lost his ability to mount any form of attack outside the city.

True to his vacillating character, after this latest setback Mulraj would again flirt with surrender. The day after the battle he would write a conciliatory letter complaining of Herbert Edwardes' conduct earlier in the execution of his brother-in-law, Lala Longa Mull, who had come to the British camp as an emissary.

> From Agnew Saheb, after I had submitted in all things and delivered up to him my fort, I received nothing but unprovoked outrage and insult – but God ordained that he should be punished by the hand of a sepoy, by whom he was wounded. If in the mutual assault which followed he was cut to pieces, I as a friend, covered his remains with a silk cloth; and in obedience to the precepts of my religion, I buried him according to the forms of his, and reported the whole circumstances to Lahore. My vakeel was imprisoned, and my despatch brought back to me unopened. What was then written is now in my possession, to prove that I am blameless. In the history of princes, it is not found that the persons of ambassadors have been outraged. It is a new practice to imprison messengers and heralds.

He offered to surrender but on similar conditions to before. However, Whish would communicate to him that he had no authority to accept anything but an unconditional surrender and that Mulraj must depend on British justice once he had given himself up.

\*\*\*

After the Suraj Khund battle, both sides again lapsed into relative inactivity. Nothing of major consequence would occur for another fortnight. Mulraj had resolved – or rather was forced by circumstances – to stand fast behind the walls of the city and it was noted he spent much time organising the strengthening of the city defences in preparation for a renewed siege. Whish, too, after Suraj Khund had resolved on no forward movement till the Bombay force joined him, although he was showing his impatience at their slow progress up country. With the more relaxed atmosphere in the British camp, and in order to occupy themselves, all sorts of games were organised to relieve the boredom till the wait for the Bombay troops was over. Plenty of games and field sports, as well as racing of all sorts, could be seen in the camp. Food supplies were of no issue. Temperatures were comfortable, hovering around the 70-degree mark during the day but falling to around 40 at night. There seemed to be some sickness in the British camp, and many had bowel complaints; it was suspected these were being brought about by the recent bad rations and food.

Three days after the battle, Edwardes, who had been asked to conduct an investigation into the recent mass defection of troops from the Kuthar Mookhee regiment before the battle, came to his conclusions. His findings were that the defections were due to the open slaughter of cows by the Muslims in the British camp. Cows being holy to Hindus, the slaughter had caused much offense to the Hindu sepoys. Edwardes had the offenders arrested and imprisoned as agreed during the Treaty of Lahore, which safeguarded the Hindu population from killing of kine. 'The latter [Hindus] have a holy horror of shedding a cow's blood, and the former [Muslims] as holy an appetite for beef. The treaty obliges me, as a magistrate in the Punjab, to enforce against our friends the most obnoxious prejudice of our enemies,' commented Edwardes. 'Still more difficult has it been, to be obliged to request Major-General Whish to forbid the slaughter of kine in his camp, in order that no hungry Mussulman detected with a steak, might tell me, that he bought it in the shambles of an European regiment.' Whish too, agreed on the ban of slaughter of cows to avoid further defections and in deference to the contingent of Hindu sepoys in the British force.

The following few weeks passed peacefully enough, with news received of the doubtful victories of Ramnuggar on 30 November and later on for Sadulpore in the north by Gough's main force. Twenty-one gun salutes were therefore fired in honour of both in the British camp. On 30 November, Whish would also receive further reinforcements of around 700 men, all from different regiments. These were the men that had originally been left behind in the march down due to illness or being on furlough. One of the group did not make it. An apothecary accompanying the force had apparently drunk too much one night and had been left behind. As he attempted to catch up, about 11 km behind the units he took a wrong turn and was cut up and shot by the locals, highlighting the danger of European soldiers travelling alone at this time.

***

The beginning of the month of December could almost be seen as the beginning of a new chapter in the conflict. The British stranglehold around the city began to tighten, with food supplies into the city being further reduced by British patrols. With the Bombay force approaching, preparations for a resumption of the siege were being progressed ever more energetically. Fresh supplies were being ferried by river to the camp. Cattle to pull the big siege guns and supplies were also being accumulated. Regarding supplies, Whish now had more than enough from the locals as well; having decided the British were much in the ascendant, they now showed great eagerness to trade.

The first major reconnaissance as part of the preparations for the renewal of the siege was carried out on 6 December. In command was Col Cheape, the chief British engineer. Two large columns were organised. A British contingent made up of a wing of each regiment with cavalry and accompanying artillery was to approach the city from the south to examine any fresh defences the garrison might have made. A second column composed of Edwardes' irregulars and British cavalry was to approach the city from the east and scout the suburbs there. Nothing of note happened, although there was firing from the city walls on any units that came too close. There were no casualties, with the suburbs, the numerous walls and the trees protecting any scouting parties well. Both columns returned to the camp at around 11 a.m. Edwardes had intercepted forty camels loaded with corn for the city and there was some skirmishing between the garrison troops who were escorting the convoy before they were repulsed. Between 13 and 16 December, other reconnaissance parties would also be despatched to explore the Seetal ke Maree and Ram Tirath areas of the suburbs as well.

The very next day, 7 December, much to everybody's surprise, it rained. What was a commonplace event elsewhere was rare at Multan. This was the first time that rain had fallen since the city had been invested by Edwardes in July.

By 9 December, such was the efficiency of the British patrols that no large supplies were now passing into the city. The price of grain in the city was said to be escalating rapidly. Several intrepid gangs continued to try and bring supplies into the city, not least for the enormous profit these brought. A large gang of banias (traders) was captured on 19 December transporting food to the city. Several camels of the garrison were captured by the 11th Light Cavalry and Jacob's Horse on the 19th also near Seetul Ke Maree in a skirmish in which two men were wounded.

One of the more interesting events during this developing blockade was the capture of a small mud fort to the north of the city on 10 December by Edwardes' irregulars. Quite a large supply of stores was found in the fort, including British Army stores of the 4th NI from Bombay from 1840, destined for the British garrison at Kabul. New clothing for troops and officers was found, complete in trunks and boxes, and all quite moth-eaten. These had presumably been sequestrated by locals as the army had marched down to Afghanistan. These were all destroyed.

So by mid-December, Mulraj and the garrison were now firmly penned in the fortress and city. Only the arrival of the Bombay troops was required for the resumption of the British siege.

# 23

# The Second Siege of Multan

Mooltan must be taken; and as matter of self-preservation the army, which has declared
its object must be met and crushed.

Dalhousie to Sir Henry Lawrence, November 1848

Seldom or never in any part of the world has a city been exposed to such a terrific
shelling as the doomed city of Mooltan. The well-served ordnance did tremendous
execution upon both houses and inhabitants; and soon the ruined streets were choked
with the mutilated bodies of the dead. The effect was highly creditable to the skill of
both artillery and engineers.

E. Buckle, Bengal Artillery

The first contingents of the Bombay force would begin drifting in on 11 December, the British
band in Whish's camp playing merrily to welcome them, accompanied by plenty of cheers from
the watching British soldiers. These units were Turnbull's battery, the 3rd NI and a detachment
of 500 of the Scinde Horse along with some 9-pounders. These were followed on the 15th by the
1st Bombay Cavalry (Lancers) while Whish sent out units to escort the British siege train, due
to arrive on the 16th by river. The bulk of the Bombay force marched into the camp between 21
and 26 December, all welcomed by the Bengal bands as enthusiastically as were the vanguard.

The hustle and bustle in the British camp further increased in mid- to late December with
numerous supplies and munitions being brought from the Ravi River, a long line of hackeries
constantly shuttling between the camp and river. Cattle were sent to the river in readiness to
drag the heavy siege pieces along with 2nd NI and Turnbull's battery escort. These had been
brought up on boats from Sukkur, 500 km downstream. The thirty guns, some of the heaviest
calibre the British owned in India, were offloaded from the boats just 10 km from the British
camp at Multan. All kinds of preparations were stepped up in the British camp in the days
prior to the move back to the city, with numerous scaling ladders ordered to be constructed in
readiness for an assault on the walls.

The issue of whether beef could be served reared its head at this time again with the arrival
of the Bombay troops. One of the points being debated around the camp was whether the war
was in fact still a war against rebels or whether this was a war against the Lahore state and its
army. If the war was indeed against the state, then the Treaty of Lahore, which observed the
prohibition of slaughter of cows and kine, no longer had to be adhered to and the Muslim
irregulars and British soldiers could eat beef to their hearts' content. The rumour was that beef
was already being served to soldiers in Gough's force. 'I write to enquire whether this statement
is correct as in that case, of course, a similar indulgence may without impropriety be extended

to the troops at Mooltan,' Edwardes questioned Currie on 18 December. Currie responded that the prohibition was still strictly in force and must be maintained, the war still being, officially at least, one against rebels against the Lahore Durbar.

With the arrival of the Bombay troops, the entire nature of the contest changed. The British section of the force, exclusive of allies, now numbered 15,000 men (roughly half being Bengal and half being Bombay troops) with sixty-four pieces of heavy artillery, and some sixty or seventy light guns. Added to these were 17,000 Muslim irregulars of Edwardes and Courtlandt and the Nawab of Bhawulpore's force with thirty guns of their own. This made a total of 32,000 troops in total, with over 150 guns, nearly half of which were the heaviest calibre.

Against this it was estimated Mulraj could muster no more than around 9,000 troops, half of questionable quality. As the shift of power towards the British continued, the less committed of the garrison had already begun deserting the city. The backbone of his force, his Sikh soldiers, thought to be 4,000 strong, were stationed in the fortress. Another 3,000 men garrisoned the city while 2,000 irregulars and mercenaries, not trusted enough to be kept in the city walls, were kept in the suburbs. These, it was suspected, could go over to the British side any time if offered a salary or simply drift away quickly now the scales had swung so decisively in the British favour.

The governor's stay in the city, while admirable, was unintelligible to many in the British camp since the coming contest would be so one-sided. A wild cocktail of rumours and differing reports from informers and deserters were coming into the British camp during mid-December about the mood inside the city on the eve of the renewal of the siege. Some rumours from deserters spoke of scarcities in the city and Mulraj's treasure being almost exhausted. Various deserters from the city were drifting into the British camp now, including two buglers on 20 December who described morale in the city plummeting and Mulraj trying to encourage his troops in vain. There was speculation he may slip away from the doomed city and join Shere Singh's army himself in the north. Others speculated he may slip across the Indus into the Derajat rather than stay and be encircled, obviating any need for a siege. These rumours were strengthened by stories that Mulraj had ordered his men to construct boats, the impression being he would use these to join Shere Singh or flee across the Chenab into the trans-Indus region before the Bombay troops arrived. Whether the deserters were saying what British ears wanted to hear is unclear.

Other reports showed a different mood. An interesting insight into the feelings of the garrison was revealed on 12 December. Several men of the 72nd NI were released from the city. They had been captured two weeks earlier while collecting wood for fire. They were asked to join the Multan force, which they did, although they had agreed to escape at the first opportunity. Their capture provided them with a chance to gauge feelings in the city. Mulraj, they declared, was busy encouraging his men to continue in the struggle. The reinforcements the British were waiting for, he said, would either not come or would be insufficient to capture the fortress and they would have to retire soon. There was confidence in the city for they reported the defences to be strong and there was belief in the city that it could not be taken.

Letters from Afghanistan also encouraged optimism within the city. On 15 December, for instance, letters from Dost Mohammad, the Kabul ruler, were intercepted by a British patrol. They intimated Dost Mohammad had already offered to either send succour to Multan or to at least offer some sort of diversion in the Derajat to draw some of the British force across the Indus. However, the main reason Mulraj was declining to surrender was supposed to be anxiety for his family. 'Moolraj is a plucky fellow,' wrote a staff officer in the British camp, 'and no mistake; he had a grand parade of his troops the other day, and roundly abused his men, who did not die at their guns but considered prudence the better part of valour. I have no doubt that he himself is really desirous to strike one more desperate blow for success. He says if he fails and dies on the field, our Government will respect his family, but if he waits the assembly of an overwhelming force, he and his will be equally involved in ruin. There is truth and spirit in these reported sentiments of his.' The staff officer would prove to be correct; over the next few days it became clear a second siege would be necessary.

***

Whish sent out orders for a resumption of the siege on 24 December, each regiment being told its position to take in front of the city walls, and thus by the evening of the 24th all was in readiness for the move. According to intelligence being brought back by deserters from the city over the days previous to the 24th, the attack was already widely expected for 25 December. 'Moolraj thinks so as it is the Eed of the Feringees, a good look out to be kept accordingly. Many desertions from the Dewan occur daily. Beyond his staunch little garrison, I expect he will have no adherents that will give us much trouble' reported the *Delhi Gazette* correspondent from a confident British camp. Desertions from the city were noted to be at an all-time high now the renewed siege was imminent. On the night of 22 December, the guns on the city walls were continuously fired for an hour. According to intelligence received later from the city in the British camp, the salute was for a supposed victory by Shere Singh over Gough or for some other good fortune. Mulraj had ordered the salute to be fired in order to encourage his men before the British ring developed round the city.

On the morning of 25 December, after a hiatus of three and a half months, Whish ordered the British force forward with a view to resuming the siege. The troops took up similar positions to the previous ones, Whish's Bengal troops to the east and northeast of the city at the Seetul Ke Maree with the Bombay troops occupying the position where Edwardes' force had been, to the left of the Bengal troops and facing the Delhi Gate and Khooni Burj, extending to the Grand Canal. Meanwhile Edwardes' force and the bulk of the irregulars and Bhawulpore force had moved to the left of the Bombay units, arcing south of the city. However, with plenty of men now for a comprehensive blockade, Whish had ordered the other irregular troops to be quartered all along the north-west and west of the city to prevent supplies entering from that direction. By sunset on the 25th, the ring of troops so familiar several months ago had reappeared round the city. Mulraj's residence just outside the city walls, the Aam Khas, was occupied by British troops again, to be used as an advance post. Being at some distance from the city guns, it suffered some shots during the next week or so, sustaining light damage. It would later become the residence of the engineer officers once the city fell and attention turned to the fort.

The British troops as they moved back found much had changed in the immediate city environs, Mulraj having kept his men busy in strengthening his position. The governor had ordered the nearby villages, already in a decrepit state after the previous siege, to be demolished to allow a clear sight of the British camp when the city was invested again. In addition much of the trees and scrub that populated the area had also been cut down and burnt. Several sand hills providing good vantage points had also been lowered to prevent British batteries being constructed which would overlook the city walls.

There had been some debate in the British camp as to which point of the city to attack first this time. Major Scott of the Bombay Engineers suggested attacking the north-eastern bastion of the citadel. Col Cheape of the Bengal Engineers said the suburbs should be captured and the city attacked first before attention was given to the fortress, a view Whish accepted; this would be the strategy pursued. His decision was perhaps influenced by the Bengal sepoys refusing to dig trenches, which would have to be excavated north of the fortress. High-caste sepoys would bluntly refuse work deemed below their caste and digging trenches was considered low-caste work.

With the decision to clear the suburbs first, the immediate task was to clear all garrison positions outside the city walls to the north, east and south-east again as before. In order to accomplish this, the British force was split into four columns to comb through this entire area simultaneously, stretching the garrison's resources. Two columns from the Bengal force and two from the Bombay force, with each assigned a sector, and with sappers attached to make entrenchments as territory was captured, were organised. A smaller force comprising a wing of the 8th Light Cavalry and the 49th and 51st NI were left to guard the camps, with the other wing of the 8th along with three companies of HM 10th comprising a reserve force. The brick kilns were to be targeted initially. Batteries were to be set up to fire on the Mundee Ava and Seedee Lall Ke Bede, the high, conical hill around 600 metres from the city walls, by noon that day. To further tax the garrison, a feint was organised for the west and north-west of the city with Edwardes troops stationed there ordered to advance around noon and to initiate a cannonade while moving towards the canal bridge near the Sheesh Mahal. By the evening of the 26th all orders were delivered as to the attack the next morning, scheduled for 11 a.m.

Edwardes' troops duly advanced for the feint on the morning of the 27th towards the bridge at Sheesh Mahal and the suburbs to the south-west of the city were systematically captured. The garrison, realising the offensive had begun, opened fire enthusiastically with the fort guns with additional parties coming out of the city to help those outside to harry Edwardes' advance. Half an hour after the first shots, heavy fighting west of the city was taking place.

With the feint in progress, the main British force on the east of the city, which had been ready by 11 a.m., began its general sweep forward at 1 p.m. Col Franks had overall command of the Bengal Division, which formed the two northern columns. Col Young with the first division was assigned the sector to the north and north-east of the city and headed a portion of HM 10th and 52nd NI. This force sheltered behind a large building and a series of large hillocks near the Eidgah before advancing under a cannonade from the fortress. They attacked the large brick kiln immediately to the east of the fortress. The right-centre column, assigned to Col Nash, was comprised of three companies of HM 32nd, six companies of the 72nd NI along with four horse artillery guns and with two 18-pounder howitzers. This contingent at the same time swept the area to the east of the fortress up to and including the right of the Mundee Ava and approached within 100 yards of the Delhi gate.

The small garrison posts and lookouts were quickly overrun. One of the prominent landmarks captured was the mausoleum of Mulraj's father Sawan Mull, a strongpoint 1 km east from the fortress, which the garrison men abandoned being too weak in numbers to hold the structure despite its strength as a defensive position. The large blue mosque was also captured. This was filled with refugees from the city, principally old men and women along with other civilians, and the British officer in charge allowed them to stay there for their safety. The houses and shops adjacent, however, were occupied by some defenders who were pushed back towards as far as the fort glacis. There were occasional rallies by the defenders. One position, a clump of trees in a garden recently taken by the British columns, was found to be occupied by only around forty British troops and was attacked by the city garrison before being driven off by reinforcements.

While this fighting was happening to the north and north-east of the city, to their south the two Bombay columns had also begun sweeping forward. The left-centre column, commanded by Brig. Capon, advanced to the area to the left of the Mundee Ava, towards the Khooni Burj, which formed the south-east corner of the city. This column consisted of five companies of the 60th Rifles and five of the 3rd Bombay NI with Turnbull's battery. Completing the attack was the left-most column under Col Dundas, consisting of five companies of the Fusiliers along with elements of the 4th Native Rifles and Bailey's battery, which advanced against the south-east and south of the city.

The right wing of the Bombay forces would capture the Mundee Ava but not before some of the fiercest fighting of the day. The Mundee Ava, being a large, sandy hill, was a natural defensive position and its height afforded a good location for a battery. The British advance was repelled once by the defenders, with Major Case ordering a retreat before the force attacking regrouped. A second attack was made, which reached the top of the hill before nearly being repelled again, although this time the garrison was overcome. Some houses and structures were found to be well defended and the British batteries were quickly used against these redoubts. By the end of that day, complete success had been achieved with all opposition swept aside and the garrison limited to the city wall and with around 200 prisoners taken. 'I hope tomorrow morning to have an 8-inch mortar battery of six pieces playing on the citadel at five or six hundred yards distance,' Whish informed the adjutant-general that evening.

Construction work on the batteries now began in earnest. Sappers and pioneers were immediately brought in, with firing from the British heavy guns commencing at dawn the very next day. Four batteries were initially set up, one to the north-east of the fortress and only 400 yards away from the structure. Here 18-pounders and six 8.5-inch mortars were placed in a battery. Mortars immediately began firing into the fort while the 18-pounder guns began the work of silencing the fort guns on the north-east, the embrasures of the fort in this location being entirely destroyed during the first few days. A large second battery was set up on the Mundee Ava, with two 9-pounders later joined by 18-pounder guns, 8.5-inch howitzers and 10.5-inch mortars. A third was set up to the south of the Mundee Ava, with a fourth targeting the extreme south-east of the city walls. Once positioned, these guns would fire continuously, night and day, till the capture of the city was effected. The only respite the city would get would be when the guns were occasionally moved forward still closer to the wall, their destructive power only increasing. 'The practice has been splendid; not a shell is now wasted as shown by the clouds of red dust that rise after a salvo of these iron monsters: every quarter of an hour we treat Moolraj to the dose, always on his bomb proofs; – twice today, we have set fire to some combustibles in his stronghold, and I hear the same has occurred in the city. Since daylight he has opened a furious cannonade on our battery from four to six guns, their artillery, their store carts, and bullocks appearing favourite objects of his attention,' wrote the correspondent of the *Delhi Gazette*. 'I think Moolraj's men are greatly dispirited since we commenced operations yesterday, for the fire from the fort has not been nearly so great as it used to be formerly, and once we get all our heavy mortars into play, I think they will be well kept alive, as there will then be a fearful cross fire into the fort. At twelve o clock to day some ten more eight-inch mortars are to open the fort and city, and then it is to be hoped that that portion of the city between the Pajawah and the citadel itself will soon be evacuated.' While this was happening, the houses in the suburbs round the guns were converted into strongholds while more breaching cannons were slowly hauled into position. Along with the batteries, trenches were thrown up for the comfort and safety of the infantry.

\*\*\*

One of the prominent civilian witnesses to the second siege of the city would be Henry Lawrence, the former Resident who had left India a year previously. As soon as news of hostilities reached London during the summer Lawrence had met with the Court of Directors in London, offering to make his way back to see if he could assist in any fashion in settling affairs in the Punjab. They were warm to the offer and Lawrence's ship left England in November, reaching Bombay on 8 December from where he sailed up the Indus reaching Multan on 28 December. He was given a tour of British positions round the beleaguered city the same day of his arrival by Whish and Edwardes.

There was a general impression that the war had been partly due to the more empathetic Henry Lawrence disappearing from the scene and that his return and friendlier approach would soothe things and bring about an end to the war. In fact there were strong rumours when his arrival was imminent that Mulraj would give himself up to Henry Lawrence, feeling he would get a fairer deal from him than with Frederick Currie. This was not the way Dalhousie felt, however, and he seemed to be irked by the influence and prestige Lawrence seemed to wield in the Punjab. Writing a letter to the former Resident on 12 December and intended to arrive when Henry Lawrence reached Multan, Dalhousie warned him that his writ no longer ran, that he had no authority to unilaterally negotiate a peace treaty to bring an end to the war without his consent.

> I have to inform you that I will grant no terms whatever to Moolraj, nor listen to any proposal but unconditional surrender. If he is captured he shall have what he does not deserve – a fair trial; and if on that trial he shall prove the traitor he is, for months in arms against the British Government, or accessory to the murder of British officers, then, as sure as I live, he shall die. But you have one answer alone to give him now – unconditional surrender. I have told you what will follow it.

Mulraj never made any approaches or indications of surrender to Henry Lawrence, and Lawrence, with the constraints put on him by the Governor-General, never made any advances towards Mulraj himself, leaving the siege to reach its own conclusion. The former Resident would stay at Multan till 2 January, witnessing the capture of the city before travelling north to join the Governor-General at Makhu on 6 January and bringing with him news of its fall. He would then travel to join Gough's army, then readying itself for the advance on Chillianwala. Returning to Lahore after the battle, Henry Lawrence thus witnessed some of the more memorable incidents of the war.

\*\*\*

The heavy imbalance between the artillery on both sides meant the city and fortress guns began to be silenced very quickly once the British heavy guns began firing in earnest. Not only that, but by the 28th it was noticed the fort guns frequently fired grape made of baked mud or simply large stones or more infrequently red-hot balls or at other times large brass or composition shells rather than more conventional shot, suggesting a shortage inside the city. As their strength faded the fortress guns did little damage, the British troops in any case being well protected inside trenches and strongholds. In contrast the British supplies were endless, being brought upriver from both Ferozepore and from supply columns from Bombay. Large quantities of guncotton had been brought by the Bombay column and were being used in the British batteries of the Bombay section of the line. This powerful new explosive, recently invented, was many times more potent than conventional gunpowder, therefore giving the British guns a much more destructive edge with every salvo.

'The Ducks [Bombay force] have been emulating us in mortar and great gun performances: they, too, have the start of us in improvements – the destructive gun cotton has been used by them with effect. At dusk yesterday we witnessed a beautiful exhibition of this invention: a broad flash intimated the discharge of the gun; this was followed by the brilliant transit of the fuse, which, on reaching its destination, was succeeded by another more vivid flash. The effect was remarkable, and must have been very disagreeably so to the occupants of the doomed city. All night our batteries played on them without intermission with shell and shrapnel,' reported the correspondent of the *Delhi Gazette* on 30 December.

The barrage from the British guns was strong and unrelenting along the wide arc of the British camp east of the city. A shell was being hurled from each of the batteries every ten minutes, while the mortar fire was almost continuous. At night, the flashes of the guns illuminated all around when fired. Adjacent to the guns were placed units of infantry to protect the batteries from excursions by the garrison. While this battering of the city defences was taking place on the east, Edwardes with his irregulars kept the garrison occupied on the west of the city with frequent diversionary attacks.

Many inhabitants of the city and suburbs could be seen surrendering during the first few days of the bombardment. Hundreds of civilians could be seen daily clambering down on ropes from the city walls during any brief periods of respite in the bombardment or at places where British guns were not stationed opposite. Once having made their way down the walls, they took shelter in the fortress ditch before taking their chances and running towards the British lines. These people were apprehended by the Bhawulpore irregulars. Those who had money and means then fled the city. Others less fortunate were seen to gradually assemble behind the British lines where a huge refugee camp began quickly materialising. The occupants of these camps were reinforced by other locals who had taken shelter in many of the large buildings outside the city by this time including Sawan Mull's tomb and the Blue Mosque. These unfortunates had been evicted in favour of the British soldiers seeking accommodation during the siege.

Over the next few days, the British siege guns were brought closer and closer to the city wall. By 29 December, for instance, two mortar batteries were firing on the citadel at 500 yards and the two southern breaching batteries of 18-pounders would open up on the morning of the 30th on the Khooni Burj and Delhi gate at a distance of only 150 yards.

The pounding of the city and fortress wasn't without incident. Work was interrupted by occasional sallies from the garrison. On the 27th for example, a party from the fort succeeded in driving out the British party from the Blue Mosque temporarily but this was subsequently recaptured. There was also some skirmishing on the 29th when Edwardes' party was attacked by the garrison. They sallied out around 1 p.m., roughly 2,000 strong. Many of them were recognised to be the Kuthar Mookhee deserters. Exiting from the Delhi gate, they moved towards the Seedee Lall Ke Bede and attacked Lake and his Daudputras before retreating back to the city. From the city walls, defiant musket fire was kept up in the face of any movement in the nearby British trenches.

'If a cap were held above the trench but for a moment, a dozen bullets came instantly whistling in; every crevice in the face of the battery was mark for a score of matchlocks; and it was curious to see (after the fall of the city) the effects of the Sikh fire. We noticed a tree on the right, in an oblique direction between the battery and the wall which was literally tattooed with musket balls; there must have been thousands lodged in its trunk and branches. Almost every bag of sand of which the battery was, in a great measure constructed had been perforated by a bullet, and indented lead balls could be seen lying about in every direction,' wrote John Jones Cole, one of the assistant surgeons with the army.

Special attention began to given to the Delhi gate and Khooni Burj, where it had been decided the Bengal and Bombay columns would attack to gain entrance to the city. Orders were given to place two eight-gun breaching batteries 100 yards from the walls. One was to face the Delhi Gate. This included the 18- and 24-pounder guns situated on the Mundee Ava. The other was halfway between the Delhi Gate and the Khooni Burj. The installation of these batteries faced as much opposition as the garrison could provide, although the British troops were well sheltered. These batteries opened up on 29 December and by the next day the guns had been moved as close as 80 yards to the city wall. At the same time ten mortars continued to play into the town, along with the howitzers and other light guns from the south-west of the city.

Whereas the fortress had been strengthened during the period of the lifting of the siege the same could not be said for the venerable city walls, as the British pounding showed. 'It is impossible to overrate the service rendered by the 8-inch and 10-inch howitzers,' remarked Major Siddons in his report of the siege. 'The walls are mostly of mud, or brick and mud; and it so happened that the part selected for the breach was very defective – a mere facing over the old wall. In this the 24-pounder shot brought down large masses; but where the wall was sound the shot buried themselves whereas the shells penetrated and then acted as small mines.'

The garrison in vain made repeated attempts to repair the breaches made by the British guns. To counter this, the 60th Rifles were stationed close by the breaches to harass and frustrate the defenders' attempts and more than a few of the defenders were shot dead in these operations to repair the wall. 'Four men who have been taken prisoners by us state that the destruction in the city been awful,' the *Delhi Gazette* correspondent noted on 30 December, as a pall of dust and smoke continuously hovered over the walled city. The granary in the fortress was known to have been hit and was on fire this day. Several small magazines had also been hit and had exploded, causing much chaos. Numerous fires beyond the capacity of the garrison or civilians to control could be seen raging through the city, the flames licking into the sky well above the city walls. While the pounding continued, irregular cavalry continued to move along the entire west of the city to both prevent any escape by the occupants away from the British guns and to stop supplies coming into the city. 'Seldom or never in any part of the world has a city been exposed to such a terrific shelling as the doomed city of Mooltan. The well-served ordnance did tremendous execution upon both houses and inhabitants; and soon the ruined streets were choked with the mutilated bodies of the dead. The effect was highly creditable to the skill of both artillery and engineers,' added E. Buckle of the Bengal Artillery.

Much worse was to come for the defenders. The location of the grand magazine (one of the Masjids) in the fort, holding an estimated 800,000–1,000,000 lbs of gunpowder, was known to the British engineers through the deserters, and at around 7 a.m. on the morning of the 30th, a time when many of the British soldiers were busy with their breakfast, a British mortar had the fortune of finding a weak point in the structure. A massive explosion, reckoned to be the largest of the nineteenth century and the like of which would only be seen again during the twentieth, signalled the destruction of the magazine. The violence of the explosion and resulting shockwave was such that many British soldiers, despite being hundreds of yards away from the fort walls, were staggered or fell to the ground, likening the feeling to a giant, irresistible force shaking them violently.

'I saw an extraordinary dense mass, black as ink, with a clearly defined outline, rising slowly out of the fort. Gradually as it rose the upper part spread out assuming the form of a gigantic tree, but losing its sharp outline in upper air till it became a dark brown cloud hanging as a pall over the fort and city. A remarkable feature was the number of eddies circling within the mass, which became visible as the body of smoke and dust became more diffused and less dense,' wrote Charlie Pollard, an officer in the Bengal Engineers. 'It was evident too that within that dark mass were certain solid bodies, whether the debris of building or human beings it was impossible to say, hurled some hundreds of feet upwards and looking like specks in the air. The fire from the batteries which had opened at sunrise suddenly ceased on both sides and a dead silence followed as all eyes were turned on the fort, watching the extraordinary, and at first incomprehensible sight. After a few moments of suspense the cry "Moolraj's magazine has exploded" ran down the trenches and was followed by a hearty ringing cheer.'

The dust, debris and smoke of the explosion was seen to rise over 1,000 feet in the air and assume the characteristic mushroom cloud seen with explosions of a later age. For a short while, the thick black smoke covered the fort like a dark canopy before the debris large and small began its descent back into the fortress, causing yet more casualties, while the remainder of the debris and smoke slowly spread out, showering both the city and British lines.

Inside the fortress, the blast's effects were terrible. The grand magazine building vanished, while many of the smaller buildings and structures inside the fortress also disappeared in that instant, and the defences adjacent to the magazine were seriously weakened. Hundreds of defenders were hurled in the air while others were buried in collapsed buildings. Some of Mulraj's own family, including his mother, became victims, as well as some of his principal officers. Mulraj himself was wounded by a fragment of a brick while standing near one of the fort guns. A report reaching the British camp a day later mentioned around 300 of the garrison being in or on top of the magazine building at the time the fatal mortar struck. Naturally, all were naturally killed. The total death toll inside the fortress was estimated at between 400 and 800 men. The remaining men of the garrison had neither the strength nor the opportunity with the continuing bombardment to attempt pulling out the bodies of the dead and so three weeks later, after the siege, as British soldiers ambled through the remains of the fortress, decaying arms and limbs could be seen protruding through the vast piles of rubble that the explosion had created.

'The damage done by that explosion is most awful: all Moolraj's family, several sirdars, the notorious Khan Singh, and numerous other rascals, with all their property &c were hurled in the air. I have also heard that the south and west angles of the fort and an angle of the city have been levelled with the ground, and the guns on those points all upset and thrown into the ditch; but there is no positive information on this point,' speculated the correspondent of the *Delhi Gazette*.

The smoke and dust made any suggestion that the massive fortress walls had been compromised impossible to verify immediately. Once the dust had settled, it was clear the walls were not damaged; at least not visibly.

In the British trenches there was much jubilation, accompanied by cheering and backslapping as the news spread. So taken aback by the explosion were the British gunners that the guns did not fire for some time as their crews stopped all work and watched the huge mushroom cloud rising into the air.

The explosion was said to have been heard over 80 km away. 'The sight was awfully grand,' wrote Whish to the adjutant-general, 'and precisely similar to that at the siege of Hatrass on the 1st of March 1817. I hope the consequence may be the same in which case the enemy would abandon the fort tonight otherwise I contemplate assaulting the city tomorrow.' The grateful general awarded the man who had aimed the mortar and did so much damage, Lt Newall of the Bengal Artillery, ten gold mohurs with three more mohurs being given him by the officer commanding the battery. Henry Lawrence, standing with Whish, was also impressed and was heard to praise profusely the men who had manned the mortar. Any hopes that the explosion would encourage the garrison to surrender were short lived, however, as no messenger with a white flag was seen sauntering out of the fortress gates. The silence of the British guns therefore wasn't permanent. 'Our batteries again opened and their fire was quickly replied to from the fort by the gallant Sikh artillerymen, who seemed not one whit disheartened by the catastrophe,' recalled infantryman Charlie Pollard.

Encouraged by the destruction of the grand magazine, British gunners firing into the fort made attempts at finding and destroying the two other remaining large magazines in the structure. Their exact locations in the fortress were well known, and not least from a high-placed officer of Mulraj, Mohammad Sadiq Khan. Khan, the governor's former aide-de-camp, had shown a distinct lack of enthusiasm for a rebellion from the time of Agnew's killing and had defected to the British. He naturally knew the fortress intimately and was used extensively by Whish for his knowledge during the siege. Despite his assistance, the British gunners had no further fortune and the two magazines survived the siege intact.

The other major news on 30 December would be a rumour in the British lines that Mulraj had buried a large amount of money in his mansion outside the fortress, the Aam Khas. There were reports it was around 3 lakh rupees and a party of diggers was immediately sent to the building to investigate these claims. Only empty bags were found, indicating Mulraj had had some wealth buried at some time but had no doubt decided the fortress would be a safer place to store it.

British guns had more luck the day following the great explosion. Around noon on 31 December, a huge conflagration was seen in the city engulfing the main food store of the city, full of an estimated 50,000 lbs of grain, many tons of oil and other supplies. This fire had been caused by the previous day's explosion and during the night had increased in size, being quite beyond the garrison's ability to extinguish. The fire would burn the whole day and night, still burning violently beyond control on the next day, the first day of 1849. So intense was the fire that it lit up the whole walled city, helping the British gunners in their aim and hampering the garrison further.

Unlike the grand explosion, this fire provoked a somewhat mixed reception in the British lines. The vast stores in the city were known to hold grain worth at least 5 lakh rupees, along with other valuables. The destruction of these valuable contents would mean rather less prize money later. There were also suspicions that much of Mulraj's other wealth and valuables was being destroyed by the intense shelling. Whish, of course, was above these considerations and therefore none of these arguments affected the gunfire still being directed at the city. As this new fire continued unabated, the Bengal and Bombay gunners carried on their bombardment seemingly in competition with each other. But the strength of the walls meant no breach wide enough had been established by the end of the year.

There was a show of defiance from the governor as the year came to a close. Mulraj would send out a message saying he had more than enough ammunition to last a year and the garrison kept up a steady fire on the British trenches with small gun and matchlock fire at the same time. The city walls were increasingly riddled with British 24-pounder shot and were clearly tottering all along the east side of the city by this time, however. At some points the wall was now little more than piles of bricks. But importantly there was no clear and wide breach through which to launch an attack, although small breaches were apparent at the Bohar and Delhi gates. The shelling was especially brisk and unforgiving on the last day of 1848.

'The showers of shells (six and eight at a time) afford a beautiful light in these dark nights; they appear like so many stars racing with each other across the hemisphere, and the rapidly succeeding explosions cause a multiplicity of sounds, there being a very remarkable echo in the suburbs,' reported the *Delhi Gazette* correspondent on the eve of the new year.

By this time all the Multan guns in the city to the east had been silenced and there was little response to the sustained British firing. The only exception was the solitary gun nicknamed 'The great Tom', placed at the Khooni Burj, which had given so much trouble in the first siege. This had been knocked out a number of times but continued to be repaired and resurrected by the defending gunners, continuing to fire defiantly at the British guns placed at the Mundee Ava.

The only other weapon being fired by the garrison at the British lines was a solitary mortar which was firing stone shots, further underlining the paucity of materials for the garrison. To the west, however the city guns pointed at Herbert Edwardes' irregulars remained active, firing away at his men and at deserters escaping by using ropes on the walls.

British shelling increased during the late evening and night of the 31st, Whish ordering a more ferocious cannonade than usual 'to bring in the new year', as he put it, and the sound of the guns rose to a crescendo at midnight, causing a huge din. 'As many as twenty shells were in the air at the same time all making their course to the devoted city,' Ryder noted in the British lines as the bombardment reached a savage peak. 'Grand and awful' was the description by a newspaper correspondent of this savage pummelling of the city at this time. This shelling continued to be helped by the fires that raged unabated in the city during the night of the 31st, brilliantly illuminating the fortress and making the use of light balls unnecessary. The joke running through the British line that New Years Eve night was that Mulraj was providing the bonfire for celebrating the coming of the New Year.

While the explosion and fire had been garnering most of the attention, the two breaches near the Khooni Burj and Delhi Gate had been given more attention and made sufficiently wide, or seemingly so, and Whish after a week's shelling therefore decided an assault would be attempted on 2 January. The bombardment of the city correspondingly began to tail off at this time – one shell being fired every minute, at other times in threes and fours every minute.

Somewhat catching Whish and his officers off-guard, the garrison made a last desperate sally on New Year's Day and opened up with as many guns as possible. Around 1,000 men ventured out of the south-west gate to fight the British irregulars stationed to the west of the city but were beaten back. 'To our great surprise the enemy have opened a heavy cannonade on them; we thought that nearly all their guns were silenced. The garrison have sworn to die at their posts, and up to the present time evince every disposition to do so; and the loss of on both sides will be great,' the *Delhi Gazette* correspondent reported on 1 January.

Whish had decided both of the main breaches in the walls would be attacked simultaneously. In line with the previous assault on the city suburbs, the Bombay and Bengal army columns would each have their own tasks. The Bengal force, consisting of HM 32nd, 49th and 72nd NI under Capt. Franks but led by a Capt. Smythe, would be under the command of Brig. Markham and would attack the northern breach at the Delhi gate. Meanwhile the Bombay force to it left, comprised of the 1st Bombay Fusiliers and 4th and 19th Bombay NI under the command of Brig. Stalker, would attack the southern breach near the Khooni Burj. Coincidentally, Major Mignon, who would lead the Fusiliers into the breach, happened to be the son of Col Mignon who fifty years previously had led the flank companies of the Bombay army at the storming o

Seringapatam. Both columns would be accompanied by a company of sappers and pioneers and an officer of the Engineers, along with a complement of twelve artillerymen armed with gun spikes. A liberal number of scaling ladders were also distributed among these troops.

The plan once both columns had entered the city was for the Bengal column to turn right and capture the area and gates towards the north and the fortress. The Bombay column, meanwhile, would turn left, fanning out to capture the Khooni Burj and the southern side of the city and its gates. It was hoped all the gates to the east and south would be captured by the end of the day. In order to facilitate the advance into the city, the commanding officers for the two columns were given maps of the city, with arrows showing where to direct the columns and which strong points and buildings were to be occupied. Strict instructions were issued to all officers to prevent any premature plundering and looting which could endanger the advance.

In addition to the two columns, many of the irregular troops who were already in the suburbs would form the reserve along with, on both flanks, two horse artillery guns and Bombay cavalry on the extreme left and Bengal army cavalry on the extreme right. These reserves would be commanded by Brig. Hervey. In order to intercept any of the garrison or other fugitives escaping from the city gates in the north of the city, more irregular cavalry with a further two horse artillery guns were situated north of the fortress.

Prior to the assault, a large diversion was also planned to the south and south-west of the city using the British allies. Lt Lake with his force of Daudputras would throw out a skirmishing force in front of the Pak gate, in the south of the city and immediately west of the Khooni Burj, where the Bombay division would be attacking. Meanwhile Courtlandt's force, stationed to Lake's left, would attack the city walls also to their front. To Courtlandt's left would be Edwardes' irregulars stretching up to the Bohar gate, the south-west extremity of the city. Thus nearly a 3 km stretch of the city walls would be under attack simultaneously at various points; this, it was thought, would stretch the resources of the garrison to the limit, allowing the breaches on the east to be easily navigated by the two British columns. Once the two columns entered the city, the diversionary forces were to be withdrawn in preparation for entering the city as and when the gates were captured and thrown open.

The British mortars and batteries were ordered to continue to fire that night and the morning of the planned attack, softening up the defences as much as possible and keeping the defenders awake and unrested.

*** 

Early on 2 January, the entire British line and its allied force were paraded in front of the British camp before being moved forward to their respective positions. At half-past one in the afternoon, orders were issued and the assault on the city commenced, with the diversionary attacks launched as planned, assisted through artillery fire along the entire British line. To the east of the city both British columns waited patiently for another hour for the defenders to thin out until, between 2 p.m. and 3 p.m., the order was given to advance to the breaches.

The Bombay brigade moved from behind the Mundee Ava, forming up around 200 yards in front of the Khooni Burj breach before continuing the advance. The road at Mundee Ava led straight to the Khooni Burj before joining the road circling the city walls.

HM 60th Rifles and British artillery with grapeshot continued to fire at the defenders in the breach area to keep them busy while the line advanced. The Bombay force managed to cross the breach without much difficulty, the few defenders found being swept aside relatively quickly.

'The breach was to our right of the Burj, a high tower and bastion on which formerly they had some heavy guns. The tower, though was much shattered without, from being stockade with thick timber and mud inside, was still a secure place of shelter for the enemy, and was occupied in strength. I can give you no accurate description of the breach we mounted. It was steep, and broken brick and mouldered dust gave beneath the feet, reminding me of the ascent of Vesuvius. We did not climb this unmolested; thick and hot the balls fell amongst us, but not a man was killed and strangely few wounded,' recorded Henry Daly, Adjutant of 1st Bombay Fusiliers.

On climbing past through the debris of the breach and into the streets behind the walls, they found themselves in a sort of enclosure, the garrison having taken time to blockade the area in makeshift fashion. A trench had been dug parallel to the breach, the other side being stockade with planks and matting. Only one exit remained, to the right via a narrow lane from which the Khooni Burj could be accessed by climbing over a low house. However, those men given scaling ladders seemed to have been held back and this caused a delay of around fifteen to twenty minutes. During this time, the few defenders on the rooftops continued firing into the waiting British troops and shot several men. Some of the streets near the breach had been blockaded as well, but once the scaling ladders arrived the force began fanning out irresistibly. The brigade was formed in three columns and each of the columns went their own separate way. The leftmost column turned left to clear the ramparts towards the Khooni Burj and the southern stretch of walls before moving out towards the Lohari gate to the west, although they would return towards the Bohar gate for the night. The Pak gate was seized by the 72nd Bengals while the 4th Rifles held the Haram gate. Thus all the gates to the south of the city were shortly in British hands with little more than token resistance. Not all went to plan despite the units following the directions on the maps distributed before the assault, for some guides had been killed and the British soldiers, oddly enough, had to ask the locals sheltering from the musket balls in their cellars the way to their destinations at various places in the warren of streets.

The centre column meanwhile pushed forward into the grain market and commercial centre of the city, meeting slight resistance. The streets they passed were seen to be literally choked with the dead, defenders and civilians alike; victims of the recent bombardment.

The right column, now headed by Lt Gray after Capt. Leith was wounded, turned right and moved adjacent to the city wall towards the point the Bengal column were to have entered. To their surprise, instead of being in front of them the Bengal column was heard moving up behind them.

\*\*\*

While the Bombay force had encountered little problem, the Bengal column attacking at the Delhi gate in the north had a very different experience. Capt. Smyth led HM 32nd who headed the column. Moving off with the troops roaring and cheering, they approached the wall but found there was no breach as reported. What had happened was that from the British position it had seemed like a breach had successfully been made. In fact the hole that had been blasted in the wall was 20–30 feet high. There was a natural incline in front of the wall topped by a mud wall 3–4 feet high followed by a dip behind and a trench around 10–12 feet deep closer to the walls which hid the natural height of the wall and gave the impression the breach was at ground level. With the breaching guns around 400 yards away from the walls it had been impossible to see beyond the incline, and with the defenders firing on anyone who came near, no reconnaissance of the ground behind the mud wall or the supposed breach had been made.

Therefore upon reaching the wall the Bengal force found passing through the breach an impossibility, even with scaling ladders. Fortunately for the attackers, the defenders were in desperate straits and were constrained by their numbers and lack of ammunition from taking full advantage of the confusion below them. Many men on the walls were seen to throw bricks and stone from the ramparts, having nothing more suitable. Nevertheless it was reported ten to twelve men were wounded or bruised by the bricks, the men continuing to stay in the exposed position as no order to retreat was issued. 'The enemy defended the breach to the utmost of their power,' recorded Corporal Ryder. 'They stood with drawn swords at the top while others kept up a regular fire and large stones, bricks with beams of timber were hurled from the summit of the walls upon us and even women could be seen loading the muskets for the men and handing them to them.'

To compound the problem, further units advanced and reached the wall and therefore a confused mass of soldiers developed below the walls, unable to gain ingress and with no orders to retreat. The matter was complicated further by the commanding officer, Capt. Smyth, being hit by one of the bricks, which delayed any decision being made. The soldiers, angry at the mistake, were heard to express much strong language at the officer of the Engineers who had expressed the breach as practicable. Eventually the order was given to retreat and to wheel to the left and use the southern breach at the Khooni Burj used by the Bombay division. The division moved south accordingly.

Upon entering this breach they moved north through the maze of streets so that they were at the Delhi gate, where they would have been had they been able to enter the breach. They too found resistance was minimal, many of the defenders having already moved into the fortress. Once inside the city the full effects of the heavy bombardment of the city were evident everywhere to the men of the column.

'Right and left before us and behind, the ground was strewed with dead; and arms and ammunition no longer useful lay scattered here and there. One gun that had been placed so as to bear upon the top of the breach was partly turned and with elevated muzzle looked as if it would willingly run away, the houses on all sides were much shattered and the streets partly filled up and in many places obstructed by the carcasses of horses and cattle. Dogs were seen in numbers lying dead; and the living were already feeding on the bodies of man and beast. The streets were dirty and disgusting; few inhabitants appeared in them and they that did looked wretched enough. Numbers of wounded were found in the houses stretched in agony on the ground,' surgeon John Jones Cole would later write.

The intense shelling had done its work, along with the fires, with collapsed buildings effectively having closed many roads. Most of the houses in the city were completely ruined and hardly any had roofs. In among the rubble could be seen hands and feet of those caught in the collapsed houses, while others lay in the streets untended.

'As we explored the different parts of the town, a death-like silence reigned in the forsaken quarters; the most intrepid were intimidated by the loneliness,' added Ryder. 'Some of the streets were so long, that we could not recognise each other at the opposite extremities – uncertain whether we were friends or enemies, we advanced towards each other cautiously. Mountains of dead lay in every part of the town, and heaps of human ashes in every square, where the bodies had been burnt as they were killed. Some were only half consumed, and were so black that it was almost impossible to tell what the materials were. Many had been gnawed and pulled to pieces by dogs; and arms, legs, heads, and other parts of the corpses lay in every place. The dead horses and beasts which lay about caused a horrid stench, and the town swarmed with millions of flies.'

The advance into the city would not be entirely straightforward. In some places defenders had barricaded themselves in houses or on rooftops. The doors to these houses were broken down with musket butts or the locks blown off before they were stormed. No prisoners were taken and all were shot, with looting taking place soon after.

Wrote Ryder:

As our fire was poured down the street into the enemy, and they were falling in numbers, intermingled with the men might be seen women and children. Their wild, terrified screams, were awful. The cries of the affrighted children, as they clung round their mothers, were equally dreadful. Grey-headed old men, with their venerable beards white with age, and their flesh deeply furrowed with the wrinkles of seventy or eighty years, whose tottering limbs stood trembling, overwhelmed by grief and age, unable to follow their families, were weeping for the ruin of their country, and lay down to die near the houses where they were born. The streets, the public squares, and especially the mosques, were crowded with these unhappy persons, who mourned as they lay on the remains of their property, with every sign of despair. The victors and the vanquished were now become equally brutish; the former by excess of fortune, the latter by excess of misery. Everyone was plundered whom our men could lay their hands upon, regardless of their pitiful cry, and in some instances were women and children shot down amongst the men. Our men now appeared to be brutish beyond everything, having but little mercy for one another – still less for an enemy; and very little pity indeed could be found in any one.

The fighting, extremely confused in the narrow streets, was made more difficult by the thousands of bodies and the huge amount of debris from the wreckage of the buildings which spread around everywhere due to the recent shelling; not a single building was in good condition. Within the maze of streets, the men of each regiment separated from one another and no semblance of order remained. Confused as to directions in the warren of streets, the British units simply followed the retreating garrison units.

'One place was fought very hard for by the enemy,' recalled Ryder. 'This was a Hindoo mosque and was occupied by a brave officer and a number of determined men. They had a colour, a very handsome one. They were attacked by a party of our men who took the colour and killed nearly all the men. The officer carrying the colour fought with it in one hand and his sword in the other cheering on his men at the same time but they were met by men equally as determined as they.' The silence was broken at intervals by the odd shell fired from the fort into the city while further away could be heard the sounds of British batteries being erected in preparation for the attack on the fort. As evening approached, the entire south-eastern half of the city had fallen into British hands, with the British standard already raised on the city walls by half-past three by the 1st Fusiliers. The Pak gate had been cleared by the Bengal sappers, the Haram gate by the Bombay sappers, and parties were organised for the night to occupy and hold the gates. As darkness fell parties were left in the advance positions while most of the troops retired to sleep in the open ground in the centre of the town.

One of the more regretful aspects to the fighting during the day had been the brutal treatment and excesses committed on some of Multan's inhabitants. Officially nothing untoward happened during the capture. 'Brig. Stalker speaks most highly of the conduct of the troops and nothing can be more honorable to their character than the humanity and kind treatment shown by them towards the unoffending inhabitants,' Brig. Dundas wrote to Whish in his report on the same day. Stalker had led the 2nd Brigade, Bombay Division into the city. But barricaded doors had been forced open and volleys of shots fired upon the civilians, frequently old men and women and children, huddled together despite the fact they were not armed. This may or may not have been British soldiers suspecting them of being combatants.

Several other men were supposed to be guilty of cold-blooded murder. Rapes were also discussed. A man belonging to HM 32nd 3rd Company, an Irishman, raped a girl, having pulled her away from her mother. With few officers, only three per hundred men, and the streets and houses hiding offences, it was difficult for the officers to prevent these atrocities. In any case many officers themselves were known to show little mercy as they burst into the houses. The sepoys were not immune to brutishness as they saw their European comrades taking advantage. A man was seen later being burnt by sepoys in the middle of firewood, heavily wounded but still alive, though he was saved in time.

Some civilians had bravely put up what resistance they could. One soldier who had entered a hovel found an old woman who had stored gunpowder in her house. As the soldier entered she threw a lighted piece of cloth and blew up the house, the soldier narrowly managing to flee the explosion. She had hoped several of the party would enter but only one had. In one of the last casualties in the city, a British soldier was shot by a female resident as he entered a house.

\*\*\*

As evening fell, the various regiments were allocated positions in the walled city to both rest and defend during the night to ensure the garrison in the fort did not attempt a surprise counter-attack in the gloom. Amid the continuing covert looting, soldiers began settling down, many burning the furniture and battered doors of dwellings for fires for cooking and warmth as temperatures fell. Others made the best of the primitive conditions in other ways, many of the British soldiers using the dead corpses littering the streets as pillows. Other unwelcome visitors, jackals and dogs, were also paying much attention and feasting on the corpses, having entered the city through the breaches and open gates by this time. As night progressed, all fighting and looting died down for the night and civilians and soldiers alike of all sides began settling down, when suddenly a huge explosion in the south of the city had the effect of unsettling everyone again. 'About 1 a.m. a most fearful event occurred. While we were lying down near the wall, a trembling of the earth, followed instantaneously by flames and fire all round. Bricks falling, houses tottering, roofs off. All was darkness, save where lurid flames were rising amongst us. We cried out to the men to stand to their arms, and remain as steady as the convulsed state of the ground would permit them. Long, awfully long, it appeared ere even the worst passed away. When it had done so, the cries of many sufferers arose on every side,' described Henry Daly, adjutant of the 1st Bombay Fusiliers. A house near one of the city gates had been used as a makeshift magazine by the garrison and had been full of gunpowder. The house hadn't been searched by the entering British columns. This gunpowder had blown up due to a spark or cinders from a nearby fire the soldiers had lit to keep warm, causing the powerful blast. 'We could not in the darkness see the havoc which had been committed, but in many places the fire which had caught pieces of wood still burned, and by its light a part of the ruin could be seen; 60 Sappers (native) had been employed at the time of the outburst in opening the gate, which had been stockaded and closed up with heavy timber beneath the archway; 35 of these were buried alive, many others escaped with their lives indeed, but with limbs desperately damaged. The 4th Rifles also were among the unfortunates; 10 of these poor fellows were killed and some

30 or more wounded. A few of the 19th NI with us were also the victims.' Twelve sappers of the Bombay force were killed, with many others badly wounded. The houses had obviously not been adequately searched, and due to this incident an investigation of the area was done and another hidden magazine was discovered close to a house that was burning. Lieutenants Pollard and Maxwell, along with some sappers, were given the task of removing the gunpowder, which was thrown over the city walls.

The night of 2 January was unusual. All guns fell silent after the fall of the city, and an unusually calm and hushed atmosphere pervaded the city. Not a gun or musket was heard that night after the explosion, something commented on by many a soldier, conditioned as they were to the constant and unrelenting fire of the big guns night and day for the previous week, along with the constant smell of powder.

***

Whish had forbidden any looting a more systematic approach could be organised by the prize agents, headed by Major Wheeler and assisted by two squadrons of 7th Irregular Cavalry. However, it was difficult to stop the common soldier continuing to look for valuables in the warren of wrecked streets and houses. A corporal was seen openly bragging about shooting an old man while he took away the little property he had, including the silver rings his wife and daughters were wearing, in very brutal fashion. He was stripped of his rank soon after for this offence. Others were robbed and anything of value that could not be carried away was destroyed rather than left. It was not till several soldiers had been apprehended and taken to the British camp as prisoners that looting tailed off. Those arrested were later flogged. At least one soldier seen pillaging was later imprisoned.

In order to prevent soldiers spiriting any wealth out of the city, guards had been put on the city gates by the prize agents. Anyone attempting to carry out items or animals was intercepted. The camp followers walking in and out of the city were all searched as well, one being shot as he refused to halt and attempted to make off with some booty. Many of the baggage cattle, mules and horses dispersed throughout the city were considered fair game and for many these became the immediate source of loot short of scavenging through the houses. The prize agents at the gates easily stopped the movement of cattle, however. A focus of attention had been Mulraj's stables, located outside the fortress in the city, where most of his collection of fine Arabs, camels and elephants were kept. Here, too, the ever vigilant prize agents had taken control. Eleven elephants from the stables were brought into the British camp as well as the selection of fine horses. One of the elephants, it turned out, was a British one captured earlier in the hostilities.

The only areas that could not be liberated of their plunder were the places adjacent to the fortress due to the fort guns facing these locations. Here plenty of animals could be seen wandering around untended. One soldier was seen to take his chance and rush in to guide back two fine horses, both of which were lost to a cannon shot from the alert garrison soldiers.

On the morning of the third, the final tally of the livestock was made. Twenty-five elephants had in total been captured, with horses too numerous to mention from Mulraj's stables. In terms of material of war, fourteen guns had also been captured in the city; the rest had been taken back into fort by the garrison, although many muskets and other weapons were seen littering the city.

The formal search for plunder would commence the following day and was as systematic and through as possible. The numerous rings and chains and jewellery worn by the dead strewed around were collected while the living residents were asked to leave their possessions and valuables behind as they were escorted out of the city. Houses were broken into and all valuables extracted. The Hindu temples in the town became a focus of attention as they housed idols made of brass or more precious metals, studded with precious stones.

Anything that had the least intrinsic value, including Qurans from the mosques, was accumulated. Hence there was the strange sight of small hillocks of books seen later at the prize agent's depots outside the city walls. Over time much cloth, including silk, was discovered and with the numerous weapons strewed around the city, considerable mountains of loot were built up over the following days, ready to be sold or auctioned off.

The civilian population was rounded up, being brought into public squares and escorted out for the purposes of extracting wealth. Each house was searched for occupants and valuables. This was a slow and laborious task as most of the residents had barricaded themselves in, closing all the windows and doors with brick and stone to prevent shell fragments and bricks flying around. Many of the civilians were extremely hungry and related to their captors they had had nothing to eat since the beginning of the siege a week earlier. The shelling had been so heavy that it had prevented anyone from going out to look for food, with most people surviving on what little they had in their own houses.

The civilians would be allowed back into the city and the suburbs round the city several days later but only to the areas lying furthest from the fortress. They were also allowed to begin repair of their dwellings. The many months of war had reduced most to penury, however, and thousands of inhabitants, now beggars, hovered round the British camp outside the city, where supplies of food were of no issue, pleading for sustenance. It was noticed all form of discrimination had ended with extreme hunger. Hindu inhabitants who would not normally touch European food as it would break caste now ate freely and alongside Muslims.

The booty in terms of money, jewellery and the numerous other valuables extracted from the broken city was estimated on 4 January to be worth over 20 lakh rupees, but still with considerable amounts coming in every hour as the city continued to be searched. This was the cue for several headmen and wealthy occupants of the city to approach Whish after the capture of the city. They offered 15 lakh rupees (around £10–12 million in today's money) if their property and the city was protected. This overture was rejected by Whish, who recognised much more could be extracted.

The prize agents would commence auctions on 5 January even as the big siege guns turned their attention towards the fortress, and the proceedings were therefore carried out amid much distracting noise and tumult. Around 200 horses in total had been captured in the city, mainly from Mulraj's stables, along with other bullocks and camels. The prices fetched were low, however, the feed of a horse and cattle being prohibitively expensive with hostilities ongoing. Most of the British soldiers were mollified by the fact that much wealth had been removed to the fortress by Mulraj and that therefore more loot would be forthcoming once the citadel itself was captured.

\*\*\*

British casualties during the assault had been relatively small. This was due both to the parlous state of the defenders and to Whish having taken all precautions to soften up the garrison and defences before the attack. Total losses in taking the city had been 350 killed and wounded (the Bombay division suffering sixteen killed and 139 wounded).

It's difficult to estimate the total civilian and garrison losses inside the city. Mulraj had retreated with his core troops into the fortress and the British found few Sikh soldiers among the captured.

'The greater portion of the prisoners we have hitherto taken are genuine Hindostanees, and in their dress and hearing very much resemble our own sepoys. It is most astonishing these men should have so warmly espoused Moolraj's cause and fought to the last: the only reason they assign for having done so is, that they strove hard, but could not get employment under our Government, and were consequently forced to enter Moolraj's service,' reported the *Delhi Gazette* correspondent. Many of the defenders had attempted to escape the city during the fighting. Wheeler's cavalry was used to capture those attempting to slip through the British lines. Despite the strong ring of troops round the city this scheme was not altogether successful, as several thousand men were known to have been successful in disappearing. The country round Multan being so cut up by nullahs, canals and other obstacles, many men evaded capture by fleeing the city through the dry canals. The darkness of the night made pursuit even more difficult and the nullahs and gardens outside the city walls provided good cover. Most, it was reported, escaped to Sirdarpore. A large body of more than 1,000 men was seen escaping and marching in disciplined fashion away from the city while the city was being occupied by British troops. Wheeler's cavalry and the four guns that accompanied it had difficulty pursuing them as the guns could not be transported across the water channels easily.

Others were less fortunate. Some of the garrison had tried to break out of the city to the west. Irregular cavalry intercepted them, with twenty of their number being killed in the fighting while the rest were taken prisoner. Some notables were captured, including a Frenchman who had been assisting Mulraj during the siege. It was speculated that this was the man who had led the Multan troops before the Suraj Khund battle. The Jemadar of the Gurkha battalion of Agnew's escort who had joined the rebellion was captured too, along with Goojur Singh, who had cut down Agnew at the Eidgah. Several other officers of Mulraj were captured as well.

So as Whish began making preparations for the capture of the fortress, the city had been quite emptied of its occupants. However, the thousands of corpses that were still strewn around the city were causing an immense odour, and a fear of disease meant steps were at length taken to bury the bodies. Some men had already been taken ill, which was generally blamed on the rotting corpses. Such were the number of casualties among the civilians that those buried, principally Muslims, were buried in shallow graves in communal areas with half the body still above ground. Consequently these corpses attracted unwelcome attention. 'The troops of jackalls which were always prowling about at night were getting quite fat,' recorded Ryder. 'With their feast of human flesh the vultures and ravens were also growing too lazy to fly away as we passed them while they were sitting upon and pecking the bodies of the dead.'

There was praise in the British newspapers both for Whish and for the stubborn resistance the garrison had made in the city's defence. It was generally accepted Whish had done the right thing by not recklessly attacking the city without pummelling its defences into dust first, thereby avoiding far greater casualties. The *Bombay Times* recorded that the city had been captured after 'after one of the most obstinate and gallant defences on the part the enemy ever recorded in our annals'.

# 24

# The Fall of the Fortress

I congratulate you and the Government of British India on the extinction of the
firebrand which raised this flame in the Punjab.

Herbert Edwardes to Frederick Currie, 22 January 1849

An assault would have been more brilliant, but I thank God it was avoided. For 3,000
desperate men must have cost us many lives.

Dalhousie, February 1849

The lull after the capture of the city was short, lasting only for the night of 2 January. The only part of the city that still remained with the garrison by the end of the previous day was the Dowlut gate area. Here a mine had been sprung on the night of the 2nd which caused casualties during an aborted British attack on the position. Early the next day, this small area between the fort and the Dowlut gate became the first focus of attention for Whish. The position was captured from the few defenders, three companies of HM 10th commanded by a Col Young scrambling over the city gate using ropes with powder bags that were used to blow up the gate from the inside. With this gate in hand, the 24-foot-deep ditch guarding the now crumbling fortress on the city side could be fully seen. The fortress guns overlooking the city could be aimed far enough down to fire into the ditch, and this was discovered by an exploring party led by a Lt Maunsell, who crossed the gate and narrowly escaped grape from a masked battery hidden by wooden palings.

Inside the fortress, meanwhile, with no hope of succour and with the city in British hands, the less committed of Mulraj's men, largely the mercenaries, began deserting. In the first few days of the shelling of the fortress, there would be a steady stream of departures. On 3 January, for example, the Eusufzye mercenaries, Muslim tribesmen from the Trans-Indus, a batch around 500 strong, expressed a wish to surrender. They sent one of their headmen, Ishmael Khan, to Herbert Edwardes. They would desert Mulraj, they said, if they were allowed to take their arms with them. Whish would not agree to the arms being retained and it was decided after negotiations they would surrender their weapons as they came out of the Dowlut gate to a company of HM 10th. They left the fortress at 4 p.m. and were escorted away from the city and allowed to return to their homes. Another contingent who had wished to leave at the same time, the Gundehpoories, were refused permission. Whish perceived them as some of Mulraj's core men. Unlike the mercenaries, these men, along with the Sikh units in the garrison, would be captured to face punitive action after the war.

The next day, the 4th, one of the chiefs of the Rohilla Afghans made his way out of the fortress with a letter signed by around 200 of his party. The letter asked that they be allowed to join the

British service with their arms. The Rohilla party in the fortress was expected to leave at some point on the 5th and one of the European regiments was ordered to be ready to receive them as they made their way out of the fortress. However, they would never appear. It may be they were convinced by Mulraj to stay longer. The British lines were still awaiting the departure of the Rohillas on the 6th but to no avail. Whish reiterated his message that anyone who wished to leave the fort could do so by the Lohari gate to the west but by the 7th all hopes of seeing this party departing the fortress were given up.

The governor, as with earlier deserters, did nothing himself to prevent them leaving, probably realising waverers and malcontents were better outside than inside the citadel. But despite this, not all the deserters got a friendly reception from the British or a warm farewell from the garrison. There was the curious sight of some fugitives being shot at and killed by both the defenders and the British. That defenders would attempt to kill any deserters was understandable. But the British units outside frequently failed to recognise deserters, thinking they were attempting to escape the British ring round the citadel. An example of this would come on the morning of 17 January when 200 Pathan defenders walked out of a gate to surrender. British guns and muskets opened up and around fifty had been killed or wounded before their intentions were identified. The remaining number were escorted out of the city and kept as prisoners in Edwardes' camp west of the city. They said more would surrender if the British would not fire on anyone coming out – for conditions in the fortress were most difficult now and the defenders were suffering severe privations.

***

Whish would use a systematic approach to reduce the fortress, and the British guns were turned in its direction with the greatest optimism that a breach in the citadel walls would be made in a matter of days. By noon on 3 January, ten 8-inch mortars were already in position within the city and commenced firing into the fortress while new batteries on the city side began to be constructed. This initial confidence was misplaced. It soon became obvious to Whish after a day or two that, despite what would be over fifty guns battering the walls day and night, a breach would not be effected soon. In fact, the guns would continue firing for the next eighteen days in preparation for an assault, a sizeable breach in the fortress walls never becoming apparent. From the 4th, trenches for the troops were therefore constructed to protect the guns, their crews and infantry from matchlock fire from the fortress. Mining towards the walls commenced.

The fire from the siege guns was continuous and deafening by all accounts. During the next few days, the garrison in the fort attempted to organise some guns to compete with the British artillery, but so accurate and overwhelming was the British fire that these were quickly disabled. Nevertheless the defenders kept up a good rate of musket fire and it was seen that as soon as British soldiers left the trenches and other shelter and ventured closer to the walls there was sure to be a hail of fire directed at them. And despite the desertions and the tightening British noose, the remaining garrison were retaining their morale well.

'Our artillery threw more shell than anything else during the night,' commented Ryder on that first night of the shelling and what could be discerned from outside the citadel, 'and we could hear their wounded groaning after our shells had exploded, when they had fallen into the fort. The night was very still, and during the time our fire had slackened, we could hear them talking, and their sentinels challenging their reliefs, as they went their rounds. We could hear one of the sentinels, upon the ramparts nearest us, singing, and he appeared quite happy, as he passed up and down on his post. We heard him call out as one of our shells was fired. This was, I supposed, to give the alarm to his comrades. We could hear them strike the hour upon their "gurrey", and their drums beat and bugles sound. Everything appeared to be going on very regularly.'

Deserters had already related the inside of the fortress was entirely wrecked. No building remained with a roof, and all was in an utter state of ruin. The defenders had been forced to take shelter as close to the walls as possible under archways and gates, these being the only places where respite was possible from the shelling. Taking this into account, and in order to increase the discomfort of the defenders, British mortars were now firing at such an angle that the shot fell either on the fort walls or just on the inside of the walls to target these small sanctuaries.

By 6 January, British mortar batteries situated in the trenches to the east of the city had begun playing on the fortress as well, while the trenches continually being extended had by this time reached the glacis of the fort. Over the next few days the big guns were inched forward and by the 8th a battery of six 24-pounders and six 18-pounders was also set up and commenced playing on the fort from the north-east. This was to draw some fire of the of the few fort guns still firing back and to effect, if possible, a breach in the north-east of the fort. By this time, a seven-piece battery of 18-pounders had been constructed only 200 yards from the fort with another for 24-pounders organised even closer. It was recorded on 9 January that an 8-inch mortar battery of six pieces on its own fired 600 shells into the fort during that day, an indication of the ferocity of the continuing bombardment.

The British bombardment would not go wholly unanswered. Sometimes the weak reply from the fort found its mark. On 8 January, a shell fired from one of the fort guns set fire to a battery of seven 18-pounders. Constructed of fascines, the wood quickly caught fire in spite of strong efforts to contain the flames. The guns managed to be extricated and the ammunition removed to nearby trenches for safety. Several men were killed during the moving of the guns by fire from the fortress.

A small breach began to be discerned on the 10th, but there was far too much brick and debris, making the height of the breach too awkward for an assault. The Engineers' recommendation was to throw shells on to the top of this breach with lengthened fuses which, when bursting, would scatter and bring down much of the earth and debris. So 10.5-inch howitzers were placed in front and to left of a battery for this purpose and began making the breach more practicable. Despite this the Engineers failed to recommend it, the loose bricks and stone forming such a steep, treacherous slope that it was thought the defenders would have too much of an advantage against an attacking column.

Firing continued through 13 January despite the day being recorded as one of the wettest yet of the siege. A huge downpour had commenced early on in the day and continuing till the night, so much so that British soldiers found themselves up to their knees in mud. It continued raining heavily during the night as well, and temperatures dropped appreciably. Due to the rain that day the shelling had slowed somewhat, but on the 14th, as the rainclouds disappeared, the ferocity of the shelling was renewed to its previous levels.

One of the more unusual and unsettling sights during these days after the recommencement of shelling was the presence of several hundred live animals in the no man's land between the fort and the British trenches in the city. This gap ordinarily contained stables for the horses and cattle of the garrison. The defenders were unable to exit the fort and reach the animals for fear of British fire and British units equally unable to approach for fear of the hail of shot from the fort. The animals therefore remained unfed and the cattle not milked, and their pitiful sounds filled the air day and night mixed in with the thunder of the artillery. Many of the animals died from starvation while some that occasionally came in view were shot by the British soldiers to put them out of their misery. Some horses were found later to have had their harnesses on them with dead garrison troops lying around, indicating there had been hurried attempts by the city defenders to either flee on the horses or bring them into the fort. The animals were found to be eating cloth and leather for sustenance, with many of the horses gnawing their way through wood in their desperation as they died.

Despite the garrison utilising debris to patch up the walls as best they could, two breaches had appeared by the end of 21 January and Whish decided that 6 a.m. on the morning of the next day, the 22nd, more than two weeks after the bombardment of the fort had recommenced, would be the time for an assault. Meanwhile, the mining had continued with vigour. The hope was the work could both destroy the counterscarp and scarp, levelling the ground as much as possible in the ditch. It was originally thought the counterscarp would be blown up by the 7th. By all accounts the soil was found to be very hard, slowing down the sapping. By 10 January, though, British engineers had reached the foot of the glacis and had sunk three mines for the purpose of blowing in the counterscarp. By the 14th, British sappers had neared the glacis of the fort on it north-eastern corner as well. Only a matter of 15–20 yards separated them from the fortress walls. Work slowed as the garrison worked equally hard to stop the progress. There were suspicions the defenders were digging a mine below the British trenches and using the ditch round the fort as cover before digging on the counterscarp. Orders were given to throw hand grenades into the ditch to prevent the defenders from operating in these positions. That there was activity going on is certain as many of the grenades yet to explode were quickly thrown back towards the British trenches. On the 17th, the large mine was exploded in the ditch to even the ground but it did not have as much success as desired. On the morning of the 19th more mines were blown and large quantities of earth thrown into the ditch in preparation for the attack. Only the scarp wall remained in any shape in front of one of the breaches now. Another mine was sprung under the ditch on the 20th.

The response from the defenders was getting weaker by the day. By 14 January most of the fort guns had been damaged or dismounted and the garrison could do little to respond to the overwhelming fire from without. Whenever a gun was repaired and brought to an embrasure, it was quickly disabled by the weight of fire from the city and outside. Ammunition for the few guns that did work was short or non-existent. One of the guns readied for firing near a gateway should the British blow the gate was later found to be full of coin, makeshift grapeshot, as resources and munitions had all but run out. The mortars in the fortress, it was noticed, fired large stones. In desperation, the defenders were resorting to throwing stones, brickbats and any other makeshift missile they could find at British soldiers, their trenches being so close now. Pots and other earthenware, leather bags or other containers were packed with powder. A lighted fuse was then attached and the pots thrown manually over the walls. From the British trenches, now close enough to hear the shouts of the defenders, the soldiers could hear them defiantly shout 'English pigs' while hurling the stones. Their plight was well known outside and while drawing sympathy also gave encouragement to the British soldiers that the end was drawing near. 'I felt for the garrison in their situation, for they were brave men and very determined still to hold out. The place now looked like an entire heap of ruins,' commented Ryder.

The defenders also made the best of what chances were afforded them organising sallies when possible. It had been noticed the British batteries were not defended as well as they should have been during the night and the guards showed complacency. On the night of 8 January, a moonless and consequently darker night, the garrison had come out in large numbers at 11 p.m. They approached the head of the sap, destroying several gabions and also attacking the lax guard of the battery. The European working party in the trench promptly fled for safety to the main entrenchments several hundred metres further behind, leaving their tools, thinking this was a major attack by the garrison. The sepoys followed suit, making no stand. The alarm was raised, though, and reinforcements quickly sent. It was a most confusing and fierce melee that followed, the night being so dark. Some of the Bombay 4th Regiment sepoys were seen to be running through the garrison party without being noticed by them and vice versa. Several of the British sepoys were shot and wounded by their own side in the darkness. It was also suggested many of the garrison took advantage of the confusion and darkness to make their way out of the city without being challenged, although others were killed in the fighting as the reinforcements drove them back into the citadel.

As if in revenge, the British guns were remanned and opened up, continuing the firing all night and lighting up the whole perimeter of the citadel. The working party would later lay the blame squarely on the Bombay 4th Regiment, who were given patrol duty at the time and who they say quickly made of when the garrison sallied out. Another sally, the last one, was made by the garrison on the 12th but was beaten back by HM 10th under Major Napier, more precautions being taken during the night following the earlier incident.

Other parties in the fortress would attempt to cut their way through the British lines. On the night of the 16th, for example, a strong party of defenders tried to make their way out in the darkness but were thwarted with many dead, the rest forced to retreat back into the citadel. On the 20th, around 300 of the garrison who had attempted a breakout were captured.

The end was near. Inside the ruins of the fortress, there was known to have been a frank meeting between the governor and his men on 18 January. All recognised there would be no succour either from Shere Singh or from Dost Mohammad despite his promises. Opinion was divided. Some of the garrison wished to continue the contest and die fighting. According to the recent deserters, the Akali Sikh soldiers were the most defiant and vociferous and were for carrying on to the death. The majority counselled Mulraj either to surrender or to organise a last major sally whereby they could attempt to cut themselves free of the British cordon and escape the city. Joining up with Shere Singh to the north was suggested. To continue the way they were and with ammunition all but finished would be a needless waste of life. One of those for a surrender was Devee Das, a high-placed and influential man, himself having around 300 men of his own in the fort. Devee Das, who used to advise Sawan Mull, Muraj's father, as well as Maharaja Ranjit Singh in former days, was heard counselling the governor to end the defence.

Intelligence of these talks reached the British lines through deserters, prompting more speculation as to how the siege would end. Some in the British camp and media speculated Mulraj would die heroically at the breach like Tipu Sultan did, for the rumour circulating round the camp was that he still firmly believed his family would be allowed to keep the family property if he died, his death being a conclusive end and sufficient retribution for the British Government. If he was captured alive, however, he would be hanged in any case but all his property and wealth would be confiscated as well, meaning financial hardship for his family. This belief, it was supposed, would goad him to continue the battle to the end. Others thought he would surrender after all. Mulraj was not a soldier, went the argument, but a bureaucrat. Rather than dying at the breach, he would hesitate to take the last step. The stories that the British heard from deserters seemed to show he would surrender. Inside the fortress Mulraj cut a very dejected and dispirited figure, many said, watching deserters lowering themselves by ropes from the walls during the lulls in the bombardment. Others related the governor as having shut himself up in one of the casemates of the fortress, leaving the garrison to continue the defence of the walls alone. Many in the British line were suspicious of these stories, suspecting the deserters of painting a deliberately rosy picture for their captors, and this was challenged as well by other captors who painted a different image. He had declined, some deserters said, to see his family for nearly a month, who were protected in a bombproof chamber underground. He also refused to speak or send messages to them, because he said it unmanned him and disturbed him in the discharge of his duties and the care of his loyal men. What was happening a few metres away inside the walls provided a lively source of discussion along the lines as the soldiers patiently waited in their trenches for Whish's orders for an attack on the breaches.

It's true to say that Mulraj had never entirely rejected the possibility of surrender after the fall of the city. On 6 January, he had sent out a messenger with two letters addressed to Edwardes and Whish. The letter contained a short message requesting a messenger be allowed out to come and relate Mulraj's position and requests. Edwardes after a meeting with Whish sent a short message back that there could be no talks until he surrendered himself. 'I have received and perused your urzee [letter]. You say you have sundry things to represent and with my leave will send a confidential person for that purpose. This I cannot assent to. It is quite impossible. The time for that was April last. You then preferred war; now go through with it or if you are unable, surrender yourself to General Whish. After that you can represent anything you like.'

Mulraj would attempt to pen a letter to Whish as well the following day, hoping he would have a softer view of talks despite Edwardes' reply. 'I ask only for my own life and the honour of my women. You are an ocean of mercy. What more need be said?' he wrote in conciliatory fashion. Whish, however, would reply in similar vein to Edwardes. 'I have received your urzee through Major Edwardes. It is impossible to grant your request to be allowed to send a confidential servant to me to make certain representations; indeed, Major Edwardes told you yesterday, that until you come in to me nothing you have to say will be listened to. You are informed that if the object of sending a confidential person is simply to state: "My master wishes to come in, and will do so at such an hour, and will come out from the fort at such a gate, and by such a road," then he may come; but if he has anything else to say, on no account send him.'

At this point, Mulraj's approach generated considerable optimism for Edwardes that the governor would surrender within a day or two, as he wrote in a letter to the Resident:

> The garrison of Mooltan is now in the last extremity. The gunners are unable to serve their guns from incessant shelling; the buildings are almost all unroofed from the same cause and afford but little shelter. Dewan Moolraj himself has sought refuge in the gateway of the Sukkee Gate and every soldier is obliged to grind the wheat for his own dinner all the flour having been blown up in the explosion of the Jumma Musjid. In this state of things, Moolraj's chief advisers are urgently pressing him to surrender and he has promised either to do so or take poison if no succour reaches him in the course of three days. I regard the present overture from Moolraj therefore as a sign that his pride is broken down at last and that he wants the courage to play out his part.

Currie quite agreed with both Edwardes and Whish, writing back stressing only unconditional surrender by Mulraj should be countenanced and that he must leave his fate to British justice. The approaches were welcomed by the newspapermen who had been present at Multan now for nearly a month and, due to the constant bombardment, had as little sleep as anyone else. 'We are all sick and tired of this Mooltan business and heartily wish it was all over,' reflected a weary newspaper correspondent at Multan. 'One thing is certain, that it could not have taken less time than what it already has, and will take to reduce this formidable fortress; and the professional opinion on the subject is that better generalship could not have been displayed by any general than by General Whish throughout this protracted campaign.'

On 9 January, Mulraj sent another messenger out of the fortress. He was taken before Whish and presented a nuzzur. The emissary was about to speak but Whish interrupted asking him to restrict himself to a simple answer as to whether Mulraj was surrendering or not and if so at what time he would come out of the fort. 'Dewan Sahib hazier hy!' ('The Dewan submits!'), the emissary declared, but he continued, 'Only hear what the message he has asked me to convey to you!' He said Mulraj had a number of questions and doubts that needed resolving regarding a possible surrender. Edwardes stopped him from speaking further and asked him whether he had authority to arrange for Mulraj's surrender or not. The messenger said he had no authority and Edwardes curtly replied back the British would listen to nothing else, leaving the messenger to return, evidently quite disappointed according to the British agent. Even as the interview was being done with the messenger, a new battery of seven 18-pounders had been set up in clear view of the emissary and began to fire away during the meeting, showing Whish would not delay the siege even for negotiations. 'I still think the Dewan will submit and avoid the last crisis of the siege,' Edwardes informed Currie confidently.

It would be a full ten days before things began to move on the diplomatic front again. Cajoled by his men to ask what surrender terms were available, another messenger appeared out of the fort entrance on 20 January. The messenger communicated Mulraj's desire to send a confidential agent for talks with Whish. Whish in response reiterated that his only wish was to see Mulraj surrendering unconditionally and that he must exit the fortress at 8 a.m. the following day. He also added any further messengers who brought any other message or documents not related to an unconditional surrender would be retained as prisoners. By now the two breaches, practicable although far from perfect, had grown, one on the south side of the fort and the other on the north. Plans were drawn in earnest to storm the fortress. Whish had decided the Bengal troops would be organised to enter the breach in the south while the Bombay troops would enter the northern breach. Further delays would not make the breaches any easier to navigate due to the enormous debris piled up, he argued. 'The delay on our part in taking this fortress has told sadly and most unfavourably against our prestige or *ikbal* as the natives say,' summed up the *Bombay Telegraph* correspondent. However, the end was near.

It seems that the final decision to surrender by Mulraj and his men was taken on the morning of 21 January. According to intelligence reaching Herbert Edwardes, Mulraj spent much of the morning convincing the garrison to continue the struggle but such was the effect of the shelling and the primitive conditions they were reduced to that his troops replied they could stand it no longer. He must either lead them out and attempt to break through the British lines or must surrender, and at length Mulraj finally relented and sent a message to Whish. At 11 a.m. on that day, two messengers were seen coming out of the fort on foot. They were taken to Whish's tent where they presented an urzee from Mulraj. These men were Dya Buksh, his vakeel, and assistant Hakim Raee. Dya Buksh had met Whish earlier, having been used as messenger on 9 January. The letter from Mulraj read as follows:

Dewan Moolraj to Major-General Whish

You yesterday ordered me to come in, and surrender before 9 A.M., but I was prevented by sickness from complying sooner. I am now ready to come in, and for this purpose have sent my vakeel to arrange with you; your slave desires only protection for his own life, and the honor of his women. The whole of this disturbance was set on foot by my soldiers, and all my endeavours failed to quell it; now however I surrender myself. I ask only for my own life, and the honor of my women. You are an ocean of mercy – what more need be said.

The whole affair originated in accident, and my own force was ready to kill and insult me; of my own free-will, I would never have done what I have; nevertheless, I confess myself an offender in every way. If you grant me my life, and protection to my women, I surrender: otherwise,

'It is better to die with honor than to live with disgrace'

You are a sea of compassion, if you forgive me, I am fortunate; if you do not, I meet my fate with contentment.

According to Whish, the paragraph beginning with 'The whole affair' was written in a different handwriting to the previous section and was written in hurried fashion. The letter it seemed was to have ended before the last paragraph. Whish immediately penned a response which was sent back by the messengers.

Major-General Whish to Dewan Moolraj

I have received your urzee. In it you write that you only ask for your own life, and the honor of your women. This is my answer: That I have neither authority to give your life, nor to take it, except in open war; the Governor-General only can do this: – and, as to your women, the British Government wars with men not with women. I will protect your women and children, to the best of my ability. Take notice, however, if you intend to come in at all, you had better do so, before sunrise to-morrow, and come out by the Dowlut gate. After sunrise, you must take the fortune of war.

The final demand to surrender before sunrise caused a minor disagreement with Dya Buksh, who had requested Mulraj should be allowed to exit the fort at 9 a.m., he and his men wishing to surrender during daylight rather than in the dark. In any case, Whish pointedly refused to give ground. 'I could not agree to so late an hour,' the general recorded. 'I told him the fire of all my batteries would continue until 5 o clock tomorrow morning and that the Dewan must at latest present himself and garrison at the Dowlut gate of the city at sun rise where arrangements would be ready to facilitate their surrender and to afford protection to their families.' Meanwhile, he told Dya Buksh, his preparations for an assault would continue in case Mulraj and the garrison changed their mind on surrender.

It was on the morning of 22 January, then, what turned out to be a wet and stormy day, that the siege came to an end. Amid torrential rain, the whole British force was assembled at 4 a.m. in the morning, prepared either to receive the surrender of the garrison or to storm the fortress. A strong guard was left for the camp and the whole force moved forward towards the fort. By the crack of dawn the entire line was ready in the entrenchments encircling the fort formed in two long lines 50 feet apart extending all the way round from the Dowlut gate. So heavy and unrelenting was the downpour during this time, the British soldiers reversed their hold on the muskets to prevent water funnelling into the barrel. The soldiers in the trenches, meanwhile stood among the water and mud. The reserve troops suffered less, sheltering in the buildings and mosques behind the front line. In these conditions the besiegers waited while the siege guns continued to pound the fortress till the last moment.

Some guns inside the fort commenced firing back at this point and for this reason it was thought that the garrison had decided against surrender. In any case Mulraj had not opened the doors of the fortress and therefore all outside readied themselves for an assault. A story ran along the British line that Mulraj would wait for the rain to stop and sunrise to arrive before coming out. Whish, perhaps hoping the furious rain would stop, making for an easier assault on the breaches, allowed for more time. Several more hours slipped by.

Finally at 10 a.m., a messenger was seen slipping out of one of the gates and signalling by hand gestures that the garrison was preparing to come out. Shortly after this, the Dowlut gate finally opened and men of the garrison began sauntering slowly out. Whish immediately gave the order for the British siege guns to cease firing.

The last casualty of the siege would occur at this point. This was of a British officer in command of one of the siege guns. His gun had just fired a shot when the order to cease fire was brought by an orderly. Thinking it was all over, he climbed on the gun to see the damage the shot had done to the wall. He was fired at and killed by a defender on the wall who saw his tormentor break cover. The British officer was later buried under the flagstaff of the fort.

One of the demands the garrison soldiers had previously made was that they should walk out with their arms, but this had been refused by Whish. So as they walked out, they were ordered to drop their muskets and swords on the fortress glacis where prize agents had quickly gathered to take control of the stock. The correspondent of the *Bombay Times* stood in the rain watching the scene of the garrison slowly making its way out of the gate.

> First appeared about 200 ill clothed, miserable wretches, who seemed broken and dispirited, then followed about 3,500 hard trained, stern, and stalwart looking men. They had defended the fort to the last, and abandoned it only when no longer tenable. They looked as if they would have fought to the death in the breaches, if such had been the will of their chief. They brought camels and horses, and large bundles of things along with them. These, together with their arms, were placed in charge of the prize agents as they passed.

Many of the men were wounded and were carried on cots by their comrades. All possessions without exception had to be deposited with the prize agents, and the men then stood in front of the fortress in the large square as the rest of their comrades continued to walk out. One of the men who came out was a European, a British soldier of HM 10th taken prisoner on 9 September when the city suburbs had been attacked by Col Pattoun. 'He looked very bad and had never been shaved,' wrote a newspaper correspondent. 'His wounds were healed but his arm was crippled and part of his toes were amputated from one foot. He had several other wounds about him. He said he had had the best of treatment until of late when he was neglected and some days he got food and some days he got none. The enemy were hard pressed and therefore could not attend to him. The poor fellow wept for joy as soon as he saw us. A crowd of men and officers soon collected round him but his colonel sent him off to camp.'

When all the defenders had trooped out, they were organised to be escorted into Edwardes' camp, there to be held as prisoners. Curiously, an exact figure was never taken of the garrison numbers. As these men stood outside the fortress, British units were readied to march into the fort to take possession. The last figures to make an appearance were the governor himself and his officers.

'At last came Moolraj, and his brethren and chiefs – the last, as became him, in the retirement,' the *Bombay Times* correspondent recorded. 'He was gorgeously attired in silks and splendid arms, and rode a magnificent Arab steed, with a rich saddle-cloth of scarlet, which bore no marks of suffering or privation. No small curiosity was experienced to discover the appearance of one who had maintained a defence, obstinate and protracted beyond any related in the annals of modern warfare. He but little exceeds the middle size, is powerfully but elegantly formed; his keen, dark, piercing, restless eyes surveyed at a glance everything around. He neither wore the face of defiance nor dejection; but moved along under the general gaze as one conscious of having bravely done his duty, and aware of being the object of universal regard.'

He wore an orange silk cloak to protect himself from the rain, wearing around his neck a gold chain and on his wrists gold bracelets with precious stones embedded. On one of his fingers he had a large diamond ring. Behind him was his head military officer along with six other officers, while two European soldiers were posted by him, one on his left and another on his right, with Major Becher, assistant quartermaster general, also positioned on his right. 'There was nothing showy or dazzling about him, and he spoke or recognised no one, but looked twice at the soldiers on each side with apparent dislike, though I did not observe a feature ruffled,' wrote the correspondent of the Calcutta *Englishman*. A European soldier was told to take hold of his horse's head as he was led through a company of British soldiers.

It was found at this point that not all of the garrison had followed orders to surrender and a few minutes of confusion followed. For there were still some Sikh artillery soldiers who, declaring they would rather die than give up, fired one of the fort guns, what turned out to be the last shot fired during the siege. This shot skimmed over the heads of some of the British soldiers outside, causing them to scurry back into the trenches. Outside of the fortress, Dewan Mulraj, on hearing the shot, stopped and asked for a piece of paper on which he wrote requesting his men still inside to surrender or their lives would be wasted for no purpose. This they would reluctantly accept, appearing at the gate a short time after the message was sent in. After this incident, once through the throng of British soldiers the governor was slowly led towards the British camp to formally tender his surrender to Whish. 'When we had got about half way to the camp, he turned round upon his horse and viewed the fort, and tears then started from his eyes and he wept much and well he might to see it then battered to a heap of ruins, while only a few months before it bade defiance to the British force and the world, and was proud of its strength and beauty,' Corporal Ryder would note.

He moved down with some dignity and in quiet fashion, with Major Becher leading the way to the British camp outside the city. Those of Mulraj's family who had stayed with him were separated from him on exit and taken to an intact house in the suburbs belonging to an Afghan merchant called Ameer Khan, to be guarded by a sepoy unit. His younger brothers Sham Singh and Ram Singh, however, were kept under guard.

A Lt Henry of the 19th Bombay NI was then given charge of Mulraj when he reached the British camp and he was led away to the Engineers' tent before being brought to Whish. The meeting between Whish and the governor was carried out in good spirits, Mulraj conversing openly, passing amusing comments and jokes with the British soldiers forming his guard. He called them good soldiers although 'nothing but beardless boys'. His officers were still attending him and were noticed to be very attentive towards him. His sword was taken from him by the British officers interpreting for him and passed to Whish, who graciously returned it to the governor. A British brigadier was seen breaking the decorum patting the governor on the back and saying he was 'a fine old cock' and that his gallantry made him deserving of honours rather than a halter.

'It now became necessary to separate him from his brethren and chiefs, and the separation is represented as having been most touching. There were eighteen of these of higher rank than the rest, who had been with him through all his adventures. They threw themselves at his feet and wept sore as they were parted from him and might not hope to see his face any more,' continued the *Bombay Times* correspondent. Mulraj was then led to one of his own country houses built in an earlier age by his father some distance from the city and a strong guard placed round it in case of any attempt at rescue by the numerous bands of disarmed former garrison soldiers and mercenaries now milling around the city suburbs and beyond. He would be given the comforts of life but no writing material nor pen. He was asked if he wished to see his family but declined the offer.

*\*\*\**

Back at the fortress, small units of British troops were ordered in to take possession of the structure and the British flag was promptly hoisted on to the walls. Some discipline was lost at this point as the more opportunistic of the soldiers scrambled to find valuables and chambers with treasure in the ruins.

'The troops now made their way in numbers into the fort and a scene of plunder is said to have ensued in the last degree discreditable to the discipline of the Bengal army. The details given by our correspondents are too distressing to be dwelt upon,' reported the *Bombay Times* as soldiers began rifling through the numerous dead defenders' clothes and pockets extracting rings, jewellery and other items before the prize agents could impose themselves and put a stop to these proceedings.

The report from Whish on 6 February would show over 38,500 shot and shells had been expended by the British heavy guns in battering the city and fortress defences, a feat that Edwardes famously had said would take just 'a few heavy guns, a mortar battery, sappers and miners' during August of the previous year. With the fortress having lasted longer than the city, the lion's share could be assumed to have fallen on the fortress. What struck observers as they entered the structure was the complete devastation caused by the heavy bombardment, the bombproof barracks of the men, the Dewar's residence and other structures inside the walls being reduced to mere shells while all ordinary buildings were entirely levelled. All around lay swords, matchlocks, muskets and pistols and other implements of war which had been thrown away once they stopped functioning. Most of the guns could be seen to have had their carriages destroyed or had been overturned by the intense British shelling. Large pieces of timber from the various destroyed buildings lay scattered everywhere, some with British unburst shells still embedded in them. Amid all this chaos, all around the inside of the fortress lay a great profusion of 18- and 24-pounder shot delivered from the British heavy guns by the thousands.

In among this carnage were hundreds of dead horses, camels, bullocks and defenders, lying everywhere in various states of decomposition while others were receiving attention from carrion and dogs. The smell of the corpses of men and animals was nearly unbearable according to early visitors. On one end of the fortress the corn stores were still on fire, apparently being so ever since 30 December, when the grand magazine had exploded.

There were still the heavily wounded of the garrison ensconced in the fortress, those too ill to be carried out. They were taken to the British hospital by Brig. Markham, who to his credit personally took interest in helping them, continuing to aid them till late in the day. Most of the guns found were heavily damaged; one of the guns was even noted to have a British ball lodged in its bore, while many others were struck on the muzzle or had their carriages destroyed. Others were broken or damaged through the middle, such had been the ferocity of the opposing fire. Despite this, nine guns, repaired and patched a number of times, had been stationed opposite the breaches that were to be stormed by the British. Short of grapeshot, the defenders had thrown small rocks along with coins, filling the guns up to the muzzle. The first party that entered therefore would have had suffered severe casualties.

In the meantime, organised parties under the prize agents who had by now taken control were arranged to search for treasure. All the moveable wealth of the city had been transferred into the underground vaults of the fortress and these it was quickly apparent were going to be difficult to access on account of the debris covering their entrances. Efforts were made to clear the debris over the next few days, and once ingress was achieved the flow of booty began. The finds included large amounts of silks, shawls, gold, silver and swords and decorated shields and muskets, precious stones, grain, sulphur, indigo along with gold mohurs. Large amounts of opium had also been stored in the vaults as well. This had been evidently used by the garrison soldiers for relieving pain of wounds as quantities of the drug were scattered around all over the fort.

The giant caves underneath the treasury building held gold and silver bullion and precious stones along with a huge amount of gold and other coinage from European countries as well as American dollars. The gold and silver was weighed and coinage counted before being loaded up on ammunition wagons. In addition there were other hidden chambers not immediately discovered and as late as December 1849, nearly a year after the fall of the fortress, 25 lakh rupees were found hidden in a vault. Along with genuine gold mohurs, surprisingly, 600 'mohurs' made of base materials were also found which escaped detection till much later. Among the finds in the vaults was also captured British loot. British baggage and captured mess stores, liquors and wines left behind after Whish had retreated to Sadulpore in September, had been moved into the fort along with sackfuls of letters captured over the previous six months, some opened, some not.

Transport of the riches within the fort commenced the day after the surrender as valuables were extracted and the initial haul took three days such being its quantity. The guarding of the treasure seemed to have been lax as some valuables were noted to have been looted by the men employed to extract the materials. Men were seen bragging in the British camp of having pilfered as much as £6,000 worth of gold, as much as they could carry physically without drawing suspicion. Many were apparently robbed, having got themselves so drunk. 'The money was so plentiful that the men would not carry copper and some of them who had got the most would not carry silver,' recorded John Ryder.

The initial plan was that the loot would be used as part payment for the expenses of the war to be extracted from the Lahore Durbar, that is, in the unlikely event annexation didn't take place. The contents of the fort after the first three days were estimated to be above £1 million, equivalent to around £80 million in today's money but with the figure being revised upwards continuously as more underground chambers were investigated over the following weeks and months.

Meanwhile, in what used to be the prison of the fortress were also found the corpses of Kahn Singh, the governor-designate for the city, and his son. Kahn Singh was found to be weighed down with so much iron he would have been barely able to stand. The pair had been killed instantly and buried by the debris of the huge explosion of the grand magazine on 30 December. Herbert Edwardes removed the gold bangles from the son and would send them to his family, with Kahn Singh being cremated with all due honour.

Over the following days, as the debris was cleared and space made, Whish ordered guns of the siege train to be moved into the fortress while also ordering the breaches in the walls to be repaired. Word to the Resident at Lahore of the surrender of the fortress was sent the same day by Herbert Edwardes. 'The flag of Old England is now flying o, in a fresh breeze, and bright sunshine, from the highest bastion of the citadel,' he wrote that day. Whish would order a royal salute to be fired on that evening at sunset to mark the occasion.

In terms of casualties, the cost on the British side had been modest due to Whish's extensive use of siege guns to pummel the defences of the city and fortress into paralysis. The avoidance of a final assault on the citadel saved more. 210 were killed with another 982 wounded during the siege. In terms of officers, thirteen were killed and fifty-one wounded. The British wounded were put on board the Beas River flats to be towed by the steamers down the river and thence to proceed to Bombay. Fifty-four guns including four mortars were taken in the citadel, some guns being of large calibre. Added to the guns captured in earlier battles with the Multan garrison, this made a total of sixty-eight.

One of the prisoners in the fort had been one of Agnew's servants and on release he led the British officers to where they had been buried. On the evening of 26 January, the bodies of Agnew and Anderson were recovered. These, although decomposed, were still recognisable, a musket ball hole being clearly visible on one of the skulls along with other body wounds. They were carried to the fort while one of the bands of the European regiments played the 'Dead March' along the way. Men of Anderson's own regiment, the 1st Bombay Fusiliers, carried him through one of the breaches in the fort walls. They were reburied the same evening in the fortress at its highest point, i.e. under the flag staff in a grave already prepared. The monument itself, on top of their tombs, would only be built in middle of 1856.

\*\*\*

Whish, previously criticised for the lifting of the first siege and for his cautionary approach, was generally lauded for his care in reducing casualties rather than insisting on a frontal assault on the fortress in the face of a determined foe. News of the surrender of the garrison reached Dalhousie on 25 January and he promptly ordered a twenty-one-gun salute to be fired from all the principal stations of the army around India to mark the occasion. After receiving reports of the fighting within the city, the Governor-General had little sympathy for the residents and would decide on an additional punitive ransom for the city over and above the booty captured. 'It is said they are finding great quantities of booty in the fort; and I have ordered a contribution from the city of 15 lacs or so. The rascals, they were in it heart and hand; and even little boys were caught perched in the trees trying to pot the officers,' he explained in his private papers. This additional money would then be added to the prize money for the soldiers. The plan never came to fruition, however, due to the impoverished state of the inhabitants after a year of war. The ransom would be quietly remitted as it was realised the city would take a long time to return to its previous prosperous state even without the added burden of the ransom. The general civilian population of the city was allowed to return on 25 January, the local kardars of the neighbouring town and districts being given strict orders to compel any former Multan residents to return to the city to quicken its return to normality.

\*\*\*

With the fortress captured and the troops rested but with orders to reinforce Gough's main force in the north as quickly as possible, Whish made immediate plans. A small force consisting of the 1st Lancers, a company of sappers and miners, a company of European artillery, two regiments of 4th and 9th NI along with two companies of golundauze along with a light field battery were left behind as garrison for the ruined fortress. Courtlandt was given charge of the city and entire province of Multan by Whish for the immediate resumption of tax collection.

The whole journey for Whish's army to join Gough's force was estimated at seventeen marches to reach Ramnuggar. The move would in fact be done in three contingents. Early at 4 a.m. on 27 January, Brig. Markham moved off with a Bengal contingent of HM 32nd Foot along with the 51st and 72nd regiments, Anderson's troop of horse artillery and the 11th Irregular Cavalry along with 400 sappers and miners. The cattle grazing around the city of Multan at considerable distances meant a delay of two days before the second and third contingents commanded by Whish and Dundas moved off. Their columns encumbered with the heavy guns would move slower. Whish himself moved off on 29 January with one brigade of infantry and ten guns (horse artillery). On the 30th, the second brigade, consisting of Mackenzie's troop of horse artillery, twelve heavy guns, the 11th Regular Cavalry, HM 10th Foot and the 8th and 51st NI, commanded by Brig. Hervey, followed in the footsteps of the first. Meanwhile Dundas (with the third contingent) would march separately on 2 February with the Bombay division (including HM 60th Rifles and Bombay Fusiliers, the 3rd and 19th NI), and 500 of the 2nd Scinde Horse.

Whish reached Ameerghur on 28 January, followed by Sirdarpore, and crossed the Chenab River to reach Jhung, a large mercantile town near the junction of the Chenab and Jhelum. Along the way he stopped at several places to reduce some minor forts. Meanwhile a bridge was built at Chinout to cross the river with the guns, a message having been received from Gough to march with all possible haste to effect a junction for the interception of Shere Singh as he may try and force his way across the Chenab towards Lahore. Whish would eventually arrive at Ramnuggar on 13 February, joining up with Gough on the 16th, with the second brigade led by Dundas three days later. Brig.-Gen. Dundas would arrive at Ramnuggar on the 18th. Meanwhile Brig. Markham had reached Ramnuggar on the 18th and would move towards Kanokee where forty-seven boats under British control were to be sent. All these contingents were in time for the final and decisive Battle of Gujrat.

# 25

# The Battle of Ramnuggar

If you see a favourable opportunity of charging, charge.
Gough to Col William Havelock, 14th Dragoons, 22 November 1848

It was a rash affair my Lord.
3rd Light Dragoon to Gough after Ramnuggar, 22 November 1848

While Whish had systematically reduced Multan and its fortress with his siege guns, things would prove considerably more complicated over 350 km to the north where Shere Singh's army would face the main British force under Gough. Three inconclusive battles had been fought there while the siege of Multan had been taking place, with the British force coming close to complete disaster in the last contest at Chillianwala.

The campaign in this part of the Punjab, where the fate of the Punjab would effectively be decided, could be said to have commenced in earnest during later October. This was when a British vanguard of the main British force, which was still being assembled at Ferozepore, moved to protect the bridge across the Ravi River to the west of Lahore. Its importance and its control lay in its allowing the British force, once assembled, to cross on to the right bank and into the Rechna doab while simultaneously preventing Shere Singh from crossing the opposite way and attempting any move on the capital. By 20 October, as the British force was still assembling at Lahore and Ferozepore, Capt. Nicholson, then at Ramnuggar, was reporting advance units of Shere Singh's army had reached Pindee Buttean with reinforcements waiting for him at Gujrat under the Sikh officer Arjun Sing. Meanwhile Ootar Singh, another Sikh commander, was crossing at Jalalpore to join up with Shere Singh with more troops. Some of these advance units were moving towards Lahore, perhaps in order to capture or destroy the Ravi Bridge. By 24 October, this advance force of around 2,000 irregulars under Sirdar Ootar Sing had reached Noorkote near Sheikhupura, only around 30 km from Lahore.

News also reached Lahore on 1 November that other units of Shere Singh's army led by Lal Singh Moraria, Arjun Singh and Jowahir Singh may be approaching Gujranwala, a major metropolis 70 km north-west of Lahore and sitting squarely in the middle of the Rechna doab, with the motive of taking the city. From Gujranwala the road ran straight to Lahore, allowing Shere Singh to advance quickly towards the capital if he should so wish.

'If Goojranwalla falls into the hands of the rebels,' the Resident advised Brig.-Gen. Cureton, in charge of the British vanguard at Lahore, 'it will strengthen the cause of the insurgents amazingly; and if they retain possession of it, we shall get neither supplies, nor carriage, from the Rechna Doab, upon which we now depend, to enable the army to move forward; it will also very much damage our credit, if these parties, which are considered our most faithful allies, are left unsupported. If your force were to push on, the insurgents would, probably, fall back: if you advance to Eminabad, which is about twenty-five miles ahead of you, you will, then, not only be able to support Goojranwalla, but will command the whole of the Doab.' Eminabad lay about 10 km from Gujranwala and would place an obstacle to his advance south as well as to allow Cureton to control the whole doab. By this time, a small Lahore Durbar force, currently stationed to guard the bridge across the Ravi, had been attacked, losing the eighteen out of the twenty-four zambarooks stationed at the bridge. The attackers had only the chance to destroy two boats, however, before British reinforcements were moved up to protect the structure. This was Brig. Godby's brigade, consisting of the 2nd European Regiment, the 70th NI and the 8th Light Cavalry along with Lane's troop of horse artillery. The bridge had been repaired the following day and a large and strong building on the right bank of the river which overlooked and completely protected the bridge from further attacks was garrisoned. The attack and the close proximity of Shere Singh's advance guard was a good reason for Currie to hurry along the British build-up. He wrote an urgent letter to Gough informing him of the need for prompt reinforcements. 'It is a bolder move of Shere Sing's than I expected and can only have been adopted by him, under the knowledge of our having no disposable troops at Lahore, and in ignorance of the cavalry being across the Sutlej at Gundia Sing Walla.' He hoped, he wrote, a faster influx of British regiments advancing on Lahore would make Shere Singh think twice about any closer approach to the capital. 'The garrison is now menaced, and hemmed in, by the rebels; and, if an attack were to be made on the cantonment of Anarkullee by the insurgents, and a simultaneous rising were to take place in the city, the population of which is all, more or less, hostile to us, and in which there are numbers ready for revolt, we should, without reinforcements, be in a very critical, as well as, in the sight of India, a very discreditable, position.'

Currie's other worry, as he mentioned, was logistics for the coming operation. Supplies for the British advance were still very short at Lahore and if Shere Singh proceeded to destroy available forage and supplies in the Rechna doab, it would make things all the more difficult when the push forward began. Fortunately for the British Shere Singh would never take advantage of the situation, using what would be his customary caution to march as far as Jalalpore on the left bank of the Chenab and arriving at Ramnuggar, where permanent camp was made. He would advance no further east. The British force protecting the bridge, meanwhile, would be joined by Brig.-Gen. Cureton, who had made his way to the capital by this time with cavalry and who camped at Shahdaree. They were also shortly joined by Major Eckford's brigade (31st and 56th NI, a light field battery, a company of artillery) on 3 November. The whole advance force protecting the bridge totalled around 7,000 men now.

Being strong enough, this British vanguard would be ordered into the doab to deny Shere Singh the centre of the territory, while Gough continued to organise his main force at Ferozepore. Cureton led the force off at 5 a.m. on the morning of 2 November towards Ramnuggar. The Ravi was crossed, with Eckford's brigade left behind to guard the bridge while the rest of the force continued on the straight road towards Gujranwala. Camp was made at the village of Baolee, 22 km from the right bank of the river. With reports of elements of the Sikh vanguard close by, the advance was continued in battle order on the next day. By the 5th, the force was closing on the city of Gujranwala where the advance was halted temporarily.

The usual confusion over irregulars would prevail in this theatre as well. On the way to Gujranwala, a body of troops around 2,000 strong was seen approaching the British force and pursued for 8 km by Cureton's cavalry under the impression they were Sikh irregulars. It was later discovered they were men of Lt Nicholson's Muslim irregulars marching to join the British force.

By this time, it had been realised that Shere Singh had no permanent interest in Gujranwala or moving towards Lahore and that the collision would occur much closer to the Chenab where the Sikh commander had established himself. At Komoke then, Cureton, instead of heading towards Eminabad and Gujranwala, accordingly took the road north-west toward the Chenab. The town of Killa Didar Singh was reached, leaving the British advance guard now only around 30 km from Shere Singh's camp to their north-west. No fighting or skirmishing had taken place at all since the crossing of the Ravi. It was noted most of the villages on the way of the British advance were already deserted as the locals had fled from the expected depredations by the army of camp followers.

It was on 5 November that news reached Cureton that the Sikh army contingents in Peshawar had finally rebelled and that Shere Singh's army would swell accordingly. More caution was now required till Gough's main force arrived. The British force therefore made permanent camp at Killa Didar Singh to await the junction with the British Commander-in-Chief, expected in around two weeks, before a further advance was organised. These two weeks would largely be characterised by general inactivity as both Cureton and Shere Singh awaited their respective reinforcements. The first casualties in this theatre occurred on 11 November when a spy from the Sikh camp was recognised but managed to effect an escape from the British camp. He was chased by four men of the native Cavalry but killed two before a third speared him.

From this position, the guns of Shere Singh could clearly be heard in the British camp as Sikh troops engaged in gun practice and fired salutes as more troops joined them. In the British camp, Eckford, who had been relieved of the duty of guarding the bridge, brought his brigade, consisting of three native infantry regiments (the 31st, 56th and 73rd) along with a battery of six guns, on 10 November. Brig.-Gen. Campbell would arrive at Killa Didar Singh on 16 November, bringing with him the 36th and 46th NI. Being the senior officer in the force now, Campbell took over command from Cureton. On the 18th, HM 61st (850 men) arrived, becoming the second European regiment in the force. The next day came Brig. Pope with 2nd Cavalry Brigade – HM 9th lancers (700 men) and the 1st and 6th Light Cavalry (a total of 1,800 men).

On 16 November this enlarged British advance force pushed further forward a short distance, reaching the vicinity of the village of Gil Wala, around 16 km from the Chenab and about equidistant from Ramnuggar and Wazirabad. Campbell himself moved his own camp westwards to Allipore, this village now becoming the most advanced British outpost, only 8 km east of Ramnuggar and Shere Singh's position. The move was to make room for Gough's main force, who could occupy the former camp at Killa Didar Singh on arrival. Extra precautions had been taken from around the 14th or 15th onwards in regard to cattle, it being dangerous to let them graze too far from the camp as they were liable to disappear. Baggage and supplies being sent to the force went under protection, and no baggage was sent in advance. Only the arrival of Gough's force was required before an advance towards Ramnuggar was organised.

In the Sikh camp, meanwhile, as the British build-up continued, Shere continued to write to his father in Hazara, urging him to hurry with his forces to join him as battle was imminent. As in the British camp, logistics were hampering progress here. Many of the Bannu and Peshawar troops who were attempting to reach Shere Singh's force were being delayed by insufficient carriage or supplies. During this time, as the two forces sat opposite each other, Shere Singh sent out various declarations around the country urging the population to rise up. Currie informed the government that Shere Singh styled his army as the 'United Khalsa, the loyal and obedient subjects of the Maharajah Duleep Singh' and claimed Duleep Singh was a virtual prisoner and entirely under the British control. The Khalsa and the Sikh religion were under threat from extermination by the British, his proclamation declared.

To counter these declarations from the Sikh camp, Currie would release his own proclamation on 18 November. This had the dual aim of discouraging recruits for Shere Singh and to bolster the official policy that the British force had entered the Punjab only to put down a rebellion against the Maharajah's government.

Proclamation by the Resident at Lahore November 18 1848
To the subjects, servants, and dependents of the Lahore State, and the residents, of all classes and castes, whether Sikh, Mussulman, or other, within the territories of Maharajah Duleep Sing, from the Beas to the mountains beyond Peshawur. Whereas certain evil disposed persons and traitors have excited rebellion and insurrection, and have seduced portions of the population of the Punjab from their allegiance, and have raised an armed opposition to the British authority; and whereas the condign punishment of the insurgents is necessary; therefore, the British army, under the command of the Right Honourable the Commander-in-Chief has entered the Punjaub districts. The army will not return to its cantonments, until the full punishment of all insurgents has been effected, all armed opposition to constituted authority put down, and obedience and order have been re-established.

And whereas it is not the desire of the British Government that those who are innocent of the above offences, who have taken no part, secretly or openly, in the disturbances, and who have remained faithful in their obedience to the government of Maharajah Duleep Sing, be they Sikh, or be they of any other class, should suffer with the guilty; therefore, all persons who are not concerned, directly or indirectly, in the present disturbances are assured that they have nothing to fear from the coming of the British army. Such persons are exhorted to remain, without apprehension, in their villages and homes, and, as loyal subjects of the Maharajah, to give every aid by providing carriage, supplies, and the like, to the army which has entered the Lahore territories, not as an enemy to the constituted government but to restore order and obedience. Furthermore all classes of the community, be they Sikh, or be they of any other caste or tribe, who merely through ignorance, may have been led away, by the false statements of the evil-disposed and insurgent Sirdars and others, and have left their homes, and assembled themselves under the standard of rebellion, are hereby admonished instantly to separate themselves from the insurgents, and to return to their villages. If they do so now, without hesitation or delay, no injury will happen to them; if they neglect this warning and advice, certain destruction will come upon them, in common with the other insurgents and rebels, and disturbers of the public peace.

In order to further allay suspicions of annexation, Currie also declared British policy to be for the support of Duleep Singh as Maharajah of the country but that the Lahore state would have to pay for the cost of this war against the insurgents. A general amnesty for all the Sikh and other troops who were joining Shere Singh at Ramnuggar was also declared if they returned home instantly. The offer was conciliatory, no doubt in the hope that this would thin the Sikh army's ranks prior to hostilities. Currie did not only target the common soldier, offering the more senior officers and sirdars who had joined Shere Singh no loss as to their landholdings.

***

1. Maharajah Duleep Singh and courtiers accompanying the Governor-General and British officers around the circumference of the city towards the Lahore fort after the arrival of the British force at the Sikh capital following the Battle of Sabraon. Sketch by Charles Hardinge, son of the Governor-General, who formed part of the Governor-General's entourage, 1847. (Courtesy of the National Army Museum)

2. Full view of the large Hazuri Bagh or garden situated between the Lahore fort entrance and the Badshahi Mosque entrance, from which this image was taken. The entire garden section, along with the Badshahi Mosque, was used to house the British garrison at Lahore after the First Anglo-Sikh War. Later on, after the Prema Plot, the fort entrance and surrounding high points were occupied. The marble Baradari was built by Ranjit Singh in 1818. (Courtesy of the British Library)

3. View from the Lahore fort looking west towards the Badshahi Mosque. Having high protecting walls, the occupied mosque formed an excellent defensive compound for a camp for the British force in the capital. To the right of the picture can be seen the Samadhi or Mausoleum of Ranjit Singh, which was only half finished at this stage. Ranjit Singh's successors had expended their energies in internal power struggles and the structure would be finished on the orders of Dalhousie after the annexation of the state. In the far distance on the top right can be seen the River Ravi, which once brushed past the fort on its west side. (Courtesy of the National Army Museum)

4. Sikh soldiers being pensioned off at the Lahore fort shortly after the First Anglo-Sikh War to comply with the new Treaty of Lahore, limiting the size of the Sikh army to 32,000 men. Sketch by Charles Hardinge, 1847. (Courtesy of the National Army Museum)

British soldiers standing sentry at
the main entrance to the Lahore fort
after the first war. Photograph by
John McCosh, 1849. (Courtesy of the
National Army Museum)

Earliest photograph taken of
Maharaja Duleep Singh, young ruler
of the Lahore state. Duleep Singh was
deposed in April 1849, shortly after
the end of the war, and given a modest
pension. He would be put under the
guardianship of Dr John Login and in
December 1849 taken to Fatehgarh, a
European colony, where he would reside
for the next four and a half years before
moving to England. Photograph by
John McCosh, 1849. (Courtesy of the
National Army Museum)

7. Gulab Singh, vassal of the Lahore state, had refused aid to the Sikh army during the First Anglo-Sikh War. He would be rewarded by Hardinge, being made the independent Maharaja of Kashmir, separated from the Sikh Empire as agreed in the Treaty of Amritsar. Charles Hardinge, 1847. (Courtesy of the National Army Museum)

8. Lal Singh, Vizier at Lahore prior to the First Anglo-Sikh War and for the bulk of the year 1846. Having aided the British in the defeat of the Sikh army, he was re-affirmed as Vizier after the war. Lal Singh would be toppled from power in December 1846 once it became known he was preventing Gulab Singh from taking control of Kashmir. (Courtesy of the National Army Museum)

Sir Henry Hardinge, Governor-General of India between 1844 and 1848. Hardinge would accompany the British force during the first war and receive the submission of Duleep Singh at Lullianee on the way to Lahore.

Sir Hugh Gough, the ageing British Commander-in-Chief, led the British force personally during the late war, nearly suffering what would have been a disastrous defeat at Ferozeshah.

*Above*: 11. Kangra fortress, October 1898. [ ] fortress formerly marked and protected th[ ] eastern borders of the Lahore state. The S[ ] governor had refused to give up his fortre[ ] in the aftermath of the First Anglo-Sikh War, hoping a stand might encourage oth[ ] rebellions in sympathy elsewhere. (Court[ ] of the British Library)

*Left*: 12. Dewan Mulraj, the reluctant rebe[ ] of Multan. The image of the governor wa[ ] taken after his surrender and while in incarceration at Lahore fort in April 1849 prior to being taken to Calcutta. The earl[ ] photographer John McCosh had not bee[ ] given permission by Frederick Currie, th[ ] Lahore Resident, to photograph the Sikh state prisoners taken during the war beca[ ] he 'didn't want the prisoners bothered' b[ ] nevertheless McCosh found the opportu[ ] Another image taken of Shere Singh and his father Chutter Singh was taken but i[ ] now missing from the McCosh album at National Army Museum. (Courtesy of th[ ] National Army Museum)

Grainy early photograph of Patrick [Va]ns Agnew, the British officer sent by [Fr]ederick Currie, the Lahore Resident, [to] effectively govern the province of [M]ultan after Mulraj's resignation. [Ag]new's unforeseen altercation with [an] unemployed soldier at the city [tri]ggered a chain of events that led [to] his death and the rebellion in the [pr]ovince. Photograph by John McCosh, [18]49. (Courtesy of the National Army [Mu]seum)

[C]ol Edwardes was the British [offic]er involved in the half-hearted [atte]mpt to stem the Multan rebellion. [In c]harge of the Derajat (trans-Indus) [regi]on, Edwardes secured the whole [area], preventing Mulraj from gaining [mer]cenaries from beyond the Indus. [He] would later cross the Indus and [appr]oach Multan with his own largely [mer]cenary army as the cautious [Mul]raj failed to take the initiative and [bega]n preparations for a siege of the [city.] Photograph by John McCosh c. [1849]. (Courtesy of the National Army [Mus]eum)

15. The Eidgah compound, lying just north of the Multan fortress, was used as a camp by Agnew and his party prior to entering the fortress the following day. It was also where he and Lt William Andrew Anderson were murdered after the altercation at the fortress. They were initially buried directly opposite the Eidgah entrance on the other side of the road to the Eidgah, essentially few metres to the right of where this picture was taken in 1918. (Courtesy of the British Librar

16. Most of the fortress walls were badly damaged during the siege, and with the heavy floods that followed shortly afterwards the decision was made to pull them down. New garrison buildings took their place during the following decades. What did survive, albeit badly damaged, were th two massive tomb structures of Shah Rukn-e-Alam, marking the westernmost point of the fortress (seen in the picture), and the Bahauddin Zakariya to the east. Both of these were repaired after the capture of t fortress. (Courtesy of the Brit Library)

17. The Shah Rukn-e-Alam structure from the same ang in the present day. The mou on which the fortress was bu can be clearly seen. Notice t date trees, of which there wa profusion all around the city

. Some remnants of the
rtress walls at Multan still
main. Notice the older,
oman-style 'Nanakshahi'
icks on the walls to the
ght compared to the more
odern bricks used on
e doorway and to its left.
urpreet Singh Anand
llection)

Khuni Burj or the 'Bloody
wer' situated on the
th-east of the old city
lls. The old city walls were
her but were lowered
er the siege by the British
thin the Khuni Burj and
er sections rebuilt having
fered damage during the
nflict. One of the breaches
de by the British force
s situated a few hundred
t north of the Khuni Burj.
xander the Great suffered
ound from a Mallian
her from the Khuni Burj
a much earlier siege.
rpreet Singh Anand
ection)

Aam Khas Bhag. The
Khas, the former
dence of Dewan
raj just outside the
ress, where he mulled
whether to support
nruly soldiers who
nded the British
ers or to hand them
no longer exists and
een replaced by a
ic garden. (Gurpreet
h Anand collection)

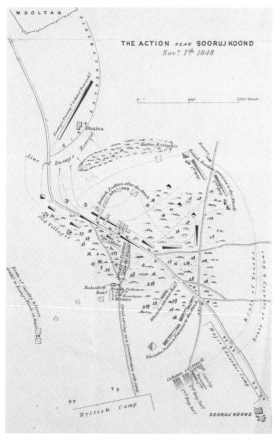

*Above left*: 21. Picture of the fortress area from the north, presumably taken very close by the location of the Eidgah and also where the British siege lines would have been drawn. The road to Lahore in the foreground, leading to the Eidgah, was used by the mob from the city to attack the Eidgah and Agnew's party. (Courtesy of the British Library)

*Above right*: 22. The British obelisk raised in memory of the two murdered officers near what would have been the eastern end of the former fortress. Picture taken 1860, photographer unknown. (Courtesy of the British Library)

*Left*: 23. Contemporary map of the skirmish at Suraj Khund by James Wyld, 20 March 1849. This battle, just to the south of the outskirts of the city, was the only time the hesitant Mulraj would personally lead his troops into battle against Herbert Edwardes.

24. A small summer house belonging to Ranjit Singh was the local landmark near the village of Ramnuggar and the battle. Situated around 1.5 km to the north-west of the village and close to the banks of the Chenab, it was utilised by British officers during the stay at Ramnuggar as a lookout post.

25. Recently renovated British graveyard at Ramnuggar containing the graves of, among others, Col Charles Cureton of the 14th Light Dragoons, Capt. John Fitzgerald of the 14th Light Dragoons and Lt Col William Havelock.

6. Grave of Col Cureton of the 14th Light Dragoons.

27. Shere Singh, commander of the Sikh army during the Second Anglo-Sikh War. Pro-British and inclined not to gamble his considerable family wealth supporting the rebellion at Multan, Shere Singh's hand was forced by the equally reluctant rebellion of his father Chutter Singh in Hazara. From a watercolour by C. Grant in *Private Letters of Marquess of Dalhousie*, 1910.

28. Chutter Singh, the Governor of Hazara province, who initiated a rebellion after cold relations with James Abbott, the British agent, led to the local Muslim tribes attacking the Sikh garrison. From a watercolour by C. Grant in *Private Letters of Marquess of Dalhousie*, 1910.

29. Maj.-Gen. Sir Joseph Thackwell, a Peninsular and Waterloo veteran who had lost his left arm at the latter battle, commanded the cavalry division at Chillianwala and Gujrat and led the British force at Sadulpore. Taken by John McCosh. (Courtesy of the National Army Museum)

30. Maj.-Gen. Sir Walter Gilbert, photographed by John McCosh *c.* 1849. Gilbert commanded a division at both Chillianwalla and Gujrat and would receive the surrender of the Sikh army at Rawalpindi rather than the Commander-in-Chi (Courtesy of the National Army Museum)

*Above left*: 31. Obelisk constructed in memory of the British dead inside the British graveyard at Chillianwala around a few hundred metres north of the village. The graveyard and monument themselves are situated on a slight mound which happened to be a Sikh outpost and where several guns were stationed prior to hostilities.

*Above right*: 32. Chillianwalla monument, Royal Hospital Chelsea, London. The obelisk by Charles Robert Cockerell commemorates the officers and men of HM 24th who died at the Battle of Chillianwala.

*Below*: 33. The British dead (excepting the officers, who were buried separately) were piled into long, parallel trenches. The camera points east, from which direction the British advance moved to capture the mound on which the graveyard is built.

34. Ancient Buddhist stupa at the village of Manikyalla, around 25 k east of Rawalpindi, alongside whic Shere Singh and his Sikh officers offered surrender of their forces to Maj.-Gen. Sir Walter Gilbert. Take Joseph Beglar David, 1875. (Courte of the British Library)

*Left*: 35. The Buddhist stupa at Manikyalla now.

*Below*: 36. The British-built Sohaw bridge across Sohan River on the r to Rawalpindi, 1885. It is difficult t work out whether the picture is ta from the east or west bank of the r In 1849, the final surrender of the of the Sikh army took place on the bank. If this is the east bank, the S soldiers were ordered to cross the in batches from their camp on the opposite bank and to lay their arm the foreground. Vice versa if the i is taken from the west bank. (Cou of the British Library)

. Fortress of Attock with
additional bridge of boats
across the River Indus. The
junction of the Kabul River
less than a kilometre
upstream of the Indus.
Gilbert managed to catch
up with the retreating
Afghan army at the Indus,
with the Afghans hurriedly
attempting to damage the
bridge. A few boats drifted
downstream but Gilbert
managed to repair the
bridge relatively quickly and
resumed his pursuit of the
Afghans. Taken by William
Baker Henry, 1870. (Courtesy
of the British Library)

Fortress of Attock and
location of the bridge
of boats in the present day.
The traditional bridge of
boats has been replaced
by modern bridges a few
hundred metres upstream.

Fortress of Jamrud,
situated at the extreme west
of Peshawar and guarding
the eastern entrance to the
Khyber Pass. Maj.-Gen
Walter Gilbert ended his
pursuit of the Afghan army
at Jamrud, having strict
orders not to continue
through the pass. Taken
by Charles Shepherd, 1860.
(Courtesy of the British
Library)

40. Mulraj in captivity at Fort William, Calcutta. Stripped of his possessions and clothes and losing weight due to self-starvation, Mulraj's heath declined rapidly after his trial. From a watercolo by C. Grant in *Private Letters of Marqu of Dalhousie*, 1910.

41. The cremation of Dewan Mulraj or the banks of the Ganges in 1851. Due t his failing health, Hardinge had agree have the ex-governor moved upcount where the climate would supposedly b more conducive to his health. He die the passage up the river.

A reconnaissance expedition commanded by Campbell towards Ramnuggar was organised on 19 November but with the same strict proviso by Gough not to engage with Shere Singh till his main force joined up, this being expected shortly. Campbell accordingly moved forward with a squadron of HM 14th Light Dragoons and one of the 5th Light Cavalry and two light guns towards Ramnuggar, passing to the left of Allipore. This and other reconnaissance missions, along with the information passed by British spies and informers, led Campbell to believe Shere Singh at this stage had only around twenty guns and 15,000 troops. Of these troops one-third were very irregular, with raw recruits and volunteers. Although deficient in guns, it was known there was no want of ammunition in the Sikh camp. Ram Singh of Bannu was supplying the Sikh force with the gunpowder and other supplies still remaining at the Bannu cantonments. Naturally this fuelled confidence in a speedy and abrupt conclusion in the British camp, for Gough was expected to have more than 20,000 men, including three regiments of Dragoons and four of European infantry, plus at least sixty guns including various large pieces.

Allipore itself had been occupied by a small Sikh garrison and Cureton had previously been fired on by Sikh guns when reconnoitring this village on the 16th. The Sikh garrison had vacated the town on seeing his considerable force approach, leaving Campbell's units to occupy it. The Sikh garrison joined the considerable remaining Sikh units on the left bank of the Chenab at Ramnuggar; Lt Chunda Singh and officers Shumshere Singh, Lal Singh and Suraj Singh Majithia were all still commanding on the left bank. By the 20th, however, almost the entire Sikh force on the left bank had crossed to the right bank to make permanent camp there, leaving only skirmishers and pickets on the left bank. There was a good supply of food at Allipore and Shere Singh seemed not to have ordered its destruction or its move to the Sikh camp. Therefore all these supplies were ordered to be transported back to the British camp. The villagers, however, proved unwilling to part with them and Campbell was forced to send a force with four guns to coax them into doing so.

Spies and informers in both camps had meanwhile begun to do their work. Some of Shere Singh's soldiers managed to intercept a letter in the Sikh camp from a British spy on 18 November. He was urging an instant attack, informing Campbell that Shere Singh was still weak and awaiting reinforcements. Around this time, two scouts that had been sent close to the Sikh camp were spotted. One was caught while the other escaped back to the British camp. In what was the typical way of punishing spies and informers, these captured men's faces were blackened and they were paraded round the Sikh camp. The British scout was later released.

Back at Ferozepore meanwhile, Gough had been making preparations to advance into the Punjab with his main force. The Commander-in-Chief had reached the British station on 5 November where news also reached him of the uprising of the Peshawar troops. He would busy himself in organising supplies for the next three days before departing. The problems the British were having with carriage and supplies were still apparent at this time. During this year there was during in the north-west of India that affected the area of Ferozepore, making supplies of all kinds more difficult to obtain than usual. The commissariat was therefore not prepared for the support of a large force at this time and was not able to supply the required ten days' supplies for a march. Even if they could, the carriage for these supplies was not available. Hence a delay longer than Gough wished was taking place.

Gough set up camp at Gunda Singh Wala on the 9th, eventually crossing the river and proceeding to Kasur on the morning of the 10th. He would not march directly to Campbell's camp, but would strike north-west to Lahore first. Gough's army was greeted with considerable ceremony as he neared Lahore on 13 November, fireworks lighting the sky as the British troops marched in. The Lahore Durbar had organised what was described in the Indian newspapers as a 'gay cavalcade' to celebrate his arrival. The Maharajah, with the Resident, the Durbar members and Sikh Commander-in-Chief Tej Singh, met him on his approach to the city. Duleep Singh gave Gough a nuzzur of 2,100 rupees while other sirdars presented highly decorated ceremonial bows and arrows as gifts. The meeting itself was short and conducted on elephants, Duleep Singh formally inviting him for a Durbar, with Gough refusing, saying his presence was required for battle but that when the war was over there would be time enough for meetings. His stay lasted for three days, the British force occupying the Anarkali area of the city, and it was not till the 16th that he and his force would begin crossing the Ravi River.

The British siege train, meanwhile, would leave Ferozepore, crossing the Sutlej on 15 November and making straight for Campbell's camp but in very ponderous fashion. It included all the heavy guns, including two 24-pounders, eight 18-pounders along with two 8-inch howitzers accompanied by a host of smaller guns and mortars and various 6- and 9-pounder guns. Each of the heavy guns required three elephants to haul them along, making for slow progress. Along with the guns were transported the parts for a large pontoon bridge. Gough, cognisant that the campaign would no doubt include the crossing of the Chenab and perhaps the Jhelum and Indus, had taken the precaution of bringing it along with the force. Although this slowed down his force further, it meant he would not be reliant on fords and the local boats for the crossing of rivers. The pontoon bridge would in fact cause more trouble than it was worth. There was also a lengthy column of camels carrying supplies as well as 800 carts of ammunition pulled by bullock, as many as could be obtained. The convoy was escorted by the 15th and 69th NI and 3rd and 9th Irregular Cavalry.

Gough's main force would be followed by more reinforcements streaming directly across from Ferozepore. On 15 November, Col Pennycuick's brigade, HM 24th, and the 22nd and 25th NI crossed into the Punjab along with Major-General Thackwell. On the 16th, Major-General Gilbert along with Col Mountain's brigade, consisting of HM 29th and 13th and 30th NI, followed them across the river.

Gough would personally leave Lahore on 16 November, crossing the Ravi and choosing the direct route across the doab rather than following Cureton's route, but travelled inexplicably slowly, taking a week to reach the Chenab. The night after crossing the Ravi he had made camp at Shah Derah, only 5 km from Lahore, before heading north-west to Pindeedoss Ke Kote, a march of 15 km. From there, the next day, a march to Burra Mullyar, a further 15 km, was undertaken with Muttah reached the next day after a 25 km march. From there he moved to Thabul, 15 km away, before reaching the British camp at Killa Didar Singh, another march of 17 km. On the 20th he reached Noewala village, 10 km south-east of Campbell's advance position.

Frederick Currie had wished to accompany Gough on the campaign himself but had decided to stay and ensure the capital stayed in British hands. 'The chiefs who remain at Lahore, professedly loyal to the Maharajah, and faithful to the British Government, are, with one or two exceptions, really disaffected, and more or less in the interest of the rebels; while some are in confinement, and under surveillance, in the fort. The desire of the insurgents to possess the person of the Maharajah is still very strong, and constant vigilance in regard to him is necessary,' he informed the government on his staying on at Lahore. In consequence, Gough had agreed to leave HM 53rd regiment at Lahore strengthening the Resident's hand but other measures were also taken to maintain British control. The fort was being enhanced with new embrasures being added all round its walls for new guns. On the south-east, the guns were placed so fire could be directed into the city as well if disturbances materialised.

Currie would, however, send his chief assistant, Mr Cocks, as political agent with Gough although the Commander-in-Chief was none too impressed with him and his stay with the army would be short. From the Durbar, a senior member was also requested to assist in supplies and carriage for the British force being organised by the Lahore Durbar. This man was Misr Sahib Dyal, who was known not to have any nationalist leanings at all.

Small units of independent Sikh irregulars had begun harassing Gough's column and the siege train as they passed through the doab towards Ramnuggar. Around fifty camels went missing, for example, the day after Gough's crossing; several of their riders were killed, although most of the camels were recovered by cavalry sent out in pursuit. Local robbers and brigands also spotted the opportunities. A general warning was given out to men not to stray beyond the pickets as casualties were taken. Local villagers also began attacking camp followers and troops. The headmen of the villages of Nurpur and Chahal along the route were later identified as leaders of a group from the village who had attacked a party of camp followers and baggage, wounding two of the men. The villages were ordered to be razed to the ground in retribution. Gough's force would finally achieve a junction with Campbell reaching Killa Didar Singh on 21 November before making camp north-west at Noewala village, just 12 km behind Campbell's advance position, with Cureton lodged at Saharun, forming a triangle of villages as camp.

*** 

The British force still wasn't complete, even with the arrival of Gough. Units under General Thackwell and Major-General Gilbert would only arrive after the coming battle, which would be fought the very next day after Gough's appearance. Neither did Gough have his siege train and its escort, which was still making its way up. Nevertheless, when his force was complete Gough could count on around 21,000 men in total. In terms of infantry he had fifteen regiments. Four of these would be European (HM 29th, 2nd European Light Infantry, HM 24th, HM 61st) with eleven being native infantry (30th, 56th, 31st, 70th, 25th, 45th, 36th, 46th, 15th, 20th, 69th). Gilbert would command the first division, with Brig Mountain commanding the first brigade (HM 29th Foot, 30th and 56th NI) and Brig. Godby commanding the second (2nd European Light Infantry, 31st and 70th NI). The second division would be commanded by Sir Joseph Thackwell. Brig. Pennycuick had charge of the 1st brigade (HM 24th, 25th and 45th NI) with Brig. Hoggan commanding the second brigade (HM 61st, 36th and 46th NI). The third brigade in this division was commanded by Brig. Penny with the 15th NI, 20th NI and 69th NI.

In terms of Cavalry, Gough could count on three Dragoon regiments (HM 3rd Light Dragoons, HM 14th Light Dragoons and HM 9th Lancers) and five of regular cavalry (1st BLC, 5th BLC, 6th BLC, 8th BLC, 11th BLC) along with four irregular units. Brig.-Gen. Cureton would be in overall command of the cavalry, with Brig. Michael White commanding the first brigade (HM 3rd Light Dragoons, HM 14th Light Dragoons and the 5th and 8th Bengal Light Cavalry) while Brig. Pope commanded the second brigade (HM 9th Lancers, HM 14th Light Dragoons and the 1st and 6th Bengal Light Cavalry) with Brig. Salter commanding the third brigade (11th BLC, 7th Irregular cavalry, 11th Irregular Cavalry). In terms of makeup of the force, the army consisted of around 5,500 Europeans with around 15,500 sepoy and native cavalry. But some of these units, as mentioned, were yet to arrive.

It was in the artillery though that Gough would have a clear advantage over Shere Singh. At his disposal, once the siege train arrived, would be around ninety guns, including sixty-four field pieces along with many 18-pounders and large howitzers. In terms of horse artillery, he had under Lt-Col Huthwaite six troops or batteries commanded by Lt-Col Lane and Majors Christie, Duncan, Waner, Fordyce and Huish. There were three field batteries under Major Dawes, Capt. Austin and Capt. Kinleside along with two heavy batteries under Major Horsford.

By this time, a reserve force was also being organised consisting of 12,000 men under Major-General Hill at Ferozepore although this would never come into play. On the other side of the Chenab in the Sikh camp, Shere Singh was fortunate to have been reinforced by the rest of the troops from Bannu by 17 November under Ram Singh, some of the sturdiest Sikh troops around. British estimates of the force under Shere Singh at this time tend to be wild and full of conjecture. These ranged from 40,000 men downwards. A newspaper correspondent present at the battle estimated 15,000 to 20,000 men judging from what he could see, the Sikh line being on the high right bank of the river and more visible. Other sources put the sum lower. A turncoat from the Sikh camp, a brother of Uttur Singh, one of Shere Singh's principal officers, defected to the British camp and told British officers Shere Singh had around 10,000 regular troops at this time, although reinforcements were coming in continuously. The number of Sikh guns was easier to estimate from the flashes of their fire during the evenings and nights in the coming days. Shere Singh had only twenty-eight guns in total at this time of varying calibre, mostly of small size.

* * *

The terrain that lay between the two armies changed greatly from east of the river where the British camp was situated towards the banks of the river opposite the main Sikh camp. In the middle of the doab and from where the British force had been advancing westwards, accounts describe the terrain as not domesticated, being under cultivation only around the villages that occasionally appeared. However this changed as one approached the Chenab, water channels making the ground much more attractive for irrigation. The area that the British had chosen for their camp had plentiful fields of sugar cane, wheat and mustard. There was plenty of forage for the army of camels accompanying the British force as well although sources mention difficulties for the British cavalry and local farmers made good profit selling the sugar cane for high prices for the forage required. From Saharun and Allipore, the British outposts, the 8 km or so towards the village of Ramnuggar was what Colin Campbell in his account would describe as 'a perfect bowling-green'. In fact the soil being dry at that time, the British guns were moved with little difficulty on the day of the battle although huge clouds of dust were kicked up.

At the western end of this flat expanse appeared the small village of Ramnuggar. The hamlet had no distinguishing features being typical of the numerous walled settlements up and down the country. What perhaps put in on the map, more than most, was the fact that Ranjit Singh had built a small summer house 1.5 km to the north-west of the village and which he frequented during the eve of his years, passing his time drilling his troops.

West of the village and up to the river, a distance of around 2 km, the terrain was quite different. Immediately to the west of the village was some high ground running parallel with the river, perhaps the ancient river bank when the river was a much larger affair. A large tope dominated the view west from the village situated midway between the river and village. The soil became gradually sandier towards the river. This wasteland was also broken by several large nullahs, dry channels of the Chenab at this time and uneven rough ground but which filled with water during the flood season. Here, there and everywhere were deep pools of river water filling indentations and ditches in the ground which hampered any passage to the river proper.

Once this sandy stretch was crossed, the waters of the Chenab River could be seen. When the river was in flood, the river channels between the village and the main stream would no doubt be full of fast-flowing water, or the whole would be submerged into one wide stream. At this time of the year, though, the river was below strength and there was just a single stream. The relative low level of the water for many years previous to this meant that a large island had appeared midstream, where an area of high ground blocked the natural path of the river, forcing the weak stream into two shallower streams which negotiated their way to the left and right of the island before joining up again downstream. Trees and bushes now populated the island.

What was noticeable was that at the left bank opposite the island there was a sharp drop of around 5 feet before a long, sandy stretch led into the waters. This considerable sandy stretch was another consequence of the low level of the river. The left branch of the river itself at the island was around 30 yards wide and quite shallow, being about 3 or 4 feet in depth. Therefore it was crossable by cavalry and infantry, although the water would no doubt hamper any crossing. The other branch of the river to the right of the island was less wide but much deeper, deep enough to make it impossible for even cavalry to cross.

One thing about the opposite bank of the right-hand stream was quite apparent to anyone standing on the left or Ramnuggar bank. 'That bank is high and commanding, and completely overlooks the ground on this side, which is a dead flat, from the high ground, a ridge of low sandhills, on which Ramnuggur stands, to the margin of the river,' commented Campbell, as well as others who had occasion to venture close to the river bank during the battle.

The advantages of this terrain close to the river hadn't been lost on Shere Singh. The high bank on the right gave his troops and guns a good position to play upon any advancing British units slowed down by sand, nullahs and the barrier of the river itself. What he hoped for was that Gough could be induced to attack his position, the bait being the units he had left on the left bank at Ramnuggar village. Meanwhile, the position at the river bank had been strengthened in anticipation of the British attack and plentiful defences had been constructed. A good description was given by Col Mountain to Dalhousie later after the Battle of Sadulpore when the Sikh position was examined.

Mountain described them to me afterwards. They were very formidable. The ford, divided by an island, was deep up to a man's breast two thirds of the way; the island was intrenched, and two batteries. The right bank was high, a quadruple intrenchment on it, with about 30 guns in battery; every tent inside had a little intrenchment round itself.

The Sikh guns too were well placed according to a soldier's letter published later in the *Delhi Gazette*. 'They displayed great skill in the manner in which they laid out their batteries and entrenchments on the opposite side. A heavy fire could have been brought on the ford each battery or line of entrenchment having been well flanked by its neighbours.' This position, described Daniel Sandford of the 2nd Bengal European Regiment as he walked through it after the Battle of Sadulpore, 'could not have been taken without immense loss. They were enormously strong; entrenchments six deep; and their magazines so constructed as to be entirely bomb-proof. The river in front was breast-high and very swift.'

Shere Singh had also kept around 4,000 irregular cavalry along with the infantry on the left bank of the river. These could retreat as and when the British line moved towards the bank and would be well supported by the batteries on the right bank and the island. In addition, there were also placed approximately 4,000 men on the island along with a battery. Gun practice prior to the battle had made clear where the Sikh guns could be effective. His main force would line up along the right bank of the Chenab to take advantage as and when required. It was known Gough had a predilection for a full-frontal assault even against strong, well dug-in positions, and the Sikh commander was confident the force he had on the left bank was strong enough to tempt the British Commander-in-Chief.

\*\*\*

Back in the British camp, as soon as Gough arrived he held a meeting with all officers and proposed an aggressive strategy, remarkably similar to the one Shere Singh had hoped for. A strong reconnaissance party would depart towards the Sikh position at 3 a.m. the very next morning to reconnoitre the land towards the river and the Sikh camp. It also had another purpose. From intelligence received, it was known elements of the Sikh army and four guns were still on the left bank and at the village of Ramnuggar, with some scout units as far east as Akalgurh. Gough thought it entirely 'necessary to drive the rebel force at this side of the river across and to capture any guns they might have had on the left bank', as he described in his despatches the day after the battle. An early surprise attack the very next morning would, it was thought, have a good chance of destroying these isolated units. After this the party organised for the ambush would push forward and provide reconnaissance up to the riverbank and hence check the practicality of using the fords nearby. To enable a swift move this contingent would be entirely cavalry, supported by artillery. Once any Sikh units had been mopped up on the left bank, the British guns, having been hauled to Ramnuggar behind the cavalry, could begin pounding the Sikh position on the opposite bank.

Thinking further ahead, Gough planned to force a crossing of the Chenab at Ramnuggar if Shere Singh was forced back, or further upstream if he wasn't. John Nicholson, who had reached Wazirabad by this time, had been busy accumulating boats at the city, 40 km upstream of Ramnuggar, for this very purpose. He had already collected twelve boats when Cureton had moved towards Gujranwala around 7 November. With these boats and the pontoon bridge that had been brought along, Gough was confident he could force a river crossing at some point or another with no great difficulty.

A strong word of warning, curiously enough, was given after this meeting but ignored by Gough. One of the locals aiding in scouting for the British force was a local Muslim chieftain of the area by the name of Suleiman Khan. He was the only person employed by Gough for help in reconnaissance of territory unfamiliar to the British officers. Recommended by a Col Garden and known as the 'prince of Kundschafters' for his reconnaissance skills, his knowledge of the local area and the terrain separating the two armies was apparently excellent. Suleiman Khan warned Gough that to enter into a battle or even a skirmish here would be folly. The soft sand and intersecting nullahs close to the river, with the river itself fordable only in select areas, would be difficult ground for combat and fit only for an ambush. Khan's advice would be ignored, and preparations continued for the push forward the next day. He was roughly treated after the battle by all accounts when his information proved correct, being demoted to scouting rather than being acknowledged.

The force to be sent would be under the overall command of Colin Campbell, with the British cavalry under the command of Cureton. Guns would be provided in the form of two troops of horse artillery (Duncan's and Warner's) along with two field batteries (Austin's and Dawes). This force, in order to move rapidly and achieve the required level of surprise, would leave all baggage and tents behind in the British camp. Meanwhile, the bulk of the force under Gough being slower would advance behind Campbell's force a few hours later with the remaining cavalry on the right with the artillery in the centre and the infantry on the left while the 12th Irregular Cavalry would cover the rear of the line. Brig. Eckford's brigade (31st and 56th NI along with some native cavalry and some artillery) would be left to protect the camp.

*** 

Orders were given that no bugles, drums or trumpets were to be sounded early next morning and complete silence was to be maintained. At 3 a.m., as planned, with no campfires to illuminate proceedings, the British column organised itself for the advance. What should have been a rapid movement, though, was unwittingly slowed by Gough himself. He had changed his mind overnight, deciding to accompany this advance force himself and take overall charge instead of Campbell. He had also decided on bringing two brigades of infantry (those of Brigs Godby and Hoggan) as well, the organisation of which delayed the move. There was still confusion in any case due to the early time of the day.

The entire column, once organised, then marched in single column, the infantry in front followed by artillery and then the cavalry. 'The morning was pitch dark when the order to move forward was given and before we had advanced a mile, cavalry, camp followers, artillery and infantry were jumbled together. At length day broke, order was restored and a report ran through the columns that Ramnuggur was in sight,' wrote an officer later in a private letter. Any element of surprise that a fast cavalry advance could have achieved, therefore, was lost as the whole force including infantry marched as one towards the river. The journey would take four hours and it was only at 7 a.m. that the British force closed in on the village of Ramnuggar. The Sikh pickets and other remaining advance units received adequate notice of the British advance and had already begun withdrawing by this time. It was apparent that there was no element of surprise left and Gough seemed to jettison the original plan at this point, deciding on camping for the night at the village in a wide arc around the hamlet. The ridge beyond the village afforded a good view across the river and the Sikh line could clearly be seen in the distance on the high bank opposite. What was immediately apparent was the difficulty in attacking Shere Singh's position with the river in the way. 'Their position is good and their guns are heavy and commanding. We have a fine view of their camp and batteries which extend a mile and a half,' wrote the correspondent with the *Delhi Gazette* accompanying the force. The Sikh line on the opposite bank only held the attention for a few brief moments though as musket fire and skirmishing broke out between the British cavalry moving past the village and the parties of Sikh soldiers moving back towards the river bank. It was the sight of these Sikh units withdrawing and the desultory firing between the two sides that triggered the conflict. Gough promptly fell back on his original plan to try and ambush all the Sikh troops on the left bank and ordered these units to be harassed and cut off as they made their way back to the river. This was a decision he would be much criticised for later as little or no reconnaissance had been made of the area near the river and the batteries of Sikh guns stationed on the opposite bank were equally obvious. Henry Havelock, who later achieved fame during the mutiny of 1857 for the recapture of Lucknow, was scathing about Gough's impulse decision to fight. In a private letter to a friend after the battle he would write,

We were provoked by the Sikh fire into a contest under every possible disadvantage, on ground where nothing but disaster could occur … As regards the operation, it must be clear to any unprejudiced person that it ought never to have been undertaken. You may remember our pickets being driven in some weeks before Sobraon; it was the commencement of the enemy's successful attempt to establish himself on the left bank. The reason which I gave then against attempting countermanoeuvres is perfectly applicable to the case of the Chenab. The enemy had a powerful artillery on the right bank, and until its fire could be subdued, were fairly to be considered the proprietors of the stream, and of as much ground beyond it as could be swept by the fire of their guns.

Nevertheless the decision had been taken and Brig. Cureton and the horse artillery troops of Warner and Lanes were ordered to be pushed forward as quickly as possible to harass the retreating Sikh troops. The response was rapid. Lt-Col Andrew Macpherson of HM 24th regiment described the enthusiasm of the British gunners to engage with the Sikh infantrymen.

> I was suddenly startled by sharp quick firing in advance, and the clatter of a battery of the old Bengal Horse artillery passing me on to the front at a gallop. Some of the drivers were smoking short pipes as well as the pace would allow. Gunners and drivers one and all, fire eating dare-devils, in buckskin breaches. The guns, their 'wheels like a whirlwind' bounding along on their deadly mission, with a hop, skip and jump. 'Hurry up' sang out a saucy gunner to us, making his horse spring to a touch from the spur and striking a rum cask with the flat of his sword blade, 'Hurry up with the grog, we have thirsty work before us. Get up behind me, old man, and come along with us if you want to see a Sikh; we'll bowl them out in a jiffey and not leave one on this side of the river for you mud crushers – Au Revoir.'
>
> Horse was tumbling over horse, there was a clashing of angry steel, a rattle of small arms, the din of sounding hoofs, the jumble of hoarse words of command from either side all making a confused noise and a babel that was heard a far, in the hush of the batteries.

Others too noticed the haste to meet with the enemy. 'It was a rush as to who should get at the enemy first,' read one letter by a soldier. Things were easy at first, but as soon as the British troops began negotiating the increasingly sandy stretches closer to the river and where larger numbers of Sikh troops were to be found, things began to get more difficult – especially as they came in range and sight of the Sikh guns on the opposite bank.

'The Sikhs had placed their guns in masked batteries, and, as you may suppose, the sudden discharge took our people by surprise; nevertheless they went on, seeing a large number of the enemy beyond the nullah. The ground was very heavy and sandy; a large portion of our cavalry got into a quicksand, and the horses, being somewhat exhausted by the march over the heavy ground, were not able to extricate themselves as soon as they might have done,' recalled an officer of the horse artillery in a letter later published in the *Illustrated London News*.

The British horse artillery guns that had accompanied the advance also reached the riverbank shortly and were unlimbered to compete against the Sikh guns on the opposite bank. The exchange became more heated now, with the Sikh pickets also reversing their motion along with Sikh troops from the right bank and the ones on the island midstream returning fire on the advancing British cavalry.

This situation was not to last long. With the twenty-eight Sikh guns against the six smaller British horse artillery guns that had been brought to the riverbank, it quickly became apparent to the British gunners that retreat was advisable. The guns were consequently ordered to limber up again and a retreat sounded. All but one of the guns and two ammunition wagons that had been brought up managed to extricate themselves and move back to safety. The problem was that the guns had been brought down a high bank of sand close to the river, and while easy to move down the slope they proved difficult to move back up again. Heavy with ammunition, they stuck easily in the sand. Soon some of the horses pulling the wagons were wounded by fire, making the task yet more difficult. As for the one gun that was also stuck, the poles of the limber were seen to have been damaged by the Sikh fire. A few minutes later the leading horse of the team was shot, making the job of extracting it impossible. This gun and the soldiers attempting to carry it clear quickly came to the notice of other Sikh gunners, who also turned their guns to this direction. At this time, as the British guns retreated, Sikh infantry and some Gorcharas, amounting to around 3,000–4,000 men, began recrossing to the left bank while infantrymen stationed on the island also made moves to cross. Colin Campbell had been made aware of the situation at the riverbank by this time and personally rode near to the riverbank to monitor efforts to extract the gun. 'We stopped while two sets of horses were sent to try and remove the gun. But these efforts were ineffectual. The truth is, the gun could only be got out of the position in which it was by cutting down the bank, or by taking the gun to a considerable distance on either side of where it was placed, in doing which, our men would have been exposed to the fire of the whole of the enemy's artillery, posted on the opposite bank, numbering 28 guns.'

A light field battery was brought up to help provide cover while the extrication process was being attempted but this had to retreat after some minutes due to the hot reception. With the effort proving ineffectual, Campbell finally rode back to get two regiments of infantry to cover the gun but met Gough along the way, who was now riding towards the river himself. Noticing the unequal contest, Gough promptly gave the order to abandon the gun, deeming it too risky in terms of lives to remove. 'It was reported to me it would occasion a fearful loss of life to bring it away,' he wrote in his despatch of the 23rd, 'which alone could be effected by manual labour and scarping the banks under the fire of even the matchlockmen on the opposite bank. I could not therefore consent to such a sacrifice.'

The gun was spiked and any British cavalry still near the river bank ordered to retreat to behind the grove of trees near the village for shelter against the Sikh fire in what looked like the end of the skirmish. This retreat now gave the Sikh Gorcharas the opportunity to harry the British units as they manoeuvred back to the village. They began quickly recrossing the river and pursuing the British units. Campbell, being made aware of this and having seen the terrain by the river, had strong reservations on resuming the struggle especially with the Sikh guns overlooking the river. As he rode back, he met Col Grant and they discussed the situation. Campbell suggested Grant ask Gough to withdraw the British force entirely from the riverbank. He also met Cureton and had a similar conversation, but Cureton expressed a much more bullish attitude about a contest with the Sikh horsemen.

> While engaged in conversation with him to this effect, I observed the 14th Light Dragoons get in movement in direction of the enemy, and I observed that they were no doubt going to engage in one of these useless encounters with the enemy in the broken ground on the banks of the river. I begged him to go and look after them, to prevent their acting wildly or foolishly. He observed that the chief ought either to take the whole management into his own hands, or leave it to those whom he had made responsible.

Gough, while willing to abandon the gun, had not been willing to end the affair entirely and was enthusiastic about another chance to destroy the Sikh units that had recrossed. It would be

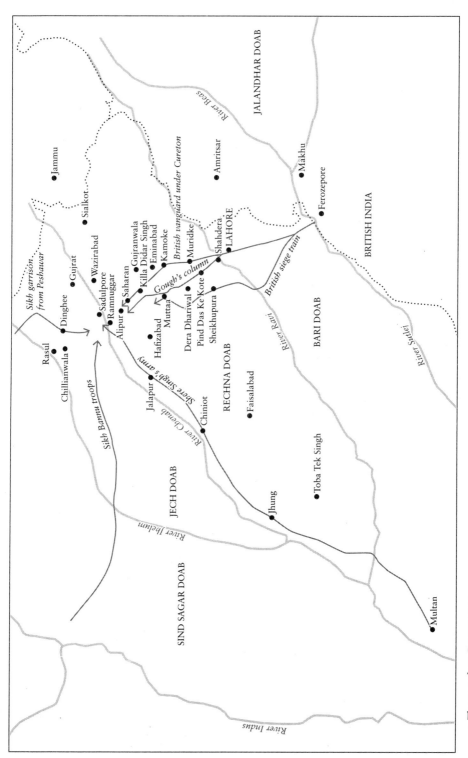

5. The march to Ramnuggar

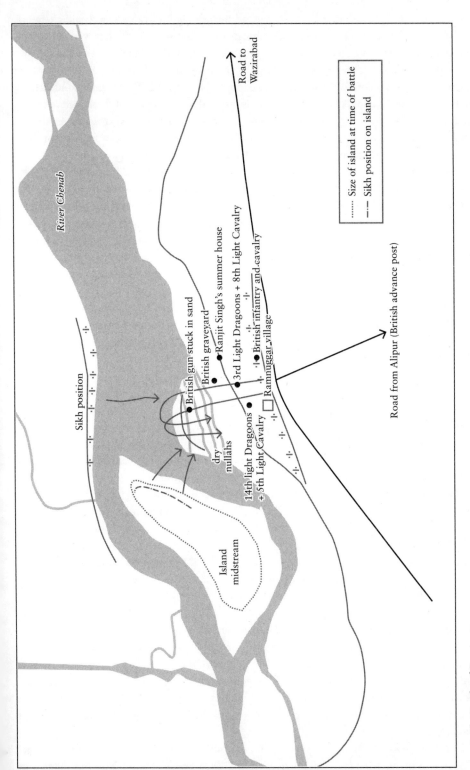

*River Chenab*

Sikh position

British gun stuck in sand
British graveyard
Ranjit Singh's summer house
3rd Light Dragoons + 8th Light Cavalry
British infantry and cavalry
Ramnuggar village

dry nullahs

14th light Dragoons + 5th Light Cavalry

Island midstream

Road to Wazirabad

Road from Alipur (British advance post)

......... Size of island at time of battle
— — — Sikh position on island

6. The Battle of Ramnuggar

the 3rd Light Dragoons under Capt. Ouvry and the 8th Light Cavalry who would charge the Gorcharas at this point first. The charge, similar to the first advance to the river, didn't go to plan. The Gorcharas in a disciplined move quickly and efficiently split into two sections to their left and right, allowing the Dragoons' charge to go unchecked and resulting in them reaching the riverbank. This allowed the Sikh guns an unencumbered view of the Dragoons and virtually all the twenty-eight guns Shere Singh had at his disposal began to play on these men. They also found themselves being the target of the many Sikh infantry that had also crossed over and had established themselves again on the left bank. The abandoned British gun had by now been taken off its damaged carriage and transported back to the right bank as a trophy.

The 3rd Light Dragoons, some of whom had entered the water, found it a frustrating time as the island in the middle of the river had high banks, making it impossible to engage the Sikh infantry. Consequently many thrashed around in the water with no great purpose or direction for several minutes while others tried to engage the few Sikh infantry men on the left bank or in the water. Some of the more courageous Dragoons managed to reach the right side of the island where they were the targets of the six guns immediately opposite them before retreating back. All this time, hundreds of Sikh infantrymen on the island peppered them with shot with impunity.

With nothing being achieved apart from presenting themselves as easy targets, the Dragoons and the 8th Light Cavalry retreated back through the water to the left bank and back towards the village. As the Dragoons rode back, several hundred of the Sikh infantrymen followed them again, bringing down more of the riders.

***

Brig. White who had led the 3rd Light Dragoons towards the river saw the impossibility of making any real gain and would proceed to retreat back to the village. But others, despite the lack of success, still viewed the Sikh troops and cavalry on the left bank as an opportunity. The return of the 3rd Light Dragoons towards the village had been keenly watched by Lt-Col William Havelock of the 14th Dragoons, and he had high hopes of scoring some success against the Sikh infantrymen where the 3rd Light Dragoons had failed. Aged fifty-five, he had not seen combat since the Napoleonic War. This campaign, according to his brother Henry Havelock, represented in William Havelock's mind his last chance for glory and he needed no encouragement at trying a charge himself. Gough, passing Havelock earlier as the engagement commenced, had given him ample encouragement: 'If you see a favourable opportunity of charging, charge,' he was heard to shout to Havelock.

'On the morning of 22 November, he seemed a good deal excited. This may be pardoned in an old sabreur, whose enthusiasm had been pent up without vent or safety valve in his bosom since the Battle of Waterloo. He is said to have worried Cureton with entreaties to be allowed to attack the Sikh horse, who were caracolling in front of the 14th, and more than once to have exclaimed, that this day "he hoped to win his golden spurs", his brother Henry recalled. Lined alongside the 14th Dragoons would be the 5th Light Cavalry under Lt-Col Alexander. As the line was being prepared he was heard to say, 'We now shall soon see whether we can clear our front of those fellows, or not.'

Not surprisingly, the 14th Dragoons would encounter the same problems as the 3rd Light Dragoons as they galloped towards the riverbank. As they struggled through the nullahs and the uneven and sandy terrain near the river, they began to be picked off by the Sikh infantry. At the bank of the river things grew progressively worse as they splashed around at the riverbank, with some of the horses swimming in full view of the Sikh line on the right bank and the infantrymen on the island. Back near the village, there was already some confusion on the advance of the Dragoons. Cureton, on hearing of the 14th Dragoons' charge, was heard to say, 'That is not the body of horse I meant to have been attacked' but it was too late. Cureton would advance towards the river to call off the attack, and a retreat was sounded.

Despite their first inconclusive skirmish at the bank, curiously there was a second charge by Havelock and the 14th Dragoons. Somewhere in the melee, Havelock was seen and heard to exclaim, 'Follow me, my brave lads, and never heed their cannon shot.' These were his last words. His orderly later recounted seeing him dead in a nullah among other dead and dying but, being wounded himself, he could not assist him in any way. His corpse was later discovered by the chaplain of the army.

While the very nature of the ground, according to some Dragoons, naturally impeded the British cavalry charge, it also paradoxically saved the 14th Dragoons and earlier the 3rd Light Dragoons from a greater mauling by the Sikh infantry. A soldier whose story was published in *The Times* described the situation: 'Had the 14th not been broken by jumping into the nullah, more than half the regiment must have been destroyed so severe was the fire as all the shot had they charged in close order would have taken effect.'

The broken ground made it equally difficult for the Sikh Gorcharas to pursue the Dragoons as they made their way back as well. The sixty-year-old Cureton was another casualty as he reached the riverbank to order the 14th Dragoons back. A roundshot had passed close to him, prompting a soldier near him to declare, 'Rather a near shave that, General.' 'Oh, I am used to it,' replied Cureton, stroking his moustache and smiling back. Several minutes later a Sikh musketman shot him; some accounts say through the head, some the chest. A certain Capt. Holmes, the commander of the 12th Irregular Cavalry, courageously attempted to retrieve his body only to get severely wounded in the chest. The body had already been stripped by nearby Sikh soldiers looking for souvenirs of a British general by the time Holmes tried dragging the corpse back. The body would eventually be brought back the day after the battle when some villagers, lured by a bounty of 300 rupees, scoured the area for British bodies.

'The guns on the opposite side of the river, and the portion of the enemy's force drawn up behind a quicksand, has been a regular trap into which we have fallen most woefully,' wrote one of the officers of the horse artillery in retrospect. That too many British casualties were being taken in the sand with no impression being made on the approach to the river was more than apparent to all, including the Commander-in-Chief. Gough would decide enough was enough and the order was given to definitely move back towards the village with strict orders that no further contests were to be sought towards the riverbank, whatever the lure.

\*\*\*

The time now was around 1 p.m. and all fighting was at an end although Sikh guns kept peppering the British troops for some time, causing some casualties among HM 61st, who had been stationed in one of the nullahs near the bank and were the last to pull back. By around 3 p.m. the whole British line had finally retired behind the sandy ridge at Ramnuggar and all guns on either side were silenced.

The decision was now made to make camp at Ramnuggar rather than making the trek back to Noewala and Saharun. Since the British camp and baggage had been left at its previous locations, the night would be spent in a most uncomfortable fashion, the soldiers having to sleep without any protection from the elements and without any food till supplies began filtering in at noon the next day. The baggage would only begin arriving on the 24th, meaning a further uncomfortable night for most with only light coverings, if any, available. The area round Ramnuggar also had other unwelcome occupants which would continue giving discomfort to the British troops during the next two weeks. 'There appears to be no paucity of white ants in this neighbourhood and their teeth have made vigorous assaults on tents settringees &c although they must be rather dry eating,' noted a letter on conditions later printed in the *Delhi Gazette*.

British casualties amounted to eleven officers killed and wounded along with 130 rank-and-file. These were naturally largely from the 14th Dragoons and 5th Light Cavalry that had charged towards the river twice. The 14th Dragoons suffered twenty-seven men killed and twenty-three wounded. The 3rd Dragoons had eight casualties. The more notable of the British casualties were Brig.-Gen. Cureton and Havelock. Havelock's corpse would be recovered nearly two weeks later on 5 December near the river and recognised with difficulty by the chaplain Revd W. Whiting, the corpse being headless and without clothes at this stage, a victim to trophy hunters and looters. Lt Hardinge, attaché to the Commander-in-Chief's staff and a nephew of Viscount Hardinge, the previous Governor-General, was wounded as well as Brig. Hoggan. Col Alexander lost an arm. Capt. Riley, Capt. Gaul and Capt. Fitzgerald all had sabre cuts, with Fitzgerald expiring later. Another two officers had musket shot wounds. In addition several artillerymen had been killed or wounded. The gun stuck in the sand was the only one lost, however, along with two ammunition wagons; in compensation, a silk Sikh standard had been captured by a member of the 5th Light Cavalry.

In his despatches, Gough attempted to put the best possible light on the events adding that 'the enemy were signally overthrown on occasion, and only saved from utter annihilation by flight', which was some way off the mark even for an official despatch. He would, however, hint at mistakes made. '[The return of the killed and wounded] I regret to say, is much greater than I could have anticipated, in a great measure, from the officers leading being unacquainted with the difficult nature of the ground in the vicinity of the river, and of which no native information ever gives you a just knowledge, and in some measure, to the impetuosity of the artillery and cavalry, who, notwithstanding those difficulties, charged to the bank of the river, thereby exposing themselves to the fire of about twenty-eight guns.'

Criticism of Gough falling into a trap was universal, whether private or public. Dalhousie was at this time still travelling up from Calcutta to Punjab and the despatch and other early news and accounts reached him on his arrival at Amballa. Unsure of the circumstances, he kept his criticism muted. 'Some blame the Commander-in-Chief, some blame Campbell and Cureton,' he informed the Duke of Wellington on 7 December 1848, largely accepting Gough's account. 'But, whoever was to blame, the result was very unfortunate. Both cavalry and artillery behaved admirably, and charged brilliantly; but they did it in unknown ground, and under the enemy's guns, and we suffered severely.'

Publicly he praised the Commander-in-Chief's conduct of the battle, considered a success. However, other accounts came to his attention in the following days. 'The despatch was followed by other letters calculated to make me very anxious as to the management of the army, and the ultimate success which would attend it in the hands in which it was,' Dalhousie mused, showing concern as to Gough's direction of the whole affair and his labelling of the contest as a success. The news-sheets too saw it for what it was and their reaction was universally unfavourable.

'We will not attempt to analyze the unfortunate proceedings at Ramnuggur, further than to say that they betrayed great preliminary ignorance on our part of the ground, and equal want of quickness in the faculty of reading ground (if such an expression be pardonable) – of taking in its features at a glance. The British horse-artillery were permitted to dip into the low sandy channels of a bight of the river swept from the opposite bank by the enemy's heavy artillery', the *Calcutta Review* opined. 'Our campaign commenced inauspiciously, without corresponding advantage over the enemy, of whose strength, or even position we were ignorant', the *Friend of India* commented. 'The movements of the Commander-in-Chief have filled with the deepest anxiety all those who have friends, relatives, and connections with the army. We can afford time, but we cannot afford a useless and wanton sacrifice of life. We have a difficult country for future operations, a brave and resolute enemy to encounter, well provided with troops, artillery and ammunition; and animated with strongest hopes of success – which our dilatory movements in reference to Mooltan have strengthened in no common degree. The whole of the Punjaub is in arms against us.'

Back in the British camp, Gough found himself at the end of a few sharp tongues from the Dragoons, who had borne the brunt of the British casualties. On one occasion on visiting the Field Hospital, he tried to gloss over the affair: 'My men, you have suffered in your arms and legs, but it was in a glorious cause', he declared to the wounded. 'It was a rash affair, my Lord', came the quick reply from one of the wounded Dragoons. Gough, taken aback by the directness of the reply, apparently left the hospital without saying another word.

Back in London, Gough's optimistic despatch would draw criticism from Lord Brougham, who wished Gough had expressed more reserve in what was plainly a drawn affair. 'When an officer in high command copying the example of Lord Nelson began his despatch with "It has pleased Almighty God to bless her Majesty arms with victory", it should be a success so great that there could be no doubt about it ... Viewed in this light the General in command of the British forces in the late engagement might perhaps have commenced his despatch in some such words as these: "It has pleased Almighty God to permit me to be out-manoeuvred by the enemy" which would have been edifying indeed.'

In the days after the action at Ramnuggar, Gough would wisely refrain from more direct charges at the Sikh position, adopting a much more patient strategy. This was to wait for the arrival of his heavy guns and his Engineers department as well as Thackwell's brigade, which was yet to arrive and which would strengthen his force further still. Offensive measures would only be taken once these units were available. He also jettisoned the idea of attempting a forced crossing of the river with the pontoon bridge or otherwise for the time being at least. The opposite bank was obviously too well defended and the river and sandy stretches too treacherous to attempt a crossing in the face of the Sikh cannon. If a crossing was to be done, it would have to be carried out up or downstream where the opposite bank wasn't being monitored so closely by the Sikh army. So for the next week or so till the British heavy guns arrived, there would only be the odd occasions of Sikh and British artillery playing ball.

Meanwhile the burials of the British dead took place the day after the battle, the service for Brig-General Cureton ending somewhat prematurely due to a false alarm as word went around that Shere Singh was crossing the river himself with his entire force. The whole British line was consequently readied. The death of both Cureton and Havelock meant some role changes would be forced on Gough. Thackwell, when he arrived, would be given Cureton's old role with Colin Campbell in turn taking Thackwell's position as commander of the third division.

One of the complaints which had resulted from the hand-to-hand combat at Ramnuggar and later at Chillianwala was the weakness of the British sword against the Sikh tulwar. The tulwar was a heavier implement, its broader back giving it more strength. On impact with the tulwar, the British sword would sometimes shatter. This had been seen too often during the recent contest and in fact during the First Anglo-Sikh War as well. In the days after the battle the Gorcharas, using the ford at Ghurree Ke-Puttan crossed the river daily for skirmishing with their British counterparts in the 3rd, 9th and 12th Irregulars. On the 24th two men of the 21st NI died and another was wounded although he managed to make it back into the camp. Fighting on the 25th between the Sikh irregulars and British cavalry again took place on the left bank. During these two days several swords had been shattered in hand-to-hand combat. It had been noticed many sepoys never used the sword, preferring to use their pistols instead, and some cavalrymen went as far as to ask if they could use the Sikh tulwars instead. This was refused by Gough, although he would later change his mind, allowing the use of tulwars to those who preferred them.

Bayonet-wielding British soldiers also had their vulnerabilities. The Sikh soldier's strategy against the bayonet was to allow the opponent to commit himself with a thrust. The Sikh soldier was typically protected with padded clothing and armour and carried shields which together made the bayonet much less potent. He then practised his counter, what the British called 'the drawing cut', grasping the bayonet and scything down on the back of the soldier's neck with the tulwar and to which he had little defence. This was seen in many individual contests during the Ramnuggar battle. For this reason British soldiers began resorting to hanging rolled cloth on the back of the shako. Others found a piece of leather gave even better protection, an idea increasingly adopted as the campaign progressed. This fashion, as Edward Thackwell, aide-de-camp to General Thackwell, would put it, partly resembled a helmet and partly a jockey-cap. 'The leather edge hanging down behind from many of these fantastic caps, gave them the appearance of those hats so peculiar to the fraternity of coal-heavers. The cap was surmounted by a white linen cover, forming a defence against the solar rays. The Generals of Divisions and their staff, adopted the prevailing fashion.'

***

Other issues to do with logistics stemming from long supply lines and the large force in the Punjab also quickly began surfacing in the British camp. Much of the British mail from the camp to Lahore and Ferozepore was disappearing as much of the doab was patrolled by Sikh units, while robbers and assorted highwaymen also took advantage of the unsettled affairs. Along with this there were already substantial losses of baggage animals. On the 24th, for instance, two elephants used for the heavy guns along with around 100 camels were driven off either by Sikh irregulars or local brigands at Akalgurh behind British lines. On 28 November it was recorded 150 camels had disappeared. On 29 November, a report came in of thirty camels of the 5th brigade having been carried off. Brig. Mountain was ordered to give chase with a force of 3rd Light Dragoons and 5th Light Cavalry and other irregulars. The chase took them to the banks of the river where Sikh guns were posted on the right bank and infantry and cavalry stationed on the left bank. Mountain declined to charge the guns – his guns being smaller – although two further wagons of ammunition were abandoned and lost.

Even if supplies were not being intercepted, the lengthy distance to Ferozepore and the lack of animals was causing delays despite the Lahore Durbar assisting with its own baggage animals. This caused some anxious moments for Gough, two days after the battle. He was told there were only four days' supply remaining for his force, which prompted him to write to the Resident that his army was in 'a most critical position'. If supplies stayed this way it would be necessary to retreat back to Lahore, he declared. Whether this was alarmist or not is unclear but supplies did eventually manage to come in in sufficient number over the next few days and weeks to allay any fears of a retreat in the British camp.

There would be an early change in the political agent accompanying the British force as well. Major Mackeson would take over the role. Gough had developed a dislike for the agent present in the camp. He would describe Mr Cocks as 'having no resources', that he was too young and that Mackeson would be preferred, arguments accepted by Dalhousie.

With the two sides being in such close proximity to each other and with soldiers straying outside the camps there was a great risk of prisoners being taken. Several workmen digging the British batteries were captured by Sikh skirmishers and cavalrymen during the last days of November. 'The enemy cross over here frequently. Their position on the other side is very strong covered with artillery', the correspondent of the *Daily Gazetteer* noted on 2 December.

Because of the extended stay at Ramnuggar, a week after the battle the British camp was already assuming a more permanent look. A high tower had been constructed behind British lines from which telescopes could be used to observe the Sikh camp on the other side of the river. Gough himself had already moved into a more comfortable tent complete with glass windows. This week-long stay, with little action beyond some skirmishing and the occasional cannonade, was not what had been expected by British soldiers, who had expected a quick conclusion once a collision with the Sikh army had been achieved. There was already a certain amount of restlessness apparent in the British camp. Supremely confident of defeating the Sikh army quickly, they were frustrated at being held at the river for what might be several more weeks while news came in daily of successful raids by Gorcharas on the British supply train and camels, many of which were being driven off every day. Conscious of this frustration, while he waited for his big guns to arrive Gough kept his force occupied with preparation on the batteries, parades and inspections. Elephants were drilled with the heavy batteries and guns and otherwise occupied in dragging dead camels and bullocks away and beyond the camp for hygiene. They were also typically used to drag the guns (each gun being hauled by three elephants) as close as possible but outside Sikh guns' range. There a team of twenty-four bullocks took over to take the guns in among the firing, bullocks being thought much less intelligent and therefore less likely to take fright with the noise of the guns and explosion.

The heavy guns that had set off from Ferozepore under Col Penny eventually reached the British camp on 30 November. They had been delayed at the fort of Jubber, midway on the route to Ramnuggar, where local Sikh commander Utter Singh had been disrupting British supplies and communications. By the time Penny had reached the fort, Utter Singh had withdrawn along with 1,300 of his men to join Shere Singh, leaving a skeleton force of around 100 men. Nevertheless, the fort was ordered to be captured. The British 18-pounders quickly began destroying the fort defences, and after the garrison surrendered Penny blew up the fort with the 7,000 lbs of gunpowder it contained. The village was allowed to be sacked by the troops, though little of any value was obtained. The capture and reduction of the fort had cost Penny three days, which meant Gough's plans to cannonade the Sikh position had been correspondingly delayed. Now the guns were present, a much fiercer cannonade against the Sikh position on the opposite bank was immediately commenced, the British guns pushed ever closer to the river as the days went past. How much damage the British guns dealt was moot, for the Sikh line was well entrenched by this stage and the Sikh guns correspondingly well protected and camouflaged.

Gough, during the days after the battle, had asked the Governor-General to designate the Ramnuggar contest a British victory for which a twenty-one-gun salute could then be ordered at British cantonments round the country. But there was some difference in opinion as to the interpretation of victory between the Governor-General and the Commander-in-Chief in what would become a running theme for the next two battles. Dalhousie would not relent on this issue and would criticise him privately on another issue. 'Wherefore the C.-in-C. 's movement was excellent, his success important, but it was not a victory, and I cannot call it so, however vexed he may be. But he is still more angry with me for another cause. When I reached Umballa, this was the state of things I found. The C.-in-C. had moved his whole army from Ferozepore to the Chenab, when commissariat and other department arrangements were incomplete, and in spite of the remonstrances of the heads of departments.' Dalhousie was of the opinion that Gough would have to demonstrate a much more clear victory before he would order a gun salute.

***

On the right bank of the Chenab, meanwhile, it is likely Shere Singh wasn't content with the proceedings of the 22nd either. Although the British had suffered losses, the general attack by the entire British force up to the riverbank he hoped he could draw Gough into had not appeared and the chance to inflict more casualties before the British heavy guns arrived had been missed.

After the battle, Shere Singh would adopt a policy of releasing his British prisoners, several men captured during the battle and afterwards in skirmishing being released on the morning of the 24th. The Sikh commander saw this as an opportunity to make a peace overture. A lengthy letter and memorial was sent from Shere Singh to Gough and Mr Cocks for the attention of Currie and Dalhousie. The memorial was long, consisting of twenty-five paragraphs, each iterating a grievance. It was signed by Shere Singh and all his officers.

The Sikh commander had written that he had no wish to fight the British and that he hoped Gough would take no further action till the arrival of his father, at which point negotiations could take place and the present state of hostilities could end amicably. He wrote that he had been driven to end his alliance with the British due to the ill faith shown by them towards him and his troops. Be that as it may, all the British needed to do now was to leave Lahore territory. If this could be agreed, he would not molest the British force as it made its way back to British territory. This would, Shere Singh wrote, 'extinguish the torch of dissension which is now lighted, and make arrangements to secure the stability of the Maharajah's kingdom, and redound to the credit of the British Government'.

In a further overture, another British prisoner, a soldier of the 2nd Bengal European Regiment, was released by Shere Singh the following day and escorted into the British camp by four Sikh soldiers. He had wandered away from the British camp beyond the pickets and was taken prisoner by a group of Gorcharas. The prisoner seemed to have provided some amusement to both camps, being none too bright. He could give no information to his questioners in the Sikh camp. 'He is such a perfect fool that they could get nothing out of him. No more can we,' wrote Daniel Sandford of the 2nd Bengal European Regiment.

Shere Singh's overture would be rejected. Gough wrote back politely, thanking Shere Singh for the release of prisoners but entirely dismissing his demands along with his request to wait until Chutter Singh's arrival. He viewed this as a ruse, with Shere Singh having no real intention of negotiating and only delaying to accumulate supplies and reinforcements. No halt would be ordered to any future British attack. Dalhousie was if anything even more adamant about refusing any overtures. 'I told them I would not treat with rebels in arms, and that I could listen to no proposal but unconditional surrender or submission. I have, however, proposed to exchange prisoners, and I have tried to bully them if they should harm the prisoners with them. I do not expect they will give them up at present, but I do not think they will harm them,' he later informed the Duke of Wellington. The prisoners being referred to were George Lawrence and his family along with other British prisoners taken at Peshawar. His answer to Shere Singh was hard and uncompromising. 'His lordship does not think the memorial entitled to any reply,' wrote his secretary in answer to Frederick Currie passing the communique, 'but, lest any misrepresentation should be made of our motives, in case no answer should be given, the Governor-General directs me to request that you will inform the memorialists that you have been instructed to state that the memorial has been received by the Governor-General, and that his only answer will be the advance of the British army.'

Currie's own answer to Shere Singh once he had received Dalhousie's reply was a little more diplomatic, although he went as far as to label them 'rebels' and would stress that 'the authority of the Government in all the provinces must be re-established before any question can be entered upon regarding arrangements for the administration of the country or other matters'. In other words, the rebels, as Shere Singh's army was termed, would have to surrender their arms before any negotiations took place. With Shere Singh entirely rejecting these demands, the stage was set for a further contest. Where and how this would be fought was unclear in the days after Ramnuggar; Dalhousie was not at all enthusiastic about Gough crossing the Chenab and further stretching his already overlong supply lines.

# 26

# The Battle of Sadulpore

The facts suppressed are so obvious and so well known, and many of the assertions
made are so suspicious, that we have preferred accepting the authority of letters from
officers with the force.

*Bombay Times*, 13 December 1848

Brave officers have fallen, but the mode of retrieving this surely lies on the surface.
I trust no attack will be made in front on Shere Singh's position.

Private letter by Henry Havelock, 7 December 1848

Given that British supply lines were already stretched and being disrupted even before
Ramnuggar, Dalhousie had decided to effectively ban Gough from advancing beyond the
Chenab and its vicinity till this matter was resolved and till the city of Multan fell, allowing
Whish's army to effect a junction with the main British force. He felt that this overwhelming
force could make short work of Shere Singh's army. The news of the Peshawar troops deciding to
join Shere Singh had only strengthened the case for caution as far as the Governor-General was
concerned. There were other compelling reasons, he thought, for caution in marching too far
west; during this time there were also revolts in the Jalandhar doab that were at risk of becoming
more serious. At the same time, Dalhousie was most anxious that Lahore should not have
an insufficient British garrison; only one European regiment and four sepoy regiments were
stationed there at the time. Keeping a hold on the Sikh capital was of paramount importance
and this hold must not be put under any danger.

'He [the Commander-in-Chief] had no reserve whatever. Between the Ravi and the Satlaj
there was not a British soldier except the garrison in Govindghar. At Firozpur there were three
native infantry regiments, instead of six, one European cavalry, and two native cavalry, as usual,'
he explained in a letter to the Duke of Wellington. Even British territory nearby was empty of
troops, Ludhiana and Amballa being quite denuded of men. Gough himself entirely agreed
with this policy. On 27 November, though, given that Shere Singh had entrenched himself on
the right bank of the Chenab and a stalemate was appearing, he wrote to Gough and granted
tentative permission to cross the river to attack the Sikh position, but to move no further west
than the right bank of the stream:

If it should appear to your Excellency that the condition of your army, in all respects,
is such as to enable you to attack Raja Sher Sing in his position with the certainty of
complete success, and without calamitous loss, the destruction of his force would be of
great importance; but I have to convey to you my request that on no consideration should

your Excellency advance with your army into the Doab beyond the Chenab, except for the purpose of attacking Sher Sing in his present position, without further communication with me and my consent obtained. The arrival of reinforcements at Multan, and the surrender of that fortress, will shortly place such an additional force at our disposal as will admit of the army advancing without exposing our present position to the imminent risk in which it would otherwise be placed.

With the authority to cross the stream, Gough felt comfortable he could successfully complete the operation in reasonable time; plans were therefore formulated for a second attack on the Sikh position. What was becoming quite clear, however, was that Shere Singh had dug in well at a most suitable location, with the river and its sandy adjacent areas preventing the British heavy guns from being hauled too close. Given that all the boats in the vicinity were on the right bank in the hands of the Sikh army as well, and that wading across the Chenab in a full-frontal assault would be disastrous, the options for Gough were limited to attempting a crossing up or downstream at a suitable location and attacking the Sikh position from the flank.

No nearby fords practical enough existed downstream but upstream there were three in close proximity. Gough had already ordered a survey of these locations, but as would be shown later this information was entirely untrustworthy; the quartermaster whose job it should have been to carry out the surveys was apparently too ill, and the persons delegated to do the job had done it hurriedly and without due attention, with Sikh troops and snipers on the left bank disrupting any comprehensive reconnaissance.

They reported that the nearest ford was at Ghurree Ke-Puttan, 10 km away, but it was known to be guarded by around 4,000 Sikh troops. Further upstream were the two other fords, Runnee Ke-Puttan, and Allee Shere Ke-Chuck, both around 10 km further on. Then there was the ford at the town of Wazirabad, 35 km up from Ramnuggar. There were boats there as well, for John Nicholson had already occupied the town with some irregulars and had accumulated seventeen boats by this time. The disadvantage in crossing at Wazirabad was the distance, a round journey of some 70 km to reach the Sikh camp on the right bank would take several days, giving Shere Singh plenty of time to respond.

Opinions were divided among the British officers at Ramnuggar. Some, including Thackwell, were of the view a full-frontal assault should still be attempted despite the attendant risks. Only four European infantry regiments were available. Splitting these and the British force by sending a contingent upstream would leave the weakened remaining force at Ramnuggar exposed to a counterattack across the river by Shere Singh. Perhaps a night attack across the river would surprise the Sikh army and nullify much of the defenders' advantage, he argued. Gough, however, would still plump for crossing the river upstream. The plan would be for a strong contingent to cross over at one of the fords, march down the other bank and outflank the Sikh line while Gough simultaneously launched a cannonade and feinted a crossing himself to tie up the bulk of the Sikh army. Both Campbell and Thackwell voiced their apprehensions about his approach again but to no avail. 'The movement,' wrote Campbell later, 'was in my view and in that of the General [Thackwell], a hazardous one, the placing of a force under 7000 in a position in which they could not be supported, and where they might be opposed by 30,000.'

A crossing at Runnee Ke-Puttan, the second ford, was deemed the most promising, the first ford being known to be guarded although the force was to confirm this and cross at the first ford if possible. If a crossing was not possible at all three fords, the force was to proceed to Wazirabad despite the delay it would cause, crossing and reaching the Sikh position in no more than two days, during which time the British heavy guns would make plenty of noise to keep Shere Singh distracted. On 30 November the last remnants of the siege train headed by Brig. Penny arrived in Gough's camp. Strung out along the road, innumerable carriages, wagons, hackeries and guns pulled by elephants continued to stream in for a large portion of the day. These heavy guns were immediately added to the batteries already pointed at the right bank and readied to pummel the Sikh position once the contingent on the right bank attacked. 'The batteries, when they open their fire, if allowed fair play, will open Shere Singh's eyes, we apprehend. In the trenches he may have seen such, but not very probably in the field,' commented the correspondent of the *Delhi Gazette*.

***

Gough chose Thackwell himself to lead the flanking contingent, comprised of HM 24th and HM 61st along with five native infantry regiments. Along with this was to come a considerable amount of cavalry including the 3rd Light Dragoons, the 5th and 8th Light Cavalry and the 3rd and 12th Irregulars. In terms of artillery there would be three troops of horse artillery (those of Christie, Huish and Warner) and two light field batteries (Austin and Kindleside) and two 18-pounders under Capt. Robinson pulled by elephants. The whole force was to total around 7,000 men. To achieve an element of surprise, the force would move that very night with the minimum of fuss and noise. Thackwell was also provided with the cumbersome pontoon bridge that had just arrived a few hours earlier, along with two companies of pioneers in case a ford could not be used for some reason. Also accompanying the force were the scouts who had done the reconnaissance of the fords earlier and who were assumed to be competent enough to guide the force. The commissariat were told only two days' rations were to be provided for this force, but no tent or bivouac equipment or other supplies. Unencumbered by baggage, it was thought this force could then move much more swiftly and covertly. The departure time was set at 1 a.m. on the night of the 30th. If surprise could be kept, Thackwell, Gough speculated, could reach a ford and be on the right bank before daylight and therefore an attack on the Sikh camp on the afternoon of the next day was a good possibility.

In the event, the departure time was not adhered to and the march was neither swift nor quiet. All campfires had been ordered to be extinguished so as not to draw attention to the move but this caused much confusion as thousands of troops and camp followers stumbled around in the pitch dark, making preparations and searching for their positions.

'We had our rations for the following day cooked in the night of 30th November, and on the 1st December at 1 o'clock we fell in without sound of bugle or noise, in order to deceive the enemy, but all our precautions was useless, for the affair was fully explained to Shere Singh by a native writer in our employ. I believe the villain has since been hung, at least I hope so,' described H. Plumb of HM 24th in a private letter. Despite the order for little or no baggage, several hundred camels still had to be readied to carry the necessary ammunition. These camels bellowed loudly as they were readied for the move and the camp followers accompanying the force also made much din, impervious to any calls to keep the noise to a minimum.

The rendezvous point for the units departing was the right flank of the British line. However, in the dark it proved difficult to organise among the labyrinth of tents and wagons. Campbell's infantry force only reached their point at 3 a.m. and it was only at around 3.30 a.m. that the column began to move. By this time the first light of the new day was ready to approach, and much of the tail of the column would be seen from across the river by Sikh pickets as they made their way out of the camp. 'We commenced our march amid the most distracting sounds,' recalled a soldier in the column, silence in the camp being conspicuously absent to the end.

***

While sound on paper, the plan to cross one of the fords proved to be anything but straightforward in practice. On the issue of the route to use it had been decided not to march down the direct road from Ramnuggar to Wazirabad due to the fact that it ran close and parallel to the river and was visible to the Sikh pickets on the right bank. Rather than the road, then, the column was to trudge through the softer ploughed (occasionally broken) ground 3 km east of the river. This naturally had the effect of greatly slowing down progress. The procedure to be followed was to check each ford to see if it could be used for a crossing and whether or not a Sikh detachment guarded the opposite bank. Locating a ford during the day was easy. Finding it in the pitch dark of the night without the use of torches was a different issue. The Chenab River between Ramnuggar and Wazirabad divides itself into several channels separated by as much as 2 or 3 km of sandbanks and treacherous quicksand. The column, when it reached each ford, would have to wait for the scouts to travel carefully through to the riverbank to see if the ford was practicable and not guarded before returning with the same care to report back. All this took time and caused delay. 'That these fords were not subjected to a minute scrutiny, in which the highest authorities should have actively participated, was afterwards deeply lamented,' Thackwell would comment later. Obscured by darkness, Ghurree Ke-Puttan, the nearest ford, was not even discovered despite attempts to locate it consuming several hours. The single main cause of slow progress, however, was the pontoon bridge being brought along in case the fords proved unfeasible. Due to its weight and size, this equipment was hauled at a very slow and stately pace and frequent stops had to be ordered as the troops outmarched the elephants pulling the equipment. In the darkness the cavalry made more ground and moved on, with two brigades of infantry going astray for a while and unable to find the tracks of the cavalry. As daylight came, all the confusion disappeared and the force moved as one.

The second ford at Runnee Ke-Puttan was finally reached at 1 p.m. but it was noticed Sikh troops guarded the other bank here as well. In any case the local villagers told the British force the ford here was much deeper than the next one at Allee Shere Ke-Chuck a couple of kilometres further although the water there was swifter so any thoughts of crossing at Runnee Ke-Puttan were abandoned as well. Thackwell and his staff personally accompanied the scouts to the riverbank at the third ford and found a similar situation as at the previous ford. 'The sand, through which the guns must pass, was very deep and heavy, and that the bullocks with the pontoon train would certainly not be able to drag the pontoons through it; and as he [the scout] had not tried the ford personally, he could not tell whether the bottom of the ford was firm enough to bear horses. The enemy, moreover, were on the opposite side, ready to oppose our passage, and in such cover as to make it difficult for our guns to drive them from it,' wrote Brig.-Gen. Campbell. There also looked to be quicksand close to the other bank. Not wishing to go all the way to Wazirabad and hoping a forced crossing could still be made, Thackwell ordered a comprehensive survey of the area but to no avail. The channels of the river made it difficult to judge whether a crossing was practical, although the water was breast-high, as one of the Engineers found. The guns could not be dragged through water greater than 4 feet in depth in safety, though, and neither could a pontoon bridge be used as it was too short to bridge even one of the streams. The area was also too sandy to secure the bridge at this point. Neither would the British guns on the left bank be able to fire on the right bank to protect a crossing as it was too far.

Things weren't going too well and Campbell, Thackwell's second-in-command recommended a return to the British camp. His reasoning was sound. A lengthy journey to Wazirabad, 20 km further up, would tire out the troops always assuming that ford wasn't watched as well. In any case the two day provisions provided, it was clear now, were simply not enough for a further march upstream and then downstream on the other bank. Thackwell, though, was firm on attempting the crossing and was confident all would go well. Nicholson had boats available and the ford at the town was known to be only around 4 feet with a hard bottom. The order was given and the column resumed its march again, the advance units finally reaching Wazirabad around 5 p.m.

Fortune began favouring Thackwell at this point. In a cardinal error, Shere Singh's pickets had neglected to travel this far upstream to watch this ford and there was no one to contest the crossing. The time of arrival, however, meant hazarding a night crossing, which was immediately commenced at 8 p.m., Thackwell deciding to benefit from the ample moonlight and a cloudless sky. Some of Nicholson's Pathans were ferried over first to ensure no enemies were on the opposite bank. Once word was received the coast was clear, the ford was assessed. It was found it stretched over three streams of the river but was around 4 feet 10 inches in depth only and could be comfortably crossed, although the final stream was more treacherous. A false step, a few feet to either left or right, and the depth plunged several feet deeper without warning. A narrow margin safe to wade through was therefore marked by stakes in the riverbed to reduce casualties.

Eckford's brigade was ordered across first to establish a bridgehead but failed. Having waded through the first and second streams successfully, they found the third to be too deep, with the stakes marking the way invisible. They therefore returned to a large sandbank between the second and third streams. This caused some confusion, especially since some commotion was now heard on the right bank. 'Just before this a zumboork was fired on the right bank,' Daniel Bamfield of the 56th NI wrote, 'but at some distance, and we did not think anything of it; but the portion of the Brigade which was still on the sand-bank, seeing us coming back, without knowing the reason, and having heard the zumboork, concluded that we had been driven back by the enemy, and many of them loaded. One or two fired in the air, but in our direction, and we heard the shot whirl above us.'

At this point more of the British line had also reached the sandbank and rather than the tired troops who had been eighteen hours in the saddle and who badly needed a rest attempting another crossing, Thackwell decided instead to bivouac on the sandbank and wait till the safety of daylight. Meanwhile the transport of the guns was effected using the boats after which some troops continued to be ferried across.

It was a cold and uncomfortable night in the middle of the river without covering or food, all the supplies still on the left bank. The severe cold and biting wind on this day forced the British detachment on the sand bank to dig holes in the sandy ground for some protection. There was no fuel for fire and in any case any light was forbidden to avoid making their presence known to Sikh pickets downstream. Sentries were placed around the bridgehead as the force was vulnerable with all the ammunition still on the left bank. Fortunately for Thackwell, no Sikh units would ever proceed to Wazirabad. Conditions for the other half of the force still remaining on the left bank were much more comfortable however with baggage and food available.

As the sun rose the next day, the crossing was resumed with the additional safety of daylight and all troops and supplies had crossed by 2 p.m. The crossing at night had taken its toll, though; three cavalrymen and four horses, along with several camp followers and a syce, had been drowned or swept away in the dark. Thackwell sent word to Gough that the force had crossed successfully, but, noticing the troops were still weary, would allow the rest of the day for recuperation, a battle being expected once the southward march was commenced. At this time the pontoon bridge, which had proved no help but much hindrance, was despatched back to the British camp at Ramnuggar with an escort of 12th Irregular Cavalry, two guns of No. 10 Light Field Battery, two companies of native infantry troops and the two 18-pounders.

On 2 December, what little food remained was consumed before the advance downstream was commenced at 6 a.m. in order of battle. The three brigades marched in columns of companies, half-distances left in front at deploying intervals. The 1st Brigade of Cavalry commanded by White and positioned on the right, and the 3rd Irregular Cavalry on the left. There were strong flanking parties and a rearguard. In front of the infantry were the skirmishers. A patrol between the river and the left of the force was kept to keep a steady distance and allow communication between any British forces marching up on the opposite bank to assist or to communicate.

It was a hot day and the marching was correspondingly slow, ensuring Thackwell never reached the Sikh camp that day as planned. By sunset only the village of Doorewal had been reached, 12 km south of Wazirabad but still around 20 km short of the Sikh camp. Camp was set up at the village and it was here sometime during the night that a shutur sowar (camel driver) arrived with a message from Gough informing Thackwell that an attack must be made the following day at the latest. Gough reiterated that Thackwell's guns opening up would be the signal for the heavy guns in the main camp to begin their fire simultaneously. Interestingly, the message also included the news that a British crossing opposite the main Sikh camp might be attempted at the same time as Thackwell attacked, some sort of secret financial arrangement with the boatmen at Ramnuggar on the right bank having been made. These men used to ferry Sikh skirmishers and cavalry across to the left bank but would now defect to the British and assist in crossing a British force, he explained. Not only that, but according to Thackwell Gough had been 'led to entertain every expectation that certain of the Sikh regiments, the Poorbeahs [Hindu sepoys from outside the Punjab] corrupted by the influence of British gold would come over to us immediately on the opening of our artillery'. With the sepoy regiments switching sides at the commencement of battle, it was hoped that a joint attack by himself and Thackwell would cause confusion in the Sikh ranks and a quick victory. 'It is much more probable that, as the event proved, the Commander-in-Chief had been duped,' wrote James Lawrence-Archer of HM 24th, later a chronicler of the war. Certainly no mass defection took place, and it was suggested later that the offer of the boatmen and sepoy regiments may have been a trick in itself by Shere Singh to lure the British infantry and cavalry into the sandy wastes by the riverbank again with no means of crossing.

British knowledge of the right bank of the Chenab and surrounding area was minimal, and Thackwell simply followed the river to his left, knowing he would hit the Sikh camp soon. At around 11 a.m., a rest was ordered and sixty rounds of ammunition supplied along with some spirits in preparation for battle. Shortly afterwards the village of Langay was reached. A long march with no food meant the troops were exceedingly hungry by this time, so much so that an officer's horse was roasted and consumed by the men of HM 61st within half an hour of its death. As they marched downstream, however, they saw well-cultivated country with fields of turnips and sugar cane. These were instantly raided by the hungry troops, which prompted the locals, worried about their crops being ravaged and their villages looted, to deliver a plea to Thackwell. They presented a nuzzur and asked if he could stop the crops being destroyed, a request to which Thackwell readily agreed, posting guards around the fields.

It was at this juncture that a messenger appeared, bringing a second letter from Gough ordering him to halt at the Ghurree Ke-Puttan ford further on where reinforcements commanded

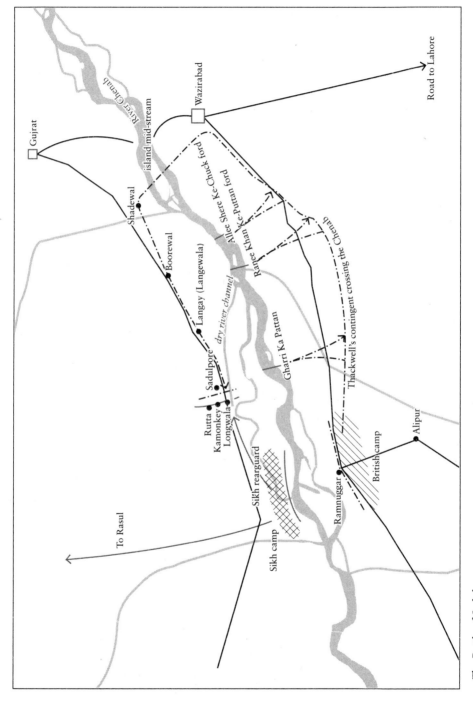

7. The Battle of Sadulpore

by Godby were to cross. Godby's contingent consisted of the 1st and 6th Light Cavalry as well as 14th Dragoons and 16th Lancers with the 2nd European Regiment and the 70th and 45th NI, which would add considerably to Thackwell's strength. On no condition, Gough stressed, should Thackwell advance and attack the Sikh camp prior to this junction of troops. The fact that Thackwell's force had no provisions left hadn't been lost on Gough and Godby's role was not just to strengthen Thackwell but to transport ammunition and food. Once Godby had reinforced him, Thackwell was given 'discretionary powers to attack any portion of the Sikh force sent to oppose him' as the situation demanded. With this in mind Thackwell therefore began advancing his line towards the vicinity of the ford where Godby was expected to cross.

\*\*\*

Unbeknown to both Gough and Thackwell, Shere Singh had already decided on abandoning his position as soon as word was brought on 2 December that Thackwell's contingent had managed to cross the river at Wazirabad. The camp was ordered to be packed in absolute silence, no hint of movement being seen in the British camp opposite. The guns facing the British position were to be held on the bank till the last minute. Rather than using his superior numbers to destroy Thackwell's force as Thackwell had feared, he retreated towards the Jhelum and thus lost the opportunity provided by the divided British force. A rearguard was organised to be sent against Thackwell headed by one of his senior officers, Ram Singh. This was moved off early on 3 December with up to 10,000 men while the move by the bulk of his forces and baggage towards the Jhelum was set in motion.

Opposite him on the left bank, Gough, expecting Thackwell's arrival at the Sikh left flank at around 3 p.m., had ordered all preparations for a forced crossing if possible with all regiments being given the facilities to spike the guns on the opposite bank. Ten spikes were issued with two hammers per troop per company. A cannonade was begun to distract the Sikh gunners as planned and the British big guns began opening up on the Sikh camp, prompting a duel which went on for most of the day. 'I directed a heavy cannonade to commence upon the enemy's batteries and encampment at Ramnuggar which was returned by only a few guns which guarded effectually the ford but were so buried that although the practice of our artillery was admirable under Major Mowatt and Captain Sir Richmond Shakespear we could not from the width of the river silence them,' Gough described in his despatch.

Unknown to Gough at this point, Shere Singh's forces had already retreated a distance of around 5 km from the riverbank and the British shells were hitting an almost empty camp, causing little damage. The few Sikh guns still stationed along the line and not readied for the move responded, however, and a British ammunition wagon was known to have been hit, causing a violent explosion.

\*\*\*

Thackwell, meanwhile, oblivious to Shere Singh's retreat and his sending a rearguard northwards to protect his move, reached the vicinity of the ford where Godby was to cross around noon. A small hamlet called Asad-Ullah-Pur (in accounts by European soldiers and officers alike invariably corrupted to Sadulpore) lay several km from the ford and Thackwell called a halt here to wait for Godby. The bulk of the British troops now took the opportunity to rest. To check on Godby's progress, Thackwell personally went up to the ford but could see no trace of British troops on the opposite bank attempting a crossing. In fact Godby would only manage to join him after the end of hostilities on that day. Similar to Thackwell, he had problems finding the ford and once found spent too much time in what proved to be an awkward crossing.

In front of where Thackwell had paused his advance at Sadulpore could be seen three more hamlets. These were the villages of Longwala, Kamookhail (Kamoke) and Rutee (Rutta), almost directly in line with each other and about 3 km away and largely surrounded by sugar cane fields. Some of the British pickets and skirmishers had already advanced to these villages and occupied them. But it wasn't long after these villages had been occupied that the Sikh contingent under Ram Singh could be discerned in the distance, having advanced the 10 km or so from the Sikh camp. Seeing the British skirmishers in the hamlets, the Sikh commander advanced with the intention of driving out the occupiers; a shell bursting in mid-air from the Sikh guns followed by round shot aimed at one of the villages brought the advance of the Sikh contingent to the attention of the British soldiers at Sadulpore. 'Some two hours passed over, when the camp-followers were seen running in great fright and immediately afterwards followed the report of artillery, the shot of which came near our columns,' recalled Colin Campbell.

This was around 2 p.m. and reports also came of advanced units of the 5th Light Cavalry being opened on by Sikh guns. The sudden appearance of the Sikh column came as a surprise to Thackwell, who had not been flagged by any of the British pickets as he was busy himself at the riverbank, anxiously scouring the other side for signs of Godby's reinforcements. At this time his force was unready for a fight, with the horses of much of the British cavalry being unharnessed and taken to the village wells nearby for watering while most of the British troops had found themselves shady places to sleep, others busying themselves washing their faces and hands after the dusty march. Campbell, with Thackwell not around, immediately rode forward towards the villages to scout the advancing Sikh line and promptly decided to send a company of infantry to each of the three hamlets to consolidate the British hold on them before they fell to Ram Singh. As this movement was happening, however, Thackwell galloped back from the ford and countermanded Campbell's order. He immediately ordered the garrisons of the three villages and all skirmishers back to the British line at Sadulpore, deciding this would be a much better position from which to form a line. Also crossing his mind were Gough's strict orders not to engage till Godby crossed. Continuing to man the three villages would have meant an immediate battle, whereas pulling back the line would allow Godby to cross in time if he was close. 'We retired accordingly in very perfect order; and, while free from the effects of musketry-fire from the sugar-fields, we obtained a beautiful open space, as smooth as a bowling-green, between us and the villages, so that if the enemy had advanced to attack us, as we had expected they would, we had an open plain, on which to advance and attack them while debouching from the openings between the villages,' recorded Campbell.

The main British line was pulled back a few hundred paces further as well. This was because the three villages had large sugar cane fields to their front, circular in form, which Thackwell realised was perfect cover for Sikh infantry, whose muskets would be in range if the present British line held its position.

With Godby still nowhere to be seen, Thackwell made preparations for a defensive battle although it was clear neither the whole Sikh army nor all the Sikh guns were present. The infantry was told to lie down flat to minimise casualties while the guns were organised to play ball.

Thackwell would post the 3rd Dragoons, 8th Cavalry and Major Christie's troops of horse artillery on the British right flank. To their left would be Eckford's and Hoggan's brigades, extended much further than normal to avoid any outflanking, with Huish's troop of horse artillery along with the two field batteries, No. 5 under Capt. Kinleside and four guns of No. 10 under Captain

Austin. On the British left were stationed Capt. Warner's troop of horse artillery, 3rd Irregular Cavalry and the 5th Light Cavalry. Brig. White, commanding the cavalry on the right, was ordered by Thackwell to retire in echelon so that the British right bent back towards the centre.

By the time the British line had been organised, Ram Singh had occupied the three hamlets opposite with infantry and Gorcharas could clearly be seen appearing on both his flanks, the bulk of them being on the Sikh left in order to outflank the British line. Shere Singh had, it was clear, sent around twenty to twenty-four guns with some 18-pounders, pretty much his entire artillery. On the Sikh right were placed around 600 cavalry that now hovered near the ford, making any potential crossing by Godby difficult. Thackwell as a countermeasure sent a wing of the 56th NI and two risallahs of the 3rd Irregular Cavalry under Major Tait towards the ford area.

At around 2–2.30 p.m. the Sikh line would commence fire for about an hour, some combatants suggesting as much as two or three hours, with battle drums and tomtoms sounding, but Thackwell declined to do the same initially; Lt-Col C. Grant, commanding the British artillery, opened up much later, with the cannonade continuing till sunset. 'At length after about two hours of this tedious sermon with such weighty arguments, our half dozen batteries opened fire, it being apparent that the Sikhs would not break cover, and I for one was much more comfortable when I felt we were returning with interest the compliments paid to us by our lively friends across the plain. Some of the enemy's spent shot, of about 6lbs weight, came slowly dribbling along the ground like cricket balls and to all appearance as harmless, A man of our "eleven" stupidly attempted to stop one with his foot, but crushing was the shock,' described Lt-Col Andrew John Macpherson.

The object of the Sikh rearguard being to cover the withdrawal, there was no real attempt by Ram Singh to advance further, apart from some half-hearted attacks or feints on both wings by the Gorcharas. On the British right, the 8th Light Cavalry and 3rd Light Dragoons along with Major Christie's troop of horse artillery kept them at bay. Meanwhile, on the left, Capt. Warner's troop of artillery was sent to the left of the line along with the 5th Light Cavalry to aid the 3rd Irregular Cavalry in response to the Sikh cavalry making moves in this direction. On both flanks there were obstacles which hindered charge or counter-charge. A large nullah on the Sikh right made things difficult while on the other flank, fields of sugar cane provided an effective block in various areas.

With both lines failing to advance things were very much at a stalemate, and as the hours ticked by Campbell would recommend to Thackwell retreating still further back. This, he argued, would lure the Sikh line into advancing and would mean Ram Singh abandoning the villages to move forward. This way, if a British attack was swiftly executed the Sikh line could be attacked without the British force having to storm the villages, which would prove much more costly otherwise. Thackwell would reject Campbell's advice, still being preoccupied with Gough's orders to wait under all circumstances for Godby to cross before taking the initiative. According to Campbell's journals, written later, he had recommended an advance twice. Sir William Napier in *The Life Sir Charles Napier* even suggested the idea was argued by Campbell no fewer than three times, something that Thackwell denied. 'The assertion that Campbell three times begged for leave to advance and take them (the guns), and then to charge (which I never heard of before), is totally unfounded in fact, for he never made any proposal to advance from the position which had been taken up by the infantry, &c,' Thackwell would reply in a letter to the author in 1857. However, Campbell stuck by his story, later describing it as a 'lost opportunity'. Pennycuick too thought the idea of a retreat followed by an advance was sound but the bulk of Thackwell's officers sided with the general. The main reason was that he had only two European regiments in the line (the rest being native infantry), which was thought insufficient a number to provide a reasonable chance of success. In addition, a considerable amount of his force was tied up in protecting the baggage which was still streaming in slowly behind the line even as the battle was taking place. The sun was setting, the gloominess increasing. With a long march prior to hostilities and the soldiers going hungry, the majority felt an advance was not appropriate.

The exchange of gunfire continued in desultory fashion, and would last till around 9 p.m. when Ram Singh retired with his force and followed the main Sikh army's path west. Thackwell in turn threw out pickets in advance of the line, with the troops told to return to their rest and sleep, quilts being distributed and camp made now that most of the baggage had arrived. Food was still not forthcoming, Godby's crossing still not having taken place. The troops made the best of the situation, with the meat of the horses killed and wounded being put to use. It was only around the time the horsemeat had been cooked and was being distributed around that shouts and cries could be heard emanating from the direction of the ford. Godby's men were finally making their way across the ford.

Godby had originally been sent on his way at 11 a.m. the same day but experienced severe problems crossing the river. News having reached the camp that Thackwell was at Ghurree Ke-Puttan, he had made straight for that ford. However, it had taken three hours to reach this position and as his brigade reached the ford at 2 p.m. the fighting had commenced and the guns could clearly be heard. The crossing was a messy, drawn-out affair, Godby facing problems similar to those Thackwell faced during his attempted crossings. Heavy carts had to be dragged over a half a mile or so of heavy sand before reaching the water. Once at the river the problems didn't stop, the pontoon bridge having its own awkward issues. After the rafts on which the bridge would rest were constructed, it was found the flow of water was too powerful for their anchors to hold them in position. Not only that but not enough anchors had been brought. Finding the bridge to be a complete loss, Godby decided on sending part of his contingent, the 14th Dragoons, back to Gough instead. Eventually, at 5 p.m. the force attempted to ferry themselves over on the rafts made for the bridge. Each raft held only twenty-five men at most, and in fast-flowing water it was slow work. By 8 p.m. only the 2nd European Regiment had crossed, with the native infantry regiments still yet to cross. The crossing being more dangerous and even slower in the dark, Godby decided to bivouac as the situation stood so half the troops joined Thackwell's force that night while the rest of his troops, principally the 70th and 45th NI, remained on the left bank to cross the next day. Fortunately for Godby, some of the boats Nicholson had at Wazirabad had been sent downstream and these now aided the crossing during the following morning. While Godby's force had been of no help to Thackwell during the skirmish, what it did do was provide him with much-needed ammunition and plentiful supplies of food.

***

Further evidence that not just Ram Singh's rearguard but the whole of the Sikh army had moved off came around midnight as a large flash and explosion was seen in the former Sikh camp both from Thackwell's camp and the main British camp on the left bank. 'The report of the explosion made the ground shake under our feet. It was like a salvo of six 24-Pounders,' recalled a newspaper correspondent with the army. This was the blowing up of the magazines in the Sikh camp by the last few Sikh troops as they left. There wasn't sufficient time to destroy the sixty-odd boats that were in the possession of the Sikh army and which were later found to be full of ammunition. These would be put to use by the British force during their crossing. By the time Thackwell's force has settled down at Sadulpore for the night Shere Singh had moved his force around 16 km inland, camping himself at the village of Jalalpore before moving on to Dinghi the next day and then heading for Rasul the day after.

***

There had been relatively few casualties on either side in the encounter. With the sugar cane field conspiring to prevent the infantry of both sides meeting, the contest was largely one of artillery. British casualties were twenty-one killed and fifty-two wounded, with forty-eight horses killed and wounded also. Most of the losses, not unexpectedly, were taken by the artillery. Three officers were among those wounded, with Capt. Austin severely wounded. The first casualty on the British side had occurred with one of the first shots fired at the British line. A sergeant laying down to rest was seen rising to his elbows to see what the commotion was about when he was seen to be hit directly in the face by a round shot, with his brains and blood staining the standard he had beside him. A horseman close to Thackwell himself had been shot through the head. A British cavalry officer was seen to have had a close escape as a round shot grazed his horse's nose, causing the horse to throw him off, but the officer was not injured badly.

Figures of Sikh casualties given tend to be impossibly high, with some speculating on as many as 1,500, although most likely they suffered similar casualties of the British. The dead were difficult to count, their comrades having thrown the corpses into the wells in the three hamlets to deny the water to the British as the Sikh line retired. 'They pretend that we have gained a great victory, but that is all nonsense. I do not believe that the Sikhs really lost more than fifty or sixty men, killed and wounded, on the 3rd of December,' Capt. Ouvry of the 3rd Light Dragoons, present at the battlefield, would opine.

***

Sadulpore was claimed as a success by both sides despite being a restrained affair. The rearguard action by Ram Singh had allowed Shere Singh to extricate his forces successfully and move towards the Jhelum River in good order without being harassed by Thackwell. Moving due west, he would set up his new camp on the left bank of the stream, close to the village of Chillianwala. On the British side, the operation had allowed a British force to cross the river with impunity although the plan to attack Shere Singh across the river in concert with Thackwell never materialised, leading to some disappointment in the British camp. Although complimentary towards Thackwell in his despatches, Gough wasn't entirely happy with his failure to exploit the situation by chasing Shere Singh's rearguard. Thackwell would later counter that he had never been given the remit to do so, having been told to wait for Godby's reinforcements before going on any offensive. Gough's despatch was nonetheless as optimistic as the one after Ramnuggar, describing the largely artillery encounter as a great victory. Magnifying Shere Singh's force to 30,000 to 40,000 men, he wrote,

> It has pleased God to vouchsafe to the British army the most successful issue to the
> extensive combinations rendered necessary for the purpose of effecting the passage
> of the Chenab, the defeat and dispersion of the Sikh force under the insurgent Rajah
> Sher Singh … The Sikhs it appears retreated in greatest disorder leaving in the villages
> numerous wounded men. They have subdivided into three divisions which have become
> more a flight than a retreat; and I understand a great portion of those not belonging to the

revolted Khalsa army have and returned to their homes thus I trust effectually frustrating the views of the rebel Shere Singh and his rebel associates.

Thackwell's more realistic despatch of events was sent by Gough to Dalhousie but was not made public until after Chillianwala. Gough's reason for delaying this report, he later stated, was that it mentioned a civilian, a volunteer by the name of Mr John Angelo, something military despatches were not supposed to do and which was regarded as a glaring informality in a military despatch.

Despite giving the skirmish a more respectable sheen than necessary, this inconclusive action, following on from Ramnuggar, had the effect of only increasing the level of criticism against the Commander-in-Chief. The *Bombay Times* more or less charged Gough with suppressing the real story with his more colourful despatches:

> The manoeuvres ultimately resorted to, showed with how small a measure of tactical skill victory without loss might have been insured; but for an uninterrupted series of blunders. Thackwell might have got into the rear of the enemy on the 2nd, with his force still fresh, while Godby and Penny were on their flanks, and our heavy batteries commanded their position in front. They might in this case have been cannonaded on all sides, and almost extinguished on the spot; as it is, they have escaped to their mountains to wear us out by a Guerilla war.

On hearing the news Dalhousie was content with the result, ending as it did with a successful crossing. 'It gives us the whole rechna and jech doab and will dispirit Shere Singh's irregular troops, who under the combined influence of retreat and a treasury at very low ebb will leave him in great numbers,' he ventured to predict to Hobhouse, for it had been heard Shere Singh was already having trouble raising sufficient funds. However a disagreement with Gough was again evident on the definition of victory. The Commander-in-Chief, being anxious to gain credit for another success, had asked for a royal salute to be fired from all British stations around the country again. The Governor-General saw it for what it was, a skirmish without a result.

'The Commander-in-Chief is vexed and angry with me because I would not fire a royal salute for this,' he confided with the Duke of Wellington on 22 December. 'I told him frankly I could not call this a victory. The turning of the position and crossing the Chenab with almost no loss was an important step gained, but it was not to be called a victory for which one would fire a royal salute. The Commander-in-Chief says the enemy lost eight guns: very likely they did lose them, but we have not found them, nor yet our own gun which they seized on 22nd November.'

Back on the left bank of the Chenab, the huge explosion caused by the exploding of the Sikh magazines had the effect of inducing Gough to ride to the riverbank with officers on the night of the 3rd to ascertain what was happening on the opposite bank. A Capt. Robbins was sent over to the other side and found the Sikh entrenchments entirely empty, confirming the Sikh army's move. With this news, another party was sent across headed by his chief engineer, Major Tremenheere, along with others. That night a crossing was ordered to be marked out in the river, long bamboos being used to mark a safe passage in the riverbed. While this was being done, an elephant was spotted approaching from the other side with four men. It turned out these men were traders, and they confirmed that the Sikh army had indeed moved off in its entirety towards Jalalpore.

With a crossing marked by dawn the next day, Major-General Sir Walter Gilbert would cross over with the 9th Lancers and 14th Light Dragoons along with some horse artillery to take possession of the old Sikh camp while a permanent bridge was ordered to be built to facilitate the crossing for the rest of the force and the heavy guns. Few if any trophies were found in the abandoned Sikh camp by the party that had crossed, just a wounded young elephant. What was found was that the water supply from the wells in the former Sikh camp were tainted with gunpowder and other pollutants to make them unusable by the new occupants.

Gough crossed to the right bank the same day, riding to Sadulpore to meet Thackwell, and expressed much surprise. 'Why, where are your guns?' he asked, referring to the plentiful captured Sikh guns he had hoped to see. Disappointed that none had been taken, but with news that the Sikh rearguard under Ram Singh was still not far off, Gough determined on making the most of the situation. Orders were immediately given to both Gilbert, with the 9th Lancers and 14th Light Dragoons, and Thackwell, reinforced as he was now with Godby's contingent, to pursue the Sikh army as far as possible and to cut off stragglers. Moving along the Jalalpore road the same day, Thackwell therefore shadowed the Sikh rearguard, following as far as Heylah, 20 km from Sadulpore, where he set up camp. Beyond Heylah, a thick belt of jungle that stretched all the way to Chillianwala and Rasul began and Thackwell considered it imprudent to continue into an area where his force could be surprised.

Heylah would prove a good advance camp; the village itself was surrounded by largely uncultivated ground, with a gap between the village and the jungle to the west. The cavalry bivouacked in the village while the infantry set up camp 8 km further behind. They had outstripped the baggage, however, and an uncomfortable time was spent during the two nights before the baggage arrived. By 8 December, more of the British infantry had begun making its way to Heylah as well.

There would be several spells of heavy rain during the middle of the month between 7 and 18 December, the downpour on the night of the 18th and continuing the following day being particularly violent. Such was the ferocity of the rain, the troops were seen using umbrellas inside their tents. The weather, while it slowed down movement, had the effect of lowering the ambient temperatures for the following days, making life more comfortable.

Gough meanwhile had crossed back to the left bank of the Chenab in order to organise the crossing of the bulk of his force, only crossing to the right bank on 18 December before visiting Heylah on 22 December. The heavy guns were laboriously transported across the Chenab on boats, reaching the right bank by the 10th. Then began the process of hauling them towards Heylah. The pontoon bridge that both Thackwell and Godby had rejected was finally laid across the Chenab but continued to be dogged with misfortune. It proved not long enough even at a narrow point of the river and had to be completed with four country boats and trestles. On 10 December, due to the heavy rains on the 8th and 9th, the level of the Chenab increased by 18 inches, which damaged the trestles on the country boat side. Only when the level of the river returned to normal levels a few days later was the damage repaired and new boats substituted. Meanwhile, a more permanent bridge of boats had already been ordered a mile upstream and would be finished shortly, at which point the pontoon bridge was finally retired to everybody's relief.

'These pontoons are at present quite useless and only an encumbrance to the army not to mention the immense cost of carrying them about,' one of the soldiers at Ramnuggar commented in a letter printed later in the *Delhi Gazette* on this unforeseen handicap, 'They are too few in number to span any of the rivers of this country the Ravee perhaps excepted … The number of the pontoons also should be increased; they should be sufficient to form a bridge at least 250 yards long. Unless such or similar improvements be made it would be much better in every way to send the pontoons into store and trust entirely to the boats of the country.'

# 27

# The Afghan Jihad

It is extraordinary how very prevalent in every quarter is the statement that the
Barukzyes [Afghan ruling family] have seized Chuttur Sing and detained him
at Peshawur.
Frederick Currie to Dalhousie, December 1848

Whenever the British feel inclined I will put an end to the feud subsisting between them
and the Sikhs and make them friends again.
Dost Mohammad, December 1848

The inconclusive exchanges at Ramnuggar and Sadulpore meant that as December progressed
and the new year approached, Gough had still not managed to destroy or even get to grips
with Shere Singh's force in a meaningful way despite being a march or two away at most for
more than a month. Meanwhile, at Multan the second siege of the city was still awaited, with
the Bombay troops making their way up. Therefore Whish's force too was largely whiling away
much of December waiting for the arrival of these reinforcements. During this time, though,
negotiations between Chutter Singh and Dost Mohammad were occurring in Peshawar; the
result would be the entry of the Afghan army into the Punjab, ostensibly to assist the Sikh army
while at the same time allowing Chutter Singh to reinforce his son's force at Chillianwala.

At this time, the most westerly strongpoint still in British hands was the fortress of Attock
on the banks of the Indus controlling the route from Peshawar to Rawalpindi and Lahore. The
fortress was held by Lt Herbert who had been deputised to hold it by John Nicholson while
he helped assist James Abbott against Chutter Singh in Hazara. The citadel was easy to defend
for an indefinite period of time given a good garrison and supplies. These Herbert had, with
the contingent of Pathans and Afghans inherited from Nicholson. Currie had asked Herbert
to hold the fortress for as long as possible for it made any possible Afghan intervention east
of Peshawar difficult. For it was known Chutter Singh had been asking for assistance from the
Kabul ruler.

During November, realising he was alone and far away from assistance from Lahore, Herbert
had managed to extract promises from the garrison they would stay loyal to him. Solemn vows
were taken on the Quran by the men, who in turn had asked for promises of good financial
rewards and protection for their families as well. These Herbert was happy to give to secure
their fidelity. Those who remained with him, he declared, to further cement their loyalty,
would be offered batta, or financial rewards similar to those which would be given the British
troops after the war. In order to eliminate any waverers or those who might sow dissent, some
of the garrison had been ejected by Herbert. This included Futteh Khan, the commander of

the garrison himself, accused by Herbert of conspiring with the Sikh army. He also offered the artillerymen who were still in the fort the option of going with him if they didn't wish to remain.

What kept the bulk of the garrison on his side in addition to the financial inducements was the belief – incorrect, as it turned out – that a British relief force would soon be on the way to Attock since Gough's army was already crossing the Chenab after Sadulpore. Around 250 km away, a relief force sent by Gough could reach the fortress in little more than a week from his new position on the right bank of the Chenab. Therefore Herbert in turn impressed these men with the belief that they would not have to hold out for long. He knew these Pathan troops were dependable as long as they were facing the Sikh force that Chutter Singh had at his disposal, which was bereft of large siege guns. What the garrison's inclinations would be if they had to face an Afghan force, Muslims like themselves and bearing the standard of Islam, was yet to be seen. But it would soon become apparent even to the Pathans that a relief force would not be sent by either Gough, who was under orders from Dalhousie not to split his force and not to leave the area of the Chenab, nor Frederick Currie, who had only sufficient troops to hold on to Lahore and no more.

Chutter Singh had attempted to lay siege to the fortress, but with only 2,000–2,500 men and around 1,000 levies at his disposal for the task according to Herbert, his resources were insufficient to trouble the British officer in a meaningful way. With eight guns in the batteries (six being horse artillery) and including a 10-inch mortar, most of his guns were unsuitable for pounding the fortress. During the month of November, therefore, with a seemingly dependable garrison and a recognition that Chutter Singh lacked the wherewithal, Lt Herbert took an uncompromising attitude towards any overtures from the Sikh governor, who had hoped to secure the fortress before joining his son. Chutter Singh had asked the captive George Lawrence to write to Lt Herbert in the hope of avoiding hostilities.

'The sirdar has sent to me, this morning, to say, that he is most anxious to save the shedding of blood,' George Lawrence wrote. 'He even promises that you and the Nezamoodowlah Mahomed Oosman Khan, shall be conveyed in safety, at once, to Lahore. Of course, situated as I am, I can give you no orders; you must be the best judge of your own position, and the means of holding it, and will, therefore, act entirely on your own judgment.'

Herbert refused the offer, declaring in his response he would only quit if orders were received from the Resident and the Durbar. This meant a stalemate held for the next few weeks, with Chutter Singh incapable of breaking into the fortress and Herbert content to defend and being too weak to make a sally in any case. So few were the besiegers, in fact, that Herbert had no difficulty in receiving and sending letters and messages to and from Lahore during the entire period between November and December. A rather half-hearted siege therefore continued while negotiations between Chutter Singh and Dost Mohammad took place for an alliance.

As December continued, however, the chances of a Sikh–Afghan alliance grew, while the probability of any sort of British relief column receded further. Disenchantment within the garrison gradually began to grow. A daily dribble of men began deciding to desert Herbert. This was entirely natural as many of these Pathans and tribesmen had relations and brothers fighting in the Afghan army and the chance to join them for plunder and loot was a greater attraction than the fast-reducing reserves of treasure Herbert had access to for salaries. In addition, food and ammunition supplies were beginning to run low and the decreasing levels of the Indus River meant obtaining water was becoming increasingly difficult from inside the fortress.

The Sikh units outside, seeing the deserters, also began expending little time firing at the garrison in order not to alienate the defenders in the hope that all would join them soon.

'It is with great grief that I report that in consequence of the non-arrival of any succour, the tenure of the fort of Attock is becoming extremely precarious,' Herbert would warn in correspondence with Currie in Lahore on 6 December. 'Serious symptoms of insubordination have exhibited themselves among the men particularly on a month's pay becoming due when it was demanded in a most unbecoming manner. I have had great difficulty in raising a loan sufficient to disburse a month's pay to the garrison and to carry on the current expenses and I fear I shall be unable to meet a second demand of a similar nature.'

By the middle of December things were coming to a head as the new accord between Chutter Singh and Dost Mohammad became known. This agreement meant the Afghan army could be seen streaming through the Khyber Pass as they arrived to take possession of the province. 'Should the Ameer bring his force either to assist or succeed that of Sirdar Chuttur Sing, I fear it could scarcely be expected that my Puthans would remain true,' Herbert continued in his warnings.

Dost Mohammad scarcely made any haste to reinforce his new ally, however, taking time passing through Peshawar city and inadvertently buying Herbert more time. The army he had brought from Kabul was largely a rabble, said to be composed of 12,000 troops, the bulk of which were irregulars although around 3,600 were drilled troops of questionable calibre. These men had little discipline and were more consumed by thoughts of plunder. With no Sikh army units remaining in Peshawar to maintain law and order, Afghan soldiers promptly began looting as they passed through the area towards Attock. News soon began spreading of the general chaos the Afghan army was causing, and reached Chutter Singh at Attock; however, reliant as he was on Afghan assistance, he was powerless to stop his new allies running roughshod over territory that had already been signed over to them.

Meanwhile, as he marched through Peshawar the Afghan ruler himself was busy writing letters to all the local tribal chiefs declaring Peshawar a province of his domain and urging them all to ally with him. 'Therefore, looking upon my country and property as your own,' urged Dost Mohammad in an intercepted letter to a local chieftain reaching Currie in Lahore, 'hasten with all speed to my presence, for the whole of my energies of lofty aim are, with the body of the men of Islam, bent on eradicating the causes of the disturbance on the part of the English, which tends to evil.'

On the evening of 20 December a letter for the garrison at Attock arrived from Sirdar Mohammad Shureef Khan, a son of Dost Mohammad and heading the Afghan vanguard, asking them to surrender the fortress. The letter said that Chutter Singh would depart and that if there was no surrender the Afghan army would conduct the siege as from now. The garrison were called to join the jihad against the British as befitting good Muslims. Herbert probably realised the game was up at this stage but would try a desperate gambit, casting doubt on the Afghan leader's motives. Assembling the whole garrison on the parade ground and reading out the letter, he asked those who wished to leave to step forward on the assumption it would be much more difficult for them to rebel on the spot. The stratagem seemed to work and none of the garrison had the courage to openly declare their sympathies for their comrades in the Afghan army. He then asked the various officers addressed in the declaration to put their seals on an already prepared and cleverly written response.

You now write, that the Ameer Saib Dost Mahomed Khan is an aspirant for martyrdom (i.e. intends to wage a war against infidels); and you call on us to join in this holy cause. Good friend! if we could see that the Ameer Saib having devoted himself to the cause of the true faith, had come in the first instance, waged war, and fought with the race of Sikhs, who are infidels – without the Book, and worshippers of idols – and, afterwards, engaged in a contest with the English (Sahiban Angrez), it would then be evident to all that this was a war for the interests of the true faith (jehad). Be assured that we also would then range ourselves in the army of the Ameer, to fight in the true cause; but as we see with our eyes, and hear with our ears, that the Ameer Saib, actuated merely by worldly interests and motives, has entered into an alliance and friendship with the Sikhs, and from a desire of acquiring new territory, has entered into hostilities with the English; in this act, we are unable to discern how the objects of religion are to be forwarded; and we, who are the servants, and are eating the salt, of the English, – how can we desire that the Sikhs should be victorious over them? At present, hostilities are being carried on between the army of the English and of the Sikhs. If the Sikhs are defeated by the English, it is our belief that, then, the Ameer Dost Mahomed Khan himself will court the alliance and friendship of the British. If the army of the English is overcome by the Sikhs, be assured, that we, who are Mussulmans, in this garrison will deliver over the fort to the Ameer.

Openly questioning the Dost's motives would buy Herbert a few more days, at least till the main Afghan army arrived at the end of December. On 26 December, though, the Afghan vanguard suddenly appeared at Khairabad, opposite Attock, and the remaining Sikh troops and guns still stationed at Attock were pulled back ready to be sent to reinforce Shere Singh at the Jhelum. On the first day of the New Year, the bulk of Dost Mohammad's force reached the right bank of the Indus and were plainly visible from the fortress, further discouraging the defenders and they openly began espousing the Afghan cause. 'It was a war of religion, and they must join his standard,' Herbert wrote on the garrison soldier's response to his entreaties. Quite apart from that, they said, the Afghan Ameer held the wives and children of the garrison and many of their own brothers were in the Afghan army. Brother would not fight brother.

With their minds made up to open the doors, the garrison sportingly allowed him the chance to escape and suggested to Herbert that now would be the best time to flee as leaving the fort would be impossible when the bulk of the Afghan army crossed the river. He could drop over the walls and attempt to make his way to the British force at Multan by river. Herbert needed no convincing. There was no money left to bribe the garrison anymore and the baniahs (shopkeepers), who had realised which way things were going, were refusing to lend him more money. He drew up plans to flee under cover of night. Along with him in the escape party would be two other Europeans, a Corporal Carthy, one of the corps of sappers and miners who had been lent to him by Capt. Abbott, and a Sergeant Salter. They would also be accompanied by some Afghans including an Afghan chief, Nizam-u-Doulah, who had decided to stick with Herbert. He immediately sent a messenger reprising Lahore of the fall of the fortress before ordering the construction of two makeshift rafts in which to float downstream.

At around midnight on 2 January, a party of around twenty Pathans who had been a sort of bodyguard started a diversion they had promised by firing at the Afghan contingents outside while Herbert's party clambered down the fortress walls on the opposite end close to the river, crossing to the right bank.

The plan was sound and Herbert's party may well have escaped had it not been for Sergeant Salter, a complete invalid. The garrison officers had advised Salter to stay to be captured by Dost Mohammad, his condition being quite severe. He would be treated well by the Afghan ruler, they assured him, and Dost Mohammad would be delighted to hold another British prisoner for future negotiations in any case. Salter, though, feared his lowly status might mean he would be disposed of instead and refused to contemplate remaining behind. The Afghans in the party helped transport Salter but it slowed progress drastically and when news reached the Afghan army of their escape, patrols were sent out. They were intercepted not far from the fortress as they slowly made their way along the right bank looking for a boat. Back at the fortress, as soon as Herbert had disappeared, the garrison promptly opened the gates to the Afghan army and Dost Mohammad's men, relieved of the duty of laying siege to the fortress, immediately turned their attention to plundering the surrounding villages. 'The Dooranees soon followed, and commenced those acts of violence and cruelty for which they are infamous, plundering the houses, and violating the kuttranies openly in the streets; that a Sikh officer, interfering to check this license, was cut down by the Dooranees, who have now exclusive possession of Attock,' Abbott at Hazara relayed to the Resident on the chaotic proceedings now descending on the area.

***

The fall of Attock meant Dost Mohammad faced no impediment in joining Shere Singh's army at the Jhelum, but this he was slow in doing. Despite the agreement with Chutter Singh and all the aggressive bluster of a jihad against the British in his correspondence with the local chiefs, no one was really sure of his motives and plans; this probably included Dost himself, as his correspondence with both Chutter Singh and the British showed. Neither was it at all obvious how much of a force Dost Mohammad would lend the Sikh army as per the agreement, if any at all. The only thing certain was his desire of permanently annexing Peshawar province, and, just as everyone suspected, he would cut a deal with either side to bring this to a success. At the same time that he held talks with Chutter Singh in Peshawar he was busy in communication with British agents as to an agreement. In correspondence with Abbott in Hazara, who happened to be the closest British agent, he wrote a conciliatory letter that while he had been approached by Chutter Singh for aid, he was happy to mediate between the two warring sides. Abbott, realising he was playing both sides, would write a cold letter back.

'He claims Peshawur, Huzara and the Derajat; says that he has sent an army to take possession and that he will afterwards be happy to reconcile differences between the British and the Sikhs,' Abbott informed the Resident. 'I bade the messenger explain to him the absurdity of joining Chutter Singh, who, if successful, would instantly exclude him from Peshawur, and, if beaten, could not for an hour save him from our vengeance.'

The general belief was that Dost Mohammad would stay in Peshawar while the Sikh and British armies fought it out, negotiating with the winning side later for the permanent possession of the province. What confused matters for a time were reliable stories from multiple sources that at one point Dost Mohammad had seized and imprisoned Chutter Singh during their first meeting together, demanding from him all his British prisoners. This, it was supposed, would allow him to bargain from a much stronger position for the Peshawar province and for friendly relations with the British. These rumours of Chutter Singh having been retained against his wishes had reached Herbert as well while at Attock, and for these reasons Frederick Currie still had considerable doubt as to a sincere alliance developing between Chutter Singh and Dost Mohammad. Dalhousie for his part learned of the entry of the Afghans into Peshawar around 5 January but was unaware of the resultant fall of Attock.

'Incredible as it may appear, there is strong reason for believing that Dost Mahomed of Cabul actually is in Peshawar, has declared against us, and assumed the government of his own province. Of course he must be kicked out of that, but you need none of you be afraid; I shall not be tempted through the Khyber Pass,' he wrote in a private letter on 2 January 1849. 'We were there once too often before. But how is it possible to reason at all regarding these people when we see the Ameer of Cabul, who knows what we are made of, and has visited the climate of Calcutta once already, idiot enough to come out of his own country against us once again?'

Cautious of the effect the entry of the Afghans could have in uniting the trans-Indus Muslim population in a general jihad, Dalhousie would pen a diplomatic letter to the Amir but to be sent in the name of the Resident to verify the Amir's motives. The letter was a subtle attempt to coax the Afghan into an alliance with the British before any open aggression had taken place.

> His Highness is aware that the British Government is now engaged in a war with the army and the people of the Sikhs, the bitter enemies of His Highness. He is aware that they are doing their utmost to injure the British power, and that they hold in captivity certain officers, their wives, and children, who have been basely delivered up to them by His Highness's brother, the Sirdar Sooltan Mahomed Khan, in violation of the rights of hospitality, in disregard of the dictates of gratitude, and in defiance of the holiest precepts of the religion he professes.
>
> The Governor-General is confident that it is to show his disapprobation of such conduct as this that the Ameer has come; that he has come to proffer to the Governor-General his assistance in punishing the treachery and violence of the Sikhs, his most inveterate foes; that he has come to declare his abhorrence of the faithlessness of Sooltan Mahomed Khan in thus delivering his guests to their enemies, and so bringing dishonor on the family from which he has sprung.
>
> The Governor-General conceives that these are the causes of His Highness's arrival but it is not well that there should be doubt between friends.

The British Government of India, he wrote, was always ready to stay on good terms with the Amir. This letter was sent along with other correspondence through Lt Taylor in Bannu, who sent one of his confidential servants to deliver it. The messenger reported back an ebullient Afghan ruler, in private at least, who seemed unwilling to make the step to open warfare against the British. He queried the messenger on British strength at various places and on the status of the war everywhere. 'Why does not he go to his own country of Calcutta; is Hindostan a small place, that he must needs set himself down in the lands of others? The Ameer reproached the guide for making himself the bearer of such messages from the English to him, which he said did not become him as a Mussulman,' Taylor informed the Resident. It was equally plain that the Dost wished not to commit himself certainly in writing. For this messenger and others had been waiting for replies for some time, being given one excuse or another by the Afghan ruler.

He would, he said, be waiting for his sons to appear and consult with them or at other times even that the right paper was not available for an official letter to the Resident at Lahore or various other excuses. 'At length one Gholam Russool, a Moonshee, told him that he was not likely to get an answer quickly from the Ameer; that if the English defeated the Sikhs, the Dost would write an answer to the effect that he was their servant to command but if on the other hand they suffered defeat themselves no answer would be give,' continued Taylor in the report. The messenger would come back empty-handed after a wait of eight days.

While Dalhousie's letter to the Ameer was being communicated to him, a letter from Dost Mohammad written to Lt Abbott appeared and was sent by the latter to Lahore. Some doubted the authenticity of this message as it firmly pushed the Ameer off the fence and in any case he would have known Abbott had no authority to make any sort of negotiation. However, Abbott was then the nearest Englishman in authority from Attock and thus an easy conduit. Writing to Lahore and awaiting the reply would have been far too slow for the Dost. In his letter he insisted that Peshawar belonged to the Afghans and that through the goodwill of the British it should belong again to his country but that he had received little understanding on this issue with the British Government in India, which had traditionally sided with the Sikh state as to its possession.

> I have brought my troops to Peshawur, for the purpose of carrying out the same object that I have, constantly, had in view, and which, at the time that I quitted Hindostan. I endeavoured to obtain, through the good will of the British; viz, the release of the country of my fathers from the hands of the Sikhs, and for such favor I should have shown unbounded gratitude. It is notorious that, in combating for the possession of Peshawur, which is the burial place of my forefathers, thousands have perished, on the part of the Affghans and of the Sikhs, and it is, therefore, the more incumbent on the race of the former to use their utmost efforts to secure it. In this matter no assistance has been received from the British.

Dost Mohammad also iterated some slights he had felt in the British attitude towards him of late. 'Subsequently, when the disturbances at Mooltan, and the outbreaks in Hazara and Bunnoo took place, Major George Lawrence gave me no information of what had occurred, and did not lead me to suppose that he considered me as his friend, nor did any other British officer write to me. My regret increased, when I considered that the British Government placed no confidence in me as their friend'. He wished peace but his price would be the possession of all the areas he had mentioned, i.e. all areas on the right bank of the Indus along with Hazara. This, he thought, must be agreeable to the British.

Whatever the case, the transfer of Peshawar into Afghan hands allowed Chutter Singh's troops and guns to reinforce Shere Singh, although he would only effect a junction after the Battle of Chillianwala. The important effect of these large reinforcements, in combination with the fall of Attock, would be a drastic increase in the pressure on Gough to jettison his slow and sure method of running of the campaign and to achieve results in much quicker time.

# 28

# The Battle of Chillianwala

… the blow should be struck with the least possible delay.
Frederick Mackeson, British political agent, 10 January 1849

We have gained a victory, but like that of the ancients, it is such a one that
'another such would ruin us'.
Dalhousie, 20 January 1849

Central Punjab is well known for its exclusively flat landscape. However, to the north, towards Jammu and Kashmir, or to the mountainous territory of the Hindu Kush in the west, foothills and uneven ground gradually begin to develop, announcing a definitive end to the plains. The wild and hilly ground running south-westwards from the town of Bhimber to the Jhelum River for a distance of 50 km or so is perhaps the southernmost manifestation of these folds in the earth. This hilly terrain has perhaps a maximum width of around 5 km but comes complete with gorges 200–300 feet deep. The nature of the ground means that to the present day there are few if any paths or tracks that traverse this area.

The Kharian Pass, running almost directly through the centre of this hilly terrain since ancient times, was the only relatively easy way through the ground to the west. The small town of Kharian, from which the pass was named, guarded the road on the east with the Jhelum 10 km west of the pass at this point. This was the more established trade route from Lahore and Gujrat and heading to Peshawar unless a traveller, or army, bypassed this ground to the south or north, paying a penalty of several days in travel. Today the ridge area has been turned into a national park, with the Kharian Pass fully utilised as part of the famous Grand Trunk (or GT) road running from Peshawar and through the Punjab.

At the southern end of the ridge on the left bank of the Jhelum nestled a string of small and nondescript villages in a rough line with the river. The village of Rasul, the northernmost, had the advantage of a ford and a ferry crossing nearby. Rasul was followed by Kot Baloch 7 km to its south, and then Chak Fateh Shah, Lakhnewala and Shaheedanwala, with Moong closer to the river. From this chain of villages, and around 7 km east of the river sat the equally unassuming village of Chillianwala on the road to Dinghee and Gujrat.

Looking west from Chillianwala towards the river it was impossible to see the other villages and the river, for a solid belt of intervening jungle stretched along the ridge southwards from Rasul. This was later reported to be as much as 3 km in depth in places, less elsewhere. Some of the participants in the coming battle would mention a large number of Keekur and kureel (caparis) trees populating this wooded line. Others mentioned babul trees and plenty of camel thorn and other bushes as many as 8 feet high. Many of the trees, moreover, were of the sort with low branches and, along with the bushes and uneven ground in parts, provided an obstacle to easy progress towards the river. Due to the denseness of these trees and bushes, visibility was reduced to no more than 15 to 20 feet in some places, although most locations allowed for several hundred feet or so. This in fact wasn't the only belt of jungle in the vicinity. While the land immediately round Chillianwala was largely cultivated, this part of the doab between the Chenab and Jhelum contained a fair amount of uncultivated territory at the time. Jungled patches began around Dinghee, around 20 km to the east of Chillianwala, gradually increasing in strength.

There also happened to be an incline from Chillianwala towards Rasul and the other villages to the west which ended in some rather precipitous riverbanks at the Jhelum. This incline was measured later as having a gradient of 6 feet for every 50 yards, presenting a relatively easy but nonetheless slowing effect for any force advancing westwards from the village. The nature of the jungle changed near its periphery towards Rasul as well. 'Here near the edge of the jungle, large pockets of dak trees (Butea Frondosa) populated the area. However they were completely denuded of foliage as a result of the continuous discharge of grapeshot from of the Sikh guns and returning British shot,' wrote a participant in the battle later. In many areas, these trees were grouped together with some density so as to preclude a passage through to the open.

Out of the belt of jungle a series of natural village ponds of water, not particularly deep but nevertheless an obstacle, could be discerned before the string of hamlets. The terrain also became rougher and fissures and nullahs were apparent with high banks before the riverbank presented itself. 'Beyond this, the ground was deeply rent, in every direction, forming precipitous ravines; while on an isolated little plateau stood the mud village of Rasul, connected with the adjacent parts by an extremely narrow neck of land, slightly protected with wood; while, on the opposite side, a deep escarpment was presented to the river Jhelum,' wrote a British officer on a reconnaissance of the area near Rasul to the north after the battle.

The area of Chillianwala was essentially a quiet backwater and held no great military advantage itself apart from the ford across the river at Rasul. The town of Dinghee was perhaps more important, being somewhat of a crossroads. From Dinghee, roads led to the Kharian Pass, to Chillianwala and Rasul and to the metropolis of Gujrat to the east. The land east of Chillianwala was largely a sandy plain and with little water apart from that available in the villages. There were few roads in this backwater between Chillianwala and the Jhelum as well. According to British accounts, there were only two paths, better described as dirt tracks, winding their way to Rasul through the trees and bushes, both being only wide enough to allow three men abreast. One was westwards from Dinghee, the other running adjacent to the Jhelum northwards behind the hilly ground.

The area made for a sound defensive position, as Shere Singh had noted after moving west from Sadulpore. With insufficient heavy guns to compete with Gough, the Sikh commander required the necessary terrain to compensate as at the Chenab. The question no doubt on his mind after Sadulpore was whether to stay on the left bank of the Jhelum or cross to the right bank, forcing Gough to cross under disadvantageous conditions. It's fairly certain Shere Singh had initially made the decision to cross to the right bank at the ford at Rasul. Things quickly changed, however. On the point of crossing, reinforcements in the form of four regiments and twelve guns sent by Chutter Singh managed to reach his son and he promptly decided that he now had the strength to make a stand on the left bank for the territory looked promising. The belt of jungled, thorny ground obscuring the view would largely negate Gough's strength in artillery. Also, any British advance would be broken up effectively during any advance through this ground. The gradual incline also gave the Sikh gunners and infantry a slightly better view than any opposing column. Gough could not attempt a flanking manoeuvre due to the high ridge north of Rasul. With his right anchored by the river, a flanking manoeuvre by the British to the south was also impossible. The Sikh commander therefore organised a long line stretching from Rasul to Moong and Lukhneewala and Futteh Shah-Ke-Chuck. This meant the line ran nearly 8 km before the battle. A strong system of defensive trenches, earthwork and breastworks was ordered to be constructed along the natural glacis which ran an appreciable way along the string of villages. The strongest section would naturally be at Rasul, and Shere Singh hoped Gough would be fool enough to attack and dash his strength on it when he eventually followed the Sikh army to the Jhelum.

Many British descriptions of the Sikh position survive and all are in consensus as to its natural strength, bolstered by manmade defences, certainly on the Sikh left, organised in the weeks before the battle. Colin Campbell, scouting the position after the Sikh army had moved to Gujrat, noted the improvements Shere Singh had organised: 'I never saw a stronger position; nor did I ever see one so well improved by works so admirably arranged, and so well adapted for the purposes of defence. It was indeed most fortunate that we had not to storm this place, for most probably we should have failed; and even had we been successful, our loss must have been frightful.'

General Gilbert and several officers toured the Sikh position extensively after the battle and mentioned a ravine around 100 feet deep in one place, presumably at Rasul, which would have been impossible to traverse. He agreed with Campbell on the defensive measures taken by Shere Singh, mentioning earthworks with ground excavated for the protection of troops from British fire and with the embrasures of the Sikh guns being protected by forked trunks of trees. Daniel Sandford of the 2nd Bengal European Regiment perhaps wrote the more comprehensive description of the northern section of the Sikh line where Gough was meant to come to grief. This too was written after Shere Singh's move to Gujrat.

From all accounts, it's a good thing for us that they have abandoned it; as, if resolutely defended it could not have been carried without fearful loss. First there was a breastwork dotted with batteries extending for a long mile. In front of this there was a deep ravine; and close on the trench, an immense barrier of thorns which must have brought up our infantry for a time; whilst a heavy fire would have been poured into them from the very muzzles of the guns; that gained there was a ravine after ravine for a quarter of a mile with only one or two narrow paths and the whole tracked by their guns on the heights. The sides of the ravine were all scarped down so as to be insurmountable; and to have toiled through these obstacles, all the time exposed to their murderous fire, would have been terrific work. At last came the village of Rasul on the summit of a crag some sixty feet high, sheer perpendicular on all sides and covered with batteries – only one narrow pass up to it, where scarce eight men could walk abreast; and this could have been destroyed by them in a short time. Of course we should have taken it if we had attacked it; but there would have been few to rejoice at the victory.

At Rasul, a ravine passed in front of the village, several hundred feet deep apparently. The only means of crossing this was a narrow wooden bridge, wide enough for a man only and too narrow for even a single horse. The village and the Sikh extreme left was to all intents and purposes unassailable from the east. Some of the Sikh batteries were known to have been placed in advance of the ravine working in concert with others to the south, perhaps to draw in the British.

Not all of the line was as impregnable as the north, however. The centre and right of the Sikh line had only the jungle to protect it, with none of the gross imperfections in the land to impede a British advance. The position in general had its faults, as well. The Sikh line was a roughly 2 km from the river and the Sikh army would need to fight with its back to the river. If the British managed to penetrate the line at any point it could spell disaster. Immediately behind the Sikh line the sharp fissures leading to the sandy banks of the Jhelum formed a considerable obstacle to a retreat under duress.

***

Back in the British advance camp at Heylah, little more than 20 km to the south-east of the Sikh camp, there was general consensus among Gough's officers, even with the sparse information available at the time of the new Sikh position, that giving battle at the Jhelum River would be foolhardy. The more vociferous perhaps were Thackwell and Major Mackeson, the political agent. These two had been leading the units scouting ahead of the British position and had taken into account intelligence received from spies. They had both declared the Sikh position altogether impracticable for an attack due to its strength. These reports served to reinforce in the Commander-in-Chief's mind, still with the bulk of the British force crossing the Chenab, of the desire to wait for a junction with Whish's force before a further advance. In any case the bridge of boats across the Chenab was still being assembled and a halt allowed the British heavy guns to be transported across to the right bank. Furthermore there was the impression that Shere Singh might simply move his army to the right bank of the Jhelum once an advance close to Rasul took place. With no boats to cross the Jhelum, moving forward would simply extend British supply lines to the Jhelum with no discernible benefit at this stage.

Obtaining water and forage for the animals, most of which had crossed to the right bank of the Chenab, was also much easier than when in the middle of the doab, where Thackwell during his reconnaissance had found water to be scarce. Moving sideways to Gujrat further along the Chenab was also mooted, allowing for easier communication with Lahore. Only the impression that any perceived reticence or lack of eagerness to advance would damage British prestige prevented this option being chosen. Otherwise it made sound sense as Gujrat was ideal for supplies, being on the direct road to Lahore. So much so, in fact, that by 12 December orders were actually given to make ready for a withdrawal to Gujrat but then countermanded. Again on 16 December, and then on the 18th and 22nd, either rumours of a move abounded or orders were spread that the army would shortly be moving to Gujrat.

The Governor-General, too, was still not inclined to have the army moving too far westward with British supply lines stretching still further, making the force more dependent on the Lahore Durbar's goodwill and supplies. However his main reason was the anxiety caused, despite the imminent arrival of the 18th Royal Irish Regiment, of only having two European regiments between Calcutta and Ambala – a distance of 1,770 km. British power was so concentrated in the Punjab now that there were insufficient resources elsewhere should an emergency arise. Already there had been ominous noises coming from Nepal of Nepalese forces being massed at the border with India to take advantage of British attention being focused on the Punjab.

'On these grounds I peremptorily ordered him [Gough] not to advance beyond the Chenab, expecting to attack Shere Singh until the arrival of reinforcements from Scinde, and the fall of

Mooltan should enable him to advance with safety and certainty of success,' he informed the Duke of Wellington on 7 December. 'The enemy is a formidable enemy, warlike in character, the whole Sikh army except two regiments has risen against us. The Sikh population, lately disciplined soldiers and dismissed, are united to them. It is not true that he has been deprived of all his guns. He has 90 pieces of artillery on his official return, besides those in forts, and plenty more will be dug up when there is occasion for them.'

Dalhousie had also had been briefed on the dangers of the terrain between Rasul and Chillianwala, and agreed with Mackeson. 'It is an ugly place,' he would write in a letter on 22 December, also sending a sketch of the future battlefield. Far better, then, to await the fall of Multan and advance only when Gough had an overwhelming force.

\*\*\*

Despite the sound reasons for not moving further west, and despite agreeing entirely with the Governor-General, Gough was never quite happy with the constraints being put on his autonomy in the field. He would harbour a certain amount of resentment at the leash and the two would exchange a decidedly cold conversation, Gough wishing for freedom to move as and when he deemed best and Dalhousie insisting it was too dangerous.

So initially at least, in the early part of December, no move forward was mooted in the British camp. Despite the lack of an advance, the army was kept in a state of readiness and with some of the heavy guns transported over the Chenab the army was prepared for an action by 11 December. The next day, the vanguard of the heavy guns convoy, principally two 18-pounders and four 8-inch howitzers, reached Heylah.

With both sides sitting in their respective positions on the Jhelum and Chenab, three more weeks would pass quietly. A prolonged period of inactivity was actually in neither party's interest; despite his strong position Shere Singh could ill afford a junction of the two British forces, and while it made sense for Gough to wait for the fall of Multan before advancing there was a growing pressure on the British commander to produce results. As the days and weeks went by a growing criticism was voiced by British newspaper correspondents as to the unreasonable delay in tackling what they felt was an undisciplined rabble camped only a couple of days' march away. British prestige in India was at stake and every day without British action tarnished it further, they argued.

Dalhousie, perhaps mindful of this criticism, would loosen the leash somewhat during the latter part of the month. By then British supply lines were much more stable, with Wheeler suppressing any uprisings in the Lahore area and beyond in Jalandhar. More importantly, perhaps, he had heard that developments across the Indus had taken place. Chutter Singh was in Peshawar and making progress in receiving aid from the Afghan ruler Dost Mohammad. It therefore made sense to attack Shere Singh's position before he received this aid and Dalhousie gave a tentative node towards a possible advance. 'Accordingly, I have authorised the Commander-in-Chief to advance to attack Sher Sing on the Jhelum, if careful consideration of these various circumstances and better information as to the position shall satisfy his Excellency that he can safely undertake such an operation, and without heavy loss, which we cannot afford.'

So on the early morning of the 19th Gough finally crossed the Chenab himself, with the bulk of his force making camp in the now deserted Sikh position on the right bank of the river. No losses had been incurred during the crossing of the Chenab apart from a few baggage camels washed downstream when exceptionally heavy rain fell between 3 a.m. and 6 a.m. that morning.

The nearby villages were given protection from the camp followers' enthusiastic plundering by units of the army. After two weeks in the former Sikh camp, on the first day of the new year of 1849, Gough advanced further to the village of Janu Ke, 7 km from the advance British outpost at Heylah.

Heylah by this time had assumed a more permanent look as more British units were moved forward and woodcutters had been organised to cut down the thick jungle in front of the British lines. Sikh guns could be heard occasionally at this position as their gunners fired off salvos for practice although neither camp was molested by attacks from the other at this stage. Further west, though, beyond the pickets and towards the river there were occasional skirmishes between British cavalry and Gorcharas. Gough had advanced certain units still further in late December with a view to setting up an advance base near the Sikh army close to Dinghee and Chillianwala 20 km north of Heylah but these had returned the same day, the position being too far from support from Heylah and therefore vulnerable to surprise attack.

There were the expected problems associated with an extended camp in one place and the reasons for not moving towards the middle of the doab put forward earlier had been sound. The position was causing difficulties in terms of logistics. These difficulties were increased by the raids of Sikh irregulars. Protecting the huge British camp was proving difficult. Large flocks of sheep and beasts of burden accompanied the army. Over 100 camels were found to have disappeared while out to pasture on 12 December alone. It was also suspected many of the camp followers who could claim compensation for lost property were covertly selling on their camels to receive compensation and then buying the camels back from the local villagers at a reduced amount, although this was never proved. On 21 December, it was noticed upwards of 200 camels out grazing had disappeared. Preventing this proved impossible, although more guards were ordered to protect the flocks. 'The cavalry are out 8 until 6 p.m. protecting the camels and camp followers. At capturing camels and Light Cavalry duties, the Sikhs beat us hollow; for every camel we take they get fifty of ours,' Capt. Ouvry of the 3rd Light Dragoons would record on the continual skirmishing for resources before and after Chillianwala.

***

In the Sikh camp, as news was received of Gough advancing his main army towards Heylah, Shere Singh would try his hand at further negotiations for a British withdrawal from Lahore territory. Major George Lawrence had been transferred by Chutter Singh to the Sikh camp at Chillianwala by 13 December and was the medium used for communication between the two camps. In order to ascertain if the British were still open to negotiations, Shere Singh would send one of Lawrence's moonshees in a preliminary mission on 16 December. Mackeson, the political agent, signalled he had no objection to Lawrence or his moonshee coming to the British camp but reiterated that the British Government would countenance no negotiations with men in arms and that nothing could be discussed till Shere Singh and his army surrendered.

Notwithstanding British coolness towards his approach, Shere Singh explained his offer to George Lawrence. If the British were interested in exchanging prisoners, he would be content to release the prisoners he held. George Lawrence and his family, along with the several other British officers and agents currently being held, would be exchanged for Shere Singh's brother and other relatives. The main purpose of sending George Lawrence, however, was to negotiate, if possible, a treaty for the withdrawal of the British force along with those stationed at Lahore back across the Sutlej. If this could be arranged, Shere Singh communicated to the officer, it would herald warm and cordial relations again between the two states. Lawrence was duly sent to the British camp to meet with Major Mackeson and the Commander-in-Chief, after which the message was relayed to Dalhousie at Makhu. On the issue of exchanging prisoners, Dalhousie was more open: 'The Governor-General is ready to assent to an exchange of the prisoners respectively held by us and by them,' the secretary to the Governor–General replied to Mackeson. 'Raja Shere Sing may accordingly be informed that on the safe return of the British prisoners and their delivery to his Excellency the Commander-in-chief, the British will deliver up the Raja's brother Sirdar Golab Sing and any others who may be in our hands belonging to that family with such other sirdars as are in our possession.' However, on one prisoner being held there could be no negotiation. 'The Maharanee Junda Khore and Raja Lal Sing whose names have been adverted to must of course be excluded from any arrangement of the above nature.' In regard to any form of negotiation or terms, Dalhousie was even more unequivocal. 'With regard to the latter proposal, I am desired to state, that the only answer the Governor-General has to give to all applications from the Sikh army, for the opening of negotiations regarding terms, is that the Government will not treat with rebels in arms. No proposal will be listened to, but that of absolute, unconditional surrender. If the surrender shall be immediate and complete, no one's life will be considered as forfeited by reason of their rebellion. If, on the other hand, the surrender shall not be immediate and complete, the sirdars and their troops must endure the consequences of their acts, and their blood will be on their own heads. From this statement, the Dewan Moolraj and his followers must be understood to be excluded.'

This uncompromising response by the Governor-General put paid to any chance of a settlement and paved the way for what would be the defining battle of the war. The overture was universally interpreted as more or less an offer of surrender by the newspaper correspondents accompanying the force at this time, and mixed with the numerous other rumours and stories drifting in from the Sikh camp via informers and spies meant there was plenty of idle gossip and speculation of one sort or another abounding in the British camp at this time of an early end to hostilities. 'Negotiations, report positively asserts, are going on between Shere Sing and our Government, by which the former is to give up his guns and munitions of war, provided he and all his followers be allowed a free pardon,' reported the correspondent for *The Mofussilite*. Other correspondents seizing on this piece of news and eager to fill their column inches made out this proved the stories emanating from the Sikh camp therefore must be true. They sent back stories invariably portraying low morale and shortages of supplies. There were rumours that the Sikh soldiers had been put on rations of one meal a day with many of the Sikh troops not having had a meal in two days. The banias in the Sikh camp had shut up shop due to the scarcity of supplies, it was said. Dalhousie, on hearing these tales, would inform the Secret Committee from his camp at Makhu on 4 January 1849: 'The enemy it is said are put to great stress for provisions and clothing and are beginning to show some indications of a desire to leave their present strong position at Moong and retire across the Jhelum.'

Other stories by spies mentioned Shere Singh's dire lack of treasure and inability to pay his troops. News came in of a contingent of several thousand Afghans along with twelve guns who had reached the right bank of the Jhelum by now but who having been told of his financial constraints were refusing to cross and join the Sikh army till they were paid in advance by Shere Singh. They had declared they would march back if the money was not forthcoming.

Perhaps because of this shortage of funds there were stories that many Sikh soldiers, thinking a British victory inevitable, wished to desert Shere Singh but were failing to find the opportunity to escape. These suspicions of low morale in the Sikh camp were fuelled by rumours of a Sikh officer surrendering early in the New Year along with thirty other Sikh soldiers. How true these rumours were is uncertain as units both regular and irregular continued to join the Sikh army before and after the battle. In addition many sepoys formerly in East India Company service but who had been made redundant due to recent cuts were found to be fighting under the Sikh standard at Chillianwala. It doubtful whether these men, more mercenary than the Sikh troops, would have stayed to fight if wages were not forthcoming. Relating to financial affairs were other stories in circulation suggesting Maharajah Gulab Singh of Kashmir was covertly assisting the Sikh commander with funds.

These stories of offers to surrender would continue into the New Year, no doubt triggered by other emissaries coming into the British camp with Shere Singh continuing to offer talks. Major Mackeson, however, continued to refuse to countenance any negotiation with 'rebels in arms' or to listen to anything but unconditional surrender as per instructions from Dalhousie. Some reports had perhaps more than a grain of truth. One was that Shere Singh was having problems in his position. The *Bombay Gazette* on 19 December reported that Shere Singh was being forced to move camp from the banks of the Jhelum a mile inland due to the same heavy rains Gough's camp had suffered recently, the deluge having swamped the Sikh defences and trenches.

***

The opening day of 1849 was marked in low-key fashion, Gough merely moving the bulk of his force to within 5 km of the advance position of Heylah where a further halt was planned till the fall of Multan. However, a sequence of events during the first two weeks of January conspired to increase markedly the already growing pressure on the British commander to achieve success in shorter time.

The first was the news that substantial reinforcements had reached Shere Singh from Multan during the first week of the year. On 21 December, Narain Singh, one of Mulraj's commanders, had left Multan to collect revenue in the surrounding area. He had a force of 3,000–4,000 men and some guns. He had been shadowed by Sheikh Imam-Ud-Deen, the ex-Governor of Kashmir, who had been ordered to intercept him or at least to prevent him from returning to Multan. Narain Singh, noting the difficulties of re-entering Multan, had instead struck northwards to join up with Shere Singh. Learning of his approach, Gough sent southwards a strong detachment consisting of the 9th Lancers and the 5th and 8th Light Cavalry along with two troops of horse artillery under Brig. White on the right bank of the Chenab to capture a fort in his path about 30 km downstream while Brig. Penny was sent with a brigade on the left bank. However, Narain Singh successfully avoided interception by either of the British columns, joining Shere Singh's in early January.

More important was the news that the fortress of Attock had fallen to the Afghans. Shere Singh, on hearing the news, ordered a salute of forty guns to be fired on the morning of 9 January to mark the occasion, clearly heard in the British camp. The news of the fall of the fortress would travel south into British India quickly. The now confirmed accord between Chutter Singh and Dost Mohammad was expected to herald both their forces significantly reinforcing Shere Singh's force.

On 6 January, meanwhile, news reached Gough and elsewhere that the city of Multan had fallen. The general impression round the British camp was that the fortress itself would only last a day or two longer. As if to take advantage of this event, the same day, Currie released another proclamation. This was the terms on which pardon could be obtained by soldiers of the Sikh army if they surrendered immediately and unconditionally. If they did, then the soldiers would be entitled to return home with impunity. The sirdars and Sikh officers who had property and land could not be guaranteed their jaghirs but would be given enough to live on and for their families. 'Let it further be observed that in order to be entitled to the terms above mentioned the submission must be immediate. No part of these terms refer to Sirdar Sooltan Mahomed Khan Barukzye.' He reiterated Dalhousie's policy. Sultan Mohammad was the brother of Dost Mohammad, who had handed George Lawrence over to Chutter Singh and whom Currie made clear would have to make separate terms.

As events unfolded all round, Gough's policy of keeping the main British force entirely static around Heylah served only to increase the clamour among the British press in India. Their impatience had been growing for some time, and they blamed tardiness and lack of vigour by the Commander-in-Chief. Attock had fallen and Chutter Singh was advancing to the aid of Shere Singh and yet the British force was lying idle, they declared in their columns. The *Bombay Times* had been one of the less forgiving newspapers regarding the lack of progress and energy being shown by the Commander-in-Chief. On 3 January they had delivered a damning verdict on his direction of the war so far:

> The Commander-in-Chief of India, at the head of 24,000 men with 100 guns, and thirty thousand others on his flanks or rear, is foiled in a skirmish which ought never to have occurred, and outmanoeuvred in a battle which ought to have closed the campaign. An enemy hardly equal to him in numbers, and with scarcely one third of his guns, – without one single European amongst them, – entraps and destroys some of the finest of his troops, defies him for a fortnight to attack them, and when the opportunity of superior numbers and discipline arrives for moving against them, retires from under our guns without leaving a shadow of a trophy, and takes up a position scarcely a march in advance, where they defy us to assail them! ... With one of the finest armies, and some of the ablest officers, under him that ever took the field, Lord Gough is compelled to remain for weeks within hearing of the Sikh artillery, not knowing how to turn himself, until reinforcements shall arrive, or the enemy retire from before him in sheer weariness.

There were, in truth, other growing pressures on Gough besides the newspaper correspondents. His uncomplaining men whiled away the time in various activities, realising a prolonged wait of several weeks was on the cards at least before the Multan force would arrive. They played cricket, wrote letters back home and enjoyed the fine weather. A popular game proved to be something called 'Long bullets', a game with strong similarities to 'bowls' and which was developed during this time in the camp. But problems typically associated with staying for a lengthy time in one place were surfacing. The detritus accumulated by a stationary army meant the British camp was getting increasingly filthy and unhygienic and suggested a move. Thousands of dead horses, bullocks and camels were strewn for miles between and around the two camps. These animals were attracting unwelcome attention, being easy food for the numerous scavengers of the area. On 1 and 2 January elements of the Sikh army had noticeably moved positions too, the lengthy stay in the location having exhausted the local forage. For the same reason, by 10 January most of the British force had been moved to Lussoorie, 10 km north-east of the previous camp. The only exceptions were Penny's brigade across the Chenab and the 13th and 22nd regiments guarding the bridge at Ramnuggar.

\*\*\*

Despite the pressure from the Indian press, Gough could only advance with the complete sanction of Dalhousie. That would change on 7 January. Dalhousie wrote to the Commander-in-Chief saying how pleased he was with progress at Multan and the fall of the city. What was required was progress on the main front. 'It would give me no less pleasure to announce a similar blow struck by you on the Jhelum,' he hinted to Gough, showing his changing view on matters. It was on 10 January that Gough received a communication from Major Mackeson giving an even stronger signal that a battle sooner rather than later needed to be fought and that there was now no need to wait for the fall of Multan. 'I would urge, in the event of your Lordship's finding yourself strong enough, with the army under your command, to strike an effectual blow at the enemy in our front, and that the blow should be struck with the least possible delay,' Mackeson requested in his communique.

Gough digested the new instructions and with the constraints taken off his actions immediately made preparations for battle, to be fought in two days' time on 13 January. A grand parade of the army was organised at the village and practice charges organised that day along with other practice by the artillery in readiness for an assault. All preparations were completed on the evening of the 11th, and at 7 a.m. on the morning of the 12th the march north towards Dinghee began. 'Concurring entirely with Major Mackeson and feeling that I was perfectly competent effectually to overthrow Shere Sing's army I moved from Loah Tibbee at daylight on the 12th to Dingee about twelve miles,' wrote Gough in his despatches of the 16th. The infantry marched in two parallel columns with the horse artillery and cavalry in single column on the left. Dinghee was reached at 2 p.m., the terrain here being open, cultivated fields, although the distant belt of jungle that would be the battlefield could be discerned in the far distance. Only around 16 km had been covered in the seven hours of marching in battle order as the heavy guns were slowly and ponderously pulled over the dirt tracks.

Gough's moves towards the Jhelum coincided with another army arriving but from another direction and on the right bank of the river. These were the troops of Gulab Singh, the ruler of Kashmir, 10,000 strong with fourteen guns under the European officer Col. Steinbach. Browbeaten into supplying help and troops and reminded of the assistance of the British in helping establish his own dominion, the ruler of Kashmir had sent a force to ostensibly assist the British. This army could disrupt Shere Singh's supply lines from the west of the Jhelum or alternatively join with Gough's force for the coming battle. The soldiers in Steinbach's force clearly had sympathies with the Sikh army, however, and Gough, anxious of the possibility of this force defecting to Shere Singh, had vigorously protested to Steinbach regarding the approach of these troops, asking him to hold them back from the immediate area. Steinbach therefore moved them back, and these troops would therefore take no part in the coming battle or *any* of the subsequent events, lying idle around 30 km upstream of Rasul for the next few weeks.

On the evening of the 12th, Gough invited all his officers to his tent to discuss the battle that would take place the next day. The Commander-in-Chief's impression, gleaned from reconnaissance over the previous weeks, was that the Sikh line was heavily overextended. Unaware of the strength of the Sikh position at Rasul, he decided on a determined attack by the road on Shere Singh's left. A successful attack and a capture of the Sikh left flank would allow an advance southwards with the rest of the Sikh line being enfiladed. This also had the merit, if it succeeded, of forcing Shere Singh away from the ford behind Rasul and preventing his force from retreating across the river. Since there were no known fords on the Jhelum further south, Shere Singh's army would be trapped in the narrow and tapering territory between the Jhelum and Chenab, an area with insufficient resources to support them. The other advantage of this plan was that the British heavy guns could be hauled along the dirt track to Rasul for the attack as opposed to being moved awkwardly through soft, cultivated country or through the belt of jungle.

More than a few soldiers and officers would comment that evening on the fact that the battle would take place on the same wooded site where Alexander the Great had locked horns with Porus, the ruler of the Punjab, over 2,000 years earlier. Capt. James Abbott, the agent in Hazara, had in fact recently written an article for the Asiatic Society of Bengal on just this battlefield. He argued that the town of Jhelum, 30 km upstream from the village of Rasul, was built on the city of Bucephalia, founded by the conqueror and where Craterus, one of his commanders, had been left holding the Greek camp while Alexander marched north to effect a crossing of the Jhelum. The village Moong just behind the Sikh line was commonly believed to be built on top of the ruins of the city of Nikaiea, founded on the banks of the Jhelum by the Macedonian after his victory. What seemed to confirm this were the many Greek coins that had been dug up bearing the inscription 'NIK' in recent years.

Others commented on the fact that 13 January was an unhappy anniversary for the British Army in India. It was on the same day seven years earlier that the final acts of the First Anglo-Afghan War had taken place, an event still fresh in British minds. A desperate stand at Gandamak had seen the last vestige of the British force that had marched to Kabul three years earlier destroyed in the mountains of Afghanistan as it attempted to move towards safety. Later that same evening the lone and exhausted figure of a certain Dr Brydon could be seen by the British garrison at Jalalabad riding unsteadily into the fort, a scene later immortalised by Lady Elizabeth Butler in her painting *The Remnants of an Army*.

\*\*\*

Gough would have just over 21,000 men with him for the battle. 16,200 of this force was infantry, of which four regiments (HM 24th, HM 29th, HM 61st and the 2nd European Light Infantry, totalling 3,200 men) were European. The sepoy regiments present were the 3th, 15th, 20th, 22nd, 25th, 30th, 31st, 36th, 45th, 46th, 52nd, 56th, 69th and 70th. In terms of cavalry, he had 5,100 men at his disposal. Three regiments of Dragoons (HM 3rd, 9th and 14th) totalled 1,500 men. Other regular cavalry units totalled 1,800 men made up of the 1st, 5th, 6th and 8th. Irregular cavalry, composed of the 3rd, 9th, 11th and 12th, added another 1,800 men.

The British line would march in order of battle towards Chillianwala and the line was organised accordingly. On the extreme of the British right would be placed three troops of horse artillery (commanded by Huish, Christie and Lane), Lt-Col Grant commanding overall. Following this would be Brig. Pope's brigade of cavalry made up of the 9th Royal Lancers and 14th Light Dragoons plus the 1st and 6th regiments of Light Cavalry (Native) for intelligence had been received that Shere Singh had strong contingents of cavalry on his left. To the left of Pope would be Sir Walter Gilbert's division. This was composed of two brigades. Godby commanded the one on the right composed of the 2nd Bengal European Regiment and the 31st and 70th NI. To his left was Mountain's brigade composed of HM 29th, plus the 30th and 56th NI. The heavy guns, which Gough always jokingly referred to as 'my politicals', would be largely positioned in the middle of the British line. These would be commanded by Major Horsford. To the left of these guns would be positioned the division of Brig.-Gen. Campbell. This consisted of Pennycuick's brigade of HM 24th plus the 45th and 25th NI, while to his left would be Hoggan's brigade of HM 61st plus the 46th and 36th NI. Thackwell would be in command of the cavalry on the British left flank. This would comprise the 3rd and 14th Light Dragoons and the 5th and 8th Light Cavalry. On the extreme left of the British line would be positioned three troops of horse artillery, those of Warner, Fordyce and Duncan under Lt-Col Brind. The 14th Dragoons would later be moved to the right flank shortly before the battle. The rearguard, meanwhile, would be composed of the 4th Brigade of Cavalry, 3rd and 9th Irregulars and the 2nd Brigade of Infantry with three guns. Brig. Penny's troops, comprising the 15th, 20th and 69th NI, would act as a reserve that Gough was quite confident would not be required. The irregular troops and the 20th NI would be assigned to protect the baggage once Chillianwala was reached.

Opposing this force, Shere Singh, 16 km to his west, was estimated to have 30,000 men although only around 10,000 of this force were estimated to be regular troops, the rest being irregulars or 'a rabble' as popularly described in the British camp. Accompanying this were around fifty guns, mostly of light calibre. Gough in his despatch of 16 January overestimated Shere Singh's resources, mentioning 30,000–40,000 men with sixty-two guns. Other sources later mention only forty guns firing during the battle and with none being heavier than 14-pounders.

A letter written three days after the battle and published later in the *Bombay Telegraph* from a combatant along with information gleaned from spies shed more light on how Shere Singh had organised his line. An officer by the name of Suraj Singh Majithia was given command of the left at Rasul with seven regiments, each 1,000 strong, and eleven guns with two mortars. To the right of Suraj Singh were five regiments and four guns commanded by Sirdar Ball Singh. Sirdar Ram Singh, Pritee Singh Kana Kutchwala and Aotar Singh held the next sections to the right, with Uttar Singh given command of the Sikh right. Shere Singh apparently stationed himself on the extreme right of the Sikh line. According to later accounts of British combatants there were several Europeans in the Sikh line, including one with a very large beard. Their nationalities were never ascertained. The line anchored at Rasul to the north stretched to the village of Futteh Shah-Ke-Chuck.

***

At 7 a.m. on 13 January, after a cessation of nearly five weeks since Sadulpore, Gough ordered the advance towards Chillianwala. A tot of rum was served to all. Colin Campbell was known to have addressed his division before setting off, giving them a stirring speech reminding them of their predecessors' exploits during the Peninsular War at Burgos and declaring he was sure they would emulate their feats later that day. No camp was left and all baggage accompanied the march. The baggage and the field hospital stores were transported in the rear of the brigades.

The country the British force passed through was still relatively open, with scattered trees till they reached Dinghee. As planned earlier, a move north was made in preparation to attack the Sikh left at Rasul and for other reasons that became apparent as he moved close to the river. 'I made a considerable detour to my right partly in order to distract the enemy's attention but principally to get as clear as I could of the jungle on which it would appear that the enemy mainly relied,' explained Gough in his despatch of 16 January.

From Dinghee, therefore, the British force moved 6 km north-westwards, reaching the village of Chota Umrao (now Amra Kalan). Here an hour or so was allowed for rest and the baggage equipment detached to remain in the village for the time being. At this point, 10 km from the Sikh line, advanced pickets of the Sikh army could be seen scouting the British movements.

At 9 a.m., the British line was ordered to advance again, moving in contiguous columns of brigades with the guns interspersed between. 'The immediate neighbourhood of Dinghee was pretty free from jungle but along the base of the sand ridge and in front of the whole of the Sikh position it was exceedingly dense rendering all military operations especially movements of cavalry or artillery most difficult and hazardous and concealing effectually the enemy's line,' noted E. Buckle of the Bengal Artillery.

For the attack on the Sikh left at Rasul, the dirt track from Amra Kalan to Rasul would be utilised as previously agreed; engineers were sent ahead and reported the road was good for the heavy guns and for an advance until they saw Sikh units in the distance, whereupon they returned. By this time it was 10 a.m., and as the advance continued down the road the Sikh batteries and camp began to be seen through the intervening trees in the distance. A few deserters and assorted camp followers from the Sikh camp were seen walking down the road at this time who informed the British pickets of the presence of the Sikh outposts in the villages of Chillianwala and Mojianwalla, around 3 km south-west of the British line. Gough, not wanting to leave any enemy units in his rear, changed plans at this point, deciding to move towards the villages first and mop up any Sikh units before resuming the advance towards Rasul. And so, after a further halt of an hour and a half to rest the troops and keep them fresh for battle, the line changed direction again, leaving the Rasul road and instead slowly moving south-westwards toward these villages.

Engineers were sent to explore the vicinity of the villages around noon, and it was found there were indeed detachments of Sikh troops with around five to six guns at Chillianwala plus some cavalry. Of these, two Sikh guns and an entrenched outpost with around 500 men were situated on a slight mound around 200 yards to the north of the village. Preparations were duly made for an attack on the village, Gough ordering ten heavy guns, including the 3rd Light Field batteries, forward along with three horse batteries. After a short cannonade lasting no more than ten minutes, the 2nd Europeans and the 30th and 70th NI were ordered to storm the village. The Sikh contingent then evacuated the village, moving back towards the main Sikh line by the Moong road. With the villages captured, the British line advanced to a position around 500 yards west of the village before stopping. There was disappointment at the lack of plunder at Chillianwala, the Sikh soldiers having left little of value. 'Some loot was taken,' one of the British soldiers recorded later. 'A looking glass falling to one doughty warrior's share, he was remarked contemplating his dirty powder-begrimed visage with evident satisfaction, "What big children soldiers are!"'

The British line now squarely faced the Sikh position rather than moving towards the Sikh left as first agreed the night before. According to Thackwell, the British line was almost as lengthy as that formed during the Battle of Waterloo but Gough still thought that he was outflanked. Whether this was founded on intelligence is unclear, but certainly with the jungle a mere 200 yards away from the periphery of the village it was difficult to tell. A temporary halt was now called while Gough searched for the highest house in the hamlet from which to survey the Sikh position over the treetops. The time now was already past 2 p.m., and, surveying what he could see of the Sikh line through the canopy of trees, a permanent halt for the day was decided, the battle to be delayed till the morning. His troops had been marching since daybreak and the short winter day would soon be over, Gough concluded. In addition there was no water to be had between Chillianwala and the Sikh positions, although there were wells in the village and Mojianwalla to its rear. Further reconnaissance was taken while there was light, with the engineers examining the terrain in front. Meanwhile the quartermasters of corps with camp colours were summoned and orders given for a camp to be made, with many of the regiments already having piled arms in anticipation.

The view of the Sikh line and camp Gough had seen through the foliage was heavily obscured and patchy despite the high position. He could see no Sikh soldiers or guns. Some of those in the British line endeavoured to get a better view of the Sikh position. One of these was Colin Campbell, who noticed a mud pillar nearby and took the opportunity to clamber on top, thus gaining possibly one of the best views from the British position.

'On looking from the mud-pillar on the right of my division, I could perceive that the enemy occupied a position of some five or six miles, at least, in extent. This position was full of troops, with the whole of their guns, between fifty and sixty,' he wrote later.

By this time, though, everyone was busying themselves with making camp. 'Arms were piled,' wrote Macpherson, a subaltern of HM 24th, 'artillery parked, horses off-saddled, the last thing anyone expected being an immediate battle'. Macpherson, also curious, looked for a vantage position and with several comrades clambered high up a tree for a better view than Campbell, as he related later.

After peering closely around, rubbing our eyes to see more clearly, 'Hallo!' cried Lutman, 'what's that yonder?' Sure enough there was something flitting to and fro, appearing and disappearing on the outskirts of the screen of jungle, which turned out to be the white turbans of the Sikhs, whom we could now distinctly see. They were bringing up their guns to enfilade the beaten tracks they knew we must traverse, should we attack. 'By jove, the place is alive,' replied Williams. Down we jumped and ran to report what we had seen ... Just then round shot came pouring into our camp ground and ere we could catch our breath, the bugles rang out 'the alarm' followed by the 'assembley' then came the hurried words of command, 'Stand to your arms', 'Unpile', 'Fall in'.

Gough had not counted on a Sikh advance post initiating the battle. As preparations for camp were being made, several shots whistled past only a few feet from Gough himself and landed well past the camp boundary flags. There's speculation as to whether these shots were fired under the orders of Shere Singh or not. It's possible the Sikh commander, having seeing the British line drawing near, was happy to begin, knowing the haughty British general would take the bait despite the disadvantage of the trees to his artillery. Other accounts later speculated Shere Singh had been more than content to let Gough encamp so close to the Sikh batteries. This meant the opportunity of bombarding the British camp during the night, inevitably causing confusion and offering little chance for the British guns to respond effectively against the Sikh troops and gunners, protected in their entrenchments. A differing account gleaned from combatants after the war mentions Gough being spotted on the housetop by a son of Shere Singh, who commanded an advance battery. Seeing an opportunity to dispose of the British general, who was in clear view, he needed no urging and had promptly moved some guns forward and fired three shots which landed close to Gough and his entourage. The enthusiasm of his son therefore frustrated Shere Singh's plan for a night cannonade and the battle was triggered prematurely, much to the chagrin of both commanders. Yet another account filtered through to the British camp after the battle that another Sikh officer, not Shere Singh's son, had ordered the premature firing and for disobeying orders was executed after the battle by an annoyed Shere Singh.

Whatever the real story, the shots from the Sikh guns had fallen comfortably within the British camp perimeter and Gough quickly realised the impossibility of staying in this position for the night. The choice was simple. Either a retreat could be called so a new camp for the night could be organised out of range of the Sikh guns or an advance for battle ordered. Perhaps bearing his character in mind, it was no surprise he opted for the latter course. The British heavy guns were immediately ordered to return the fire. This had the effect of drawing the fire from all the batteries in the Sikh line as well. This along with a body of Gorcharas advancing toward the British line excited the Commander-in-Chief still further. A smart cannonade between the rival guns now ensued for around twenty to thirty minutes while the British line was organised for an advance.

By this time it was 3 p.m. and only an hour or two of daylight remained. Some of his officers, nonplussed by the decision to fight, would strongly advise a retreat to a safer camp area and deferring the battle till the next day. However, irritated by his officers' presumptuousness along with the spectacle of Sikh cannon shot falling round him, he apparently refused to consider this option, going as far as to say, according to a newspaper correspondent standing in close proximity, that 'the first officer who presumes to advice, he will put him in close arrest'. Neither did he appear to wish to listen to the political agent Major Mackeson, who approached him with similar words of caution. 'His answer to my agent was, "I am C.-in-C. of this army and I desire you to be silent,"' complained Dalhousie later in correspondence with the Secret Committee. According to Lord Gifford, who was standing close to Gough and who related the story of the battle later to Dalhousie, the Commander-in-Chief in conversation with a brigadier was frank about his impulse to do battle. 'Indeed, I had not intended to attack to-day, but the impudent rascals fired on me. They put my Irish blood up, and I attacked them.'

While these discussions were being taken at his vantage point on top of the village house, the gunners of both sides continued exchanging shot. They had their own difficulties in judging distance with the intervening jungle. The gathering darkness helped in some fashion. The flashes of the Sikh guns could be seen through the foliage as light became progressively dimmer, giving indication of the location of the Sikh artillery and vice versa, although little or no damage was recorded in this opening exchange. While this had been going on, the infantry had been told to lie down to escape the worst effects of the guns. Gough ordered a concentration of fire from his big guns at the Sikh middle, this being where the flashes showed most of the guns were placed.

As the ammunition began to run out, Gough would give out orders for a general advance. And therefore it was at around 3:30 p.m., with the sun low on the horizon, that the general British advance began towards the river. Campbell was ordered to advance at the same time as Gilbert and Pope. Thackwell on the left was given free rein to decide his policy depending on the conditions and resistance he met. All the troops marched in line with no reserve apart from Brig. Penny's brigade, to be stationed at Chillianwala village. From here on, there would be contrasting fortunes for each of the British brigades as they pushed forward, the belt of trees precluding any effective communication or action in concert and making the battle a series of individual struggles.

*\*\*\**

The advance on the British right by the cavalry began in high spirits as orders were relayed to Pope to move forward. He was heard to call on his men to 'Come on' as the trumpets sounded. His division answered with a cheer and moved off with perfect precision. With the British right moving first, followed a short while later by Gilbert's division to his left, in theory an echelon formation should have developed. The roughly 5 km separating the Sikh line from the British should have posed no problem in clear terrain. However, the natural obstruction of the jungle as Pope advanced conspired to make his line more and more ragged as they worked their way through the trees. Each man was only able to see a few metres to either side and the ends of the line were out of sight to each other, making it impossible to maintain order.

The Sikh line was still believed to be longer by Gough, and so as Pope advanced some squadrons were told to turn right in order to stop an expected flank attack but most of the division advanced ahead. In the confusing circumstances of the jungle, Pope's cavalry imperceptibly drifted to their left, however, and into the path of the artillery between themselves and Gilbert's division, advancing a few hundred metres behind at that time. In fact, some of the cavalry drifted far enough to be directly in front of Gilbert's advancing line, reducing the extent of the British line and proving an obstruction for Gilbert's men later.

The selection of Pope to lead was an error on the part of Gough. He was a sick man and by some accounts suffering from rheumatic issues. The veteran had not been feeling well that day and could not mount his own horse without help from three or four men and a chair. No doubt if the advance had gone well he would have been treated as a hero for his gallantry on the day. With what was about to happen, however, the choice of Pope would be criticised later. He had never commanded a brigade under fire.

Midway during the advance, Pope managed to get into a personal contest with a Sikh skirmisher, the result being a severe wound in the face from a sabre. Disabled from the wound, he would arrive back in the village and would play no further part in the proceedings. A short distance from the Sikh line a temporary halt was called as his injury was made known to his officers before the advance was continued. Importantly there seemed to be some confusion as to who would take command in Pope's absence and a lack of communication with the soldiers on this issue.

Havelock commented later on the fact that the forest here was quite thick and that no skirmishers for some reason had been sent forward to warn of an advance by the enemy. In addition, he commented, 'No reserve, second line, or supporting column provided against temporary reverse, though this is an indispensable rule in cavalry arrangements, and not only did the extended line overlap the infantry, but the line was by the trees and clumps of brushwood speedily broken into an infinite series of small sections doubled behind each other.'

According to the letter of a non-commissioned officer of the 14th Dragoons, the 1st and 6th Light Cavalry and the 14th Light Dragoons advanced in a line two deep, not realising that the British guns were now behind them as the bushes were too high even for a man on horseback. The gunners presumably had no clue that the cavalry was in front of them by several hundred yards, either. In this rather confused fashion, Pope's men, minus their leader, continued the advance at a slow trot, negotiating their way through the thorny bushes when Sikh Gorcharas ordered to attack by Shere Singh were seen thundering towards them from the front. This attack by the Gorcharas came as a complete surprise, there being no skirmishers in front. What happened next was the cause of much discussion and recrimination for years to come, with a huge number of alternate explanations being put forward.

With Pope *hors de combat*, there had still been no effective transfer of command. Some would claim the order 'Threes about' was given out by an officer, the command to retreat, and was the reason for the rapid retreat by the 14th Dragoons. According to Lord Gifford, one of Gough's aides at Chillianwala, a private apparently was blamed by others nearby who heard him shout, 'The Sikhs are in our rear—threes about,' at which point the turning and the confusion caused by the jungle led to the panic in the line. Other witnesses argued a sergeant-armourer of the 14th

Dragoons shouted the command. Interestingly, some combatants, like a certain Geo Pocock, whose account was published in one of the newspapers in March 1849, later blamed Pope, saying he was still on the field despite his wound at the time and personally gave the order to retire.

> This old Pope, he was up in front of the brigade and he got a — in the back of the head that took his — half off and stunned him, so he didn't know what he was doing. He gave the trumpeter the order to sound Retire, and I have heard that he told the natives in Hindustani to retire. I know very well that I was on the left of my regiment in among them cutting away like old boots and I heard the native cavalry officers give them the order to retire to the rear by threes from left of squadrons, and at the same time was just got into them. Me being on the left could hear this order give to them. I began to look two ways for Sunday.

Gough would later state in his despatches that 'some order or misapprehension of an order' had caused their flight, which put the blame on Pope although he wasn't named. Pope in turn would write protesting to Gough on this point, dismayed he was implicated when he claimed he was being transported back to the village at the time.

Still others blamed Col Bradford of the 1st Light Cavalry, who was the senior officer after Pope's injury. He disagreed that any verbal order to retreat was issued at all, by him or by any other officer. Letters by him and several members of the Dragoons later written to the *Calcutta Review* and printed in November 1850 and to the *The Englishman* in June 1849 attempted to clear his name and that of the Dragoons and tell a different story. Bradford claims he was only made aware of Pope's injuries when the brigade had finally rallied near the village of Chillianwala and therefore he did not have the authority to order any retreat. According to Bradford, it was sheer panic due to the attack by the Gorcharas that was to blame.

> I solemnly declare that I gave no order to retire, either to my own, or to any other regiment; nor did I hear such an order given; and the first intimation I had of the retreat of the brigade was, having it pointed out to me by one of my own officers, when we were in the midst of, and actually engaged with, the advanced party of the Ghorechurras; after which my whole energies and attention were necessarily directed to my own regiment, then giving way.
>
> My trumpeter sounded the bait and rally repeatedly, which had the effect of halting the three troops of my own regiment engaged, and other squadrons; but, our flank being by this time turned by the Ghorechurras, the retreat was continued, in spite of my exertions to stop it.

According to a letter by Bradford later to a Capt. Ferguson, there was an engagement with the Sikh cavalry and the retreat wasn't purely impulsive.

> A number of single handed encounters with the enemy then ensued. I observed officers and men of the 14th dragoons and light cavalry engaged with the enemy, and the same was going on on our right along the line, but very shortly the troops, without any order, went about, and without any apparent reason the whole line galloped to the rear, nor could all the exertions of the officers arrest the panic. The halt was repeatedly sounded by my trumpeters, and at one time there appeared a prospect of stopping the disorder, and

bringing back the men to the charge, but the appearance of the enemy on the flank sent the whole of the troops in one mass to the left; nor could the men be halted until they formed in rear of the guns.

Both Col Bradford and Col Lane would write to Col Pope later expressing their versions of what happened. Sensing some of the blame falling on him again, Pope forwarded these letters to Gough, asking to be publicly exonerated for having given any order to retreat. Gough would reply rather coldly through the Adjutant-General that he 'accepted the denial' but didn't extend any sympathy. He also didn't go as far as publicly withdrawing the version he had written in his despatches either. None of these accounts, of course, gave any credit to the Gorcharas who had swept through the jungle and who now drove the Dragoons back towards the village.

Whatever the situation and sequence of events, this was the beginning of what Havelock would describe later as a 'panic as shameful as that of Preston Pans'. The Dragoons raced back down towards the village with little discipline, followed closely by the Gorcharas in hot pursuit. According to Bradford, the Lancers positioned to the right of the Dragoons also ran but they didn't exhibit the 'intense panic', as he put it, of the Dragoons. If Pope's division had not overlapped the British guns, specifically the horse artillery of Major Christie and Gilbert's men advancing to their left, the confusion would have been limited. This was not the case, however. As the two lines of horsemen, intermingling in some places due to their close proximity, raced towards the village of Chillianwala, they confused the British artillery and wagons that had been advancing a few hundred metres behind the horsemen, some of the crew of the twelve guns being sabred and the rest of the crews being thrown into disarray. 'They were so crowded among the guns that the gunners could not unlimber. The result was that the enemy's cavalry got among our guns and cut our men down, right and left. The — never drew rein until they got right through the general hospital in the rear, knocking over the doolies and everything that came in their way. What caused this panic no one knows,' a private letter from the battlefield later revealed.

Some of the gunners were trampled down by the British cavalry themselves and others by the Gorcharas, including Major Christie and many of his gunners. Tumbrils were seen being upset by both sets of cavalry as they thundered through the jungle. Any British gunner, even if he had had the opportunity, could not have fired for fear of hitting their own comrades at this point. All six cannon were abandoned by the gunners in the panic, although two would be recovered later.

Lt Cureton, the son of Brig.-Gen. Cureton who had died at Ramnuggar, was one of those despatched by the advancing Sikh cavalry, his horse becoming unmanageable during the confusion. Meanwhile Major Ekins, Deputy Adjutant-General, who was delivering an order to the brigade, was caught in the melee and badly wounded. Major Chester, a friend of his near the scene, attempted rescuing him but Ekins, realising anyone attempting to help him would be courting death, waved him off. Chester saved himself, although Ekins was found dead later. Lt Dundas and Lt Manson were also killed during this time.

Further confusion was to follow. The British field hospital had been set up a few hundred metres behind the advancing line. Major Matthew Smith of HM 29th happened to be in the hospital at the time it was being readied in anticipation for receiving the wounded.

At 3:30 p.m. an order came for the brigade to charge, away they went with all the dash of British dragoons while the surgeon and myself were giving directions to have our appliances brought up from a short distance behind. We has scarcely given our directions, the brigade had not gone two minutes when to my utter confusion the whole brigade came tearing back in the wildest disorder and before I could spring in to my saddle, I was surrounded by those who were fleetest in flight. I enquired the cause, could get no answer, and as those behind the foremost were coming on in mass I called upon our surgeon.

Both the British cavalry and the Gorcharas now raced through the British hospital, upsetting wounded soldiers and causing panic among the numerous camels and other pack animals. Various wounded and camp followers were trampled by the stampede of hundreds of mounted horses through the tents. Others who had managed to gain some sort of warning of the retreat managed to gain protection by climbing trees or by hiding in undergrowth and escaped injury.

The panic infected the complement of doctors and orderlies in the hospital, with surgeons mounting their horses and joining the fleeing soldiers. Some of the surgeons had been busy with those who had been wounded early on. A Dr Mc'Rae, a large and powerful man, was seen to be picking up a patient whom he flung on his horse before joining the retreat. Many would escape death, for the attention of the Gorcharas was on pursuing the Dragoons rather than the hospital occupants. Joining this mass of men fleeing to the rear were the thousands of camp followers who had drifted up to help in the hospital among other duties.

One of the more publicised stories of the confusion in the hospital involved the Revd Whiting, the army chaplain who was present when the Dragoons rode through. He was seen warding off the panic-stricken camp followers with a long bamboo, possibly a tent pole, as they trampled down tents in attempts to escape to Chillianwala village with little regard for the wounded lying in and around them. His action, Thackwell declared later, was 'worthy of a field-officer's batta!' Whiting would narrate a more controversial and widely circulated story after the battle. He declared he had held a loaded pistol to a fleeing officer's head (whom he did not name) and threatened to shoot him dead to make him halt, but that the officer was resistant to the threat and, shaking him off, would continue his run down the incline. Others would swear they saw Whiting remonstrating against other officers also as they fled the field.

This tale was challenged by various officers of the 14th Dragoons later and he was asked to retract it. In his letter to *The Mofussilite* Whiting, perhaps under pressure, would do so, changing his story to a milder version. Rather than the Dragoons causing havoc as they passed through the field hospital and knocking over the doctors and dhoolies containing the wounded and dying, he claimed it was the panic-stricken camp followers who did the damage. Regarding holding a pistol to the officer's head, Whiting wrote that he had just waved it around but not in a threatening way and not specifically at any officer.

That I did stop a small body of HM 14th Dragoons is true, and a large body of others who had equally no business where they were; but I used no threatening language which would have been alike foolish and unnecessary, for on receiving the word, the men instantly fronted and formed, listened in silence to what I had to say to them, and then with the other fugitives following in their rear, moved through the jungle quietly and steadily to their proper station. I need hardly say that no officer of HM 14th was with them. I mean commissioned officers.

There were other stories of officers behaving dishonourably as well. The retreat of the Dragoons had come to the notice of Gough by this time. He immediately sent Major Nicholson, then acting as one of his aides-de-camp, to help rally the retreating columns. Nicholson would see several officers running along with the men and in response approached and grabbed one of the officers by the collar to interrogate him about his conduct. The officer, apparently either from fear or lack of breath, failed to answer. Nicholson tried to instil some discipline into the man by shaking him but without success. Tiring of his lack of success, he then pushed him back among the fleeing column, telling him to 'go with his fellow-poltroons'.

Others like Thackwell largely dismissed stories like Whiting's as nonsense and there was a general consensus that most of the officers did their utmost to prevent the panicked retreat, initially at least, a view borne out by the casualty statistics in which officers suffered out of proportion. 'Many officers exerted themselves to stop the retreat,' Col Bradford would explain later, but the panic was too great. Bradford himself several times ordered a nearby trumpeter to sound a halt and rally repeatedly but to no avail; the pursuing Gorcharas too close behind to allow for a stand to be organised in any case.

The Dragoons soon cleared the belt of jungle and appeared to the right of where the British Commander-in-Chief happened to be situated with his staff before galloping on towards the village. Seconds later the Sikh cavalry appeared out of the jungle and halted just several hundred metres away from Gough. Only a small escort of cavalry was present near Gough and these were promptly moved forward in case of an attack, although their numbers were far too small to challenge the Gorcharas. A staff officer in Gough's group described those vital few seconds.

> The old chief [Gough] and the whole us were completely exposed to the Gorchurrahs who came within fifty yards of us but in consequence of the jungle were not aware of the prize within their reach; and two guns happening to come up at the moment – God knows how or why – the horsemen were driven back by the first discharge. Had this not providentially occurred we should all have been 'gone coons', as nothing, I am sure would have persuaded Lord Gough to budge an inch.

Having possibly run clear of their officers and with no clear orders to attack, the Sikh cavalry eschewed the chance of attacking Gough's small group and returned back to the Sikh line, giving the British Commander-in-Chief probably the closest escape of his life. There was some suggestion that the Gorcharas may have thought this all too easy a victory and that the retreat of the Dragoons may instead be a trap. Meanwhile, behind Gough and near the village, order was finally restored in the Dragoons by their officers.

Not all the British units on the right had fled, it was later found. These included two squadrons of 9th Lancers and two of the 6th Light Cavalry previously left defending the extreme-right flank along with Dawes battery. The firing of the battery and the cover of the forest prevented its isolated position being known to the Sikh line, thus preventing an advance which would most certainly have captured the isolated unit. Much praise would be directed towards Dawes after the battle for preventing a complete collapse of the British line on the right. Afterwards Godby on the left would thank Dawes for his remaining on the field. 'Captain Dawes, I am happy to have this public opportunity of thanking you, for saving my Brigade,' he was heard saying to Dawes in public. Gilbert, who was leading the division to the left of Pope, was also profuse in his praise. 'Dawes! Thank you for saving my Division!' he shouted loudly on seeing him after the battle.

*\*\*\**

Pope's confused retreat would have implications on Gilbert's division, advancing to his immediate left. When the advance began, the 2nd Bengal European Regiment, the 31st and

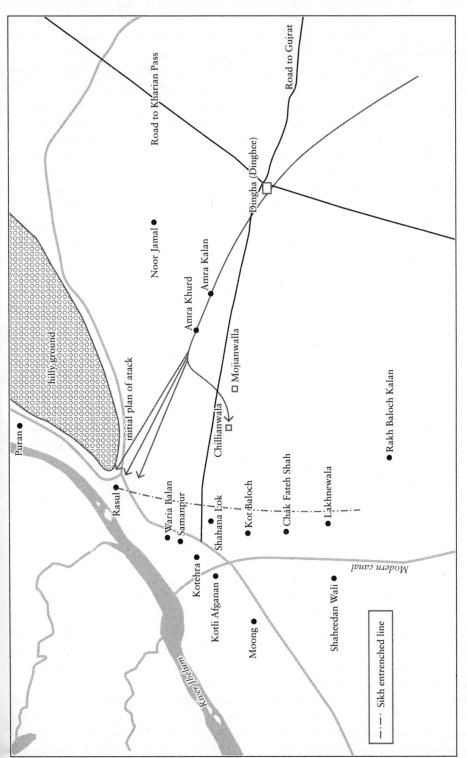

8. The Battle of Chillianwala

70th NI, commanded by Godby were positioned to the left of Pope's cavalry. With Pope's cavalry unintentionally veering left during the initial advance, they found themselves a few hundred metres behind the British horse instead of to their left as the British line became increasingly compressed. As they approached the Sikh line through the jungle, cries of shouting and fighting could be heard in front of them and moments later they saw elements of Pope's cavalry nearest and overlapping Gilbert's line threatening to mow down some of the advancing infantry, principally the 70th NI. Unfazed, most of Gilbert's division continued its advance and reached the Sikh line where fierce hand-to-hand fighting erupted along the division's whole length. The 2nd Bengal European Regiment had the most success, capturing and spiking four Sikh guns in some of the most confused fighting on the day. In the jungle no line was apparent and the brigade found they had to face all four directions at various points, some Sikh units having successfully outflanked the brigade. 'A large body of the enemy had turned our flank in the jungle, and got between us and the rest of the troops,' described Daniel Sandford, a soldier in the 2nd Bengal European Regiment, referring to the Gorcharas who had been pursuing Pope's men and who were returning up the incline. 'Another party was on our left, and we found ourselves with our light field battery, completely surrounded, and alone in the field. The fire was fearful; the atmosphere seemed alive with balls; I can only compare it to a storm of hail. They sang above my head and ear so thick, that I felt that if I put out my hand, it would be taken off. A man was knocked over on either side of me, and I expected every moment to be hit, so incessant was the storm of balls.'

\*\*\*

If the fighting was difficult for Gilbert's division, it was much worse for Campbell's brigades to their left. This division was situated directly to the left of the village before the advance. To Campbell's left were three troops of horse artillery along with White's brigade of cavalry. Between the two brigades was situated battery No. 5 of artillery, along with six 9-pounders. Campbell had decided he would remain and advance with Hoggan's brigade on his left while Pennycuick would command his own brigade. Campbell records that the terrain ahead of him was 'wood, dense and thick', similar to what was in front of White, and therefore any officer could only manage one brigade at best. 'I was told by the staff officer who brought me the order to advance that the three troops of horse-artillery on my left would support my advance,' recorded Campbell. He was also led to believe the division would be supported by horse artillery guns under Col Brind.

Campbell's division began the advance at the same time as Gilbert's to his right. A staff officer had ridden up to Campbell with instructions to use a silent approach, attacking the Sikh line with bayonets only. The reason for this was the supposed gap in the middle of the Sikh line; a silent approach could take advantage of this. Another reason for this tactic surfaced later, though. Pennycuick, in his conversations with Gough a few days earlier, had discussed tactics to be used in the coming battle. The topic of HM 10th's advance into the Sikh line at Sabraon during the First Anglo-Sikh War had somehow arisen during these dialogues. Pennycuick had expressed a wish to emulate the feat and Gough apparently could not praise this enough and had given the appropriate blessing, the fact that this middle section of the Sikh line was supposedly poorly manned no doubt helping the decision. But there would be few similarities between Sabraon and the Sikh line lying in front of his brigade now. At Sabraon, HM 10th had attacked the weakest section of the Sikh line, bereft of guns, over a clear piece of ground. Here the brigade was attacking a section well manned and well guarded by guns through difficult terrain. In addition the brigade would advance without the benefit of accompanying flanking artillery. 'Why the batteries attached to this brigade were left in the background, is a question which must be left to Sir Colin Campbell and Lord Gough,' mused Thackwell after the battle. 'We do not undertake to state what the exact nature of the order was; but, it is very manifest, that neither the Brig. General, nor his brigadiers, regarded the artillery as necessary; in other words, the contempt of the enemy was not confined to poor Pennycuick.'

The reason for the lack of guns, again, was speculated to have been the element of surprise. In addition, some of the combatants later related that there was confusion as to whether the brigade was asked to attack the Sikh line or merely to advance but not attack till ordered. On the day, with reference to Gough's instructions, Campbell rode towards Pennycuick's brigade before the advance and a stirring speech was delivered of the exploits of HM 24th during the Peninsular War.

'He told us, how on one occasion, when some corps, of which the 24th was one, were ordered to carry a position at the point of the bayonet, it was the only corps that obeyed the order, doing its part without firing a shot,' an officer wrote later. 'You must not fire, steel must do the work,' Campbell summed up loudly to reinforce the point before he rode back towards Hoggan's brigade. 'Let it be said that the 24th carried the position and guns at the point of the bayonet, without firing a shot.' In conversation with another officer after the battle, Campbell would go some way to admitting this policy was an error: 'I am sorry I said it. It would have been better to have sent in a volley or two before storming the guns.'

Not that the fault was entirely his. It was said that Pennycuick, anxious to make the feat of capturing the Sikh line in front of him more memorable, even forbade the priming of muskets so no fire could be returned rapidly even if circumstances dictated it. Others disagree with this, although the order to avoid fire is not disputed. Pennycuick was in charge of HM 24th, which comprised nearly half of his force at around 1,100 men, with the 45th NI to its left and 25th NI to its right comprising around 600 men each. HM 24th incidentally were the only regiment on the battlefield with chacos and full dress. Sergeant Thompson of the regiment recalled a confident Col Brookes addressing the regiment before the advance. 'Men, we are going to charge the mound, and, by the grace of God, we shall gain a glorious victory!'

Some accounts mention that Brookes, with the Grenadier Company in skirmishing order in front, would wave his sword over his head, which was a signal to move in double time. However, Lt-Col Howell Paynter declared that they continued walking rather than moving in double time. Whatever the case, a cheer went up along the line as the brigade commenced its advance. They happened to be accompanied by a deer in front of their line by the name of 'Billy', a regimental pet and apparently a great favourite of the men. Mowatt's field battery was positioned between Pennycuick's men and Hoggan's brigade to his left, with companies of skirmishers leading the advance.

As expected, the brigade would face awkward terrain similar to that faced by Gilbert's division to their right and had correspondingly similar difficulties. As they marched through the undergrowth, the jungle seemed to get thicker and the ground more uncompromising. Some overlapping of the companies began to take place and disorder was apparent. Many of the men complained later of the loose, thorny hedges which tended to cling on to clothing as the men moved through, making the advance difficult. Many of the men of HM 24th found their chacos being knocked off by the low branches as well. As Capt. Hamilton described in a letter to the *Calcutta Review* later, 'It was soon anything but a line – marching through thick jungle, having to clear our way through enclosures of thorns, how could it be otherwise than broken? We could see no distance to our front. Our light companies were ordered to skirmish, but not to fire.'

Because of the jungle, the left of the brigade could not hear or see what the right was doing. Despite the confusion, there was an upbeat feeling and confidence through the line, the men cheering loudly every time the Sikh guns in front of them fired despite men already falling. Campbell would concede the terrain was more difficult for Pennycuick's men than for Hoggan's brigade.

> I accompanied the left brigade. The wood was thick in front of both brigades, but it offered many and more serious obstacles to the advance of poor Pennycuick's, the line formation of which was exceedingly disordered and broken, the companies in many places being obliged to reduce their front to sections; whilst the regiments, during this state, were exposed to the fire of fifteen or eighteen pieces of artillery placed on a mound immediately in their front, from whence the advance of H.M's 24th and the other two regiments could be plainly seen, although the battery was concealed from the view of our men by reason of their being below it, and owing to the thickness of the jungle. H.M. 24th advanced at a rapid rate, and preceded the native corps on either flank. These corps, I am told, crowded in upon the 24th to escape the fire of the artillery, and by this means got mixed up with that regiment, adding much to their confusion.

The original plan was for this brigade along with Hoggan's and Mountain's brigades to its left and right to emerge from the jungle and attack simultaneously, but the poor visibility through the trees frustrated this at an early stage and all attempts to move in concert failed. HM 24th, as it turned out, would move much faster than the other regiments. Increasingly in a huddle rather than a line, the brigade continued until the jungle could be seen to clear. The men of HM 24th, as they approached the end of the belt, encountered some denser sections of trees. In avoiding these, they found themselves bunched up even more when they came out in the open. These denser sections the Sikh gunners already knew about; they had anticipated the points from which British troops would appear, and the Sikh guns were trained accordingly.

Another 50 metres later, the brigade was out in the open and could see the Sikh line stretching to the left and right. The trees and bushes that confused the British line, though, had also served to protect them from the worst of the Sikh shot. Coming into the open allowed the brigade as it filtered out to get its bearings but also exposed it to the withering fire from the Sikh gunners, who had now changed to grapeshot, only 300 yards to the front while the Sikh musket men finally found something to aim at and began peppering the British line.

The brigade appeared tired, having negotiated their way through the trees. In conversation with Lt Bowie and George Lawrence later, Shere Singh, who happened to be opposite the brigade at this time, related the soldiers of HM 24th 'panting like dogs in chase' when they broke into the open area. There was one other obstacle before a clear run at the Sikh line. These were the stretches of shallow water in front. In order to avoid these, the brigade found itself bunching up still further. Much of the brigade would approach no closer than the periphery of the jungle, however, for the fire from the Sikh line was so severe that the British line was thrown entirely into confusion. The Sikh guns opened up with grape and canister with such precision and rapidity that whole sections of the line began to be swept away before any attempt at advance. Some British troops as they moved out of the jungle swore they saw Europeans among the Sikh line manning and helping direct the artillery, possibly French.

'My company was near the centre where the Colours were as a target to aim at. One discharge of grape seems to have swept away my right section – for a moment I am alone, still unhurt,' wrote a soldier of the 24th. The centre companies in fact would be largely annihilated, only the side ones reaching the Sikh line. All order disappeared at this point, with the 24th regiment breaking into several scattered groups. Some of the groups bravely attempted to attack the Sikh line while others withered in the storm. One of the casualties in this fire as they advanced was Brig. Pennycuick. Pennycuick had dismounted earlier according to Major Matthew Smith, perhaps due to having his horse shot underneath him, and continued on foot with his men.

They got under a tremendous fire of round shot and grape – the regiment was at the charge pace – and when within some 50 yards of the guns, a seargeant saw the brigadier stagger and put his hand to his body, just below the breast. He and another went up to him to offer assistance – but he declined it saying – 'go on with the regiment'. Shortly after, a private soldier seeing that he was wounded went to him, and he accepted his assistance – two seargeants then joined him – and he said 'I am badly wounded, take me to the rear' – they saw that he was bleeding profusely from a large wound in the body – and rapidly losing strength – these three men conveyed him towards the rear, and shortly found that he was dead.

Those that did follow the order to charge meanwhile had quickened their pace and advanced. The grenadier company on the right were the first to reach the Sikh line, where the fighting was fierce. 'At the battery, the Sikhs fought like fiends, struggling on the bayonets, and while impaled, slashing at our men with their keen tulwars as long as life lasted – dying with a scowl of hatred,' wrote another soldier. Others noted too the Sikh soldier's willingness to trade a bayonet wound for the return chance to swing the tulwar at the heads of the British soldiers. Some of the brigade led by a Capt. Travers managed to capture and spike several guns. On seeing his line wavering, Shere Singh, who had purposely hidden some of his best men behind a depression a few metres behind the Sikh line, ordered his reserve to advance and reinforce the main line. This turned the contest definitively in the Sikh line's favour and precipitated a retreat by the entire British brigade. 'Close to the position it received a deadly shower of grape, and, while shattered by its fatal effects, was torn to pieces by a close fire poured in by the Bunnoo troops from behind a screen of jungle. The native regiments, when they came up, were unable to restore the battle. The brigade was thrown into utter confusion. The most desperate efforts of the officers availed not to restore order,' Havelock would describe later. A rapid retreat of the regiment down the incline was the consequence.

'Our regiment at this time was in the greatest confusion possible, no man knew his place nor was there any one to tell you. The enemy's cavalry charged on us and their solid squares of infantry formed up in rear of their guns let a regular volley into us, and with the cavalry made a tremendous charge upon us. Our brigade retired in disorder, the cavalry at our heels, cutting every poor fellow that was wounded or exhausted with running to the rear. We had no support, not so much as a gun or a dragoon. Awful indeed was the slaughter in our regiment,' wrote Pte H. Plumb of HM 24th.

One of the reasons mooted later for the retreat of HM 24th not being stemmed was, as Plumb had written, the lack of British guns in support. According to the chronicler James Lawrence-Archer, who later met Lt Sweton Grant of HM 24th, the orderly officer to Brig.-Gen. Campbell on the day of the battle, Campbell had realised the mistake of not posting any batteries in this section of the line. He had sent Grant to search for them but by then it was too late and Grant in any case had no luck tracing them in the jungle.

At the same time as HM 24th were clearing the jungle, a few hundred metres to the left the 45th NI had also been advancing. They were close enough to HM 24th and sought to coordinate their charge with them. Through the trees a few hundred metres away, however, it was difficult to see what was happening to the extreme left of HM 24th. As the 45th emerged into the clearing, they noticed three guns had been situated directly opposite them. A charge of sorts would take place according to Capt. Hamilton of the 45th, but they had been looking to HM 24th to lead the way: 'We were under the impression that the Europeans were merely taking breath, and would immediately make the final spring; but the enemy's fire had been very severe, and, as it was concentrated on the Europeans, they could not stand it, but broke and made off for the village. The 45th N. I. followed their example. It was not to be expected that natives would stand, when Europeans would not.' The 45th began to retreat back into the jungle. To add to their discomfort, Shere Singh ordered a charge by the Gorcharas along with an advance by some of his infantry. A rapid retreat from the brigade now began down the hill. What would save the brigade from worse casualties was the advance of Mountain and Hoggan's brigades on either side of them. Many of the Sikh cavalrymen and infantry pursuing had to turn left and right to protect their own flanks. The Sikh contingents who began a pursuit were seen to return to bolster the Sikh line as the other British brigades advanced through the jungle. Some of the retreating troops of the 45th, on seeing Hoggan advancing through the jungle to their left, joined up with him and thus prevented a complete rout in this section of the line.

From the list of fatalities it was obvious here, too, that the British officers attempted a determined effort to prevent a collapse. Thirteen officers in total fell under the attack from the Sikh line with another ten wounded from a full complement of twenty-nine that had commenced the advance. The brigadier, colonel and major of the brigade would all fall. Pennycuick had already fallen. His seventeen-year-old son, also of HM 24th, was killed as well when he saw his father's body and challenged the advancing Sikh infantrymen nearby. His officers Sgt McCabe and Sgt Stocken attempted to bring his body back but the rapid retreat allowed no opportunity and his corpse was dropped. Col Brookes, who had assumed command on Pennycuick's death, was also killed. He had recently transferred from HM 69th Foot. Major Painter was shot through the lungs and, although he managed to ride away, later succumbed to his wounds. Capt. Williams was badly wounded. Feigning death, he managed to survive and slipped back into the British camp. Major Harris, described as 'a tall portly old officer' who was severely fatigued and scarcely capable of walking, was seen at the retreat being cut down by a Sikh sowar with one blow of his tulwar. Lt Thelwall, a mounted orderly officer in Pennycuick's brigade, was also wounded but saved by a fortunate occurrence. He was shot in the thigh. With his horse shot under him as well, he lay there as the Sikh line advanced, expecting to meet his maker shortly. However, a horse that he had recently sold to Major Harris, who had already been slain, recognised its previous owner. Thelwall wasted no time in seizing the opportunity, mounting the horse and promptly riding back towards the village. A senior officer wounded during the retreat, on passing another wounded officer as the men pushed back, was heard to exclaim, 'This is a bad day for the 24th.'

The retreat of this brigade along with the repulse of Pope on the right had begun filtering through to the camp at Chillianwala by now, and panic had begun spreading through the camp followers as the staff of the field hospital were seen fleeing towards the village and camp. It was found the bheesties (water carriers) were spreading the news of the British repulse rapidly and the camp followers were in turn being infected with more panic. There were murmurs among the camp followers: 'The English are beaten and the Sikhs are coming,' was heard being shouted.

Rather than trying to rally in the jungle, which was proving fruitless, some officers were of the opinion a rally would be better attempted on open ground closer to the village. In due course the brigade would arrive back at the village of Chillianwala and the officers remaining exerted themselves to bring about some order. There followed a hasty reorganisation of the battle line. An officer finding a colour sergeant ordered him to stand twenty paces off and shout to his company (naming its number) while the officer did the same. The calls by the officers hastened the troops towards the officers. The officer was then heard to have 'told them off' while the remnants of the regiment drifted in through the undergrowth and trees.

At this stage, an officer on a grey charger was seen riding past the regiment. 'Save yourselves! Their Cavalry are upon you!' he shouted to them as he passed them by. The fleeing officer was never named in any account. He was known to be a good officer and was promoted later, awarded the Companionship of the Bath, his name appearing in Gough's despatch. Despite the rider's suggestion, order had been largely re-established and a fresh line organised. A Capt. Blachford, the acting field officer for the day, who had not joined in the previous advance, was now given the command. 'I found myself senior officer on the field with only seven officers to command,' Blachford would write later. Managing the line as best he could, he led it back toward the Jhelum, the orders he received being to support Gilbert's division to the right of their original position where some Sikh batteries were to be attacked. As they advanced they could see corpses of HM 29th and 56th NI round them. It was too late, however. When the regiment and the remainder of the brigade reached its position, most of the fighting had ceased. The two shots marking the end of the battle would come from the Sikh guns as the 24th reappeared through the jungle.

*** 

Hoggan's brigade, situated to the left of Pennycuick and led personally by Sir Colin Campbell, had more success and the battle on this section of the line was much more evenly balanced. Campbell had decided to deliberately march at a much slower rate given the obstacle of the jungle in front and thus his brigade managed to approach the Sikh line in a more organised fashion, although much later than Pennycuick's men. HM 61st were situated in the middle of the brigade, flanked by the 36th NI on the right and the 46th on the left. In this condition, and showing no tiredness due to their cautious advance, they emerged from the wooded area to face the Sikh line. Owing to its position, Campbell's brigade would contest with the flank of Shere Singh's centre units. Campbell brought up his left in order to outflank the Sikh line and turn it. The brigade managed to reach the Sikh line at various points and spiked several guns. However, sharp conflict broke out everywhere along this line. It is known that units of HM 61st had to face several directions during the fight, indicating Sikh troops themselves attempting to outflank the British line. Word had reached Campbell by this time of the repulse and retreat of Pennycuick's brigade, and to his credit he managed to move HM 61st to the right in good order. Four of the Sikh guns were captured along with those spiked.

An unlikely event occurred on this section of the field while HM 61st were moving to their right. A Sikh officer rode to within a few feet of the regiment through the jungle and the din of the battle and calmly observed the British movement and its troops. He then rode back just as calmly. So assured and confident was he that the soldiers of the regiment believed him to be on their side. It was only when he had ridden back close to the Sikh lines that it was realised who he was and the British muskets opened up – rather too late, as it turned out.

'The contest here,' reported Thackwell later, 'was more equal, and better maintained than in any other quarter.' Although some guns had been spiked, the Sikh line in due course pushed back the British, recapturing the guns. 'We found the enemy posted on an open space on a slight rise. He had four guns, which played upon us in our advance; a large body of cavalry in the immediate front of the 61st, and a large body of infantry immediately on their left, and opposite to the 36th N.I. The four guns were on the right of the infantry, and played upon the 6Ist and the 36th N.I in their advance. The 36th N.I. went at the infantry, and were repulsed; while the 61st moved gallantly and steadily on the cavalry in their front, which steadily and slowly retired.'

As HM 61st continued to move forward Campbell ordered them to fire on the retreating Sikh cavalry, which had the intended effect. However, the advance of the 36th NI had completely failed. Meanwhile, Sikh gunners had manoeuvred two guns towards the right flank of HM 61st in order to enfilade the line while protected by Sikh infantry in the process of advancing against the now retreating 36th. From the right of HM 61st, the guns were only 30 yards away and ready to pour grape into the British line. This forced Campbell's hand and his immediate right was turned to face and charge the two guns, which were captured. The Sikh units that had followed the 36th were now forced to retreat themselves as Campbell's right advanced diagonally and opened fire on their flank and rear. 'In the meantime, the remainder of the 61st was formed upon the two right companies; and the officers of the 36th, with myself and other officers, tried to get the 36th to re-form upon the 61st, which we could not succeed in doing. The men were all talking together; many firing in the air, and all in confusion.'

In some of the most see-saw action of the battle, Sikh gunners would again approach the confused mass of men of HM 61st and 36th with two guns and open fire, prompting Campbell to perform the same manoeuvre as before to protect the 36th and continuing the diagonal advance on the Sikh line. 'After the capture of the second two guns, and dispersion of the enemy, we proceeded rolling up the enemy's line, continuing along the line of their position until we had taken thirteen guns, all of them at the point of the bayonet by the 61st,' wrote Campbell.

Holding the advantage, Campbell would continue the advance till he met Mountain's Brigade further to the right. This was therefore the most successful British action of the battle and quite critical in making up for the collapse elsewhere. The 46th NI, meanwhile, on HM 61st's left, had been attacked by Sikh cavalry and there was heavy fighting. In this confused fighting the guns that had been taken by HM 61st were captured again by the Sikh army, Campbell having moved the regiment to the right and being unable to either take them away or leave a detachment for their protection.

***

On the extreme left of the British line were stationed White's cavalry under the general command of Thackwell, along with three troops of horse artillery under Lt-Col Brind to their right (and to the left of Campbell's men). These men faced the Sikh commander Uttar Singh, who was thought to have several regiments of infantry and cavalry and around twenty guns. It would be Uttar Singh who attempted taking the initiative first by advancing the Gorcharas. The British line was well organised by Brind, who prevented the Gorcharas penetrating the line by opening up accurately with the British guns. However, the gap between Campbell's division and White's cavalry presented opportunities for the Sikh cavalry, who turned to their left to outflank

Campbell, further confusing the fight. Campbell was now engaged on three fronts: front, flank and rear. In addition, some of the Gorcharas outflanked Thackwell on his left. Thackwell in response divided his forces, with three squadrons of the 5th Light Cavalry and the Grey squadron of the 3rd Light Dragoons under Capt. Unett ordered to attack the flanking Gorcharas. Success brought them closer to the Sikh guns, but as they pushed forward they began to take more casualties.

'The 5th cavalry, in spite of their officers, came back in confusion, and intense was our anxiety about the fate of the 3rd Light Dragoons. At length they emerged covered with glory! Two officers were wounded – the gallant Unett and Stisted – and the loss among the men amounted to 46 killed and wounded!' reported one newspaper correspondent.

The rest of his force Thackwell had kept for a full-frontal assault. The bulk of the 3rd Light Dragoons and the 8th Light Cavalry was ordered to charge. The Sikh guns were served well here and along with the Sikh musket men, the British cavalry refrained from approaching too close to the Sikh line. 'It is an undeniable fact that the enemy ended the ball on the left,' concluded Thackwell. 'The precision of the Sikh fire on the whole was admirable; they disabled some of our guns and wagons. Loose horses, both British and Sikh abounded in all parts of the field.' The battle in this sector continued in desultory fashion, petering out into a virtual stalemate.

***

Back near the village, Gough was receiving regular news from all sectors and the desperate situation in some quarters was perhaps more obvious to him than to the some of the brigade commanders and officers in the jungle. Shortly after the British line had reached the Sikh line, a staff officer rode up to Gough to tell him Pope's brigade on the right had been repulsed and were retreating. Just a few minutes later, evidence of this retreat became apparent as the brigade rode back through the jungle and galloped by Gough's right and on to the village pursued by the Sikh Gorcharas. Shortly after this came news of the repulse of HM 24th with heavy casualties, and Pennycuick's brigade began to filter out of the jungle. With no news of a breakthrough from his left flank either, where Thackwell was holding his own, things looked grave. Thinking to use Penny's reserve brigade to bolster the line, Gough had ordered them in as soon as news of the repulse of Pennycuick's brigade was brought in.

These men, however, had got confused in the jungle and had instead veered right to join Gilbert's division, thus leaving almost the entire centre of the British line exposed, although neither Gough nor Shere Singh realised it at the time. Gough was seen disappearing into the wooded belt several times during the battle to examine the British line personally, something that would draw criticism later. It delayed vital decision-making and it was debatable how much he could see of what was happening in any case. 'His lordship fancied himself at Donnybrook Fair and was in the thick of it in the melee and lost to sight,' one soldier who would note sarcastically in a private letter.

By this time it was 5 p.m. and darkness was rapidly gathering pace with the fear of a Sikh counter-attack real and strong. 'If they had been enterprising and could have perceived the extent of their advantage, they would assuredly have thrown themselves on us; but the jungle which had befriended them in the commencement of the actions now formed a protection for us,' Thackwell wrote. Gough too was cognisant of the vulnerability of the British line and in one of his rides into the jungle had taken the opportunity to discuss the situation with Campbell. Campbell suggested a retreat to Chillianwala rather than continuing an attack that had clearly failed at many points. On the extreme right of the British line only the token force of Lane's batteries now stopped the Sikh line from advancing and outflanking the British line. In addition the British troops were tired and no water was available on the battlefield, with camp followers having fled. With all troops including the reserve committed, there were no more troops to bolster the line if required.

Gough took a strong stance against a retreat, initially at least. 'What! and leave my wounded to be massacred? Never!' he declared to Campbell. Nevertheless Campbell's argument was sound. To stay on the battlefield for the night would mean the British troops would be harassed all night by the Sikh guns. They would be deprived of any sleep, food and water before hostilities erupted again the next morning. Campbell also reminded Gough the baggage lay largely unprotected at this point to the east of the village, an opportunity for the Sikh cavalry that would be obvious as soon as daylight arrived. The best thing would be to retreat to the village, he reiterated, where a reorganisation of the army could be attempted, something clearly not possible in the jungle. Gough at length took the advice and finally a decision to entrench the entire force back at Chillianwala village was taken.

With the order for the British line to retreat given, this effectively signalled the end of the battle. So dark was it now, though, with no campfires having been lit on either side, that the wooded terrain caused an entirely disorienting effect for many soldiers and there was general confusion as to which way to move. Campbell had anticipated this situation to an extent and had told an engineer officer to take the bearing of the village of Chillianwala before darkness settled completely, and thus many of his brigade were faced towards the right direction although other soldiers in other brigades suffered more, sauntering off in confusion to the north or south. The British pullback suffered no added discomfort from the Sikh line. Thackwell was correct in that Shere Singh, unable to see through the jungle, had no inkling of the advantage he held along several positions along the line. Instead he merely ordered his line to hold their positions, with a general order to pick up the wounded and secure the Sikh cannon.

*\*\*\**

The British camp had not been organised prior to the battle, all the baggage having been left several miles to the east of Chillianwala village. So as the British troops trudged back to Chillianwala, they found they would have to bivouac without any shelter in the cold. The lucky few who reached the village occupied the deserted village houses, the vast majority having to make do with sleeping outside. By this time a drizzle had commenced, gradually increasing in strength till around 8 p.m. when it would develop into a fierce rainstorm, adding to the discomfort of those attempting sleep in the open. Adding to this was the lack of water available in the village, which turned out to have few wells, and the bulk of the soldiers settled down for the night thirsty. A British doctor in the camp described the situation:

> The night that followed this dreadful day was the most miserable of my life. The troops all huddled together without order, and the tents and baggage nowhere to be seen. Some of us sat for the early part of the night upon some guns, and – when it began to rain, which it did heavily toward midnight, we sought the shelter of an adjacent village, where in a mud hut of diminutive dimensions, we found a most motley assemblage congregated in the dark, and where we passed the night in a crouching position with my back to the wall, for there was not room to lie at length on the mud floor … In this position we spent the

night; the longest I ever experienced. No one spoke, every one was occupied with his own reflections, longing for the light of the morrow, and listening to every sound that broke the stillness of the night. Had the Sikhs been an enterprising enemy (which they are not), and come down upon us that night, our troops could have offered no resistance and must have fallen an easy prey … Amongst the latter I recognised the Adjutant-General, Judge-Advocate-General, Quartermaster-General, Brig. Penny, &c.; not one of them appeared to know what had become of the Commander-in-Chief for some time. At length we heard of his having passed the night in another village about a mile off. I had had no food since six a.m. on the previous day, save a crust of bread the Col had given me.

Gough, it turned out, in the confusion had stationed himself at Mojianwala, 1.5 km further east of Chillianwala village. As some semblance of order was established later that night, work began and camp equipment was extricated from the baggage train while the surgeons began commencing with amputations and the other assortment of operations required on the wounded. The chaos caused by the darkness would only really become apparent as the sun rose the next day. Despite Gough thinking he had put some distance between his army and the Sikh line, both camps were dangerously close; at times it was unclear whose campfire belonged to whom. It was found, for example, that Pope's second cavalry brigade's pickets had their rears pointing towards the Sikh line for much of the night, the pickets vigilantly watching the British units at Chillianwala instead. Other regiments in the pitch dark had not organised any pickets at all.

Later during the night an alarm was raised and there was an assumption Shere Singh may have ordered a general advance. Huish's troops heard or saw what they thought was horse artillery approaching in the distance and preparations were made for a defence. It was found, however, to be the elements of the 3rd Dragoons out scouting for food and water.

Among those resting in the British camp were some of the first casualties of the battle during the capture of the village. These included some Sikh soldiers seen by Thackwell as he rode through the masses of men finding some place to rest for the night.

In front of the village of Chillianwala lay a wounded Sikh, who had been abandoned by his comrades. He was attired in the usual Khalsa infantry uniform – a red coat of an old European pattern, with white stripes of braid across his breast, and facings of a different colour: a white turban and loose blue trousers completed his costume. His handsome features were adorned with the usual thick black beard, whiskers and moustache. A cannon ball had shattered his thighbone, and to alleviate his pain, he was seeking relief by taking bhang (Indian hemp) a quantity of which seemed to be in his pockets. Another officer has described him making a desperate effort to collect his dormant energies, and convulsively grasping at a tulwar lying within his reach, but his strength failed.

***

British casualties had been significant. In a battle which had lasted scarcely three hours, 586 had been killed with 1,641 wounded. There were also 104 missing at this stage. This made a total of 2,331, plus 176 horses. These statistics were only rivalled by those of the Battle of Ferozeshah three years earlier. Many of the casualties were European, recognisable by their Albert hats. It was a common saying in Sikh cantonments that without European troops the native sepoys would not last an hour in the Punjab and consequently in battle Sikh gunners and infantrymen preferred to turn their attention towards European soldiers. Sepoys would, when they saw British troops being beaten, retreat alongside them in any case, so it was a belief that had more than an element of truth in it.

The greatest losses were suffered by HM 24th. Altogether the regiment, which had gone into action with 31 officers and 1,065 NCOs and men, had 13 officers and 225 men killed, 9 officers and 278 men wounded, in all nearly half its strength. This was a loss greater than any regiment in the history of British involvement in India, barring the catastrophe of the retreat from Kabul. Curiously, an antelope nicknamed Billy that was used as a mascot and walked in front of HM 24th during its advance towards the Sikh line survived; perhaps Sikh musket men avoided firing on the animal. Billy would later receive a medal for the campaign, tied with a ribbon round its neck. Of the sepoy regiments, the 30th suffered the most, losing a third of its strength. The accompanying regiments to HM 24th, the 25th and 45th, suffered losses as well, being driven back at the same time. The 25th lost three officers and 201 men killed and wounded, the 45th four officers and 75 men.

In total, eighty-nine European officers had been casualties (twenty-two killed and sixty-seven wounded). The notable among the dead included General Staff Brevet Major C. Ekins, Deputy Adjutant General of the Army, and Lt Cureton of the 14th Light Dragoons. In addition to this, six British horse artillery guns had been captured including three of Huish's guns on the British right and one of Christie's. Ammunition wagons of several of the corps had also been lost.

HM 24th had lost a standard, the queen's colour. Both the 25th and 45th NI regiments lost all their standards, eight in total being lost in the battle. The 56th lost initially two standards, although one was recovered. The standard recovered had originally been taken by the 56th from the Mahrattas at Maharajpore and was always carried along with their other two banners into battle. This banner, a distinctive one made of yellow silk with a red cross and bearing in the upper quarter a naked dagger, was recovered by the 70th NI of Godby's brigade.

A large reward was offered for the queen's colour standard of the 24th initially, the impression being that camp followers of either side might have spirited it away. Thousands were seen criss-crossing the battlefield in large numbers during the night, stripping away the clothes and possessions of the dead men of both sides. When no one came forward, it was thought it had been picked up by Sikh soldiers. The captured Lt Bowie, along with George Lawrence and other European prisoners, after the battle was shown the British guns and standards captured during the battle by Shere Singh. 'He never showed us the 24th colour,' Bowie wrote. The conclusion in the British camp was that it may have been dropped into one of the pools near the Sikh line. One account mentioned the staff of the standard being broken and that it was picked up by a Private Martin Connolly who was subsequently killed.

The Sikh army's losses were higher in guns, the number captured by the British being twelve; however, they were generally of a lower calibre than the British guns, being mainly 6-or 7-pounders. Six of the guns had carriages and limbers, another six lacking limbers. Various other items had been captured, including two ammunition carriages, one platform cart, 144 cartridge liners fixed to shot, 16 cartridges unfixed and 18 port fires. Other guns had been spiked but had been recaptured by the Sikh soldiers and would be repaired for use at the coming Battle of Gujrat. There are no real figures as to Sikh casualties, although it was later suggested with little foundation that 3,000–4,000 casualties were had by the Sikh army as well. This was in the same ballpark as the British casualties. The bulk of the casualties had been at the Sikh line and it's safe to say no genuine estimate survived, the men being cremated by their comrades.

\*\*\*

The weather would effectively decide the course of things over the next few days. The day after the battle, 14 January, was a wet and gloomy one although the daylight, such as it was, dispelled the confusion of the night. Communication between Gough and his officers, scattered about the field and the two villages, began to be re-established early in the morning. Trumpets were sounded and the troops assembled and organised. With the heavy rain showing no respite, an extremely melancholy atmosphere prevailed and was increased by an awareness of the invidious task ahead: collecting the dead and wounded scattered between the two lines. The rain would continue heavily till the evening of the 15th and then intermittently onwards right into late January. The 22nd and the 23rd would be especially noted for unusually heavy downpours all day – rain so heavy and noisy that neither camp, it was speculated, would have been able to hear the opponent's guns firing had they bothered to fire in the deluge. Whatever temporary advantages Shere Singh had immediately after the battle therefore vanished in these continuous downpours and any immediate renewal of the contest, mooted or not by either side, was postponed indefinitely.

Early that morning a twenty-one-gun salute from the Sikh camp was heard, signalling success in the battle. This was initially assumed to be guns firing on the British camp and it was assumed Shere Singh had ordered an advance, causing momentary disorder. Gough himself was content with no renewal of warfare, the British troops having had the minimum of sleep and being exposed to incessant rain the entire night. Gough and Major Mackeson rode up a nearby hill later that morning for reconnaissance, both hoping they could see the Sikh army retreating so that a victory, albeit technical, could be announced that day. However, the Sikh camp was still there in the same position. Large funeral pyres were already being prepared along the line for the Sikh casualties, although the rain made the process of cremation difficult.

The bad weather also had the effect of delaying the distribution of the British baggage. It was only around 11 a.m. when tents were finally available for the majority of the troops. Most of the troops, with protection from the elements now, went straight to sleep and would be awakened only during that evening. Food, too, the first available since early the previous day, was also available but the continuing deluge meant little preparation could take place for the next two days and raw food had to be served, contributing to the dismal atmosphere in the British camp.

\*\*\*

Following the battle, several unusual orders were given by Gough. No doubt aware of the bad press the repulse along with heavy casualties would generate, instructions were given that no private letters were to be allowed out of the camp until after his despatch on the battle had been sent. The short note he sent to Dalhousie prior to the official despatch was a highly optimistic one considering the previous day's events. Shere Singh, he said, had been entirely defeated and driven back at every point. The enemy had lost many guns and had been forced to relinquish his entrenched position. The ban on the sending of letters unsurprisingly turned out to be a complete failure. There was silence in the newspapers for the three days it took for the mail to reach their destinations before the flood of individual stories hit the front pages. These stories of the battle from both the common soldier and officers alike overshadowed and told an entirely different tale to the Commander-in-Chief's official despatch.

The second and more curious order of the day was that the consumption of beef was entirely forbidden and no kine was to be killed in the British camp. Henry Lawrence after Bhyrowal had respected the Sikh Government's ban on the eating of beef to placate the Hindu population and British troops stationed at Lahore had refrained from eating beef accordingly. However, this was a grey area for the British force that had entered the Punjab from British territories under Gough. In the tense situation that followed in the days after the battle, Gough may have been anxious that the sepoys, largely Hindus, who formed the bulk of his force may turn on their British colleagues or defect, while things were so finely balanced, similar to events at Multan before Suraj Khund. The sepoys knew just as well the precarious state the British force had been in during the battle and it may have been thought that cows being slaughtered under their noses might prove too much. Gough could ill afford to lose his sepoy regiments at this time.

***

On the evening of 14 January, the collection and burial of the British dead finally commenced. Four companies of Europeans, 200 sappers and miners and two troops of native cavalry accompanied by camels to transport the dead and wounded were despatched towards the battlefield. Along with them went Revd Whiting to carry out the religious rituals. Meanwhile, Brig. White's cavalry were sent to collect any guns abandoned by the Sikh army. The rain made the work awkward, and as the parties traversed the jungle the corpses lying on the battlefield proved to be a powerful reminder of the horrors of war. One soldier passing through where HM 24th had retreated the previous day recorded what he saw.

> The scene of the retreat of this regiment presented a melancholy spectacle on the morrow. The pallid, ghastly colour of the bodies of the English soldiers formed a strange contrast to the dark hue of the natives. Many were already stark naked. The attitudes of death were various—an arm might be seen lying at a considerable distance from its body, severed by the sword or round shot. Many corpses lay with throats cut, whilst all were more or less mutilated. Many men arrested attention who, with their arms directed upwards, appeared to have been in the act of warding off the blows of the enemy with their muskets when the vital spark deserted them. Prince Albert hats and military shoes might be seen in all directions, strewing the ground in great abundance; they afforded splendid booty to the needy camp followers.

Sikh parties too were traversing across the field at the same time with similar objectives. Each allowed the others to take away their dead without obstruction or violence. The only visible exceptions were British dead lying too close to the Sikh line, to which Sikh officers refused access as intelligence could be gained of the Sikh position in the process.

The officers' corpses as they were brought in were laid in the officers' mess tent until the evening. The Pennycuicks, both father and son, were brought back in a single dhoolie. Multiple bodies were lashed to the camelbacks with ropes or suspended on the sides. As the dead continued to be brought in, it was deemed inappropriate to do so in such fashion. Many of them, quite naked, already half-eaten or molested to some extent by vultures and carrion, had assumed a ghastly appearance. The decision was therefore taken to bury the corpses on the battlefield where they lay. The British officers killed would be buried separately, twenty-five in a mass grave with another thirteen of the HM 24th in a separate trench. Brig. Pennycuick and his son were buried in their own separate grave. The lower-ranking soldiers were buried in the other trenches. There was one exception; the men of Christie's horse artillery had written asking permission for Christie to be buried with the men of his own troop. The chaplain had agreed to the request. Upward of 200 Europeans were thought to have been buried on the field by the end of the second day after the battle, with the bodies of the sepoys cremated in Hindu fashion.

Due to the extended task of fetching the dead, the compilation of the casualty list would take several days. The long trenches in the new cemetery were finally closed on the 16th, three days after the battle. Auctions of the possessions of the dead officers and soldiers were begun on 19 January. 'Sales are going on, daily, of dead officers' effects, which go for one eighth of their value – a piece of injustice both to a man's friends and to his creditor's. But it can't be helped,' bemoaned Daniel Sandford of the 2nd Bengal European Regiment. Sandford's regiment had lost their treasure chest, canteen and band instruments too, items that were no doubt being auctioned in the Sikh camp at the same time.

Most of the British wounded went without treatment as the field hospital had been destroyed along with most of its supplies during the retreat. In the dark and stormy conditions of the night, extracting the apparatus from the baggage east of the village proved time-consuming and difficult. Medical supplies and apparatus gradually drifted in over the next morning, and the process of treatment began in earnest for the wounded. The doctors worked incessantly, one recording in his diary that he had had nothing to eat for two days and three nights and that he had neither slept nor changed his clothes during this time. 'I assure you the fight of the 13th was as nearly proving another massacre of a British army as possible,' he wrote in his private letters. The continual downpour of rain didn't help either, and the doctor noted the risk of exposure for the troops in the cold and rain.

The baggage animals, given the least priority, were brought in on the evening of the 14th. The cattle were in stressed conditions themselves, not having been milked for over thirty hours. The other casualties of the battle, the hundreds of dead camels and numerous cavalry horses lying around the site, were another issue entirely. An ugly stench arose in the following days and weeks from these carcasses, but they were left where they fell despite fears of disease spreading during what would turn out to be an extended stay at the battlefield for both armies.

\*\*\*

The matter of the precipitous retreat by the 14th Dragoons hadn't been forgotten and would provoke much debate and criticism in the British camp. It was said that it was the horse artillery who first asked for a court of enquiry into their conduct during the battle. The day after the battle an enquiry was in fact organised, but behind closed doors. What happened and what conclusions were arrived at were not revealed but it was decided no further action would be taken. This left the whole matter in limbo, allowing a somewhat cold feeling to prevail against the Dragoons in the British camp over the following days. The colonel of the 14th Dragoons, addressing his men, was known to have told them they 'had behaved in a dastardly manner, and the less they said about it the better'. Macpherson of HM 24th would record an anecdote of a conversation between a party of his regiment and a Dragoon that was indicative of the general mood. The party happened to be digging the entrenchments round the camp when a couple of Dragoons exercising their chargers passed by. 'Ah! You chaps, what are you making that deep ditch for?' questioned a horseman while twisting his moustache. 'Well I don't rightly know,' replied one of the men, annoyed at the rough questioning, 'but I'm told it is to put the cavalry in the next time we fight.'

Dalhousie himself would be quite indignant at the way the 14th Dragoons and 9th Lancers had fled during the battle and wished for a proper investigation into the whole affair, with culprits punished and those innocent cleared. However, in his despatches Gough exonerated the larger part of the 9th Lancers as they had been with Col Lane. He also explained his desire to forego any further enquiry above and beyond the one on 14 January, remarking that even if blame could be put on an officer it would not have justified the disorderly behaviour of the troops on the day, when all attempts to restore order failed. Dalhousie would back down when faced with this argument.

\*\*\*

Conscious of a possible counter-attack as and when the weather cleared, for it was known Chutter Singh would shortly be arriving with reinforcements for his son, Gough ordered the British engineers to mark the ground for a defensive encampment with fortifications. All jungle and general brushwood close to the village was to be cleared to a distance of a mile to allow a clean line of fire. Gough had decided on a large square defensive perimeter encompassing the villages of Chillianwala and nearby Mojianwala, 2 km directly to the east. A mound facing the Sikh lines was utilised and some of the heavy guns were placed in battery to sweep the area between the lines. Trenches would be dug all around the encampment with advance earthworks dug for the pickets in what incidentally would be the first time any British army had ever entrenched itself on the subcontinent in this manner. A strong redoubt was also ordered to be constructed facing the Sikh lines on the right flank, around a quarter of a mile from the main camp as this was thought to be the position an attack was most likely to emanate from. The redoubt was to be populated with some field pieces and later a light field battery and several companies of infantry. Immediately behind it in the square position would be two troops of horse artillery with some 9-pounders. 'Our left beyond the village [Chillianwala] was slightly retired in an oblique direction,' recalled Capt. Buckle later of the British camp during the following days. 'The park was in rear of the mound. As the enemy became stronger and more threatening several changes took place. The whole of the left was thrown back so as to unite the village of Mojawala in rear of camp with the front face and our right flank was also connected with the village by a rear face; thus our camp formed an irregular quadrilateral figure or rhomboid and four pieces of heavy ordnance were placed near Mojawala.'

Work commenced in earnest on the building of the redoubt on the British right on the 18th and would be carried out on a twenty-four-hour basis. 500 men were constantly at work on the structure with a similar number relieving them at midnight to continue on the work during the night. Parallel to this, other defensive structures were also being assembled with the use of hired labour with sepoys guarding the workmen. By the 21st, trenches and breastworks had been established all around the British camp complete with batteries at strategic positions. A vigilant lookout was kept night and day as a Sikh attack was not unexpected.

In addition to these preparations, a series of small artificial hillocks sprang up facing the Sikh lines in front of the British square, each constructed by a different regiment for the purpose of watching the enemy lines over the brushwood and intervening jungle. Gough had started the trend by ordering that one be made for him. With nothing to do over the coming weeks except wait as neither army advanced, the regiments vied with each other as to who could make the tallest to while away the time. Sitting on top of these artificial hillocks and gazing at the Sikh line in the distance became a popular pastime in the British camp.

Gough realised over the following days that the British position wasn't particularly good. The camp did not traverse any roads and was not near plentiful water. The village of Chillianwala, while having one or two wells, did not have sufficient for the roughly 100,000 soldiers, camp followers and animals there. The only thing that alleviated the lack of water over the next week or so was the sheer amount of rain that fell during the remaining part of the month, which turned the hollows in the ground in the vicinity into small lakes and thus provided ample drinking water for horses and cattle. Fodder would also run short, with grazing areas being exhausted by the animals as the days ticked by. They would have to be grazed further away, with all the attendant dangers of the animals disappearing. In addition, the Sikh army already controlled the northern positions of the site (the hilly areas), making the harrying of British lines, grazing herds and supply convoys easier. As the days dragged on, Gough would therefore show an inclination to retreat to Dinghee, 12 km east of his current position. Dinghee was closer to the British lines of communication, with good roads connecting it to Gujrat and on to Lahore. Supplies could be better protected as well. Water was much more abundant at Dinghee, with numerous wells, as it was a far larger settlement than Chillianwala. Even better, he reflected, would be a move back to the old Sikh camp at Ramnuggar. The camp was already being used as a British base, two regiments and a few guns guarding the bridge. The other alternative, as before, was to move towards Gujrat, which was on the direct road to Lahore and made supplies yet easier to protect.

Henry Lawrence, present in the camp, was strongly against any move towards the east and dissuaded Gough from this course. Any retreat from Chillianwala in whichever direction, he argued, would confirm the events of the 13th as a British defeat, damage British prestige and increase Sikh morale. Despite the logistical difficulties it was paramount to maintain this position, he advised. The Commander-in-Chief would, however, face criticism from certain quarters regarding the defensive setup. Some deemed it too defensive, allowing the Sikh army too much foraging space. A line facing the Sikh army would have been more suitable, with the British left resting on Chillianwala and the right at the village of Kokri, close to the hilly area and where a large mound formed an admirable anchor for the right flank. If a strong position was also taken on the hills above Kokri then this would entirely deny Shere Singh forage for animals and would block the road to Gujrat, cutting off supplies from the north.

Arguments over positions and entrenchments aside, Gough had by this time sent urgent messages to Lahore with a view to drawing in more reinforcements. Since HM 24th and the 30th and 56th NI were too crippled to be of further use, especially in terms of officers, Gough ordered these regiments back to Lahore. In return Brig. Wheeler's force, around 6,000 men in Jalandhar, was ordered to join him. HM 53rd regiment, around 600 strong, the only European regiment hitherto stationed at Lahore to hold the Sikh capital, was ordered to join the units at Ramnuggar and every soldier within a day's march of his force was to be sent for. In order to compensate, Dalhousie would order two companies of HM 98th Foot (part of his own camp) to Lahore to take the place of HM 53rd. 'I am determined that whatever risks are run elsewhere, none shall be run in the face of the enemy,' Dalhousie wrote, concurring entirely with Gough. Sir Dudley Hill's army of reserve, 8,500 strong, all sepoy regiments at Ferozepore, was also ordered to be ready to move on Lahore to strengthen the British hold on the capital, news of the recent reverse already having spread round the country. Meanwhile 500 British troops were mustered from Madras to come up as well with the sanction of Dalhousie.

\*\*\*

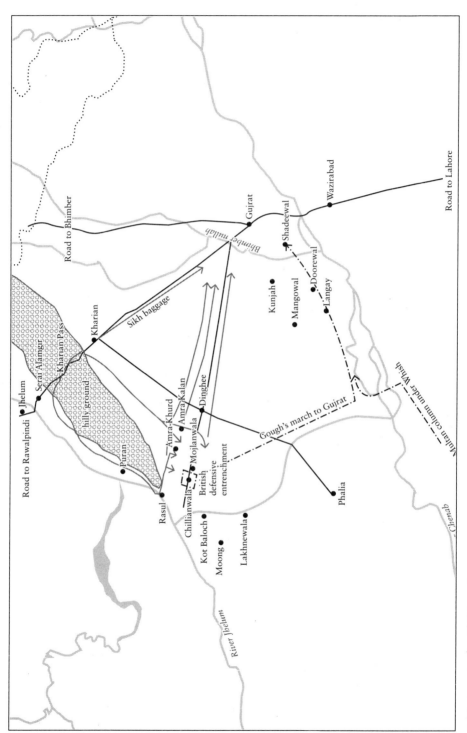

9. Movements after Chillianwala

In the Sikh camp, meanwhile, the battle had been seen as an undoubted victory. Shortly after the battle Shere Singh would release George Lawrence on parole for eight days for a trip to Lahore to meet his brother Henry. His meeting with Gough and Mackeson in the British camp before he travelled to Lahore provides a glimpse into the Sikh soldier's view of the battle. Gough queried the mood in the Sikh camp, expressing surprise that they were jubilant. He alleged as many as thirty or forty of the Sikh guns had been spiked and that they occupied the ground of the Sikhs. 'Yes but they say you did not occupy the ground you had gained, and that the guns you had taken and spiked were retaken in consequence; and that they took up a position stronger than before,' retorted George Lawrence. He would also confide in Gough that there was a strong surprise in the Sikh camp that he had not made the best use of his heavy artillery despite the jungle.

Gough would write his despatch in the most optimistic fashion again, describing what could only be called a complete victory at Chillianwala. 'The enemy, who defended not only his guns but his position with desperation,' he wrote, 'was driven in much confusion and with heavy loss from every part of it and the greater part of his field artillery was actually captured.' No mention was made at all of the British reverses. Only the fall of night and the cover of the jungle, he continued, allowed the Sikh army to recover their guns and regain its poise, otherwise British bayonets had been irresistible. 'The victory was complete as to the total overthrow of the enemy and his sense of utter discomfiture and defeat.'

There would be several days before the real story reached the newspaper editors around the country. This was time enough for Dalhousie to use Gough's official despatch to release a public proclamation on 17 January which announced rather confidently the victory and 'that on the afternoon of the 13th inst. the troops under his command attacked and entirely defeated the Sikh army under Rajah Shere Singh in its position near the river Jhelum. The action was obstinately and severely contested. The enemy was in great force and occupied very strong positions. They were driven back at every point with the loss of many of their guns and by the latest intelligence relinquished all the positions in they had been entrenched.' In addition, to celebrate the 'victory', the Governor-General ordered a twenty-one-gun salute to be fired from every principal British military station in the country.

Gough's despatch fooled no one, least of all the population around the Punjab. On 18 January, Henry Lawrence, who had been present with the army during the battle, travelled back to Lahore to resume his position as Resident on 1 February. As he approached the Ravi to cross into the city he noted the brigadier in charge talking of breaking the bridge across the Ravi in case Shere Singh marched on Lahore and of bricking up the gates to the city, an indication of the uncertainty of the times. Inside the city he saw scenes of open elation in the streets at Shere Singh's success, raising British anxieties of an insurrection in the capital. The fact that HM 53rd had been pulled from the capital to reinforce Gough simply reinforced the truth in the minds of the common man. Lord Gifford, meanwhile, left the British camp on the 19th, heading straight to the Governor-General's camp at Makhu to supply him a candid story of the late battle.

Neither did Gough's despatch fool the British newspaper correspondents with the army, who had witnessed it all at first hand. Over the next few days and weeks the newspapers launched a frenzy of attacks on the Commander-in-Chief and his tactics during the battle. A correspondent had already written from the battlefield on the 16th, his letter reaching Delhi on the 19th and setting the tone for the criticisms in the *Delhi Gazette*:

It indeed has been a sad business, and it is impossible to predict when our mishaps, and such fearful butchery and wanton sacrifice of lives will end or stop under such an incompetent Commander in Chief. Unless the Governor-General recalls Lord Gough to the provinces, the chances are he will not only lose the splendid army under his command (which he has already done his best to cripple and weaken), but he will so compromise the Government, that the most serious apprehension may be entertained as to the ultimate result of this contest … With so tremendous a park of artillery and supply of mortars as that at his disposal it might have been imagined that rather than stand still he would have endeavoured to approach their position by regular parallels and covered ways as in case of siege our ordnance could have told on them fearfully at a range to which their shot could not have reached.

The matter of Gough's impulsive insistence on fighting when the Sikh round shot had landed close to him was particularly ridiculed. A proper understanding of the terrain in front was lacking and it was obvious insufficient reconnaissance had been carried out before blundering straight for the Sikh line. The *Bombay Times* was even more candid in its opinion. 'Not, since the destruction of the garrison of Cabul,' it declared, 'has so heavy a catalogue of blunders and misfortunes been carried home from India as that which the present mail conveys; we have, for the first time since 1842, to give particulars of the annihilation of half regiments, from the sheer mismanagement of the commanding officer.'

The *Bombay Telegraph* was equally critical of Gough's tactics. It declared 'the opinion to be almost universal that the terrible slaughter during the engagement is attributable in a great measure to the want of forethought judgment and tactical skill on the part of the Commander'.

The *Mofussilite* was one of the few that praised the Sikh force rather than attributing the defeat entirely to Gough's flaws. 'The great mistake which Lord Gough has made – and he has not been singular – is the under-rating of the Sikhs as an enemy. In the common acceptation of the word, they are not "natives". They are a disciplined and a brave foe. Of their bravery let us instance the fact, that they met the charge of H.M's 24th, and seizing hold of the foremost muskets with their left hands, cut at the men who carried them. With a foe like that to contend with, it is impossible for any General to oust them from a position without losing very heavily. Much more might have been gained with much less loss; but it is wrong to lay all the blame on the Commander-in-Chief.'

In Britain, where the news would only reach two months later, there was similar consternation at the heavy losses. Gough was playing with the lives of the soldiers, declared *The Times*. 'The disaster has thrown the successes into the shade, and the impression made upon the public mind is stronger than that caused by the Kabul massacre,' Hobhouse informed Dalhousie on 7 March. The Duke of Wellington, on hearing the news from Dalhousie, would, like the Governor-General, publicly support Gough. The loss was severe, he said, but fortunately the fall of the Multan fortress (news of which had also reached London) had offset this. If the fortress had had to be stormed, he declared, then casualties would have been large and thus many British lives had been saved despite what had happened at Chillianwala. Privately he was much more hawkish, and within forty-eight hours of the news of the 'victory' reaching London he, along with Government ministers and the head of the Army, were of the opinion that Gough must be replaced immediately by Charles Napier. 'If you don't, I must,' the Duke of Wellington declared to Sir Charles Napier, insisting he go out to India.

Meanwhile, the atmosphere in the Governor-General's camp at Makhu was correspondingly gloomy. Both Henry Lawrence and Lord Gifford, present at the battle, had given the Governor-General a frank analysis of the battle. According to a camp officer present in their conversations the impression they gave was that 'the Sikhs, in every sense of the word, licked us, and if their cavalry had only gone on, must have routed us and taken the Commander-in-Chief and Staff prisoners,' referring to the incident where the Gorcharas had advanced close to Gough. In light of Gough's despatch, however, Dalhousie, in an attempt to make the best of things, believed the less said about the battle the better. He also stayed civil with the Commander-in-Chief, going as far as commending him on the 19th for his victory. Privately, though, he was furious and his correspondence over the next few weeks showed a heavy loss of confidence in the Commander-in-Chief. On 20 January he wrote a downbeat account of the state of affairs prevailing in the British camp.

"I regret to say that every man in the army, generals of divisions, officers, Europeans and sepoys, have totally lost confidence in their leader, loudly proclaim it themselves, and repeat it in their letters to their friends. For some days, a very unhappy and discouraging gloom prevailed in his camp, aggravated by torrents of rain which deprived the men of food, rest and shelter. It is with pain, but I state my opinion, that I can no longer feel any confidence that the army is safe from disaster in the hands of the present commander-in-chief, and add, that there is not a man in India, who does not share that feeling with me and yet I am in so false a position that I cannot remedy this evil which I see.' Frustrated at the setback at Ramnuggar and now at Chillianwala, he went as far as hinting at a possible resignation in his private papers at the 'incapable instruments' (referring to Gough) that had been forced on him. His own reputation was being tarnished, he bemoaned. 'My best hope now is, that he may be able to keep his army unharmed until the Mooltan force can join him.'

Over the following weeks, he increasingly brought Gough's conduct of the battle and the war in general into question in his private letters and with the Duke of Wellington. The decision he would make, mulling over the battle, was that Gough must not cross the Jhelum and must wait near the Chenab for the Multan force to reinforce him. If Shere Singh crossed the Jhelum someone else would take charge of the army, his correspondence hinting at Gilbert. The excuse, Dalhousie confided to the Duke of Wellington, would be that he would insist on the British headquarters staying east of the Jhelum, meaning indirectly that Gough, being C-in-C, would also necessarily have to stay east of the Jhelum himself, having to delegate command of any force crossing the river to another man. This was the most delicate means, Dalhousie thought, by which he could relieve Gough of effective command. Meanwhile he would insist on Gough waiting for Whish's force to turn up before another contest and would insist on the use of his far superior artillery. 'If he disregards in his obstinacy these means again, if he again fights an incomplete action with terrible carnage as before, you must expect to hear of my taking a strong step; he shall not remain in command of that army in the field,' he wrote bluntly.

There were other fears as well as far as the Governor-General was concerned. The recent reverse meant the possibility of a 'grand alliance' against the British developing as news of Chillianwala spread. The roughly 10,000 men and fourteen guns of Gulab Singh west of the Jhelum along with the 12,000-strong Afghan force under Dost Mohammad at Attock could reinforce Shere Singh to destroy Gough's crippled force before Whish could reinforce him from Multan. This was already thought of as probable and many, like Havelock, felt it a bad policy to continue to have two separate forces in the Punjab after Chillianwala. Havelock argued that Whish and Gough should instead join up forces before the fall of Multan. A single large army, either at the Jhelum or at Multan, rather than two separate forces, would be more efficient and safer in the light of things.

There were other attendant risks arising as well on another border of British India. This was the potential threat from the Nepalese, whom it was suspected might take advantage of

British strength, being largely diverted to the Punjab. It was noticed the Nepalese were forming a military camp close to the border with British territory capable of holding 12,000 soldiers, presumably in preparation for an invasion should further misfortunes fall on Gough's force. Supplies were also being collected. The official reason for these military preparations was that the headquarters of the Dinapore Division of the British force had recently been moved too close to the Nepalese border and that the Nepalese Government felt it had to take the same precautions. In concert with this, it had been reported that Nepalese leader Jang Bahadur had begun moving thirteen regiments and forty-one guns close to the border. The excuse would be that he was on a shooting expedition, although the sheer numbers made this a little suspect. The danger of any Nepalese invasion would fall away later, a fever having spread among the Nepalese troops. Jang Bahadur himself had fallen ill and it was heard with some amusement that the British Resident himself was giving him quinine pills.

\*\*\*

A period of relative inactivity now followed despite these preparations and calls for reinforcements, allowing both sides to lick their wounds. This did not mean there was an entire absence of violence, however. From the day after the battle till Shere Singh would depart for Gujrat nearly a month later, there was desultory skirmishing almost every day. Sikh pickets would harass their British counterparts, with British supply columns being a particular target. On 25 January, there was a false alarm in the British camp at around 2 p.m., with rumours of the entire Sikh army advancing, and the British force was readied. But miserable weather was returning, and from 10 p.m. it kept raining heavily all night, dispelling any notions of battle in the near future. The frequent rumours of a Sikh attack led Gough at this stage to keep half the army prepared at all times. A few days later, the order went out for British soldiers to sleep in their clothes. It was agreed that in the event of an attack the signal would be three guns firing from the mound in front of the British positions, on which signal all soldiers were to turn out. On several days, in fact, Shere Singh had brought the whole Sikh line out but more frequently there was skirmishing on the right of the British line near the redoubt. The 9th Lancers were stationed nearest the Sikh camp and would receive daily alarms of the approaches of Sikh troops, and the British horse artillerymen accompanying the Lancers took to sleeping with their boots on as the alarms, both genuine and false, became frequent.

The prolonged stay near Chillianwala would mean frequent supply columns for the British camp but forage for animals was nevertheless fast becoming a problem. Gough was sending one or two regiments of cavalry daily towards Ramnuggar and Wazirabad, 60 km away to the east and across the Chenab. The Chillianwala area was simply unable to support the many hundreds of thousands of camels, sheep and beasts of burden and other livestock brought in by Gough's army and these animals were by necessity allowed to graze over a wide stretch, many miles from camp. Some flocks were having to be grazed as far as Gujrat 40 km away. Many of these camels, easy prey for locals and Sikh pickets continued disappearing. Losses skyrocketed during the coming days and weeks as guarding this considerable number of animals was impossible. The capture of livestock and supplies forced Gough to keep certain sections of the cavalry and artillery saddled the whole night as attacks were almost constant, especially during the night when gloom covered the doab.

'Sometimes his [Shere Singh's] whole line turned out,' wrote Edmund Buckle of the Bengal Artillery, 'but more frequently he brought small parties into the jungle below Rasul and then attacked our right wing, which was frequently on the alert. But the Sikhs gave us the greatest annoyance by capturing our baggage cattle. This they did frequently, and we were obliged to send out very strong parties of cavalry to protect them. Our horse artillery too, had very fatiguing work, guns being frequently out with detachments sent to protect convoys of grain &c. These had to make long harassing marches and latterly it became necessary to send out parties of cavalry and horse artillery to reconnoitre the country in our right rear.'

A large skirmish occurred on 30 January. The British had a considerable number of camels grazing in a certain area behind British lines which were driven away by the Gorcharas. On 1 February, a detachment of troops was sent to protect a large convoy of supplies coming in to the British camp from Ramnuggar. The detachment, consisting of two squadrons of 14th Dragoons along with two squadrons of 8th Lancers and four guns, had another objective as well. They were to take the Sikh guns captured on the 13th to Ramnuggar for safekeeping before bringing the convoy in. The convoy consisted of 2,500 camels packed with new provisions along with 15 lakh rupees for the payment of troops. This convoy, which reached the British camp on 5 February, had sufficient supplies to provide for Gough's army for two weeks. Another large convoy would reach Gough on 10 February, eliminating all worries as to supplies and ammunition for the time being.

There was considerable suspicion among the British officers at this time that the camp followers were giving vital information to locals or to Sikh irregulars regarding foraging locations for the coming days, allowing them to carry off the animals where the guard was most lax. The locals were then selling the animals back to the British commissariat at a high rate, the profits being shared between the parties. Sufficient evidence was found against one of the camp followers who had employment in the commissariat, a certain Jootee Persha, and he was the first to be arrested and charged. Other arrests were made. The chief Gomashteh or agent used for the purchase of livestock was said to have made a huge fortune in the transactions although he was not implicated in the racket. The day after the battle, a moonshee in the British camp was also caught sending information to the Sikh camp. He was discharged from British service with back wages, a generosity which caused rather a stir in the camp, where stiffer punishment was expected. Informers were rife in both camps too, it being unusual to find enough proof against them, but on 5 February a high-profile informer, a *babu* (clerk) working in Gough's own office, was discovered who had been sending over a copy of every order of the Commander-in-Chief since the campaign began. His messenger had been apprehended slipping out of the camp with documents. The *babu*, perhaps having been tipped off about his servant's arrest, showed a clean pair of heels and managed to effect an escape to the Sikh camp before he could be apprehended.

There were other issues to do with logistics coming to the fore as well. Bearing all these in mind, on 28 January Gough declared private camp followers and personal servants would not henceforth be allowed to buy their food from the camp bazaar. They would instead need to purchase their provisions in the local villages regardless of the high prices. This was prompted by reports that camp followers were buying suspiciously large quantities of provisions in the British camp which were then promptly being sold on to the Sikh army at inflated prices through middlemen, depleting British stocks but enriching the camp followers.

As the threat of an advance by Shere Singh receded, the embattled British Commander-in-Chief finally began to receive some good news near the end of the month. The deluge had continued on the morning of the 26th and some parts of the British camp were seen to be as much as a foot deep in water, making life difficult. Through this swamp a messenger appeared with the news of the fall of the fortress of Multan on 22 January and Mulraj's status as a prisoner in the British camp. This was the cause of much celebration in the British camp and Gough promptly ordered a royal salute to be fired.

***

Things hadn't been entirely rosy in the Sikh camp during the days after the battle either. A British sepoy released and used as a messenger a few days after the battle brought back news that there were difficulties in the Sikh camp as well, with Sikh casualties dying as there were insufficient doctors to attend to the wounded. However, Shere Singh received a strong fillip shortly after the battle. His father, Chutter Singh, reached Chillianwala on 16 January with around 10,000 men followed shortly by Akram Khan, the son of Dost Mohammad, with around 1,500 irregular Afghan cavalry, all the force that Dost Mohammad had given so far. The Afghan force was rumoured to be commanded among others by three Europeans, former privates in the 44th Regiment who had remained in Kabul and converted to Islam. The *Delhi Gazette* also commented on rumours from spies in the Sikh camp that the elderly Chutter Singh, never in good health, had been further incapacitated in recent weeks. He had therefore retired from all military decisions and leadership, leaving his son to decide on the campaign while he concentrated on civil duties and supplies for the Sikh army. To celebrate his arrival Shere Singh would order the firing of a royal salute for his father and a parade of the entire army, something that would cause a false alarm in the British camp. These additions to Shere Singh's force raised the possibility he would attack the British camp soon, although this proved not to be the case.

On the same day, perhaps thinking the well-publicised arrival of his new reinforcements was an opportune moment to make another attempt at negotiation, Shere Singh sent back two Lancers who had been captured in the recent battle as an overture. With them they brought a friendly letter from the Sikh commander. Shere Singh reiterated he was not the aggressor in this war. If the British would leave Lahore and the Punjab he would not harass the British force in their move back to British territories and there would be warm and amicable relations between the two states as before. Gough would send a reply thanking Shere Singh for the kind treatment of the prisoners and their release but refused to be drawn on wider issues. The released Lancers, meanwhile, were the talk of the camp all day for they came back with tales of being well befriended. They were amply wined and dined, with champagne and brandy to drink. They had been carried out of the Sikh camp by servants in palkis (palanquins) with their scarves tied round their heads in turban fashion, causing much mirth in the Sikh camp according to the Lancers. They were given 10 rupees (more than a month's wages) each by Shere Singh at departure and were apparently reluctant to come back given the kind treatment. The stories seemed to scotch the many and varied rumours of extreme food shortages in the Sikh camp. 'We wonder what they would have done if they succeeded in capturing Lord Gough. Where do they get champaign with which they regale their prisoners?' commented the *Bombay Telegraph* later on the treatment of the prisoners.

As the days went by, Shere Singh would write to Gough again on 27 January with a more ebullient letter than before. He had decided to release Lt Herbert with Lt Bowie on parole to the British camp. The Sikhs, he said in the note, would not surrender, or serve the British in any way. Neither would they hold land under British supremacy. A British withdrawal from the Punjab was the only way for peaceful and friendly relations. If the British would not agree to this, then they had better come and fight; the Sikh army was ready in position. 'I am perfectly certain, however that the Sikhs will entertain no terms with us except they are based on our quitting the Punjab and retiring across the Sutlej: this is a sine qua non with them,' wrote a British correspondent on the field on 16 January. However, Gough too would refuse to budge an iota from British policy and replied that only offers of an unconditional surrender by the Sikh army and the surrender of all guns would be considered. This uncompromising stance was fully backed by Dalhousie on hearing of Shere Singh's proposals on 5 February: 'First, because their demands are preposterous; second, because any compromise would in the eyes of all India now be confession of inability to conquer, or compel. I give one reply: "Unconditional submission to British power, but I will not forfeit your lives, and not compel you to starve."'

Interestingly, the overture from Shere Singh was seen by some in the British camp as a *ruse de guerre*. It was thought he was waiting for more Afghans to join him and possibly still more reinforcements and was only using the negotiations to buy more time himself. There is no doubt, however, that his excess caution after the recent battle may have provoked some doubt in the Sikh camp. This unease increased on the news of the fall of Multan fortress reaching the battlefield. It was thought on the British side that about 4,000 sepoys who had been fighting on the Sikh side were ready to desert. Major Mackeson had written to them telling them they would be well received if they laid down their arms at certain prescribed pickets. This never happened but there were other defections, the most prominent being that of Elahee Buksh, the talented Muslim commander of the Sikh artillery. A handsome man with a smallish beard and dressed in Afghan fashion, he rode into the British camp on the 17th accompanied by twenty-five gunners with similar views and gave himself up to Major Mackeson. Buksh was an energetic man, as accounts of that time reveal, and a big loss to Shere Singh. His knowledge of the state of the Sikh army and artillery was invaluable to Gough. He also knew the area well and the strengths of the Sikh position. Buksh would help the British much in gaining supplies in the coming weeks. As a reward he was given command of a fort and 200 soldiers behind British lines.

His defection didn't faze Shere Singh. Frederick Currie would write of letters by Shere Singh to Sheikh Imam-Ud-Deen at Multan continuing to urge him to join the Sikh standard. These the Sheikh forwarded to Currie without fail. Others in the Sikh army also wrote to the Sheikh including Bedee Bikram Singh, who had escaped from the Jalandhar area to join up with Shere Singh. An interesting letter is preserved from him to the Sheikh and was forwarded to Currie a few days after the Shere Singh letter and sent to Dalhousie by the Resident on 25 January.

Bedee Bikrama Sing to Sheik Emamooddeen.

All the Hindoos and Mussulmans of the country, considering what is due from them as loyal subjects, and upholders of their respective religions, have assembled together. Dost Mahomed also, esteeming the friendship of the Sirkar of more value than worldly matters, is marching hither with his army. Sirdar Sooltan Mahomed and Peer Mahomed Khan, although formerly enemies to the State, have also thought the time opportune for establishing friendly relations. I have brought about this result, and doubt not that they will continue to abide by my suggestions. They have, accordingly, set up their standard, and have been admitted to the holy Punth of the Khalsa. It is matter of astonishment that you, who have received so many favors from the Sirkar have not also joined us. Since life is short, it is not becoming in you to forget what is due from you.

Although it was unnecessary for me to write to you, yet in consideration of your former services, I have thought it proper to do so. The time is auspicious, and if you are inclined to act with wisdom and with loyalty, you will insure advantage to yourself. If you will not join us, unite yourself at least with Sirdar Narain Sing. I need not write more, as you are a well wisher of, and faithful to, the Sirkar, and will forget the services you have rendered, of late, to the British.

\*\*\*

The arrival of February brought about a sudden and definitive end to the rainy period after the battle. It also brought about a new initiative by Henry Lawrence, who had now retaken his role of Resident at Lahore. This was triggered by a friendly letter from Chutter Singh at Chillianwala, the last overture before the Battle of Gujrat. The letter was sent in the hands of Major Lawrence, Henry Lawrence's brother. Chutter Singh would write about the warm relations he had always had with Henry Lawrence, stating that he was ready to consider Henry Lawrence's advice as to bringing the war to an amicable conclusion.

Henry Lawrence in return would pen a conciliatory response that matters could be resolved and the status quo within the Punjab resumed if the Sikh army laid down its arms. This was sent to the Governor-General's camp for approval, but the declaration penned made it quite clear that the British would not annex the Punjab, in stark contrast to the hard stance Dalhousie had chosen. Dalhousie always took the greatest exception to British agents deciding policy by themselves. This had happened several times since the start of hostilities. Herbert Edwardes had without sanction offered terms to Mulraj. John Nicholson had written to Shere Singh offering terms. James Abbott in Hazara had in correspondence invited Dost Mohammad to assist the British. It was with anger that Dalhousie responded quickly to another unsanctioned initiative. Dalhousie wrote a strong letter back remonstrating against the soft tone of the wording.

I can by no means consent to the promulgation of it, and regard it as objectionable both in the matter of it and in the manner. It is objectionable in matter, because from the terms in which it is worded, it is calculated to convey to those who are engaged in this shameful war an expectation of much more favourable terms – much more extended indemnity of punishment than I consider myself justified in granting to them. It is objectionable in manner, because (unintentionally, no doubt) its whole tone substitutes you personally, as the Resident at Lahore, for the Government which you represent.

It is calculated to raise the inference that a new state of things is arising, that the fact of your arrival with a desire to bring peace to the Punjab is likely to affect the warlike preparations of the Government, and that you are come as a peacemaker for the Sikhs, as standing between them and the Government. This cannot be. I cannot permit that any one word shall be said or any one act be done which shall give the faintest reason for any one to entertain the notion—a notion entirely false—that the views and the policy of the Government of India are dependent upon the particular agent who may be selected to represent them at Lahore … There must be entire identity between the Government and its agent, whoever he is; and I repeat that I can permit nothing publicly to be said or done which should raise the notion that the policy of the Government of India or its intentions depend on your presence as Resident in the Punjab, or the presence of Sir F. Currie instead.

The British policy on the future of the Punjab was not to be declared until the war was over and the Punjab in British military possession. This wrap on the knuckles of the former Resident had the desired effect and forthwith Lawrence ignored the elephant in the room, the issue of annexation, and would essentially tow Dalhousie's line of promising as little as possible. Dalhousie's attitude no doubt was made firmer by the news arriving of the fall of Multan fortress and the fact that Whish's troops were already marching north to join and reinforce Gough. 'Lawrence has been greatly praised and rewarded and petted, and no doubt naturally supposes himself a king of the Punjab; but as I don't take the Brentford dynasty as a pattern, I object to sharing the chairs, and think it best to come to an understanding as to relative positions at once. It will soon be settled,' Dalhousie wrote. Lawrence's new declaration of 5 February, which was subsequently passed to the Sikh camp, was therefore much more equivocal as to what would happen to the Punjab, promising little more than life and subsistence for the men of the Sikh army.

> A proclamation was issued by Sir F. Currie on 18 November last. I now again make known, by order of the Governor-General, the terms on which alone pardon may still be obtained. They are, first, unconditional surrender; it being understood that no man's life shall be forfeited for the part he has taken in hostilities against the British Government.
>
> Secondly, that the soldiers now in rebellion shall, on laying down their arms, be permitted to return to their homes, and to remain there in security; and that those Sardars who possessed Jaghirs shall not be entirely deprived of the means of subsistence. Let it be further observed that, in order to be entitled to the terms above mentioned, the submission must be immediate. No part of these terms refer to Sardar Sultan Mahomed Khan Barakzai.

In line with the Governor-General's wishes, along with the declaration Henry Lawrence would therefore include a strong and cold letter.

> My advice is, that which has already been given to you, on the part of the British Government, viz, immediately, on receipt of this letter, to deliver over to Major Mackeson, the British officers, ladies, and children, at present in confinement; and secondly, to come yourself into the British camp, trusting to the mercy of the Governor-General.
>
> Inclosed is a copy of a proclamation this day issued by me, under orders from the Governor-General.
>
> No more can be promised to men with arms in their hands.

Even as these letters and discussions were passing between Lahore and the Sikh camp, though, Shere Singh had made the decision to move from his present position. On 2 February Shere Singh had moved some of his forces onto the hills north of Rasul and on to Puran village. Three days later, on 5 February, Shere Singh would move more of his forces to the east of Rasul so they faced the British camp to the north. Three shots were fired from the British cannon, the signal for a general turnout, as it was thought a battle was imminent, but Shere Singh was too cautious to attack the entrenched camp.

Some said the reason for this move was that the recent influx of reinforcements made the present position too cramped. This was especially so for the animals in the Sikh camp, which had to be grazed across the river and on the narrow stretch of land north of Rasul, whereas the British had the whole doab to themselves. Others said it was the problem of supplies which forced his hand. Most of these had to come by more tortuous routes, the bridge and ford across the river and north from the ford at Jhelum village. What was generally accepted albeit in retrospect was that it was a major mistake for him to ever move from the strong position at Rasul, a position which would have been difficult to take even if Whish had reinforced Gough. It may have been that on hearing of the fall of Multan and the approach of Whish's column Shere Singh decided to take a gamble before the two British forces combined. This gamble was an attempt to lure Gough into attacking him again, failing which a march to Lahore would be arranged.

As he faced the north of the British camp, the Sikh baggage as well as the bulk of his troops would be moved up north towards Puran and through the Kharian Pass and south again. This meant a march of around 70 km, but with jungle to the north-east of Rasul his move was largely screened from British eyes. The movement in fact would not be seen from the British side until the Sikh troops had made their move and positioned themselves a few kilometres north of the British camp.

Gough immediately ordered a meeting with his officers and Major Mackeson. There was a large convoy from Gujrat due at this time and currently heading toward the British camp, and Gough supposed this must be the target. Some of his officers, including Campbell, thought otherwise. 'I looked upon the move of the enemy behind the hills, which screened the operations from our view, as intended for future offensive operations against our right flank and rear; but the Commander-in-chief thought otherwise, though a movement on our part to our right, to Khoree or Dingee, which I deemed prudent and advisable, especially as the enemy had moved the larger portion of his army to his left, could not be regarded as a movement in retreat.'

As Campbell pointed out, Shere Singh was now able to advance and attack the rear of the British position or attack the supply convoys coming east from Gujrat. Major Mackeson agreed with Campbell and suggested a move back to Dinghee to protect the British supply lines but in such a fashion as to avoid a battle before Whish arrived. Gough, though, continued to disagree, preferring to defend in the entrenchment instead. Grant, the Adjutant-General, concurred with Gough that there should be no move till Whish's force could join them. He argued Shere Singh would not continue further east, the Rasul position being so advantageous to the Sikh commander that this must merely be a ruse. What they all agreed on was that Shere Singh offering battle was an attempt to force the issue before Whish came up and therefore it was best to avoid taking the bait and stay on the defensive.

To ensure Shere Singh could not march to Lahore, Gough issued orders to have the fords across the Chenab watched and guarded. In addition orders were given to bring all cattle and baggage in, which were to be placed behind the centre of the British line. The British force was kept under arms overnight in case of a night attack. With Gough's deciding to stay put, by 6 February Shere Singh sat with his army to the right and rear of Gough's position at a distance of some 10 km, with Sikh cavalry occupying Dinghee.

This new position made life more difficult for the British grass cutters, who were used to bringing forage for the animals in the direction of Dinghee, and skirmishing increased particularly near the village of Chak Memori, lying north-east of the British square and in British control. The reason for this was that Chak was the only nearby source of water for the British apart from the few wells at Chillianwala and thus needed to be controlled. Flocks of goats taken to the village for water and wrongly taken beyond the picket lines for grazing would frequently disappear. On 6 February, for example, it was noticed that a whole flock had been taken by Sikh skirmishers.

Shere Singh would make another half-hearted effort to draw out the British force on 11 February. The Sikh army was moved to Burra Oomrah, barely a couple of kilometres away from the British camp. This information was received at 10.30 a.m. in the British camp. The three signal guns at the front mound were fired as usual and the whole British force turned out. Shere Singh now had two columns, one at Rasul threatening the northern face of the British camp and one at Burra Oomrah threatening the north-east and east. He again failed to order an advance, though, hoping Gough would make the move and leave the entrenchment. The two lines faced each other for two to three hours before Shere Singh withdrew back to Dinghee. There was speculation later in the British camp that this was never an offer of battle but simply a ruse to cover the move of the Sikh army baggage towards Gujrat. If this was truly the strategy then it worked, for Gough would have no chance of trailing and harrying the Sikh rear.

Early at 3 a.m. the next day, 12 February, British pickets heard a gun firing in the Sikh camp, which turned out to be the signal to move to Gujrat. An hour later the Sikh army definitively moved off eastwards in what was considered a superlative manoeuvre, the campfires both at Dinghee and Rasul being left burning to disguise the move and no hint of a move being given. A Major McCurdo recorded,

> A gallant officer who was prisoner in the late campaign told me that the march of the Sikh army from the neighbourhood of Chillianwala to Goojerat was one of the best executed, and most magnificent manoeuvres he ever witnessed. Drawn up in order of battle, facing the British camp, Shere Singh first passed his baggage well to the reverse flank of his intended march; he then commenced his march preserving order of battle, every battalion keeping its place and alignment for a distance of twenty miles! So perfectly was the order of battle preserved, that the British captive believed our army must have been marching close and parallel to that of the Sikhs, instead of being as it was on the day quietly in camp at Chillianwala!

Once the move was recognised, a party of thirty men were organised under a European officer to gather the rotting corpses of the British soldiers still lying untended in what was previously no man's land while Gilbert was ordered to reconnoitre the former Sikh camp to ensure no Sikh troops remained. His opinion, on coming back, was that it was fortunate that Shere Singh had vacated his position, the position being so strong. This surprised Gough and prompted him on the morning of the 13th to go in person to inspect the former Sikh line. There were still some occupants of the camp. Shere Singh had left behind around 2,000 of his wounded at Rasul and the other villages nearby. Gough in a kind gesture would order some flour and other provisions to be sent to these men. It was also discovered that not all the Sikh army had departed eastwards. Attar Singh, one of Shere Singh's officers, had crossed the Jhelum with six to twelve guns and up to 5,000 men but for what reason was not known at this point. It was speculated his job would be to protect the fords across which Shere Singh might retreat across the Jhelum. Outgunned even at Chillianwala, the lessening of his artillery strength while Gough's was to increase markedly on the arrival of Whish's guns would make the disparity in firepower even starker in the next contest. By the morning of the 13th, British patrols found all Sikh units had disappeared beyond Dinghee and the Kharian Pass area too. The day was also marked by the arrival of the very first troops from Multan, Brig. Cheape arriving with a portion of the cavalry contingent of the Bombay force. He had conducted a series of forced marches in order to reach Gough while Whish was still bringing up the bulk of his troops in a slower convoy a few marches behind.

Colin Campbell's view was that Shere Singh's move towards Gujrat and Wazirabad was a ruse and mere pretence of a move towards Lahore, devised to entice Gough into a battle before the

Multan troops arrived. 'My own idea is, that this is a mere threat, with a view to get us to divide our forces, so that we may not have all our Europeans and guns in the battle which must take place in a few days, and which will decide in whose hands the empire of the East is to remain; for that is the point at issue, and by the result of the approaching conflict will this point be settled.' Gough, however, was confident he would not need to fight as Shere Singh would never be able to cross the Chenab for a force of HM 53rd, the 13th NI and 12th Irregular Cavalry under Lt-Col Byrne was already marching to Wazirabad on the right bank and opposite Gujrat where the Sikh army was most likely to attempt a crossing. These units would in fact arrive just in time to see preparations by Sikh units on the other side getting ready to cross.

Plans were made to follow the Sikh army. Gough had initially wanted to move to Gujrat on 14 February, and orders were given accordingly. The main delay, however, involved bringing in the vast herds of camels from the grazing grounds to which they had been sent early in the morning. Therefore the move was delayed for another day. At 4 a.m. on the 15th, then, after camping more than a month at Chillianwala village, the entire British force moved off eastwards towards Sadulpore. It was around this time, as the army moved back eastwards, that a seemingly innocuous piece of news belonging to another chapter of history reached Chillianwala. Scant attention was given to the news that Dara Bakht, the heir to the Mughal throne, had died in Delhi. Dara Bakht would in due course have become the ruler of what remained of the Mughal Empire, essentially the capital Delhi and its outskirts. His death would initiate intrigues and machinations in the capital which would presage the Indian Mutiny of 1857.

A second event as the two armies moved towards Gujrat, one which certainly garnered more attention from Dalhousie, was a kidnap event at Makhu. Normally little happened in the Governor-General's camp apart from the stream of messengers passing between the camp, Lahore, Ferozepore and Gough's camp. However, in early February Dalhousie found himself the focus of a Sikh kidnapping plot. Makhu was situated on the border with Punjab and was close to the Sabraon battlefield, near the banks of the Sutlej. Dalhousie opted to stay at the border as moving further back into British territory would stretch the lines of communication with Gough and the Resident at Lahore while entering the Punjab itself would require a strong force to protect his camp, and these troops would thus be denied to Gough. His camp at Makhu had little protection beyond the ordinary peacetime guard – many of whom, curiously, were Sikh – and the possibility of a strongly armed band wishing to abduct him was realistic. 'It would have been a bonny job to have had to swap me for the Maharanee!' he mused in his private papers on 5 February after the plot was uncovered and the planned terms were exposed.

# 29

# The Battle of Gujrat

If he [Shere Singh] stands a fight he must, humanly speaking, be smashed.
Dalhousie, 19 February 1849

The cannonade was the most magnificent I ever witnessed, and as terrible in its effect.
Gough, Gujrat battlefield, 26 February 1849

The dual error of abandoning his strong position at Rasul and allowing Whish to reinforce Gough without a struggle provoked much discussion about Shere Singh's intentions. James Lawrence-Archer of HM 24th, later a chronicler of the war, even hints at treachery on the part of Shere Singh, although this is unlikely. An alternative reason was put forward by Sir William Francis Patrick Napier, author of the *Life of General Sir William Napier*: Shere Singh had decided on crossing the Chenab and marching to Lahore, he argued, because he was confident he would be joined by the army of Maharajah Gulab Singh along with the rest of the army of Dost Mohammad. Dalhousie apparently told Charles Napier later that he had definitive proof Gulab Singh had promised to do so, although this help would never materialise.

Whatever the case, advance units of the Sikh army would begin reaching Gujrat on 12 February with the bulk of the army arriving by the 14th. The town was captured and prisoners made of the several hundred Afghan irregulars employed by Capt. Nicholson to man the town fort. Only one of the Afghans escaped and he promptly went to the British camp at Chillianwala to report on the Sikh occupation of the town. Across the Chenab River, there was consternation that Shere Singh, little more than 5 km from the river, might be able to effect a crossing. The Afghan contingent left by Nicholson at Wazirabad on the opposite bank sent a message to Gough's camp that they would attempt a defence for some days if Shere Singh managed to cross over to the left bank provided there were moves by the British force towards Gujrat. Otherwise, they declared, they would be forced to surrender or abandon the town. At Lahore, meanwhile, rumours had circulated that Shere Singh after outflanking Gough had already crossed the Chenab and was assumed to be in full march upon Lahore. This prompted preparations by Brig. Godby to meet any emergency and the British garrison was put on alert.

This would never be a crossing, however. Shere Singh found the fords were already vigilantly guarded by several British detachments and with all boats in the vicinity in their command and on the left bank. Three native regiments and cavalry had been stationed at Ramnuggar at this time and had been moved up to block the fords. Around 500 of Shere Singh's troops managed to cross the Chenab opposite Gujrat to the right bank but were driven back by Col Bryne, in charge of preventing a crossing. Reconnaissance of several points up and down the river from Gujrat was also ordered by Shere Singh but these too were well guarded. If his destination was indeed

Lahore, then a forced crossing would surely have been the right thing to do. However, the Sikh commander hesitated and the opportunity disappeared. With Gough already pursuing him by this stage, staying and fighting on the plains of Gujrat now became his only option.

\*\*\*

George Lawrence, who had by now returned from his parole at Lahore, had a meeting with the Sikh commander at Gujrat as the army settled into its camp. He brought the letter and proclamation from Henry Lawrence with him but Shere Singh appeared unfazed. He said hoped to negotiate a better treaty. The Sikh commander had confidence his force could stand up to the combined armies of Gough and Whish, but George Lawrence was equally confident he had lost his opportunity. 'Shortly after my arrival in their camp, Shere Singh took me up to the roof of a house in Gujerat, and pointing out, with evident pride, his army of 60,000 men and 60 guns, drawn up in the plain before us, exultingly asked me what I thought of them, and how I supposed the British army would meet the attack of such a superb force. I told him very plainly that if he had 200,000 instead of 60,000, they would avail him nothing in the day of battle against our troops.' On being shown some horsemen manoeuvring in the distance, Lawrence would ask who they were. Shere Singh would explain they were the cavalry of Dost Mohammad, who had thrashed the British and expelled them from Kabul. George Lawrence, who was perhaps more cognisant of the value of Afghans on the plains, would reply, 'No Affghans, either horse or foot, ever thrashed us in Cabul. We were beaten by cold and starvation. But as for these fellows I know them well, and depend upon it, fine looking body as they are, they will be your destruction; they will be the first to fly, and then your men, who otherwise would fight well, will follow their example.'

Despite George Lawrence's words and the little fortune in negotiations so far, Chutter Singh and son would continue attempting a settlement while preparing for battle. After discussions with their officers, it was decided that another attempt at diplomacy would be made. George Lawrence would be sent again, this time on eight days' parole to Lahore. Chutter Singh informed him that if the British won the battle that would undoubtedly be fought in the next few days there would be no need for him to come back and that he would arrange for Mrs Lawrence and the other British prisoners to be released. George Lawrence, however, to his credit promised not to break his parole and gave his assurance he would return to the Sikh camp whatever the circumstances.

\*\*\*

One of the talking points in both camps ever since Chillianwala and before had been the inability of Gough to bring his clear superiority in terms of heavy artillery to advantage. Shere Singh in his evening conversations with his British prisoners frequently brought up this issue. 'We used to have a visit each night from Shere Singh, who conversed very freely, and expressed his great surprise that we did not make much more use of our splendid artillery than hitherto, instead of depending so entirely as we seemed to do on our infantry, which, he let us know, his soldiers had much less dread of than our guns,' recalled George Lawrence after the war.

The Sikh soldiers too were open about the situation, perhaps more open than they should have been. Mrs Lawrence, who was being held at Sukhoo, would hold similar dialogues with the Sikh soldiers present in the fort. She would mention in her letters to Major Mackeson while imprisoned that the soldiers fully considered themselves equal to British soldiers. The only apprehension among the Sikh soldiers regarded the preponderance of heavy guns in the British camp. Mrs Lawrence would beg Mackeson in her correspondence to persuade Gough to use the heavy guns in a future contest. These feelings weren't restricted to the Sikh camp, being prevalent in the British camp as well. Gough's officers, anxious of the continuing casualties during the campaign (especially of the European contingent), would advise him of the benefits of using his heavy artillery to its maximum potential instead of relying as previously on his infantry. 'We had too much slaughter of human life at Chillianwala, without due precaution having been taken to prevent it by the employment of our magnificent artillery,' wrote Colin Campbell during the days before the Battle of Gujrat. 'Having felt this strongly, and having expressed it to the Commander-in-chief in warm terms, I determined to employ this weapon against the enemy to the fullest extent, whenever we should again come in contact with them, and I did so, accordingly, in the battle of Goojrat.'

George Lawrence, who had by this time set off again to try a negotiated settlement, would reach Gough's camp on 17 February before returning to Lahore on the 19th and then travelling to Ferozepore to meet Dalhousie. Here he would relate Shere Singh's bemusement, similar to Dalhousie's, on Gough's failure to exploit his one overwhelming advantage. 'Placed as the armies are,' Dalhousie wrote on 21 February, incidentally the same day as the Battle of Gujrat, 'the commander-in-chief ought literally to exterminate the Sikh army. The whole body of his officers have told him that if he will only use it, he can destroy them with his artillery alone. The general of artillery, Elahee Buksh, who came over from the Sikh camp, told him so, to his Excellency's great dissatisfaction. Major Lawrence told him that Shere Sing and the very Sikhs in their camp said so to him. Three days ago he had urged on him the use of his heavy guns as to the right method and the commander-in-chief angrily replied: "No it is not; the bayonet's the thing, and I shall use the bayonet."'

Dalhousie would write hinting strongly of his frustrations at Gough's tactics so far and saying different measures should be taken. The enormous baggage that Gough's army had accumulated, which was hampering his movements as he followed Shere Singh eastwards, was a sore point. Dalhousie had urged Gough to jettison much of it, which included double sets of tents, the whole headquarters' records and even various printing presses which accompanied the force, but to no avail. Gough had agreed and replied he would shed this excess load, but had not followed up. But the suggestion that he had not been using his artillery wisely was his main issue. 'I wrote to the C.-in-C.,' Dalhousie had written on 13 February, 'as I felt myself bound to do, strongly impressing upon him the necessity for using the vast means he had, and warning him at once against the past, and of what I expected for the future. By my word it was time for me to do so.'

Dalhousie's letters infuriated Gough in turn, and although he held his tongue in public he would privately threaten to resign. However, the combination of all these entreaties from the Governor-General and his officers did change his mind, as would be seen in the coming battle. For this reason, the Battle of Gujrat would later be labelled the 'battle of the guns'. In fact, so chastened was the Commander-in-Chief that when a colonel was seen to declare to him he was confident he could storm the Sikh position in front of him using the bayonet, he was heard to reply, 'That is the very thing I do not want you to do.'

On the issue of further negotiations there would be no progress. George Lawrence in his talks with Dalhousie had communicated to him that Shere Singh was willing to release all prisoners he held immediately if this would help in bringing about an amicable agreement. Dalhousie, fully confident that Gough's heavy guns would triumph on the plains of Gujrat, had decided to defer any further communication till after the battle.

***

The British force reached Mukhnawala before moving to Lussoorie by 2 p.m. on the 15th, a march of 20 km on a route that was quite difficult as it went through jungle. From there a move was made to Suparee, where it was learned Shere Singh had definitely camped at Gujrat. By this time a fierce heat had begun developing over the Punjab, far different from the cold deluge of the previous weeks after Chillianwala. On the 16th the British force continued heading slowly for Gujrat, the deliberate slow pace being to allow the rest of the Multan contingent to achieve a junction before the battle. In addition, rather than using the road to Dinghee and then taking the direct road to Gujrat a more circuitous route was decided on by Gough, moving towards Sadulpore to the east. Therefore he would approach Gujrat from the south rather than from the east. This allowed communication via the bridge at Ramnuggar and would allow British units watching the river crossings an opportunity to join up before the battle. So massive were the supplies and paraphernalia in the British camp now that Gough had finally decided to take Dalhousie's advice and jettison as much of the baggage as he could to travel lighter and faster. The number of camp followers had been savagely reduced before the move to Gujrat, along with baggage reductions. As an indication of the changed circumstances following this decision, it was found 8,000 fewer camels were now required.

Gough moved northwards from Sadulpore on 17 February, reaching the vicinity of Kunjur (Kunjah) on the 19th, around 12 km southwest of the Sikh army's position. Here elements of Whish's force joined Gough. Whish had marched north, moving in parallel on the left bank of the Chenab, reaching Ramnuggar before crossing over to join Gough's force. One brigade of infantry along with ten horse artillery guns came in with Whish himself the night of the 18th. The 19th brought Dundas's column as well – HM 60th and the 1st Bombay Fusiliers and 32nd Bombay Infantry, along with the Scinde Horse and a troop and battery of horse artillery of twelve guns. A slow advance was continued to the village of Shadiwal, closer to the Chenab, on the 20th, in order to give the Multan column soldiers time to recuperate after their long march, Gough having decided to give battle the next day. Gujrat was only 8 km away and the Sikh army's positions round the town could be clearly seen from the top of high houses in the village. The last of the British troops from Multan (Brig. Markham's brigade) filtered in on the 20th as well, giving Gough his full complement of troops for the battle the next day. On the same day, Lt-Col Byrne, who commanded the units on the left bank of the Chenab, was also ordered to cross downstream with two corps of infantry and four guns, leaving two regiments of irregular cavalry behind to man the crossings.

***

Situated on a flat expanse, Gujrat town only had two natural features in its vicinity. These were two nullahs flowing round it, one on the east and the other (much larger), the River Dwara, to the west. The channel to the west was dry at this time, with the smaller one to the east being wet. Apart from these two obstructions there were no other imperfections in the ground and there was consequently no difficulty for any sort for manoeuvres. 'The field of battle was a vast plain of boundless extent, Salisbury plain ten thousand times magnified, but much flatter: such ground for cavalry and artillery was never seen,' wrote Henry Aimé Ouvry, Capt. of the 3rd Light Dragoons. What gave the battlefield a quite picturesque look were the far-off foothills and snowy mountains that signalled the beginning of the high land towards Kashmir, with the Pir Punjal mountain range, 18,000 feet high, clearly visible as a magnificent and mesmerising backdrop.

The morning of 21 February, a day that would decide the future of the Punjab, was by all accounts sunny with a slight breeze discernible. 'At half past seven o clock,' says Gough in his official despatch, 'the army advanced with the precision of a parade movement', eventually reaching within gun range of the Sikh line by 8:30 a.m. Before reaching the vicinity of Gujrat the army crossed the nullah which ran west of the Gujrat, the stream veering south-east after passing the town to join the Chenab River. The terrain south of Gujrat which the army passed through in full battle order was some of the most beautiful cultivated land of the Punjab. Around and about were plentiful sipoo, siris and babool trees, with the land carpeted by young corn, 6 inches in height at the time. In the far distance, in front of the town of Gujrat and all around, could be seen the Sikh camp with a myriad of tents striped red, white and blue.

Shere Singh, on seeing the British advance, had formed a line with the bulk of his troops situated a mile or so to the south of the town and between the two nullahs. Meanwhile, his cavalry formed up on both flanks on the other sides of the two nullahs. On the right of the Sikh line to the west of the large nullah, the Gorcharas had been placed on a gentle rise which gave no advantage. Alongside them was the contingent of 1,500 Afghan horse led by Akram Khan, son of Dost Mohammad, still the only Afghan assistance to appear so far. On the day, the line extended a little further than the British line. The nullahs gave little advantage over a frontal assault from the British approaching from the south, although they protected his infantry from a flanking manoeuvre. In front of him were situated several villages. Two of these, Greater and Smaller Kalra (Burra and Chota Khalra), the Sikh commander had garrisoned with some of his infantry. Varying estimates were given of the strength of the Sikh army with Shere Singh. Some say as many as 60,000 men were present while others numbered it at 50,000, although these numbers were probably inflated. What would play more of a role in the battle was the strength of the Sikh guns, which were known to total fifty-nine on the day.

In the British camp, the battle plan had been decided the previous night. The Bombay contingent were to fight on the left wing while the Bengal troops formed the right wing, with cavalry on each flank and the heavy guns interspersed in the middle. More specifically, Brig. White's cavalry (3rd Light Dragoons, HM 9th Lancers, 8th Bengal Light Cavalry) and the Scinde Horse under the overall command of Thackwell would hold the extreme left. To their right would be Dundas, commanding the Bombay division comprising of HM 60th, 1st Bengal European and the 3rd and 19th Bengal NI. In front of this division would advance Duncan and Huish's troops of horse artillery. To the left of the nullah but touching it would be Campbell's division. Carnegie's brigade (HM 24th, 25th and 27th NI) was positioned adjacent to the nullah, with McLeod's (HM 61st, 36th and 46th NI) to their left and with Hoggan's brigade (69th and 45th NI, 6th and 5th Bengal Light Cavalry) held in reserve by Campbell.

Campbell was given orders by Gough not to cross the nullah but to stay on its left until instructions were otherwise given. The idea was for the whole line to move forward when the opportunity came and Campbell to be supported by the heavy guns on the right of the nullah. In keeping with this, Campbell would place two guns of the No. 10 Light Field battery adjacent to the nullah alongside HM 24th. In front of the two brigades would be skirmishers supported by Nos 5 and 10 Light Field batteries and twelve 9-pounders. These would move in line with the skirmishers to their left belonging to the Bombay Division.'

To Campbell's right was Gilbert's division, which would be situated in the middle of the two nullahs. Mountain's brigade (HM 29th, 56th and 30th NI) would line up on the right of the nullah with Penny's brigade (2nd Bengal Europeans, 70th and 31st NI). Kept in reserve would be Hervey's brigade (HM 10th, 52nd and 53rd NI). Most of the heavy guns, eighteen in number, would be placed here as well, being placed to the left and right wing of Gilbert's division.

To the right of Gilbert would be Whish's division. These had an additional brigade of infantry under Brig. Markham (HM 32nd, 51st and 72nd NI) as reinforcement. Three troops of horse artillery fronted this division – Fordyce's, Mackenzie's and Anderson's – and No. 17 Light Field battery under Dawes protected the line. Lane and Kindleside's horse artillery formed a reserve. Gough would put Brig. Hearsey's (3rd Irregular, 9th Irregular) and Lockwood's (HM 14th Light Dragoons, 1st, 11th and 14th Bengal Light Cavalry) cavalry on his extreme right along with Warner's troop of horse artillery. To protect the British rear and baggage, Gough would leave the 45th and 69th NI along with the 5th and 6th Light Cavalry under Lt-Col Mercer.

All in all, more than twenty battalions of infantry and some ten regiments of cavalry were formed in a line. This was a force which by general consensus was the most powerful army ever fielded by the East India Company in India. It would be strengthened by the greatest accumulation of guns as well. With Dalhousie and his officer's advice ringing in his ears, Gough had decided to make full use of the artillery and a total of 106 guns of varying calibre were pushed forward. The bulk of the heavy guns were placed in the middle. Each of the brigades as it advanced had its own artillery in front of itself, the heavier guns, drawn by elephant, being in the centre of the British line while horse artillery was stationed on the two flanks. 'With my right wing I proposed penetrating the centre of the enemy's line,' the British Commander-in-Chief wrote, 'so as to turn the position of their force in rear of the nullah, and thus enable my left wing to cross it with little loss, and in co-operation with the right to double upon the centre the wing of the enemy's force opposed to them.'

With that in mind, the British line was pushed forward. An hour and a half after beginning their march the British skirmishers arrived within the range of the Sikh guns and the British columns were deployed into the line. What followed was a textbook example of how to use overwhelming artillery to the best advantage. As the British line approached it was the Sikh guns that opened up first, but the British line, being out of range of these mainly lighter guns, received no damage. On the other hand, the Sikh line was in range of the British heavy guns and Gough halted the line instantly for the artillery to do its work while the skirmishers pushed forward. At 8.30 a.m., the eighteen heavy guns Gough had at his disposal began firing at a range of 1,500 yards with the lighter guns following a few minutes later from a distance of 800 to 1,000 yards, the smaller guns gradually being pushed forward to around 600 yards from the Sikh line.

'I halted the infantry just out of fire and advanced the whole of my artillery covered by skirmishers. The cannonade now opened upon the enemy was the most magnificent I ever witnessed,' wrote Gough in his despatch of the battle. By around 9 a.m., ninety-six of the British guns began battering the Sikh position in earnest, continuously and without pause for nearly four hours, systematically destroying the Sikh artillery and defensive positions while the lighter Sikh guns could do little in response. It was estimated each of the big British guns was firing at the rate of forty rounds per hour at their peak, the gun crews pausing briefly only if the guns were showing signs of overheating. 'The Sikh guns were served with their accustomed rapidity and the enemy well and resolutely maintained his position but the terrific force of our fire obliged them after an obstinate resistance to fall back,' Gough recorded. Shere Singh had no option but to pull his line out of range. This action would only prompt Gough to push his guns forward an equal distance and continue pummelling the Sikh line. The Sikh artillery was knocked out within the opening two hours. 'Ninety six of our guns "opened the ball", and played the very deuce with the enemy. The latter's artillery was well and pluckily served, but their gunners were all shot down, the carriages of their guns knocked about, and their horses, bullocks, buffaloes, etc all killed,' a soldier wrote in a private letter. 'I saw one team of six bay horses lying in their harness, regularly riddled by our shrapnel. Men also with their heads blown off by our big shot.'

Another hour passed, the fire of the British guns systematically booming away at the Sikh line without answer. 'It was an interesting and magnificent sight, to watch the beautiful and correct practice of our artillery,' wrote R. W. Bingham, Quartermaster Sergeant of the 30th NI. 'Not a shot or shell was thrown away, as tumbrils were blown up, one after the other, guns overturned, or huge gaps made in the enemy's ranks. By our shot and shell, the gunners were encouraged in their exertions, by repeated cheers from their infantry brethren, while John Sepoy was in extacies and extolling the "bundobast" to the skies.' The word 'bundobast' means arrangements.

Conscious that he needed to take the initiative, Shere Singh ordered a charge by his cavalry on his right and left. On the right the Gorcharas attacked first, joined by the Afghan horsemen. Advancing against a heavy battery, the Afghans were hit by a shell. 'The effect of the shell bursting in the midst was to cut a gap, just as if one had taken a bite out of a biscuit,' wrote a British gunner. Losing heart, the Afghan horse wavered and turned tail. The Gorcharas, noticing their allies charging away, did the same. In order to push his advantage, Thackwell would order the Scinde Horse and a squadron of the 9th Lancers to advance and a charge was made upon the retreating Afghan horse and Gorcharas, while to the left of them the British guns continued to pummel the Sikh cavalry at an angle. The charge dissipated the Gorcharas, who crossed to the east of the nullah near the Baradari, leaving the Sikh right entirely exposed albeit protected by the nullah to an extent. The first to run from the field, as predicted a few days earlier by George Lawrence, were the Afghan horsemen, whose destination now seemed to be Kabul. Paired with Shere Singh's orders to pull back slowly under the intense fire of the British artillery, this had the effect of unsettling the entire Sikh right.

Dundas, commanding the British left, advanced his troops, the 60th Rifles and the 3rd troop of horse artillery under Major Blood, in advance of the main line. There was precious little to do as the entire Sikh right folded. 'The division kept gradually advancing without firing a shot, the enemy moving off so fast we could not reach him, the artillery taking every advantage of opening its fire that was afforded,' Dundas reported. The line as it advanced passed through the Sikh camp, passing round the west of the town. 'The ground at the first was studded with bushes and hedges of prickly pear which caused some delay in getting through and on reaching the open country again not a sign of the enemy was to be seen. Two guns were abandoned by him on this side of the town. Not a casualty occurred in the infantry division or in the troop with the exception of two horses.'

To the right of Dundas were Campbell's two brigades, situated also to the west of the Bhimber nullah or river. The fighting here was almost entirely an artillery affair. As with the rest of the line the advance was systematic, the Sikh line gradually being forced back by the paralysing fire of the British guns and many of the Sikh infantry taking shelter in the nullah. The nullah, bisecting both the British and Sikh line was quite open to being enfiladed by the British guns. There was an attack of sorts on Campbell's men by the Sikh line here but in disorderly fashion. 'As we advanced, an effort was made by some of the principal chiefs to bring forward their cavalry to attack the advancing line; but it was evident from my position, from whence the movement could be seen in flank, that the willingness was confined but to a few hundreds.

These were in front, following their chiefs, who were leading. The horsemen in rear of this more willing body evidently went forward reluctantly. The infantry, who had taken shelter in the nullah, accompanied this movement in a very disorderly and tumultuous manner,' described Colin Campbell. Campbell, sensing the opportunity, ordered his artillery to turn left and fire on the flanks, essentially enfilading the advancing body of cavalry while the Bombay columns to his left fired directly ahead. This caused the cavalry to retire across the nullah. Campbell would then turn his guns to fire on the massed Sikh infantry in the nullah. 'I received orders to storm this nullah; but to have done so with infantry would have occasioned a very useless and most unnecessary sacrifice of life. And seeing that this end could be obtained by the use of the artillery without risking the loss of a man, I proceeded upon my own responsibility to employ my artillery in enfilading the nullah; and after succeeding in driving the enemy out of every part of it, I had the satisfaction of seeing the whole left wing of our army, including my own division, pass this formidable defence of the enemy's right wing without firing a musket or losing a man,' he continued.

So unequal was the contest here that the infantry columns of Campbell had no occasion to fire a shot, the British artillery fire doing all the work as it had done to his left. Eventually Campbell's division did cross the nullah, moving east of Gujrat, leaving the Bombay Division to move to its west before linking up again on the other side of the town after having cleared the town.

One of the more memorable incidents of the battle occurred opposite HM 24th as it advanced towards the village of Lundpur. A battery of eight Sikh heavy guns opposed the brigade here, but were quickly targeted by the British guns opposite.

On the smoke clearing away, it was seen that of the eight Sikh guns, seven were dismounted, the eighth being untouched. Round after round was ineffectually fired at this single gun, which could not be silenced. It continued to play steadily on our line, even when we had advanced up to grape distance. The gunners serving it were gradually either killed or wounded, or had retired, until at last only one fine old Sikh artilleryman was left. Single handed, he persisted. I must mention that the Sikhs were accustomed to stop the vent with a heavy damp sand bag, not as we do with the thumb, hence his ability to work alone. He fired several rounds on our advancing line, himself the target for shot, shell and musketry. When our men were getting very close, he hurriedly attempted to ram down a charge, possibly belonging to one of the dismounted guns, and too large for his, as it jammed in the bore, and rendered the gun useless. Seeing this, he turned towards our advancing force, made a profound salaam, and then walked quietly away, as if he were on his own parade ground. Our men, observing his marvellous coolness, could scarce forbear from cheering him. I hope sincerely that the fine old boy lived for many years afterwards to tell the tale. It would have been a thousand pities had this gallant gunner been killed. The daring deed was done just in front of the 24th regiment.

Most of the hand-to-hand fighting would be largely confined to the British right, in front of Gilbert's division. The 3rd brigade, consisting of the 2nd Europeans and 31st and 70th NI under Brig. Penny, faced the village of Burra Kalra while Brig. Hervey's men faced Chota Kalra, 1.5 km further to the east. Both of the villages had Sikh troops stationed in them. Gilbert was given the order to advance and subsequently Fordyce's horse artillery and Dawes's field battery in front of his brigades was moved forward. These were targeted by two Sikh batteries from either side of the village of Burra Kalra and a heavy fire was exchanged. Burra Kalra was captured after some brisk fighting by Penny's brigade. It appeared to be unoccupied and Gilbert ordered his infantry forward, but upon them reaching the village a sudden fire broke out upon then from loopholed village houses which were taken by the 2nd European Regiment, albeit with casualties. Meanwhile, the other village, Chota Kalra, was also attacked at the same time by Brig. Hervey's brigade. Brig. Hervey would draw up his force with horse artillery on either flank for the attack. This movement made a gap in the British line and Whish pushed up Markham's reserve brigade to avoid the Sikh cavalry taking advantage, which they were seen to be preparing to do. Capt. Warner was ordered forward to open fire on the Sikh troops to the east of Chota Kalra. 'But as they returned a heavy fire within accurate range, I changed position left back and the horse artillery ceased firing. The enemy's horsemen now appeared in great force on our right threatening to turn our flank. So I changed front to the right. Captain Warner's guns opened with great effect upon the horsemen and turned them but they only retired a short distance and then a regiment of their regular cavalry moved round by a circuitous route and got completely into our rear', wrote Brig. Lockwood. Commanding the cavalry on the British right, Lockwood proceeded to detach three guns and a squadron of the 16th Dragoons plus a corps of irregular cavalry under Major Christie, who then drove off the attack by the Sikh cavalry. Two troops of horse artillery under Lt-Col Brind previously held in reserve were now moved forward to enfilade some Sikh guns on the Sikh left now that the cavalry had been driven off.

Brig. Hearsey commanded the 4th Cavalry to the extreme right of the British line. This was the only unit to the east of the Katella Nullah on the east of the town. A Sikh regiment faced Hearsey after the cannonade along with cavalry on the Sikh left. Hearsey would move the horse cavalry along with a squadron of HM 14th Dragoons and a squadron of irregular horse towards the Sikh line with the horse artillery keeping the Sikh line at bay. In order to avoid the artillery and to outflank the British right, the Sikh Gorcharas would in response move further to the right and circle round to the south. To counter this, Hearsey wheeled his irregular brigade to face east. He would be joined at this stage by Brig. Lockwood's brigade and three additional guns. The move by Lockwood to the right meant a gap now appeared in the British lines between Lockwood and Gilbert's division and the Gorcharas made an attempt to enter this gap. Hearsey immediately moved some of his irregulars from the 3rd and 9th Irregulars in this direction, which prevented any intrusion. This was the last attempt by the Gorcharas to try and break the British line.

With the villages cleared, Gough maintained his original strategy of bombarding the Sikh line as Shere Singh continued to pull back. No respite was given from the shelling. 'The heavy artillery continued to advance with extraordinary celerity, taking up successive forward positions, driving the enemy from those they had retired to, whilst the rapid advance and beautiful fire of the horse artillery and light field batteries, which I strengthened by bringing to the front the two reserved troops of horse artillery under Lieutenant Col Brind, Brig. Brooke having the general superintendence of the whole of the horse artillery, broke the ranks of the enemy at all points', Gough continued in his despatch.

As most of the Sikh force had evacuated the town, moving past its northern outskirts, British troops were organised to move in. The eight gates of the walled town were occupied and manned to stop any Sikh units still inside the town from leaving. HM 32nd along with the 36th and two companies of the 51st NI under Lt Wallace were ordered into the town to eliminate any opposition. The town fort, a modest structure which had been garrisoned by eighty men, surrendered but there was isolated fighting elsewhere, Sikh soldiers being holed up in various

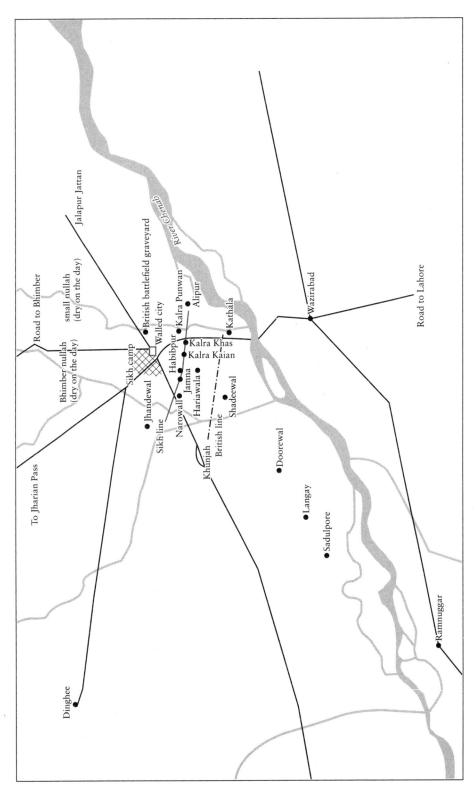

Jalapur Jattan

small nullah (dry on the day)

British battlefield graveyard

River Chenab

Road to Bhimber

Bhimber nullah (dry on the day)

Walled city

Sikh camp

Kalra Punwan

Alipur

Kathala

Wazirabad

Road to Lahore

Kalra Khas

Habibpur

Kalra Kaian

Jhandewal

Jamna

Sikh line

Narowall

Hariawala

Shadeewal

British line

To Jharian Pass

Khunjah

Doorewal

Langay

Sadulpore

Dinghee

Ramnuggar

10. Battle of Gujrat

buildings. The largest resistance was at a Hindu temple where a core of around 200 Sikh soldiers had barricaded themselves. It was captured with thirty to forty Sikh soldiers killed and the rest taken prisoner.

*\*\*\**

Taking full advantage of Shere Singh's discomfort, Gough continued to push his force on past the town and the Sikh camp with his guns moving in prefect order and continuing the bombardment without respite. This could not continue indefinitely, and by 1 p.m. the Sikh line was breaking up and the battle effectively finished. North of the town, the Sikh troops had retreated through their own camp. Most of the Sikh guns, either destroyed or disabled, were being left behind and as the line retreated through the camp a bare minimum of the entire baggage and ammunition behind could be taken. Units began fleeing with what they could. 'I may here observe that all the enemy's tents were left standing near the Barra Durree and on the Sikh right of the town with probably much baggage in them all of which were probably plundered by the camp followers,' recalled Thackwell in his despatch on the advance of the Dundas's Bombay troops west of the town. British camp followers, sensing profit, began quickly filtering on to the field before the last firing had died down. Meanwhile, Campbell would circle past round the east of the town, passing through the abandoned Sikh camp on this side with both wings meeting up on the north of the town. The rapid advance of the British line through the Sikh camp meant many Sikh camp followers fell victim to the shot or were simply left behind in the confusion by others. One British soldier wrote an encounter on passing through the camp:

> The most heart rending sight of the day was one I witnessed in the tent I entered. There on the ground, bleeding to death lay a young mother; her leg had been carried off by a round shot, and the jagged stump protruded in a ghastly manner through the mangled flesh. She held a baby to her breast, and as she bent over it with maternal anxiety, all her thoughts seemed to be of her child. She appeared totally regardless of the agony she must have been suffering, and to think of nothing but the poor infant, who was drawing its nourishment from her failing breast. I gave her some water, and she drank it greedily, raising her large imploring eyes to my face with an expression that was heart rending to witness. I was obliged to leave her and go on with the regiment, but the remembrance of that sight will live with me until my dying day.

The Sikh army now split up into several portions and began a confused retreat. Some of the baggage and ammunition wagons that had been retrieved from the Sikh camp could be seen either standing or their contents strewn along the road for approximately 19 km towards Bhimber as Sikh troops desperately fought to bring along as much as they could while being harassed by the fast advancing British line. British units would push on for the rest of the day, chasing the Sikh units till dusk drew an end to the day's proceedings. Gough, meanwhile, intending to apprehend the remnants of any Sikh units in the area, issued a proclamation warning the inhabitants of Gujrat town to the effect that if any residents were found harbouring or assisting Sikh soldiers a fine of 200,000 rupees would promptly be imposed on the town.

*\*\*\**

The total British casualties for the battle would be modest. 92 were killed (including 5 officers) and 682 wounded. Consistent with the fact that the contest was almost entirely an artillery affair bar the fighting at the two villages, the British casualties from the artillery arm were greater in proportion. Most of the infantry casualties were suffered by the 2nd Bengal European regiment, which took part in fighting at the village of Barra Kalra in conjunction with the 31st and 70th NI. The 2nd European Regiment suffered 8 men killed and 135 wounded, the 31st 11 men killed and 131 wounded and the 70th 10 killed and 40 wounded. In the 4th Brigade, to their left in the line, HM 29th lost only 2 men and 6 wounded, the 30th having 3 men wounded while the 56th NI had only one wounded.

For the Sikh army, while the losses in men weren't calculated, forty-three of the fifty-nine guns were abandoned on the field. Gough was confident more would be captured or left behind as he planned to pursue the broken sections of Shere Singh's army the next day. 'Immense quantities of ammunition and ordnance stores of every description have been destroyed and I am making every exertion to collect that which was left concealed in the different villages,' Gough wrote in his despatch. All the standing camp had been left behind. Added to this was almost the entire complement of cattle and ammunition. Meanwhile, looting in the former Sikh camp began in earnest, curious British soldiers and camp followers alike searching through the tents for valuable items. Exploding ammunition tumbrils and wagons ended the search for several of the less careful. One soldier who had picked up a shot while searching a tumbril for loot passed it to a comrade who threw it into a nearby wagon full of shot and powder. As the shot flew in it hit another shot, creating a spark which blew the whole ammunition wagon. One man was killed instantly and a group of soldiers nearby were badly wounded. The Commander-in-Chief happened also to be nearby but far enough away to avoid being wounded. Despite these death-defying searches, the prize agents and their assistants, unfortunately for the looters, had begun moving in and all items looted had to be surrendered. This included men taking the many fine Arabian horses and camels laden with cashmere shawls worth significant amounts.

Intelligence arrived around this time of Sikh units in the nearby villages having in their possession seven more guns, and a party of 1st Light Cavalry with Capt. Nicholson in command was sent to capture these. The party also captured two other guns in another village a few miles further. HM 24th, meanwhile, were ordered to pursue the Sikh troops heading towards the Bhimber Pass and Kashmir along with some native regiments and would return after two days with another two guns captured. Thackwell at this time sent Brig White to the villages to the left of the Jhelum road, where large quantities of baggage were also captured. Here the bulk of the British troops stopped to reorganise, although cavalry and horse artillery continued the pursuit till night.

This close pursuit meant more Sikh casualties as British troops pressed close on the back of the retreating Sikh contingents. 'The cavalry lads say, in every field some twenty or thirty were shot down,' related a private letter from a combatant. 'Arms, chogas, shoes &c. were lying in hundreds all about, having been thrown away by the fugitives in order to travel lighter. The pursuit stopped only when the artillery horses were quite done up.' Thackwell himself would continue the pursuit to Sainthul, 24 km from Gujrat, before returning at 10 p.m. Major Blood's troop of horse artillery accompanied Thackwell as he continued the pursuit, as recorded by Major Leeson:

I proceeded accompanied by Lieutenant Hamilton and my staff. After proceeding at a trot and gallop for about nine miles we joined the Cavalry Division and soon joined the enemy's rear and at a distance of about 400 yards opened fire with manifest good effect; they were then attempting to carry three guns and a considerable body of cavalry were hovering round to afford them protection. This they were unable to effect as our well directed fire soon obliged the enemy to abandon their guns camels carts bullocks &c and a great proportion of their baggage which fell into our hands. The enemy still continuing to retreat in a most disorderly manner, we advanced at a gallop for about three miles and again opened fire with such effect that they were compelled to abandon another gun. We again advanced some distance further and were halted by order of the General commanding who proceeded and at a quarter to five PM we began to fall back towards the camp which we reached at half past three o clock PM.

# 30

# The Surrender

… old whitebearded men, going about weeping and sobbing like children.
Mrs Lawrence, Sukhoo Fort, February 1849

I had not time to procure money, ammunition, or provisions,
and I was in want of all three.
Shere Singh, Rawalpindi, 14 March 1849

The Sikh army's retreat from Gujrat was initially a confused flight, with units moving off in three directions. The Afghans had already fled while the battle was being fought, making off towards Peshawar by the Jhelum road to the Kharian Pass. Some of the Sikh contingents took the road north towards Bhimber, later linking up with Shere Singh past the Jhelum. Other smaller, scattered groups headed towards the various surrounding villages north and west of Gujrat to gain some respite. Shere Singh with the bulk of his troops would begin retreating up the Jhelum road himself. There was little attempt to rally his forces, and in the confusion much of the baggage and a huge amount of munitions and material had been left behind. There would be no immediate surrender, however, and his immediate thought was to cross the Jhelum or pass the Indus into Peshawar and gain some time to reorganise his force. There he hoped he could gather more resources and cast new guns for another stand. In his conversations with his British prisoners during the next few weeks, he frequently considered crossing the Khyber Pass into Afghanistan with his army as well. The hope here was that his nominal ally Dost Mohammad would help finance and re-equip his army.

In the British camp, Dalhousie made it equally and amply clear to Gough that the advantage accrued at Gujrat must not be allowed to dissipate and that the Sikh army must be pursued as forcefully as possible to prevent a rally and to help bring the war to a definitive and quick conclusion. 'I am well aware that the season is advancing, and that the difficulties of military operations in the hills may possibly be very great. Nevertheless, it is of such vital importance to crush the resistance of the Sikhs, and, at once, and effectually, to break up their combination with the Mahomedan power which has taken possession of the territories on this side of the mountains, that the operations of the present campaign against them must be prosecuted vigorously, and without cessation, so long as it is possible for us to do so. There can be neither concession nor compromise,' he made clear to Gough.

The British Commander-in-Chief needed no prompting from the Governor-General and made plans accordingly. However, he would not be given the chance to receive any possible surrender himself. Dismayed at Gough's performance during the previous battles, the Governor-General had already decided to restrain him from commanding in any future contests. Dalhousie insisted in diplomatic fashion that the main British camp should remain at Gujrat, which by convention would tie Gough himself to the town. The Commander-in-Chief responded gracefully by busying himself after the battle organising posts all along the fords of the Chenab to prevent Sikh units crossing the river and heading eastward. He also organised the destruction of the magazines in the now deserted Sikh camp, although curiously the Sikh dead were not allowed to be disposed of; they would remain littering the battlefield for many days after.

Early on the 22nd, the day after the battle, three British columns would leave the British camp to pursue the various sections of the Sikh army. The first column, headed by Brig.-Gen. Colin Campbell with infantry, was directed towards Daulut Nuggar, a town 20 km northwards on the route to Bhimber and the hill country. Campbell set off around 2 p.m. with his division accompanied by HM 9th Lancers and the 8th Light Cavalry and would succeed in capturing and bringing in nine Sikh guns that had been abandoned close to the town. A further two abandoned guns were found further on, bringing the total captured at or after Gujrat to fifty-three. The second column, a smaller portion of cavalry under Col Bradford and Capt. Nicholson, was directed to scour the nearby hills for Sikh stragglers and other units.

The third column, by far the largest and a sizeable portion of the British force, would trail Shere Singh with a view to pushing him into surrender. The command of this column was given to Gilbert. Following receipt of his orders, Gilbert assembled his force of around 10,000 men and twenty-four guns in readiness for the pursuit. The infantry comprised both sections of the Bombay and Bengal infantry. The Bengal contingent included HM 29th Foot, 2nd Bengal European regiment along with the 30th, 56th, 31st and 70th Native regiments. From the Bombay contingent were present HM 60th Rifles, 1st European Fusiliers along with the 3rd and 19th Native regiments. The force was also accompanied by three companies of Bengal Sappers and Pioneers and a company of Bombay Sappers and Miners. In addition to this, HM 14th Light Dragoons, along with the 3rd Irregular Cavalry, 9th Irregular Cavalry and the 11th Irregular Cavalry and a detachment of Scinde Horse would be present.

22 February, a hot, dry day, saw Gilbert begin the pursuit. Huge columns of dust were thrown up by the cavalry as covered a distance of 35 km on the first day. However, it soon became clear to Gilbert that Shere Singh had not gone directly through the Kharian Pass, instead veering off towards Dinghee and Rasul. The Sikh commander's plan quite possibly was to cross the Jhelum at Rasul if not to reoccupy his old and sound position. With that in mind, Gilbert reached Dinghee at speed with his Bengal troops while the Bombay units trailed behind. The weather in the evening of that day rapidly deteriorated, with a storm developing. This would continue all night and the next day, whipping up huge amounts of dust and hampering both armies in their movements.

At 6 a.m. the next day, despite the dismal conditions, Gilbert reached Rasul before veering north towards Aurangabad as news came in that Shere Singh was crossing the river opposite Jhelum town instead. By the afternoon that day he reached the village of Pooran, where various traces of the former Sikh entrenchments could still be seen from the earlier battle. Here villagers told the British column the last remnants of the Sikh army, around 1,000 men with four guns, had passed through just a few hours before Gilbert. Aurangabad Serai, a couple of kilometres from the Jhelum, was reached at 3 p.m. despite the weather making a further downturn. 'We were now saluted with a tremendous storm of rain and hail, which speedily wetted us to the skin; and, what was worse, froze us to the bone; while to mend the matter, the hail and sleet beat full in our faces and almost blinded us. It continued, without intermission, until 3 p. m. by which time we had reached the banks of the Jhelum, which runs in a narrow but rapid stream, about two miles from the pass,' recorded R. W. Bingham of the 30th NI.

As his force entered the town, British pickets brought back the message that the last remaining Sikh units were still in the process of crossing the Jhelum. Hoping to interrupt their progress, Gilbert rode ahead with just the HM 14th Light Dragoons, the 11th Irregular Cavalry and Fordyce's troop of horse artillery. He met with no fortune, for as he reached the riverbank the Sikh troops could plainly be seen already on the right bank, in the process of burning a large batch of the roughly 120 boats used for the crossing.

The Sikh troops were evidently making camp in the town of Jhelum, seemingly ready to contest a British crossing, with batteries being constructed on the right bank. Gilbert in his despatches noted the number of Sikh troops on the opposite bank to be around 20,000. 'I was not able to distinguish any of them dressed in red and I am therefore disposed to think the force was entirely composed of irregular troops,' he recorded. The regulars had in fact crossed earlier and were ensconced in the nearby village. Gilbert counted upwards of nine guns with them, although the local villagers later gave information that this force had approximately twenty guns. With no boats available and the nearby fords guarded, there was no possibility of crossing the swollen river, and therefore Gilbert set up camp at Aurangabad to wait for Shere Singh to vacate the right bank. The pause at the Jhelum would stretch for several days and gave the trailing Bombay units a chance to catch up with his advance force. This halt also allowed another arrival at the Jhelum. Major George Lawrence, who had been released on parole by Chutter Singh before Gujrat, had left Lahore on the 22nd. He would reach Gough's camp at Gujrat two days later, where he wrote to Shere Singh requesting to rejoin the Sikh army. Leaving the British camp on the 25th, he reached Gilbert's force at the Jhelum the next day. A ceasefire was arranged on that afternoon with the guns on both banks falling silent to allow the emissary to cross over and complete his promise of returning. A volley of six shots were fired by the Sikh gunners at Gilbert's men before George Lawrence began crossing; although it was not apparent then, these would be the last shots fired in this war.

'The Sikhs were on the right bank, and both armies were firing into each other,' George Lawrence wrote. 'As I went down alone to the bank of the river to join Shere Singh, I waved a white handkerchief as a signal for a boat to ferry me across. One immediately was sent, the firing ceasing on both sides until I landed. I then joined the sirdar, and surrendered myself in terms of my parole, much to Shere Singh's surprise, and that of the Sikhs, who cheered me long and loudly, applauding me for returning to them, now that they had been defeated.'

The news George Lawrence had brought from Lahore wasn't good, however. The Governor-General's attitude was unwavering, especially now that a decisive victory had been gained at Gujrat. In addition, Henry Lawrence had sent a separate ultimatum as regarding the British prisoners.

To Sirdar Chuttur Sing, the Sirdars, Officers and Soldiers in arms against the British Government.

If within eight days Major Lawrence, Lieutenants Bowie and Herbert, and Dr. Thompson, and the ladies and children now in captivity, are not made over in safety to one of the British camps, I will send Sirdars Golab Sing, Nar Sing and Bishen Sing and the other Sikh prisoners now in confinement at Lahore, also their families and the families of such other rebels as may fall into my hands, to Hindostan. Such will be the first step taken; the next will depend upon circumstances. You should understand that this proclamation is made by order of the Governor-General, and will be thoroughly carried out.

Golab Singh was the younger brother of Shere Singh who had been in incarceration in Lahore since the previous year on Frederick Currie's orders. Nar Singh was another relation. This ultimatum had been given in response to news that Shere Singh was contemplating crossing into Afghanistan along with his British prisoners. Dalhousie was most anxious about the English prisoners falling into Afghan hands. He hoped the threat of exile in British territory for the relatives of the Sikh commander might cause him to consider giving up his prisoners in case he crossed the border.

Recognising the anxiety in the British camp over the prisoners, Shere Singh became curious as to the best offer the British might make. George Lawrence was sent back across the river twice to negotiate and to open up a dialogue. What he wanted, the Sikh commander told Lawrence, was complete immunity for his soldiers, a cast-iron guarantee in writing that he and his father would not be exiled abroad or imprisoned and an assurance that he would not be held to account for any of their past actions. He also wanted it clear they would not be held accountable for the finances of the war or for any other situation prior to that. In other words, he wanted no punitive action at all. If these conditions were acceptable to the Governor-General then Shere Singh would contemplate a surrender that might be to the satisfaction of his men, who were very much for continuing the conflict. George Lawrence's crossing of the river to discuss matters with Gilbert resulted in nothing more concrete or promising. Gilbert replied that he had no power to negotiate but that his message would be passed to Mackeson, who would in turn communicate his message to Henry Lawrence and the Governor-General.

Dalhousie would make one concession requested by Shere Singh: their lives would not be at risk and they would not be forced into any sort of desperate existence. In addition, a fair pension would be awarded to allow them to live out their existence in a decent if modest manner in their home village and property. This was assuming they gave up their prisoners as per the earlier proclamation. There would be criticism from certain quarters later for this show of leniency. However, the Governor-General had no wish to chance the British prisoners being given over to the tender mercies of the Afghans, especially George Lawrence, who had already suffered captivity after the First Anglo-Afghan War. 'If I had refused, and they [Shere Singh and Chutter Singh] had retired into Cabul with the British prisoners, &c., as they said they would, and as they would have done, what would England have said of me, who had allowed our name to suffer such a reproach, and had brought on us either further war or deeper disgrace for so trifling a matter as the sirdars being put under surveillance in the Punjab instead of in the provinces?' he would later write.

Meanwhile, in the Sikh camp George Lawrence did his best to dissuade the Sikh commander from contemplating crossing into Afghanistan himself. He told Shere Singh that the alliance with the Afghans was dubious at best and that only treachery awaited him when he and his army reached Kabul. It was far better to negotiate terms with the British, who would be sure to honour any agreement made. 'I told them that once in the power of the Afghans, I was certain, from my knowledge of the people, they would be considered and treated as prisoners, and probably forcibly converted to Mahomedanism. These arguments I could plainly perceive produced a deep effect on the minds of the sirdars, who were perfectly aware I had not by any means exaggerated the risk they would incur by placing themselves in the power of the Affghans.'

Shere Singh would ignore the British ultimatum for more than a week, however, continuing to head west. One thing that may have swayed his decision for the time being was the prospect of reinforcements to the tune of 5,000 men and six guns. This was the force he had unwisely detached and left on the right bank of the Jhelum when marching from Chillianwala to Gujrat.

By the night of the 26th, therefore, the Sikh batteries at the river were vacated and all Sikh units had resumed their march westwards from the Jhelum toward the Bakrala Pass.

The next day, British pickets found the right bank quite deserted. Gilbert, realising the Sikh army had left, immediately made preparations to cross and continue the pursuit. A ford 8 km upstream with an island in the middle was utilised, the depth of water there being only 3 or 4 feet, while a portion of Gilbert's troops crossed the river at his original position, utilising the few boats that had been discovered over the previous days. It was a difficult crossing, the river swollen with heavy rains, and the entire crossing ended up taking several days. Several camels complete with the supplies they carried were washed away by the powerful current. Many of the Sikh wounded were found at the village of Jhelum on the right bank and at nearby Puckowal, having been left behind by Shere Singh to facilitate quicker movement. A substantial amount of ammunition (9,000 rounds) for his guns had been abandoned too, along with two brass mortars, suggesting he was short of carriage.

It was only on 1 March, after the awkward crossing, that Gilbert could resume trailing the Sikh army. An advance force by this time led by Lumsden and Nicholson had taken possession of the fortress of Rhotas. Gilbert initially seemed at a loss as to the direction Shere Singh had taken at this point. 'Of the movements of the Seiks, I know little; the villagers report them to have gone to Rowill Pinn [Rawalpindi] with only five guns and that the Mussalmans have risen and thrashed Chutter Sing and many other things which are to be doubted,' he wrote, deciding to continue due west towards the Bakrala Pass, this being the obvious route for Shere Singh. His officers were of the opinion Shere Singh would make a stand at the pass, a couple of days' march from Gilbert's present position. This narrow pass had a long, steep and winding entrance, with the road leading up to it being difficult, making hard work of transporting the guns. The officers felt that a few boulders could quite easily and effectively block the pass, thus making the location ideal for a defensive stand. Gilbert disagreed. He believed the Sikh force to be too disorganised and weak at this stage to make any stand at all. Otherwise, he argued, the position on the right bank of the Jhelum would not have been deserted by Shere Singh. He was convinced the Sikh commander would retreat further west, towards the Indus or across to Peshawar, as rapidly as possible.

One of the advantages for Gilbert in the delay before crossing the river was that it gave more time for reinforcements to join him, his force now numbering 16,000 men and forty guns. But after crossing the river, and despite the open and cultivated country that now stretched before him, the British general found progress was slower than expected; in his fast march to the river he had outrun much of his own supplies and ammunition. Another factor was that portions of the road after the Rhotas fort had been deliberately destroyed by gunpowder. These had to be repaired before Gilbert's carriage could pass and therefore it was only on 5 March that the British advance units reached the village of Dhuneeal. In order to allow supplies to catch up, therefore, Gilbert decided to set up camp at the village for several days before continuing.

What he had suspected about the Bakrala Pass proved true. The Sikh commander had opted not to make a stand there at all, instead putting as much distance as possible between himself and the pursuing force. It took Gilbert's column two days to traverse the pass before reaching the village of Tamieh Koh near the Horsa River on the other side, soon arriving at Pucka Serai, 25 km further down the road. Pucka Serai was a village on the banks of the Sohan River named after an ageing red-brick serai (inn) in dilapidated condition on the right bank of the river.

It was at this time, on 5 March, when all felt Shere Singh would continue to proceed to Peshawar and beyond, that dramatic news filtered into the British camp that the Sikh

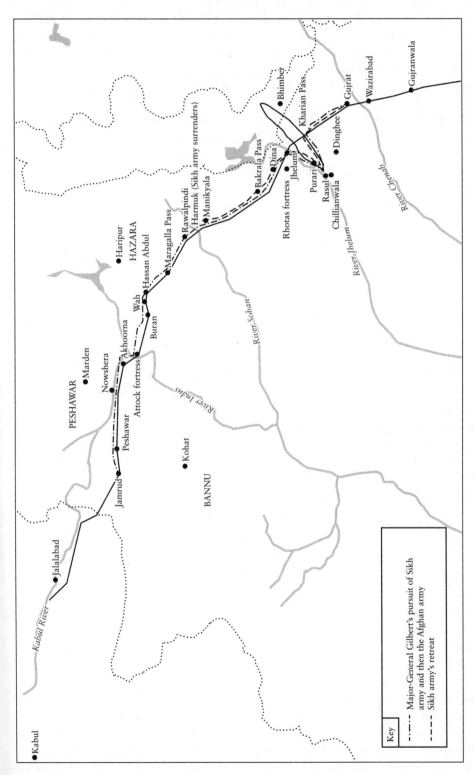

11. The surrender

commander, now at Rawalpindi, had decided to ask for terms with a view to surrender. This was confirmed later that day when several of Shere Singh's officers, including General Boodh Singh, rode into the British camp at Tamieh Koh to ask for talks. There were several reasons for this sudden change. The truth was that Shere Singh's situation had been getting rapidly worse by the day. With Gilbert pursuing him with all speed there had been no time to accumulate supplies and ammunition, and what few supplies had been successfully brought along from Gujrat were being rapidly exhausted. Many of the men had had nothing to eat for several days. On top of this came the news that two different forces were moving to block his passage across the Indus. James Abbott, the British agent in Hazara, had successfully blocked the Margalla Pass with his Muslim tribesmen levies and four guns. Although these tribesmen could be tackled, it looked like the route further west would also be blocked by Gulab Singh's forces, who were nearing the Indus. The Maharajah of Kashmir, with his new enthusiasm for working with the British after the decisive battle at Gujrat, had ordered the commander of his force, Steinbach, to work much more closely with the British. With this in mind a British officer, Lt Robinson, had already been sent to guide the force so that it worked in concert with Gilbert's force and movements. Shere Singh could expect little help from Dost Mohammad's forces, who had continued to flee westwards and were close to crossing the Indus at this time. With his path westwards cut off, continuing the conflict without provisions or sufficient guns and ammunition would be pointless.

Still, the Sikh commander took another three days to weigh up his options. The final decision on capitulation in the Sikh camp was likely made early on 8 March after a long meeting by Shere Singh with his officers. The decision was then communicated to the soldiers, who apparently gave him a hostile reception as he went round the camp. 'I accompanied these two leaders [Chutter Singh and Shere Singh] when for the last time they went down the ranks of their army,' recalled George Lawrence later as father and son communicated their decision to rank and file. 'The soldiers were infuriated, and heartily abused them for having sold them to the Feringhees. It was perhaps fortunate for the sirdars that they took the precaution of making me walk between them and their troops, as otherwise some of the soldiers might probably have used violence to them.' News of the disastrous defeat at Gujrat had spread, and with rumours of the surrender there had been much consternation and dismay among the Sikh troops scattered round the forts and towns. The wife of George Lawrence, detained at Sukhoo fort along with Bowie and others, later described a great commotion when news of the defeat reached the fort. Some of the older troops took it most gravely, 'old whitebearded men, going about weeping and sobbing like children'.

Despite the reservations of his soldiers, the formalities of surrender were organised the same day. The British prisoners were released, Mrs Lawrence and her children with an escort being sent first to the British camp. Later that day Shere Singh, accompanied by the rest of the prisoners, rode into the British camp to talk terms. With him was one of his officers, Lal Singh Moraria, along with around 450 soldiers. His arrival and escort aroused much curiosity, crowds of British soldiers gathering round the Sikh commander and his retinue as he was led to Gilbert's tent. The British soldiers found many of the Sikh soldiers who accompanied Shere Singh carried trophies of Ramnuggar and Chillianwala, British saddles, bridles and reins on their horses. One man of the 14th Dragoons saw a bridle marked with the name of his friend D. Lacey, killed at Ramnuggar. The rider who had slain the Dragoon was relieved of the equipment immediately. A friendly atmosphere otherwise prevailed, with British soldiers crowding round the group to discuss affairs and ask how the Sikh officers and soldiers were faring. 'I had a long talk with a fine, soldierly looking old man who had been a colonel in Ranjit Singh's time,' Henry Daly of the 1st Bombay Fusiliers remembered. 'He was one of the many Sikhs who went over to Sher Singh and forsook our people at Attock. He was particularly intelligent, very friendly and frank; deplored the state of the country and their own impoverished condition, contrasting it with what they held in the Maharajah's day. He at once admitted having joined Shere Singh in the hope of restoring the falling time.'

Shere Singh would be led into Gilbert's tent. Here he made a last attempt to extract some concessions, hoping the handing back of prisoners had softened the British stance. For his men he wanted eight months' back pay along with the free pardon. Unless Gilbert agreed to this, his men would refuse to surrender their arms and would prolong the war into the hot season that the Europeans dreaded. This condition Gilbert would not countenance, knowing well the troubled state of the Sikh army. He countered that Multan was captured during the hot weather and that the British army therefore had no anxiety of the coming heat. An immediate and unconditional surrender was demanded. If another shot was fired the offer of his and his father's lives being spared would be withdrawn. Unable to extract any more concessions, the Sikh commander finally agreed to an unconditional surrender. He would stay the night in the British camp, returning to Rawalpindi the next day to organise matters. This did not stop Gilbert continuing his advance to the Sikh camp at Rawalpindi, moving to the village of Manikyalla, around 50 km south-east of the city, the same day.

Here at the village, in front of which some of the surrender scenes would be conducted, a tall and well-built Buddhist stupa that had managed to stand the test of time dominated the landscape. Nobody had managed to fathom the function of this structure at the time. Reaching 80–100 feet high, it was believed to be the tomb of an important person, or even royalty. Many of the British soldiers whiled away the hours in camp clambering over the mound and speculating on its origins. The locals told them it was the tomb of a Greek general, while others, including Major Napier, suggested it was an ancient temple. Some suggested it may be the ruins of ancient Taxila or a burial mound which no doubt held great treasure. The huge number of pigeons that populated the ruin and area were targeted by the hungry soldiers and turned into snacks while others bought Greek, Persian and Bactrian coins turned up by the local farmers during their cultivation.

Gilbert had specified to Shere Singh the manner of giving up arms, and at Manikyalla the first batches of Sikh soldiers were arriving to give up their weapons. These included Sirdar Khan Singh Majithia, a senior officer who came in with 1,000–1,200 of his men and some guns to surrender. These men were asked to lay down their arms in front of their former prisoners George Lawrence and Lt Herbert. The camp at Manikyalla turned out to be short-lived, though. The distance between the two army camps was nearly 20 km. British camp followers were taking advantage of this distance, descending in large groups on the area between the two armies and plundering any possessions and money that remained to the Sikh soldiers after they had surrendered their arms and waited by the roadsides. News had also reached Gilbert of fiery meetings and vacillations among the Sikh officers and soldiers, who were dismayed at the surrender and refused to contemplate giving up their arms. For the double reason of maintaining a semblance of order and applying pressure on the Sikh units, the advance was continued another 15 km to the little village of Harmuk on the banks of the River Sohan on the outskirts of Rawalpindi. Now just the stream and a few kilometres separated the two camps and the proceedings could be better managed. Here, Shere Singh and his father who had returned to the Sikh camp would accompany the first contingents of their men coming in to surrender.

'The father's features are fine; he looks a noble. He appeared sorrowful and worn, his head was almost concealed. Not so the son, who keenly eyed the soldiers who thronged the banks to see them pass. The Sher even tapped his forehead and salaamed to them. They were both well-mounted,' noted Henry Daly. The next day, the 12th, was wet and cold. A large portion of the Sikh army, one division in all, marched in and laid down their arms under the supervision of Bombay native regiments. 'Their horse artillery were well turned out,' wrote Henry Daly. 'Some had as many as eight horses, others six in each gun; every horse a rider. The harness appointments bore traces of having been good. The artillerymen were well dressed too, although somewhat worn. Two of our guns which were lost at Chillianwalah were amongst those given up.'

Forty-two guns were handed in, surprising the British officers as they had expected the Sikh army to have been in a more parlous condition in terms of artillery. Included in these were some fine brass 12-pounders and a beautiful howitzer manufactured in Paris. This had been brought over by the famous General Ventura as a present for one of Ranjit Singh's sons in earlier years. What ammunition remained was also handed over, to be blown up later.

The British troops were ordered not to enter the city of Rawalpindi itself, Gilbert wishing to keep his troops and the Sikh soldiers apart in case of violence as many groups of Sikhs now roamed around instead of heading off home. All along the side of one thoroughfare to the city could be seen Sikh soldiers resting on the verges of the road. Most said they had no food and most had no more than five or six rounds left for their muskets. Others who had already surrendered were bereft of arms and watched with glum faces as the British soldiers marched by. On the 14th Gilbert gave a two-hour deadline to the bulk of the Sikh soldiery as they were still hesitant to give up their arms, ordering them to comply and surrender their weapons. Once this deadline passed, the British guns would be advanced across the stream and would begin firing grape into the Sikh camp. The threat cajoled most into surrender and no further violence occurred, the rest of the soldiers soon ambling across the ford at the river to surrender their arms.

A full 16,000 men would surrender at the River Sohan. The proceedings were done with silence but with ceremony. The Sikh soldiers were walked in small detachments to the British camp. Here a long line of sentries was drawn up through which the Sikh soldiers had to pass. At the end of the line a roughly 45-foot square was marked out, behind which Gilbert, the British commanding officers of divisions and brigades and their staff stood watching in silence. Into this square the Sikh soldiers were asked to throw their muskets and tulwars and other weapons, a scene that would be replicated on the campaign medal for the war. Once such a heap – a confusion of muskets, swords, pistols, spears and blunderbusses as well as bugles, drums and army standards – had achieved a height of roughly 4 feet, a fresh square was begun. Once this was done the soldiers were directed to another line of sentries ending at a table behind which Mr Cocks, the Resident's assistant, and Lt Nicholson sat. Noting that the Sikh soldiers were hungry, Gilbert, either through generosity or to prevent the soldiers raiding villages on their way home, had ordered a rupee to be offered to each man once he surrendered his arms to support him on his journey home. At this table they were given the rupee and allowed to return home unconditionally as per the agreement with Shere Singh. Many British troops and officers vividly recalled the scenes of surrender they saw at the river, with no animosity displayed by either side in the ritual. 'They are undoubtedly a fine and brave people,' wrote Colin Campbell, who had arrived in the British camp by this time and who was witness to the nearly silent scenes. One of those he saw surrendering was a priest or chaplain of the Sikh army who addressed Campbell in a loud and firm voice after dropping his weapon. 'The injustice of the English drove me to take up arms. They confiscated my property in the Jullundur Doab, amounting to 5 lakh rupees annually. Poverty, starvation, and want of ammunition have obliged me to surrender. These wants have brought me here. But for these wants, we should have again tried the fortune of war. I do not regret what I have done; and I would do the same to-morrow if it were in my power.' Campbell in turn was gracious towards the Sikh soldiers. 'There was nothing cringing in the manner of these men in laying down their arms,' he wrote. 'They acknowledged themselves to have been beaten, and that they gave in because they were starving. They were without money, food, or ammunition. There was nothing offensive in their manner in saying these things.' The priest, perhaps because of his age or rank, was offered a chair by Gilbert among his staff and watched the rest of the surrender ritual with the British officers. Many of the older veterans of Ranjit Singh's time were seen to be especially tearful, uttering cries of anguish as they lay down their arms. Others made salaams to their weapons before throwing them on the pile. One soldier was seen quietly laying his shield, sword and musket on the pile, then joining his hands together and saying, 'Aj Ranjit Sing mar gaya' – 'today Ranjit Singh has died'. Another soldier was seen sadly muttering, 'Mera kum hogaya' ('my work is finished now') before walking away with no interest in the rupee being offered by the British.

Once the entire infantry had surrendered their weapons, the Sikh cavalry, around 10,000 strong, were then invited to hand in their weapons. They would ride in two and threes, throwing their arms on heaps which grew to 8–10 feet high and covered 20 square yards each. 'Some of the old veterans of Ranjit did it with a very bad grace,' recorded R. W. Bingham, though some were more placid in their conduct. Others showed a quiet defiance. 'One old Goorcharrah drew his sword, knelt down and kissed it, and then with tears in his eyes, laid it gently on the pile, as if it had been an infant; and walked mournfully away refusing to take the rupee which was tendered to him by our politicals.'

After the Sikh soldiers surrendered their arms, there was open fraternisation between Sikh and British soldiers. John Nicholson had occasion to talk to one of the Sikh soldiers he recognised from an earlier time and the conversation provided a glimpse of the desperate straits the Sikh army had been in in the last few weeks as supplies ran out. 'How is this, friend?' he said, striking up a mocking conversation. 'Did you not say you would drive us all into the sea? Your Guru should have advised you better.' The soldier replied 'Ah! Sahib, there's no striving against Fate. There's no fighting upon a diet of cabbage. Just you try it yourself, sahib.' The soldiers had been subsisting on a bare diet of raw carrots, cabbages and turnips for the last two months. Others in conversation with the British soldiers voiced their determination for continuing the fight but were firm in their belief that to have gone on to Kabul as Shere Singh was contemplating would have courted certain catastrophe. 'What could we do? Dost Muhammad, now that disaster had befallen us, would give us up!'

The cavalrymen were obliged to surrender their horses as well, and their attachment to their steeds made for more emotional scenes. One of the anecdotes of the time was related by Neville Bowles Chamberlain to Lord Dalhousie in his camp in 1851. 'One of them, who had been obliged to sell his favourite steed, reined up its head, and, fastening the reins on the peak of his saddle front, addressed the animal in touching terms. He recounted the battles and adventures which they had shared together, and lamented the evil fate which had now befallen them. He claimed to have been a good and kind master, and, wishing of the horse a continuance of such treatment, he salaamed to it and bade it good-bye with perfect gravity and sorrowful demeanour.'

All in all around 15,000 rupees were expended in this exercise, suggesting 15,000 soldiers accepted the offer, the other 5,000-odd either refusing any help from the victors or quietly making their way home, avoiding British patrols. Half of the men who surrendered were in uniform, suggesting the others were irregulars of various kinds. The men were largely Sikhs although sepoys, Rajputs and Muslims were aplenty in this force.

Shere Singh and Chutter Singh and his entire coterie of officers were the last to give themselves in. The party included Lal Singh Moraria; Arjan Singh; Khan Singh Rosa, and his son Bootah Singh; Sultan Mohammad, the brother of Dost Mohammad; General Bahadur Sing; Dewan Kishen Koar; Dewan Hakeem Raee; Ootar Singh; and Bikram Singh Bedi, who had begun his own insurrection in the Jalandhar but had joined Shere Singh after its extinction. Not all surrendered. Prominent among the latter was the famous preacher Bhai Maharaj, who escaped to continue a guerrilla war against the British. Col Richpaul Singh, a principal officer of Shere Singh who had counselled heavily against surrender, also made his escape.

The Sikh guns surrendered, which surprisingly included several 18-pounders, were placed in regular order at the height of the hill next to the river. The guns were in addition to the sixty-two captured in the Multan theatre (although some sources mention around fifty). Twelve were taken at Chillianwala, fifty-two at Gujrat, seven after Gujrat at Bhimber and two found abandoned at Jhelum. Another fifty-two were found hidden in the fort of Gobindgarh, with two guns taken from the fort of Chiniot, five from the fort of Jubba and one recovered by Mackeson. Another twenty-five to thirty guns were stationed at Lahore fort and were also now forfeit. All in all these totalled almost 270 pieces either taken or forfeited during the entire war. These in addition to the 253 taken during the first war made over 500 pieces, the full complement Ranjit Singh had so assiduously built up over the years. Two regiments of irregular cavalry were given over to protect the surrendered arms till they were disposed of. The British standards captured at Chillianwala had also been asked for and given up.

In his conversations with Gilbert after the surrender, Shere Singh revealed much of what he'd been thinking and planning over the last few weeks. He had, he said, intended to make a stand at the Jhelum but feared Gilbert crossing at another point. Thinking the river would prevent a British crossing for at least a week, he had then determined to make a stand at the Bakrala Pass, the week's respite allowing him to source more ammunition and guns. Gilbert, though, had crossed quicker than he had expected and the idea in any case was not popular with his officers. He had finally decided on a stand at Rawalpindi but Gilbert had marched too quickly for him to gather more resources. 'I had not time to procure money, ammunition, or provisions, and I was in want of all three, but had you given me another week's respite, I should have been able to fight you; as it was, my men were on the brink of starvation, and my ammunition at so low an ebb, that it would not have sufficed for an hour's action.' In this situation, and with his path west being blocked, surrender was the only option to avoid unnecessary casualties.

While most of the soldiers were allowed to return home, Chutter Singh and Shere Singh along with Aotar Singh (Shere Singh's brother) and his senior officers would suffer the humiliation of being escorted to Wazirabad, where they were required to tender their submission to Gough personally before being taken to Lahore. There they would be held till a pronouncement by the Governor-General on their fate was issued.

***

Despite the British precautions many of the Sikh soldiers managed to carry their arms home, bypassing the British patrols all around the area; others preferred to sell their arms to British soldiers or camp followers they encountered, generating money for food for their passage home. These new owners, though, had to hide their trophies as organised patrols looked out for this illegal trade; it was strictly forbidden to purchase arms from Sikh soldiers, Gilbert's instructions being that all Sikh weapons and other trophies of war would be sold at auction later, the money generated going towards batta. Various amusing stories circulated later in the British camp about soldiers hiding their new trophies to escape the scrutiny of the patrols. Many took to hiding swords or matchlocks under uniforms or coats. One soldier of HM 60th was caught with two tulwars he had bought, hiding one in each leg of his trousers. Although he was seen to have awkward movements, he had escaped further scrutiny until he waded over the river ford; his wet trousers betrayed him, the cloth clinging to the swords and showing their shape underneath, much to the patrol's amusement. Another was challenged by Nicholson. Wishing not to use deceit, he gave up a sword in the hopes that Nicholson would be generous enough to allow him to keep it despite the ruling. Nicholson refused rather brusquely, but the man got his revenge – he was later seen with four swords under his cloak, having picked them up from one of the piles of surrendered weapons when the guards weren't paying sufficient attention.

The camp followers too were busy buying arms from the Sikh soldiers. A water carrier who had accumulated ten tulwars was found to have secreted them in his mussuck, or water bag, by the patrols. The bags were empty of water, which would have effectively hidden the swords and he was forced to hand them over. A brigade major took sympathy and allowed him to keep one, but the rest were confiscated. Others, wiser soldiers avoided the dragnet by heading off to Rawalpindi in the opposite direction from the British camp, thereby avoiding the patrols. The same went for the Sikh horses, which were going cheap and whose trade the patrols found more difficult to prevent. Once someone had purchased a horse it was difficult to prove he had obtained it from a Sikh sowar and the reply invariably was that the horse had been bought off such-and-such person or dealer, which was difficult to verify. It's quite possible these explanations were entirely true, of course, although stolen horses were known to go for a song.

With all the arms surrendered, auctions for the more valuable and prestigious items were begun the very next day. (Lesser valuable equipment was allowed to be taken away for fixed sums or gratis if heavily damaged.) 'Some of the swords, matchlocks, &c which had been surrendered at Manikyalla were sold by auction, and realised high prices, as everyone was anxious to have some memorial of so gallant a foe. Many of the match-locks were curiosities, as they had double locks, also a pan and nipple, so that they could be used either as flint or as percussion pieces. The plan was certainly a very ingenious one. The barrels were very handsomely damasked and gilt, but all fetched prices far beyond my means; I however managed to secure a very good sword at a reasonable rate,' R. W. Bingham wrote.

News of the Sikh army's surrender would reach Dalhousie three days later at Ferozepore, and he immediately ordered a salute of twenty-one guns to be fired from all British military stations in India to mark the occasion and the effective end of the war. The larger portion of the Sikh guns (111 in total) he would order to be taken to Calcutta. Two of the finer guns were sent post-haste to Calcutta to be shown in events marking the victory while the others would make their way down in slower fashion after the summer heat was over. However, Gilbert's auction of the prestige items had come too prematurely for Dalhousie's liking as none of the choice items had been retained. 'I had reserved the best of the captured guns for the Queen, in case she should wish to have some,' wrote Dalhousie later, 'and in consequence of orders sent to me I am now trying to recover some of the arms and armour taken at Goojerat. The Government has none, and if I get it at all, I must purchase it from fellows who have got hold of it.'

\*\*\*

All that was left to bring the campaign to a conclusion was the nominal work of chasing the Afghan army back into Afghanistan or destroying it if it attempted a stand. Gilbert had been authorised to continue across towards Peshawar and up to the Khyber Pass with this objective in mind. 'No apology of any kind will now be accepted. He [Dost Mohammad] has chosen to defy our power and must abide the consequences,' Dalhousie had written on 7 March. Dost Mohammad had by now fled with his army to Attock, around 100 km ahead of Gilbert. This distance had made the Afghans complacent, though, and in recent days they had not made the expected rapid crossing of the Indus and subsequent march towards the Khyber. Gilbert was therefore confident he could catch up with them if a strenuous effort were made. The day after the surrender, and with his troops rested, he therefore commenced a brisk advance, marching to Janee-ke-Sung on 15 February. Wah, near Hassan Abdul, 35 km north-west of Rawalpindi, was reached the next day. It was at this town that news came in at around 4 p.m. that the Afghans had not yet destroyed the bridge over the Indus either. Attock being around 50 km away, Gilbert decided on as rapid a march as possible on the chance the bridge could be captured intact. At 6 p.m. on the 16th his force moved off from Wah, reaching Buran by midnight, a move that totally exhausted his force and the artillery horses. Determined not to waste any time, a short two hours for rest and sleep for both men, horses and cattle was ordered before the pursuit was renewed. It was severely cold and uncomfortable during the night, with frost covering the ground. Nevertheless, by marching all night he managed to reach Shumsabad by daybreak. Leaving the main force of infantry behind at Shumsabad to rest and taking just his Dragoons and horse artillery, he quickly raced towards the Indus. This fast pace tired even the cavalry and artillery horses, and they gradually fell behind. By the time Gilbert reached Attock and the banks of the Indus at 11:30 a.m., he was therefore accompanied only by his staff, Major Mackeson and around forty cavalrymen who had managed to keep up. 'The fort of Attock, I found to be evacuated and the rear guard of the Affghan army was in the act of crossing the bridge of boats. Our troops had hardly shown themselves when the bridge was broken up and many of the boats allowed to float down the river,' noted Gilbert. The Afghans had panicked as they spotted Gilbert and his coterie, not realising he was accompanied by only a nominal force with the bulk of his men still some miles behind. A hurried attempt at destroying the bridge of boats had ensued, which was not altogether successful. Only four of the boats nearest to the right bank were burned and the centre ropes cut. With the bridge still tied on the left bank this had the effect of swinging the string of boats outwards due to the current, although several of the boats broke free and commenced floating down the river. Some of the boats were captured almost immediately by Gilbert's men, with seventeen being in hand shortly.

With the bridge eminently repairable and British artillery closing in, the Afghans made only a pretence of a stand on the right bank. Three batteries had been set up, comprising around ten guns in total with another two guns placed in the fort of Khyrabad plus some infantry and cavalry supporting the guns. There were a few desultory exchanges between Afghan Jezailchees and British units, with Afghan guns on the riverbank and the fort opening up. The fire from both sides was kept up for two to three hours, little damage being sustained by either side. The British horse artillery had arrived by about 1 p.m. and began returning fire, hastening the Afghan departure from the right bank. By 4 p.m. the advance guard of British infantry, having been rested, also appeared at the riverbank.

There was no chance of crossing the river immediately without additional boats, a process that was expected to take 2 to 3 days, and therefore Gilbert set up camp 3 km north of Attock on the banks of the river in an open space. The next day an attempt was made to cross without a bridge, using the boats only. Orders were given to the 30th and 56th NI but so swift was the current that the boats made no progress, only one company making it across. Therefore Gilbert would revert back to the original plan and Nicholson the political agent was ordered to manage the building of the bridge. Nicholson in turn cajoled the native ferrymen and villagers into helping with the construction, helped by a 500-rupee reward. By midnight a makeshift structure had been readied, and two boatloads of Guides had crossed over with baggage by 4 a.m. Three cast-iron guns abandoned by the Afghans in their hurry were captured on the right bank, although they had taken care to destroy the carriages.

By 9 a.m. on the 19th, all the British force had crossed the Indus. The westward march continued. A fast march meant 50 km was covered towards Peshawar city, and the route along the way was found to be littered with much of the Afghan baggage left two days earlier as their force made all haste to cross back into Afghanistan. By now the whole vale of Peshawar could be seen, surrounded on all sides by hills. Some of the local villagers informed Gilbert that the Afghans in their rush had lost another four guns on crossing the Kabul River. Attempting to retrieve these proved impossible as they were found to have sunk deep into the mud of the river. Here it was also learned the Afghan army had split in two – one force retiring by following the valley of the Kabul River while the other went to Peshawar town before going up the Khyber. Gilbert would make his camp at Akhoorna, 16 km west of Khyrabad and 16 km east of Nowshera on the banks of the Kabul River, planning on entering the city of Peshawar the next day. However, the Afghan army was beyond reach.

The news from Peshawar disappointed Dalhousie, who had hoped to destroy the Afghan ruler and his army to provide a final flourish to the campaign. He had been confident that the Afghans could be stopped from fleeing back to Kabul by the local tribesmen and then obliterated by Gilbert. In order to facilitate this, British agents had already been busy beyond the Indus building relations with these people and promising large rewards for successfully obstructing and halting the Afghan retreat through the Khyber Pass. 'I hardly think they [the Afghans] will fight. My savages in the Khyber swear they will stop them. If they do I have promised the beasts a lac of rupees, and if they succeed, the Afghans will be tremendously pounded. I hope all will be over by next mail,' Dalhousie wrote confidently on 23 March. But either the lure of money had been dangled too late, giving the tribesmen insufficient time to organise themselves for an ambush, or the tribesmen had decided to opt for their own co-religionists. Whatever the case, Dost Mohammad's force passed through back to Kabul without any problem, with the local tribal chiefs making the excuse that Dost Mohammad had retreated far too rapidly to allow them to organise a proper defence of the passes.

Dost Mohammad's worries weren't entirely over after reaching Kabul. News would reach Lahore a few weeks later that there had been some considerable dread in the city that a punitive expedition would be launched by the British in retribution for the Dost's alliance with the Sikh army. Many residents still had the British retribution after the debacle of the First Anglo-Afghan War a few years earlier fresh in their minds and feared a similar response to the recent war. They need not have worried, as Dalhousie in any case had no intention of renewing Anglo-Afghan hostilities across the pass.

Gilbert, meanwhile, would reach the town of Nowshera on the 20th and the city of Peshawar on the 21st. He had ordered a further hurried march in order to prevent the Afghans sacking the city before they vanished. This scheme proved largely successful, for Peshawar escaped a systematic plundering, the Afghans having only two days' advantage over Gilbert. The citizens had closed the gates on their approach, and with Gilbert coming up behind them the Afghan army only had time for some desultory looting outside the city walls before being forced to move on. Many of the garden houses and mansions outside the city walls had fallen victim to their rapacity, however. The British force set up camp to the north-west side of the city, hoping to use the old Sikh army cantonments. These were found to be burnt down by the Afghans and the timber from these building had already been carried off by the locals, presenting a ruined and melancholy appearance. The house formerly occupied by Major Lawrence had also been burned to the ground, its ruins still smoking.

The local inhabitants were happy to see the British column, having been the under the short but savage control of the Afghans. They were seen to come out of the city in droves to welcome Gilbert's force. At various places roses were thrown on to the British column, with the inhabitants wearing their best clothes and happy countenances as they cheered the force in. Many crowded round the army, making the best of the commercial opportunity. Hundreds of stalls opened up near the British camp selling butter, milk, fruit, iced sherbet and a myriad of other things that were eagerly bought by men unused to good living over the past month of fast marching. The British soldiers also availed themselves of the pleasures of Peshawar, there being many shops and eating places, with silk cloth and turquoise stones being popular as souvenirs.

Pausing for several days' rest at Peshawar, Gilbert would continue to advance as far as Jamrud fort at the mouth of the Khyber Pass before calling a final halt. Camp was set up 6.5 km short of the famous fortress. This effectively signalled the end of the British advance and Gilbert's field force was officially broken up on 1 April, with the general leaving for Lahore the following day after a week's stay sampling the pleasures of the beautiful vale. The bulk of the troops would stay at Peshawar as garrison for the time being, with some returning to British provinces. The Bala Hissar fortress outside the city was occupied by the British garrison, and on 3 April the British flag was raised for the first time and a royal salute fired from its walls, bringing things to a definitive conclusion and perhaps prematurely proclaiming the Punjab to be British territory.

Despite the initial welcome, the British troops would find the friendship of the local tribesmen as ephemeral as the Sikh army had before them. Several ominous developments early on signalled the need for vigilance and a permanent and strong hand in the valley for the ninety-eight years of British rule that were now beginning. British soldiers were warned off seeing the Khyber Pass, the area being infested with brigands and unruly tribesmen. Two British officers curious to see the pass had ridden the short distance after the British arrival at Jamrud but had been chased by tribesmen hiding in nearby caves anxious to make them prisoners for ransom. Trouble was also already brewing with other tribes. It was found that some local Afridis had already killed several of the British force as they made their way from Peshawar to the British camp a few days after the force's arrival, bringing an end to the friendly state of things.

Back at Ferozepore, as soon as news of Gilbert reaching the Khyber Pass and the British flag being hoisted at Peshawar reached Dalhousie on 23 March, he promptly directed all principal British Army stations around the country to fire another twenty-one-gun salute to officially mark the end of the war.

# DISSOLUTION

*Sab lal hojea ga* [All will be red soon].
Ranjit Singh before his death on seeing a map of India with
British possessions marked in red

We must resolve on the entire subjection of the Sikh people and on its extinction as an
independent nation.
Governor General Dalhousie's dispatch to Secret Committee, 7 April 1849

# 31

# Annex It Now

In order to prevent a confused interregnum in the Punjab now that the war was over, Dalhousie had been urged by all to declare his intentions quickly. Although it was well known that he had already privately decided on annexation of the region, for the past six months the façade of the British Government helping put down a rebellion against the Maharajah had been maintained to prevent Shere Singh's declaration of a national war against the British ringing true. Indeed, none of the Governor-General's public utterances revealed anything of his inner intentions at any time. This policy had been in alignment with the views of the Secret Committee: 'We strongly incline to the opinion that you would do well to refrain, in the first instance, from any public announcement of future intentions. It would be as well to defeat the Sikh army first as to declare annexation at this point would only play into the hands of Shere Singh,' they had advised on 24 November.

Now, with the conclusion of the war and the surrender of the Sikh army, there was no need to maintain the pretence of putting down a revolt. As the months went by, this lack of disclosure had in any case become somewhat redundant; all had come to the conclusion, whether Sikh or British, in the Punjab and beyond, that the British Government would annex the state. Whether all would be swallowed or just the richer and more manageable portions of the state was a matter for discussion. Some argued that the entire east of the Punjab from Multan would be annexed, with the Indus as the new frontier of British possessions. The area west of the Indus, too troublesome to police and providing too little revenue in exchange, could possibly be offered to Dost Mohammad on the agreement he would police the tribes in the trans-Indus belt and prevent incursions over the British frontier. The fortress of Attock therefore would become the westernmost point of the British Empire, garrisoned by a strong force. Whatever the strength of this argument, Dalhousie had by this time decided to swallow the whole of the Punjab up to the Khyber Pass and including the tribal areas, a move that future rulers of India would perhaps rue over the next hundred years.

\*\*\*

Reginald Bosworth Smith in his book *The Life of Lord Lawrence* records a conversation between John Lawrence and Dalhousie on the issue of the Punjab as news reached Lahore of Shere Singh handing over his prisoners and agreeing to surrender. 'What is to be done with the Punjab now?' asked the Governor-General, certainly in a rhetorical sense as his feelings on the subject were now clear. 'Annex it now,' came the terse reply from John Lawrence, who knew Dalhousie would not veer from a decision already made. Dalhousie continued the conversation, posing the problems associated with the approach. 'Annex it now; annex it now; annex it now,' was the answer from John Lawrence, fortifying Dalhousie's mind on the subject. Other authors dispute this conversation, arguing it was inconsistent with John Lawrence's views. Whatever the case, Dalhousie formally told Henry Lawrence of his decision the next day. These discussions on the future of the Punjab were supposed to include Henry Lawrence as well but he was otherwise indisposed. It has been said that he missed the meeting deliberately since Dalhousie had already made his mind up and that his only role, being heavily against annexation, would have been to put forward unsuccessful arguments, a role he was loath to take.

Dalhousie had been discussing the future of the Punjab with the Board of Control from as early as August the previous year, annexation being a constant issue. From Hobhouse he had already received reassurance and support back in October as the news of Shere Singh's defection and the declaration of a general war had been pronounced. Hobhouse would on 23 October 1848 communicate to Dalhousie that he had consulted Lord John Russell on the issue of annexation and that he was against this step but that if Dalhousie were to argue for annexation and commit himself to it then the 'the most favourable construction would be put upon your proceedings' and that any further propping up of the Sikh dynasty would be abandoned in favour of clear and direct British rule. As the war came to a close, Hobhouse did in fact advise Dalhousie to wait before declaring annexation but in vain; Dalhousie countered that to wait several months would only result in confusion, anarchy and renewed resistance to British rule. An immediate decision was therefore desirable.

Hardinge, the former Governor-General, would agree with Dalhousie once his decision had been made but many others were convinced of the injustice of annexing an ally and friendly state and of punishing the Lahore Government for the tardiness the Resident had shown in tackling the nascent rebellion at Multan. There was also the injustice of deposing Duleep Singh through no fault of his own and at such a tender age. These critics included Henry Lawrence, who had never seen any wisdom in swallowing up the Punjab. To Dalhousie's accusation that the war had been started by the Sikhs at Multan, his view was quite the opposite – that none had been Sikhs, neither Mulraj nor the assassin Ameer Chund who had attacked Agnew. He reserved some sarcasm for Dalhousie's assertion that there was the most bitter animosity against the English in the Lahore Durbar.

Although most of the British newspapers showed a broad agreement to the annexation of the Punjab, some opposed the move. The *Calcutta Star*, for example, sided with Henry Lawrence, declaring the growth of the insurrection could only be blamed on the lack of energy shown by the British Government in putting down the insurrection in its early stages. 'To seize the country because of a rebellion of which we ourselves were the leading cause would be violating the first principle of law which forbids men to take advantage of their own transgressions,' it declared.

After the declaration of annexation Dalhousie would justify himself by writing a strong and lengthy polemic against the Lahore Government on 7 April 1849, sensational in its content and arguing numerous points against the Durbar and the Sikh army to the Secret Committee in his final justification for his policy.

> We have been, for the second time, engaged in war with the most formidable enemy we have yet encountered in India. They have resisted us through the course of a protracted and severe campaign. The Ameer of Cabool, proclaiming himself the Apostle of Islam, and calling on all true Mussulmans to unite in a holy war against the English, has joined his ancient enemies, in order to a combined attack upon us ... if we do not thus reduce

to absolute subjection the people who have twice already rudely shaken our power in India, and deprive them at once of power and of existence as a nation; if concession or compromise shall be made; if, in short, the resolution which we adopt, shall be anything less than full assertion of absolute conquest of our enemy, and maintenance of our conquest hereafter, – we shall be considered, throughout all India, as having been worsted in the struggle.

Despite the British Resident leading the Lahore Government, he blamed the weak Durbar entirely for the war. Many were secret nationalists and falsely held their hands up in impotence when the Multan outbreak occurred, declaring they could do nothing. These were allies, he said, who were not worth having if they could not control their own soldiery. It was not possible to form a Sikh government from the feeble materials present and Muslim control of the Punjab could not be countenanced. 'The advantages, which we hoped to derive from such a Government, were the existence of a friendly Power upon our frontier; one which, from national and religious animosity to the Mahomedan Powers which lie beyond, would be an effectual barrier and defence to us,' he explained, 'but we have now seen, that the hatred of Sikhs against the British exceeds the national and religious enmity of Sikhs against Affghans.'

On the matter of finances, he noted the Durbar were supposed to have paid 22 lakh rupees per annum as payment for the stationing of British troops in Lahore and for the payment of loans made to allow for the discharging of the soldiers. This he said had grown to 50 lakh rupees. Not a rupee had been paid. As regards the Sikh army, Dalhousie argued that the real reason for the war was to expel the British from the Punjab and to destroy British influence. The Sikh army, he said, would be forever hostile to the British and the 'whole Sikh people throughout the land as one man have risen in arms against us and for months have been carrying on a ferocious war for the proclaimed purpose of destroying our power and exterminating our race'.

Not only this, but there had been calls for help to other neighbouring states – to Afghanistan, to Kashmir, to Rajputana – to assist in destroying the Firangis. As regards the notion of continuing the Sikh monarchy, he brushed away all objections relating to the youth and innocence of Duleep Singh, going as far as to question whether he really was the son of Ranjit Singh.

By maintaining the pageant of a throne we should leave just enough of sovereignty to keep alive among the Sikhs the memory of their nationality and to serve as a nucleus for constant intrigue. We should have all the labor, all the anxiety, all the responsibility which would attach to the territories if they were actually made our own while we should not reap the corresponding benefits of increase of revenue and acknowledged possession.

He argued that a precedent for this had been set after the first war when Duleep Singh's government had waged war against the British. The Maharajah had been even younger then and had been deprived of the rich provinces of Jalandhar and Kashmir by the previous Governor-General. He was older now and the argument had even less merit. Duleep Singh's government had promised after the Treaty of Lahore that if there was misrule he would be held responsible and so he must accept British punitive measures.

Much of Dalhousie's argument was well wide of the mark. What he had entirely chosen to ignore was that the state, to all intents and purposes, was being led by the Resident and that the Maharajah, being in a minority, was under the protection of the British Government.

Furthermore, the British Government was being paid to keep security and as such the Multan uprising should have been put down by the Resident as per the agreement. His assertion that all the chiefs of the Punjab had risen against the British was patently untrue as well. As recently as 15 January 1849, Currie had sent Dalhousie a long list of Durbar members and other notables who had not joined Shere Singh, whatever their inner sympathies. These included Raja Tej Singh, Raja Deena Nath, Sirdar Utter Sing Kaleewala, Sheik Imam-Ud-Deen and Fakeer Nur-Ud-Deen, all senior members of the Lahore Government, along with a host of lesser notables. In fact, thirty-four of the leading officials of the country did not side with Shere Singh, twenty-eight being Sikh, two Muslim and four Hindus. This included Bhai Nidhan Singh, the senior minister of the Sikh religion. What had initiated the war wasn't a deep ambition within the Sikh Government to throw off British interference but British tardiness in allowing a small rebellion triggered by local soldiers' fears for their livelihoods to grow into a war of independence waged by Sikh regular troops. His comments on the matter of payments from the Lahore Durbar into British coffers was in error as well; as recently as 23 February, Currie, as head of the Lahore Government, had transferred 1,356,837 rupees into the East India Company treasury. This had reduced the debt owed to the company from the previous 40 lakh rupees to 27 lakh rupees. In fact, Currie had in the same report expressed his satisfaction at how things were going.

***

Any arguments for and against annexation were moot in any case, with the decision already having been made. Dalhousie had decided against going to Lahore himself for the formal announcement of annexation and formalities, deputing Mr H. M. Elliot, the foreign secretary of the government, to deliver the deathblow. On 26 March 1849, he wrote to Elliot briefing him to inform the Durbar that the decision to annex had been taken, that the Punjab would now be a portion of the British Empire and that all state property must be surrendered. A declaration had been prepared which was to be read out to the Durbar. If the Durbar members acquiesced in everything, then he could offer a financial settlement, i.e. a pension, for the Maharajah on the 'relinquishment, for ever, of all title to the sovereignty of the country, a surrender of the property of the state, and of the gem called Koh-i-noor (respecting which it was specified that it should be given up to Her Majesty the Queen)'. Promises would also be made to the Durbar members that they could retain their jaghirs and titles. 'If any resistance should be attempted,' continued Dalhousie, 'or, if application for, or acceptance of, the terms should be declined, the Resident, on your intimation thereof, will proceed to take such measures as may be necessary, at Lahore, for carrying the resolution of the Government of India into immediate effect; and you will issue the Proclamation above mentioned accordingly. The Resident will take every proper precaution for providing against the possibility of disturbance, on the intentions of the Government of India being made known.' In other words, annexation would still take place regardless of their views. However, Elliot was to warn them that their jaghirs and titles could not be guaranteed in this case. Dalhousie assumed this financial inducement would encourage their participation in the winding up of the state in an organised fashion. In regards to the possibility of any disturbance once the news spread, a brigade of troops in addition to those already in Lahore had been summoned for arrival on the 28th, the same day as Elliot's arrival.

Elliot's own impression was that the Lahore Government members would not submit meekly to the request for cooperation in the annexation process. Reaching Lahore, he would hold a meeting with both of the Lawrence brothers on the matter. Both were firmly of the same opinion, voicing the view that the Durbar members were already treated with barely concealed contempt by the Lahore public and recognised as the Resident's creatures. To put their signatures to the end of the state would be too much even for them to swallow. Henry Lawrence also seems to have persisted in his argument over the presentation of the annexation document to the Durbar, prompting Elliot to request that Henry Lawrence should put his point of view in writing to the Governor-General, which served to effectively silence him.

Elliot's plan was to address the members in separate groups, any group bravado therefore being dissipated. Tej Singh and Dewan Deena Nath were summoned first. If these two leading members accepted the British decision, the lesser members of the Durbar would likely put up no resistance. Tej Singh, well aware of the purpose of the meeting, would initially make excuses for not attending, as related by Elliot:

> The Raja, at first, excused himself, on the ground of sickness and I should have, consequently, gone to his house, had I not been apprehensive that any exhibition of undue eagerness might have been interpreted into too great a desire to obtain his concurrence. It was then intimated to him that, as my mission was urgent, and could not be accomplished without him, he should come to the Residency, unless he really was seriously ill. Upon this, he came, his looks giving no warrant for his excuses; and was accompanied by Dewan Deena Nath.

Elliot explained at length the reason for the meeting to the two Durbar members. The Punjab was to be annexed and this decision was beyond negotiation. It was now up to the Durbar members to decide whether they would cooperate. If they were in agreement with the British Government, their jaghirs would be safe. If they did not cooperate, Elliot could guarantee nothing. Tej Singh was noticeably nervous and more talkative than usual, Elliot noticed, and in an outpouring criticised Shere Singh heavily for having brought matters to this state. '[Tej Singh] acknowledged that the British Government had acquired a perfect right to dispose of the country as it saw fit and recommended that it should declare its will without calling upon the Council to sign any conditions,' Elliot wrote. This was an obvious ploy to avoid the odium from the general public at having signed away the country's existence. Elliot realised this and was insistent a decision be made either agreeing or disagreeing with British intent. The signatures of the Durbar members were required if they submitted to the Governor-General's dictum but not if they disagreed. In other words, they needed to make their stance public.

Dewan Deena Nath at this point noted the severity of the terms. Elliot had earlier told them the Maharajah would have to leave the palace and live elsewhere outside of the Punjab in British Hindustan. This he demurred on, saying he found it difficult to accept. Elliot replied that not only the Maharajah but all members of the royal family and relatives were to be moved out of the palace and fort. These would now be used by the new British administration. This prompted a discussion on where in India the Maharajah would reside. Elliot had mentioned that the Deccan would be the destination. This did not go down well with the two men, and after some further discussion it was decided it would be a place 'which would not be further east than the Ganges'. Hardwar and Allahabad were mooted as well as other Hindu holy places. 'They seemed to be thankful for this as a concession,' Elliot noted. The 10,000 rupees per month proposed for Duleep Singh's pension was readily accepted without any discussion.

The last thing the two asked about related to personal interests. They asked whether their jaghirs would be hereditary if they assented to signing the documents that Elliot had laid before them. 'Certainly not,' replied Elliot, explaining there would be no change but that it would be left to the officers assigned to the task of looking at whether jaghirs were already hereditary or not. Mindful of the consequences if signatures were not forthcoming, both now promptly put pen to paper. Elliot observed that Dewan Deena Nath did so with reticence and some sorrow, and Tej Singh with none at all.

With the signatures of these two being received, the only other two Durbar members in Lahore, Fakeer Nur-Ud-Deen and Bhai Nidhan Singh were summoned. Upon being told of the other two assenting, these two promptly signed the paper. Henry Lawrence and Elliot then both countersigned the paper. The other Durbar members' signatures were not required for the winding up of the state, apparently. Elliot told the four Durbar members, the declaration of annexation would be formally declared the next day and therefore a Durbar was to be organised for 7 a.m. in the morning where the Maharajah's signature would also be obtained in public. The whole business of discussing and obtaining the assent of the Durbar members for the termination of the state had lasted barely two hours and Elliot and Henry Lawrence now busied themselves on the preparation for the Durbar the next day with orders given for the British troops to be readied in case of any disturbance in the city.

\*\*\*

Early the next day, 29 March, Elliot travelled to the palace with Henry Lawrence and various other Europeans of the Residency along with a bodyguard of troops. They were met by the Maharajah at the fort gate. The communication regarding the annexation had seemingly already been spread by the Durbar members. Large numbers of people, of both low and high station, Sikh and European, had crowded into the Durbar hall of the fort where the joint entourages of the Maharajah and Elliot's party filed in. British soldiers lined the walls round the room. Elliot and Lawrence guided the Maharajah to the front of the assembly, and once all were seated the proceedings were commenced. The Governor-General's note of annexation was read out in Persian, being translated later into Hindustani.

The British had shown moderation in not annexing the country after the first war and treaties of friendship had been signed, it said, and all promises faithfully kept. They had tamed the army. The sirdars themselves had invited the British to govern the country till the Maharajah had come of age. But the blame for the current war Dalhousie put squarely on the Sikh Government. The annual debt to the British Government of 22 lakh rupees agreed after the first war had not been paid and had now increased to 50 lakh rupees. To this amount the British Government would add the cost of the war just fought. British officers had been killed and the Lahore Durbar had not made reparations for these actions, declaring it had no control over its army. Many prominent sirdars had joined the enemy in the war against the British, and the Sikh army itself was led by a member of the Durbar.

Punishments and benefits alike have failed to remove the inveterate hostility of the Sikhs. Wherefore, the Governor-General, as the only effectual mode which now remains of preventing the recurrence of national outrage, and the renewal of perpetual wars, has resolved upon declaring the British sovereignty in the Punjab and upon the entire subjection of the Sikh nation whom their own rulers have long been unable to control, who are equally insensible to punishment or forbearance, and who, as past events have now shown will never desist from war so long as they possess the power of an independent kingdom.

And that was that. Bar a tame question from Dewan Deena Nath hoping the Maharajah would receive a generous settlement, the formalities came to a close. No further questions or issues were voiced. The signatures of the agents of those members of the regency who could not attend were then also added to the papers. A witness recorded Deena Nath murmuring as the signings were going on that the British had killed 2 lakh Sikhs and had ended up seizing the state. The Maharajah was the last to sign. 'The alacrity with which he took the papers when offered to him,' noted Elliot, 'was a matter of remark to all, and suggested the idea that, possibly, he had been instructed by his advisers that any show of hesitation might lead to the substitution of terms less favourable than those which had been offered.'

Through the ceremony, Duleep Singh had kept his gaze on Elliot but showed no hesitation in signing. A copy was then handed to the Maharajah and the British party without any ceremony took their leave. Only Dewan Deena Nath was seen to shed any tears at the passing of the state, with the other members of the Durbar displaying apathy and indifference. 'The general indifference exhibited has been remarked upon in other accounts than that of Mr. Elliot,' remarked Dalhousie on the events later. 'Except Deena Nath, the only persons who exhibited signs of dejection and regret were the two Lawrences, whom, principally in reference to the past, I had previously placed at the head of the new Government.'

The British flag was hoisted on the fort as the assembly made its way out and a royal salute fired. A declaration for public consumption had also been prepared, similar to the note read out in the Durbar. In addition, it declared, all jaghirs and property of any of the sirdars who had fought against the British would be confiscated. Various forts would be occupied by the British Army, all other fortifications round the country would be destroyed and any defiance or violence attempted would be punished with severity. Elliot would return to Dalhousie's camp at Makhu the day after the last Durbar to reprise the Governor-General of the previous day's proceedings, following which Dalhousie sanctioned a royal salute to be fired from all the principal British stations round the country to mark the annexation of the Punjab.

\*\*\*

The celebrations to mark the annexation were not limited to the British cantonments. Many of the more obsequious in Punjab determined on making the best of the new situation as well. As the British colours were hoisted at the fortress of Gobindgarh at Amritsar by Col McSherry, local Sikh dignitaries of Amritsar asked to attend the ceremony as a show of support, presenting nuzzurs to the colonel. They also requested permission to illuminate the whole city. 'It is a most strange feature in this most strange series of events, view it as you will,' McSherry wrote to Col Benson of their request. Tens of thousands of lamps were lit all around the city and at the Harminder Sahib, the Golden Temple, to mark the event. McSherry's letter related the extravagant festivities organised in the city by the local administration the following day on the arrival of news of the annexation.

> Last evening, between the hours of half past six and eight o' clock, this city was illuminated by rich and poor, by Hindoos as well as Mahomedans, in honour of their joy and approbation in coming under British dominion. Some of the officers from the garrison of Govindgurh, who went to witness it said they had never seen the like before. The great temple, as well as the steps leading down to the Pool, in the centre of which the temple is built together with the causeway of white marble, which leads to the temple, and

the houses around the grand square in which the Holy Pool stands, were all one mass of light; and the effect was grand indeed and most imposing. The whole population was out of doors to witness it. The Akhalees and Sikhs vied with the Khetrees in evincing their loyalty and their allegiance to the new state of things; and last, though not least, the priests of the temple, in their sacerdotal dress, and with their long beards hanging down, chanted hymns of praise and thanksgiving, in honour of their country's having come under British rule and government. It was a sight to be witnessed once in a century.

The same joy would be shown in the western provinces as British officers – now to be the rulers, commissioners and deputy commissioners of the Punjab rather than political agents – fanned out again over the coming weeks, this time to take overt and unchallenged command of the country. George Lawrence was one of them, travelling back to Peshawar in April 1849, where he was met with much joy by the Muslim population. Whether it was genuine or false is hard to say. On 29 June 1849, a large deputation sent by Maharajah Gulab Singh, now a fast friend of the British Government, appeared at Calcutta with presents to extend congratulations on the recent success of the British in Punjab.

The population of Lahore and its surrounds apparently took the events much more soberly, and were by all accounts not afraid to show their anger at the declaration of annexation. As a precaution, HM 32nd, due to be transferred to Jalandhar on 2 April, was ordered to stay resident in the city for the time being. What was left now was to bring about the end of the Sikh administration and replace it with a British board of control, and organisation began for this immediately. These administrative changes would receive less attention, fading into the background as attention turned to the forthcoming trials and exiles of the main actors in the recent war.

# 32

# Trials and Exiles

An insurrection such as theirs can hardly be called treason.
Hobhouse to Dalhousie, 24 March 1849

I can't hang him, but I will do what he will think a thousand times worse: I will send him across the sea, what they call 'the black water' and dread far more than death.
Dalhousie, 5 February 1849

Curiously, the only major figure to elude British punitive action after the war, albeit in anonymity, was the person who could be said to have instigated the whole thing. Ameer Chund, the cannabis addict and ex-soldier who had casually assaulted Patrick Vans Agnew at the gates of the Multan fortress nearly ten months previously, was never apprehended. Chund was one of the soldiers who had retreated inside the fortress after the fall of the city. Despite the strong British ring round the citadel, he was said to have made good his escape several days before the final surrender.

Two other main figures had refused to surrender at Rawalpindi with Shere Singh's army and had made good their escapes, but they had less fortunate endings. One of these was a colonel by the name of Richpaul Singh, the only officer of Shere Singh's army not to hand himself in at Rawalpindi. He had gone on the run hoping to raise another insurrection and would lie low for around a year, evading British attention. He was seen by informants in July 1850 close to his home and was reportedly well armed. A party was sent against him but they found him dead, possibly by his own hand as he realised all avenues of escape were closed.

The other person who remained for some time at large was Bhai Maharaj, the famous preacher. He too, like Richpaul Singh, had disappeared after the surrender at Rawalpindi to carry on a guerrilla struggle. 'One actor is wanting, Bhaee Maharaj Singh, the soi-disant Gooroo who began the row, and is preaching rebellion now. I have offered 10,000 rupees for him (not dead or alive, as the newspapers say). He is a pestilent vagabond; and if I catch him, he shall be hanged, and so meet with his longstanding deserts,' an impatient Dalhousie had written on 15 December 1849, nine months after the end of the war. It was imperative for the British to capture him because of his influence among the common people and his ability to raise headlines that tended to embarrass the British authorities. Bhai Maharaj had travelled to Jammu after the war with the few men he had, making his hideout at a place called Dev Batala. During this time he made strenuous efforts to recruit the discharged Sikh soldiers of the former Sikh army and approached other nationalists whose land and jaghirs had been confiscated by the British. Bhai Maharaj would continue writing to the neighbouring powers for help during this time as well. Gulab Singh and the Maharajah of Bikaner are known to have received letters from the preacher. He would also write letters to Dost Mohammad seeking help and funds.

To generate money in the meantime he had launched an attack on the Government treasury at Bajwara, making off with the stored treasure, and was planning attacks in Jalandhar. What made his capture difficult for the British, as before, was the continuing sympathy and influence he had with the local people. He was invariably tipped off as in the previous year about any posse organised to apprehend him. During November 1849 he had secretly moved to Jalandhar, where he made plans to attack some British cantonments as well. He appeared briefly in the open at Sham Chaurasi village in Hoshiarpore, where he declared there would be another uprising against the British on 3 January 1850.

Dalhousie's substantial bounty, when announced, would pay dividends quickly. The British Deputy Commissioner of Jalandhar, Henry Vansittart, was given information by a local on 28 December that the preacher was passing through his area of Adampur between Hoshiarpore and Jalandhar along with some followers. The preacher's intention was to recruit the Sikh soldiers currently joining the British East India Company's army in the locality. Vansittart quickly organised a force and rode to intercept Bhai Maharaj. Seven of his men managed to escape as they saw the police riding up but Bhai Maharaj and twenty other followers were captured. They were unarmed at the time although one of the men charged the force with an axe and was shot and wounded. Bhai Maharaj's arrest closed a chapter, with all the main characters (apart from Ameer Chund) either dead or in British hands. 'Thus, within eighteen months after the close of the war, every single man who was reckoned dangerous to the State has been disposed of; not one is at large; for even Narain Singh, a second-rate villain, who escaped the other day, has again been recaptured,' Dalhousie wrote triumphantly on 4 August 1850 in correspondence with East India directors.

***

With the principal actors apprehended, retribution was considered. What would complicate matters here was the technical definition of the conflict. Had the conflict officially been a war between the Lahore state and the East India Company, or a rebellion against the Lahore state backed by British Government of India? On this decision rested the status of the prisoners – whether they should be considered traitors to the Lahore state and the British Government or simply nationalists fighting a good fight against an encroaching British Empire. This confusion would colour the proceedings and meant that many would face exile or imprisonment rather than hanging. While the bulk of the rank and file of the Sikh army, including many officers, had been allowed to return home, those higher up the ranks and others known to be openly unhappy with British power or involved in any plotting were to be held for the time being. These Dalhousie declined to make a judgement on till reports on the siege and the prisoners were received from Herbert Edwardes at Multan.

The only person who would receive capital punishment would be Goojur Singh, the killer of Patrick Vans Agnew at the Eidgah at Multan. He was among the prisoners of war taken after the fall of the fortress and would be the first to be tried. Dalhousie would take a special interest in Goojur Singh, ordering him to be tried in an open court in Multan. He was to be tried 'as a principal in the murder and as aiding and abetting in its perpetration', Dalhousie further mentioning that the process should be carried out by a special military court to be composed of two British and two Indian commissioned officers along with a Sikh colonel who had not joined the insurrection with another European officer acting as president. He stipulated that the sentence must be submitted to him before being carried into execution, with the trial to be carried out without further delay.

On 3 March, six weeks after his capture, the trial of Goojur Singh commenced. Being an open affair, it attracted a large audience of curious city people. Three witnesses were called for questioning from among the assorted moonshees and servants Agnew and his party had with him at his death in the Eidgah. Wuzeer Ali, on being questioned, confirmed he had witnessed Goojur Singh wounding the officer before cutting off his head. Ramjee Mull, another servant, testified he saw the defendant riding around Multan on Agnew's horse and wearing his pistol in his belt. Bunsee Dhur was also present at the Eidgah when Goojur Singh decapitated Agnew and present also at Mulraj's residence when he presented the officer's head to the governor. The evidence of these three witnesses was deemed sufficient and the trial finished the following day. A guilty verdict was delivered on 15 March. He was sentenced to be hanged and orders were received from the Governor-General, who concurred with the decision, that the execution was to be carried out as soon as possible in public with due care to avoid any public disturbance taking place.

Henry Lawrence was of the firm opinion that Goojur Singh should be executed at Lahore but agreed with Herbert Edwardes' suggestion that it would be more symbolic to carry it out at the same place where the two British officers were killed. So it was decided the gallows would be constructed at the Eidgah at Multan. A British eyewitness recorded the final moments of Goojur Singh.

> At the appointed time, the company of rifles arrived and formed a line facing the Eedgah; but outside the compound, some hundred yards or so, at about ten minutes to seven o clock. No. 5 light field battery, being out for exercise, passed close to the gallows, Lieut. Keir in command. It was an imposing sight, for the battery is in first rate order, both men and horses. At seven o' clock precisely, the murderer ascended the ladder, which was no very easy job, seeing that it was some dozen feet long, and at an elevation of about forty degrees. However, Goodhur Sing walked, or rather crawled, up very quietly, and stood still until the rope was adjusted, and on a given signal the drop fell, and the scoundrel was launched into eternity. He was a poor, miserable looking wretch, middle-aged with jet black hair and a long beard. Major Edwardes was present at the execution and superintended it in his official capacity.

The bulk of the Sikh army prisoners taken at Multan and Rawalpindi but who had been retained were split into three groups. The rank-and-file soldiers or 'lesser prisoners' who were considered dangerous and were to be kept incarcerated were sorted into one group. The second, 'intermediate', group comprised lower-ranking leaders in the war such as Bhai Maharaj, Ram Singh Pathania and Narain Singh, a highly placed officer of Mulraj, plus the various petty rulers of the hill states and other senior officers of the Sikh army. The third group was comprised of the high-profile state prisoners including Mulraj, Shere Singh, Chutter Singh and Sultan Mohammad, the brother of the Afghan ruler Dost Mohammad and some other high-profile officers.

For the large number of rank-and-file prisoners taken Dalhousie had declined to make a judgement till detailed reports of each prisoner were received from Herbert Edwardes so the appropriate punishment could be awarded. Many of those deemed less important, the 2,000 irregulars who lived in the Manjha and Jalandhar territories and had enthusiastically come down to fight at Multan, would eventually be released although they were required to give security, in other words a sort of bail money, as assurance for future behaviour. Those financially unable or unwilling to procure the necessary security were sentenced to hard labour (although without irons) among the jails of British India for one year.

The prisoners that were retained included those soldiers who had formed Agnew and Anderson's force and who had deserted him at the Eidgah. The Resident's opinion was that they should be sentenced to hard labour in irons, working on the resurrection of the fortress and other city defences along with the public buildings destroyed in the recent siege. Their sentences were decided to be between two and five years depending on their crimes and station in life. A portion of these prisoners were also to be put to work on local roads and canals damaged during the recent siege.

Of the second group of prisoners, intermediate in terms of importance, varying levels of leniency or harshness were shown. Bikram Singh Bedi, the priest who had helped organise insurrection in the Kangra and Jalandhar areas and had surrendered to the British at Rawalpindi with the Sikh army, was one of those shown more leniency. He was to spend the rest of his life on parole at Amritsar on a modest British pension, his property and wealth having been confiscated. Several of the other rajahs who had rebelled in the Jalandhar area with Bikram Singh Bedi would be exiled to Almora.

The rest of the soldier prisoners, however, would be transported en masse to British territories, firstly to the fortress at Allahabad and either imprisoned there or scattered between the prisons at Agra or Chunar fortress or further afield to Fort William at Calcutta to serve out lengthy prison sentences. Ram Singh Pathania, who had given the British considerable trouble in the Jalandhar and hill areas, was one of those taken to Calcutta. Sentenced to life imprisonment outside India, he was then deported to Rangoon in Burma. He would die in a British prison on 11 November 1856. Ram Singh would have the distinction of being one of the few rebels who is still remembered to this day. At Dussehra, the Hindu festival, ballads of Ram Singh are still sung by folk artists all around the districts of Himachal Pradesh, whence he hailed. In addition, a fair is held in his name at Dhaula Dhar near Shahpur Kandi on 17 August, where armour and a sword allegedly belonging to the local hero are put on display.

As for the contingent retained at Allahabad, the authorities found them hard to manage. By September 1850, there had been a number of attempts by the prisoners to escape and by external groups to set them free. There were some rather improbable rumours that Maharani Jind Kaur was actually funding these attempts from Nepal, despite the fact she had had her wealth confiscated at Benares. Several people had been arrested in the town and found to be holding large amounts of money, too large to be explained easily. Also, certain staff in the prison had been bribed to allow in persons to converse with the prisoners and various letters were discovered. The guard was changed and strengthened and a watchful eye kept on future proceedings by British authorities. In another incident, an outside group was found to have paid 600 rupees to a woman who supplied butter to the entire garrison to convince her to poison the food. 'The Sikh prisoners at Allahabad are unpleasant guests and keep the garrison in a constant state of anxiety,' wrote one newspaper correspondent on 3 September 1850. 'The people of the Punjab are not like the timid Bengalees and will require, we fear, for many years to come, an anxious supervision.'

Perhaps because of the large native garrison at Allahabad, it was decided to transfer almost the entire contingent to Fort William, the facilities there being more secure and with more

European guards. 'Repeated attempts to tamper with their guards have been detected and it seems to have been thought that the fortitude of the sepoys of the 61th BNI would not be able to resist much longer the allurements held out to them by the friends of the prisoners who appear to be well provided with money,' the *Bengal Morning Chronicle* explained in somewhat amusing fashion during October 1850.

They were transported on a vessel towed by steamer along the Ganges with thirty-eight other officers and prisoners of the Sikh army, including Narain Singh. The journey to further incarceration was not without incident, however. Realising the chances of escape at Calcutta would be minimal and that any opportunity had to be taken sooner rather than later, Narain Singh busied himself formulating an escape plan. It had been noticed that that the eighteen guards on board exhibited much confidence in the chains binding the prisoners and consequently were less alert than they should have been. Loaded muskets were also piled up on board under no guard. The prisoners had their hands and feet shackled to a long chain fixed at both ends but were released in batches during the afternoon for their daily ablutions. The chance came on 22 June 1850, a few hours downstream of the city of Patna. Narain Singh and several others were freed. On seeing a good opportunity, Narain Singh gave out a low whistle, the agreed sign, and the gang of ex-soldiers quickly overpowered the inattentive guards and grabbed the muskets neatly stacked up close to them. With their chained comrades also freed, and all now armed with their recently acquired weapons, the rest of the guards on the vessel were also attacked and disposed of, although not before two of the prisoners were shot dead. Two guards were wounded severely and seven less so in the fight before the vessel was captured. Meanwhile, the European officers, alerted by the firing of muskets, ran the steamer aground in case it was commandeered before they too were overpowered. This only allowed the prisoners to escape to land more easily, and it wasn't long before they were gone. In their hurry they had not checked the vessel properly; it happened to be carrying much government treasure to Calcutta. The crew of the ship, though, were relieved of all money they possessed, amounting to around 200 rupees. The alarm was duly raised by the crew and Narain Singh was among twenty-four of the thirty-nine recaptured; the rest, it was supposed, made their way north and reached sanctuary in Nepal for they were not seen again. Perhaps as further punishment, those recaptured upon reaching Calcutta were sent overseas to the usual destination of Singapore.

Another batch of prisoners, 264 strong, who had been transferred to Agra proved equally adept at creating difficulties for their captors. These were soldiers primarily of Narain Singh and Ram Singh Pathania. They were immediately put to work digging a tank close to their jail with a strong guard watching over them. On 5 April 1850, after returning to the jail following the day's labour, one of their leaders, a Heera Singh, approached the guards at the prison gate to monitor their alertness and on finding it propitious called the other prisoners over. The party then grabbed six muskets which had been left unguarded in a tent approximately 50 feet from the gates where the guards were. According to *The Mofussilite*, the prisoners while eating their dinner 'suddenly attacked, with a strong hand, the guard placed over the inner gate of the jail, possessed themselves of their arms, and then rushed forth to effect their escape by a wicket-gate, from which they were driven back by an armed party from the main-guard firing upon them, killing and wounding some forty of the insurgents'.

Other prisoners then grabbed bricks and stones and began pelting the guards while others were released from their cells, and an attempt was made to scale the walls on the other side of the fort. Here they were fired on by the subedar and his men, who foiled the escape attempt. Having just two muskets, they were gradually pushed back into the prison complex and many of the prisoners were shot dead or wounded. Some were killed or wounded after they had surrendered to angry guards. By nightfall, when all resistance had been put down, three doctors were called in.

The number of prisoners killed amounted to thirty-two, with forty-one wounded, some mortally. Heera Singh, the man who had triggered the attempt, was one of the dead. The ringleaders, sixteen in number, were put in double irons. Many of them had been already sentenced to life imprisonment with labour. 'I may state,' wrote the Inspector of Prisons to the government on the escape attempt, 'that this is the third attempt made by these Seikh prisoners, once at Lahore, a second time en route, and from the spirit now shown, have no doubt that a fourth attempt will shortly be made.' The loss of life among the prisoners, he wrote, was due to the guards continuing to shoot even after the prisoners had stopped all resistance. Some of the prisoners nevertheless managed to escape during the confusion.

\*\*\*

One of those transported overseas would be the preacher Bhai Maharaj. Bhai Maharaj was initially kept in the Jalandhar civil jail, but was taken along with a batch of prisoners to Allahabad and then on to Calcutta for exile to Singapore. Along with him came a disciple, a man named Khurruck Singh. What had been noted by European visitors to Bhai Maharaj during his time at Jalandhar was the reverence showed by everyone towards the man, even by the guards at the jail, who bowed as he was led into his cell. This inspired a belief that the guards may try and aid the prisoner. Vansittart also wrote to the Commissioner of Jalandhar, D. McLeod, the following day to warn of the hundreds of people daily collecting outside the jail. 'The Gooroo is not an ordinary man. He is to the Natives what Jesus Christ is to the most zealous of Christians. His miracles were seen by tens of thousands, and are more implicitly relied on that those worked by the ancient prophets.' His case must be dealt with quickly, he recommended, for there was apprehension a riot to free him might ensue, with the guards being overwhelmed. The district magistrate quickly organised the preacher's custody to be transferred to the military authorities, and he was then moved to Lahore in readiness for a move to Calcutta and possible overseas exile.

Unlike the high-profile state prisoners Shere Singh, Chutter Singh and Mulraj, who would also be transported downstream later, Bhai Maharaj was less protected from onlookers at the various cities and towns his retinue passed as they travelled down country. Crowds of curious people turned up, looking at him and his fellow prisoners as if they were wild animals on show. Bhai Maharaj, realising he would be exiled abroad, would also try and escape at Gunga Sagur while being transported down the Ganges. A European sergeant and ten European privates had been assigned to guard him on the boat being used for transport. By chance the sergeant had gone down to check on the prisoner and found Bhai Maharaj had successfully removed three bars of his cabin window but was yet to dive into the water.

Bhai Maharaj never deigned to speak much to Europeans and this continued on his arrival at Calcutta. During June 1850, Dalhousie commissioned an artist to make portraits of both Mulraj and Bhai Maharaj while they were both captive at Fort William. The artist was perhaps the only European to grow close to Mulraj and to a lesser extent Bhai Maharaj, requiring by the nature of his work to have extended stays in their cells. He had been given all privileges to meet the prisoners whenever he desired. On entering Bhai Maharaj's cell, the artist would invariably find him seated on the ground in a corner looking towards the wall and praying continuously.

He would move so little that it was difficult to tell he was alive. The guards informed him Bhai Maharaj never turned to look at anyone entering but would stay facing the wall and praying. Khurruck Singh, his disciple, the artist described as 'a fine, stout young fellow who being unhappily found in the Gooroo's society (and perhaps offering resistance) was arrested with him, and alike condemned to banishment – a stout opponent, no doubt, with a blade in his hand, but otherwise a peaceful, good humoured, contented mortal'. Unlike Bhai Maharaj he knew Hindustani, but spoke little. 'Yes, during some seven visits I paid him, he opened his lips twice; once to ask (Khurruck Singh interpreting) whether I was taking all who had come down, and whether Moolraj also was to be sent over the "kala panee" (black waters – the sea); and, on a second occasion, to complain by one brief monosyllable of pain or weariness of standing.'

Bhai Maharaj was in heavy chains during their meetings in his cell, with a sentry with bayonet always standing over the two during their sessions. Sentenced to overseas exile, he was put on the *Muhmed Shah*, reaching Singapore on 9 July 1850 along with Khurruck Singh. There he would be transferred to Outram jail, where he was put in solitary confinement. The conditions he was kept in were unpleasant. The windows had been walled up, rendering the 14-by-15-foot room dark, dank and dingy. He would survive three years of this treatment, by which time he had gone blind through cataracts and had developed a cancerous tumour on his tongue along with rheumatic swelling on his ankles and feet. The sympathetic civil surgeon of Singapore, realising the prisoner was in terminal decline, wrote a recommendation that Bhai Maharaj be allowed out of his cell and into the open and fresh air occasionally to relieve the tedium of staying in the cell during his last days. The Government of India would refuse the request. On 5 July 1856, Bhai Maharaj died a painful death. Swellings on his neck and tongue had made it difficult for him to swallow food. He was allowed to be cremated outside of the jail complex by his follower Khurruck Singh, who also expired soon after. Local Hindus, mainly Tamils from south India resident nearby, would begin to treat the location of his cremation with much reverence and soon many Hindus, Sikhs and Muslims would come to pay their respects at the spot, a tradition that continues to this day.

The prisoners at Allahabad and Agra, meanwhile, would meet others already serving time for plotting against the British prior to the war. These included prisoners involved in the Prema Plot, who were treated considerably more harshly, only seeing their release from hard labour in prison in 1869. Some British sepoys also faced punitive action. These were the sentries at Chunar fort found guilty of carelessness in allowing Jind Kaur to escape in disguise. A Havildar and two sepoys had been charged. The officer was reduced to the rank of a common soldier and sentenced to six months' imprisonment. Sir Charles Napier, the new Commander-in-Chief, however, thought the sentence too light and ordered a revision in the decision. It was eventually decided hard labour for a year would be more fitting. The Havildar, however, had had an excellent record prior to this infraction and the court recommended mercy, which the Commander-in-Chief accepted. The sepoys were to be dismissed, but the sentence was officially listed as one year's hard labour.

\*\*\*

It would be the third category of 'state prisoners' that would naturally garner the most attention. From his surrender at Multan, Mulraj would go through a much more eventful period before his eventual incarceration at Fort William. The same day that he heard of the fall of the fortress, Dalhousie had ordered the governor be brought to Lahore. Frederick Currie had expressed his opinion that evidence would be sufficient to convict Mulraj if he was brought to trial, and certainly as an accessory to the murders of the two British officers. He could also be put on trial for rebellion against the Lahore Durbar and possibly for organising rebellion not only in Multan but further afield in the British provinces, some of his letters to other rulers in India having been intercepted. Dalhousie would entirely agree with the Resident. In the meantime, before Mulraj was transported to the capital, Dalhousie ordered the commandant of the fortress to keep him under guard in strict fashion with only European guards being employed until decisions as to his future were taken. A few weeks into his imprisonment a stricter vigilance was requested by the Governor-General, who ordered the separation of the governor from much of his entourage and other assistants along with family and servants. Henceforth Mulraj would be kept in relative isolation, and visits were curtailed. 'The Dewan must not be permitted to have any train except a few personal attendants and effectual precautions must be taken for his safe custody,' Dalhousie wrote to the Resident on 25 January. 'You will direct Major Edwardes to make temporary provisions for the lodging of the women; they must not be allowed to remain in the fort.' Three weeks later, more instructions arrived for the Resident. 'It would appear that Moolraj enjoys more liberty than is expedient. His Lordship requests that every precaution may be taken, and that if there should appear to be any reason for believing that his servants are conveying letters to and fro, they should be punished, and replaced by others of Lieutenant Henry's own selection.'

The family were set free and given accommodation outside the city, although a watch would be retained on them. Mulraj's journey to the capital began early at 5 a.m. on 15 February. His party and escort took the road north to Lahore, which happened to pass between the Eidgah and the graves of Agnew and Anderson who had been buried a few metres to one side. The open graves of the officers could be seen on the right of the road as the party passed, the bodies having been recently disinterred for burial in the fortress. With war still continuing in the north, Mulraj was given a strong escort of cavalry from Multan to thwart any attempt of rescue. The Resident always suspected the native guards were susceptible to bribery or sympathetic towards Mulraj and took care accordingly. In any case, for part of the way the party escorting Mulraj would accompany Whish's force, moving north to join Gough's army.

Mulraj's convoy parted ways with Whish's column at Ramnuggar, heading east to Lahore. This part of the journey was to be done with Mulraj being transported in a Durbar carriage for rapid transit rather than by elephant, again to discourage any rescue. A period of rest was taken at Akalgurh, 8 km from Ramnuggar, using a house that belonged to Mulraj himself before the final leg of the journey to Lahore, which was reached late the following day. The plan had been to hold Mulraj at Lahore for two to three days before transferring him to the fortress of Gobindgarh while the Governor-General decided his fate, although this never took place; Mulraj would be retained at Lahore along with all the other state prisoners, this being deemed more convenient.

An important discovery into the extent of his relationship with Dost Mohammad had been discovered by British soldiers during his transportation to Lahore. Mulraj kept a cushion with him at all times for his own comfort, and this aroused suspicion. The cushion was taken from him and found to have gold coins and some letters and documents hidden within. The more interesting of these were his correspondence with the Afghan ruler, some as late as 22 December. Dost Mohammad had written strongly urging Mulraj to hold out, assuring him he would send assistance and stating the British were suffering severely themselves. They were vulnerable to the severe temperatures at Multan and would be forced to lift the siege again if he could but hold out until the hot season, he argued. While the gold coins could be used to bribe his captors, it's less clear why Mulraj had brought along the letters which failed to aid his cause and merely implicated Dost Mohammad. Perhaps he hoped to use the letters as a bargaining counter later in his trial, implicating his untrustworthy friend in return for a lighter sentence.

Mulraj's entry into Lahore as prisoner was organised with some fanfare by the British authorities. A procession of highly placed sirdars with a British captain and a brigadier rode out to meet the convoy. Mulraj entered the city riding an elephant with a British political officer keeping visible guard over him while large city crowds watched the scene. In fact there was some criticism in certain circles later that he had been treated more as a prince for his entry into the city rather than as a captive. Temporary lodging was made for him in a tent in the Baradari garden opposite the palace gates where he was kept under constant supervision till accommodation in the fortress was made available. He also generated a large amount of curiosity and interest among the Europeans and British soldiers in the capital who came to meet and gawp at the ex-governor.

Whatever his kind treatment so far, and despite Whish's promise of his life during surrender, Mulraj was fully cognisant he was to be put on a show trial shortly and had taken the precaution of bringing as many documents for his defence with him as he wished. Included within these was the letter sent by Patrick Vans Agnew exonerating him of any responsibility for the attack on the British officers in the Multan fortress. It was said that he also had papers from members of the Lahore Durbar asking him to hold out against the British, although as yet no names had been leaked. Like the letters in his cushion, these perhaps were to be used as bargaining chips for he had received little help from the individuals who had egged him on to continue the struggle.

On 29 March, Mulraj in his temporary accommodation outside the fort entrance received many more curious visitors than before, for this was the day that Duleep Singh signed away his kingdom in Durbar. The fortress was visited by hundreds of Europeans who took the time to meet him as he departed the palace. Reports by those who saw him present similar accounts of his demeanour and outlook. 'When I visited him, he would not say much but kept muttering about the "Will of God", fate &c. He was sitting with a small hookah and one attendant to fan him: and was very dirty and not a soldier at all,' described Capt. Henry Ouvry, who took time to converse with fellow prisoners Shere Singh and his father as well.

Mulraj was right in assuming the Governor-General would decide on a trial with capital punishment considered. Dalhousie's excuse for brushing aside Whish's promise of life would be that new evidence and correspondence had been discovered in the fortress ruins which implicated Mulraj further than previously thought.

It came out on this trial [Goojur Singh's] (though the investigation was directed solely to the question of the prisoner's guilt), that the Dewan Moolraj had taken a much more prominent part than was supposed, in the attack on the Eidgah, which led to the murder of the British officers. The question of Moolraj's complicity had already been looked into by Major Edwardes, with considerable care; and much very pertinent evidence had been collected on the subject, principally from Moolraj's servants, and persons least likely to inculpate him. Sir Henry Lawrence gave his opinion, in concurrence with Major Edwardes, that a strong prima facie case was made out against Moolraj. The perusal of these papers, and of the evidence given on the trial of Goodhur Sing, has greatly weakened the favorable impression which various circumstances had created in my mind relative to Moolraj's innocence of the deaths of Mr. Agnew and Lieutenant Anderson, and has renewed my original belief in his complicity with the actors in that horrible scene, and his consequent guilt.

His intended trial provoked much discussion in both the local and European community, there being even more technicalities involved than for other prisoners and not least for the fact his trial would form a great precedent. This would be the first time a 'foreigner' of such a high rank as governor (for he was a governor of a province of the state of Lahore, not of British territory) would be tried before a purely British court for a rebellion that was technically against the state of Lahore, not the British Government of India. It was well known that the when news reached Lahore of the deaths of the two British officers, Frederick Currie had written advising the Governor-General that 'Dewan Moolraj is an officer of the Sikh Government; he is in rebellion to the Sikh durbar and the orders of that Government from which coercion must come'. He was in essence answerable only to the Lahore Durbar. Under the laws of the Lahore state, the accusation that he was an accessory before and after the act was not a capital offence.

As regards the actual murders in the Eidgah, the only thing going against him was the reward he gave to Goojur Singh for bringing Agnew's head; however, the crime had been committed by that time. It was also accepted he was under duress from his own soldiers, a 'victim of circumstance' as the court would point out, and never had the freedom of will during those vital few hours in the fort and after, his life being entirely in the hands of unruly soldiers. His soldiers had rebelled before and there had been threats to kill him. So although he could have been tried on the basis of treason or leading a rebellion against the Lahore State, the idea that he was guilty of murder himself was laughable to many. Despite these arguments, already around the city many held the impression that the decision to hang him was a fait accompli. The prospect of the British Government bringing him to trial simply to see him acquitted was deemed remote by most.

Others felt Dalhousie should and would honour Whish's pledge of life at the final hurdle. That Mulraj had no reason to rebel was generally accepted since he had offered to resign prior to events. The fact that he transferred large portions of his wealth to Amritsar and Lahore before the murders also pointed to his innocence. Mulraj certainly seemed to have garnered a fair amount of sympathy among the British press in India by this time. His spirited resistance against superior forces and the civil and mild manners he showed visitors while being held prisoner counted in his favour. There were mutterings in the press that he was being treated too harshly, a guilty verdict and death penalty being expected. The general feeling was that his hand had been forced by his unruly soldiers but that he had stoically made the best of the situation. The *Friend of India* described him as no murderer but 'rebel by accident', arguing he had little control of his soldiers and had chosen the more heroic and manly route than fleeing the citadel and his own men's whims at the first opportunity. The paper believed that his gallant defence entitled him to be treated 'not only with consideration but distinction'. Other newspapers argued Chutter Singh had disposed of Col. Canora but had been released on parole and that surely Mulraj, who had no immediate hand in the murders of the British officers at Multan, should receive similar treatment. Back in London, the East India Company directors too were inclined to allow Mulraj the benefit of the doubt prior to the trial. 'You will see that we threw out a hint in our Secret Letter that if you can spare the life of Moolraj, we shall not be sorry for the clemency.' Hobhouse wrote to the Governor-General on 24 February that 'there is a very general feeling here that the man has fought a good fight and the general impression is that he was not guilty of treachery or had any secret intention of murdering your officers'.

If Mulraj was to be spared his life, Shere Singh and his father should be treated in the same clement fashion. 'As regards the sirdars, Shere Singh and the rest, they must be treated, I presume, like enemies in the field, and not as traitors with a rope about their necks. An insurrection such as theirs can hardly be called treason. It is a rebellion for a whole people and must, of course be put down by sword and gun, but I do not hope that you will like to bring the rope in the accident to play.'

The trial of Mulraj, an open one, would be held in the Diwan-I-Aam or Durbar Hall where Ranjit Singh formerly held court. A raised platform had been constructed in the hall for the members of the commission, the counsels for the defence and prosecution and Mulraj himself. There would be chairs filling the hall for spectators wishing to witness the proceedings. Mulraj would be tried by a commission of three consisting of a Mr R. Montgomery and Brig. Godby and a Mr C. G. Mansell as president. Owing to Brig. Godby being unavailable due to sickness, his position would be taken by Mr Bowring later. According to the *Delhi Gazette*, the prosecution had arranged no fewer than 300 witnesses against Mulraj. To counter this Mulraj had expressed a desire for a European to represent him, feeling perhaps this would give him a better chance. He showed a strong preference for either John Lawrence or, surprisingly, Major Edwardes, against whom he had fought these past months. He was told this was impossible, a decision which seemed to dismay him, but a Capt. Hamilton would volunteer his services to the governor.

The trial began on 31 May 1849 after delays of one kind or another and with considerable interest from the public, the hall being full of 'common' people although there were some sirdars of rank who had come to witness the proceedings along with various curious Europeans. British troops lined the sides of the hall as Mulraj was escorted into the hall by soldiers of the 98th regiment and given a seat near the president on the platform. His expression was described as one of a careworn man wracked with nervousness, and apart from brief conversations with his vakeel during the proceedings he appeared to show as little interest as a man expecting to be found guilty would. The captivity and associated anxieties regarding the trial had taken a great toll on his health by this time. He had a tired gait and his face looked sallow, his legs very thin. Only his eyes showed liveliness. He was seen to brighten up as he passed a British officer who had escorted him from Multan and with whom he had formed a friendship during the journey. He saluted him with enthusiasm.

With the normal etiquette of the trial dispensed with, the three charges that would be brought against the governor were read out: that he had aided and abetted in the murder of the two officers, that he had been an accessory before the fact inasmuch as he had instigated his troops in the murder of Agnew and Anderson and that he had been an accessory after the fact in as much as he had rewarded the murderers. Rather than speaking, Mulraj with a wave of his hand pleaded 'Not Guilty' to all these charges.

Mr Bowring then proceeded to address the court in Hindustani, arguing that Mulraj's behaviour prior to the day of the officer's deaths was suspect. He had greeted Anderson several months earlier on his visit to the city by riding out several miles from the city to welcome the officer himself but had not followed this practice on the more recent visit, betraying his aggressive intentions. Bowring made quite plain the fact that Mulraj had rewarded the killers of the British officers.

The trial would last till 22 June, with proceedings occurring for fourteen days. Eleven witnesses – some trustworthy, others decidedly partisan – would eventually be brought forward during this time. Capt. Hamilton handled the defence with great panache, pointing out to the court the personal qualities of Mulraj. His mild nature and the courteous way he presented himself and went about his business was not the stuff of assassins, he declared. Was there 'ought of ferocity in that countenance?' he asked, passionately pointing to Mulraj. He had been made to change his allegiance under duress by his soldiers and could on no account be seen as guilty of treachery himself. He argued the reforms that had been effectually forced upon him by John Lawrence had soured the relationship between him and the Resident. That he had resigned as governor because of these reforms also weighed against the possibility of any designs or plots. In fact, he had gone so far as to pay up all arrears owed to Lahore and had transferred some of his private wealth to Amritsar – a sure sign against him having rebellion in mind. Capt. Hamilton also went through in considerable detail the brusque fashion in which Agnew had dealt with the governor. The fact that he was not going to be exempt from judgment based on complaints by his enemies or the public, and the insistence that he pass on accounts over which he had no control, made before his rise to governorship, had hardened the governor's mind against the British officer. Mulraj had no desire to be at the mercy of any his inferiors, some of whom harboured deep animosity against him for his autocratic rule. He disputed the assertion that he had rewarded Ameer Chund. Hamilton also argued that the mob who had turned up at the Eidgah to dispose of the British party were not led by or organised under the direction of Mulraj or any of his senior officers. They were simply a mob. Hamilton's most powerful argument, however, was that Agnew in his letters before his death had put no blame on Mulraj for the attack. Agnew had written of tumult and mutiny by the garrison, not of a plot or rebellion.

After generating much interest during the first few days, the trial quickly lost its hold on the casual observer after the first week. By the last day, when the court opened at an early hour, few people were seen to come and watch the proceedings. Around twenty-five civilians and officers could be seen dotted around the room. Mr Bowring delivered a lengthy speech before the court was closed. After a recess, the court reopened at 11 a.m. and Mulraj was brought forward to hear his sentence. The charges were read out and Mulraj was seen to shake his head at all three but without attempting to speak. The court found him guilty of all charges, the sentence being death. Execution would not be carried out until the Governor-General had pronounced on the case.

The judges remarked on his character at the end of the trial:

> Moolraj would seem by nature and habit to possess more of a mercantile than a martial character ... From the evidence of the above witnesses, and from the general probabilities of the case, the attack at the fort seems to have been regarded by Moolraj as hopelessly compromising him with the British authorities. Taking his position as it stood at noon on the 19th of April, he seems, on a deliberate calculation of chances, to have come to the conclusion that, in the then state of affairs, he had more to hope from the fears of the English than from their mercy. He headed an armed movement as his best policy, and the death of the officers was completed in due pursuance of his hostile proceedings. He yields to the circumstances of his case, and draws new vigour and determination from his isolated position.

A recommendation for mercy would, it was declared, be forwarded on the grounds that Mulraj was 'a victim of circumstance'. Mulraj betrayed no emotion according to eyewitnesses, hearing the verdict with silence. Later, according to a correspondent of the *Delhi Gazette* covering the trial, he seemed to have had second thoughts. 'It seems that Moolraj, although apparently indifferent to the proceedings of the trial, while they were going on, became painfully alive to the real peril of his situation when the sentence was pronounced, and abstained from food for three entire days after the closing of the court; he then addressed himself to the task of aiding in the preparation of a memorial to the Governor-General, which was in time to accompany the copy of the entire proceedings that was forwarded to his Lordship by express on the 28th June.'

Much public and media opinion, as before the trial, was against the verdict. Mulraj had clearly not murdered the officers himself or indeed ordered them killed. Agnew's own letter to Mulraj, shown in court, had cleared him of any involvement in the attack. Neither was there in his mind a wilful and premeditated destruction of life, part of the definition of murder in British law. Certainly the court's decision that he was a 'victim of circumstance' was inconsistent with the definition of murder. It was also obvious too that some of the witnesses were plainly against Mulraj; the defence had been carried out very well by Hamilton and there was a widespread belief that an English jury, uninfluenced by close proximity to the happenings, would have acquitted a man known to be in the hands of a turbulent soldiery.

Dalhousie, taking into account the feelings of the directors in London, would give in to the court's recommendation of mercy although he was determined on harsh measures. 'I can't hang him, but I will do what he will think a thousand times worse: I will send him across the sea, what they call "the black water" and dread far more than death,' he wrote. On 31 July, Mulraj was accordingly brought back to the Am Khas in the fort of Lahore and informed he would instead face life imprisonment in close confinement overseas, usually meaning Singapore. Hindus at that time had a general dread of travelling overseas, an action which they thought led to losing their caste. Mulraj would register a protest at this, but to no avail. Leg irons were ordered to be put on him for the duration of his stay in Lahore. By this time several newspaper correspondents had managed to interview him, and all noted the continuing sharp drop in his health. He would be visited by Dalhousie in December 1849 while waiting to be transported to Calcutta. Dalhousie noticed the same fading strength. The ex-Governor of Multan appeared to Dalhousie as 'a small-limbed, slight-made man, his face gaunt and haggard, and rendered more wild by the peculiarity of one eye being much smaller than the other. The expression of the mouth was gentle, and his countenance, by the aid of fine teeth and a long black beard, would have been attractive but for the peculiarities described. As it was, the haggard features, the worn emaciated fingers, and frame tottering from weakness, even as he sat, were painful to look upon.' Mulraj was spending much of this time in prayer and fasting, which was further accelerating his deterioration. Cognisant of his situation, Dalhousie promised him medical examination and attention at Calcutta before his exile.

On arrival in Calcutta he was transferred to Fort William, where quarters had been readied for him. During his travel down country and in his first few weeks at Calcutta, Mulraj was reported to have dropped two stone in weight and to be in very low spirits. Never an imposing figure, Mulraj's decline reduced what little physical presence he had. A newspaper correspondent who witnessed his party reach the city reported as follows.

I was never so completely disappointed as in Moolraj, the much talked about hero of Mooltan. He landed at Prinsep's Ghaut escorted by the town major (Major Bidulph) and another officer having a file or one or two dozen soldiers surrounded by whom he, with Gooroo Bhai Maharaj Singh and Kurruck Singh conveyed in palkees entered the fort, the place of their present destination. My ideas of the man were very high. I had expected to see a well-built personage, of a commanding aspect, clean complexion, a princely appearance and of course respectably garbed; but what was my surprise when I beheld a common-looking man, of an effeminate make, somewhat pulled down in flesh from fear and grief as well as the penance he is said to be doing to himself by abstinence! His costume was a plain white cotton trouser and a banian of the same; his complexion is dark, and his deportment so sluggish that one would be led to suppose he was incapable of exerting any activity even on great emergencies. The only mark of intelligence visible in his physiognomy was the indication which his small twinkling eyes gave of their cunning; otherwise all was blank and unreadable.

Due to Mulraj's waning health, Dalhousie would never follow through on his decision to send the ex-governor abroad into exile; his stay in Fort William prison was made permanent in September 1849. Despite his condition, he still valued freedom. Shortly after his arrival, Mulraj attempted to buy his escape from one of the sepoys with a pair of gold bangles, the only items of any value he had been allowed to retain in prison. The sepoy informed his officer and the bangles were confiscated. Two European sentries guarded him instead of sepoys following this incident.

As with Bhai Maharaj, Dalhousie had commissioned an artist to make portraits of Mulraj while captive at Fort William. Mulraj's ill health led the artist to estimate his age at forty-five years, much higher than his thirty-three years. He did manage to draw Mulraj into conversation, albeit infrequently, the discussions being usually on weighty issues.

'You have drawn many faces; did you ever draw the face of God?' Mulraj asked him once.

'No,' the artist replied. 'God is a spirit, and not confined to one place; He is in all places.'

'How do you know that if you have never seen him?' Mulraj replied.

Other conversations were about mesmerism or hypnotism, while other discourses led to lively if friendly debate. Once the artist brought a globe and map of the world, the discussion being on the geography of the planet. Mulraj didn't believe much of what he saw. A devout Hindu, anything on the map or globe not in accordance with his religious beliefs would see him invariably utter, 'But it is written in our shastras …' before expounding the Hindu explanation of nature and geography.

In May 1851 authorities uncovered an audacious plot by sympathisers, perhaps unaware of his inexorable decline, to rescue the ex-governor from Fort William. 4 lakh rupees had been accumulated by the group, with 700 armed men to be used in the operation. The plan was to blow up the nearby arsenal. While troops were then diverted to extinguish the flames, a large body would attack the less well-manned fort and rescue Mulraj. He would then be secretly moved to Nepal. As with any plot of this size, informers were aplenty and much of the correspondence fell into the hands of the government.

In mid-1851, Dalhousie assented to a plan to move him to a milder climate away from the sea air of Calcutta, somewhere upcountry, which it was thought would be beneficial to his health. His new abode would be the Allahabad fortress and he departed under escort on 26 July. He would never reach his new prison, dying at a place called Parputpore near Buxar in Bengal province on 11 August 1851 while being conveyed up the Ganges. He was allowed to be cremated on the banks of the river, consistent with his Hindu beliefs. 'Moolraj is dead,' wrote Dalhousie on news reaching him at Simla in early September 1851, 'and burnt by the Ganges so that his worst fears were not realised, and one of his best hopes fulfilled.' His immediate family and those of his father Sawan Mull were given modest pensions following his death.

***

Shere Singh and his father would be brought back to Lahore under escort from the Gujrat battlefield after submitting their surrender to Gough personally. Dalhousie, as with Mulraj, had determined to take a hard line on father and son despite Henry Lawrence advocating a lenient stance. 'Chuttur Sing and Shere Sing cannot be allowed to live at home and weave treachery at leisure,' he wrote back to the Resident, dismissing Lawrence's arguments over their honourable treatment of the British prisoners. In one of the last Durbars held at Lahore before the state was annexed, the Sikh commander would be brought in and warned publicly by the Resident as requested by the Governor-General. 'His treachery to the state, and to the British Government, was so great that he deserved condign punishment, but that the promise to spare his life would be kept and some small allowance made for his support,' Lawrence wrote later of his address to Shere Singh during the Durbar. He was told to dismiss all his followers and to give up any and all arms, following which he would be allowed to reside at his home village of Attari as agreed with Major Mackeson. However, he and his father would not be allowed to leave the village without permission. The only exceptions would be made for health reasons. He would be allowed to ride up to a radius of 3 miles from his home.

There were other strict conditions, too. They would be kept under constant surveillance by unarmed guards in the village. They were also not to have any correspondence with anyone else involved in the recent war, including Sikh officers who had served under them. Anyone who visited them must be reported to the British authorities in Lahore. Their servants were registered and no others allowed. As far as money was concerned, the entire family wealth and jaghirs, amounting to 11 lakh rupees, was confiscated and an allowance of 240 rupees a month was given them for their subsistence in exchange. Any infraction of these conditions, any attempt to escape or any plotting against the British Government, would mean the allowance would be withdrawn and more punitive measures taken. 'If they run away, our contract is void. If they are caught, I will imprison them. And if they raise tumult again, I will hang them, as sure as they now live, and I live then,' he informed Henry Lawrence. Shere Singh responded in the Durbar by expressing his gratitude at the concession of the allowance and the liberty to live on parole in his home village. On 8 March, after being duly warned of their future conduct, Shere Singh and his father left for their village. Meanwhile, other officers and followers of Shere Singh were given similar instructions and smaller allowances. Sultan Mohammad, the brother of Dost Mohammad who had taken George Lawrence and his family captive at Kohat, was told to reside at the village of Bhyrowal, not far from Shere Singh's village.

Not everyone was happy with parole being given to the father and son. *The Times* in London along with others would suggest this agreement was misplaced and that not incarcerating Shere Singh only strengthened the possibility of a third Anglo-Sikh war. 'With 240 a-year as his all, paid monthly, what could Shere Singh do, if he did escape, among a disarmed population surrounded by a large British army?' was Dalhousie's irritated reply in his private papers on 10 July 1849. 'Pooh! folks at home have not recovered their pusillanimous terror after Chillianwala. If it were not for the fresh access of hysteria which the report would bring on at home, I wish to goodness they would run away. I should save their pensions like that of the Maharanee. They know very well if they do they will receive no mercy; and Moolraj's trip across the "black water" will be a wholesome reminder.'

This wasn't the way things would stay, however, for Shere Singh began somewhat recklessly breaking the stringent conditions imposed on him. In April of that year, just a few weeks after his arrival at his home village, there were reports he had left the village without telling British authorities. John Lawrence on travelling to the village found these reports false, although as the year progressed he found other things that aroused his suspicion. One of the conditions of the men's stay at home was that they must refrain from inviting or meeting anyone at Attari. In the month of September, it was noted they had fed 100 Brahmin priests on the eclipse of the moon, a religious custom. These men were suspected of being messengers between Shere Singh and his former officers, on parole in Sealkote and Amritsar. 'Brahmins and barbers, the two classes of people who are usually engaged in all kinds of intrigues, have been repeatedly seen at Attari,' warned John Lawrence in a letter to the Government of India, recommending action be taken. Alongside this, there were rumours they were carrying correspondence or messages to and from Dost Mohammad and Gulab Singh in Kashmir as well. On hearing of these infractions, Dalhousie decided he had sufficient reason to break the agreement and to pass more punitive measures on father and son. 'On this I ordered their arrest. They will of course plead religious observances. But this is a futile plea here. In the first place, no religious observances require such an assemblage. In the next place, these Brahmins are notorious as the intriguers through whom every political machination is carried on in India. Lawrence at that time prohibited such assemblages, and this is well known to Shere Singh, who was one of the Regency that issued the order. I have said before that I did not fear anything these men could do. But I am glad they have committed themselves, for now I shall "mak' sicker" [make sure] by sending them to the provinces, and men's minds here and in England will be quieted.'

A strong party headed by John Lawrence, doab commissioner Mr R. Montgomery, deputy commissioner Major Edwardes and Lt Hodson of the Guide Corps, with Capt. Skinner and the 14th Irregular Cavalry and some Pathan horse, marched down to arrest them at 1 a.m. on 1 September. They reached Attari at daybreak and surrounded the village and its mud fort. Other units and two guns were prepared in case Shere Singh and followers resisted but the arrest of father and four sons passed without incident. 'The whole were mounted on horseback without the least delay, and hurried into Lahore, where Dr Login added them to his "rare collection of celebrated characters", reported the *Daily Gazette* in colourful fashion. The prison in the Lahore fort would be where they would reside for the rest of the year while Dalhousie mulled over incarceration at Calcutta or exile abroad.

Hodson and Skinner's irregular cavalry and the native infantry remained behind with men to search the rest of the village for incriminating documents and letters. An extensive search was carried out, and arms and correspondence of a suspicious nature, including some with Dost Mohammad, was uncovered. There were rumours that it was Gulab Singh himself who tipped off the British to ingratiate himself after the suspicions he had been under during the war. He is reported to have received a letter suggesting another insurrection and requesting his assistance. This letter he had sent to Henry Lawrence, hurrying the arrests. Whether Shere Singh seriously contemplated another uprising bereft of any resources and money was moot – the papers had made up their minds. In response to these findings, his village fort was ordered to be blown up.

The Sikh commander and his father weren't the only people arrested on that day. Two other parties were organised to arrest other notables including Sikh army officers Lal Singh Moraria and Surat Singh Majithia near Amritsar and Diwan Hakeem Rai at Sialkot, all suspected of communicating with Shere Singh. All would be incarcerated in the Lahore fortress for the rest of the year under the watchful of Dr John Login, the commandant of the fortress. Their transfer meant all the important Sikh state prisoners were in one location for the last time. Their accommodation, like that of Mulraj, who was a fellow prisoner at this time, was comfortable.

Like Mulraj they had many European visitors; Capt. Ouvry of the 3rd Light Dragoons was one such visitor and records an interesting conversation of a rather Victorian flavour.

He was sitting in his tent, and afterwards, his father Chutter Singh and his younger brother came in. I commenced by asking him in Persian, if he had my horse which I lost at Chillianwala, in his camp. He advised me to go and look about. I broke down in my Persian and he smiled and said that he thought my knowledge of Persian was 'bisear kum' that is to say, very small, so I then spoke to him in Hindustani. He was highly amused at my holding my glass in my eye. I lent it to him and he tried, without success, to keep it in his eye; while an old man who was present said that there was 'Jaduee' in it, that is to say, magic. The very same thing occurred when I was with Goolab Singh in Cashmere, and his son made the same remark. All these Easterners believe in magic. We then talked of the late battles, and I was loud in my praises of the gallantry of the Sikhs. He said that all was written in the Book of Fate. I told him that such might be quite true, but that if he had taken the trouble to read what was written therein he would not have come to grief. He replied that it was not given to mortals to read therein. 'There you are mistaken,' I said, 'any wise man can read pretty distinctly in the Book of Fate,' provided he uses the intellect that nature has given him. Pointing to my horse, I asked him which would win a race, say of five miles, a man mounted on the horse against one on foot? Of course, the man on the horse would win, they all, at once exclaimed, but they could not see the application. So I explained: 'You are of a race intellectually inferior to Europeans; you cannot even make an iron shell; your guns are inferior, and you cannot fire them quickly enough and your army is incapable of discipline.' How then could you suppose that you would succeed in a struggle where all the disadvantages are on your side? They were all silent, but Shere Singh said, 'You have spoken the truth,' but one thing I added for their comfort. 'Notwithstanding all that I have said of Feringhi superiority, the rule of the English will not be permanent, that is plainly written in the Book of Fate. In this world nothing is lasting, and there is no more hope for nations than there is for individuals.'

Dalhousie also took the opportunity to meet them during his tour to Lahore in December 1849. The Governor-General was interested in the way they were being treated and if they had any requests or complaints. He gained a positive impression of Chutter Singh who showed a respectful but manly bearing 'without the least approach to supplication, far less to servility'. Chutter Singh greeted and talked with Dalhousie in friendly fashion and made no request or complaint, quietly 'returning to his cell with dignity'. The son's conduct was more conversational, Shere Singh striking him as someone with an intelligent countenance. He spoke with a mild voice according to the Governor-General. Dalhousie asked him also if he had any requests or complaints. Shere Singh replied that if he was to be kept as a prisoner perhaps he could be allowed to go hunting once a while, in keeping with his passion. Dalhousie's message to them as with Mulraj was similar – that he could concede nothing on their incarceration and possible exile but would look into any complaints they may have over their treatment and would consider any other concession they may wish for. Further he had decided to restore some of their property and wealth to avoid destitution for their families. He also assured them good living quarters in Calcutta.

The plan was to send all the high-profile state prisoners held by Dr Login at Lahore to Allahabad under tight security before their dispersal to various prisons or to exile. This included

Chutter Singh, Shere Singh, his brother Aotar Singh along with 'lesser' prisoners like Lal Singh Moraria, Mehtab Singh Majithia and Dewan Hakim Rai. The prisoners were slowly transported down to Calcutta via Delhi on 1 February. Unlike the convoy of lesser prisoners sent earlier, this batch of important state prisoners was accorded much better treatment during the journey. The tents they were given had furnishings and they were allowed to walk around the camp during the evenings. 'No persons are allowed to pass into the tents or to stand in front of them to gratify their curiosity by staring them out of countenance,' noted a correspondent of the *Delhi Gazette* visiting the party. The party would arrive at Allahabad on 12 March 1850.

Chutter Singh and his sons were kept back in Allahabad while other Sikh prisoners, including Mulraj, were sent to their various destinations at Calcutta, Chunar and Agra. During their stay in the city fortress it appears an attempt was readied in the city to free father and son. Some of the servants of Shere Singh, accompanying the party who resided outside the fortress prison, were seen exchanging signals and fraternising with other Sikhs in the city. The fort had a complement of 120 sepoys and 150 raw British recruits who were not able at this stage to handle muskets properly. The plotters felt that if an element of surprise was exploited and the guards were sufficiently lax, the fort could be stormed and the guards overpowered with sufficient men. However, extra precautions were taken by the prison authorities on the plot being discovered. The next day, the commissioner of Allahabad, a Mr Lowther, was told by informers that a large group of Sikhs (1,300 Sikhs in the city) had accumulated outside the city in order to storm the fort. The fort doors were immediately closed and all persons not part of the garrison were ejected. Forty rounds of ammunition were supplied to each soldier. Two European soldiers were placed on Shere Singh and Chutter Singh along with two sepoys. These measures warded off any planned attack.

On 17 January 1851, Chutter Singh and Shere Singh, along with the other prisoners, were transferred to Fort William, Calcutta under a strong escort. The decision to exile them to Singapore never came to fruition. 'We are glad to find that Lord Dalhousie had no part in a measure which is so severe and unnecessary an aggravation of the punishment inflicted on the sirdars. The sentence moreover as regards Chutter and Shere Singh is opposed to English views, both of justice and humanity. If the sirdars are to be punished as rebels, they ought to be tried as Moolraj was; and if they are state-prisoners, the Court has no right to sentence them to transportation,' wrote the *Friend of India* rather sympathetically.

The following year, public attention was drawn further east as the Anglo-Burmese War broke out. In July 1852 Shere Singh and Chutter Singh both volunteered for service in the conflict and offered to help recruitment of Sikh soldiers in return for freedom, but this offer was not accepted. Many of their former soldiers had now entered into the East India Company's forces by this stage in any case. However, Dalhousie's attitude towards father and son had begun to soften by this time. Perhaps because of their offer of help, it had been decided by mid-1852 that they would be released on the termination of the war in Burma. The delay till the end of the war was because it was thought dangerous to free them while war was continuing. The Sikh soldiers in Burma, it was thought, would develop nationalist feelings on seeing their former Sikh commander at liberty to lead them again. Many of the other Sikh officers incarcerated after the war were now given their liberty as well, although they were informed they were on parole and must move no more than 2 to 3 miles from their homes.

Shere Singh and Chutter Singh were later allowed the privilege of leaving the jail on a carriage three times a week escorted by a British officer and armed guard. This was extended to a daily trip in May 1853 by order of the Governor-General. In January 1854, Shere Singh and his father were finally set at liberty but with conditions on their movements. They were to remain in Calcutta where they would remain under surveillance. Pensions were given to them sufficient to allow them to live with their families, who had made their way down from the Punjab. Chutter Singh was awarded 8,000 rupees per month, Shere Singh 6,000 rupees, and smaller amounts went to their followers. In July 1857, while still in Calcutta under watch, with the Bengal sepoy mutiny breaking out, Shere Singh would again offer his services to the British Government in return for complete liberty. He would be glad, he said, to lead the Sikh soldiers being recruited in the Punjab during the siege of Delhi, going as far as to suggest leaving his family as hostages as proof of his fidelity. However, these offers were again refused by the British Government.

# 33

# Those Who Cling to the Ancien Régime

I should say that for camp-equipage old Ranjit's camp was the very finest and most
sumptuous among all the Princes of India!

John Login to Lena Login, 22 May 1849

The last symbol of Sikh supremacy in the Punjab is about to pass away. The coinage of
Ranjit Singh and his successors is to be called in with the least practicable delay.

*Lahore Chronicle*, April 1850

A grand ball was held by Gough on 1 May 1849 at Bentinck Castle in Simla in honour of
Dalhousie and to celebrate the success of the recent war. All the developing friction between
the two following Chillianwala had been forgotten by this point and it was an occasion
for much backslapping. Two of the finest Sikh guns taken during the war, with carriages
decorated in brass and steel, were brought into the building. They were hidden from
Dalhousie's view by being placed inside a choice tent taken at Gujrat belonging to Sirdar
Ram Singh, one of the Sikh generals. Some of the Sikh standards captured had been brought
and placed in the room and alongside the tent were drawn British artillerymen in full dress
to add to the occasion.

Lord and Lady Dalhousie on arriving were conducted to the raised platform by the tent
and Gough made a speech congratulating Dalhousie on the conquest of the Punjab, which he
ventured to predict 'would prove hereafter one of the brightest and most valuable additions to
our eastern empire'. The tent was then drawn open and the guns inside presented to a beaming
Dalhousie. The Governor-General, forgetting all doubts he had ever had in his mind over the
ageing Commander-in-Chief, returned the compliment, declaring 'it had been Lord Gough's
good fortune to conduct to a successful termination two of the most arduous campaigns
recorded in the annals of British India, and that against an enemy, than whom one more skillful,
more enterprising, or more endued with soldierly qualities had never opposed us in the field'.
The festivities, ceremonies and dancing would continue late into that night.

Years before his death, Ranjit Singh had been shown a map on which substantial areas of the
Indian subcontinent had been marked in red. On asking what this meant, he was told the areas
in red were British conquests. After gazing at the map for a while, he had famously muttered,
'*Sab lal hojeaga*' to his courtiers, meaning 'All will be red soon'. Whether he meant the Punjab
too would disappear into the maw of the East India Company or whether he meant the rest of
India was never clarified. Ten years after his death, and with the trials of the main protagonists
beginning, the army and state that he had created so assiduously began to be dismantled and the

dispersal of its assets organised immediately in preparation for the new British administration in Lahore.

***

After the declaration that the Punjab was annexed, disarmament of the Sikh soldiery and civilians alike around the Punjab was commenced. In accordance with this, Dalhousie would immediately send forth instructions as to the surrender of all weapons in the area between Lahore and Ferozepore as a precursor to further disarmament elsewhere. Over the following days and weeks, action was taken to bring this about. A Major Mayne, the commandant of Dalhousie's bodyguard, was deputed for this operation. Within a few days, 5,000 arms including firearms, swords, lances along with five guns had been confiscated or handed in. Dalhousie was particularly anxious to target the Bari doab, 'where the Sikhs are most martial and turbulent' as he put it. There were reports of isolated fighting in parts, although when a strong force was sent the villagers acquiesced grudgingly.

Six weeks after the declaration of annexation it was announced by the British authorities in Lahore that all weapons between the Beas and Indus rivers must also be surrendered. Furthermore it was now illegal to either sell or manufacture or to be engaged in the sale of arms throughout the Punjab. The walls of villages and towns also must be deconstructed. The trans-Indus and Peshawar regions were excluded from this new law, the area being so lawless it was felt villagers here required arms and village walls to protect themselves from robbery, rapine and murder. The news was communicated to every village and town, with the headmen responsible for the handing over of all arms and with the police from the major cities responsible for enforcing it.

Over the coming months, 119,796 pieces of arms of all descriptions were handed in to the arsenals of Lahore including fifty-five more guns of various descriptions, sizes and vintage, 34,815 matchlocks, 106 zambarooks along with 44,283 swords and tulwars and 11,573 lances. The better of the muskets and matchlocks were given over to arm the local police forces, with many of the tulwars, lances and other arms melted to make, among other things, fetters for use in the city prisons. The *Lahore Chronicle* of 10 August 1849 reported a total of 956 persons caught and punished for possession of arms between May and August, the three months following the declaration. Many of the weapons, like those taken at Gujrat, were sold off to sepoys and British soldiers as trophies, the going rate for a Sikh tulwar, matchlock or shield being eight annas, while others were sold off in British territory. There was, however, certain disquiet in certain circles regarding this policy as the sale was open to robbers and people of unsavoury nature as well as honest civilians.

In the middle of 1850, attention would turn to the Lahore fort and the eviction of its royal residents. Many of Ranjit Singh's wives and his son's wives still occupied the fort, being quartered in the Sheesh Mahal building. These were now pensioners of the British Government and plans were drawn to send the ladies back to their towns and villages of origin. In July 1850, since the work on the new cantonments at Mean Meer had been halted, the plan had been to turn the Dewan-i-am or Great Hall of Audience, where Duleep Singh formerly held Durbar, into a hospital. It was mooted that the European artillery could meanwhile be quartered in the Sheesh Mahal apartments, but Dalhousie disagreed with turning the palace building into a barracks; the buildings would be left to the civil authorities.

***

Perhaps the most potent and visible symbol of the Sikh state was its coinage, and this would begin to disappear during the middle of 1850 as well. 'The last symbol of Sikh supremacy in the Punjab is about to pass away,' the *Lahore Chronicle* mused on the event. 'The coinage of Ranjit Singh and his successors is to be called in with the least practicable delay, to be assayed and melted down at Lahore, and forwarded for recoinage to Calcutta or Bombay, as soon as sufficient amount of Company's coin can be obtained to replace that about to be withdrawn from circulation. We suspect that, desirable as the alteration will be, sometime must elapse before a complete change can take place, and that, unless a period be fixed within which only the Nanuckshaie rupee is to be considered a legal tender, a considerable number will be retained by those who cling to the ancien régime with a lingering hope that Sikh supremacy may once more be in the ascendant.'

All Sikh coinage dated between 1814 and the present time would be exchanged, it was declared, one East India rupee for one Sikh rupee. Coins from Ranjit Singh's earlier days and from before the nineteenth century, particularly gold or silver coins, were to be assessed by their intrinsic value. The Punjab had a vast diversity of coins which logged in financial form the various changes of power in the Punjab over the previous century and a half and thus each coin had to be assessed. The coinage in circulation dated back to the Mughal period, with Persian coins of Nadir Shah, others of the Afghan Zeman Shah and current coinage from Afghanistan all in use across the state. This was more so in the trans-Indus region, where around twenty-eight different types of coinage were commonly in circulation. The gold coins would be difficult to assess. The Hari Singh Kashmir gold currency, for instance, was worth sixty-six of the company's rupees, with other gold coins being as much as a hundred rupees depending on their purity. The Nanukshahi gold rupee had a purer metal than the East India Company's counterpart and thus was valued higher and had fifty different variations. In total there were sixty-one different denominations, which flummoxed most people and aided only the crafty moneychangers, who alone could accurately measure the amount of gold in each. All these were ordered to be disposed of and the single currency of the company introduced. The process of gradual exchange would take several years, with Sikh coinage being collected and melted down well into 1853 while the British mints at Bombay and Calcutta sent East India coinage stamped with the queen's image in the other direction. By the mid-1850s, Sikh coins had become a rarity.

\*\*\*

What would invariably garner most attention from European visitors to Lahore was Ranjit Singh's collection of gemstones and other treasures, one of the most impressive collections of the nineteenth century, kept in the Toshakhana, the royal treasury. This had been relatively untouched during the late convulsions of the state, although the more easily convertible gold bullion and money had all long gone. Stored in the Motee Mandir were numerous state jewels, diamonds and gold pieces in the form of rings, necklaces and other jewellery. Also present were dishes, plates, cups and water pitchers used in banquets and made of gold and silver. Other items included Ranjit Singh's entire baggage with a vast amount of richly decorated cashmere cloth tents lined with satin and velvet and their equipment and fine carpets matched with tent poles made of solid silver and gold along with numerous valuable horse and elephant trappings. In terms of cloth there were Kashmir shawls and numerous royal robes of the Maharajah and princes, valuable Persian and Bokhara rugs and fine carpets. A summerhouse made entirely out of silver was also logged. Ranjit Singh's fondness for weaponry meant the building contained ceremonial swords of all descriptions along with valuable armour and arms of all kinds. Also present were the weapons of past Sikh heroes and generals, some still caked with their blood.

Then there were the items of historic value the ruler had acquired over the years. The wedding garments of his mother and father lay in the Toshakhana. Also present was the sword of the legendary Persian hero Rustam, which Ranjit Singh obtained from Shah Shuja, along with the Maratha ruler Holkar's sword, as well as the sword of Wazir Fateh Khan, the founder of the Barakzai royal family at Kabul. He had also acquired Shah Shuja's magnificently embroidered state pavilion.

There were also religious artefacts stored alongside the numerous items of state property. These included the *kulgee* (headgear plume) of Guru Gobind Singh, the last Sikh Guru, and his shoes, shorts and walking stick. He also had several locks of the hair of the Prophet Mohammad. Then there were more modern treasures and gifts from other rulers. There were valuable gifts, including a beautiful portrait of Queen Victoria, given him as presents by past Governor-Generals and other rulers from Russia, France, Persia, Afghanistan and other Indian royalty. The most valuable items in the treasury was unquestionably the famous Koh-i-noor diamond, which had its own guardian. Also stored was the Darya-i-noor (river of light), a sister diamond with a surface as broad as that of the more famous Koh-i-noor. But the most noticeable item in the Toshakhana was the gold throne of Ranjit Singh himself. The whole horde of jewels and diamonds on their own was estimated to be worth £2 million (approximately £160–180 million in today's money) without taking into account any historic significance. This did not include treasures like the Koh-i-noor and the Sikh and Islamic relics, whose status made valuations impossible.

Two of the first to see the treasures had been Dr John Login, the well-travelled Scottish Presbyterian surgeon who had been employed in the recent war for his services, and his wife Lena. On 2 April 1849, four days after the declaration of annexation in the last Lahore Durbar, Dr Login had been appointed the 'Killah-ke-Malik' or governor of 'the citadel of Lahore and all it contains' also being later given the job of Postmaster General of the Punjab. This powerful and unique position put him not only in charge of the Lahore treasury, the royal stud and all the military supplies inside the fortress but all the thousands of residents of the palace as well. This included thirty-three Maharanis, widows of Ranjit Singh and his deceased sons, and all the paraphernalia associated with the royal establishment including six sets of courtesans, five full bands of musicians and 130 concubines still resident in the fortress. In addition he was in charge of thirteen political prisoners, their numbers to be supplemented later by Shere Singh and Chutter Singh as well as Mulraj. He also had charge of Dewan Mulraj's family as well as several princes of the royal family of Afghanistan. Others of lesser station included the female servants of Maharani Jind Kaur, who had been separated from her after exile. Most importantly it put him in charge of its principal resident, the young Maharajah.

Login would spend an enormous amount of time with Duleep Singh later, but the more recognisable responsibility he would have in the first few weeks would be to take care of, catalogue and assess the worth of the Lahore treasury. The diamonds of Ranjit Singh were typically kept wrapped in rags which were themselves placed in velvet purses. These could be found dispersed all over the Toshakhana in no particular order. Wooden boxes were initially ordered by Login to place the entire collection of gems in order and value.

The wealth of the Toshakhana was a talking point among Europeans passing though Lahore, who always asked Login for guided tours of the treasures, seen as one the highlights of a visit to the city. Lena Login's cousin Col Robert Adams, afterwards second-in-command of the Guides, and deputy commissioner at Peshawar, on being shown the treasury passed comments similar to other visitors who saw the Toshakhan:

> I wish you could walk through that same Toshkhana and see its wonders; the vast quantities of gold and silver; the jewels not to be valued, so many, and so rich; the Koh-i-noor, far beyond what I had imagined; Ranjit's golden chair of State; silver pavilion; Shah Soojah's ditto; Relics of the Prophet; Kulgee plume of the last Sikh Guru; sword of the Persian hero Rustum (taken from Shah Soojah); sword of Holkar, etc.; and, perhaps above all, the immense collection of magnificent Cashmere shawls, rooms full of them, laid out on shelves and heaped up in bales it is not to be described!

The man formerly in charge of the Toshakhana had been Misr Makraj, the treasurer, whose family had been the guardians of the Koh-i-noor for three generations. On being asked to give up the diamond to Dr Login, Makraj, either through superstition or servility, commented to Login on the curse of the diamond and how glad he was to be free of the responsibility. 'The Koh-i-noor had been fatal to so many of his family that he had hardly hoped ever to survive the charge of it!' Login would write. Stories of this alleged curse would soon reach England as well, where they received wide circulation.

Login formed a team to help him in investigating the Toshakhana contents in reasonable time. This consisted of some European assistants and a sergeant of the horse artillery present in the fort along with four other European writers and various assorted moonshees. In order to ready the jewels for disposal, which would undoubtedly happen, many of the items the precious stones were set into were ordered by Login to be destroyed after their precious stones and metals had been removed. Also to be included in this haul was the personal property of Duleep Singh, estimated to be worth £250,000 (£20 million in today's money) for he would only be allowed to keep items to the value of £20,000 for his much reduced future establishment in British territory along with a small portion of state property. Login had picked out a few tents and jewels from the vast collection he would be allowed. During this process of extracting precious stones from their settings, one of the largest emeralds ever seen was almost thrown away when one of the many royal saddles to be disposed of wasn't examined properly. The giant stone had been assumed to be a large piece of green glass, being far larger than the usual size of emeralds.

Just as with the status of the prisoners, the windfall of the treasury prompted considerable discourse both in India and in London as to the technicalities of its status. The fact was that the Lahore treasury had always been in British control since the Treaty of Bhyrowal and thus had not been taken in conflict, and therefore it could not count as booty. Therefore many of the regulations related to spoils taken in war did not apply. In the House of Lords on 26 May 1849, Lord Ellenborough, an earlier Governor-General, argued Dalhousie had no right to choose the means of disposal since Her Majesty's troops had been used as part of the army during the late war rather than just East India Company troops. This precluded him from having sole authority over the decision and meant the entire contents of the Toshakhana should be put at the disposal of the queen. Failing this, he argued that the collection should be sold with the prize money obtained added to the six month batta that the troops would be receiving.

Dalhousie's opinion was that the treasury could not be considered as part of the prize money as it was not seized in combat unlike the treasure seized at the fall of Multan which could be considered rightful booty. He also argued though that HM troops had been used previously in campaigns where the East India Company appropriated all booty for itself and thus this was no precedent. The batta should be sufficient for the army, he argued. Lord Ellenborough's pronouncements, Dalhousie wrote in his private letters on 10 July 1849, were 'a pitiful act of popularity-hunting'. The Lord Chancellor concurred, pronouncing that the jewels and state property had been under the guard of company troops for the entire period of the war and that a subsequent declaration of war did not affect the treasury's status, that it did not belong to the Crown, nor had the Crown any right to it and therefore neither did the army any right to it as booty.

There was also the question of who would receive a share of the prize money from the capture of Multan. While the army at Multan would naturally receive their share, Gough argued the army that had faced Shere Singh also deserved to have a share of the booty from the city. It was thought that only the soldiers present during the second siege would be eligible. If, however, all were eligible then the share for each would go down drastically.

Disposal of the treasures from both cities would be done in measured fashion. The Multan items would be auctioned off first. Almost a year after the end of the war, on 13 February 1850, disposal of the best of Mulraj's jewels from the fort treasury commenced. The jewellery would be sold in ten lots. The *Indian Times* reported the prices being realised 'for the jewels were considered very good, being in some circumstances considerably higher than the market value'. The centrepiece of the auction and the item which garnered the most attention among his other pearl and emerald necklaces was one of Mulraj's favourites, described by the *Indian Times* as 'being composed of 180 of the rarest large white whole pearls, far surpassing any like number ever offered for public sale here – being all of a select kind and forming the necklace daily worn by the Dewan Moolraj previous to the time he surrendered to the British authorities. The pearls were of the whitest and rarest description and altogether the necklace was said to be the handsomest ornament ever exhibited in Calcutta.' It was bought by a merchant, Gooroopersaud Shaw and Co., for the princely sum of 14,940 rupees. This was followed by Mulraj's other emerald and pearl necklaces and turban ornaments. The auction attracted various wealthy merchants and traders from around the country as well as Europeans.

'The prices realised for the jewels were considered very good, being in some instances considerably higher than the market value. The pearls were of the best description, particularily Moolraj's necklace which as will be seen below fetched a handsome price,' wrote a newspaper correspondent. The larger Lahore section of the treasure Dalhousie would auction off as well, and this occurred in November 1852 in Calcutta, with the proceeds going into East India Company coffers rather than to the Crown. This would include Duleep Singh's private property, jewels, gold silver plate, his wearing apparel and household furniture. These auctions would exclude the more conspicuous and valuable of Ranjit Singh's collection. They would also exclude one of the legacies of the deposition of Duleep Singh and his aborted marriage with Chutter Singh's daughter. This was the considerable amount of wedding clothes readied for the bride. These clothes Dalhousie intended to be sent to London as the queen had expressed a strong wish to inspect the wedding apparel.

The famous throne of Ranjit Singh Dalhousie would keep, for the time being at least. He would chance to use the throne when meeting the Sikh Maharajah of Patiala, a strong British ally, on 28 October 1851 to impress both him and his entourage in a reception at Pinjore. A specially commissioned engraving showing the entry of the recently captured Sikh guns in Calcutta was given to the Maharajah along with other gifts. Ranjit's throne would be later despatched to London, where it would find its eventual resting place in what would become the Victoria and Albert Museum.

The Koh-i-noor, formerly in the peacock throne of the Mughals, then in the treasure boxes of Nadir Shah and the Afghan Shah Suja before being confiscated by Ranjit Singh, was for a time put up on public display in Lahore for European visitors. Three viewings were organised per week for the curious between the hours of 8 a.m. and 10 a.m. However, its eventual destination was to be across the ocean. 'It is a superb gem,' Dalhousie remarked simply upon first gazing at it. He had decided to take it to Bombay personally for shipment to England. Dalhousie was given the diamond on 7 December 1849 and would keep it in a small leather bag made by Lady Dalhousie. On receiving the diamond, according to Gough Dalhousie went into another room and tied it round his waist under his clothing in a small leather bag. This leather bag then was sewed into a Kashmir belt that Dalhousie used to wear. He had taken quite a shine to the diamond by this time and kept it with him day and night. The only persons who knew he had the diamond always with him were his wife and a Capt. Ramsay. At night his two dogs Baron and Banda guarded his camp bed and the jewel. The only time it left his belt was when he rode though some wild country near Dera Ghazi Khan during his trip downstream to Bombay when he thought it best to leave it with Capt. Ramsay while out riding.

The diamond was taken on board the steamer HMS *Medea* by Lt-Col Mackeson and Capt. Ramsay on 6 April 1850. Stored in an iron box which itself was inserted into a despatch box, the diamond was carried aboard in innocuous fashion by the officers, even the ship's captain, Commander Lockyer, being ignorant of the cargo. The ship nearly met disaster twice, adding some weight to the reputed curse on the diamond for the more superstitious. Cholera broke out on the ship and, needing supplies, the crew made an unscheduled stop at Mauritius. The locals, being told of the outbreak, refused to go near the ship and opened fire, threatening to sink the ship unless it moved off. Following this the ship had to navigate through a severe tempest that raged for nearly twelve hours. The steamer eventually made it to Plymouth with the diamond being offloaded at Portsmouth. The Koh-i-noor was handed over to the chairman and deputy chairman of the East India Company in London, and on 3 July 1850 the deputy chairman personally travelled to Buckingham Palace to officially hand over the gem to the queen. 'The Koh-i-noor is at present decidedly the lion of the Exhibition,' *The Times* commented when it was put up as an exhibit at the Great Exhibition of 1851. 'A mysterious interest appears to be attached to it, and now that so many precautions have been resorted to, and so much difficulty attends its inspection, the crowd is enormously enhanced, and the policemen at either end of the covered entrance have much trouble in restraining the struggling and impatient multitude.'

***

Along with the currency, the other, more visible symbol of the state, the Sikh army, was no more. Large numbers of soldiers who had not joined the 'rebel' army were available as a fresh new supply for the East India Company forces. These men were summoned to Lahore and offered service in the British forces, with pensions offered to those not required for service. There was some anxiety mixed with a generally welcoming and enthusiastic attitude to this recruitment. The official circular produced by the adjutant general's office and sent to the various commanders of divisions at the time provides interesting insight into the feelings prevalent at the time. 'No Sikh is to be required to cut either his beard or the hair of his head and all who enter the service with the kis [uncut hair] are to be required to continue to wear the hair after that fashion,' declared the first directive, a clear one as the soldiers' freedom to practice their beliefs. The second revealed more insecurity: 'Not more than 200 Punjabees are to be introduced into a regiment and not more than 100 of them are to be Sikhs,' it explained. It was hoped the dilution of Sikh soldiers within the regiments would minimise any nationalist tendencies or any possible attempts at renewed insurrection. The third directive reinforced the second: 'The Sikhs are on no account to be formed into a distinct company but are to be interspersed in equal proportions throughout the several companies of corps.' The fourth once more encouraged the keeping of the Sikh traditions and culture: 'Every countenance and encouragement is to be given to their comparative freedom from the bigoted prejudices of caste, every means adopted to preserve intact the distinctive characteristics of their race, their peculiar conventional and social customs and commanding officers must exercise strict, unceasing watchfulness and the firm intervention of their power to prevent all bullying and browbeating of the Sikhs by the other classes of the regiment and to crush all schemes and attempts to persuade the Sikh to abandon the social peculiarities of his class for the tenets and customs of strict Hindooism.' The fifth directive, that 'the Pahol or religious pledge of Sikh fraternity is on no account to be interfered with', recognised the enormous feeling of camaraderie among the Sikh soldiers. The sixth directive, that 'in the early part of their instruction, the Sikhs are to be drilled in distinct squads and the greatest care and circumspection is to exercised in the selection of instructors as regards equanimity temper and superior intelligence and they are to be warned and cautioned against the use of abusive or language the cane or of any violent or rough treatment whatsoever', was a submission to the fact that Sikh soldiers and Punjabis previously in the Sikh army rarely respected or showed a servile nature to superior officers who abused their privilege. The essence of these instructions therefore was that the recruitment of Sikh soldiers was welcomed but that they were to be kept in small numbers and distributed throughout the force till a level of trust had taken root.

There were sharp differences between the Sikh soldiers and the Hindu and Muslim sepoys, and there was a perception in high circles that the sepoys would dislike the Sikhs, who ate both pork and beef, which the Muslim and Hindu sepoys avoided because of their own religious constraints. Also, having no caste loyalties, the Sikh soldiers had no hesitation in drinking and eating from the same utensils as other castes as opposed to the Hindu soldiers, who would only share implements with their own caste. This, it was supposed, would therefore bind them to their British officers who had no qualms either on these points. The numbers of Sikh soldiers began to climb as the former Khalsa soldiers found they were being welcomed into the British army. 'There are now 70 Sikhs in this regiment and if officers were allowed to exercise a choice in the matter they would gladly fill the ranks of the entire corps with the sons of the Khalsa who transcend the Hindostanees by far in all the essential qualities of soldiership,' gushed the *Delhi Gazette* on the Sikh recruits into the 13th NI. 'For prompt and cheerful obedience no less than for superiority in bone and sinew they are unmatched except by British troops and almost the only question to be determined now is that of their ultimate fidelity to their present masters. Amongst those eating the company's salt in the 13th are men who have fought against us through both campaigns and who curse to this hour the treachery of their leaders; but the instinctive love of war as a profession combined with the pressure of necessity has brought them to seek service in the ranks of their late enemies; and it may be that if occupation and a vent for their daring valour can be found by the British, the hopes and aims of the more mercenary fighter may take the place of their ardent nationality and religious zeal.'

The *Friend of India* suggested Indian policy should match that used elsewhere, with former enemies happily enlisted by the British Government to serve in their forces, sometimes even before the conflicts had finished, as in the Gurkha war. The people of India felt no patriotism, it declared, and were happy to fight under the banner that paid them. But it also felt that the

Sikh soldiers must be dispersed in small bodies across India to prevent danger. 'At the same time we introduce a new element of safety into our own army which has hitherto been rather too exclusively composed of men of class and region. We have now Hindoos and Mahomedans, Goorkahs and Sikhs mingled in our army at this Presidency and we are no longer at the mercy of a body of men who from community of lineage, religion habits and feelings might form into formidable combinations,' it declared on 19 April 1851.

The *Englishman*, though, was heavily against the recruitment of Sikh soldiers, arguing there was a strong chance of Sikh soldiers betraying their new masters. 'There is much more nationality among the Sikhs than there has been amongst the several conquered tribes of Hindoostan,' it declared. 'The Sikhs on the contrary are an eminently national people and notwithstanding the defeats they have experienced at our hands have still the spirit of nationality strong upon them. Indeed this spirit is perhaps as fresh with them now as it was in the days of Ranjit. The glory of the Khalsa is the same cherished object in Sikh minds which it has ever been. The Sikhs are no longer dominant it is true but have they abandoned therefore the hope and desire to be so? Not if we have read their character right. To our thinking then a force composed of such materials is not to be trusted with the task of preserving order and quiet in the Punjab.'

That being said, the *Englishman* recognised the ex-soldiers of the Sikh army had to be given employment and that if employed it was best to station them outside the Punjab where there would be less danger of mutiny. 'If managed they may make not only good but even faithful soldiers to our government but do not try their fidelity too sorely and at the first outset by employing them in the country of their birth and amongst the scenes of the exploits of the Khalsa.' However, all arguments and resistance to the enlistment were quickly forgotten on the outbreak of the Anglo-Burmese War in 1852, when plenty of ex-Sikh army veterans, eager to hold the musket again, would volunteer and show complete fidelity to the East India Company.

*** 

Dalhousie would tour the newly annexed Punjab as a part of a grand tour in late 1849 and this proved to be the last time the semblance of Sikh power would be on display. Dalhousie set off on his tour from Simla on 1 November, travelling through to Ludhiana before crossing into the Jalandhar doab and reaching Kapurthala. The Raja of Kapurthala had helped the Sikh army in the first war but had stayed neutral in the recent war and Dalhousie presented him with a khillut (robe of honour) as a gift for his neutrality. On 20 November he crossed the Beas River, reaching Amritsar on 22 November. The population and officials of the city put on a great show and Dalhousie took the time to meet local dignitaries. 'I was very anxious to see the interior of the shrine [of the Golden Temple], and I confess that I saw no reason why I should not comply with the form prescribed and cover my shoes with a sock before entering the precincts of the temple, like everybody else,' he wrote. However, Mr Saunders, the local British official, suggested that to take off or cover his shoes would be to show too much compliance and concession to Sikh wishes and would give a negative impression of British power and authority. Dalhousie accepted the advice reluctantly and declined the opportunity to see the temple.

His interest meant he would follow his own wishes the next time he came to Amritsar. A trip to the nearby Gobindgarh fortress, now populated with a British garrison, on the outskirts of the city was organised instead before a return to see Amritsar and the Golden Temple from afar, illuminated in the evening for his honour. He travelled through the narrow streets of the city and through a friendly crowd, with no rude or abusive language heard. 'Five hundred times over any man among them might have shot me that night, for I could almost have shaken hands with the denizens of the houses on either hand as I passed; and there would not have existed the smallest possibility of detection. Yet not one rude word was heard, not a single sound of discontent,' he recorded.

Reaching Lahore on 28 November 1849, he entered with much fanfare and was greeted by a large cavalcade of Sikh sirdars along with John Lawrence and other dignitaries and the members of the board of control. A grand parade of British garrison troops numbering 8,000–9,000 men was conducted under the walls of the fort. Visits to the tomb of the Mughal Emperor Jahangir and other landmarks were arranged during his stay. The highlight of the stay was the inspection of Ranjit Singh's treasury with Lady Dalhousie, who had accompanied him on his tour and took a special interest in the jewels on display.

There was a reminder that Bhai Maharaj, lone of all the Sikh leaders, had not been caught at this point, with the arrest of some of his followers during Dalhousie's stay in Lahore. At this time Mulraj, Shere Singh and his father had been brought back to Lahore and the city was well lit in celebration of the Governor-General's visit by the local Sikh city chiefs. Dalhousie was shown around the city in a large procession. 'The camp was pitched just under the walls of the citadel of Lahore, a fine mass of building, and as I knew that Chutter Singh, and Shere Singh, and Moolraj, our prisoners, as well as the little Maharajah, were looking down upon us, the sight was rather a fine one in sentiment as well as in gay externals,' recorded Dalhousie. Shere Singh and Mulraj watching the sight as prisoners rather than as guests was symbolic perhaps, but whether they saw anything was moot as the dust was so tremendous by Dalhousie's account that he himself could not see the end of the British lines from the middle, all being conducted in confusion. The Governor-General would be shown the city, with city chiefs garlanding him numerous times and large crowds developing along the route to see and salaam him as he passed through. 'Immense crowds were present, there was not so much as a mischievous boy out of his place, and perfect silence prevailed, except when they saw me, when salaams resounded wherever I passed. I am not stupid enough to suppose that this is really attachment to our rule, but it shows their submission, that they are cowed and thoroughly in hand. Only eleven years ago, the English, guests of Ranjit Singh, and protected by his guards, were pelted through the streets of Lahore: is it not marvellous that such a change should be effected, on such a people, in such a time?' he wrote on 15 December on his visit through the old Sikh capital.

The main event of importance was a reception for Dalhousie, with the Governor-General meeting Duleep Singh for the first time. The Maharajah greeted him in the English language being taught to him at the time. 'I am very happy to see you here,' he said at their meeting, from which sprouted a good friendship. Duleep Singh, now pensioned off, would shortly be sent to Fatehgarh in British territory along with the only remaining prince of royal blood. This was Shiv Deo, the son of Maharajah Shere Singh, one of Duleep Singh's predecessors. One of the other festivities at the former capital included the investitures of Major-General Gilbert, while other officers were given the Order of the Bath. Some of the former Durbar members were also honoured, with Sheikh Imam-Ud-Deen being given the title of Nawab. The ceremony was carried out in Dalhousie's state tent with over 300 of the high and mighty from both Sikh and British society present, including Duleep Singh.

A day before his departure to Multan on 8 December, Dalhousie took possession of the Koh-i-noor which was to be shipped to London. The journey south, executed in leisurely fashion, meant the Governor-General's party reached Multan on 29 December with his camp set up in close proximity to the Eidgah and in sight of the gallows where Goojur Singh had been hanged and which still stood as a warning to any would-be insurrectionists. Dalhousie was shown around the city and the much-battered fortress and expressed his opinion that it was no surprise the fortress had withstood so much punishment. He also visited the temporary tombs of Agnew and Anderson along with the resting place of Montizambert, an old school-fellow, before ordering a monument to the officers be built over them. His last stop was at the Blue Mosque before leaving for Bombay and Ceylon, the next steps on his grand tour.

Dalhousie would visit Lahore again at the end of the following year. Faithful to his interest in Ranjit Singh, Dalhousie during his travels in the Punjab set up his camp at Ropar on 2 November 1850. This was the spot where the Maharajah met a previous Governor-General in what was termed a second Field of the Cloth of Gold for its magnificent spectacle. One of the more unfortunate features of the internal wrangles that plagued the Lahore state after Ranjit Singh's death was the slow construction of his mausoleum. Despite its modest size, the structure was only half complete by the time of the British annexation. Dalhousie inspected the building and showed a lively interest in completing the project and under his orders the preservation and completion was planned at British expense. Along with this he also ordered the maintenance of the Mughal Emperor Shah Jahan's tomb just outside the city along with the famous Shalimar gardens. He seemed to enjoy the pomp and visits by this stage. 'To-morrow I have a durbar for the sirdars here. All these pomps are grievous wasters of time. However, it will be the last I shall ever see. At times I do not feel quite sure whether to be glad or sorry in that conviction, for I like these Sikhs, they are fine manly fellows.'

# 34

# Twelve Years in Nepal

It is also to be hoped that happier times may come and that you may again
visit your home when an impartial investigation into your case will show the world
that you are innocent.

Jeebun Singh to Jind Kaur, July 1848

An appeal to the Court of Directors of the East India Company, to the British
Parliament, and to Her Majesty in England, is now the only course which remains
open to your Highness.

Mr Newmarch to Jind Kaur, early 1849

With the Lahore state being wound up in the months after the surrender of the Sikh army, the only matter unresolved was what to do with the leading figures of the royal family, principally the mother-and-son combination of the queen mother, Jind Kaur, and Maharajah Duleep Singh, who had been separated from each other for nearly two years now. Events would take unexpected turns for both during the next few years. The Maharani was already in British custody, having been exiled to Benares. After her arrival at the city on 2 August 1848, the expectation was she would retire and fade into obscurity on the modest pension allowed her. Her feisty nature nullified the likelihood of this happening, however, and as the war progressed in Punjab so began a contest of a different and legal nature in Benares, ending abruptly in her escape from British custody and sanctuary in Nepal.

Jind Kaur had been given a large residence in Benares, or rather a gilded cage, where only the servants were allowed ingress and egress by the British guards, and it soon became clear the Maharani would refuse to be passive about her effective imprisonment. She had already been busy making legal preparations to challenge the restrictions on her freedom before her arrival, in fact. She had employed one Jeebun Singh, a lawyer based in Calcutta, as one of her vakeels to assist her. Residing in the heart of the capital of British India, he became an important link for her to the outside world. Realising his shortcomings in the English language, Jeebun Singh had taken steps to employ a European solicitor, a certain J. Newmarch Esq., an attorney of the Calcutta Supreme Court, to assist in her case. Together these two men had taken up the challenge to have her released from effectual house arrest as war broke out in the Punjab. Since Newmarch did not know Punjabi or Persian and the Maharani could not speak English, a translator, a certain Behari Lall, had also been hired who had managed to pick up English from the local European priest, Revd Sandby. This made communication between Newmarch and his client much easier.

Jeebun Singh had written a letter to Major G. H. Macgregor, the agent placed in charge of Jind Kaur at Benares, for the attention of the Maharani when she reached the city. The letter informed her that he would, along with Mr Newmarch, be looking after her case. She should not worry, Jeebun Singh had written, about the allegations being made about her. News stories had arisen while she was being transported down to Benares that she was the prime instigator for the Multan uprising. Newmarch had been going through the documents that had been sent to the British Government in London related to the Punjab. These indicated an unfriendly attitude on the part of the Resident and a desire to deprive her of power *before* any accusations of her plotting against the British control in the Punjab had ever been made and in fact when she was in close alliance with the British. This would be much in her favour when publicised. She had also never broken the treaties with the British in any fashion. He was confident that she would be freed from captivity and that she would be allowed to return to the Punjab to resume her previous role and position. Regardless, they would take her case as far as they could, even if it meant bringing it to attention overseas.

I beg to add my humble assertions of devotion to your cause, and to entreat my Royal Mistress not to allow confinement and exile to damp her courage, and induce the acquiescence of despair. God is merciful and the clouds of your misfortune must be dispersed. Patience is necessary in the time of distress, as considerable delay must be apprehended, as the proceedings of English law are always dilatory. I hope, however, that, in the course of five or six months, you may obtain redress. If the local Government is unfavourable to you, justice may be obtained by an appeal to England. I have been told by Mr. Newmarch, that a proclamation was made at Lahore, that, if any letter containing any intrigues be detected, addressed by your Highness to any person of your country, the rigor of your treatment will be much more increased; but, as you never were, nor are, inclined to have recourse to such unworthy means, I am not at all uneasy at it.

Both Jeebun Singh and Newmarch had already begun writing to the Government of India regarding the issue of her exile from the Punjab during June 1848, even before she had arrived at Benares, but had been told they must follow protocol and go through the offices of the Resident in Lahore. In addition, once she reached Benares correspondence must be directed firstly to Macgregor, in whose custody she had been placed at Benares. They could not deal directly with the government. In order to build his case, Jeebun Singh wrote to her asking if the conditions she was kept in were comfortable, how many servants she was allowed, whether she had access to all her personal possessions and jewellery, and whether the British agent was treating her kindly. There were also issues regarding how much of her stipend she was being allowed. He also reminded her that Macgregor had been given liberty to read all her correspondence from him and Newmarch by the government.

Things didn't go well from the beginning with Macgregor. Her guardian and jailor in one, he seemed to have quickly taken a heavy disliking to the Maharani. Macgregor also had reservations about her vakeel. Receiving Jeebun Singh's letter on being allowed access to the Maharani, Macgregor immediately cast doubt on Jeebun Singh's character. 'I think, that I should relate what I know of his character. He was looked upon by Sir Henry Lawrence, then the Resident at Lahore, and by all of the principal Chiefs of the Lahore Government, as a person disaffected towards the Durbar, and inimical to the interests of the British Government, reposing much in the confidence of the Maharanee, and plying her with those evil counsels which have, doubtless, in no small degree contributed to her downfall, from the high position she once held at Lahore, to her present confinement and exile at Benares,' he wrote on 29 July. 'I conceive that such a person should not be permitted, either in person, or by attorney, to have access to the Maharanee Junda of Lahore.'

The Governor-General, already less than sympathetic with the Maharani's plight, concurred entirely. On no account, he ordered in response, should Jeebun Singh be allowed to visit the Maharani. She must choose another vakeel if she wished a vakeel's services at all. The consequence of this was that Jeebun Singh's role was severely limited, leaving Newmarch in future to largely deal with her case in person. Not that it was easy for Newmarch himself; he found he had to cross several hurdles before he was allowed to see his client. Therefore there was a delay throughout August and continuing into September where nothing of consequence could be done for his client.

\*\*\*

It was only in October 1848 that Newmarch with his interpreter was finally allowed to see the Maharani. Beginning on 4 October and ending on 12 October, Newmarch conducted a series of interviews with her in the presence of Macgregor, taking down all relevant information from the period of her brother's demise (i.e. the period several months before the outbreak of the first war) till the present time. Jind Kaur gave him a lengthy and detailed account of all that had been happened since then and related her correspondence with Henry Lawrence and his brother John. 'She dwelt much on the severity of her imprisonment in the fort of Sheikhoopoor and on the nature of her rigid confinement now at Benares and also on the hardship of having been deprived of all her jewels and valuables on her arrival here,' Macgregor would report to the government of these sessions.

From what he had learnt, Newmarch in turn would draw up a letter to be sent to the Governor-General in her name, the contents of which she had read and approved. The letter sent on 12 October was an impassioned plea to have her situation re-examined. Newmarch complained of the treatment she had been faced with and requested her case to be re-examined urgently for she had been exiled from the Punjab and incarcerated with constant surveillance for no given reason. He also asked for an increase in her much-reduced monthly allowance. She was a Maharani, and mother of the Maharajah, and needed to live a lifestyle as befitted her status and not that of a prisoner, he argued. The current meagre allowance merely lowered her in the eyes of her servants and prevented her purchasing the items necessary for her station in life. Although she had clothes, as a monarch it was customary for her to purchase some new clothes every month. She had already had to reduce her retinue quite considerably, and cutting back further would simply loosen ties with the servants she had left. She could barely afford to pay for her vakeels at this time and he asked the government to release a further sum of around 750 rupees per month from her confiscated wealth to enable her to do all the above in easier circumstances. On the issue of her confiscated property, Newmarch requested an inventory of all that had been taken from her including her jewellery. With reference to the recent claims by Lahore Durbar members that she had taken state property, he asked to be told if there were any claims so they could be contested if necessary.

A look at the list of Jind Kaur's monthly expenses that Newmarch drew up for the government to argue his case gives an interesting picture of her reduced circumstances at this time. Her allowance was a modest 1,000 rupees per month, but her food expenses including for her servants (including the interpreter, a bheestie, four syces, ten bearers for a palanquin with four bearers for her servants, four cooks and twelve female servants) and feed for horses and oxen, etc. totalled 1,490 rupees. She had a retinue of around seventy servants which cost an additional 718 rupees. This totalled 2,208 rupees, which meant she would have to cut her staff and costs by more than half to stay within her means and avoid debt. But to do so, Newmarch argued, she would be left with a retinue unbefitting her status as a Maharani of the Punjab. As it was, she had no money for warm clothes for her and her servants for the coming winter.

Macgregor, not unexpectedly perhaps, was against an increase in her monthly allowance. He argued that anything she required could be managed through her confiscated wealth and any extra provisions like the warm clothing he would see to himself. If she was allowed an increase he felt 'she would then be able to save money out of her monthly allowance which might be applied by her to some improper purpose', as he advised the government on 23 October. The answer to Newmarch from the government on 5 November, following Macgregor's advice, was that her allowance would not be raised and that she must live within the reduced means. The warm clothing was allowed, however, the funds to be made available under the management of Macgregor as he had requested. There was further bad news for the Maharani, the message from the government stating that it saw no need to re-examine the measures taken against her by the Lahore Durbar and that therefore the Government of India declined to renew any investigations into her present situation.

As the year came to a close, an unfazed Newmarch then moved for habeas corpus in relation to her virtual incarceration, making an application to the Supreme Court in India in Calcutta to have her case brought before the tribunal. He told his client he was confident of success on this count. The fact was that she was being held without any charges, confirmed by Major McGregor when Newmarch had gone to visit her. Newmarch had asked on what grounds she had been imprisoned and Macgregor had simply said she was being detained due to instructions from the Governor-General, instructions which he refused to show. He had admitted he was ignorant of any charges or reasons for her detention. He did not believe there were any charges, in fact. She was simply being held due to the suspicions of the Resident at Lahore, although investigations were currently going on regarding her involvement in any intrigues against the Lahore and British Government in India. This was confirmed by Jind Kaur in their meetings in December 1848, Jind Kaur had also complained of no charges having been made; she hadn't even been questioned at any point. She would protest to Newmarch that she was a subject of the Lahore state and that therefore there was no reason that the British Government could hold her in British territory in any case. The Treaty of Lahore had said there would be perpetual peace between the two states and the 15th article of the treaty declared the subjects of one state visiting the other would be placed on the footing of the most favoured nations. Disregarding this, she had been most shabbily treated and imprisoned. The war that was going on now was not the decision of the Lahore Durbar or hers and hence there was no reason for holding her in custody.

The court's response would not be encouraging. Although the two states were allies and on good relations, this did not mean that individuals were necessarily friends. The Maharani had been imprisoned by the Lahore state (albeit headed by a British Resident) on the grounds of her association with enemies of that state. The court had no jurisdiction regarding enquiries into acts taken at Lahore. It could simply deal with her status on arrival in British territory, which was that of a prisoner, a state agreed on by both Lahore and the British Government during a time of hostilities. 'She is a state prisoner detained by the authority of the Governor-General and though not taken in arms her status under the circumstances of her detention appears to us not different from that of a prisoner of war ... The conduct of the Governor-General in so dealing with state prisoners is exempt from the jurisdiction of this court as well as of the courts of the Honourable the East India Company. For an oppressive use of this power which is not to be supposed probable the remedy would be by application to a higher though distant authority. It appears that this lady who is not a subject who owes not even a temporary allegiance, who is brought into this country a prisoner of state during actual hostilities and so remains, hostilities still raging, can claim no right to this high prerogative writ grantable as of right to a subject for the vindication of that liberty which the English law gives to all resident where it prevails.'

Her state therefore technically was as an 'alien enemy and a state prisoner'. With this avenue closing as well, Newmarch gambled on making the issue as public as possible to garner public support for her case. An open letter addressed to the Governor-General was sent to the *Englishman* newspaper, one of the more widely read publications, in support of her case. The editorial column of the *Englishman* and of the *Calcutta Star*, which was also taking an interest in the case of the Maharani, proved to be favourable to her cause. The Maharani had been arrested and detained, he wrote in the letter, on mere suspicion and there had been no hard evidence uncovered of her plotting against the Government of India or the Lahore Durbar. Rather than being against the British presence in the Punjab, Jind Kaur had instead always been for the maintenance of British troops at Lahore to control the turbulent soldiery. Despite this the British Government had concluded a treaty behind her back, with the Durbar pensioning her off with a modest sum. He asserted that Jind Kaur had in fact warned the Resident of the Prema Plot when he had approached her secretary. His main plea on her behalf was the fact that she had been exiled from Lahore and kept in close supervision and then taken to British territory on the outbreak of war without ever being charged with any crime. Despite this, and despite Newmarch and Jeebun Singh making applications to clarify why she was being imprisoned, the Government of India was refusing to renew investigations into her case. Newmarch then denounced the government's treatment of the Rani as unjust and unfair and said he would continue to assist his client till her case was put before the British Parliament and public.

Conscious of keeping her morale high, Newmarch wrote to Jind Kaur an encouraging letter on New Year's Day 1849 as to the sympathy of the European public in India.

> It will also be gratifying to your Highness to learn that, since the publication of my letter, I have received assurances from persons in almost every rank of society in Calcutta, of their sympathy in your Highness's misfortunes, and their conviction that, on an appeal to England, the cruel measures pursued towards your Highness by the Indian Government arising out of delusion and timidity, will be reversed, and your Highness restored to the regency of the Punjab.

Following up on this, and hoping to escalate matters, Newmarch would advise her to send a power of attorney for execution by the Maharani should she be in favour of his suggestion that steps should be taken in England. 'An appeal to the Court of Directors of the East India Company, to the British Parliament, and to Her Majesty in England, is now the only course which remains open to your Highness,' he summed up. The catch in all this was the cost. In order to increase their chance of success and to ensure a speedier progress, it would be necessary for him to go to England to conduct these affairs. This would mean him leaving his affairs in India for an extended time and thus losing new business as well as taking on the costs of being in England. His costs he estimated would be 50,000 rupees, a sum that would need to be paid in advance of his leaving the shores of India. This was a huge amount, quite beyond the ability of the Maharani to pay. But Newmarch suggested if she was in broad agreement, the large expenditure would justify the increase in chance of release. There was the possibility that the government would allow her to sell a portion of her jewels presently confiscated to pay for her costs, although the mere threat of taking the issue to England may bear results. Newmarch also addressed the issue of how much information his client in her captivity was allowed to receive. The news in several newspapers and editorials on her case and plight in addition to the open letter in the *Englishman* which he had sent to Maharani Jind had been refused by Macgregor, who argued references to the Governor-General had been 'couched in very disrespectful terms' in these open letters by Newmarch and therefore could not be passed on to the prisoner. His policy after querying by Newmarch was backed by government. On 23 January an uncompromising message was received by Macgregor. 'The Government will not permit one of its own subjects, through its own officers, to transmit, to a state prisoner, letters, and documents, containing reflections on the public policy pursued by the Government, which are quite unnecessary for the transaction of business between his client and himself. The Governor-General, therefore, declines to sanction the delivery to Her Highness of these papers, or of the printed letter alluded to by you.'

So as matters stood, Jind Kaur could not be given access to the opinions and news concerning her in the media. Neither was her appeal to the High Court successful and nor was she likely to receive any new support from either the Lahore Durbar or the Resident. Realising that all Newmarch's approaches were also doomed to failure in the face of an uncompromising Governor-General, Jind had already decided to try a direct attempt herself with a letter to the government on 15 January. She had always been a supporter of the British, she declared, but had suffered the most at their hands. Still, despite the recent treatment, she was willing to work for the benefit of the British and assist in ending the current war and punishing those warring against their authority.

> My wish is to requite the British Government, for the good it has done me: how is this to be effected? Why, in this manner: send me back to the Punjab, and I would repress anarchy, and restore good Government. I would advance the interests of the British Government. The British should confide in me; I am a person of integrity, and never tell falsehoods.
>
> If the British would send me to the Punjab, I would settle the affairs of that country in four months, and in such a manner as to meet the approval of the British. If it pleased the British, I would make prisoners of the evil-disposed persons, and cause them to be slain: in fact, I would, in no way, act contrary to the wishes of the British: by sending me back to the Punjab, they would see how wisely I would administer the affairs of that country: What good has arisen from keeping me a prisoner? All has gone wrong in consequence. People should regulate their actions, so as to derive some good from them: make use of my services; and the interests of the British Government would thereby be promoted.

She mentioned the fact that she had a large amount of wealth, 52 lakh rupees in assets and cash in Sheikhupura before it was extracted from her at Benares. She had never used this wealth against the British. 'If the British desire to avail themselves of my services – which might prove most beneficial to their interests – now is the time to consider the matter, while misrule prevails throughout the Punjab: should they be suspicious of my intentions, let them be assured that I entertain no evil designs whatever, and should promote their interests.'

She criticised Chutter Singh for having given over Peshawar to the Afghans which she would never have done. Other parts of the Punjab too may be handed over to the Afghan ruler, she warned. 'Those who resolve to die fighting cannot be taken alive and the British may fight many battles but the Sikhs will never submit to their rule. If the British desire to settle the country, let them send me thither, and I will rule the country on their terms'. Dalhousie would forward her letters on to the Secret Committee on 7 February 1849 and apprised them of her and her lawyer's ambition to take her case to England. Meanwhile a rather terse reply designed to end all discourse was sent to the Maharani care of Macgregor on 31 January. 'The letter from the Maharanee calls for no answer'.

\*\*\*

Nothing of note would occur for the remainder of the month of February as Newmarch and Jind Kaur mulled over the weighty and expensive issue of taking the case to England. It's known despite the heavy precautions taken by Macgregor to vet the letters and information being passed to her that either through her servants or by secret communication she was aware of how the war in the Punjab was going. Not only that but she managed to slip out letters to her sympathisers. She also managed to send messages to Chutter Singh and Mulraj during the month of March 1849 at least once. These messages were, unfortunately for her, intercepted. Two horsemen were seen one day crossing into the Punjab on 1 March 1849. Their eastern Indian features marking them out as different and their movements seen as suspicious, they were pursued. One managed to escape but one was captured and arrested. Papers were found on the man along with two amulets. A letter secreted inside jewellery was a common form of carrying confidential information. The amulets carried a letter each for Mulraj and Chutter Singh. They were dated two months to the date the horseman was captured, around the time it would take a horseman travelling from Benares, so the letters were presumably written early in January, prior to Chillianwala. Frederick Currie had no doubt the letters came from Jind Kaur. He had, he explained, shown them to Mr Bowring, his assistant, who had seen many of the Maharani's letters she had sent to the previous Residents and knew her writing nuances. Bowring was positive these were genuine. The letter, a diatribe rather than any discussion of plots and intrigue, allowed Jind Kaur to vent her anger and frustration at the British for her incarceration and encouraged Chutter Singh to humiliate the British prisoners already taken.

By the grace of the holy Gooroo, written by the Maee Sahib to Chuttur Sing.
I am well and pray for your welfare also. A hundred praises on your bravery. I am unable to bestow sufficient commendation on it; as long as the earth and heavens exist, so long shall people continue to utter your praises. You have settled matters with the British, right well.
They quake and tremble through fear of you and have lost all their ascendancy. They have abandoned eating their food, and their tongues falter. Be confident and firm. The English have no troops, so exert yourself to the utmost.
Give the British, whom you have taken prisoners, one hundred blows each a day; blacken their faces; and placing them on donkeys, parade them through your camp; cut off their noses also; by these means, in a short time, not one of the British will be left in the land. Do not interfere with the Hindostanees, but proclaim, by beat of tom-tom, that all who will enter the Maharajah's service shall be rewarded.

Collect together 1000 or 2000 able bodied men, and having disguised them as fakeers, send them across [to Calcutta]. Instruct them to watch the British during the day and to kill them at night. The British have no troops in this part of the country, certainly not more than 1000 or 2000 men, and at night are accustomed to sleep with no one near them. Be confident. The British do not molest me at all, being afraid to do so.

The other letter being addressed to Moolraj was a copy of the above. The intervening time between her writing the letters and the horsemen messengers being captured had seen the fall of Multan and the battles of Chillianwala and Gujrat, bringing an end to the war and making the message redundant. A further letter from her to Shere Singh was also intercepted. In this she informed Shere Singh there was a crore of rupees hidden at Sheikhupura which he could use to pay his troops. This money was shortly confiscated by the British. These intercepted letters, sent to the government on 19 March, ten days before annexation ended any little chance of leniency by the British Government and in fact provided the excuse for further drastic action against her. The decision was taken to put the Maharani under official incarceration.

The immediate pretext though would be an incident relating to one of her servants who managed to escape the strict guard and disappear. This, it was decided, was a trial run for the Maharani herself to escape British custody and Macgregor immediately sanctioned the transfer of Jind Kaur to the fortress of Chunar, the usual jail for state prisoners, the move taking place on 6 April.

Realising she would probably spend the rest of her days in the prison, and with no expectations of release despite the legal efforts of Newmarch, Jind Kaur looked to other means of escaping British custody. The ladies of the time normally were in purdah (face veils), and thus the Maharani was never asked to show her face on arrival at Chunar and the days after. Occasionally her voice was heard, but in recent days the guards had noticed it had taken on a different tone, attributed by the person under the veil to a cold she had contracted. In fact Jind Kaur had escaped. One of her servants, known by the name Seenawallee, meaning seamstress, who was allowed in and out of the prison had exchanged clothes (and face veils) and taken her place while the Maharani in her servant's clothes had walked out of the fortress. The plan had nearly come to grief; one of the guards had initially challenged the 'seamstress' and refused to allow her to leave the fortress but had been convinced by her other servants that she had always had the right to enter and exit the fortress to visit her mistress. She was challenged again by the guards on the outer gate but the Havildar had shouted out all was fine. The next day Seenawallee (or what appeared to her but was another servant) appeared again asking for entry to the fort so that the guards' suspicions were put to rest. As the real seamstress took the place of the Maharani in her cell, Jind Kaur was already well on her way north to Nepal. The charade continued till the 19th, when her servants, confident that her royal mistress had a good start, made public their ruse.

The escape prompted much speculation in the papers. Some, refusing to believe in the servants' accounts, speculated she had escaped even earlier during the preparation for her removal to Chunar. According to the story written by the *Benares Recorder*, she had escaped the same afternoon as her arrival on the 6th and that she had very definitely reached Chunar. Others speculated she had escaped several days after being transferred. The matter would prove unresolvable due to the face veils she and her accomplices had always worn. Jind Kaur had coolly left a note in her cell:

You put me in the cage and locked me up. For all your locks and your sentries, I got out by my magic ... I had told you plainly not to push me too hard – but don't think I ran

away, understand well, that I escape by myself unaided … When I quit the Fort of Chunar
I threw down two papers on my gaddi and one I threw on the European charpoy now
don't imagine, I got out like a thief.

Jind Kaur travelled rapidly under the disguise of a pilgrim, crossing the 480 km and the border
and reaching Kathmandu by the 29th of the same month, where she applied for sanctuary. Back
at Benares, the Rajah of Betteeah, who had been encamped near Benares at the time of her
escape, was immediately put under suspicion of having given her aid. Two suspicious parties
had been seen with some palanquins belonging to the Raja carrying his wives to Allahabad
and a boat was also seen travelling rapidly down the river from his camp. The rajah's party
was put under surveillance, although nothing could be proved. The successful escape from the
fortress and travel to Nepal raised many eyebrows considering the level of security that she had
been placed under. 'The planning and execution of her escape and her journey to Nepaul,' the
*Bombay Times* declared, 'disclose a degree of ingenuity and enterprise on her part and that of
her abettors, as well as a want of care and circumspection on ours, we were not at all prepared
for. That the Light of the Harem, so famous for her profligacy and beauty, should for such a
length of time have successfully enacted the character of saint, seems the strangest of all her
transformations.'

In the cool climate of Simla, where Dalhousie was situated at the time, there was also surprise
and the Governor-General, although irritated at her escape, after reflection was confident no
disadvantage would result now the war had ended. 'Thence she effected her escape alone,
nobody knows how. It seems impossible that it could have been done without the connivance of
her guard, and a Committee of Inquiry is now going on … I have confiscated her 9 lacs worth of
jewels, and she has no money of her own, so that she can't do much harm. If she flies to Nepaul
and keeps quiet there, it will be a clear gain, for she will lose her pension, of course. If she goes
to the Punjab she can do no great mischief there now. Three months ago it would have been
less agreeable.'

Jind Kaur's sudden appearance in Kathmandu along with a request for asylum would worry
the Nepalese Government and put them in an awkward position. The Nepalese Prime Minister,
Jang Bahadur, was equivocal towards her. While apparently well pleased to hear of the defeat
of the Sikh army at Gujrat, he was known to have expressed a dislike to the recent behaviour of
the British Government towards Jind Kaur herself. Her previous treatment and then attempted
incarceration in Chunar he had said was 'a blot on the British escutcheon', and was the only case
he knew where British generosity had not been extended to a vanquished foe. However giving
her asylum meant relations with British India might suffer. Nepal was already in thrall to the
British at this time and the Prime Minister was nervous about giving her sanctuary. Asylum had
been asked for, however, and it was a custom to grant it. But if he had to hand the Maharani
back to the British at any point this would involve a loss of face. When news of her having
arrived at Nepal reached Dalhousie, he, understanding the Nepalese predicament, would refrain
from asking for her repatriation. A warning was sent out instead. 'I have not,' he wrote on the
matter, 'the least intention of going to war with Nepal for the Maharani Janda, so I have told the
Court of Nepal that I do not meddle with her; but that, as she is a bitter enemy of the British
Government, I hold Nepal, as a friendly power, responsible for her engaging in no intrigues
against us and doing no mischief, while she is in their territory.'

Jind Kaur would be given a modest allowance by the Nepalese Government for a stay that
would turn out to last twelve years. Jind Kaur would have long, frank conversations during

these months and years with Jang Bahadur in which she always protested she had been well disposed to the British. Only their meddling in Lahore affairs and the raising of her enemies like Tej Singh to great honour had made her an enemy. Her enemies, she said, had the ear of the Resident, which they used to the full extent to poison him against her. She had lost none of her fight, however, and was optimistic of a return to an independent Punjab, as evidenced by the story of a Capt. Shepherd stationed at Kathmandu. Summoned by the Prime Minster one day, she was asked about the future of the Punjab. Jind Kaur replied that it was predicted in the Sikh Granth (holy book) that one day she would return and that her son Duleep Singh would be a sovereign again. The Prime Minister was less impressed, replying, 'When you had treasure, troops and munitions of war at your command you could not hold the country and now that you do not possess a single tulwar it is absurd to think that you will ever recover it from its present possessors.'

Far from the opulence of former days, she nevertheless had comparative freedom in Nepal compared to the prison of Chunar. And this would have been the end of her story had it not been for her son, now older, requesting the opportunity to get together with his mother, an event which would lead to her residing in faraway London in the twilight of her years. Prematurely aged, half-blind and relatively young at forty-six, she passed away in 1863.

# 35

# The Black Prince of Perthshire

To-morrow we are to dine with little Duleep Singh, who is becoming more and more European every day, and was very anxious that I should do so.

Dalhousie, 26 December 1851

...he has been fairly rescued from those influences which warp the minds of the Porphyrogeniti of the East.

*Friend of India*, 17 March 1853

Almost at the same time as Jind Kaur's escape from Chunar to sanctuary in Nepal, the declaration of the annexation of the Punjab was being announced and her ten-year-old son Duleep Singh was being pensioned off. In her absence, John Login and his wife were appointed as British guardians of the Maharajah. Allowing the youngster to live his life in private and free of surveillance was out of the question for Dalhousie, who was anxious not to have him reared on stories of his lost throne and empire. The role of a guardian was therefore to look after the affairs of Duleep Singh while still a minor and secondly to ensure he did not become the focus or inspiration for further unrest should it occur.

Login would have an easy time in keeping the young Maharajah away from Sikh influence. The child was heavily traumatised by the palace coups and violence in the months before the First Anglo-Sikh War had broken out. An example of this was when he was being taken through Lahore by Login when they happened to pass the spot where his Uncle Jawahar Singh had been assassinated by the Sikh army nearly three years previously. He pointed out the exact spot where the incident happened and where he had watched from the howdah of his elephant, going as far to name the mahout who had been managing the elephant on that day.

These strong memories and the general fear of being murdered had alienated him from the court and servants that surrounded him. He had also been alienated somewhat from his mother, complaining at times to Login that she used to beat him every day. Login's friendship and kindness towards the impressionable youngster therefore quickly paid dividends and they rapidly became good friends, Login having a strong and increasing influence over the child. He also moved into the palace himself at this stage, with apartments adjacent to Duleep Singh's. 'He soon had a door of communication opened between his rooms and the Maharajah's apartments, as he found his charge was happier when he knew he had him always within call. He gravely informed his new Governor that he would not trust himself again amongst the Sikhs, and declined to go out for a ride or drive unless he was with him,' Lady Login would write of their early relationship.

Duleep Singh quickly began losing his family ties, virtually adopting the Logins as a surrogate father and mother. As mentioned by Henry Elliot to the Lahore Durbar, there always had been a plan to move Duleep Singh into a residence away from the Punjab after his deposition. No date had been planned as yet by Dalhousie. The pace of change was quickened, however, by a plot by nationalist elements to spirit Duleep Singh away from British hands during December 1849 when Dalhousie's first visit to Lahore was ongoing. Some of the irregular troops who were guarding Duleep Singh had been bribed and the plan was to take him while Dalhousie was conducting a review of the British troops in Lahore and where consequently most of the British troops, security and attention would be focussed. But some of these men informed their British officers and subsequently nine plotters were arrested. The suspicion for financing the operation was put on Duleep's mother, now in exile in Nepal, despite the fact she had little financial resources at this time. 'The Ranee has been at her tricks again, and again she has been foiled. Her agents are evidently not as clever as she is,' the *Delhi Gazette* reported. 'Some of her emissaries have been at Lahore tampering with the men of Prendergast's Irregular Cavalry Corps. But who as in Wheeler's Regiment, proved true, and gave notice of the intrigue to their commanding officer; the result has been the same. None of the intrigants have been caught in the city. And all of them are ci-de-vant "Kommedans" of Ranjit's better time, or in the employ of his successors.'

In order to prevent any similar plots in future and to remove any focus for revolution, plans were put in motion to remove all possible heirs to the throne of the Punjab to a secure British colony with a heavy guard. The place chosen was Fatehgarh, 700 km from Lahore, situated on the Ganges. Fatehgarh was a mainly European colony where they could be guarded with ease and any Sikh or other strangers turning up easily spotted. On 21 December, with a strong escort of artillery, cavalry and infantry, Duleep Singh set off to his new place of residence, never to return to the Punjab. He was accompanied by his guardian Login. Also accompanying him was the only other possible clamant to the former throne, Shahzada (Prince) Sheo Deo Singh, the son of Maharajah Shere Singh, the murdered former half-brother of Duleep. He was even younger than Duleep at six years of age, and his mother Rani Duknoo, refusing to part with her son, would be allowed to stay with him along with her uncle and brother. A small village of bungalows had been allocated for the party at Fatehgarh, with each bungalow having its own enclosure. Duleep Singh had the largest house followed by the Logins, with another being occupied by Sheo Deo and his party. Sikh priests had been found to be unwilling to travel the large distance with him to Fatehgarh and most of his Sikh companions were discouraged from coming along, so it was no surprise that the youngster quickly fell under the influence of the European society in the town.

'Everyone was struck with the young Sikh Sovereign's charm of manner; his geniality and love of truth, and his straightforwardness was very unusual in an Oriental,' Lady Login would remark during his stay at Fatehgarh. Even at that young age, however, he had some sense as to who he was and what had occurred in the Punjab recently. An amusing tale was related by Lady Login of how Duleep Singh once, after playing in the rain, refused to change into dry clothes despite the insistence of Dr Login, his argument being the Treaty of Lahore allowed him to do as he pleased.

Duleep Singh settled into a rather indolent life at Fatehgarh, with a leisurely daily routine organised by Login. In the early morning or evening, the Maharajah would go for his daily ride. This was either on his horse, an elephant or on other occasions his carriage, driven by an English coachman accompanied by Sheo Deo and other European boys of the settlement. A Sikh guard and a detachment of the Governor-General's bodyguard plus Skinner's irregulars in their saffron uniforms accompanied him at all times. This was followed by studies and exercise during the day where a teacher, Mr Guise, was put in charge of him and his education. Duleep developed a good friendship with an English lad and apparently did well in his studies, especially in English, with a friendly rivalry between him and the young man. Games were organised for Duleep including hide and seek and blind man's buff, which he and the boys of his age found delightful and in which all the adults joined. The evening was reserved for formality and Duleep Singh continued to hold a miniature court with the odd remnants of his courtiers who had been allowed to accompany him. These were Dewan Ajoodeah Pershad, Fakeer Zehoorudin, Sirdar Boor Singh Butaliwallah, along with several others who appeared in full dress and stayed with the deposed monarch for several hours before retiring. Some of the formalities of a court were still allowed him – the courtiers on entering his presence shouted 'Maharaj!', and the same on leaving with Duleep with the ex-monarch sitting impassively. Very occasionally he was allowed out of Fatehgarh, once to Agra to see the Taj Mahal and other sights. His courtiers, meanwhile, according to Lady Login spent their time endlessly discussing and disputing with her and her husband in friendly terms the meanings of the treaties of Lahore and Bhyrowal which together had deprived him of power.

By August of 1850, eight months after his departure from Lahore, as his few courtiers dropped away and his memories faded, Duleep Singh fell further into the European ways of the local British society. Eating beef was frowned upon in the Sikh society in deference to Hindu sentiments, the cow being seen by Hindus as sacred. There were rumours in the newspapers that he had begun emulating the Europeans in the habit of eating beef. What was certain was the all-pervading Christian influence in the place and he must have felt out of place on the Sundays as all the people he knew disappeared to attend the service in church. One of his native companions chosen for him and who had a strong impact on him was a Brahmin called Bhajan Lal. Lal had been studying in the local city high school and although not baptised was to all intents a Christian. Lal soon enjoyed the confidence of the prince and would ply the young Maharajah with stories from the Bible with all the fervour of a convert. Duleep gradually took up the ritual of going to the church services, trooping along with the Europeans and Indian converts in order not to be left behind to his own devices and soon after began showing a desire to convert to Christianity, to the apparent consternation of the non-Christian Indian staff and servants. Dalhousie's own view was that he was privately content at Duleep's decision although no pressure must be applied to encourage him in this direction. His conversion was to the benefit of the British and to the detriment of those seeking the resurrection of a Sikh dynasty and empire. 'My little friend Duleep has taken us all aback lately by declaring his resolution to become a Christian,' wrote Dalhousie in March 1851. 'The pundits, he says, tell him humbug; he has had the Bible read to him, and he believes the sahib's religion. The household, of course, are in a grand state. Politically we could desire nothing better, for it destroys his possible influence for ever. But I should have been glad if it had been deferred, since at present it may be represented to have been brought about by tampering with the mind of a child. This is not the case, it is his own free act, and apparently his firm resolution.'

By the end of the year Duleep was attending the daily Login family prayers at the Login house as well. By the end of the following year, 1852, at barely fourteen years of age he was seen openly clutching a Bible and prayer books and had decided to make his wish to become a Christian public. This wish was fulfilled several months later. On 8 March 1853, as the Anglo-Burmese War took much of the public attention, the chaplain of Fatehgarh, a Revd W. J. Jay went through a modest ceremony whereby the youngster underwent conversion to another faith. Duleep

Singh's own house was used and a large audience of Europeans civilians, military officers and some American missionaries along with Duleep's own servants witnessed the process.

There was some doubt and regret even among the European community that he should convert at this tender age with no opportunity for mature thought. Many felt that he should have been advised to consider this action at a later age and that his conversion might create discontent in the Punjab. A teenage prince had been extracted from his family and all he knew and was vulnerable to influence if not to pressure, depending as he did on the same people for all his wants and finances. Others, more zealously Christian, supported his conversion and felt at his age he was quite old enough to make his own decision. Among these was the Archdeacon of Calcutta, John Pratt, who argued he had not been encouraged by Login but had become disgusted by his own countrymen due to the assassinations and intrigues. It was an informed decision and entirely his own, he argued. There was support in some of the newspapers as well, lauding him as the first Christian prince on India and defending the event. 'A lad of this age in India is a man, with as great a capacity for estimating the merits of different creeds as he is ever likely to possess. From the time that he was placed under the charge of Dr Login, his education has been carefully provided for; and the boy who, when rescued from Lahore, could not even read, is now almost English in language, ideas and feelings. His conduct with reference to the ceremonial salutes, and his visit to the Governor-General are sufficient proofs that his judgment is not beneath his acquirements, and that he has been fairly rescued from those influences that warp the minds of the Porphyrogeniti of the East,' pontificated the *Friend of India* on 17 March 1853. 'His conversion will at least save the palace Futtehgurh from becoming like that of Delhi, a place whither evil naturally seeks shelter; and a native Christian noble, with vast wealth, may accomplish far more good than a hundred ordinary converts.'

After his conversion, and bereft of any real responsibilities and direction as he grew older, Duleep Singh showed an increasing interest in visiting and donating large sums to Christian charities. He would establish relief societies at Fatehgarh, giving control of these to the American missions present. He would also support ten village mission schools in the Fatehgarh area. He was at this time suspected to be spending around a tenth of his pension on the causes of the Church and related charities and schools. He had also redoubled his requests to see England and Europe, having expressed a strong interest in going to England for some time, ostensibly in order to improve his mind with travel. Dalhousie was wary of allowing him to do so. 'He is wild to be allowed to do so, not that he wishes to be made a fool of, like the Rajah of Coorg, or Jung Bahadur, but because his fancy is to be European in all his tastes, and he is dying to see Europe and all its wonders. He told me he used to dream every night that he was visiting the Duke of Wellington. That dream, unhappily, can never come true.'

The duke had died already, but nevertheless he sanctioned the trip after a time and preparations were made for Duleep Singh's voyage to England. Duleep left Fatehgarh for the final time on 5 March 1854, reaching and staying in Government House, Barrackpore in early April where he dined with Dalhousie before sailing for England on 19 April 1854. Accompanying him was his party of officers and Login, along with a superb Arab charger for riding. He was treated with honour by the various British authorities at each port meeting and dining with the Governor of Malta as he crossed the Mediterranean. At Gibraltar a salute was fired in his honour. On board the *Columbo*, he occupied himself by playing chess with fellow passengers before reaching Southampton on 18 June 1854. Two weeks later, on 1 July, he was presented to the queen, who had so much curiosity about the Maharajah from the Punjab. The queen and

Prince Albert would provide him with suitable accommodation in Wimbledon and showed him much kindness.

Given a pension and with no responsibilities, Duleep Singh would settle into the life of a country squire, whiling away the years in spendthrift and reckless abandon first in Scotland, where he earned the title the 'Black Prince of Perthshire', and then later in Thetford in Norfolk. It was only much later in his life that he would come to regret the indolence of these years and go chasing after the empire that he had lost as a youth. He would die an obese but still young man in his fifties in a downmarket hotel in Paris.

# THE BATTLEFIELDS

The soil appears made of lead; bullets strew the ground like pebbles.
British officer's letter, *Delhi Gazette*, 25 January 1849

The fortress as it stood when we attacked it, never can exist again.
Dalhousie, 21 January 1850

# 36

# Multan after the Battle

On 23 January, the day after the surrender of the fortress garrison and the end of the siege of Multan, Major Wheeler was deputed to search for the hidden riches inside the fortress and city. As an assistant he had an aged and bedridden *mistree* (builder) from the time of the previous governor, Sawan Mull. The *mistree* had been in charge of the construction of the subterranean storehouses and treasuries of the city and fortress along with its hidden vaults and so had valuable information. He agreed to help on being offered a substantial sum for his assistance in locating the wealth. The main underground structures were built inside the fort but their entrances were by now heavily covered by debris which took several days to clear before ingress could be achieved. Silk cloth and Kashmir shawls in large amounts, accumulated over the time of Sawan Mull and his son, along with ghee and grain were discovered in addition to stores of indigo and opium worth substantial amounts. Money was also found. It was estimated 2–3 lakh rupees alone had been blown up during the pounding the fortress had taken.

'In the mint, a pretty good amount of silver and gold coin was found. Moolraj's house and the neighbouring Toshakhana [treasury] contained a great quantity as also many valuable swords and rich property of every description,' wrote an officer who left one of the more comprehensive descriptions of what he found in a letter to the *Delhi Gazette*:

> The fort is reduced to such a heap of ruins that it will require many months to excavate and remove the fallen houses. The site of the explosions is marked by a long deep pit around which buildings are piled on buildings; scarcely one brick remains on another. Corpses, carcasses of animals and every description of property strew the ground; the stench within the citadel is dreadful; there must be hundreds of men buried in the rubbish. The piles of huge stone shot have been hurled to a great distance and the contents of large bomb proofs showered far and wide upon the occupants of the place. The Bahawul Huk shrine is reduced to a mere wreck but that of Shah Rookn Alum has been more fortunate; it has escaped with only a few scars … Within the courtyard of this shrine there is a newly-built range of bombproof barracks; in these, some valuable property has been stowed away. Moolraj's house appears to have been once a good substantial one. It is unroofed, and the walls are knocked to pieces with our shells; he appears to have vacated it long ago. There is a large garden with raised walks, which appear to have been nicely laid out. Between this and the before mentioned tomb there is an enormous domed magazine, surrounded by a dry ditch several feet deep. A trench has been cut to communicate with it underground, and the surface being closely packed with logs of timber, a mine is suspected; double sentries have been placed as a precaution against accidents. The stables, godowns, and arsenals are built in long ranges behind the citadel wall; they are mostly protected by domed roofs of considerable thickness, but our shells have penetrated them, and set fire to the contents; many dead and wounded men, on charpoys were found in them. In a large timber yard, wheels for guns of all sizes, and Zumbooruk saddles, newly made, are lying about in great profusion.

Near the ramparts were two of the furnaces for producing new guns. The mould of a large cannon was lying nearby in such a fashion that it was obvious the garrison were in the process of manufacturing it before the order to surrender. Everywhere loose gunpowder abounded in holes in the ground. This gunpowder made walking through the structure a danger, with logs of wood and other material still being on fire. Camp followers were by now spreading through the city and fortress scrambling for booty, either ignorant or indifferent this danger. Several small explosions had already taken place and various people badly burnt although there were no deaths. 'The soil appears made of lead. Bullets strew the ground like pebbles; the supply would have lasted for years had the garrison held out; cannon-balls are equally common, from those stone ones of Brobdingnagian proportion, to the Lilliputian for one pounders,' the officer continued.

One of the more poignant discoveries made in one of chambers in the fortress was the remnants of Kahn Singh, the would-be new governor killed during the grand explosion. There was always a suspicion as to which side Kahn Singh had taken. Edwardes among others had suspected he had had sympathies with Mulraj all the way through. He had speculated the new governor had asked to be kept in chains as a ploy. This was to fool the British so that his jaghirs and wealth would not be confiscated by the British Resident. Otherwise, he argued, surely Kahn Singh would have been killed along with Agnew and Anderson at the Eidgah. Despite this far-fetched theory, he was kind enough to give him the benefit of the doubt in death. 'After the fall of the fort, his body was dug out, and was found so heavily ironed, that it must have been impossible for him to walk. His little boy had been apparently sleeping beside him on the bed; and the attitudes of calm repose in which both remained even in decay, showed that they had never awakened, but passed with awful suddenness from sleep to death. Under these circumstances, I thought it right to adopt the most charitable construction of the Sirdar's conduct, caused him to be buried with all honour, and sent the gold bangles which were on the arms of his son to the surviving members of the family.'

By this time, the treasure in some of the concealed underground chambers had been found and over the next few days tumbrils were sent into the fortress to collect and transport the gold coin – said to be worth between three or four crore rupees. Some places where money and wealth was strongly rumoured to be kept were only known to Mulraj, who it was suspected would use this knowledge as a negotiation point for a lighter sentence. The total booty in the fort at this point, excluding the hidden chambers, stood at £1 million (approximately £80-100 million in today's money). Since Multan was the territory of the Lahore state, it was supposed it would be passed to Lahore in the first instance before being diverted into company coffers to meet the expenses of the war.

Two distinct types of booty were captured, the main haul from the city and the second haul from the fortress. The sale of the booty from the city would on its own raise nearly 12.5 lakh rupees. Mulraj had a substantial amount of gold in the fort and had been minting his own gold coins to the value of 20 lakh rupees to pay the troops. Curiously, much of this Multan coinage was already finding its way as far as Ludhiana and other British territories owing to the pay of the irregulars from afar who had joined his banner. Even more curiously, several samples of Mulraj's gold coins were known to have been reached as far as England by the end of the war. Mulraj in turn had various foreign currencies in his treasury, gold dollar coins from America being part of the haul discovered. 'Daily discoveries were being made in the fort and the prize prospects were looking up thanks to Major Wheeler and Capt. Hobson of the Bombay division whose experience renders them au fait at the task,' the *Delhi Gazette* would report.

Even before the fall of the fortress, attempts were being made to revive the city. By 7 January, Courtlandt had been placed in charge of the broken city and its surroundings with the order to re-establish order and encourage the city dwellers and shopkeepers to return to their abodes. He was only partially successful, with people none too enthusiastic to re-enter a metropolis that was in such ruin. Meanwhile the clearing of the city began to gather pace, with corpses removed and the rubble filling the city taking attention. The trenches and approaches dug by the British force were ordered to be filled in and bridges over the canals repaired.

Dalhousie had initially decided that the city must pay a fine in the form of increased taxation for a set number of years. With Multan entirely on its knees and commerce at a standstill during the following months, it was realised the ransom imposed would never be paid and moreover would hamper recovery of the city as many of the merchants, fearing the heavy tax, were reluctant to return. The demand was reduced to 20 lakh rupees, but general feeling was that even 15 lakh rupees would not be raised, such was the devastation.

***

Command of the fortress would be given to Major Scott of the Bombay Engineers, whose job it was to resurrect its defences. This meant filling in the breaches and repairing the ditch scarping, etc. A fuller report was requested from Scott in due course, the Governor-General wishing to make a decision on whether the money and effort required to repair the fortress was reasonable or whether the structure should be razed to the ground instead. Based on his report, it was initially decided to repair the fortress as far as was practical.

The ruins would not survive long. Clear weather characterised the following few months at Multan but heavy rains inundated the area in the second half of the year. After an unusually hot day, 16 August 1849, large storm clouds began to gather, and soon after it began to rain heavily, with 3 inches of rain recorded during the first night. The rain continued unabated, so much so that the whole area around the city resembled a giant lake after a few days. The fort walls and many of the buildings, already having sustained heavy damage from the British guns and the magazine explosion of 30 December, were vulnerable. Several sections of the walls round the city fell during the rains, burying some unfortunate victims of the garrison. The walls and the domes of the fortress especially were thought to be near to collapse and the British troops began moving out, preferring to live in tents than chance being entombed by the collapsing walls. Four of the domes of various fort buildings would fall in, it was noted, nearly killing a sepoy who had taken shelter there despite the risks. As the rains continued many of the mud walls round the city began dissolving as well. Nevertheless, the fort, being built on a height, was still in a more comfortable position than the city itself and its surroundings. People could be seen gathering on high points all around the city.

'The destruction to the fort has been very great and we are at present on an island all around being flooded,' wrote one of the men of the garrison. So heavy was the inundation that the ditch began filling with water, affecting the counterscarp. The brick walls of the fort, with the ground around them dissolving, were expected to collapse in various parts. But it wasn't the walls but the Muslim shrine inside that collapsed first on 17 August. 'At 10 this morning we were all startled by what at first was thought to be an earthquake but it was soon discovered that the enormous dome of the beautiful shrine of Bhawul Huk (injured by our shot), had fallen in with a noise like thunder; fortunately the fakirs were all at a distance; it is now a perfect heap of ruins. Another fall of rain will lay the famous fort of Mooltan flat, being built on an old site, perfectly honeycombed in all directions; it is dangerous to ride about, the earth everywhere giving way. A Major of artillery and his horse were nearly swallowed up in one of these immense fissures, and several small treasures have been discovered to the prize agent by the ground opening,' wrote one of the soldiers stationed in the city.

The firing of gun salutes was prohibited at this time in the fort in case the vibrations or noise should trigger a further fall of the walls. On 23 August 1848, what had been expected for some time finally occurred. A strong current from the river broke its banks and swept up towards the fortress, completely inundating the ditch and triggering the collapse of large sections of the bastions and walls, also destroying the huts of the sepoy garrison outside the fortress walls. Despite the dangerous condition of the structure, it happened to be the only place above water and so had drawn the other sections of the garrison of the city. By the following day water began making its way into the fort itself despite its high position. The horses of the cavalry were seen swimming off to high points outside the city. 'The whole country was one magnificent lake studded with innumerable islands on which the people and their live stock sought refuge boats and rafts being the only means of communication,' a major of artillery lamented. No such flood had come before within living memory in the city.

Dalhousie visited Multan in the early days of January 1850, when the city had recovered somewhat from the recent flooding. 'The visit to Mooltan was interesting, as you may well conceive. My camp was pitched alongside the Eidgah where poor Agnew and Anderson were murdered, and the gibbet on which retribution was inflicted on their murderers still stood before the gate. The marks of the bombardment were still ruinously evident, and the fort stood a crumbling mass. The inner line of fortifications may be made serviceable again; the fortress as it stood when we attacked it, never can exist again. It was like a story-book, seeing the Sikhi gate, and the Ram Teerut, and the Blue Mosque, and all the places one had read of from day to day with intense interest, and it was difficult to realise the hard matter of fact to oneself.'

He was fortunate enough to see the city and fortress in its present incarnation, complete with battle damage, for further misfortunes would hit the city a year later. A substantial earthquake was experienced by the city on the night of 9 January 1851. It was described by one of the European residents as one of the most violent he had witnessed in India and which further undermined the remnants of the fortress. Finally, in mid-1852, with the fortress walls in ever more parlous condition, the decision was taken to demolish the structure entirely, it being considered in too precarious a state.

## Multan Now
### The fortress (30.198320°N, 71.473051°E)
Owing to its demolition very little of the fort now exists, although the two shrines of Hazrat Bahauddin Zakariya and Shah Rukn-e-Alam positioned inside the former walls give telltale indications of the eastern and western extremities of the fortress. The position of the former fortress being on an elevation, there are good views of the city from the mound. Roads allow an easy exploration of what would have been the structure's 2 km perimeter. None of the old structures inside the fortress survive, although many are easy to imagine. The garrison barracks lined the fortress walls while Mulraj's residence was roughly in the middle of the fortress.

*Tomb of Shah Rukn-e-Alam (30.199178°N, 71.471699°E)*
The tomb was situated just inside the westernmost part of the former fortress. Its dome could be seen from outside the walls during the time of the siege and in turn provided the defenders with a good view of the besiegers.

*Bahauddin Zakariya (30.200666°N, 71.476457°E)*
The shrine was situated just inside the eastern end of the Multan fortress. The structure was completely destroyed during the siege but was subsequently restored.

### The fortress gates
*Position of the Sikhi gate (30.198569°N, 71.477181°E)*
The Sikhi gate was situated on the east of the fortress, being used to gain entrance into the fortress after passing through the Dowlut gate of the city walls.

*Position of the Rehri gate (30.195601°N, 71.474065°E)*
The Rehri gate was directly connected to the Delhi gate.

*Position of the De (or Delhi) gate (30°11'55.07"N, 71°28'14.76"E)*
Only this gate, the westernmost of the four, survives, although in a new incarnation.

*Approximate position of the Khidri (Khizri) gate (30°12'4.18"N, 71°28'29.99"E)*

### Internal road through the fortress (30°11'55.02"N, 71°28'15.89"E)
The fortress was bisected from west to east by a road connecting the De gate to the Sikhi gate.

### British memorial obelisk (30.198715°N, 71.474845°E)
The obelisk in memory to the two murdered officers made of sandstone rises 50 feet high. The inscription on the monument is by Sir Herbert Edwardes. The obelisk was constructed sometime after 1864 for it doesn't feature in descriptions of the city before this date.

During the period after its construction it formed the centre of a garden complete with waterfalls and pavilions, although these have long since disappeared. A visitor to the monument mentions the foundations of the obelisk having been weakened during the laying of the garden, with the podium and the steps having begun to decay from their pristine condition after 1864.

### Surya Sun Temple (30°12'1.25"N, 71°28'36.84"E)
Remains of the old Hindu temple situated inside the fortress and used by Mulraj for worship.

### Qasim Bagh stadium/approximate position of the Jami Masjid (or Grand Mosque) (30°11'50.79"N, 71°28'27.64"E)
The mosque building was used as the main magazine inside the fortress. Its destruction signalled one of the largest explosions of the nineteenth century.

### Old road connecting Rehri gate to Delhi gate (30°11'34.30"N, 71°28'36.56"E)
The old road in the walled city still exists and was the one of the routes used by Mughal rulers to enter the fortress, being the direct route from Delhi.

### The Esplanade (30.196276°N, 71.472456°E)
The area between the citadel and the city walls was formerly a channel of the Chenab River but had long been dry. The space next to the fortress walls was occupied by stables for cavalry horses as well as the several hundred kine and beasts of burden used by the garrison. The space is now used by the Hussain Agahi main road, part of the road system circling the position of the former citadel.

### The walled city
*City walls*
The city walls encompassed the old city, which lay directly south of the citadel. The higher parts of the original wall round the city, 40–50 feet high, were demolished in 1854, the walls being restricted to 10 or 12 feet in height for purposes of sanitation.

*Chowk bazaar road (30°11'33.79"N, 71°28'21.44"E)*
The main commercial thoroughfare of the walled city, running north to south, bisected the city from the Haram gate to the Rehri gate.

### The city gates
The Bohar, Haram and the Delhi gates were rebuilt later in the century and are therefore not original.

*The Daulat gate (30.197692°N, 71.478627°E)*
This gate has now entirely disappeared and the location is only marked by the nearby tomb of the Muslim saint Pir Doulat Shah, from whose name the gate took its name and which still draws devotees.

*The Delhi gate (30.192186°N, 71.478083°E)*
The breach of the Delhi gate during the siege meant the complete destruction of the original gate and one of the oldest landmarks of the city. The city walls in the vicinity of the gate were noted to be around 30 feet in height. The gate was rebuilt after the war, its purpose being as a memorial to the fighting during the war. The design was of a European style with small gothic windows. The gate is similar in construction to the Bohar and Haram gates but with a wider span. It is now a freestanding structure bereft of its connecting walls.

*Khooni Burj (30.187390°N, 71.475206°E)*
The Khooni Burj (or bloody tower) received plenty of attention during the siege and was a few hundred feet south of one of the two breaches made in the eastern walls of the city during the second siege.

*Approximate location of south breach (30°11'17.84"N, 71°28'32.75"E)*
The breach in the walls during the second siege of the city was made a few hundred feet north of the
Khooni Burj.

*The Pak gate (30.188329°N, 71.472671°E)*
The tomb of the Saint Hazrat Musa Pak Shaheed from which the gate took its name lies 300 feet from the
gate location itself.

*The Haram gate (30.190145°N, 71.469422°E)*
The gate providing ingress from the south of the city.

*The Bohar gate (30.193692°N, 71.465221°E)*
The Bohar gate to the south-west of the city was extensively damaged during the siege and entirely
demolished in 1854 as the city revived. A new gate, a double-storey structure with castellated towers, stands
in its place.

*The Lohari gate (30.197926°N, 71.468538°E)*
The Lohari gate was demolished in 1854 and replaced with a plainer double-storey structure.

**Outside the walled city**
*The Eidgah (30.210778°N, 71.478873°E)*
The mosque where the two British officers were killed by a mob stands around 1.5 km due north of the
Dowlut gate area.

*Eidgah road (30.203570°N, 71.479719°E)*
The road north to Lahore leads from the east of the fort to the Eidgah and was used by Agnew to return to
the Eidgah. The same road was used to escort Mulraj to Lahore after his surrender.

*Approximate former burial place of Agnew and Anderson (30.211324°N, 71.481295°E)*
The two officers were initially buried by Afghan merchants a few feet to the right of the road leading to
Lahore and opposite the Eidgah.

*Tomb of Sawan Mull (30.200429°N, 71.487927°E)*
The tomb of Mulraj's father was used by British troops as a shelter during the siege. It escaped significant
damage from the guns due to its distance from the fort.

*Aam Khas (30.197481°N, 71.481923°E)*
The Aam Khas, formerly the residence of Mulraj outside the walled city, is now a garden with none of the
original buildings surviving.

*Tomb of Shah Shams Tabraiz (30.201120°N, 71.484042°E)*
The tomb was used as a shelter by British troops during the siege.

**Related locations in Multan province or nearby**
*Leiah (30.961609°N, 70.941557°E)*
Leiah was held by a kardar of Mulraj but was captured by Herbert Edwardes early on in the
campaign. A desultory battle was fought outside the city between a Mulraj contingent and
Edwardes, ending in a victory for the British officer.

*Jhung (31.265719°N, 72.313488°E)*
Passed by Shere Singh on his way north to Ramnuggar after leaving Multan. The city was partly sacked in revenge for the inhabitants assisting the British in their attempts to capture or kill Bhai Maharaj.

*Toulumba (30.524802°N, 72.239871°E)*
The city was passed by Agnew's retinue on the way to Multan and was where his party received the first warnings of the mutinous nature of the garrison at Multan.

*Dera Ghazi Khan (30° 2'52.39"N, 70°38'39.38"E)*
The city close to the right bank of the Indus was captured by Herbert Edwardes prior to his crossing the Indus to join forces with the Bhawulpore forces before a push towards Multan.

*Dera Ismael Khan (31°49'56.32"N, 70°54'8.36"E)*
News of the Multan emeute was given to Hebert Edwardes when he was situated in Dera Ishmael Khan.

**Battle of Kyneerie**
Kyneerie was the first battle to be fought by Mulraj and Edwardes and ended in a defeat of Mulraj's force.

*Khangurh (29°54'50.16"N, 71° 9'34.55"E)*

*Shujabad (29°52'49.87"N, 71°17'41.73"E)*
Town which fell to Edwardes after Kyneerie after his march north towards Multan.

*Shujabad Fort (29°52'52.15"N, 71°17'35.32"E)*
Fortress of Shujabad which fell to Edwardes after Kyneerie.

*Tibiwala (29°57'10.07"N, 71°19'32.52"E)*
Town and fort which fell to Edwardes after Kyneerie.

*Secunderabad (29°57'57.27"N, 71°21'37.38"E)*
Town on the way north towards Multan and which fell to Herbert Edwardes.

**Battle of Suraj Khund**
*Suraj Khund village (30.132354°N, 71.441971°E)*
Suraj Khund was the third battle between Mulraj and Edwardes' forces. Whish and Edwardes' force was drawn up to the north of the village.

*Suraj Khund tank (30.132196°N, 71.441183°E)*
An important and historic holy Hindu lake which Dewan Mulraj used to visit during Dussehra, a Hindu festival.

*Wollee Mohammed's Canal or Grand Canal (30.133209°N, 71.444098°E)*
The Multan force was drawn up on the east of the canal prior to the battle with Edwardes.

**British areas of importance**
*Ferozepore (30.964499°N, 74.609805°E)*
British cantonment nearest to Sikh territory and from where the bulk of the troops set out for Multan and later to counter the Sikh army under Shere Singh.

*Makhu village (31.108110°N, 74.976556°E)*
Village used as camp by Dalhousie on reaching the Punjab. It lies around 10 km south-east of the battlefield of Sabraon, the last battle of the First Anglo-Sikh War.

*Bhawulpore (29.397100°N, 71.670483°E)*
Muslim state on the left bank of the Sutlej which was friendly towards the British and which aided in the siege of Multan.

*Simla (31.104453°N, 77.172718°E)*
The summer capital of British India.

*Sabathu (30.975466°N, 76.990247°E)*
One of the northernmost British cantonment towns during the Anglo-Sikh wars.

# 37

# The Chenab Jhelum Theatre

Went over the field of battle. A good many bodies: all Sikhs;
very handsome men – many very old.

Colin Campbell, Gujrat battlefield, 26 February 1849

Such are the horrors perpetrated by man for a few miles of land, a quibble in a treaty, or a short-
lived glory. God! how is glory obtained, that men should be so proud of it!

Daniel Sandford, Chillianwala battlefield, 12 February 1849

No monument was ever planned for either Ramnuggar and Sadulpore or even Chillianwala after the
conflict. The popular opinion, to which Dalhousie subscribed, was that a monument to the war should be
constructed on the battlefield of Gujrat where the war was won. Nevertheless, a monument would appear at
Chillianwala in due course and with the sanction of the Governor-General on his second visit to the Punjab
in late 1850. The suggestion for the construction of a wall around the British graveyard first appeared in
the *Delhi Gazette*:

> A correspondent has addressed us on the subject of protecting, in some suitable manner, the graves
> of the brave men who fell at Chillianwala, and whose mortal remains, interred in a comparative
> wilderness, have been hitherto, necessarily, left exposed to the attacks of the beasts of prey that
> abound there as well as in other parts of India. The suggestion made by our correspondent and
> supported by a donation of 16 rupees, is one deserving the attention of the friends of those who died
> nobly doing their duty on the battle field. The enclosure required is, we believe, not a large one, and
> the addition of a small stone obelisk, with the names of those who lie buried within the enclosure,
> engraved thereon, would not very materially increase the expense, and hand some permanent record
> of the battle of Chillianwala down to posterity.

By July 1849 a 4-foot wall had already been constructed around the graves at Gujrat, paid for by officers
of the engineers and artillery, and a similar wall was begun at Chillianwala. In April 1850, an account by a
visitor to the Chillianwala graveyard appeared in the *Bombay Times*:

> The wall around the graves is complete and it appears a solid and durable structure of considerable
> architectural beauty. The gateway is in keeping with the other portions of the structure, and when
> a suitable gate is added will doubtless have all the effect that could be wished. The intended site of
> the obelisk (which is I believe to be of solid stone) is traced out, and the foundation is partly dug.
> I trust I am right in saying partly, because in my humble opinion it should be at least three times as
> deep as it is as present. If the funds have anything to do with the depth of the foundation, I would
> suggest that the shaft be left out of the plan for the present, and the foundation and base made as
> solid as possible. I feel a conviction that should larger funds be required, they will, on representation

from the proper quarter, be readily advanced. There are, if I counted aright fifty-one graves within the wall distinctly visible.

Only one of the tombs, that of Lt Aurelian Money of the 25th BNI, had an inscription at this time. Other graves had been given little attention, the graves of Pennycuick and his son for instance having merely a covering of loose red bricks to mark the spot. 'The situation of this graveyard is particularly well calculated for the erection of a lasting memorial, for it consists of a mound of considerable extent, with a binding soil, and no lodgment for water. The wall at present, cased as it is with white chunam, can be seen for a very considerable distance; and when an obelisk is added, it will be visible for many miles around,' opined another visitor in the *Bombay Times*, adding that the obelisk to be raised would have been better at Gujrat.

7,000 rupees had already been spent on a monument by the end of December 1850, with another 3,000 required to complete it although these funds seemed to be in short supply. Dalhousie showed little interest in its completion, despite promising to donate a sum out of his own private purse. 'His lordship declines to lend any aid on the part of Government, thinking that "so expensive and conspicuous a monument", if erected at all, "would be more appropriate for Goojrat than Chillianwallah", reported the *Delhi Gazette*.

By the end of May 1853, despite financial constraints, the grey sandstone Chillianwala monument was nearly completed. It stood 70 feet high on its mound and, being 120 feet higher than the surrounding area, could be seen at a considerable distance. There were apparently insufficient funds to inscribe the names of the British dead on the monument which was the original plan and there were calls in certain quarters from interested parties that extra funds should be raised by a penny subscription to complete the work, although nothing would come of this.

### Before the War
*Attari village (31.599263°N, 74.605597°E)*
The home village of Chutter Singh and Shere Singh and where they were allowed to stay after the war under strict conditions. They were later arrested and incarcerated at Fort William, Calcutta.

### First Anglo-Sikh War battlefields
*Mudki (30.808466°N, 74.844379°E)*

*Ferozeshah (30.878754°N, 74.787568°E)*

*Bhudowal (30.859908°N, 75.746990°E)*

*Aliwal (30.944525°N, 75.611408°E)*

*Sabraon (31.137914°N, 74.871189°E)*

### The British advance to Lahore
*Crossing of the Sutlej (30.993016°N, 74.549251°E)*
The British force crossed by pontoon bridge at the Gunda Singh Wala ford opposite Ferozepore.

*Kasur (31.121788°N, 74.451363°E)*
The town and its fort was occupied by the British force as they advanced towards the capital.

*Lullianee (31.252829°N, 74.420471°E)*
Village en route to Lahore where Duleep Singh was brought to tender submission to the British Governor-General.

*Khana Kutch (31.351910°N, 74.373497°E)*
Village used as encampment by the British force en route to Lahore.

*Bhyrowal village (31.394383°N, 75.073855°E)*
The treaty which effectively signed away the independence of the country was signed by the Lahore Durbar and Hardinge at the small village near the Beas River that Hardinge had made his camp during late December 1846.

**Lahore and main sites around the Punjab**
*Fort and palace (31.588399°N, 74.314083°E)*
The fort, which functioned as the seat of power of the Sikh government and palace for the Sikh Maharajas, was originally constructed by the Mughal Emperor Akbar.

*Athdara (31.589699°N, 74.313391°E)*
Pavilion inside Lahore fort commonly used by Ranjit Singh for holding court.

*Ranjit Singh's mausoleum (31.589196°N, 74.311308°E)*
The founder of the Sikh state was cremated in 1839, with his ashes stored in the mausoleum opposite the fort and palace.

*Akbari gate (31.588488°N, 74.312575°)*
The Akbari gate was the main fort entrance and which was used for all formal occasions.

*Baradari area outside the fort (31.588407°N, 74.311750°E)*
The area between the main entrance of the Lahore fort and the Badshahi Mosque was occupied by the British force immediately after the first war. The occupation continued till the end of the war and annexation when the troops were moved into the fort.

*Badshahi Mosque (31.588160°N, 74.310133°E)*
The main mosque of the city, opposite the Lahore fort, had been built by the Mughal Emperor Aurangzeb and was latterly used as stables and encampment for Sikh troops. The structure was also occupied by the British garrison after the First Anglo-Sikh War.

*Walled city (31.581737°N, 74.319659°E)*
The old city was enclosed within the 6 km perimeter walled area to the south and east of the adjoining fort.

*Shalimar Gardens (31.586957°N, 74.382133°E)*
Pleasure gardens used by Mughal emperors and latterly Ranjit Singh and the Sikh nobility around 7 km east of the walled city. The Prema Plot, a failed scheme to kill the Lahore Resident and main members of the Lahore Durbar, was to have been executed at the gardens in February 1847.

*Tomb of Anarkali (31.567395°N, 74.300631°E)*
The tomb was used as an office by Henry Lawrence during his period of Residency at Lahore.

*Bridge across the Ravi River (31.611309°N, 74.299280°E)*
The main crossing point, the location of bridge of boats across the Ravi was situated directly opposite the fort. It was approached by advance units of Shere Singh's army but secured by the British garrison in the city prior to the advance into the Punjab.

**Amritsar**
*Harimandir Sahib (31.619907°N, 74.876554°E)*
Harmandir Sahib (commonly referred to as the Golden Temple), the most important of the holy places of the Sikh faith.

*Gobindgarh fortress (31.626953°N, 74.860330°E)*
The fortress doubled as a second treasury for Ranjit Singh and garrison for the city of Amritsar. The fort was capture by ruse on orders of Frederick Currie as war began breaking out after the defection of Shere Singh and his men.

**Kangra**
*Kangra fortress (32.087427°N, 76.253732°E)*
The citadel which protected the easternmost possessions of Ranjit Singh. The fortress, being situated in the Jullunder doab, was to have been ceded to the British after the Treaty of Lahore but the Commandant of the fortress refused to hand over control, only doing so when sufficient siege guns had been brought to bombard the structure.

**Sheikhupura (31.711429°N, 73.997515°E)**
One of the main provincial towns of the Punjab and situated 30 km due west of Lahore.

*Sheikhupura fort (31.708892°N, 73.990239°E)*
The Maharani of Lahore, Jind Kaur was held prisoner in the fortress of Sheikhupura before being exiled into British territory after the breakout of hostilities.

**The Jalandhar Rebellion**
*Pathankot (32.264432°N, 75.644788°E)*
The small fort and police station of Pathankot was twice attacked by Ram Singh Pathania during his rebellion.

*Dulla Dher (32.222064°N, 76.221655°E)*
Ram Singh Pathania set up his rebel camp in the Dulla Dher hilly area during early 1849.

*Shahpur Kandi (32.382819°N, 75.675966°E)*
Ram Singh Pathania would attack the small fort at Shapur Kandi during his uprising. He was also finally apprehended by the British authorities just a few miles from the fort.

*Nurpur (32.302954°N, 75.880509°E)*
Petty state from which Ram Singh Pathania originated.

*Ram Singh's redoubt near Nurpur (32.278374°N, 75.883346°E)*
Large hilly area which was made rebel camp by Ram Singh. The whole area was subsequently blockaded by the British but Ram Singh managed to escape with most of his followers.

*Bassa village (32.272463°N, 75.872507°E)*
Major Fisher commanded the 15th Irregular Cavalry and the 16th to the south and south-west at the villages of Bassa and Jach during the attempt to capture Ram Singh in his redoubt near Nurpur.

*Jach (32.280851°N, 75.862086°E)*
See above.

*Deena Nuggar (32.131717°N, 75.467669°E)*
The town was a stronghold of Bhai Maharaj where he received plenty of sympathy from locals.

*Mukerian (31.952814°N, 75.613399°E)*
One of the British garrison towns in Jalandhar and from where troops were sent to combat Ram Singh Pathania.

*Hajeepore (31.974055°N, 75.753503°E)*
Area under the support of the rebel Bedee Bikram Singh.

*Chakki (Chukki) River (32.326180°N, 75.800908°E)*
River flowing through the Pathankot area.

*Teerah Sujanpur (31.832706°N, 76.500110°E)*
The small area under the control of the rebelling Raja of Katoch.

**Hazara province**
*Haripur (33.998066°N, 72.936823°E)*
Main administrative city of Hazara province during the Anglo-Sikh war period and where Chutter Singh, the nominal governor of the province had his camp.

*Abbottabad (34.145352°N, 73.213194°E)*
City founded in January 1853 and named after James Abbott, the effective governor of the province between the Anglo-Sikh wars.

*Shirwaun (34.203321°N, 73.069626°E)*
Town where James Abbott had made his camp before and during the troubles in Hazara.

*Hassan Abdul (33.822037°N, 72.686857°E)*
Major city en route to Peshawar from Rawalpindi on what would become the Grand Trunk road.

**Peshawar province**
*Peshawar town (34.014924°N, 71.584196°E)*
The main administrative centre of Peshawar province.

*Nowshera (34.016132°N, 71.973931°E)*
Large town to the east of Peshawar. The location was famous for a battle between Sikh and Afghan forces in March 1823 in which the Afghan influence was finally ejected from the province.

*Jamrud fort (34.003134°N, 71.378768°E)*
Historic fortress built to protect the Khyber Pass on the Peshawar side.

*Bala Hissar fort (34.012477°N, 71.570049°E)*
Ancient citadel of Peshawar town.

*Kohat city (33.585845°N 71.439606°E)*
Sultan Mohammad Khan, brother of Dost Mohammad, ruler of Kabul, was the Sikh-appointed governor of Kohat province. Sultan Mohammad Khan would transfer George Lawrence and his family and other European prisoners to Chutter Singh after the conflict broke out in Peshawar.

*Fortress of Attock (33.891834°N, 72.234880°E)*
The fortress of Attock guarded the passage over the Indus on the Peshawar to Lahore road. It was held by Lt Herbert and a garrison of Afghan irregulars till the arrival of the Afghan army under Dost Mohammad into Peshawar in early January 1849 after which the Afghan garrison surrendered.

*Indus River bridge of boats location (33.893853°N, 72.233021°E)*
The bridge of boats was formerly close by and under the guns of the fortress of Attock, just a few hundred metres downstream of the two modern bridges.

*Khairabad (33.894712°N, 72.229155°E)*
Town situated on the right bank of the Indus and opposite the fortress of Attock. The Afghan army in its retreat after the Battle of Gujrat attempted a nominal stand on the right bank here against Gilbert's force before continuing their retreat back to Kabul.

*Kabul River's junction with the Indus (33.890973°N, 72.207869°)*

*Entrance of Khyber Pass (34.006132°N, 71.307962°E)*
Traditional entry point into Peshawar and India for Afghan and other invaders.

## The Main Battlefields
### Battle of Ramnuggar
### *British march to Ramnuggar*
*Shahdara (31.620845°N, 74.282147°E)*
Situated on the right bank of the Ravi River, Shahdara village was used by Gough as first encampment in the Rechna doab after his crossing of the stream.

*Muttaa (Mattoo) (31.986343°N, 73.991327°E)*
This village is mentioned in accounts as a stop by Gough and the main British force prior to Ramnuggar.

*Dera Dhariwal (31.798298°N, 74.034725°E)*
This village is mentioned in accounts as a stop by Gough and the main British force prior to Ramnuggar.

*Kot Pindee Dass (31.706390°N, 74.181972°E)*
This village is mentioned in accounts as a stop by Gough and the main British force prior to Ramnuggar.

*Killah Didar Singh (32.134933°N, 74.011943°E)*
The village was used as an advance outpost by the British vanguard before being used as camp by Gough and the main British force prior to the battle.

*Alipur (32.266838°N, 73.814789°N)*
Allipur (or Allipore) village was the advance British outpost commanded by Colin Campbell which along with Noewala and Saharan formed a triangle of villages occupied by the gathering British force immediately prior to the Battle of Ramnuggar.

*Noewala (32.176930°N, 73.877783°E)*
See above.

*Saharun (32.226193°N, 73.891453°E)*
See above.

**The battlefield**

*Ramnuggar village (32.328695°N, 73.779737°E)*

Ramnuggar (literally meaning abode of Ram) has since partition been changed to the more Islamic name of Rasulnuggar. The village was occupied by Sikh pickets prior to the battle.

*Baradari (32.336854°N, 73.791982°E)*

The ruins of Ranjit Singh's Baradari or small summerhouse lie a 1.5 km upstream of the village. The baradari was used by British officers after the Battle of Ramnuggar.

*Large island midstream separating left and right banks of the Chenab (32.343869°N, 73.751171°E)*

With much water of the Chenab being diverted for irrigation, the Chenab River is now a shadow of its former self. The island opposite Ramnuggar dividing the Chenab into two streams that was occupied by Sikh troops has therefore grown substantially with the drop in water level.

*Belt of sand on the left bank of the Chenab (32.341478°N, 73.771208°E)*

The large belt of sand on which the cavalry of both armies retreated and advanced several times during the contest.

*Position of the Sikh army (32.365443°N, 73.749735°E)*

The bulk of the Sikh force under Shere Singh was dug in on the right bank of the Chenab opposite Ramnuggar.

*Ramnuggar British cemetery (32.336755°N, 73.791646°)*

The graveyard, surrounded by a T-shaped wall, contains, among others, the remains of Col Charles Cureton of the 16th Light Dragoons; Capt. John Fitzgerald of the 14th Light Dragoons, wounded in the battle and died four days later; and Lt-Col William Havelock. It also contains the grave of Subedar Mir Ali Sirdar Bahadhur of the 8th Light Cavalry.

**Battle of Sadulpore**

**Thackwell's crossing and route to Sadulpore**

*The three fords*

The British intention was to force a crossing of the Chenab River using one of the three fords between the British camp at Ramnuggar and Wazirabad. In the event, Thackwell's contingent had to utilise the ford at Wazirabad while only Godby with additional troops would manage a crossing at Ghurree Ke-Puttan.

*Ghurree Ke-Puttan (32.384918°N, 73.867108°E)*

The ford utilised by Godby's reinforcements was a few hundred metres downstream from the village of Sadulpore on the right bank.

*Approximate position of Runnee Ke-Puttan (32.409110°N, 73.983052°E)*

The second ford upstream from Ramnuggar was guarded by Sikh pickets on the right bank and was therefore not used.

*Approximate position of Allee Shere Ke-Chuck (32.422498°N, 74.001611°E)*

The third of the three fords upstream from Ramnuggar was also considered unusable by Thackwell.

*Thackwell's crossing point at Wazirabad*

Thackwell's advance force crossed at Wazirabad, utilising the large sandbank midstream to camp overnight before completing the crossing the next morning. Again, due to the lessening of the river waters the sandbank has significantly grown in intervening years.

*Wazirabad town (32.443140°N, 74.115995°E)*
One of the main provincial towns of the Punjab and situated on the main route from Lahore to Rawalpindi, this town adjacent to the Chenab was one of the main crossing points, having local ferry boats along with a nearby ford.

*Doorewal (32.465356°N, 73.961925°E)*
*Khojanwali (32.447532°N, 73.927231°E)*
*Langay (32.443423°N, 73.910823°E)*
After crossing the Chenab, Thackwell utilised the dirt track running parallel to the river from Shadiwal to Sadulpore, passing the villages of Doorewal, Khojanwali and Langay (Longwala).

### The battlefield
*Sadulpore (or Sad-Ullah-pur) village (32.420302°N, 73.868591°E)*
The British line under Thackwell was formed a few hundred metres to the west of the village.

*Ratti Pindi village (32.431178°N, 73.841851°E)*
Formerly occupied by British pickets, as were the villages of Kamoke and Longwala, Ratti Pindi was occupied by Sikh troops and formed the left of the Sikh position.

*Kamonkey village (32.424322°N, 73.845316°E)*
The village formed the centre of the Sikh line.

*Longwala (Long) village (32.416257°N, 73.849768°E)*
The village formed the right of the Sikh line.

*Nullah on the right of the Sikh line (left of the British line)*
The nullah made it difficult for Sikh and British cavalry to attack each other from their flanks on the Chenab side.

### Battle of Chillianwala
British advance towards Chillianwala
*Heylah (32.488612°N, 73.658879°E)*
An advance outpost was organised at Heylah village the day after Sadulpore by Thackwell with much of the British force moving to the village in the following days.

*Lussoorie (32.521427°N, 73.747696°E)*
Camp for most of the British force was moved to Lussoorie, around 10 km north-east of Heylah, during early January 1849.

*Loha tibba (32.510199°N, 73.771251°E)*
The village was used as camp by Gough prior to the Battle of Chillianwala.

*Dinghee (32.641686°N, 73.719465°E)*
Town reached en route to Chillianwala as the British force marched north-westwards before changing direction towards Amra Kalan.

*Amra Kalan (32.665371°N, 73.670047°E)*
*Amra Khurd (32.673480°N, 73.655668°E)*
The route Gough used to advance to Chillianwala passed the town of Dinghee, Amra Kalan and Amra Khurd before changing direction towards Mojianwala and Chillianwala.

*Chillianwala village (32.657434°N, 73.603903°E)*
*Mojianwala (32.654729°N, 73.622915°E)*
Chillianwala and Mojianwala villages were Sikh outposts prior to the battle with several guns stationed at Chillianwala. The positions were evacuated by the Sikh pickets as the British force changed direction to clear the villages before the battle. The British baggage was left at Mojianwala village.

### The battle
*Rasul (32.708649°N, 73.574867°E)*
*Kot Baloch (32.648184° N, 73.554253°E)*
*Chak Fateh Shah (32.633394°N, 73.553940°E)*
*Lakhnewala (32.615288°N, 73.557217°E)*
The village of Rasul formed the anchor for the left flank of the Sikh army, with their position stretching along the villages of Kot Baloch, Chak Fateh Shah and Lakhnewala.

*Moong (32.647103°N, 73.509848°E)*
The village of Moong, thought to be built on the ancient Greek ruins of the city of Nikaiea, was situated just behind the Sikh lines.

*Hilly high ground protecting the Sikh left flank (32.706209°N, 73.587381°E)*
A long, thin stretch of hilly ground bisected only by the Kharian Pass stretched towards the town of Bhimber and protected the Sikh left from being turned.

### After the battle
*Approximate British defensive position to the north of the main camp (32.683622°N, 73.607398°E)*
Gough had ordered a defensive position manned by guns to the north of the main British camp to protect against Sikh encroachment and skirmishers from the direction of Rasul.

*The Chillianwala monument (32.662377°N, 73.606011°E)*
Obelisk constructed in memory of the British fallen at the battle.

*Chillianwala cemetery (32.662174°N, 73.606049°E)*
The cemetery contains the bulk of the British dead although a considerable number were buried where they fell. Three large rectangular strips mark the area where the rank and file were buried, with the officers' graves in separate locations.

*Alexander monument (32.664856°N, 73.408630°E)*
A modern construction by the Pakistan Government marking the crossing of the Hydaspes (Jhelum River) by Alexander the Great.

*Puran (32.768820°N, 73.622535°E)*
Village between the Jhelum and the hilly ground through which Shere Singh and his army passed on their way to face the British from the north.

*Kharian Pass (32.834177°N, 73.828986°E)*
Formerly a narrow and difficult pass through the hilly stretch of ground linking Lahore and Gujrat to Rawalpindi across the Jhelum.

*Kharian village (32.815072°N, 73.865204°E)*
Village adjacent to the pass and from which it derives its name.

*Chak Memori (32.677311°N, 73.634437°E)*
Prior to moving to Gujrat, Shere Singh passed through the Kharian Pass to the village of Chak Memori to threaten the north and east sides of the British entrenchment.

## Battle of Gujrat

*Doorewal (32.465346°N, 73.962563°E)*
Rather than following Shere Singh directly, Gough marched his force towards the Chenab prior to the Battle of Gujrat in order to first achieve a junction with Whish's force marching north from Multan. Much of Whish's force joined Gough near Doorewal village.

*Khoonjah (Kunjah) (32.529583°N, 73.973510°E)*
The village of Kunjah en route to Shadiwal was reached by the British force the day before the Battle of Gujrat. The last remnants of Whish's force joined Gough's army at Kunjah and Shadiwal.

*Shadiwal (32.511717°N, 74.034118°E)*
Shadiwal village was made the British camp the night before the Battle of Gujrat.

*Haryawala (32.536467°N, 74.059372°E)*
Village situated just behind the British line during the Battle of Gujrat.

## The battle

*Eastern nullah (32.535990°N, 74.103642°E)*
Both the Sikh and British lines straddled the eastern nullah flowing due south into the Chenab. The nullah was dry during the battle.

*Bhimber nullah or River Dwara (32.545366°N, 74.019211°E)*
The Bhimber nullah, much larger than the eastern nullah, was also dry during the battle.

*Barra Kalra (Kalra Khas) village (32.545323°N, 74.090150°E)*
*Chota Kalra (Kalra Kalan) (32.545958°N, 74.075227°E)*
The two villages of Barra Kalra and Chota Kalra were a few hundred metres ahead of the main Sikh line and were occupied by Sikh contingents during the battle.

*Lundpur (Habibpur) (32.548920°N, 74.058908°E)*
*Lala Chak (32.536588°N, 74.043008°E)*
*Narowali (32.549299°N, 74.034723°E)*
These villages, situated just a few hundred metres in advance of what was the main Sikh line, are not mentioned in contemporary accounts and are therefore possibly new villages.

*Old walled section of the town (32.573152°N, 74.078220°E)*
Some contingents of the Sikh army after the retreat would pull back into the walled section of the town and its fortress, positions which the British force would have to storm.

*British graveyard (32.580244°N, 74.098187°E)*
British graveyard containing the graves of the casualties suffered in the battle.

## The surrender

*Daulut Nuggar and road to Bhimber (32.746892°N, 74.079300°E)*
Some of the Sikh army contingents retreated down the road to Bhimber after the Battle of Gujrat, with some of the Sikh guns being captured at Daulut Nuggar.

*Road to the Kharian Pass and Rawalpindi (32.607327°N, 74.033297°E)*
Gilbert expected Shere Singh to retreat down this direct route to cross the Jhelum after his defeat at Gujrat but the Sikh commander chose to move back towards Chillianwala instead, perhaps hoping to cross by the ferry or ford there. He seemed to have changed his mind later, marching by the side of the Jhelum past Puran and on to Serai Alamgir for the crossing of the river.

*Puran (32.768996°N, 73.621913°E)*
Passed by Shere Singh and his army as they headed towards Serai Alamgir to cross the Jhelum and chase Gilbert with his British force.

*Serai Alamgir (32.906265°N, 73.750446°E)*
The ferry at Serai Alamgir connected the road from Gujrat and Rawalpindi. The boats here were used by Shere Singh to cross before being burnt. Gilbert in turn crossed by a ford a few kilometres upstream when the Sikh army had vacated the right bank.

*Jalalpore (32.648647°N, 74.055901°E)*
Village on the road to Daulut Nuggar and where several Sikh guns were abandoned and captured.

*Jhelum town (32.935736°N, 73.729170°E)*
The right bank of the Jhelum River adjacent to the town of Jhelum formed the Sikh camp for several days after the crossing of the river while negotiations for a possible surrender were taking place with Gilbert, whose force had reached the left bank. Shere Singh subsequently left his wounded in the town, which has now expanded to the banks of the river.

*Serai Alamgir (32.906763°N, 73.750058°E)*
Gilbert camped at Serai Alamgir opposite the Sikh army position till after Shere Singh's departure towards Rawalpindi, when a crossing by a ford was made a few kilometres further upstream.

*Rhotas fort (32.968340°N, 73.579699°E)*
Sixteenth-century fortress built on orders by Sher Shah Suri and commanding the road to Peshawar and Rawalpindi. After crossing the Jhelum, Shere Singh continued along the road to Rawalpindi passing the Rhotas fort before heading down the road for the Bakrala Pass.

*Bakrala Pass (33.060906°N, 73.468070°E)*
A narrow and difficult pass through a mountainous area and where Gilbert expected Shere Singh to make a stand.

*Bakrala village (33.096466°N, 73.450334°E)*
Village to the west of the pass from which the pass takes its name.

*Manikyalla (33.454920°N, 73.246270°E)*
The village of Manikyalla, a camp for Gilbert's force, was where Shere Singh first arrived to negotiate a surrender of his forces.

*Manikyalla Buddhist stupa or tope (33.448087°N, 73.243396°E)*
The surrender of the first portion of the Sikh army was done in front of the large and still extant Buddhist structure just outside the village.

*Left bank of the River Sohan, outside Rawalpindi (33.536248°N, 73.112715°E)*
The left bank of the river where the road to Rawalpindi crosses the river was the location for the final surrender of the bulk of the Sikh troops. Sikh troops were led in batches across the river from the Sikh camp

on the outskirts of Rawalpindi and ordered to lay down their weapons in large heaps before the watching British officers.

*General Gilbert's Camp, Harmuk village (33.538489°N, 73.148162°E)*
Gilbert set his camp for the final surrender on the large meadow on the left bank of the river on the right of the road leading to Rawalpindi.

*Last Sikh camp (33.577858°N, 73.075895°E)*
Most of the Sikh troops camped on the road and on the outskirts of the city of Rawalpindi during the period before the surrender.

*Rawalpindi (33.625682°N, 73.082207°E)*
Ancient city of Rawalpindi on the route from Lahore to Peshawar.

**Gilbert route to Peshawar**
The route followed by the Afghan army and latterly by Gilbert in chasing them from Rawalpindi to the Khyber Pass.

*Jani Ka Sang (Sangjani) (33.675309°N, 72.851527°E)*
Village en route to Peshawar passed by Gilbert in his mission to intercept the Afghan army.

*Margalla Pass (33.705099°N, 72.823465°E)*
The Margalla Pass (literally meaning cut-throat pass) is the main route through the hilly area west of Rawalpindi.

*Wah (33.770386°N, 72.739715°E)*
The village of Wah was passed by Gilbert's force en route to Peshawar.

*Hassan Abdul (33.820355°N, 72.689144°E)*
Ancient city en route to Peshawar.

*Shumsabad (33.895933°N, 72.415749°E)*
Town passed by Gilbert's force en route to Peshawar.

*Attock fortress (33.891775°N, 72.234610°E)*
The fortress was formerly held by Lt Abbott before the Afghan garrison defected to the Afghan army. Gilbert on reaching the fortress on the banks of the Indus found the Afghan army had just finished completing their crossing.

*Position of former boat bridge across the Indus (33.894001°N, 72.233105°E)*
The bridge of boats was situated directly under the guns of the fortress. The Afghan army attempted to destroy the bridge on seeing Gilbert's advance force on the left bank of the Indus but only managed to destroy several boats. The bridge was later repaired and used for crossing by Gilbert.

*Khairabad (33.897159°N, 72.228169°E)*
The town and fortress of Khairabad are situated on the right bank of the Indus and opposite the fortress of Attock. The town was briefly occupied.

*Gilberts camp at Indus (33.905965°N, 72.282119°E)*
The British camp was situated, for a few days, a few kilometres north of Attock fortress while the Afghans still held the right bank.

## Peshawar
*Akhoorna (34.002756°N, 72.124925°E)*
Small town of Akhoorna, a crossing point for the Kabul River, was passed by Gilbert en route to Peshawar town. The Afghan army during their own crossing several days earlier here had lost some guns which Gilbert was unsuccessful in retrieving from the river, the pieces having sunk too deeply into the mud.

*Nowshera (34.016914°N, 71.976566°E)*
The plains outside the town of Nowshera were the site of a major battle between the Sikh and Afghan armies in the contest for Peshawar. The town was passed by Gilbert en route to Peshawar city.

*Peshawar city (34.010560°N, 71.573991°E)*
Key garrison city of Peshawar province situated around 30 km from the Khyber Pass and former summer capital of the Afghan rulers.

*Bala Hissar fortress (34.012301°N, 71.570049°E)*
Peshawar city fortress rebuilt by the Sikh general Hari Singh Nalwa in 1834.

*Jamrud fortress (34.003172°N, 71.378472°E)*
Frontier fortress guarding the entrance of the Khyber Pass.

*Entrance of Khyber Pass (34.002931°N, 71.318906°E)*
Route used to gain ingress into Peshawar from Kabul.

## Outside the Punjab
*Fort William, Calcutta (22.557265°N, 88.337805°E)*
Mulraj and Bhai Maharaj were both incarcerated at Fort William after the end of the war.

*Benares (25.306783°N, 83.002606°E)*
Place of exile for Jind Kaur after exile from the Punjab.

*Chunar fortress (25.125660°N, 82.874683°E)*
The fortress cum prison was where the Maharani was transferred to from Benares although she escaped quickly receiving sanctuary in Nepal.

*Fatehgarh (27.363808°N, 79.633985°E)*
The European settlement by the Ganges and the home of the deposed Duleep Singh after being removed from the Punjab.

# Appendix A

# Treaty of Lahore (9 March 1846)

Whereas the treaty of amity and concord, which was concluded between the British government and the late Maharajah Ranjit Sing, the ruler of Lahore, in 1809, was broken by the unprovoked aggression, on the British Provinces, of the Sikh army, in December last; and whereas, on that occasion, by the proclamation, dated 13th December, the territories then in the occupation of the Maharajah of Lahore, on the left or British bank of the river Sutlej, were confiscated and annexed to the British Provinces; and since that time hostile operations have been prosecuted by the two Governments; the one against the other, which have resulted in the occupation of Lahore by the British troops; and whereas it has been determined that, upon certain conditions, peace shall be re-established between the two Governments, the following treaty of peace between the Honourable East India Company and Maharajah Dhuleep Sing Bahadoor, and his children, heirs and successors, has been concluded on the part of the Honourable Company by Frederick Currie, Esquire, and Brevet-Major Henry Montgomery Lawrence, by virtue of full powers to that effect vested in them by the Right Hon'ble Sir Henry Hardinge, G.C.B., one of her Britannic Majesty's Most Hon'ble Privy Council, Governor-General, appointed by the Honourable Company to direct and control all their affairs in the East Indies, and on the part of His Highness Maharajah Dhuleep Sing by Bhaee Ram Sing, Rajah Lal Sing, Sirdar Tej Sing, Sirdar Chuttur Sing Attareewalla, Sirdar Runjore Sing Majeethia, Dewan Deena Nath and Fakeer Nooroodden, vested with full powers and authority on the part of His Highness.

Article 1. There shall be perpetual peace and friendship between the British Government on the one part and Maharajah Dhuleep Sing, his heirs and successors on the other.

Article 2. The Maharajah of Lahore renounces for himself, his heirs and successors, all claim to, or connection with, the territories lying to the south of the River Sutlej, and engages never to have any concern with those territories or the inhabitants thereof.

Article 3. The Maharajah cedes to the Hon'ble Company, in perpetual sovereignty, all his forts, territories and rights in the Doab or country, hill and plain, situated between the Rivers Beas and Sutlej.

Article 4. The British Government having demanded from the Lahore State, as indemnification for the expenses of the war, in addition to the cession of territory described in Article 3, payment of one and half crore of Rupees, and the Lahore Government being unable to pay the whole of this sum at this time, or to give security satisfactory to the British Government for its eventual payment, the Maharajah cedes to the Honourable Company, in perpetual sovereignty, as equivalent for one crore of Rupees, all his forts, territories, rights and interests in the hill countries, which are situated between the Rivers Beas and Indus, including the Provinces of Cashmere and Hazarah.

Article 5. The Maharajah will pay to the British Government the sum of 60 lakhs of Rupees on or before the ratification of this Treaty.

Article 6. The Maharajah engages to disband the mutinous troops of the Lahore Army, taking from them their arms and His Highness agrees to reorganise the Regular or Aeen Regiments of Infantry upon the system, and according to the Regulations as to pay and allowances, observed in the time of the late Maharajah Ranjit Sing. The Maharajah further engages to pay up all arrears to the soldiers that are discharged, under the provisions of this Article.

Article 7. The Regular Army of the Lahore State shall henceforth be limited to 25 Battalions of Infantry, consisting of 800 bayonets each with twelve thousand Cavalry – this number at no time to be exceeded without the concurrence of the British Government. Should it be necessary at any time – for any special cause – that this force should be increased, the cause shall be fully explained to the British Government, and when the special necessity shall have passed, the regular troops shall be again reduced to the standard specified in the former Clause of this Article.

Article 8. The Maharajah will surrender to the British Government all the guns – thirty-six in number – which have been pointed against the British troops and which, having been placed on the right Bank of the River Sutlej, were not captured at the battle of Subraon.

Article 9. The control of the Rivers Beas and Sutlej, with the continuations of the latter river, commonly called the Gharrah and the Punjnud, to the confluence of the Indus at Mithunkote and the control of the Indus from Mithunkote to the borders of Beloochistan, shall, in respect to tolls and ferries, rest with the British Government. The provisions of this Article shall not interfere with the passage of boats belonging to the Lahore Government on the said rivers, for the purpose of traffic or the conveyance of passengers up and down their course. Regarding the ferries between the two countries respectively, at the several ghats of the said rivers, it is agreed that the British Government, after defraying all the expenses of management and establishments, shall account to the Lahore Government for one-half the net profits of the ferry collections. The provisions of this Article have no reference to the ferries on that part of the River Sutlej which forms the boundary of Bhawulpore and Lahore respectively.

Article 10. If the British Government should, at any time, desire to pass troops through the territories of His Highness the Maharajah, for the protection of the British territories, or those of their Allies, the British troops shall, on such special occasion, due notice being given, be allowed to pass through the Lahore territories. In such case the officers of the Lahore State will afford facilities in providing supplies and boats for the passage of rivers, and the British Government will pay the full price of all such provisions and boats, and will make fair compensation for all private property that may be damaged. The British Government will, moreover, observe all due consideration to the religious feelings of the inhabitants of those tracts through which the army may pass.

Article 11. The Maharajah engages never to take or to retain in his service any British subject – nor the subject of any European or American State – without the consent of the British Government.

Article 12. In consideration of the services rendered by Rajah Golab Sing of Jummoo, to the Lahore State, towards procuring the restoration of the relations of amity between the Lahore and British Governments, the Maharajah hereby agrees to recognise the Independent sovereignty of Rajah Golab Sing in such territories and districts in the hills as may be made over to the said Rajah Golab Sing, by separate Agreement between himself and the British Government, with the dependencies thereof, which may have been in the Rajah's possession since the time of the late Maharajah Khurruck Sing, and the British Government, in consideration of the good conduct of Rajah Golab Sing, also agrees to recognise his independence in such territories, and to admit him to the privileges of a separate Treaty with the British Government.

Article 13. In the event of any dispute or difference arising between the Lahore State and Rajah Golab Sing, the same shall be referred to the arbitration of the British Government, and by its decision the Maharajah engages to abide.

Article 14. The limits of the Lahore territories shall not be, at any time, changed without the concurrence of the British Government.

Article 15. The British Government will not exercise any interference in the internal administration of the Lahore State, but in all cases or questions which may be referred to the British Government, the Governor-General will give the aid of his advice and good offices for the furtherance of the interests of the Lahore Government.

Article 16. The subjects of either State shall, on visiting the territories of the other, be on the footing of the subjects of the most favoured nation.

This Treaty consisting of sixteen articles, has been this day settled by Frederick Currie, Esquire, and Brevet-Major Henry Montgomery Lawrence acting under the directions of the Right Hon'ble Sir Henry Hardinge, G.C.B., Governor-General, on the part of the British Government, and by Bhaee Ram Sing, Rajah Lal Sing, Sirdar Tej Sing, Sirdar Chuttur Sing Attareewalla, Sirdar Runjore Sing Majeethia, Dewan Deena Nath, and Faqueer Noorooddeen, on the part of the Maharajah Dhuleep Sing, and the said Treaty has been this day ratified by the seal of the Right Hon'ble Sir Henry Hardinge, G.C.B., Governor-General, and by that of His Highness Maharajah Dhuleep Sing.

Done at Lahore, this ninth day of March, in year of Our Lord one thousand eight hundred and forty-six; corresponding with the tenth day of Rubbee-ool-awul, 1262 Hijree, and ratified on the same date.

(Sd.) H. Hardinge (L.S.)

(Sd.) Maharajah Dhuleep Sing (L.S.)

Bhaee Ram Sing (L.S.)

Rajah Lal Sing (L.S.)

Sirdar Tej Sing (L.S.)

Sirdar Chuttur Sing Attareewalla (L.S.)

Sirdar Runjore Sing Majeethia (L.S.)

Dewan Deena Nath (L.S.)

Faqueer Noorooddeen (L.S.)

# Appendix B

# Treaty of Amritsar (16 March 1846)

The treaty between the British Government on the one part and Maharajah Gulab Singh of Jammu on the other concluded on the part of the British Government by Frederick Currie, Esq. and Brevet-Major Henry Montgomery Lawrence, acting under the orders of the Rt. Hon. Sir Henry Hardinge, G.C.B., one of her Britannic Majesty's most Honorable Privy Council, Governor-General of the possessions of the East India Company, to direct and control all the affairs in the East Indies and by Maharajah Gulab Singh in person – 1846.

Article 1 The British Government transfers and makes over for ever in independent possession to Maharajah Gulab Singh and the heirs male of his body all the hilly or mountainous country with its dependencies situated to the eastward of the River Indus and the westward of the River Ravi including Chamba and excluding Lahol, being part of the territories ceded to the British Government by the Lahore State according to the provisions of Article IV of the Treaty of Lahore, dated 9 March 1846.

Article 2. The eastern boundary of the tract transferred by the foregoing article to Maharajah Gulab Singh shall be laid down by the Commissioners appointed by the British Government and Maharajah Gulab Singh respectively for that purpose and shall be defined in a separate engagement after survey.

Article 3. In consideration of the transfer made to him and his heirs by the provisions of the foregoing article Maharajah Gulab Singh will pay to the British Government the sum of seventy-five lakhs of rupees (Nanukshahee), fifty lakhs to be paid on or before the 1st October of the current year, A.D., 1846.

Article 4. The limits of territories of Maharajah Gulab Singh shall not be at any time changed without concurrence of the British Government.

Article 5 Maharajah Gulab Singh will refer to the arbitration of the British Government any disputes or question that may arise between himself and the Government of Lahore or any other neighboring State, and will abide by the decision of the British Government.

Article 6. Maharajah Gulab Singh engages for himself and heirs to join, with the whole of his Military Forces, the British troops when employed within the hills or in the territories adjoining his possessions.

Article 7. Maharajah Gulab Singh engages never to take to retain in his service any British subject nor the subject of any European or American State without the consent of the British Government.

Article 8. Maharajah Gulab Singh engages to respect in regard to the territory transferred to him, the provisions of Articles V, VI and VII of the separate Engagement between the British Government and the Lahore Durbar, dated 11 March 1846.

Article 9. The British Government will give its aid to Maharajah Gulab Singh in protecting his territories from external enemies.

Article 10. Maharajah Gulab Singh acknowledges the supremacy of the British Government and will in token of such supremacy present annually to the British Government one horse, twelve shawl goats of approved breed (six male and six female) and three pairs of Cashmere shawls.

This Treaty of ten articles has been this day settled by Frederick Currie, Esq. and Brever-Major Henry Montgomery Lawrence, acting under directions of the Rt. Hon. Sir Henry Hardinge, Governor-General, on the part of the British Government and by Maharajah Gulab Singh in person, and the said Treaty has been this day ratified by the seal of the Rt. Hon. Sir Henry Hardinge, Governor-General. Done at Amritsar the sixteenth day of March, in the year of our Lord one thousand eight hundred and forty-six, corresponding with the seventeenth day of Rubee-ul-Awal (1262 Hijri).

(Signed) H. Hardinge (Seal) (Signed) F. Currie (Signed) H. M. Lawrence

# Appendix C

# Treaty of Bhyrowal (16 December 1846)

ARTICLES OF AGREEMENT concluded between the BRITISH GOVERNMENT and the LAHORE DURBAR on 16 December 1846

Whereas the Lahore Durbar and the principal Chiefs and Sirdars of the State have in express terms communicated to the British Government their anxious desire that the Governor-General should give his aid and assistance to maintain the administration of the Lahore State during the minority of Maharajah Dulleep Sing, and have declared this measure to be indispensable for the maintenance of the Government; and whereas the Governor-General has, under certain conditions, consented to give the aid and assistance solicited, the following Articles of Agreement, in modification of the Articles of Agreement executed at Lahore on the 11th March last, have been concluded on the part of the British Government by Frederick Currie, Esquire, Secretary to Government of India, and Lieutenant-Col Henry Montgomery Lawrence, C.B., Agent to the Governor-General, North-West Frontier, by virtue of full powers to that effect vested in them by the Right Honorable Viscount Hardinge, G.C.B., Governor-General, and on the part of His Highness Maharajah Dulleep Sing, by Sirdar Tej Sing, Sirdar Shere Sing, Dewan Deena Nath, Fukeer Nooroodeen, Rai Kishen Chund, Sirdar Runjore Sing Majethea, Sirdar Utter Sing Kaleewalla, Bhaee Nidhan Sing, Sirdar Khan Singh Majethea, Sirdar Shumshere Sing, Sirdar Lall Sing Morarea, Sirdar Kehr Sing Sindhanwalla, Sirdar Urjun Sing Rungurnungalea, acting with the unanimous consent and concurrence of the Chiefs and Sirdars of the State assembled at Lahore.

Article 1. All and every part of the Treaty of peace between the British Government and the State of Lahore, bearing date the 9th day of March, 1846, except in so far as it may be temporarily modified in respect to Clause 15 of the said Treaty by this engagement, shall remain binding upon the two Governments.

Article 2. A British officer, with an efficient establishment of assistants, shall be appointed by the Governor-General to remain at Lahore, which officer shall have full authority to direct and control all matters in every Department of the State.

Article 3. Every attention shall be paid in conducting the administration to the feelings of the people, to preserving the national institutions and customs, and to maintaining the just rights of all classes.

Article 4. Changes in the mode and details of administration shall not be made, except when found necessary for effecting the objects set forth in the foregoing Clause, and for securing the just dues of the Lahore Government. These details shall be conducted by native officers as at present, who shall be appointed and superintended by a Council of Regency composed of leading Chiefs and Sirdars acting under the control and guidance of the British Resident.

Article 5. The following persons shall in the first instance constitute the Council of Regency, viz., Sirdar Tej Sing, Sirdar Shere Sing Attareewalla, Dewan Deena Nath, Fukeer Nooroodeen, Sirdar Runjore Sing Majeethea, Bhaee Nidhan Sing, Sirdar Utter Sing Kaleewalla, Sirdar Shumshere Sing Sindhanwalla, and no change shall be made in the persons thus nominated, without the consent of the British Resident, acting under the orders of the Governor-General.

Article 6. The administration of the country shall be conducted by this Council of Regency in such manner as may be determined on by themselves in consultation with the British Resident, who shall have full authority to direct and control the duties of every department.

Article 7. A British Force of such strength and numbers and in such positions as the Governor-General may think fit, shall remain at Lahore for the protection of the Maharajah and the preservation of the peace of the country.

Article 8. The Governor-General shall be at liberty to occupy with British soldiers any fort or military post in the Lahore territories, the occupation of which may be deemed necessary by the British Government, for the security of the capital or for maintaining the peace of the country.

Article 9. The Lahore State shall pay to the British Government twenty two lakhs of new Nanuck Shahee Rupees of full tale and weight per annum for the maintenance of this force, and to meet the expenses incurred by the British Government. Such sum to be paid by two instalments, or 13,20,000 in May or June, and 8,80,000 in November or December of each year.

Article 10. Inasmuch as it is fitting that Her Highness the Maharanee, the mother of Maharajah Dulleep Sing, should have a proper provision made for the maintenance of herself and dependants, the sum of one lakh and fifty thousand rupees shall be set apart annually for that purpose, and shall be at Her Highness' disposal.

Article 11. The provisions of this Engagement shall have effect during the minority of His Highness Maharajah Dulleep Sing, and shall cease and terminate on His Highness attaining the full age of sixteen years or, on the 4th September of the year 1854, but it shall be competent to the Governor-General to cause the arrangement to cease at any period prior to the coming of age of His Highness, at which the Governor-General and the Lahore Durbar may be satisfied that the interposition of the British Government is no longer necessary for maintaining the Government of His Highness the Maharajah.

This agreement, consisting of eleven articles, was settled and executed at Lahore by the Officers and Chiefs and Sirdars above named, on the 16th day of December, 1846. (Sd.) F. CURRIE H.M. LAWRENCE (Sd.) Sirdar Tej Sing (L.S.) Sirdar Shere Sing (L.S.) Dewan Deena Nath (L.S.) Fukeer Nooroodeen (L.S.) Rai Kishen Chund (L.S.) Sirdar Runjore Sing Majethea (L.S.) Sirdar Utter Sing Kalewalla (L.S.) Bhaee Nidhan Sing (L.S.) Sirdar Khan Sing Majethea (L.S.) Sirdar Shumshere Sing (L.S.) Sirdar Lal Sing Morarea (L.S.) Sirdar Kher Sing Sindhanwalla (L.S.) Sirdar Urjan Sing Rungurnungalea (L.S.) (Sd.) Hardinge (L.S.) & (Sd.) Dulleep Sing (L.S.)

Ratified by the Right Honorable the Governor-General, at Bhyrowal Ghat on the left bank of the Beas, twenty-sixth day of December, One Thousand Eight Hundred and Forty-Six. (Sd.) F. CURRIE, Secretary to the Government of India

# Appendix D

# Exile of Maharani Jind Kaur

A General Proclamation for the information of the Chiefs of the Lahore Durbar, the Priests, Elders and People of the Countries belonging to Maharajah Duleep Sing.

Lahore, August 20 1847

THE Right Honorable the Governor-General of India, taking into consideration the friendly relations subsisting between the Lahore and British Governments, and the tender age of Maharajah Duleep Sing, feels the interest of a father in the education, and guardianship, of the young Prince.

With this end in view, it appeared to the Governor-General to have become absolutely necessary to separate the Maharajah from the Maharanee, his mother; an opinion in which the Durbar perfectly coincided: accordingly, on the 19th day of August 1847, Her Highness left the palace of Lahore, and was taken to Sheikhoopoor.

The reasons for this step are shortly these: First, that at the time of the making of the Treaty of Bhyrowal, it vas considered necessary to exclude Her Highness the Maharanee from all share in the administration of public affairs; and that she should have a separate maintenance appointed her, to enable her to pass the rest of her life in honorable retirement. Notwithstanding this, Her Highness has, ever since, been intriguing to disturb the Government, and carried her opposition to the Ministers so far as quite to embarrass and impede the public business.

Secondly. The Maharajah is now a child, and he will grow up in the way he is trained. It was only too probable, therefore, that his mother would instil into him her own bitter feelings of hostility to the chiefs, and that he would have thus grown up at variance with the Sirdars and Ministers of his kingdom. This could not be allowed. The young Prince should be reared up in the cultivation of every natural and acquired excellence of mind and disposition, so that, at the expiration of the present treaty, peace should be preserved, by the kindly understanding existing between the Maharajah and all classes of his subjects, a blessing which could not be hoped for, if the young Prince remained with his mother.

Thirdly. So long as Her Highness the Maharanee occupied the Lahore Palace, strangers visited her without restriction, and every seditious intriguer who was displeased with the present order of things, looked up to the Queen-Mother as the head of the State; some of them even went so far as to plan the subversion of the restored Khalsa Government.

Let all ranks, therefore, rejoice throughout the kingdom, that the Right Honorable the Governor-General of India has so much at heart the peace and security of this country, the firm establishment of the State, and the honor of the Maharajah, and his Ministers.

# Appendix E

# Shere Singh's Letter to Lahore Resident

Raja Shere Sing and the Sirdars of his Camp to the Resident at Lahore.

Ramnuggur November 24 1848

THE British have obtained for themselves a far spread reputation, by the kindness they have shown, in bestowing upon various illustrious persons extensive revenues; as, for instance, the King of Lucknow, for whose support a large sum was settled, which he is allowed to enjoy in peace and security, and in no instance has any breach of faith taken place.

Maharajah Ranjit Sing, till the time of his death, preserved an undiminished friendship with the British, for the space of thirty-five years, in which he was imitated by Maharajah Khurruck Sing, Koonwur Nao Nehal Sing, and Maharajah Shere Sing. After the Sutlej campaign, in which the Khalsa army suffered a becoming punishment, for having broken the friendship which, till that time had subsisted, the Governor-General, having at heart the welfare of the Maharajah's kingdom, made a new treaty.

It is strange, indeed, that notwithstanding the efforts of the Khalsa, and the good faith of the British, the present disturbances have taken place. The reason, however, is to be found in the evil dealing, and faithlessness, of the members of the Durbar, who have neither regarded the credit of their own kingdom, nor respected the good name of the British.

Should the British desire to know the whole particulars, they will find them in the annexed points, which will clearly show the origin of all the disturbances which have arisen. When these remarks are taken carefully into consideration, and with a view to the stability of Maharajah Duleep Sing's kingdom, and the preservation of the good name of the British, these disturbances will, immediately be put a stop to.

**Annexed Points**

Maharajah Ranjit Sing preserved an unbroken friendship with the British, for the space of thirty five years, without regard to expense, or loss, to himself. At the time of the Cabool campaign, he deputed Koonwur Nao Nehal Sing and the principal Sirdars of the State, to accompany the British troops to Peshawur, with orders to afford every possible aid and assistance. This he did, under the impression that it would tend to strengthen the friendship which existed between him and the British Government.

In like manner, Maharajah Khurruck Sing and Koonwur Nao Nehal Sing kept up the friendly relations which had existed previously; on Mr. Clerk sending for the Ghilzies, they were immediately forwarded under the care of Fakeer Azeezooddeen; and subsequently, on Mr Clerk's request, Sirdar Sooltan Mohammad Khan was sent to him, by Koonwur Nao Nehal Sing's orders, under charge of Dewan Hakim Raee.

Subsequently Maharajah Shere Sing sent his troops under Sirdar Golab Sing Povindea to accompany the British army to Cabool; while, at the same time Koonwur Purtab Sing and Raja Golab Sing were deputed to Peshawur to give assistance in procuring supplies ammunition &c. This friendly aid was given, until the arrival of the British troops at Ferozepore.

In the treaty made with Maharajah Ranjit Sing, it was arranged that the Sikh Government should have permission, on giving notice to the British Government, to send 200 or 300 sowars and a gun across the Sutlej to punish refractory zemindars. On one occasion, Sirdar Joala Sing Purdhania accompanied by 1,000 sowars and two guns crossed the river, and inflicted such severe punishment on the people of Kotkupoora, that, from that time no one dared to create a disturbance.

In the time of Maharajah Duleep Sing, Dewan Hakim Raee, with 100 sowars, was sent across the river, for the purpose of repressing the disturbances then existing beyond the Sutlej, and putting a stop to the prevailing system of murder and highway robbery. In the meantime, an insurrection arose among the Khalsa troops, and Raja Heera Sing was killed. An additional 100 sowars were sent to the assistance of Hakim Raee, who was unable to deal with the zemindars. As this was imagined to be contrary to the treaty, they were not suffered to cross and their officers were maltreated. In consequence of this, the revenue of the Cis-Sutlej States, estimated at eighteen lakhs was lost and the authority of the Sikh Government over the country was put an end to, by the interference of the British Government, who disregarded the terms of friendship which formerly existed.

When the Sikh army heedless of the tender age of the Maharajah, and the respect due to the Maharanee, marched, without leaders, and contrary to the counsels of the Sirdars across the river, they were defeated, and overthrown by the British, who advanced to this side of the Sutlej and encamped at Kussoor. Raja Golab Sing, Raja Deena Nath and Bhaee Ram Sing waited on the Governor-General, and explained the disobedience of orders of the Sikh army, upon which his Lordship, in consideration of the helplessness of the Maharajah and the Maharane, directed that the sum of 2 and a half crores of rupees should be paid to defray the expenses incurred in the war. As the Maharanee and Maharajah had nothing to do with what had taken place, which solely originated with the army, who had been punished for their temerity this arrangement of the Governor-General could merely have been to attain certain ends. If the army had not been sufficiently punished, the Governor-General should have inflicted further castigation upon them. That man is not a friend who assists merely in the time of strength and power; but his friendship is to be depended on, who takes your hand in the moment of weakness.

When the Maharajah went to Lullianee to pay his respects to the Governor-General, Raja Golab Sing, Raja Deena Nath, Bhaee Ram Sing and Sirdar Chuttur Sing offered several suggestions regarding the sum demanded but in vain. At last, it was settled that the Cis Sutlej States and Jalandhar doab should be made over in payment, and that one and a half crore should be paid by three instalments of 50,00,000: the first in Phagoon, 1902; the second in Chait, 1903; and the third in Chait, 1904. After the arrival of the Governor-General at Lahore, this arrangement was broken through, and the Kohistan country and Cashmere, were taken, in lieu of one crore, and the gold and silver in the Toshakhana seized in payment of the remaining 50,00,000 rupees.

The Hill country and Cashmere were made over to Raja Golab Sing, who, by the favor of the Sikh Government, was raised from a humble to a lofty position, and who, forgetting what was due from him as a servant of the State, set himself up in an independent sovereignty. It cannot be believed that such an arrangement showed any regard for the previous friendship with Maharajah Ranjit Sing, or for securing the stability of Maharajah Duleep Sing's kingdom. However, not one of the Durbar offered any opposition to the wishes of the British Government.

The British Government, professing a wish to reduce the expenditure of the Maharajah's kingdom, which would indeed have been an act, in accordance with the friendship so long preserved with the Sikh Government, made the following reductions, entailing a loss to the State of seventy lakhs:

1. Twenty two lakhs. for the support of the British troops.
2. Thirty Lakhs, remitted to the zemindars on the former revenue.
3. Eight lakhs, on account of expenses of the various criminal jurisdictions, fixed at four lakhs, and which previously used to pay to the Government four lakhs, in excess of their expenditure.
4. Eight lakhs, lost in the remission of the customs dues.
5. Two lakhs, expended in erecting buildings, making roads &c.

From the above statement, it is clear that the British Government, acting on the suggestion of evil-disposed persons, have never had at heart the welfare of the Maharajah's kingdom.

Considering the above mentioned loss to the revenue, of seventy lakhs, and the straitened condition of the Maharajah, as to money, and even clothing, it is impossible to imagine that friendship could have guided the views of the British Government. It can only be supposed that, being led astray by evil councilors, they have forgotten what was due to their good name, and their position, as supporters of the Maharajah's kingdom.

Maharajah Ranjit Sing, collected, in the government Toshakhana, great quantities of gold and silver articles, and various kinds of clothing, which he was in the habit of sending to the British Government, and distributing to the troops and Sirdars, and from which the State derived great credit and importance. The whole of these have been sold.

It should, also, be considered what sum of money was in the Motie Mundir treasury, when the British arrived at Lahore, and what sum is in it now. Not-withstanding, the Resident having expressed a wish that it should become as full as formerly, there is now nothing left in it.

The British Government, have imprisoned, and sent off to Benares, the Maharanee, mother of the Maharajah, whom it would have been befitting to have treated with the respect due to those of her sex, who are accustomed to remain in privacy and retirement. Since her departure, no advantage has been gained in settling the affairs of the kingdom, and the treatment she has experienced shows but little friendship on the part of the British.

The whole of the people of the Punjab, whether high or low, have been dispirited by this conduct; and the Sirdars, who voted for her expulsion from the country, did so, solely to protect their own dignity and honor, and to meet the wishes of the Resident. How could her well-wishers dare to express their thoughts?

Raja Tej Sing, whose incapacity was well known to Maharajah Ranjit Sing, and who only received an appointment in the army, on account of the Maharajah's affection for Jemadar Khosal Sing, has been promoted to the highest station in the kingdom, notwithstanding that he never led the troops of the Khalsa, as Sirdar Golab Sing Povindea, Umeer Sing Man or General Sooltan Mohammad Khan, has done, and, in no instance, has been known to display any ability, or courage, or to have been entrusted with any share in the government of the country.

Again, Mool Sing, who was a common moonshee on thirty rupees a month, in the service of Sirdar Hure Sing and, subsequently, in that of Jemadar Khosal Sing, has been raised to a position of great importance, and is entirely in the confidence of the Resident. This has greatly grieved, and disgusted, the Sirdars and others.

Dewan Moolraj, whose father Sawun Mull, for many years ruled the province of Mooltan, with great reputation, and whose good service has frequently been mentioned, and praised, by the British, seeing the disorder that prevailed in the kingdom, sent in his resignation; and on Mr Agnew's being deputed to receive charge of the province from him, made over the fort, and all its ammunition and stationed that officer's guards inside. By chance, a wretched soldier, without the instigation, or advice of the Dewan, murdered Mr Agnew, and by degrees, the affair acquired its present importance. The sepoy is, to this day, a prisoner in the fort.

By the evil counsel of Tej Sing, a force was sent against Bhaee Maharaj Sing, who was a faker,and the spiritual preceptor of the Khalsa, and who, in no way, interfered with the affairs of government; and the villages of Kariala &c were burnt and sacked. This was pure oppression and tyranny, and has excited the indignation of the whole of the Khalsa.

Many Sirdars, who were of great consideration in the time of Maharajah Ranjit Sing, have through the instigation of Raja Tej Sing and Mool Sing, been degraded, imprisoned, and even hung; receiving a severe punishment for even a trifling offence. This treatment has caused great apprehension to both Hindoos and Mussulmans, who fear lest they should incur similar undeserved punishment.

The affair in Hazara originated solely in the injustice and oppression exercised by Captain Abbott against Sirdar Chuttur Sing; much might be said on this point, but it is not necessary to allude to all the particulars, at present, at full length.

Notwithstanding that the British Government has nothing to do with the management of affairs in the Punjab, not a single order is issued, except when bearing the Resident's signature.

This is contrary to the spirit of the treaty, made by the British Government with the Lahore State.

Although the army of the Khalsa received severe punishment at the hands of the British, Raja Tej Sing proclaimed, in open Durbar, that the hair and beards of all the Khalsa should be cut off. Such a speech was highly offensive to the Sikhs and has caused general indignation.

In every former, and in the present treaty, it was stipulated that the crime of cow killing should be severely punished. In Maharajah Ranjit Sing's time the penalty was hanging; and in the code promulgated by the British, the punishment is imprisonment, for life, or for a term of years. No punishment, however, is inflicted upon those who transgress in this point, which is clearly contrary to all notions of friendship, and is in opposition to the faith of the Khalsa.

In Peshawur, Major George Lawrence, through enmity, and opposition to the Sikhs, removed the guns from the Khalsa troops, and collected 4000 or 5000 of the Moolkias to attack them at night, whereas the Sikhs had never disobeyed, or acted contrary to his orders.

When Raja Shere Sing, with the Sirdars and the troops, were deputed to Mooltan, to assist Major Edwardes, they implicitly followed the directions of that officer in no way deviating from his orders. In fact, Major Edwardes, in writing to the Resident, expressed his approval of their behavior. In accordance with Major Edwardes' orders. Soojan Sing, Alloowalla, who was a Sirdar, was blown away from a gun, notwithstanding that such condign punishment is opposed to the customs of the Khalsa. By this conduct, they hoped to have obtained credit for themselves, but instead, they became objects of suspicion and want of confidence, which was shown by Major Edwardes directing the Sirdars to remove their troops to a distance from the British camp. Consequently, all the troops became dispirited and grieved, and at length, resolved to join Dewan Moolraj. Had Major Edwardes not shown this want of confidence, the Sikhs would never have gone over.

Major Edwardes wrote to all the Puthan zemindars, on the other side of the Indus, directing them to join him to oppose the Sikhs and promising to remit to them seven years revenue; and, also made over to the people of Bahawul Khan the districts that he obtained possession of, in the Mooltan territory.

This conduct has greatly irritated the Khalsa.

When the insurrection took place among the troops at Mooltan, Sirdar Shumshere Sing Sindanwalla and Sirdar Ootar Sing Kaleewala, in company with the other Sirdars, came to an agreement, in Raja Shere Sing's tent to go over to Moolraj; but after having joined the Dewan, they seized an opportunity of escaping, and instilled into Major Edwardes the confidence that he formerly had in them.

Much might be said, as regards Futteh Khan Towanah having, by the instigation of Major Edwardes, imprisoned Ram Sing Chappeewalah, and planned the murder of the officers of the Bunnoo troops, but there is not room to dilate on this subject.

Should you have any wish to examine, more fully into the points above mentioned, in which the grievances of the servants of Government, and of the Sirdars of the State, are set forth, further particulars shall be given; and it is, to be hoped that after a careful consideration as to which side is in the right, you will be enabled to come to such a decision as may extinguish the torch of dissension which is now lighted, and make arrangements which will secure the stability of the Maharajah's kingdom, and redound to the credit of the British Government.

# Appendix F

# Notice of Annexation of the Punjab

For many years, while the wisdom of Maharajah Ranjit Sing ruled the people of the Punjab, friendship and unbroken peace prevailed between the British nation and the Sikhs.

The British Government desired to maintain with the heirs of Ranjit Sing the same friendly relations they had held with him. But the Sirdars and Sikh army, forgetful of the policy which the Maharajah's prudence had enjoined, and departing from the friendly example he had set, suddenly crossed the frontier, and without any provocation, made war upon the British power.

They were met by the British army – four times they were defeated – they were driven back with ignominy across the Sutlej, and pursued to the walls of Lahore.

The Maharajah Duleep Sing tendered there, to the Governor-General of India, the submission of himself and his chiefs, and implored the clemency of the British Government.

The Government of India had acquired, by its conquest, an absolute right to subvert the Government of the Sikhs, by which it had been so grossly injured. But, in that time of victory, it showed the sincerity of its declarations, and gave signal proof of the moderation and forbearance by which its policy was directed.

The kingdom of the Punjab was spared: the Maharajah was placed on the throne of Ranjit Sing; and treaties of friendship were formed between the states.

How have the obligations of these treaties been fulfilled?

The British Government has with scrupulous fidelity, observed every promise which was made, and has discharged every obligation which the treaties imposed upon it.

It gave to the Maharajah the service of its troops. It afforded him the aid of its treasures in his difficulties. It meddled with none of the institutions, or customs, of the people. By its advice to the council, it improved the condition of the army; and it laboured to lessen the burdens, and to promote the prosperity, of every class of the Maharajah's people. It left nothing undone which it had promised to perform; it engaged in nothing from which it had promised to abstain. But there is not one of the main provisions of those treaties which the Sikh Government and the Sikh people have not, on their part, faithlessly and flagrantly violated. They bound themselves to pay an annual subsidy of twenty-two lakhs of rupees. No portion whatever has at any time been paid.

The whole debt due by the state of Lahore has increased to more than fifty lakhs of rupees; and crores have been added by the charges of the present war. The control of the British Government, which the sirdars themselves invited, and to which they bound themselves to submit, has been rejected, and resisted by force.

The peace and friendship, which were promised by the treaties, have been thrown aside. British officers, in the discharge of their duty, have treacherously been thrown into captivity, with women and children.

Other British officers, when acting for the Maharajah's interests, were murdered by the Maharajah's servants, after having been deserted by the Maharajah's troops.

Yet for these things, the Government of Lahore neither inflicted punishment on the offender, nor made reparation for the offence. It confessed itself unable to control its subjects. It formally declared to the British Resident that its troops would not obey its command, and would not act against the chief who had committed this outrage against the Government of India.

Not only did the army of the state refuse thus to act, but it everywhere openly rose in arms against the British. The whole people of the Sikhs joined in its hostility. The high Sirdars of the state have been its leaders; those of them who signed the treaties of peace were the most conspicuous in its ranks; and the chief by whom it was commanded, was a member of the council of regency itself. They proclaimed their purpose to be the extirpation of the British power, and the destruction of the British people; and they have struggled fiercely to effect it.

But the Government of India has put forth the vast resources of its power. The army of the Sikhs has been utterly discomfited; their artillery has been captured; the allies they invited have been driven from the Punjab with shame; the Sikh Sirdars, with their troops have surrendered, and been disarmed; and the Punjab is occupied by the British troops.

The Government of India repeatedly declared that it desired no further conquest; and it gave to the Maharajah, by its acts, a proof of the sincerity of its declarations.

The Government of India has sought, and desires no conquest now.

But, when unprovoked, and costly, war has again been wantonly renewed, the Government of India is bound, by its duty, to provide for its own security for the future, and to guard effectually the interests and tranquillity of its own people.

Punishments and benefits alike have failed to remove the inveterate hostility of the Sikhs. Wherefore, the Governor-General, as the only effectual mode which now remains of preventing the recurrence of national outrage, and the renewal of perpetual wars, has resolved upon declaring the British sovereignty in the Punjab, and upon the entire subjection of the Sikh nation – whom their own rulers have long been unable to control, who are equally insensible to punishment or forbearance, and who, as past events have now shown, will never desist from war, so long as they possess the power of an independent kingdom.

The Governor-General of India unfeignedly regrets that he should feel himself compelled to depose from his throne a descendant of Maharajah Ranjit Sing, while he is yet in his early youth.

But the Sovereign of every State is responsible for, and must be affected by, the acts of the people over whom he reigns.

As in the former war, the Maharajah, because of the lawless violence of his subjects, whom his Government was unable to control, was made to pay the penalty of their offence, in the loss of his richest provinces, so must he now be involved in all the consequences of their further violence, and of the deep national injury they have again committed.

When a renewal of formidable war by the army, and the great body of the Sikhs, has forced upon the Government of India, the conviction that a continuance of Sikh dominion in the Punjab is incompatible with the security of the British territories, the Governor-General cannot permit that mere compassion for the prince should deter him from the adoption of such measures against the nation, as alone can be effectual for the future maintenance of peace, and for protecting the interests of the British people.

# Appendix G

# Terms Granted to Duleep Singh on Annexation

TERMS granted to the Maharajah Duleep Sing, Bahadoor, on the part of the Honorable East India Company, by Henry Miers Elliot Esq., Foreign Secretary to the Government of India, and Lieutenant-Col Sir Henry Montgomery Lawrence, K.C.B. Resident, in virtue of full powers vested in them by the Right Honorable James, Earl of Dalhousie, Knight of the Most Ancient and Most Noble Order of the Thistle, one of Her Majesty's Most Honorable Privy Council, Governor-General, appointed by the Honorable East India Company to direct and control all their affairs in the East Indies; and accepted, on the part of His Highness the Maharajah, by Raja Tej Sing, Raja Deena Nath, Bhaee Nidhan Sing, Fakeer Nooroodeen, Gundur Sing, Agent of Sirdar Shere Sing Sindunwala, and Sirdar Lal Sing, Agent and Son of Sirdar Uttur Sing Kaleewalla, members of the Council of Regency, invested with full powers and authority on the part of His Highness.

I. His Highness the Maharajah Duleep Sing shall resign for himself, his heirs, and his successors, all right, title, and claim to the Sovereignty of the Punjab, or to any Sovereign Power whatever.

II. All the property of the State, of whatever description, and wheresoever found, shall be confiscated to the Honorable East India Company; in part payment of the debt due by the State of Lahore to the British Government, and of the expenses of the war.

III. The gem called the Koh-i-noor, which was taken from Shah Shooja-ool-Moolk by Maharajah Ranjit Sing, shall be surrendered by the Maharajah of Lahore to the Queen of England.

IV. His Highness Duleep Sing shall receive, from the Honorable East India Company, for the support of himself, his relatives, and the servants of the State, a pension not less than four, and not exceding five, lakhs of Company's Rupees per annum.

V. His Highness shall be treated with respect and honor. He shall retain the title of Maharajah Duleep Sing, Bahadoor; and he shall continue to receive, during his life, such portion of the above named pension as may be allotted to himself personally provided he shall remain obedient to the British Government; and shall reside at such place as the Governor-General of India may select.

Granted and accepted at Lahore, on the 29th of March, 1849 and ratified by the Right Honorable the Governor-General on the 5th of April, 1849.

| | |
|---|---|
| DALHOUSIE | MAHARAJAH DULEEP SING |
| H. M. ELLIOT | RAJA TEJ SING |
| H. M. LAWRENCE | RAJA DEENA NATH |
| | BHAEE NIDHAN SING |
| | FAKEER NOOROODEEN |
| | GUNDUR SING |
| | Agent to Sirdar Shere Sing, Sindunwala |
| | SIRDAR LAL SING |
| | Agent and Son of Sirdar Uttur Sing, Kaleewala |

# Selected Bibliography

Abbott, Capt. James. *Some accounts of the battlefield of Alexander and Porus*. Calcutta: Baptist Mission Press, 1849.

Abbott, James and George Lawrence. *Journals and diaries of the assistants to the Agent, Governor-General North-West Frontier and Resident at Lahore 1846-1849*. Allahabad: Pioneer Press, 1911.

Ahluwalia, M. L. *Maharani Jind Kaur*. Amritsar: Singh Brothers, 2001.

Allen, Charles. *Soldier Sahibs*. London: John Murray, 2000.

Allen, Wm. H. *Allen's Indian Mail*, Volumes 3–15. London: Wm. H. Allen & Co., 1845–1857.

Arnold, Edwin. *The Marquis of Dalhousie's administration of British India*, Volume 1. London: F. Shoberl, 1862.

Baird, J. G. A. *Private letters of the Marquess of Dalhousie*. Edinburgh: William Blackwood and Son, 1910.

Bamfield, Christian and Mrs Daniel Bamfield. *Extracts from letters to Mrs. Bamfield from her husband, during the second Seikh war ... also, the subsequent letters of her son*. Bath: C. W. Oliver, 1854.

Barnes, George Carnac. *Report on the settlement in the district of Kangra in the Trans-Sutlej states*. Lahore: Hope Press, 1862.

Bell, Major Evans. *Retrospects and prospects of Indian policy*. London: Trubner & Co., 1868.

Buckle, Capt. E. *Memoirs of the services of the Bengal artillery*. London: WM. H. Allen, 1852.

Burton, Reginald G. *The first and second Sikh wars*. India: Government Central Branch Press, 1911.

Campbell, George Douglas. *India under Dalhousie and Canning*. London: Longman, Green, Longman, Roberts & Green, 1865.

Campbell, Sir George. *Memoirs of my Indian career*, Volume 1. New York: Macmillan and Co., 1893.

Cavenagh, Orfeur. *Reminiscences of an Indian official*. London: W. H. Allen, 1884.

Cole, John Jones. *A sketch of the siege of Multan*. Lahore: Sang-E-Meel Publications, 1849.

Daly, Major Hugh. *Memoirs of General Sir Henry Dermot Daly*. London: John Murray, 1905.

Edwardes, Herbert and Herman Merivale. *Life of Sir Henry Lawrence*. London: Smith, Elder and Co., 1872.

Edwardes, Herbert B. *A year on the Punjab frontier in 1848–49*, Volume 1 and 2. London: Richard Bentley, 1851.

Edwardes, Michael. *The necessary hell, John and Henry Lawrence and the Indian Empire*. London: Cassell & Company Ltd., 1958.

Edwards, William. *Reminiscences of a Bengal Civilian*. London: Smith, Elder and Co, 1866.

Gambier-Perry, Ernest. *Reynell Taylor A Biography*. London: Kegan Paul, Trench, & Co., 1888.

*Gazetteer of the Kangra District Part 1 Kangra 1883–1884*. New Delhi: Indus Publishing Company, 1884.

Gill, Avtar Singh. *Maharaja Dalip Singh cheated out*. Ludhiana: Jaswant Printers, 2007.

Gough, Charles and Arthur Innes. *The Sikhs and the Sikh Wars*. London: A. D. Innes & Co, 1897.

Hamilton, Henry B. *The Puggrie Wallahs, The 14th (King's) Light Dragoons in India during the Second Sikh War & the Indian Mutiny, 1841–1859*. London: Longmans,Green and Co., 1901.

Hardinge, Charles. *Rulers of India: Viscount Hardinge*. Oxford: Clarendon Press, 1900.

Hasrat, Bikrama Jit. *The Punjab papers*. Hoshiarpur, Punjab India: V. V. Research Institute Press, 1970.

Hodson, George H (ed.). *Twelve years of a soldier's life in India*. London: John W. Parker and son, 1859.

Humbley, W. W. W. *Journal of a Cavalry officer*. London: Longman, Brown, Green and Longmans, 1854.

Innes, Lt Gen. J. J. McLeod. *Sir Henry Lawrence, the pacificator*. Oxford: Clarendon Press, 1898.

Kasturi, N. *History of the British occupation of India*. Calcutta: R. Chatterjee, n.d.

Knollys, Hope Grant and Henry. *Life of General Sir Hope Grant V1: With selections from his correspondence*. Edinburgh and London: William Blackwood and Sons, 1894.

Lawrence, George. *Reminiscences of forty-three years in India*. London: George Murray, 1875.

Lawrence-Archer, James Henry. *Commentaries on the Punjab campaign 1848–1849*. London: W. H. Allen, 1878.

Lee, Harold. *Brothers in the Raj*. Oxford: Oxford University Press, 2002.

Lee-Warner, Sir William. *The Life of the Marquis of Dalhousie*. New York: Macmillan and Co Ltd, 1904.

Login, Lady. *Sir John Login and Duleep Singh*. London: W. H. Allen, 1890.

Lumsden, General Sir Peter. *Lumsden of the Guides*. London: John Murray, 1900.

Mackenzie, Helen Douglas. *Life in the mission, the camp, and the zenáná; or, Six years in India*, Volume 2. New York: Redfield, 1853.

Mahajan, Jagmohan. *Circumstances leading to the annexation of the Punjab 1846–1849*. Allahabad: Kitabistan, 1949.

Malcolm, Thomas and Rev. Caeser Caine. *Barracks an battlefields in India*. London: C. H. Kelly, 1891.

Malleson, Col. G. B. *The Decisive Battles of India from 1746 to 1849*. 1885.

Marshman, John Clark. *Memoirs of Major-General Sir Henry Havelock, K. C. B*. London: Longman, Green, Longman and Roberts, 1860.

Maude, Edwin. *Oriental campaigns and European furloughs*. London: T. F. Unwin, 1908.

Mountain, Armie Simcoe Henry. *Memoirs and Letters of the Late Colonel Armine S.H. Mountain, C.B.: Aide-De-Camp to the Queen and Adjutant-General of Her Majesty's Forces in India*. London: Longman, Brown, Green, Longmans & Roberts, 1858.

N. M. Khilnani. *British power in the Punjab 1839–1858*. Bombay: Asia Publishing House, 1972.

Ouvry, Henry Aimé. *Cavalry Experiences and Leaves from My Journal*. Lymington: Chas. T. King, 1892.

*Papers relating to the Articles of Agreement concluded between the British Government and the Lahore Durbar on the 16th December 1846*. London: T. R. Harrison, 1847.

*Papers relating to the Punjab 1847–1849 Presented to both Houses of Parliament by Command of Her Majesty, May 1849*. London: Harrison and Son, 1849.

Paton, George. *Historical records of the 24th regiment, from its formation, in 1689*. London: Simpkin, Marshall, Hamilton, Kent, & co, 1892.

R. W. Bingham. *General Gilbert's raid to the Khyber. A personal narrative*. Calcutta: W. Thacker and Co. St. Andrew's Library, 1850.

Rait, Robert S. *The life and campaigns of Hugh First Viscount Gough Field-Marshall*. Westminster: Archibald Constable and Co. Ltd., 1903.

*The Calcutta Review*, Volumes 5–16. Calcutta: Sanders, Cones & Co., 1846–1851.

Roseberry, J. Royal. *Imperial rule in Punjab*. Riverdale, Maryland: The Riverdale Company, 1987.

Ryder, Corporal John. *Four years' service in India*. Leicester: W. H. Burton, 1853.

Sandford, Daniel A. *A Journal of the Second Sikh War: the Experiences of an Ensign of the 2nd Bengal European Regiment During the Campaign in the Punjab, India, 1848–49*. Leonaur Ltd, 2007.

Scott, Donald & Arthur Swinson (eds). *The memoirs of Private Waterfield*. London: Cassell & Company Ltd, 1968.

Sethi, R. R. *The trial of Raja Lal Singh (The Lahore Minister)*. New Delhi: Nirmal Publishers and Distributors, 1986.

Shadwell, Lawrence. *The Life of Colin Campbell, Lord Clyde*. Edinburgh: W. Blackwood and sons, 1881.

Singh, Bawa Satinder. *Hardinge Letters 1844–1847*. London: Royal Historical Society, 1986.

Singh, Bawa Satinder. *The letters of the first Viscount Hardinge of Lahore to Lady Hardinge and Sir Walter and Lady James*. London: Royal Historical Society, 1986.

Singh, Bawa Satinder (ed.). *My Indian peregrinations*. Lubbock, Texas: Texas Tech University Press, 2001.

Singh, Ganda (ed.). *Private correspondence relating to the Anglo-Sikh Wars*. Amritsar: Sikh Historical Society, 1955.

Singh, Ganda. *Some new light on the Treaty of Bharowal*. Amritsar: Khalsa College, 1941.

Singh, Nahar. *History of Koh-i-Noor, Darya-i-Noor, and Taimur's Ruby*. New Delhi: Atlantic Publishers and Distributers, n.d.

Smith, George. *Twelve Indian Statesmen*. London: George Murray, 1897.

Smith, Reginald Bosworth. *Life of Lord Lawrence*. London: Smith, Elder and Co., 1883.

Swinson, Arthur and Donald Scott. *The memoirs of Private Waterfield*. London: Cassell & Company Ltd, 1968.

Thackwell, Edward Joseph. *Narrative of the second Seikh war, in 1848–49*. London: Richard Bentley, 1851.

*The Indian News and Chronicle of Indian Affairs*. London, 1849.

*The North British Review*, Volumes 9–12. London: Hamilton, Adams & Co., 1848–1849.

Thorburn, S. S. *The Punjab in peace and war*. Edinburgh and London: William Blackwood and Sons, 1904.

Trotter, L. J. *The Life of John Nicholson*. London: John Murray, 1897.

Trotter, Lionel James. *The history of the British Empire in India*. London: Wm. H. Allen and Co., 1866.

Walsh, Revd J. Johnston. *A memorial of the Futtehghur Mission*. Philadelphia: Presbyterian Board of Publication, 1858.

Wylly, H. C. *The military memoirs of Lieut.-General Sir Joseph Thackwell*. London: John Murray, 1908.

Younghusband, Col G. J. *The story of the Guides*. London: Macmillan and Co., 1908.

*Letters and Documents*
National Army Museum
British Library
National Archives of India

*Websites*
http://hansard.millbanksystems.com/index.html

# Index

Also available from Amberley Publishing

'A detailed study of an important but largely forgotten campaign'
JOHN KEAY, *INDIA: A HISTORY*

# THE FIRST
# ANGLO-SIKH
# WAR

## AMARPAL SINGH

Available from all good bookshops or to order direct
Please call **01453–847–800**
**www.amberley-books.com**